The Mystery Of The Historical Jesus

The Messiah in the Qur'an, the Bible, and Historical Sources

Louay Fatoohi

Luna Plena Publishing   Birmingham

© 2007 Louay Fatoohi

All Rights reserved. No part of this book may be reproduced, translated, stored in a retrieval system, or transmitted by any means, electronic, mechanical, photocopying, recording, or otherwise, without written permission from the author.

First published: September 2007

Production Reference: 1010907

Published by:
Luna Plena Publishing
Birmingham, UK.
www.lunaplenapub.com

ISBN 978-1-906342-01-2

Cover design by:
Mawlid Design
www.mawliddesign.com

Front cover images:

A 12th-13th century Qur'anic manuscript in Maghribi script (courtesy of www.columbia.edu/itc/mealac/pritchett/00xcallig/sultanate/quranspain/quranspain.html). These are the shown verses: "So be dutiful toward Allah and listen [O you who believe]; Allah does not guide the rebellious people (5.108). On the Day when Allah will assemble the messengers then say: 'What answer were you given [to your calls to people to worship me]?' They shall say: 'We have no knowledge; You are the Knower of the unseen' (5.109). Lo! When Allah said: 'O Jesus son of Mary! Remember My favor on you and on your mother, that I have supported you with the Spirit of Holiness, [making you] speak to people in the cradle and when middle-aged; and that I taught you the Book, Wisdom, the Torah, and the Injīl; and that you create out of clay the figures of birds'" (5.110).

A 13th century Greek Gospels lectionary manuscript (courtesy of *The Center for the Study of New Testament Manuscripts* www.csntm.org).

A 13th century Hebrew Old Testament manuscript (courtesy of *The Schøyen Collection* schoyencollection.com).

About the Author

Louay Fatoohi was born in Baghdad, Iraq, in 1961. He obtained a BSc in Physics from the College of Science, University of Baghdad, in 1984. In 1992, he and his wife Shetha moved to the United Kingdom where they have settled. He obtained his PhD in Astronomy from the Physics Department, Durham University, in 1998.

The author of several books and many articles in Arabic and English, Dr Fatoohi is particularly interested in Qur'anic exegesis (*Tafsir*), history in the Qur'an, and comparative religion. His books include *The Prophet Joseph in the Qur'an, the Bible, and History* and *Jihad in the Qur'an: The Truth from the Source (2nd Edition)*.

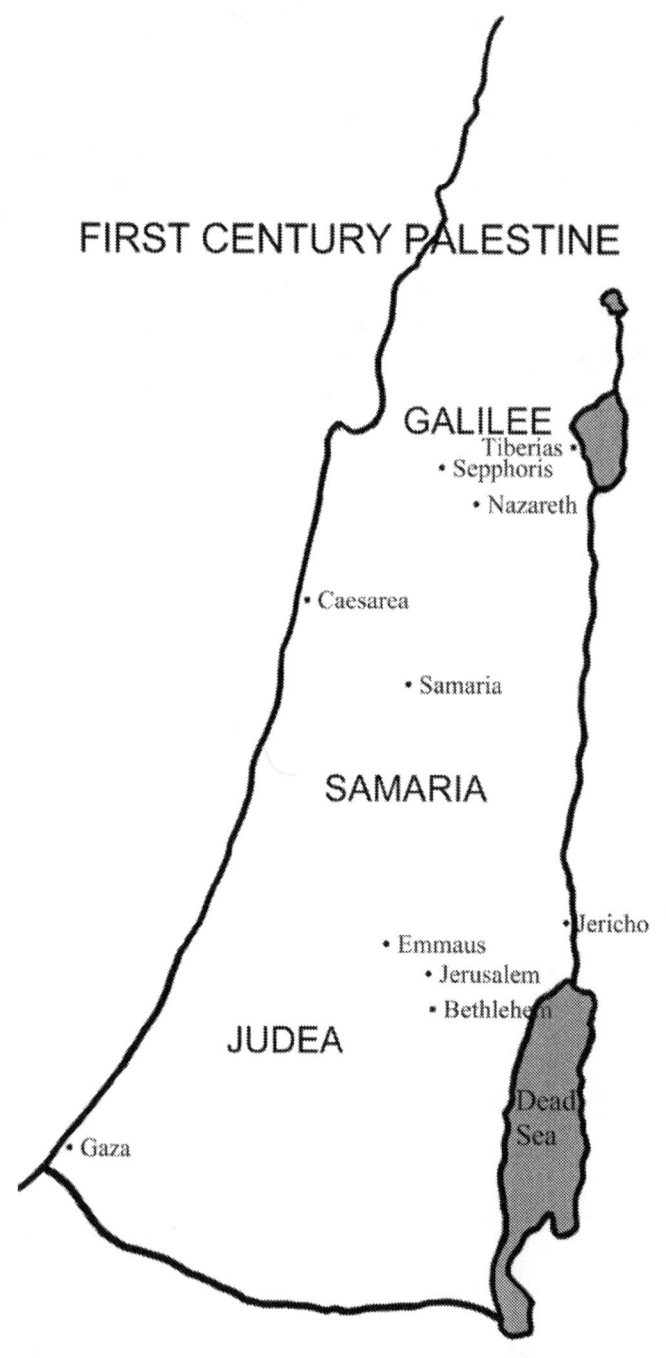

Contents

Preface 1

Introduction 5

1. Approaches to the Study of History in the Qur'an and the Bible 11
   1.1. The Secular Approach 11
      1.1.1. The Unavailability of Independent Evidence 12
      1.1.2. Similarities Between the Bible and Other Sources 13
      1.1.3. Similarities Between the Qur'an and Jewish and Christian Writings 18
      1.1.4. The Question of the Paranormal 19
   1.2. The Biblical Approach 20
      1.2.1. Internal Biblical Discrepancies 21
      1.2.2. Unfactual Biblical Statements 23
      1.2.3. The indefinability of the "Bible" and "Scripture" 23
      1.2.4. The False Superiority of the Canon 26
   1.3. The Secular-Biblical Approach 28
   1.4. The Qur'anic Approach 31
      1.4.1. Islamic Sacred Texts 31
      1.4.2. The Authenticity of the Qur'an 33
      1.4.3. The Qur'an and Other Scriptures 35
      1.4.4. Contextual Displacement as a Form of Scriptural Textual Manipulation ... 38
      1.4.5. Refuted Accusations 40
   1.5. The Approach of This Book 41

2. Mary Before the Annunciation 45
   2.1. Mary Before the Annunciation in the Apocrypha 45
      2.1.1. The Account of the Gospel of the Birth of Mary 45
      2.1.2. The Account of the Infancy Gospel of James 46
      2.1.3. The Account of the Gospel of Pseudo-Matthew 47
   2.2. Mary Before the Annunciation in the Qur'an 48

3. Prophet Zechariah: Mary's Guardian 57
   3.1. Zechariah in the New Testament 57
   3.2. Zechariahs in the Apocrypha 59
   3.3. Prophet Zechariah in the Qur'an 60
      3.3.1 Prophet Zechariah in Chapter 3 (The Family of 'Imrān) 61
      3.3.2. Prophet Zechariah in Chapter 19 (Maryam) 66

4. Prophet John 73
   4.1. John the Baptist in the New Testament 73
   4.2. John the Baptist in History 78
   4.3. Prophet John in the Qur'an 79

5. More Than Annunciation 87
   5.1. The Annunciation in the New Testament 87

5.2. The Annunciation in the Apocrypha 88
5.3. The Annunciation and the Inducement of the Virginal Conception According to the Qur'an 90
   5.3.1. Gabriel's Visit and the Inducement of the Virginal Conception in Chapter 19 91
   5.3.2. Gabriel's Visit and the Annunciation in Chapter 3 95

6. The Virginal Conception 99
6.1. The Virginal Conception in Christian Sources 100
6.2. The Arguments Against the Virginal Conception 101
   6.2.1. The Scriptural Arguments 101
      6.2.1.1. Unknown Story 102
      6.2.1.2. Contradictory Accounts 108
      6.2.1.3. Different Infancy Narratives 110
   6.2.2. The Historical Arguments 111
   6.2.3. The Scientific Arguments 113
6.3. The Accusation of the Illegitimacy of Jesus 114
6.4. The Qur'an's Affirmation of the Virginal Conception 117

7. The *Rūḥ* (Spirit) 121
7.1. The Hebrew *Ruach* in the Old Testament 121
7.2. The Greek *Pneuma* in the New Testament 122
7.3. The Arabic *Rūḥ* in the Qur'an 124
   7.3.1. Gabriel 124
   7.3.2. The Spirit of the Creation of Man 127
   7.3.3. Inspiration 134

8. Joseph: Mary's Husband? 137
8.1. Joseph in Christian Sources 137
   8.1.1. Joseph and Mary 137
   8.1.2. Joseph and Jesus 139
8.2. The Non-historicity of Joseph According to the Qur'an 143

9. Did Jesus Have Brothers and Sisters? 145
9.1. Paul and Jesus' Brothers 145
9.2. Jesus' Brothers and Sisters in the Gospels 146
9.3. The Church and Jesus' Brothers and Sisters 148
9.4. James 150
   9.4.1. Paul and James 151
   9.4.2. James in Other New Testament Books 154
   9.4.3. James in History 156
9.5. The Qur'an's Implicit Rejection of Jesus' Siblings 163

10. Jesus' Birth 165
10.1. Jesus' Birth in the Canonical Gospels 165
10.2. Jesus' Birth in Apocryphal Sources 170
10.3. The Star of Bethlehem 171
10.4. Jesus' Birth in the Qur'an 173
10.5. Birth Under A Palm Tree 180
10.6. Jesus' Date of Birth 186

11. Massacre of Truth 195
11.1. Herod's Massacre in Christian Sources 195
11.2. The Non-historicity of Herod's Massacre According to the Qur'an 199
11.3. A Massacre That Never Was 201
11.3.1. The Scriptural Arguments 201
11.3.2. The Historical Arguments 205
11.4. The Massacre That Did Happen 207

12. Was Jesus A Nazarene From Nazareth? 215
12.1. Jesus' Birth and Growing up places 215
12.2. "Nazarene" in the New Testament 218
12.3. The Nazarenes of the Qur'an 224

13. The Messiah 231
13.1. The Messiah in the Old Testament 231
13.2. The Christ in the New Testament 236
13.2.1. Self-proclamation and the Public Acceptance of Jesus' Messiahship 236
13.2.2. Faces of the Messiah 238
13.2.2.1 Son of David 238
13.2.2.2 Miracle Worker 239
13.2.2.3 King of the Jews 242
13.2.2.4 Founder of an Imminent Kingdom 246
13.2.2.5 Salvational Figure 247
13.2.2.6 Suffering Messiah 248
13.2.2.7 Virtuous Teacher 249
13.2.3. The Messiah's Entry into Jerusalem 249
13.3. *Al-Masīḥ* in the Qur'an 251

14. The Divine Son of God That Jesus Never Was 257
14.1. The Jewish "Sonship of God" 257
14.2. The Christian "Sonship of God" 259
14.2.1. Sonship of God, Messiahship, and Miracle Working 260
14.2.2. Sonship of God and Blasphemy 261
14.2.3. Christian Sons of God 263
14.2.4. The Unique Son of God 264
14.2.5. The Eternal Son of John 268
14.2.6. When Did Jesus' Sonship of God become Special? 270
14.3. The Prevailing of the Johannine Theology 272
14.4. The Trinity 275
14.5. Son of Man 278

15. The Human Jesus 287
15.1. Muslim Messenger and Prophet 287
15.1.1. Islam 287
15.1.2. Messenger and Prophet 290
15.2. Human Servant of God 293
15.3. Forerunner of Prophet Muhammad 295

- 15.4. The Exclusiveness of Divinity 297
  - 15.4.1. The Oneness of God 297
  - 15.4.2. No Offspring of God 299
  - 15.4.3. False Sonship of God 303
  - 15.4.4. The Fallacy of the Trinity 309

16. Miracles 313
- 16.1. Wonder Workers at the Time of Jesus 313
- 16.2. Jesus' Miracles in the New Testament 321
  - 16.2.1. The Categories of Jesus' Miracles 322
    - 16.2.1.1. Healing Miracles 323
    - 16.2.1.2. Nature Miracles 325
    - 16.2.1.3. Prophecies 326
    - 16.2.1.4. Clairvoyance 327
  - 16.2.2. Different Gospel Accounts 327
  - 16.2.3. The Significance and Purpose of Miracles 330
  - 16.2.4. Miracles and Faith 334
  - 16.2.5. Miracles between Publicity and Secrecy 338
- 16.3. Jesus' Miracles in Apocryphal Writings 342
- 16.4. Jesus' Miracles in the Qur'an 346

17. The *Injīl* (Gospel) 357
- 17.1. The Term "Gospel" Before and After Christianity 357
- 17.2. The Injīl: Jesus' Divine Book 363
- 17.3. The Meaning of "Injīl" 364
- 17.4. The Paraclete 369
- 17.5. The Injīl and the Law 377
  - 17.5.1. Jesus and the Law in the New Testament 377
  - 17.5.2. The Injīl's Modification of the Law 382

18. The Crucifixion in the New Testament and Historical Sources 389
- 18.1. Inconsistencies in the New Testament Accounts of the Crucifixion 390
- 18.2. Historical Problems in the New Testament Accounts of the Crucifixion 404
- 18.3. Who Killed Jesus? 409
- 18.4. The Crucifixion in History 414
- 18.5. Alternative Scenarios 428
- 18.6. The Date of the Crucifixion 432

19. The Qur'an and the Cross Fiction 435
- 19.1. The Fiction of Jesus' Crucifixion 435
- 19.2. The Crucifixion of Jesus' Substitute 439
- 19.3. After the Crucifixion 445
- 19.4. The Theology of the Crucifixion 453
  - 19.4.1. The New Testament and Theology of the Cross 453
  - 19.4.2. The Qur'an's Rejection of the Theology of the Cross 459

20. A Second Coming? 467
- 20.1. The Second Coming in the New Testament 467

    20.1.1. The Unfulfilled Imminence of the Second Coming 469
    20.1.2. The Second Coming and Other Apocalyptic Events 475
    20.1.3. The Dangerous Politics of the Second Coming.. 477
  20.2. The Second Coming in Sayings Attributed to Prophet Muhammad.. 478
  20.3. The Qur'an's Silence on Jesus' Second Coming 483

21. Christians in the Qur'an 493
  21.1. The Oldest Roman Mentions of the "Christians" 493
  21.2. Christians in the Qur'an 494
    21.2.1. The *Ḥawāriyyūn*.. 495
    21.2.2. The *Naṣārā*... 499

22. The Qur'anic Historical Jesus 509

Appendix A: History in the Qur'an 513

Appendix B: Apocryphal Gospels 519
  The Infancy Gospel of James 519
  The Gospel of the Birth of Mary 522
  The Arabic Gospel of the Infancy... 524
  The Infancy Gospel of Thomas 525
  The Gospel of Pseudo-Matthew 526

Appendix C: Abbreviations 529

References 531
  Modern Works.. 531
  Classical and Ancient Writings.. 535
  Religious Texts... 537

Index of Qur'anic Verses 539

Index of Biblical Passages.. 543

Index of Other Religious Texts 551

Index of Ancient Texts.. 553

Index of Names and Subjects... 554

Preface

My interest in Jesus is not new. It started as far back as I can remember. I was born to an Iraqi Christian family — a Catholic father and Orthodox mother. My parents were not particularly religious and by no means regular Churchgoers, but they had a strong awareness of their Christian identity, as did their three children.

With religion rarely a topic of discussion at home, my Catholic primary school ensured that I was influenced by Christian teachings and the stories of Jesus. I was around 8 years old or so when my fascination with Jesus led to an encounter with him in a dream which I still remember vividly. I saw myself walking with him hand in hand on an endless beautiful green plain. He looked like his images. He did not speak to me, nor I to him. That dream left me with a special feeling of satisfaction.

In my last year in the Catholic school, I received the Sacrament of the First Eucharist. I considered that day to be the best and happiest of my life. Someone — possibly one of my parents — then told me that this is how Napoleon Bonaparte also felt about his first Eucharist. This reassured me that although I was only 12 years old, this feeling was unlikely to change. I continued to attend church and take the Holy Communion regularly for a couple of months before my interest started to wane.

Leaving the Catholic school and joining a state run intermediary school marked a significant change in my contact with Christian practices and teachings. There was not much of a Christian atmosphere at home — apart from the icons on the walls, attending the church for social functions each now and then, and, of course, celebrating Christmas and Easter — and now there was no Christian teaching at school either. Those three years were marked by more of a loss of interest in religion than any change in my religious views. I still considered myself a Christian, but did not really care much as to what that meant.

But things were to change at high school, where I became friends with someone who held Marxist views and, expectedly, did not believe in the existence of God. The fact this friend came from a Christian family must have made it easier for me to examine my Christian faith. We used to spend many hours discussing various topics of interest. I did not find myself particularly interested in this friend's political views, although socialism appealed to me, but I found myself gradually getting closer to his dismissive views of religion. By the time I joined university, I had labeled myself an "atheist."

In my second year at university I befriended a very different person. He was a very liberal Muslim with a strange mix of intelligent insights and outlandish views supported by an unenviable amount of self-righteousness. This friendship gave me another opportunity to reexamine my beliefs. I had never considered Islam seriously. What I knew about Islam was largely the myths that I was taught at home, which were popular among other Christians. One of these claimed that

Muhammad was taught the Qur'an by a renegade Christian priest called Baḥirā. Later I discovered that the oldest surviving biography of Prophet Muhammad presents this priest as a solitary monk whom the young boy Muhammad met when he was in the company of his uncle on a commercial journey to Syria. Baḥirā identified Muhammad as the awaited future Prophet.

My close friendship with this person, which replaced my friendship with the Marxist, made me take Islam, and more specifically the Qur'an, seriously and study it, although not in a systematic way. In the first year of this friendship I read the four Gospels critically and wrote a critique of them. This short revisit of Christianity confirmed to me the unreliability of the Gospels and my earlier decision to reject it. But this time I was not to go back to atheism but to enter reassuringly the new world of the Qur'an.

This is how my gradual conversion to Islam started. By the time I was 23 years old or so, I could describe myself as a Muslim, although more so intellectually than in practice. The Qur'an took center stage in my life and, among other things, renewed my interest in Jesus. While it speaks highly of all prophets, it paints a particularly venerable picture of Jesus and presents him as a unique prophet, but this image is very different from the divine Jesus of the New Testament. This book is an expression of my lifelong fascination with Jesus.

But I did not write this book only because of my personal interest. True, I enjoy writing books, but I can motivate myself to write a book only if I believe it can be a genuinely new contribution to the available literature. And this book is no exception. Let me explain why I believe that this book is a new addition to the literature on the historical Jesus and not a rewrite of something already available.

Numerous books and articles have examined the historicity of the Jesus of the Gospels. Some endorse his image in the New Testament, others accept parts of it and reject others, and yet others draw completely different pictures of this intriguing man. There is even a small minority of writers who have gone as far as suggesting that there was never a Jesus in history! Depending on the backgrounds, goals, and trainings of their respective authors, these works relied on the New Testament, Christian sources, Jewish writings, or other historical sources, or on combinations of these writings. The Qur'an is rarely mentioned, let alone seriously considered, by the mainly Western authors of these writings. The explicit or implicit reasoning for this neglect is the perceived historical worthlessness of the Qur'an.

There have also been a few studies that considered the Qur'anic Jesus from a Christian point of view. One such study is *Jesus in the Qur'an*, which was first published in 1965, by Professor Geoffrey Parrinder. This Methodist minister had the commendable goal of bridging the gap between the Qur'an and the Gospels and wrote a very sensitive and sympathetic book. But his method was to show that the differences of the Qur'an with the Gospels are either due to misunderstanding

Qur'anic verses or such passages targeting non-canonical or "apocryphal" Christian concepts not what the New Testament says.

Another study that may be worth citing is Kenneth Cragg's *Jesus and the Muslim: An Exploration*, first published in 1985. Bishop Cragg focused on clarifying for Muslims the misunderstanding of their scripture of Christian theology.

In addition to the fact that both of these studies are written from a Christian perspective, both of them are religious studies that do not consider independent sources. Reading the Qur'an from the New Testament's point of view is interesting, but what history says about the New Testament is at least not less so.

Muslim scholars have also written quite a lot about Jesus. But, contrary to their Western counterparts, they focused mainly on the Qur'an and other Islamic sources. The Christian image of Jesus is often cited to be dismissed, usually on the basis of what Islamic sources say, but at times because of its incoherence and internal discrepancies. Like Western scholars who have ignored the Qur'an, Muslim writers have ignored independent historical sources.

This book fills a gap in the literature on the historical Jesus by considering simultaneously the Qur'anic account of Jesus' life, its counterparts in the Gospels, and historical sources. As I explain in more detail in Chapter 1, the book sets out to show that, unlike the New Testament stories, the Qur'anic statements about Jesus are consistent and can be reconciled with what we know from history. Put differently, this book is an attempt to know the historical Jesus by studying both the Qur'an and history.

My original plan for the book was to focus on studying the Qur'anic account in the light of history and to cite the New Testament as little as possible. I thought there were already numerous studies that examine the Gospel accounts in their own right and in the light of history. But as I started writing the book I found it difficult to adhere to the original plan. One reason is that presenting the accounts of the Gospels alongside that of the Qur'an is itself useful in showing significant differences between the two. It would make the message of the book clearer to the Christian, Muslim, and other readers.

Of course, it is the reader who will ultimately judge how much this book has succeeded in what it set out to do. But I sincerely believe that the attempt was more than worth doing. I also hope that others will follow suit and study the historical Jesus from the Qur'anic perspective.

I mentioned earlier the critique of the Gospels that I wrote about 26 years ago. It was useful to me then, but I did not do much with it until 6 years later when I used it to impress my future wife, Shetha. Neither she nor I had any idea at the time that 20 years later I would be presenting her with a much more substantial study to read and critique. This book has benefited immensely from Shetha's extensive comments on two earlier drafts. She has also given me a lot of editorial help with the book. As ever, she has given me all the help I asked for. Her contribution to this book, as it is to my other works, is invaluable. I cannot thank her enough.

My close friend Howard Hall has also kindly acted as a reviewer on the book. His thoughtful comments and suggestions helped me spot and remedy gaps in the book. He also highlighted weaknesses that I needed to address. I am indebted to Howard.

I have also got used to the help of my close friend Tariq Chaudhry with reviewing my writings. Tariq read thoroughly an earlier draft of the book and added many comments. These comments allowed me to make the text read better and clearer. I would like to thank Tariq for his help.

These three generous reviewers have helped me to greatly improve the book. Any oversights and mistakes that are in the book are mine, and mine alone.

Readers are welcome to email me any feedback and comments on the book at fatoohi_louay@gmail.com.

Introduction

Christians believe that the New Testament authors wrote their books under the guidance of God. They consider the Qur'an to be the handwork of Muhammad, probably written with the help of others who had knowledge of Jewish and Christian scriptures and apocryphal writings. Because some statements in the Qur'an resemble passages in non-canonical writings, it is claimed that the latter are among the sources used by the Qur'an's author. Because these apocryphal writings, by definition, are considered inauthentic and inferior to the New Testament, the Qur'an stands accused not only of copying texts, but also using the wrong ones.

The Qur'an, on the other hand, claims that the Torah, which God revealed to Moses, and the Injīl, which is Jesus' divine book, were changed by the Jews and Christians. The Five Books of Moses in the Old Testament and the Gospels in the New Testament are very different books that have almost nothing of the original revelation. Additionally, the Biblical books are not necessarily more accurate or factual than apocryphal sources, and a non-canonical book may have a seed of truth that is missing from the canonical writings. The view that the canonical Gospels are superior to the apocryphal ones is not a statement of fact but an expression of faith.

Similarly, the centuries-old popular perception in Western culture that the Gospel accounts of Jesus are confirmed by history — and thus all different accounts, such as the Qur'an's and apocryphal sources' are unhistorical — is nothing more than an urban myth. It would come as a big surprise to many to know that there are only a few mentions of Jesus in historical sources from the first century CE, and that this information cannot be shown conclusively to be independent of Christian influence. Not even the most famous incident of the crucifixion has testimony in history that can be confidently described as independent. What most people believe about Jesus is derived from the Gospels, which ultimately won the battle against the many other alternative gospels that were available in the first few centuries after Jesus as they became "canonized." The reliability of this belief depends very much on the credibility of the Gospels, and these are anything but credible sources. The perception that history supports the Gospel accounts of Jesus' life is an instance of confusing assumptions with facts and mistaking tradition for history.

This book presents an alternative history of Jesus based on the Qur'an. It also reads the New Testament, relevant apocryphal writings, and history in the light of the Qur'anic account. But does not this *assume* that the Qur'an is a reliable book? It does, but then Jesus' history cannot be studied without starting from a major assumption. What is the difference, then, between an image of the historical Jesus that presumes the reliability of the Qur'an and one that assumes the reliability of the New Testament? The Qur'an provides a coherent and consistent image of Jesus, whereas the Gospels draw conflicting images. In fact, the image of Jesus even within any one Gospel is inconsistent. Furthermore, the Qur'anic image makes much more sense of the limited historical information on Jesus than his images in the Gospels do. This approach, which I call the "Qur'anic approach," is discussed in detail — along with alternative approaches to studying the historical Jesus, including the "Biblical approach" — in Chapter 1.

The book makes every effort to clearly state its assumptions and to distinguish between the scriptural passages and independent facts it cites and their interpretations. It discusses in detail not only its arguments, but also counterarguments. This should make it easier for the reader to assess the strength of the arguments of the book and to pursue different lines of interpretation of those passages and facts if she so wishes.

The book should be suitable for both the general reader and the specialist. It is intended to appeal to Christians, Muslims, people of other faiths, and the non-religious. It is for anyone who is interested in the historical Jesus. It does not require prior familiarity with the Qur'an or the Bible.

This book is a complete study of the Qur'anic Jesus in the sense that every verse that talks about him directly or indirectly is analyzed. The same applies to the verses that talk about his mother and two other relevant figures, Zechariah and his son John (the Baptist).

I have chosen to avoid studying other Islamic literature, including the sayings of Prophet Muhammad. As I explain in the first chapter, this literature is extremely unreliable. I cite a few alleged Prophetic sayings in Chapter 20, but mainly to show problems they have.

I need to explain some of the stylistic choices in the book. Each Qur'anic verse has been followed by a combination of two numbers identifying its *sūra* (chapter) and its position in that chapter. For instance, the combination 5.110 refers to the 110th verse of the 5th chapter.

I have consulted some of the available English translations of the Qur'an, but the translations I used are mine. I had to use my own translations of the Qur'an because translation is an act of interpretation, reflecting the translator's understanding of the text. Translations of all other cited Arabic texts are also mine.

I have also added in square brackets any explanatory text needed to clarify the translation. Round brackets have been used to add alternative texts, such as the English meaning of a term that is cited in its Arabic origin.

A number of different printing styles are used in the book. A special font has been used for the Qur'anic text and another for the canonical and apocryphal Jewish and Christian scriptures. Roman transliterations of Arabic terms are in italics.

When I needed to cite a passage that exists in Mark and any or all of the other three Gospels, I chose Mark's version. Also, when quoting from more than one Gospel I cited Mark first, followed by Matthew and Luke, and finally John. This reflects the consensus that Mark is the earliest Gospel, which Matthew and Luke are partly based on, whereas John is the latest.

Finally, I would like to give a quick overview of the chapters of the book. A brief, but still more detailed, summary of the content of each chapter has been added to the beginning of each one.

Chapter 1 identifies and discusses the main approaches in studying history in the Bible and the Qur'an. This introductory chapter is necessary to clarify what assumptions are employed by each approach. It also shows the main problems with what I term as the secular, Biblical, and secular-Biblical approaches before introducing the Qur'anic approach, which is followed in this book.

Chapter 2 focuses on Mary's childhood — that is, before she received the news about her conception of Jesus. As this period of Mary's life is not covered in the Gospels, the chapter focuses only on apocryphal writings, along with the Qur'an's account.

Zechariah is the subject of Chapter 3. He is portrayed as a priest in both the Gospel of Luke and apocryphal gospels. The Qur'an states that Zechariah became Mary's guardian.

Zechariah is also the father of John the Baptist, who has a distinct presence in the story of Jesus in Christian sources. John is the subject of Chapter 4. Like his father, John is also a prophet in the Qur'an.

In Chapter 5 we study the delivery of the news to Mary about her miraculous conception or the "annunciation," which is confirmed in Christian sources and the Qur'an. This is one of the events that the Qur'an recounts in more detail.

The virginal conception is then looked in Chapter 6. This particular miracle has become one of the most disputed aspects of Jesus' story, with those who deny that it happened or could have happened seeking supportive arguments from the Gospels themselves, history, and science. The Qur'an unequivocally confirms that Mary's conception of Jesus was virginal.

The Gospels of Matthew and Luke agree that the Holy Spirit was involved in Mary's virginal conception. The Qur'an gives a different role to Gabriel, who is described a "Spirit," in this miracle. Chapter 7 examines the concept of "spirit" in the Jewish, Christian, and Islamic scriptures.

The exact relationship between Joseph and Mary has been the subject of so much debate. Joseph is the subject of Chapter 8. There is no such figure in the Qur'anic story of Mary and Jesus. The Qur'an also strongly implies that Mary never got engaged or married.

Another controversial topic that is related to that of Joseph is Jesus' brothers and sisters. These are references to them in the Gospels and Paul's letters. Whether they are meant to be Jesus' siblings or not, Chapter 9 shows, has had scholars argue for centuries. There is no mention of any sibling of Jesus in the Qur'an, and its implication that Mary never got married means that Jesus had none.

Jesus' birth is recounted only in two of the four canonical Gospels. These accounts and the significantly different one of the Qur'an are discussed in Chapter 10. The possibility of dating of Jesus' birth is also discussed.

Matthew and apocryphal gospels claim that King Herod the Great committed a massacre of small boys to ensure the death of baby Jesus whom he saw as a threat to his reign. Chapter 11 looks critically at these accounts. No such massacre is recorded in the Qur'an.

The New Testament calls Jesus a "Nazarene." This term appears in the plural only in the Qur'an. Chapter 12 examines the differences between the meanings of this term in both sources.

While Judaism does not accept that Jesus was the Messiah, both Christianity and Islam do. The different images of the Messiah in the Old Testament, New Testament, and the Qur'an are discussed in Chapter 13.

The form of Christianity that prevailed is the one that declared Jesus to be divine. Chapter 14 studies the divine qualities that the New Testament confers on Jesus and discussed how this man was turned into a god.

Chapter 15 focuses the light on the human image of Jesus in the Qur'an. His deification is completely rejected by the Qur'an. Judaism also does not believe in the divinity of other than God.

The Gospels, apocryphal gospels, and the Qur'an all attribute many, albeit different, miracles to Jesus. These wonders are discussed in detail in Chapter 16.

Contrary to what Christian sources say, the Qur'an says that God revealed to Jesus a book called the "Injīl." It also suggests that this is the real meaning of the term "gospel." These and other aspects of Jesus' book are discussed in Chapter 17.

Chapter 18 studies the account of Jesus' crucifixion in the New Testaments. It also examines the reliability of the records of this alleged event in early non-Christian sources.

Jesus' death on the crucifixion is denied in the Qur'an whose alternative account of what happened to Jesus is discussed in Chapter 19.

Christian and Islamic sources, but not the Qur'an, expect Jesus to return before the end times. The second coming is the subject of Chapter 20.

Having studied what the Qur'an says about Jesus in the previous chapter, Chapter 21 focuses on what the Qur'an says about Christians.

Chapter 22 is a recap of the story of Jesus as this book has presented it.

The book has three appendices. Appendix A is an introduction to the Qur'an's characteristic style in recounting history. Appendix B introduces the five apocryphal gospels that were often used in the book. The last appendix is a table of the abbreviations used.

The modern, classic, and apocryphal sources that the book cited are all included in the references.

Finally, for the reader's convenience, the book has five separate indexes for Qur'anic verses, Biblical passages, other religious texts, ancient texts, and names and subjects.

1

Approaches to the Study of History in the Qur'an and the Bible

Almost any study of history in the Bible and the Qur'an follows one of four main and distinct approaches, which I will call *secular, Biblical, secular-Biblical,* and *Qur'anic*. Although each of these approaches has its own assumptions and methods, the chosen approach is not something that researchers always make clear. It is also not uncommon for studies to show a mix of approaches and confused methodology, which is what the secular-Biblical approach is. While general and not specific to the topic of this book, the subject of the different approaches is crucial to examine before we embark on a study that discusses history in the Qur'an, the Bible, and other independent sources.

In this chapter, I will explain those four main approaches and the different assumptions each employs. I will examine three flawed assumptions that are often used by secularists when studying the scripture. I will then discuss four arguments that undermine the fundamental assumption of the Biblical approach: its inerrancy. I will also show how the Biblical approach has improperly been used to study the Qur'an — something that we will see examples on through the book. I will then move to discuss the natural development of the hybrid secular-Biblical approach which is the result of rejecting the inerrancy of the Bible but accepting the historical accuracy of parts of it, although researchers disagree on which Biblical statements are historical.

I will then introduce the Qur'anic approach, which is the approach that this books takes, and discuss its fundamental assumption: the absolute verity of the Qur'an. I will discuss the main arguments against this assumption. Specific Qur'anic claims about Jesus will be discussed in their respective chapters. The main conclusion of the book is that the historical Jesus is to be found in the Qur'an, not in the New Testament or any alternative purely secular or secular-Biblical history.

1.1. The Secular Approach

I mean by secular the approach that does not give the Bible or the Qur'an, or to that matter any other religious text, special credibility because of its religious nature. The secular approach would not consider, for instance, the history of Moses in the Bible or the Qur'an factual just because it is related in either or both of these books. Both books are treated like any other ancient sources whose accounts may or may not be accurate, and the credibility of these accounts would need to be considered on their merits. This may very much sound like an *objective* approach and one that impartial scholars would take. But not founding a study on religious beliefs is no guarantee of genuine objectivity. While a secular researcher would not start off with a fundamental religious assumption, he may well use a variety of assumptions when dealing with various questions. The objectivity of any secular research is thus equally susceptible to the researcher's non-religious biases and assumptions, and these can translate into flawed methodology and unbalanced arguments and conclusions.

I will discuss three general flawed, yet popular, assumptions found in secular studies of history in the Bible and the Qur'an. What makes these assumptions particularly poor is that they are often treated more like indisputable facts.

1.1.1. The Unavailability of Independent Evidence

The first assumption is that *the unavailability of evidence on the historicity of characters and events in the Bible means that these characters never existed and these events never happened.* For instance, archaeological excavations have failed so far to unearth any find that mentions main Biblical figures such as Abraham, Moses, and Joseph. Suggesting that the only, or even the most plausible, conclusion is that these figures are unhistorical is misleading. What is found by way of archaeological excavation depends not only on whether what is being looked for had existed one day, but also on many other factors, such as whether one is looking in the right site, the excavated area is large enough to yield significant findings, the site is being dug deep enough and, above all, the sought remnants have resisted falling victim to erosion in the first place. This is why in this context an *argument from silence is no argument*, and *negative evidence is no evidence.*

Egyptologist Professor Kenneth Kitchen notes that "time and again in Old Testament studies, we are told that 'history knows of no such person' as, say, Abraham or Moses, or '.... of no such events' as the battles of Genesis 14, for example." He rightly comments that such sweeping statements reflect "the ignorance not of 'history' personified but of the person making this claim." He gives a number of examples to stress the incompleteness of the current knowledge of the history of the ancient Near East, warning against rushing into premature conclusions about Biblical figures that are not yet attested in archaeological finds (Kitchen, 1977: 48).

There are many examples where historical records were treated with much suspicion for a long time because there were no archaeological findings to support them. Some excavations then brought to light supportive evidence for those ancient records. One example mentioned by Kitchen is that of the city of Ebla:

> Until 1975, Ebla was nothing more than a shadowy name: a once-prominent north-Syrian city along side many more, such as Aleppo, Carchemish, Emar and the rest. If anyone *before* 1975 had stood up and dared proclaim that Ebla had been the centre of a vast economic empire,

rival to that of Akkad, under a dynasty of six kings, he or she would have been dismissed with derision. History "knew" of no such sweeping dominion, no such line of kings, no such preeminence. But since 1975, of course, the archives exhumed have changed all that. (Kitchen, 1977: 48)

This is why *absence of evidence is not evidence of absence*.

1.1.2. Similarities Between the Bible and Other Sources

The second widespread, albeit unproven, assumption is that *similarities between Biblical historical accounts and different stories mentioned in earlier sources mean that the Biblical accounts are unhistorical*. This assumption takes two forms. **First**, the Biblical story was somehow copied from or based on the similar, earlier stories. **Second**, similar stories appear in different cultures because they are the product of the creative imagination of man, which is the same across cultures and traditions. These common literary themes or "motifs" are seen as having no historical background. Both forms of the assumption are fundamentally flawed.

From a nonbeliever's point of view, it is *possible* that a Biblical story was influenced to a small or great extent, directly or indirectly, by older stories, or that both were influenced by other, earlier sources. It is also *possible* that a Biblical story was completely created by the Biblical writers in the same way that similar stories were developed in other cultures. These *possibilities*, nevertheless, tell us nothing about the historicity or otherwise of the account under consideration. Whether a story is historical or not should be determined, as is the case with any historical claim, by examining the reliability of the available records, independent historical evidence, and any indications to the occurrence or non-occurrence of the story. Otherwise, any historical story that appears in more than one culture may be said to have been fabricated by its respective culture, and there would be no criteria for separating stories that reflect history from those that do not. A story about a heroic action is not necessarily unhistorical because of similarities with the story of another hero in a different culture. There are numerous similar stories from completely different cultures that are all known to be historical. Let me expand on this important point with examples.

In an ancient Egyptian story from around the 12th century BCE known as *The Story of Two Brothers*, the elder brother has a house and a wife, and the younger, stronger brother is responsible for doing the hard work in the field. One day while working in the field, the two brothers ran short of seed so the elder one sent his younger brother home to bring some more. At home, the wife of the elder brother tried to seduce her brother-in-law. When he rejected her advances she complained to her husband that his younger brother wanted to seduce her and that he beat her when she repelled him. The angry husband decided to kill his younger brother, but the latter was told of his brother's intention by two cows so he ran away. The story contains much more details and continues with many elaborate episodes (*ANET*, 1950: 23-25).

Scholars (e.g. Irvin, 1977; Pritchard, 1950: 23; Thompson, 1977: 155) have noted that the literary motif of the "spurned seductress" also figures in the Biblical story of Prophet Joseph where he rejects the invitation of his lord's wife to commit adultery. The Egyptian story is itself linked to a yet older Hittite story. What makes any attempt to establish any direct or indirect link between the story of Joseph and the Egyptian story almost meaningless is the fact that the "spurned seductress" theme has always existed in real life. A man's rejection of a woman's sexual advances is something that happened in the past, is happening today, and will continue to happen in the future, everywhere. Using the theme of the "spurned seductress" to reach any conclusion about the historicity or non-historicity of Joseph's story, or that particular part of it, is untenable.

One common flaw in motif studies is that while they focus on the shared elements in stories, they do not properly and adequately appreciate the many more and substantial differences between those stories. For instance, the theme of the "spurned seductress" aside, the story of Joseph and the *Story of the Two Brothers* have hardly anything else in common. There are numerous differences between them and they consist of entirely different episodes. If the element of "spurned seductress" is considered sufficient to trace Joseph's story to the ancient Egyptian story, then any two stories could probably be linked with each other in some way.

I should also note in this particular example that while the Biblical story of Joseph may have been written around 10th century BCE, the story itself is supposed to have happened in the 16th century BCE, i.e. it predates the Egyptian story by a good few centuries.

Another observation that I would like to make is that there are authors who wrote in their novels and fiction about events and inventions that happened later. For instance, novelist Jules Verne (1828-1905) is known to have described future inventions, such as "flying machines," and achievements, such as "moon landing." The fact that these were motioned in novels and fiction, which are the equivalent of myths and legends in the ancient world, did not mean that they could not happen. Similarly, the existence of ancient stories about people with unusual abilities similar to those that modern technologies have granted all of us, such as the ability to fly, is no reason to reject the verity of these technologies. Let's look at the following *predictions* that were made almost half a millennium ago by the well-known English soothsayer Mother Shipton (ca. 1488-1561):

> Beneath the water, men shall walk
> shall ride, shall sleep, shall even talk.
> And in the air men shall be seen
> in white and black and even green.
> ....

For in those wondrous far off days
the women shall adopt a craze
to dress like men, and trousers wear
and to cut off their locks of hair.
They'll ride astride with brazen brow
as witches do on broomstick now.

And roaring monsters with man atop
does seem to eat the verdant crop
and men shall fly as birds do now
and give away the horse and plough.
....
When pictures seem alive with movements free
when boats like fishes swim beneath the sea,
when men like birds shall scour the sky
then half the world, deep drenched in blood shall die.

This poem is strikingly accurately descriptive of modern technological achievements and lifestyle changes. The fact that centuries ago someone predicted, guessed, or whatever the right term is, technologies, social, and behavioral changes that have become an intrinsic part of modern life has no bearing on the reality of these modern developments.

One particularly impressive instance of a written story that described in amazing accuracy future events concerns the drowning of the Titanic. In 1898, that is fourteen years before the Titanic sank, an American writer called Morgan Robertson wrote a novel called *Futility* about a giant liner that, in addition to being considered unsinkable like the Titanic, had many amazing similarities with its future, real-world counterpart. Both liners were British, made of steel, had 3 propellers, could make 25 knots, had 2 masts, and had 3,000 passenger capacity. Robertson's vessel was 800 feet, only 82 feet shorter than the Titanic. The imaginary liner had 24 lifeboats, and the real one had 20. Both had room on lifeboats for only less than half of their passengers. Both supposedly unsinkable liners set sail in April on their maiden voyages from Southampton to New York when they struck an ice berg and sank. The point of impact of both vessels was the starboard. The collision of the fictional liner took place at midnight, and that of the Titanic 20 minutes before midnight. Finally, Robertson's liner was called the Titan! With these amazing similarities, no wonder that after the sinking of the Titanic in 1912 Robertson's novel was republished, this time under the title *The Wreck of the Titan*!

The stunning similarities between the fictional story of the Titan and the real one of the Titanic have been the subject of argument between those who believe Robertson's story was precognitive, i.e. had paranormal elements to it, and those who seek more rational interpretations and consider the whole episode no more than a strange cluster of coincidences. This difference is a moot point for our current discussion. Regardless of how Robertson conceived his story, the fact that he did is what interests us. The reality of the story of the Titanic is beyond any doubt, and no reasonable person would suggest that the authenticity of that disaster should be questioned because an earlier novel had remarkable similarities with the story of the doomed ship!

Some may argue that the situation is different when a specific concept or story episode in the Bible appears not only in one or two, as in the examples above, but in *many* older and different cultural traditions. The presence of a story detail or plot in *many* different sources is taken to mean that it *must be* a natural product of man's way of thinking and imagination or widespread copying, and cannot be a reflection of an event that has really taken place. For instance, it is often pointed out that the concept of "virgin birth" is found in one form or another in the tradition and myths of many ancient nations that lived before Jesus, and it is thus concluded that the New Testament story of the virgin birth of Jesus is yet another variation of that product of the imagination of man or a copy of an earlier story. Mary's miraculous conception of Jesus is considered as no more rooted in reality than any of the similar fictional virginal conceptions.

It is misleading to call this a conclusion. This is an assumption. Unless it can be shown how imaginative thinking created and developed the specific instance of that concept or story, or prove that it was an act of copying similar accounts, it remains an unproven hypothesis. The repeated imagining or copying of a concept or an event by different individuals or groups of people does *not necessarily* mean that this concept could not be true or that this event could not happen in reality. Human imagination knows no limit, and with a history as long as that of man and the number of different traditions and cultures that man created, it should not surprise us to find that all kinds of thoughts and stories have been repeatedly fancied, in various places and at different times. This repeated appearance is no firm evidence of the non-historicity of those stories. Later in the book, I will discuss specific applications of this shortcoming of the secular approach to details of the story of Jesus, including the virgin birth. Here, I will discuss this flaw in the secular approach in the case of the concept of "flood."

The concept of a devastating "deluge" that leaves only a few people alive is found in the tradition of most cultures and civilizations. In a comprehensive study, Theodor Gaster (1969) reviewed variations of this story in the tradition and literature of the people of Mesopotamia, Egypt, Greece, Europe, India, Eastern Asia, Indonesia, New Guinea and Melanesia, Polynesia and Micronesia, Australia, North America, Central America and Mexico, and South America. Some cultures had several versions of the story. Clearly, some of the many flood stories are adaptations of each other, but equally certain is the fact that at least some of them must have been developed separately. A flood was so frequent an event in many places of the ancient world that it goes against common sense to suggest that all those accounts were mythical and could not have originated from real events of flood. The likelihood is that some accounts may refer to one particular flood, while others are based on different floods. The accuracy of these flood accounts is open to questioning, however, as ancient people in general tended to exaggerate and give events mythical or paranormal dimensions borrowed from their cultures.

A story of a major flood is also recorded in the Bible. Seeing the earth full of corruption and violence, God told Noah that He decided to destroy the earth and its inhabitants with a massive flood. God commanded Noah to build an ark to save him, his wife, his sons, and his daughters-in-law. He also ordered Noah to take on the Ark a male and female of every living species. When the flood started, the populated Ark was driven to the top of a mountain called Ararat. After the forty days that the flood lasted, Noah sent out a raven, and then a dove on three different occasions to test whether the water had dried up. When the third dove did not come back he concluded that it must have found a dry place, so he, his family, and the animals left the Ark (Gen. 6-8).

The Mesopotamian story of the flood is found in the Epic of Gilgamesh, the fullest version of which is found in an Akkadian recension from the 7th Century BCE, but fragments of versions of the story date back to at least one thousand years earlier. Gaster (1969: 82) claims that the Mesopotamian story is "undoubtedly the primary source" of the Biblical version of the flood. It is true that there are striking parallels between the Mesopotamian account and the Biblical story, which probably means that the Biblical story was influenced by its Mesopotamian counterpart or that they both were influenced by a common source. But this does not mean that the flood itself did not happen and that the Bible is not reporting a real event. It may not have happened exactly as described in the Bible or the Epic of Gilgamesh — and some of the details in the two accounts do look quite mythical — but there is every reason to believe that the story is based on a real flood. It would be actually odd if such a flood never took place. Once it is accepted that the flood has probably happened, there is suddenly far less pressure and justification to attempt to prove that the Biblical account is *completely* unhistorical.

Some may argue that cases such as those of the Titan/Titanic and the deluge are fundamentally different from the concept of virginal conception and other details in the story of Jesus in that the latter are *paranormal* in nature. This objection is invalid in this context, because the point of discussion here is not whether paranormal events can or cannot take place. The issue under discussion is whether the existence of older, similar versions, whether few or many, of a concept or story necessarily means that the latter is unreal or unhistorical.

It is important to stress here that the fact that some historical claims in the Bible have been shown to be wrong or inaccurate still does not justify the use of any of the two assumptions above.

1.1.3. Similarities Between the Qur'an and Jewish and Christian Writings

The third flawed assumption of the secular approach has caused the Qur'anic account of history to be almost completely ignored. It states that *most of the Qur'an's accounts were borrowed from similar stories in the Old and New Testaments and other early Jewish and Christian writings*. Similarities between Qur'anic texts and the Old and New Testaments and other early Jewish and Christian scriptures are usually taken to indicate that the Qur'an is no more than an inaccurate and distorted reproduction of stories and passages from those sources. This argument is taken, even by religious people, as evidence that the Qur'an *obviously could not have been revealed by God*. Differences between the Qur'an and those earlier sources, and Qur'anic material that cannot be linked to these writings, are both viewed as content that was authored by Muhammad alone or with the help of others. Biblical historical accounts are considered superior to the Qur'an's, even when no extra-Biblical evidence lends support to those accounts. While Biblical stories and details are given the chance to prove their historicity, Qur'anic stories are simply ignored.

The view that the Qur'an has derived its material from the Bible renders Qur'anic historical accounts worthless in studying history. As a result, studies of Biblical history and characters have systematically ignored the respective Qur'anic accounts. I would like to mention one example.

Hundreds and thousands of articles and books have been published on the Biblical account of the exodus of the Israelites from Ancient Egypt and how it relates to the history of that period as known from other sources. These writings show researchers desperately clinging to a shred of pottery unearthed from an ancient site or arguing the reading and/or translation of a few hardly legible words from an ancient inscription to prove one point or another. The Qur'anic story of the exodus, however, has been singularly neglected. Scholars do not even bother to show why the Qur'an's account should be dismissed. To the best of my knowledge, our 1999 book that compares the Qur'an's story with its Biblical account and examines both in the light of known history was the first, and probably still the only, dedicated study in English on the subject.

Let me give an example from that particular history. One difference between the story of Moses in the Qur'an and the Bible is the presence of a high ranking figure in Pharaoh's court called "Hāmān" in the Qur'an's version. Biblical scholars have noted that while the Biblical story of Moses does not have such a character, there is a Hāmān in the court of the Persian king Ahasuerus in the Biblical Book of Esther. It is suggested that the appearance of Hāmān in the Qur'an was the result of a misreading of the Bible which moved him from the court of Ahasuerus to the Egyptian court of Pharaoh. This is what *The Encyclopedia of Islam*, for instance, states in its entry for "Hāmān": "name of a person whom the Kur'an associates with

Pharaoh, because of a still unexplained confusion with the minister of Ahasuerus in the Biblical book of Esther" (Vajda, 1971: 110).

This statement has a number of problems. **First**, there is no evidence that the Qur'an's Hāmān was a reproduction of the Biblical Hāmān. **Second**, it ignores the possibility that there was someone called Hāmān in the Egyptian court of the Pharaoh in question. **Third**, it does not consider the possibility that it is the Bible which wrongly depicted Hāmān as the prime minister of the Persian king Ahasuerus. What is particularly telling is that the Book of Esther has long been known to contain serious historical problems. This Biblical book is considered so unhistorical that one study has concluded that it is "best seen as a historical novella set within the Persian empire" (Levenson, 1997: 25).

Additionally, the Bible is known to have anachronous problems — placing characters in the wrong historical periods and places. For instance, Pharaoh Shabtaka (ca. 697-690 BCE) appears in the Table of Nations (Gen. 10:7) as a Nubian tribe" (Redford, 1992: 258). **Fourth**, there is good reason to believe that if Hāmān ever existed, then he would have lived in Egypt, as his name sounds Egyptian. There is a detailed discussion of the Hāmān issue in the forthcoming revision of our book on the Israelites' exodus from Egypt.

I should emphasize again that the criticisms above are not targeted at the secular approach's legitimate attempt to subject historical claims in the Bible, the Qur'an, and any other source to unbiased examination and assess any account on its merits. They rather expose biases and use of unfounded assumptions that go against the declared aim and methods of this approach.

1.1.4. The Question of the Paranormal

There is one last point that I need to mention before moving on to discuss the Biblical approach. Many secular researchers reject out of hand any paranormal account, on the assumption that the paranormal does not exist. This stance is in total opposition to the Biblical and Qur'anic approaches which accept that miracles and supernatural events can take place. Needless to say, if paranormal events, such as miracles, cannot happen, then clearly the Bible and the Qur'an would be left with little credibility. Many of their claims and stories would have to be understood in a way different from how they are explained by the two books. For instance, Mary's conception of Jesus would be explained as the result of a normal relationship with a man rather than a miracle whereby a woman was made pregnant by divine intervention without the involvement of a man. On the other hand, if the paranormal and supernatural can take place, then this fundamental fact would always need to be considered by secular researchers when dealing with various Biblical and Qur'anic accounts. So a virginal conception, for instance, would not be dismissed simply because it is paranormal.

Rejecting the paranormal, however, is not really as simple and straightforward as many secularists claim. It is highly misleading to claim that it is unscientific to accept the paranormal and supernatural. The paranormal is a complex topic where science, philosophy, and anecdotal evidence have been used to support opposing views. While this subject has implications for the current study, it falls outside the scope of the book. It has been and is set to continue to be addressed by numerous books and articles, which the reader can consult for further reading. While leaving aside the question of the paranormal, this book will nevertheless present both religious and secular views, i.e. views that accommodate the paranormal and others that do not, but without discussing whether the paranormal can or cannot happen. The Qur'anic approach that the book takes, however, accommodates the paranormal.

1.2. The Biblical Approach

This is a faith-driven approach that considers the Bible, in both parts the Old and New Testaments, to be the Word of God. Consequently, the Bible's account of history is considered to be completely factual. The researcher who adopts this approach seeks to understand any extra-Biblical historical fact in line with what the Bible says. This reconciliation process may require coming up with a particular reading or interpretation of the Biblical text or the fact.

Setting out from the assumption that the Bible is a divine book, Biblicists who follow this approach clearly disagree with secularists who claim there are inaccurate and wrong information and internal inconsistencies in the Bible. Such claims are dismissed or explained away one way or another. Biblicists share with secular researchers the view that the Qur'an is based on the Bible and other Jewish and Christian sources and is not an independent source. In his classic book *The Original Sources of Islam*, which typifies the Biblical approach, Reverend William Tisdall has this to say:

> Arabia was a refuge for not a few heretics of different sects; and it is clear from the Qur'an (as we shall see) that, whether in written form or not, many of the mythical stories which are contained in the apocryphal Gospels and other similar works, together with certain heretical views on various subjects, must have reached Muhammad and have been accepted by him as true. (Tisdall, 1905: 140-141)

I criticized the adoption of this view by secular researchers because it is an unfounded assumption that goes against the claimed objectivity of that approach. The Biblical approach cannot be similarly criticized for its adoption of this view, because this view is a natural conclusion of the more fundamental assumption of this approach that the Bible is wholly accurate and truthful. As the Qur'an has similarities and differences with the Bible, it is natural for those who believe that the Bible is the Word of God to conclude that the Qur'an must have used material from the older book. Tisdall's words are a logical conclusion of the fundamental assumption of the Biblical approach.

What deserves criticism, however, are those not uncommon Biblical studies that try to show that the claim that the Qur'an has borrowed its content from other sources, including the Bible and other Jewish and Christian sources, is an *impartial* conclusion. Such studies often use double standards, applying one standard to the Qur'an and another to the Bible. Let me give an example. One popular claim among followers of the Biblical approach is that the Qur'an's claim that Jesus was born under a tree was borrowed from Buddhist and Greek sources. They point to the story of birth of Buddha and that of the Greek god Apollo both of whom are claimed to have been born under a tree. What these studies do not do, however, is to point out that many more similarities have been noted between the story of Buddha and the accounts in the Gospel, including sayings and events! The Biblical story of the birth of Moses in the 13th century BCE also has similarities with the birth of King Sargon of Akkad who lived 11 centuries earlier. If some similarities between the Qur'an and other sources mean that the Qur'an misappropriated material from those sources, then surely the same should be concluded about the Bible which contains details that resemble older historical writings.

I have already pointed out that such comparisons and conclusions are simply misleading. Claiming that the Qur'an is an unauthentic source because of the assumption that the Bible is the Word of God is one thing, and presenting that claim as an impartial conclusion or cold fact is another.

Obviously, one cannot object to the process of drawing a logical conclusion from a fundamental assumption, but it is perfectly legitimate to securitize the assumption itself and its application. It is equally logical to test any conclusion on its merits and draw inferences about the validity of its underlying assumption. In the course of our study of the story of Jesus in the Bible, the Qur'an, and history, we will carry out both tests. We will examine the Biblicists' assumption that the Bible is the Word of God and its logical conclusion that the Qur'an has misappropriated material from the Bible and other Jewish and Christian sources.

There are four main arguments that opponents of the Biblical approach make.

1.2.1. Internal Biblical Discrepancies

There are many clear discrepancies within the Bible, some of which we will encounter in this book. These contradictions can be found even within the four Gospels, which are our main sources on Jesus' life in the New Testament. These differences touch on various parts of these books and, accordingly, Jesus' life. I would like to highlight here one major difference, which is that between the Gospels of Mark, Matthew, and Luke, on the one hand, and the Gospel of John, on the other. Because of their similarities to each other, the former three have become to be known as the "Synoptics," which is derived from the Greek for "view together," as scholars could study them in parallel columns. John has substantial and irreconcilable differences with the Synoptic Gospels:

> It is impossible to think that Jesus spent his short ministry teaching in two such completely different ways, conveying such different contents, and that there were simply two traditions, each going back to Jesus, one transmitting 50 per cent of what he said and another one the other 50 per cent, with almost no overlaps. Consequently, for the last 150 or so years scholars have had to choose. They have almost unanimously, and I think entirely correctly, concluded that the teaching of the historical Jesus is to be sought in the synoptic gospels and that John represents an advanced theological development, in which meditations on the person and work of Christ are presented in the first person, as if Jesus said them. (Sanders, 1995: 70-71)

The label "Synoptic" should not give the wrong impression that Mark, Matthew, and Luke are consistent with each other. We will see that there are numerous disagreements between these three books, and even within each. The common use of the singular term "Gospel" to refer to the four Gospels in the sense of implying that they tell a coherent story is completely misleading. There are different Jesuses in the different Gospels, and there is more than one Jesus in any one Gospel.

Additionally, New Testament scholars do not consider the three Synoptics as equally independent sources. Mark, which is the oldest of the four canonical Gospels and dated to around 70 CE, is thought to have been used by the authors of Matthew and Luke when writing their own Gospels. These two Gospels, which are believed to have been composed around 80-90 and 70-100 CE, respectively, are also thought to have used, besides Mark, another source that is not existent anymore. The latter has become known as Q from the German word "Quelle" for "source." Thus, only Q and Mark are independent sources. While this "two-source hypothesis," as is known, is not accepted by everyone, it has been the predominant source theory for over one and a half century. The author of the Gospel of John is thought to have written it at the turn of the 1st century CE.

Another important fact to stress here is that the four Gospels are very different from the other equally important set of New Testament books: Paul's Epistles. These are the earliest books of the New Testament and were written over a period of 10 years, with the first of them, 1 Thessalonians, written around 50 CE. Unlike the Evangelists, Paul shows almost no interest in Jesus' life, focusing only on developing a theology based on the death and resurrection of the Messiah.

1.2.2. Unfactual Biblical Statements

Archaeological excavations in Palestine, which started in the 19th century, have revealed inaccurate and wrong historical information in the Bible. The Biblical account of times, places, and events has substantial differences with the picture painted by archaeological finds and historical records. We will address some of these untrue Biblical claims that relate to the story of Jesus in this book. Naturally, followers of this approach have attempted to explain away such problems in a number of ways, including providing a new interpretation of the Biblical text or disputing the significance of finds. The attempts to explain away Biblical internal discrepancies or reconcile Biblical text with extra-Biblical evidence have different degrees of plausibility and credibility. Other than the followers of the Biblical approach, scholars are unanimous that the Bible contains clear inaccuracies and mistakes.

Our growing knowledge about 1st century Judaism and Palestine has also shown that certain historical claims in the Gospels are wrong. We will study some of these later in the book.

1.2.3. The indefinability of the "Bible" and "Scripture"

The third argument targets the most fundamental assumption of this approach as it questions how "scripture" has become identified with the "Bible," and highlights the fact that the term "Bible" is almost indefinable. Contrary to what the Biblical approach implies, the term "Bible" does not mean the same thing even to its believers. There is disagreement not only over the authenticity of specific passages in certain Biblical books, but also on which books constitute the *official Bible* or "canon." Certain books that are considered canonical by some denominations are noncanonical or "apocryphal" for others. As many as seven books in the canon of the Catholic and Orthodox churches — Tobias, Judith, Baruch, Ecclesiasticus, Wisdom, First and Second Maccabees — as well as certain parts to the Books of Esther and Daniel are considered apocryphal by the Protestants. The Catholics and Orthodox call these seven books "deuterocanonical" or the "second canon," because they were declared canonical only as late as the 16th century by the Council of Trent. These books are rejected by the Jews also. The Jewish Bible does not contain any of the Christian New Testament books.

Of particular interest here are passages that New Testament books present as quotations from the scripture but which cannot be found in the Old Testament of any group. One instance is found in this passage from the Gospel of John: "let the one who believes in me drink. Just as the scripture says, 'From within him will flow rivers of living water'" (John 7:38). This quote is nowhere to be found in the Old Testament. Another example comes from the Epistle of James: "do you think the scripture means nothing when it says, 'The spirit that God caused to live within us has an envious yearning'?" (Jam. 4:5). Later in the book we will examine in more detail such quotations. Either the writers of these New Testament books were mistaken in attributing those passages to the scripture, or they meant by the term "scripture" writings other than the Old Testament. Both possibilities seriously undermine the Biblical approach.

The confusion over the meaning of the term "Bible" is not confined to the Old Testament but covers also the other half of the Bible, the New Testament. As Christian writings are our main interest in this book, I will focus on them in the rest of this section.

The classification of which books are canonical and which are not was a centuries-long political process that involved considerable conflicts between many groups and individuals. For almost 150 years after Jesus there was no "canon," and many books were adopted and discredited by various Christian groups over the centuries before we ended up with the current canon. The first attempt to produce a Christian canon was undertaken by Marcion in the middle of the 2nd century. Marcion's set of sacred texts included only 10 letters of Paul and a form of the Gospel of Luke. He completely dismissed the Old Testament. Many scholars believe that it was Marcion's canon that prompted concerned Christians, who did not agree with Marcion, to establish what ultimately became the New Testament. By around the end of the 2nd century an increasing number of Christians were claiming that Mark, Matthew, Luke, and John were *the authentic Gospels*. But the first Christian mention on record that the New Testament consists of the 27 books that we have today dates as late as 367 CE in a letter from Athanasius, the bishop of Alexandria, to the Egyptian churches. Tens other books that were considered sacred by various groups for centuries failed to make it into the canon.

Although the label "apocrypha" has come to imply inauthenticity, inaccuracy, and little value, this is actually the modern meaning of this term. Many books that are derogated as apocrypha were for centuries revered by so many early Christians. In her book *Studies in the Gospel of Thomas*, R. M. Wilson says the following about the ancient meaning of the term "apocrypha" (from the Greek ἀπόκρυφος for "hidden"):

> The Greek word Apokrufos did not always have the disparaging sense which later became attached to it. In Gnostic circles it was used of books the contents of which were too sacred to be divulged to the common herd, and it was in fact the heretical associations which it thus came to possess which led to its use as a term of disparagement. In the Nag Hammadi library, for example, one document bears the title Apocryphon or Secret Book of John, another that of Apocryphon of James, and several Gnostic gospels contain solemn warnings against imparting their contents to any save the deserving, or for the sake of material gain. (Wilson 1960, pp 11-12)

It is with such facts in mind that we need to think of the value and implications of apocryphal writings.

Decisions by powerful men ultimately determined which books formed the canon. But copying and translating the early manuscripts also played a major role in defining the canonical text. Until around the first third of the 4th century, manuscripts of the Christian books were being produced by amateur copyists for their fellow believers. These amateurs were far more likely to make unintentional mistakes than professional scribes, and their beliefs often made them deliberately change the text they copied. The conversion of the Roman emperor Constantine to Christianity in 312 led to massive conversions to the faith, including many highly educated and skilled people. In 331, the emperor commissioned Eusebius, bishop of Caesarea, to produce 50 copies of the Bible to send to the main churches. This major work must have been undertaken by professional scribes.

The fact that there were significant differences between the different copies of any one Christian book was well known to the early Christian scholars. This is how the 3rd century father Origen complained about the corruption of the Christian manuscripts:

> The differences among the manuscripts have become great, either through the negligence of some copyists or through the perverse audacity of others; they either neglect to check over what they have transcribed, or, in the process of checking, they make additions or deletions as they please. (Origen, *Commentary on Matthew*, 15.14; cited in Ehrman, 2007: 52)

New Testament scholars always knew that there were many textual variants in the available manuscripts, but the seriousness and enormity of the scribal changes remained well underestimated and understated for many centuries. This changed in 1707 when Oxford scholar John Mill published his edition of the Greek New Testament. Over the course of 30 years, Mill studied about 100 manuscripts, citations of New Testament texts by early Church fathers, and various versions of the New Testament. He found a staggering 30,000 textual variants (Ehrman, 2007: 84)!

This figure shocked many people then, but it can be equally shocking to many today. Mill's study still had limitations. He knew only Latin, in addition to Greek, so he did not consider manuscripts in other ancient languages; he was not completely comprehensive; and he did not report all his findings, such as changes of word order. Also, while Mill had access to only around 100 manuscripts, today we have around 5700 Greek manuscripts that range from some that contain the New Testament in its entirety to others that are only very small fragments. Also, today there are about 10,000 Latin manuscripts, as well manuscripts in other ancient languages, such as Syriac and Coptic. Finally, there is large literature of Church fathers quoting New Testament manuscripts they had access to. So how many textual variants do we know of today? This is how Professor Bard Ehrman, a leading authority on early Christianity, sums up the situation in his brilliant book *Misquoting Jesus*:

> Scholars differ significantly in their estimates — some say there are 200,000 variants known, some say 300,000, some say 400,000 or more! We do not know for sure because, despite impressive developments in computer technology, no one has yet been able to count them all. Perhaps, as I indicated earlier, it is best simply to leave the matter in comparative terms. There are more variations among our manuscripts than there are words in the New Testament. (Ehrman, 2007: 89-90)

Ehrman confirms that most of these variants are negligible: "of all the hundreds of thousands of textual changes found among our manuscripts, most of them are completely insignificant, immaterial, of no real importance for anything other than showing that scribes could not spell or keep focused any better than the rest of us." But he warns that "it would be wrong, however, to say — as people sometimes do — that the changes in our text have no real bearing on what the texts mean or on the theological conclusions that one draws from them. We have seen, in fact, that just the opposite is the case" (Ehrman, 2007: 207-208). Another important point to note is that for a long time, earlier editions and translation of the New Testament did not use the best ancient manuscripts. For instance, the King James Bible was based on an inferior form of the text.

Given the fundamental differences between Christians since the early days of the faith on which texts belong to scripture, the flawed political process of establishing the canon, and the unreliability of the copying and translation of the text, the term "Bible" is extremely difficult, in fact impossible, to define and highly unconvincing as a referent to the "scripture." It does not really matter whether the first Christian texts were inspired by God or not. We do not have those texts; what we have today is substantially edited and changed texts.

1.2.4. The False Superiority of the Canon

This leads us to the fourth argument that questions the validity of the Biblical approach: a canonical book is not *necessarily* more authentic, historical, or accurate than an apocryphal book. The process that resulted in the inclusion of some books but not others in the canon could not have guaranteed that the superior books were canonized. Similarly, the popularity of any version of a text in any book provides no assurance whatsoever that it is more reliable than other variants of that text.

Commenting in their book *The Historical Jesus* on the early Christian books, New Testament scholars Gerd Theissen and Annette Merz state that: "Historically, it has been recognized that the Christianity of the church, to which we owe the selection and establishment of the canon, is the result of a lengthy process within which other traditions, with writings which similarly went back to the beginnings, were excluded." They go on to cite Walter Bauer's *Orthodoxy and Heresy in Earliest Christianity*, which was first published in 1934, which showed that "in some areas like Egypt and East Syria (Edessa), forms of Christianity later regarded as heterodox chronologically preceded the 'orthodox' communities. 'Catholic' and 'heretical' views existed side by side for decades in the same communities in Asia Minor and Macedonia, before orthodoxy established itself under Roman influence in the second century" (Theissen & Merz, 1999: 23). They stress that "the idea that the originally pure apostolic teaching was *later* distorted by heresies is a dogmatic construct. 'Orthodoxy and heresy' developed chronologically in parallel, and each borrowed from the other. The groups which were later excluded as heretical also (at least in part) refer to the earliest Christian traditions and developed these in accordance with their needs — here in principle they were no different from the 'orthodox' communities" (Theissen & Merz, 1999: 21).

The untrue claim that the canonical Gospels represent the earliest form of Christianity is usually coupled with the equally wrong claim that the noncanonical writings are far more legendary and fanciful than the canonical sources. For instance, the Methodist minister and author of *Jesus in the Qur'an* Geoffrey Parrinder describes them as follows: "The book of James is one of the oldest Christian apocrypha, upon which many others depend, adding to its stories. Most of this must be regarded as legend, and there is little evidence of any historical fact apart from that which is derived from the Gospel" (Parrinder, 1995: 65). The assumption that early, noncanonical writings have no value whatsoever, or even less value than canonical books, is not borne out by facts. A genuinely objective approach would be, as Theissen and Merz stress, to apply the same critical standards to all books. They draw attention to the fact that "the Synoptic Gospels, too, contain 'legends' and 'fantastic narratives.' Distinction should always be made only on the basis of individual texts — independently of whether they belong in the canon" (Theissen & Merz, 1999: 21).

This fourth and major argument against the Biblical approach has been totally overlooked by Biblicists, as shown in this sample quotation from Tisdall:

> Muhammad seems to have learnt what little he knew of our Lord and His Apostles from very unreliable hearsay. We shall see that the agreement in detail between what the Qur'an relates on these subjects and what may be found in apocryphal and heretical literature is very remarkable. Here again Muhammad seems to have had a wonderful talent for rejecting the true and accepting the false, just as in the case of the Jewish traditions. (Tisdall, 1905: 142-143)

Preferring the canonical to the apocryphal books and declaring the former as *the* authentic ones, or even *more* authentic, are faith-driven and cannot find support outside the realms of faith. This is one reason why this book pays almost as much attention to relevant apocryphal books as it does to the canon. The other reason is that the Qur'an is accused of borrowing from the apocrypha, as suggested by Tisdall.

It is not possible to even argue that the canonical Gospels were written by more reliable authors than those of the extra-canonical gospels, as the identities of those authors are unknown. The names associated with those books are conventional and do not reflect knowledge of their authorship. The four Gospels appear to have been quoted in the 1st half of the 2nd century, but always anonymously. They start to suddenly appear titled around 180 CE, but by then there were many gospels, not only the four that were eventually canonized (Sanders, 1995: 64). Probably certain names were associated with the Gospels to differentiate them from and position them as superior to other, competing writings. Professor Ed Parish Sanders (1995: 65) convincingly argues that "It is unlikely that Christians knew the names of the authors of the gospels for a period of a hundred years or so, but did not mention them in any of the surviving literature (which is quite substantial)". Also, had the author of any of these Gospels been a credible firsthand observer of the events or a disciple of Jesus he would have undoubtedly made this clear to distinguish his Gospel from competing writings and add credibility to it.

1.3. The Secular-Biblical Approach

In an informative summary of the history of research into Jesus' life, Mark Allan Powell (1999: 18-36) identified four different stages. In the first stage, before the Enlightenment, scholars adopted what I have labeled as the Biblical approach. The truth of the Bible was taken for granted, but the fact that the New Testament contains four different *historical* accounts of Jesus had to be addressed. Writers focused their efforts on reconciling the accounts of the Gospels. The earliest such attempt was undertaken as early as the middle of the 2nd century CE by an Assyrian called Tatian, who was a student of the Christian apologist Justin Martyr. About 100 years after the earliest Gospel was written, Tatian produced a harmony of the four Gospels in one continuous narrative which he called *Diatessaron* or "four-in-one." Gospel harmonies would not qualify as *historical* research in the modern sense of the word.

The second stage, which came after the Enlightenment, is when scholars started "the quest for the historical Jesus," writing biographies or "lives" of Jesus. A life of Jesus might harmonize the four Gospel accounts, but it has three major differences with the earlier harmonies. **First**, it painted a particular image of Jesus, such as seeing him as "social reformer," and interpreted the Gospels in line with the adopted image. **Second**, Gospel material that was incompatible with the hypothesized image was excluded, implying that this content is incorrect. **Third**, the image of Jesus was not drawn exclusively using Gospel material, but incorporated also the author's assumptions and thoughts to fill in gaps about things such as Jesus' motivations and goals. The rationalism of the Enlightenment also introduced suspicion about Jesus' miracles. Powell (1999: 19-25) reviews briefly some of the most important works of the hundreds of lives of Jesus that were produced, most of which were written in the 19th century.

The third stage began early in the 50's of the 20th century. It did not produce Jesus lives, but the "new quest," as this phase is known, focused on identifying what is historical from what is not in the Gospels. The historicity of Jesus' reported sayings and deeds was checked using the growing knowledge of the time of Jesus provided by historical and archaeological research. New discoveries allowed better and more accurate understanding of Jesus' time, and that was reflected in the research into his life.

Early in the nineties of the 20th century, a new approach to researching Jesus' life emerged, which Nicholas Thomas Wright, the bishop of Durham, calls the "third quest." This kind of research stressed Jesus' 1st century Jewish background and portrayed him as an eschatological prophet. Wright believes that the new quest and the third quest can coexist as two different strands of research into Jesus' life.

Excluding the phase of Gospel harmonies, which completely adhered to the Biblical approach, "Jesus' lives" ushered the beginning of the gradual attempt to make Jesus' life and the Gospels the subject of proper historical research. This may suggest that academic research into Jesus' life has been moving progressively from the realms of religion and theology into that of science and history. This is only partly true. Modern scholars are surely far more aware of the difference between religious beliefs and cold facts than their predecessors, but this is no guarantee that their conclusions and theories are driven by objective facts only. Let me give an example.

Apart from a minority of scholars who strictly follow the Biblical approach, Biblical scholars, like some lay believers, concede that little or much of the historical information in the Bible is wrong. Yet this realization does not seem to have done much to weaken the acceptance of many of Biblical theology. This position is rather illogical and untenable. The fact that many verifiable historical statements are wrong or inaccurate means that the Bible is unreliable, and that theological statements, which are by nature unverifiable, are possibly or even likely to be also flawed or inaccurate. If the history in the Gospels is wrong, then there is no reason to believe that theological arguments they make or statements they attribute to Jesus cannot be similarly untrue or at least inaccurate.

One view that was developed to reconcile the fact that the Bible contains incorrect historical information with the faith in the verity of the religious doctrines and claims of this book is to suggest that history did not mean to those ancient authors what it means to us today. Historical accuracy, it is claimed, did not matter to them as it does to us today. Surely modern historians are more attentive to details and accuracy, but all evidence suggests that the ancient authors of the Bible did mean by and large to report what they believed took place.

Geza Vermes, a prominent authority on the historical Jesus, criticizes the refusal of a large number of New Testament experts to accept that "the Synoptic evangelists were popular story-tellers" and their preference to consider them mainly as "conveyers of a doctrinal message disguised as history." He attributes this tendency to continued influence by the famous dictum of the German scholar Rudolf Bultmann who stated in 1926 that "we can now know almost nothing concerning the life and personality of Jesus, since the early Christian sources show no interest in either." Bultmann also attributed the impossibility of this knowledge to the "fragmentary and often legendary" nature of those writings, as well as the absence of other sources (Bultmann, 1958: 8-9). Vermes then goes on to make this strong argument:

> This view is inspired, I fear, more by a learned Christian believer's disinclination to face up to the real Jesus than by the nature of the Gospel evidence itself. If the evangelists had intended to report, as Bultmann and his followers claim, not the life, ideas and aspirations of Jesus, but the doctrinal message corresponding to the spiritual and organizational needs of the primitive church, they would have been better advised to adopt the more suitable literary form of letters, tracts, or sermons than to write a fake biography. (Vermes, 2000: 147)

The power of Vermes' arguments can be easily seen if we compare Paul's writings with the Gospels. The former was completely interested in Christological theology, so he wrote letters that focused exclusively on developing and promoting his theological arguments. It is not only that he did not seek to use history to build his theology around it, but he completely ignored it, because it was not necessary. Contrary to Paul, the Evangelists focused mainly on Jesus' history, although they, and in particular John, showed also interest in theology and at times manipulated the history they reported to reflect that theology. But had any of them been interested in only promoting his theology and not also presenting a history of Jesus, his writings would have been much more like Paul's and certainly not like the Gospel he wrote. Also, the Gospels are full of historical details that have no clear theological function.

Another interesting indication that the Gospels were meant to report Jesus' history comes from Matthew. This Evangelist was so keen on showing that certain episodes in Jesus' life fulfilled Old Testament prophecies about the Messiah. Yet he had to present non-prophetic passages as prophecies, change prophecies, or take them out of context in order to make them appear applicable to Jesus. In other words, he was so convinced that he was reporting Jesus' real history that he manipulated Old Testament passages to make them predict and confirm that history.

Also, Luke was absolutely clear that he reported Jesus' history in his Gospel:

> Now many have undertaken to compile an account of the things that have been fulfilled among us, like the accounts passed on to us by those who were eyewitnesses and servants of the word from the beginning. So it seemed good to me as well, because I have followed all things carefully from the beginning, to write an orderly account for you, most excellent Theophilus, so that you may know for certain the things you were taught. (Luke 1:1-4)

His other book, Acts, is also a book on history, although of the disciples and apostles.

Vermes is probably right about Bultmann's continued influence, but on a more fundamental level the view that the Gospels are not books of history is driven by a desire to maintain the credibility of its theology, after its history lost credibility. This view is an attempt to avoid the fact that the wrong information in the Bible poses a problem not only for those who are fascinated by the history it contains, but equally to the believers in the religion it promotes. Scholars who adopt this view often end up rewriting an alternative history to that of the Gospels in order to reflect their, essentially, theological image of Jesus. I am calling this approach "secular-Biblical" because it borrows from the secular and Biblical approaches.

Interestingly, if the Bible's authors did not mean to talk about history as we know it today and that they used historical stories *symbolically* to convey particular messages then other parts or much of the Bible, including its theology, might also be *symbolic*, meaning that they do not mean what they appear to mean.

1.4. The Qur'anic Approach

Unsurprising, this approach is based on accepting the Qur'an's claim to be the Word of God which Muhammad received and communicated, without any change, to people. It seeks to understand history and everything that the Qur'an addresses in line with what this book says.

1.4.1. Islamic Sacred Texts

The Qur'an is not the only text that is considered sacred in Islam, but there are compelling reasons for focusing on the Qur'an only in this book.

There are three kinds of texts that Muslims consider sacred. The **first** is the Qur'an, which is believed to have been preserved as it was revealed by God to Muhammad.

The **second** category comprises the reports about what the Prophet Muhammad said, did, or approved of. These texts, which are significantly larger in size than the Qur'an, are known as *ḥadīth* (saying, news, report, or narration). These highly venerated texts are considered by most Muslims as essential to understanding the Qur'an, and they form the basis for a good deal of the Islamic laws. The subcategory of *ḥadīth* (plural *aḥādīth*) that is relevant to our study here is the sayings that are attributed to the Prophet. While the Prophet is believed to have spoken and acted under the guidance of God, his words are not considered to be God's. They are the utterances of a human being expressing divine revelations to him.

Another difference with the Qur'an is that the Prophetic sayings are not necessarily reported exactly as the Prophet spoke them. For instance, a saying may be found in more than one wording in the same book, and yet in other different variations in other books. This difference is considered by Muslim scholars as an attribute of Prophetic sayings. I think this view is a reaction to the natural, serious implication of this observation: these textual differences undermine the reliability of the reported Prophetic sayings.

Different writers are bound to produce slightly or significantly different reports of the same event or saying, and some of these changes can compromise partly or completely the accuracy of the report. We will see examples of this when we study how the different Evangelists reported a certain event or saying and when we look at some Prophetic sayings in Chapter 20.

The simple fact is that any writer who undertook the extremely difficult task of compiling the sayings of the Prophet many decades after his death could not have ensured that his compilation contained only accurate or even authentic sayings. For instance, the Sunni authoritative compilations of Prophetic sayings, which are Al-Bukhārī's and Muslim's, were written over two centuries after the Prophet. The process of compiling the Prophetic sayings and its unreliability may be compared to the unreliable process of forming the canon and classifying the rejected texts as apocrypha.

Unsurprisingly then, unlike the Qur'an which has preserved its original text and whose authenticity is accepted by all Muslims, the sayings of the Prophet are the subject of so much disagreement. All Muslims accept that whatever Prophet Muhammad said is absolutely true and must be followed by all Muslims, but there is sharp disagreement on what he exactly said. Scholars of the two major branches of Islam disagree on which compilations of Prophetic sayings are authoritative. Many sayings that are accepted by Sunnis as authentic are rejected by Shias as fake, and vice versa. Scholars within the same branch have also disagreed on the authenticity of some sayings. These differences exist between scholars of even minor denominations. This serious problem with the sayings literature makes the term *ḥadīth* almost as indefinable as the term "Bible" is.

There is a **third** but much smaller corpus of literature known as *aḥādīth qudsiyyah* or "sacred sayings." These are considered to be, like the Qur'an, divine revelations that, unlike the Qur'an, the Prophet expressed in his own words. The *aḥādīth qudsiyyah* are subject to the same controversy as the Prophetic sayings.

The Qur'an is not only theologically, being the exact words of God, unique and distinct from the *ḥadīth* and *aḥādīth qudsiyyah*. The history, authenticity, and consistency of the Qur'an's text also set it aside from the other sacred texts, as we shall see in the next section.

This book will focus completely on the Qur'an, citing some Prophetic sayings only at times for specific purposes.

1.4.2. The Authenticity of the Qur'an

The existence of only one version of the Qur'an's text attests to its authenticity. The full strength of this argument becomes clear only when we consider the major doctrinal and political differences between Muslims.

Even though scholars from different denominations have always had differences about the *interpretation* of the Qur'an, they are unanimous in their acceptance of the authenticity of its text. Contentious Prophetic sayings are often used by different scholars to interpret Qur'anic passages differently, but the Qur'an itself unites scholars of different denominations and convictions. It is impossible to exaggerate the significance of this consensus given that some of the interpretational differences are very serious and reflect fundamental doctrinal divisions.

The serious division over the succession of Prophet Muhammad, which gradually developed into the major doctrinal and political split between Sunnis and Shias, ensued immediately after the Prophet's death. Had different Muslims believed in different versions of the Qur'an, no one could have managed to destroy all those copies and make every Muslim keep, read, and pass on the same Qur'an. It would have been practically impossible. Also, had there been any real doubt about the authenticity of the Qur'an at any point in the past 14 centuries, it would have been inevitable that those doctrinal differences would have resulted in the spread of different versions of the Qur'an. Each doctrine would have had its own version of the Qur'an to support its views — just as different Christian denominations and sects had and have different versions of the scripture — rather than rely completely on different interpretations of the same version. No attempt by any secular or religious authority could have ensured that only one version of the Qur'an survived, if there were more than one in circulation. Any such attempt would have failed as the Church — despite its enormous, peaceful and violent, efforts down the centuries — failed in unifying Christians around one set of books.

Also, Arabs before Islam were very skilled in memorizing poetry, and they utilized this skill after their conversion to memorize the Qur'an by heart. Memorizing the whole Qur'an is still a common practice among Muslims and believed to be a source of blessings. There were numerous "memorizers," or *ḥuffāẓ* as they are known in Arabic, of the Qur'an since the time of the Prophet, and it is these who were usually sent out to spread the message of Islam. Had people memorized different versions of the Qur'an, no one could have removed those *virtual* copies. That would have been even more difficult than the impossible task of removing all physical copies of any different version of the Qur'an. It would have been inevitable that at least some of those memorized versions would be written down and distributed. No one and no measure could have prevented that.

According to old Muslim historians, Abū Bakr aṣ-Ṣiddīq (632-634 CE), the first caliph or ruler of Muslims after the Prophet, officially compiled the Qur'an in one written volume. Many, and perhaps most, people used to have parts of it in written form, and some had complete copies of it. The third caliph, 'Uthmān bin 'Affān (644-656 CE), sent out copies of the complete Qur'an to the various Muslim lands. 'Uthmān is said to have undertaken this action after the spread of Islam in non-Arabic speaking lands, because he and others were concerned that inaccurate versions of the Qur'an could develop in those areas because Arabic was not the first language of those people. The idea was to have all existing copies of the Qur'an burned and new copies of the master copy made and distributed. Some western scholars try to present this as an attempt by 'Uthmān to impose one Qur'an instead of the several versions that were in existence. In addition to the practical impossibility of this task which I have already explained, there is another equally important argument that completely undermines this suggestion.

Abū Bakr and 'Uthmān were both at the center of the schism between the Sunnis and Shias. There is no way that the Shias, who did not accept either of the two caliphs as a legitimate successor of Prophet Muhammad, favoring the Prophet's cousin 'Alī bin Abī Ṭālib, could have got rid of their Qur'ans for one compiled and approved by Abū Bakr and distributed by 'Uthmān. Even after 'Alī (656-661 CE) succeeded 'Uthmān he never distributed a different Qur'an, and no new Qur'an ever appeared. Indeed, 'Alī is said to have been consulted by the caliphs on the compilation and distribution of the Qur'an. Had there been any doubts about the official version of the Qur'an, different versions would have inevitably appeared. The major differences between Sunnis and Shias have been centered on interpretations of some verses, but not on whether there are missing verses from or inauthentic verses in the Qur'an. A good and concise work in English on the history of the written text of the Qur'an is Ahmad Von Denffer's (2000) *Ulūm al-Qur'an: An Introduction to the Sciences of the Qur'an*. A much more detailed examination of this subject, but in Arabic, can be found in Muhammad Az-Zarqānī's (undated) *Manāhil al-'I'rfān fi 'Ulūm al-Qur'ān (Sources of Knowledge of the Sciences of the Qur'an)*.

This is a *rational* discussion of why the Qur'an we have today must be the same original text that Prophet Muhammad communicated to the early Muslims. This is the view of the overwhelming majority of not only Muslim but non-Muslim scholars also.

This unique phenomenon is also predicted in the Qur'an but explained as a *divine miracle*:

Surely it is We who revealed the *Dhikr* (Qur'an), and surely, We are its Guardian (15.9).

Surely those who disbelieved in the *Dhikr* when it came to them [were wrong]; and surely it is an impregnable Book (41.41). Falsehood cannot come to it from anywhere; [it is] a revelation from One who is Wise and Praised (41.42).

These verses do, among other things, set the Qur'an aside from the Jewish and Christian scriptures which the Qur'an claims were not the subject of a similar divine protection so were tampered with.

Judaism and Christianity are not defined by the words and acts of Moses and Jesus only. The holy books of both religions are written by other figures, although the writers are said to have been guided spiritually when writing those books. The credibility of these books, and ultimately the religions they represent, depends very much on the credibility of those authors also, not only of Moses and Jesus.

This is a fundamental difference between Islam and the other two great religions. The credibility of the Islamic faith rests solely on the credibility of the Qur'an and the prophethood of Muhammad. Muhammad claimed to have received the Qur'an from God and that neither he nor anyone else contributed to it. The Qur'an is the only divine text in Islam. No spiritual experience of any other Muslim figure, ancient or modern, constitutes part of the faith, and no other writings have a claim to inerrability — not even the words attributed to Muhammad or the *aḥādīth qudsiyyah*, which were reported down the centuries by numerous people. The fact that Muhammad's prophethood is the only foundation of Islam is manifested in the fact that the following two verses form the declaration of faith in Islam: "There is no god save Allah" (37.35, 47.19) and "Muhammad is the messenger of Allah" (48.29).

1.4.3. The Qur'an and Other Scriptures

The Qur'an says that it is the last of a number of books that God revealed to various Prophets before Muhammad (570-632 CE). These books include the "Taurāt (Torah)", which was revealed to Moses, and the "Injīl," which is the book that God gave to Jesus and which we will discuss in detail in Chapter 17. Coming from the same, divine source, these books carry fundamentally one and the same message. They all called people to worship the one and only God, whose Arabic name in the Qur'an is Allah, and to do good deeds in preparation for the Day of Resurrection when the pious get rewarded in paradise and the disbelievers are punished in hell. It is no surprise, then, that part of the message of the Injīl is to confirm the divine source of the Torah, and part of the message of the Qur'an is to confirm the Torah and the Injīl:

And We caused Jesus, son of Mary, to follow in their (the prophets') footsteps, confirming that which was revealed before him in the Torah, and We bestowed on him the Injīl wherein is guidance and a light, confirming that which was revealed before it in the Torah, and as a guidance and an admonition to the Allah-fearing (5.46).

He has sent down to you [O Muhammad!] the Book with truth, confirming that which was revealed before it, and He sent down the Torah and the Injīl (3.3) before it; and He sent down the criterion [of judgment between right and wrong] (3.4).

The fact that the Qur'an confirms the message of the Torah and the Injīl implies that its teaching has similarities with both books. The Qur'an also covers, though briefly, the life of some of the prophets who are mentioned in the two earlier books, so the stories of these prophets are another area of similarity.

The Qur'an tells us that the Torah and the Injīl were available to the Jews and Christians, whom the Qur'an call "People of the Book" in reference to the revelation of divine books to them, of the Arabian peninsula at the time of the revelation of the Qur'an (see also 2.44, 2.113, 5.43):

Say [O Muhammad!]: "O People of the Book! You follow no good till you observe the Torah, the Injīl, and that which has been revealed to you from your Lord"; and surely that which has been revealed to you from your [O Muhammad!] Lord shall make many of them increase in insolence and disbelief, so do not be sad for the disbelieving people (5.68).

The Qur'an says that the two books were not readily accessible to people though. This may mean that these books were made inaccessible to non-Jews, but it is more likely that it means that the religious authorities considered access to these books part of their special privileges and kept them away from people in general. They would reveal parts of the book that served their needs but conceal the parts that did not suit them (see also 2.140, 2.159, 2.174, 3.71, 3.187):

They do not make a proper estimate of Allah's status when they say: "Allah has not revealed anything to a human being." Say [O, Muhammad!]: "Who, then, did reveal the Book which Moses brought — a light and a guidance to people — which you make into [separate] sheets which you show while you conceal much, and you were taught what you and your fathers did not know?" Say: "Allah," then leave them playing in their muddle (6.91).

O People of the Book! Our Messenger has come to you, expounding to you much of that which you used to hide of the Book, and forgiving much. Here has come to you a light from Allah and manifest Book (5.15).

One mistake that some make when reading these and similar verses is to conclude that the Old Testament and the New Testament are the Torah and Injīl, respectively. There are major differences between these two books, on one hand, and the Bible and other early Jewish and Christian writings, on the other. The

Qur'an tells us that Israelite priests tampered with the Torah which God sent to them (also 2.75, 4.46, 5.41):

> And among them are illiterates who know not the Book but only imagine it in line with their wishes, and they only guess (2.78). Woe, then, to those who write the book with their hands and then say "This is from Allah" to get a small price for it; therefore woe to them for what their hands have written and woe to them for what they earn (2.79).
>
> But because of their breach of their covenant We cursed them and made their hearts hard: they altered words from their contexts, and they forgot a part of what they were reminded of; and you [O Muhammad!] will continue to discover treachery from them, save a minority of them; so pardon them and overlook [their misdeeds]; surely Allah loves those who do righteous deeds [to others] (5.13).

Verse 3.78 below seems to refer to changing the Injīl, as the next verse mentions the wrong development of the image of Jesus from a human being to divine:

> And surely there is amongst them a party who distorts the Book with their tongue that you [O you who believe!] may consider it to be part of the Book, when it is not part of the Book, and they say: "It is from Allah," while it is not from Allah, and they tell lies about Allah whilst they know (3.78). It is not [possible] for a human being to whom Allah had given the Book, Wisdom, and Prophethood, that he should then say to people: "Be my servants rather than Allah's"; but rather [he would say]: "Be faithful servants of the Lord by virtue of your constant teaching of the Book and of your constant study thereof" (3.79).

The Qur'an refers to *two different kinds of texts* that were treated as divine by Jews and Christians at the time of Prophet Muhammad: first, Torah and Injīl texts; second, other writings that were either partially based on the divine books or completely written by man. Some of those unauthentic sources were considered by some as part of the Torah and Injīl.

This is the Qur'an's explanation of the differences and similarities it has with the Bible and other early Jewish and Christian writings. The similarities point to texts that were revealed by the one and only source of all divine books, God, and were not changed by man. The differences are the result of changing the original text of the Torah and Injīl by man or the introduction of man authored texts. This is the Qur'anic perspective which most secular and Biblical scholars consistently ignore when stressing the popular view the Qur'an *must* have appropriated content from the Bible and other Jewish and Christian sources (e.g. Mourad, 1999).

The Qur'an pointed out 14 centuries ago what historians, archaeologists, and even Biblicists started to accept only 2 centuries ago: even if the Bible is seen as *partially* accurate, it cannot be considered as *totally* correct. In religious terms, it cannot be the work of God who never errs. I have already presented in my discussion of the Biblical approach some of the facts and arguments that not only show the man-driven process of compiling the Bible, but also show problems in that book.

Some Qur'anic verses have similarities with canonical and apocryphal passages. According to the Biblical approach, this not only confirms that the Qur'an was copied from Jewish and Christian writings, but also that the author of the Qur'an could not differentiate between authentic and unauthentic sources, thus copying from apocryphal sources also. I explained earlier why any attempt to distinguish between the canon and apocrypha in terms of accuracy and authenticity, claiming that the canonical books are superior, is unfounded and misleading. It is perfectly logical to argue that *a particular canonical book* is more accurate than *certain apocryphal writings*, but it is baseless to suggest that *all canonical books* are more accurate or authentic than *all apocryphal books*.

From the Qur'an's perspective, any similarity it has with parts of other books, whether canonical or not, indicates that those parts have genuine divine origin, even if the books are largely written by man. If an apocryphal book contradicts a canonical source but agrees with the Qur'an, then it is the apocryphal account that is considered authentic. This is one reason why this book shows almost equal interest in the Qur'an's similarities with both canonical and apocryphal sources. The special emphasis put on Paul's Epistles and the Gospels in certain chapters reflects the special role of these writings in introducing and spreading certain concepts and their particularly high influence on Christianity.

1.4.4. Contextual Displacement as a Form of Scriptural Textual Manipulation

The Qur'an attributes the inauthenticity of the Bible to two forms of textual manipulation by the latter's authors, editors, and copyists: textual addition and textual corruption. These two explain the differences between the Qur'an and Jewish and Christian sources.

Textual addition denotes the practice of adding passages that were never part of the revealed divine book, so they are completely the creation of their respective authors. These are also likely to have been modified, deliberately or inadvertently, by later editors and copyists. We have already seen a Qur'anic verse that criticizes "those who write the book with their hands and then say 'This is from Allah' to get a small price for it" (2.79). Examples of added texts include the passages that promote Jesus' divinity. These were never part of the Injīl and where added by their respective authors and editors (see Chapters 14 and 15).

Textual corruption, on the other hand, signifies the practice of changing original divine texts. Any passage that was developed from one that was in the original divine book is an instance of textual corruption. This may involve deleting parts of the original passage or adding to it. This is one verse that confirms that the Biblical authors *altered* the divine text:

Do you [O you who believe!] hope that they would believe with you when a party from among them used to hear the Word of Allah and then alter it after they had understood it, knowingly? (2.75).

One example of textual corruption in the Bible is its description of the image in which God created man. This is what the Old Testament says:

Then God said, "Let us make mankind in our image, after our likeness, so they may rule over the fish of the sea and the birds of the air, over the cattle, and over all the earth, and over all the creatures that move on the earth." God created mankind in his own image, in the image of God he created them, male and female he created them. (Gen. 1:26-27)

The Qur'an only says that God gave man a good image, without relating it to the image of God — a concept that does not make sense in the Qur'an, because "there is nothing like Him" (42.11):

It is Allah who has made for you the earth as a resting place, and the sky as a canopy, and has shaped you, making your shapes good, and has provided for you sustenance, of things pure and good. Such is Allah your Lord. So blessed is Allah, the Lord of the peoples (40.64).

The statement that God made man look good which was in the original Torah was changed by the Old Testament authors to another that states that God created man in His own image.

There is one form of textual corruption that is particularly relevant to this book and to any comparative study of history in the Qur'an and the Bible. This type of textual corruption denotes the instances where a character, event, or statement appears in one context in the Qur'an and in a different context in other sources. I will call this form of textual corruption "contextual displacement."

One example of contextual displacement is found in the Biblical book of Esther. The story of Esther is known to be unhistorical, so it must have been invented by its authors, i.e. it is a textual addition. But the story has a Hāmān who is described as the prime minister in the court of the Persian king Ahasuerus. A character with the same name appears in the Qur'an as a high ranking minister in Pharaoh's court. This is an instance of contextual displacement where a character has been moved by the Biblical authors from one context to another.

Contextual displacements are seen by followers of the secular and Biblical approaches as proofs that the Qur'an has *copied inaccurately* from those sources. The Qur'an's explanation is that it reports the true contexts, and that any different contexts in Jewish and Christian writings resulted from changes made to the Torah, Injīl, or other divine revelations. In other words, these are the result of the Bible's editors moving figures, events, and statements from their correct, original contexts.

In the case of Hāmān's identity, for example, the Qur'an's story was revealed by God and is therefore true, whereas the Biblical identification resulted from moving Hāmān from the story of Moses, which was part of the Torah to a completely different story.

The Qur'an uses the Arabic verb *ḥarrafa* — which means "alter," "change," or "move away from" — when talking about the tampering that the Torah and Injīl were subjected to. Interestingly, in three of these verses, the verb is used in combination with the Arabic word *mawāḍi'* which means "contexts" or "places" (also 15.13):

> Allah best knows your [O you who believe!] enemies. Allah is sufficient as a Guardian, and Allah is sufficient as a Supporter (4.45). [Your enemies] from among the Jews who alter words from their contexts (4.46).

> O Messenger! Let not them grieve you, those who vie one with another in the race to disbelief, among those who say with their mouths: "We believe," but their hearts did not believe, and of the Jews who listen to falsehood, listen to other folk who have not come to you [who] alter words from their contexts (5.41).

Displacing words and changing their contexts or "contextual displacement" is what these verse talk about. We will discuss in this book a number of contextual displacements in the story of Jesus.

1.4.5. Refuted Accusations

The Qur'an also deals with the various accusations that were made against Prophet Muhammad by people who did not believe that he received the book from God. One charge was that the Qur'an, which was considered as a collection of ancient stories, was being taught to Muhammad by some people, and that he was having it written down for him:

> And they [the disbelievers] say: "[The Qur'an is] stories of the ancients that he [Muhammad] has got them written, as they are read out to him morning and evening" (25.5).

Another verse responds to a specific form of this accusation which identifies a certain non-Arab — probably a Jew or Christian — as Muhammad's teacher:

> Say [O Muhammad!]: "The Spirit of Holiness (Gabriel) has revealed it (the Qur'an) from your Lord with the truth, that it may establish those who believe and as a guidance and good news for the Muslims (16.102). Certainly We know that they say: "It is a man that teaches him." The tongue of the man to whom they attribute the Qur'an is foreign, yet this is clear Arabic tongue (16.103).

This particular accusation is likely to have been leveled at the Prophet by Jews and Christians who did not accept that he could have received revelation in the same way that their prophets did.

Other charges, which probably came mainly from the polytheistic Arabs, included accusing Muhammad of making up the Qur'an out of confused dreams; authoring it; and being merely a poet, a madman, or a soothsayer:

> They (the disbelievers) say: "Nay, it (the Qur'an) is Medleys of dreams! Nay, he (Muhammad) has made it up! Nay, he is a poet! So let him bring to us a sign as the former [Prophets] were sent with" (21.5).
>
> And they [the disbelievers] say [to Muhammad]: "O you to whom the *Dhikr* (Qur'an) has been revealed, you are a madman!" (15.6).
>
> Therefore continue [O Muhammad!] to remind; for by the grace of your Lord, you are not a soothsayer or a madman (52.29).

One Qur'anic response to these claims is the fact that Muhammad had not read or written a book in his life, so he could not have copied the Qur'an from another source:

> You [O Muhammad!] did not recite before it (the Qur'an) any book, nor did you write one with your right hand, for those who rejected you to have doubts (29.48).

This is usually taken to mean that Prophet Muhammad was illiterate.

Muhammad could not have studied any book, let alone the *many* Jewish and Christian sources that he is alleged to have used in authoring the Qur'an. Whether he could have obtained those books at all is yet another problem that is also often glossed over by his accusers. Later in the book we will come across many instances where a Qur'anic story has both similarities and differences with its Jewish or Christian counterpart. If the similarities are claimed to have resulted from Muhammad having direct access to the Jewish or Christian source, then how can one explain the differences? Surely copying parts of a story from an old source and authoring the others would not have helped Muhammad convince the believers in that source or the disbelievers of Arabia! The fact that the Qur'anic version makes more historical sense and is more consistent is yet another problem that the copying theory cannot explain.

1.5. The Approach of This Book

Having introduced the main approaches to the study of history in the Bible and the Qur'an and explained why it is important to understand what approach a study takes, I need to make it clear that this book follows the Qur'anic approach. Any information in the canon, apocrypha, and history that is relevant to the subject of this book will first be presented and then explained from the Qur'an's point of view.

Presuming that the Qur'an is the Word of God, this book seeks to show the consistency of the Qur'anic story of Jesus and its alignment with historical facts. It also compares the Qur'an's consistent account of Jesus' life with the problems that the same story has in Christian sources.

There are many who argue against the assumption that the Qur'an is the Word of God and claim that it was copied from Jewish and Christian sources. There are a number of theories as to how the Qur'an could have borrowed from other sources, but there is no shred of material evidence that this happened. Additionally, the fundamental assumption that the Qur'an is the Word of God cannot be rejected on the basis of the history of the text in the same way that the equivalent assumption of the Biblical approach can. The history of the Bible and that of the Qur'an are very different. The Qur'an was revealed over 22 years (610-632 CE) and the revealed text did not go through any development or change.

The ultimate test for the assumption that a book is the Word of God is that it must be free of inconsistencies, inaccuracies, or mistakes. If the book is found to contain any of these flaws, then it cannot be attributed in its entirety to the all-knowing, unerring God.

Verifying the accuracy of some Qur'anic statements by comparing it with established facts, say historical or scientific, is not an approach that can be applied to every statement in the Qur'an. In fact, it can be used with only a relatively small number of verses, because most of the Qur'an talks about unverifiable metaphysical and theological issues. For instance, the Day of Resurrection and the afterlife are major themes in the Qur'an, with numerous verses dedicated to them. Yet there is no way to verify these future events. Similarly, statements about God and spiritual beings, such as the angels, are also unverifiable. This is why the belief in the Qur'an, or the Bible to that matter, cannot be completely justified rationally and would always involve accepting claims that cannot be attested, i.e. an element of faith. The Qur'an stresses in many verses that faith involves belief in the *ghayb*, a term that may be translated as "the unseen" or "unknown." Words that share the same root with *ghayb* include *ghāba* (became absent; disappeared) and *ghā'ib* (absent). One quality of the pious is that they "believe in the unseen" (2.3). Statements about the "unseen" cannot be verified, but others can.

While it is not possible to found the belief in the Qur'an completely on reason and material evidence, because of the statements about the unseen, examining the accuracy of verifiable statements can be used to check the reliability of the book. If verifiable statements are found to be wrong or inaccurate, then clearly the Qur'an cannot be the divine or accurate book it claims to be. At best, it would be a text based on revelation, but which has been edited by man — something similar to what happened to the Bible. In this case, the unverifiable statements in the Qur'an also might well be wrong or inaccurate. This situation would undermine the Qur'anic approach completely. On the other hand, if the verifiable statements pass every test, then one can justifiably conclude that there is increasing probability that the Qur'an is the Word of the unerring God.

Books such as the Bible and the Qur'an are far more than historical records of events and characters. Each book provides a panoramic view of this world and its history, and specific events that it mentions are used to develop that overall picture. Each book sets out to answer questions about the meaning of life and the main forces behind this continually changing world — covering its past, present, and future. So in addition to the smaller historical and scientific details that can be tested against external evidence, the global view of each of these books is also something that must be considered. The secular approach also produces global views. The question is then which of the competing views makes more sense of this world, its history, and its various phenomena.

As it follows the Qur'anic approach, this book will argue that the historical Jesus is that of the Qur'an, and that his real role in history is accurately explained by the Qur'an's view of the world, not the view of the Bible or any secular approach. However, it will consider in detail the arguments of the other approaches and any counter argument to the Qur'anic approach.

I will make every effort to differentiate between bare facts and their interpretations according to the Qur'anic approach. These facts can then be looked at by others to examine the validity of the given interpretations and test whether a different approach gives better interpretations of these facts. I will point out the similarities and differences between the Qur'an and relevant Jewish and Christian sources, and I will explain and relate them to established historical facts, using the Qur'anic perceptive. It is then to the reader to decide whether this Qur'anic interpretation of history is more consistent, convincing, and in line with established facts, or other alternatives, including the Bible's.

Let me repeat again, this book does not claim to be a dispassionate, neutral study of Jesus' history. I am not sure that such an attempt is possible at all anyway. Nevertheless, I will ensure that I make my assumptions clear and differentiate between facts and their interpretations, allowing the reader to decide whether the arguments of the book are likely or unlikely, credible or absurd.

2

Mary Before the Annunciation

Our study of Jesus' life starts with the infancy story of his mother. Except for a few disparaging remarks in Jewish literature which we will study later in the book, Jesus' mother is mentioned only in Christian sources. None of the four canonical Gospels talks about Mary's birth. In fact, none of them contains any information about the life of Mary before the annunciation of Jesus. However, detailed accounts are given in Apocryphal gospels of Mary's miraculous birth and childhood.

The much briefer Qur'anic story of Mary before her conception of Jesus has similarities and differences with the apocryphal accounts. We will note these as we compare both accounts.

2.1. Mary Before the Annunciation in the Apocrypha

We will focus here on three apocryphal sources: *The Gospel of the Birth of Mary*, *the Infancy Gospel of James*, and *the Gospel of Pseudo-Matthew*. These three books have similarities, but they also contain very significant differences. This is why although some scholars consider the first two as one and the same book (Ehrman, 2005: 63), I will treat them as two different sources in this book. The Infancy Gospel of James is believed to be earlier than the Gospel of the Birth of Mary, but I will start with the latter because it focuses on Mary. Appendix B contains more information on the apocryphal sources used in this book.

2.1.1. The Account of the Gospel of the Birth of Mary

This Gospel tells us that a Joachim and his wife Anna led a very pious life, but after twenty years of marriage, they were still with no children. They vowed that should God give them any child, they would devote it to His service.

One day Joachim went with some of his tribe to Jerusalem to give offerings. He was reproached by the high priest Isachar for failing to parent a child for Israel. Worried that his companions might ridicule him for what the high priest said to him, Joachim did not return home but went to stay with some Shepherds.

While there, an angel appeared to Joachim to give him the good news that God has listened to his prayers and shall give him a child. He told Joachim that his wife was going to give birth to a female and that they shall call her "Mary." Confirming the vow that Joachim and his wife had made, the angel said that Mary shall be devoted to the Lord from her infancy. Mary would be clean, pure, and dedicated to the worship of her Lord. The angel also told Joachim that Mary would give birth whilst a virgin to the son of God, Jesus.

Another angel appeared to Anna and gave her the good news about Mary. The angel informed Anna that Mary would remain in the temple to worship the Lord until she reaches the years of discretion. The angel also stressed that Mary shall give birth while still a virgin to someone who would be the savior of the world.

Events unfolded just as the angel had foretold Joachim and his wife. Anna gave birth to a girl whom they duly called "Mary."

When Mary was three, her parents took her to the temple to be brought up there with other virgins. She stayed there until she was 14, at which point the high priest — whose name the text does not confirm — made a public announcement that all virgins who had arrived this age, and thus were mature, must leave the temple and try to get married in keeping with the custom.

All virgins of the temple obeyed the high priest's order, except Mary. She said that she and her parents had decided to devote her to the Lord, and that she had vowed not to get married for the sake of the Lord.

Unwilling to make someone break a vow to the Lord or allow virgins to stay in the temple beyond the allowed age, the high priest sought council from God. He was directed to a prophecy by Isaiah regarding whom the Virgin (Mary) should get married to. According to this prophecy, all eligible bachelors who are decedents of David should bring their rods to the altar. The man on whose rod a dove will sit is the one who should marry Mary. Thus, Joseph, an old man from the bloodline of David, was chosen.

After the ceremonies of betrothal were over, Joseph returned to his home city of Bethlehem to prepare his house for the marriage. Mary returned to her parent's house in Galilee.

The book then covers in the last three chapters Mary's conception of Jesus, which we will study in Chapter 5.

2.1.2. The Account of the Infancy Gospel of James

The story of the birth of Mary in this Gospel has considerable similarity with its counterpart in the Gospel of Mary.

When Joachim tried to offer his gifts to God on a day of celebration, he was rebuked by the high priest, who is named Reuben here, for offering gifts yet not having offspring. Saddened by what happened, Joachim went into solitude in the wilderness, vowing not to return home until God had shown mercy to him.

Anna, Joachim's wife, was doubly upset by her infertility and thinking that her husband had died. But an angel appeared to her to tell her that she, although old also, was going to conceive and give birth to a child that the whole world will speak about. So she vowed to devote the child to the Lord. Another two angels then appeared to Anna to tell her that her husband was coming home. An angel also appeared to Joachim and told him that his wife will conceive. Nine months later, Mary was born.

When Mary was 3 her parents took her to the temple and left her there to worship the Lord. She stayed there until she was 12 when the priests met to discuss what to do with her, as they thought had arrived the age when she could defile the temple — the menstruation age. It was decided that the high priest, Zechariah, would stand at the altar and consult God about the issue.

An angel appeared to the high priest and told him to call together all the widowers and that each of them should bring his rod. The Lord would then give a sign as to whom Mary should be betrothed to. A dove proceeded out of Joseph's rod, which was the sign that he was chosen to be Mary's husband. Joseph argued that Mary was too young for him, but he was advised by the high priest to obey the order. Joseph took Mary to his house and left her there as he had to go and mind his building business.

In chapter 9 of this gospel, the account of the annunciation starts.

2.1.3. The Account of the Gospel of Pseudo-Matthew

This book also starts with a very similar story of Joachim and his wife Anna. It mentions their sense of humiliation for not having a child after 20 years of marriage, the rebuke of the priest Ruben to Joachim for his childlessness, and the visit of an angel to Joachim to tell him that his wife has miraculously become pregnant. One noticeable difference in this part of the story is that Anna is said to have conceived although Joachim had been away from her for five months. While the text does not state that explicitly, it suggests that the pregnancy of Anna had some similarity with the future pregnancy of her daughter Mary.

Unlike the Gospel of the birth of Mary and the Infancy Gospel of James, this gospel does not tell us that Mary was taken to live in the temple, but the story later clearly suggests that she was living in the temple. When someone approached the high priests about marrying Mary to his son, she said: "It cannot be that I should know a man, or that a man should know me" and she affirmed that she "should not know a man at all" (PsMatt. 7). She is later quoted to have said that she had devoted herself to the Lord from her infancy: "I am known by Him to whom from my earliest years I have devoted myself. And this vow I made to my God from my infancy, that I should remain unspotted in Him who created me, and I trust that I shall so live to Him alone, and serve Him alone; and in Him, as long as I shall live, will I remain unpolluted" (PsMatt. 12)

When Mary was fourteen the priests wanted to have her married and leave the temple. The high priest, who is called Abiathar in this book, called on all men who did not have wives to bring their rods to take part in the choosing of Mary's husband. Joseph won the lottery and took Mary with him home, but did not marry her.

This gospel then starts in chapter 9 talking about the annunciation.

2.2. Mary Before the Annunciation in the Qur'an

The Qur'an gives a very brief account of the story of the birth of Mary, whom it calls "Maryam" and highly venerates. While the Qur'an confirms some of the details in the apocryphal gospels above, it contradicts them in various other details. It must be stressed here that *every Qur'anic verse differs from the corresponding apocryphal accounts in at least some details*, as we shall see. I shall point out such similarities and differences as I comment on the Qur'anic text.

The Qur'an does not say whether the conception of Mary's mother was miraculous or not, and it does not confirm the apocryphal gospels' claims that she was barren (e.g. BirMary. 2:5; InJam. 2:1, 3:1) or old (BirMary. 2:9; PsMatt. 1). While the Qur'an does not name Mary's mother, it calls her father "'Imrān" (3.35). This is one difference between the Christian writings and the Qur'an.

There is a verse in which Mary's people address her as "sister of Aaron" (19.28). When relating a person to his/her people, the Qur'an describes that person as *akh* (brother) or *ukht* (sister) of that people. This is one example:

> The people of Noah rejected the messengers (26.105). When their *akhūhum* (brother) Noah said to them: "Will you not be dutiful [toward Allah]?" (26.106).

Thus, "sister of Aaron" means that Mary was a descendant of a famous grandfather known as "Aaron." Exegetes believe it is Prophet Aaron, Moses' brother. I will explain later this phrase and the confusion of the Qur'an's critics who consider it a mistake (pp. 176-177).

The Qur'an's brief account of Mary's birth starts with this verse:

> When the wife of 'Imrān said: "My Lord! I vow to consecrate to You that which is in my womb, so accept it from me. You are the Hearer, the Knower (3.35).

The words of Mary's mother "that which is in my womb" indicate that she did not know the sex of her child. This contradicts the account given in the Gospel of the Birth of Mary which claims that the angel had told Joachim: "Anna your wife shall bring you a daughter" (BirMary. 2:9), and told Anna: "a daughter will be born to you" (BirMary. 3:2). The Infancy Gospel of James, on the other hand, indicates that Mary's parents were not aware of the sex of the child, as shown in Anna's following prayer: "As the Lord my God lives, whatever I bring forth, whether it be male or female, I will devote it to the Lord my God and it shall minister to him in holy things, during its whole life" (InJam. 4:2). This is also shown in the dialog between Anna and the midwife: "And when nine months were fulfilled to Anna, she brought forth, and said to the midwife, 'What have I brought forth?' And she told her, 'A girl'" (InJam. 5:6-7).

The vow of Mary's mother to consecrate her child to God probably means dedicating the child to live in a worshipping place. This agrees with the apocrypha. The Old Testament has the story of a childless woman called Hannah who vowed to dedicate her son to God if He would give her one: "O Lord of hosts, if you will look with compassion on the suffering of your female servant, remembering me and not forgetting your servant, and give a male child to your servant, then I will dedicate him to the Lord all the days of his life. His hair will never be cut" (1 Sam. 1:11).

The Qur'an states that the decision to offer Mary to the worship of Allah was taken by her mother. This might well mean that Mary's father was probably dead. He actually never appears in the story. This contradicts the account given in the Gospel of the Birth of Mary. The latter states that both Joachim and Anna had vowed to offer Mary to the temple should God favor them with a child: "But they vowed, if God should favour them with any issue, they would devote it to the service of the Lord; on which account they went at every feast in the year to the temple of the Lord" (BirMary. 1:6). It claims in another place that this matter was confirmed by an order from an angel who appeared to Anna: "She shall be, immediately upon her birth, full of the grace of the Lord, and shall continue during the three years of her weaning in her father's house, and afterwards, being devoted to the service of the Lord, shall not depart from the temple, till she arrives to years of discretion" (BirMary. 3:3).

The Infancy Gospel of James differs with the Gospel of the Birth of Mary and agrees with the Qur'an, stating that it was Anna who, having been told by an angel about her conception of a child, took the vow to dedicate her child to the temple (InJam. 4:2).

Of the two different accounts of the two gospels, the Infancy Gospel of James seems improbable. It is very unlikely that Anna would take such a major decision about her child on her own without the participation of her husband. The Gospel of Pseudo-Matthew also has Anna alone making the vow (PsMatt. 2), but that is because her husband had disappeared five months earlier.

Another similar difference between the apocryphal gospels is seen with respect to the naming of Mary. According to the Gospel of the Birth of Mary, the name "Mary" came in an order from the angel who said to Joachim: "Anna your wife shall bring you a daughter, and you shall call her name Mary" (BirMary. 2:9), and to Anna: "a daughter will be born to you, who shall be called Mary, and shall be blessed above all women" (BirMary. 3:2). The claims that Mary's name was given by an *order from the angel* and that *both of her parents* named her accordingly are also stressed later: "So Anna conceived, and brought forth a daughter, and, according to the angel's command, the parents did call her name Mary" (BirMary. 3:11). Conversely, the Infancy Gospel of James tells us that it was Anna who called her new born daughter "Mary": "And when the days of her purification were accomplished, she gave suck to the child; and called her name Mary" (InJam. 5:9). The Gospel of Pseudo-Matthew also identifies Anna as the person who named Mary: "After these things, her nine months being fulfilled, Anna brought forth a daughter, and called her Mary" (PsMatt. 4). While not as illogical and significant as the implicit claim that Joachim was not involved in the decision to dedicate his daughter to the Lord, it still looks odd that Mary's name was chosen by her mother only.

The Qur'anic story continues as follows:

> When she gave birth to her, she said: "My Lord! I have delivered a female." Allah knows best what she delivered. The male is not like the female. "I have named her Mary. I commend her and her offspring to Your protection from accursed Satan" (3.36).

The Qur'an here contradicts the Gospel of the Birth of Mary but supports the other two gospels that it was Mary's mother who named her. However, it has one major difference with the two apocryphal books which gives its version of events the consistency and harmony that the Infancy Gospel of James and the Gospel of Pseudo-Matthew lack. Unlike these two, the Qur'an does not state that Mary's father was alive at the time of naming Mary. It implies that Mary's father was already dead, as the vow to dedicate her to God was made by his wife only.

The name of Mary's father, 'Imrān, occurs in the Qur'an in three verses, albeit none in reference to him directly, but to people related to him:

> Allah chose Adam, Noah, the family of Abraham, and the family of 'Imrān above all nations (3.33).
>
> When the wife of 'Imrān said: "My Lord! I vow to consecrate to You that which is in my womb, so accept it from me. You are the Hearer, the Knower (3.35).
>
> And [Allah set forth an example] Mary, daughter of 'Imrān, who guarded her private parts, then We breathed therein of Our spirit. And she believed in the words of her Lord and His Book, and was one of the obedient (66.12).

The statement "I have delivered a female" is consistent with Mary's mother's statement "that which is in my womb" in verse 3.35, as both indicate that she did not know the sex of her child before birth. Her words that the newborn turned out to be female suggest that this had implications for her vow to dedicate her child to the worship of God. Perhaps, it was unusual, or even unheard of at all, that a female should be dedicated to live in a temple. The apocryphal gospels that we discussed earlier suggest that young girls could be dedicated to the worship of God in the temple, but they had to leave before they start menstruating so that they do not defile the place. In Judaism, after the end of the menstrual period, the woman must take a purifying ritual bath known as "Mikvah." The briefness of the Qur'an does not allow us to favor a particular possibility.

The Qur'anic context of the clause "the male is not like the female" reveals that the similar passage in the Infancy Gospel of James was displaced from its original context. The apocryphal book attributes the following prayer to Mary's mother: "As the Lord my God lives, whatever I bring forth, whether it be male or female, I will devote it to the Lord my God and it shall minister to him in holy things, during its whole life" (InJam. 4:2). This is one example of the *contextual displacements* I discussed in §1.4.4 where a figure, statement, or event appears in different contexts in the

Qur'an and Jewish or Christian writings. A statement to the same meaning as "the male is not like the female" would have been found probably in the Injīl, but by the time it made it into the Infancy Gospel of James it had been displaced from its original context as an observation by God to a statement by Mary's mother. Another element of textual corruption in the Christian version is the suggestion that Mary's mother vowed to dedicate her child to temple regardless of "whether it be male or female."

The verse then tells us that Mary's mother went on to pray to God to protect Mary and, significantly, *her offspring* from the seduction of Satan. Whatever *consecrating Mary to God* meant, it clearly did not imply that Mary was never going to get married.

There is a beautiful contrast between the words of Mary's mother "I have delivered a female" and God's emphatic statement "Allah knows best what she delivered." The mother's words implicitly concede that the good that she had in mind for her child was not going to materialize, or at least not fully, because of the gender of the child. As if replying to those words, God's statement, which emphasizes His absolute knowledge of what really happened and the limitedness of the knowledge of Mary's mother, subtly refers to the great status that He had ordained for the newborn girl. While the mother wanted her child to serve God *like any of those dedicated to His service*, He wanted to make the child a female to raise her to *a unique status that no other woman would ever achieve*. He conferred more good on Mary than her mother had wished for her. In addition to the piety and purity that God bestowed on Mary, He chose her to be the virgin mother of one of His greatest prophets, Jesus the Messiah.

This interpretation is confirmed by another observation. Rather than comparing the female with the male — which is what would have been expected, as it is the female who was being discussed — it is the male who is being compared with the female. Mary's mother was saddened because *the female is not like the male*, but God emphasized the good news in the fact that *the male was not like the female*, as if He said and *no male is like this female*.

Aṭ-Ṭabāṭabā'ī's has cited this peculiar comparison to reject the claim of some exegetes that the clause "the male is not as the female" is part of the prayer of Mary's mother not part of God's parenthetical speech. Aṭ-Ṭabāṭabā'ī has noted that had that been the case, Mary's mother would have instead said something such as "the female is not as the male," as it is the female whom she was talking about and would have been comparing with the male, not the other way around.

A minority of exegetes have read the Arabic word *wadha'at*, which means "she delivered," as *wadha'tu*, which means "I have delivered." This reading is admitted by the fact that the change in reading requires changing only two diacritical signs but no letters. These signs were not used in the early manuscripts of the Qur'an. According to this alternative reading, the changed clause "Allah knows best what I have delivered" would be part of the prayer of Mary's mother. This reading is very unlikely because this prayer would refer to God in the third person yet the prayers that surround it address Him directly, using "My Lord" and "Your protection." Also, this reading would probably imply that the clause "the male is not like the female" is also spoken by Mary's mother, yet we have already seen that this is not the case. I therefore think that *wadha'at* is the correct reading. The sentences "Allah knows best what she delivered. The male is not like the female" are parenthetical and attributed to God, although they fall in the middle of the prayer of Mary's mother. It is common style in the Qur'an for God to comment on details of an account as He relates it.

The Qur'an then goes on to talk about Mary's childhood:

> Her Lord accepted her with a good acceptance, made her grow a good growth, and made Zechariah her guardian. Whenever Zechariah went into the sanctuary where she was, he found that she had sustenance. He said: "O Mary! How did this [sustenance] come to you?" She answered: "It is from Allah. Allah gives to whom He pleases without measure" (3.37).

God "accepted" Mary who was dedicated to Him, and He brought her up as a righteous person. It is not clear how old Mary was when God "made Zechariah her guardian." None of the canonical or apocryphal gospels mentions this custody, though some of them mention a certain Zechariah, but in different contexts. We will discuss this in more detail in Chapter 3.

There are two possible interpretations for why Zechariah became Mary's guardian. **First**, this guardianship is the result of Zechariah being in charge of a temple and looking after Mary when she lived there. In this case, the appearance of Zechariah in Mary's life would have been triggered not by the death of her mother, but by her joining a place of worship and her need to have a spiritual guide. This does not necessitate that Zechariah or his wife was related to Mary.

The **second** possibility is that, already a half-orphan when born, little Mary later lost her mother also, so Zechariah started to look after her. This implies that he or his wife was probably related to Mary in some way, although he had to fight off the attempts of others to become Mary's guardians, as we shall see in verse 3.44. I find this possibility more likely for two reasons. **First**, it is difficult to see how a stranger, even if well respected, could have been allowed to adopt the little child instead of one of her relatives. **Second**, verse 19.16, which we will study later, states that Mary secluded herself "from her family" to worship God. The term "family" suggests that she was living with relatives rather than strangers.

The clause "whenever Zechariah went into the sanctuary where she was" indicates that Mary was living in some kind of solitude, dedicating herself to the worship of God in what looks, at least in atmosphere, like a temple. The Arabic term *Miḥrāb*, translated as "sanctuary," may suggest that she was indeed in a temple which Zechariah was probably in charge of.

On many of his visits to Mary in the sanctuary, Zechariah found food with her. Zechariah's question about how Mary got the food suggests that there was something *miraculous* about her having that food. This is also confirmed by Zechariah's reaction in the next verse, 3.38 where, having listened to Mary's wise reply, he asked God to give him and his barren and old wife offspring — something that can happen only by a miracle. The miracle that Zechariah witnessed happening to Mary prompted him to ask God to give him offspring by a miracle, as He gave Mary food miraculously.

Some exegetes have suggested that the kinds of food Zechariah used to see with Mary were not available at that time of the year or could not have been from that region. It is equally possible that Zechariah's surprise was at the fact that the food was not something that he, or whoever was supplying Mary with the food, could have given her, for instance, because it was not food that they had prepared. Aṭ-Ṭabāṭabā'ī has cleverly noted that the Arabic word for sustenance occurs in the indefinite form *rizqan* rather the definite *ar-rizq*, suggesting that this food was not something that Zechariah was familiar with.

Mary's wise but vague reply, "it is from Allah. Allah gives to whom He pleases without measure," seems to confirm the interpretation that the food was not brought to her in a normal way.

Interestingly, the Infancy Gospel of James states that, having been taken by her parents to stay in the temple, Mary "received her food from the hand of an angel" (InJam. 8:2; see also 10:9 and 11:9). The Gospel of the Pseudo-Matthew (6) has yet another version, saying that Mary "did not retire from praying until there appeared to her the angel of the Lord, from whose hand she used to receive food," and that "she refreshed herself only with the food which she daily received from the hand of the angel." The virgins who were with Mary also said that "daily does she receive food from the hand of the Lord" (PsMatt. 10). This is another contextual displacement where a statement that was originally made by Mary, as the Qur'an confirms, appears as an observation made by the author of the gospel in the case of the Infancy Gospel of James and by the author and other virgins in the case of the Gospel of Pseudo-Matthew.

Verses 38-41 then divert to talk about Zechariah and the good news that he received about the birth of his son John. We will study these verses in Chapter 3.

In verse 42 the Qur'an returns to talk about Mary. The interception of the verses about Zechariah indicates the lapse of a period of time between the dialog about the miraculous food and the events related in 42 and following verses. This passage of time is also confirmed by commencing verse 3.42 with the article *idh* (when), which is used in the Qur'an to start a new context, often indicating a different time, as explained in Appendix A:

> And when the angels said: "O Mary! Allah has chosen you, purified you, and chosen you above the women of all nations (3.42).

The Qur'an always talks about "angels" not "an angel" delivering messages, although the voice that Mary heard is likely to be of one of the angels. Only Gabriel is mentioned as an individual messenger in the Qur'an, as we shall see later. The Qur'an contains a number of stories about how God sent groups of angels to deliver messages, such as the group of angels that visited prophets Abraham and Lot (11.69-83, 15.51-74). There is a verse in the Qur'an which probably means that angels are sent in groups to deliver God's messages:

> Praise be to Allah, who has created the heavens and the earth, and who has made the angels messengers — with wings — two, three, and four; He increases in creation what He pleases; surely Allah has power over all things (35.1).

I favor this reading over the alternative reading where the phrase "two, three, and four" refers to the wings not the messengers.

It is likely that this good news was conveyed to Mary by a number of different angels on more than one occasion. So this verse does not refer to only one event in which Mary was spoken to by the angels, but to a number of such events. Note that Mary was already used to receiving food miraculously, so seeing angels, listening to them, and being at the center of miracles was not an uncommon experience for her. The Gospel of Pseudo-Matthew (6) states that the angel spoke to Mary daily.

The second choosing in verse 3.42 may be just a confirmation of the choosing that is mentioned earlier in the verse, but it is more likely that the two signify two different divine acts of choosing of Mary. The first seems to be God's choice of Mary to be one of His most dedicated servants. He then refers to the purity that He conferred on Mary, as He protected her from sins. Finally, God declares that He chose her over all women. There is no indication in the Qur'an that Mary was better than *all* other women, i.e. was nearer to God than all, so this must refer to her conception of Jesus. This miracle is certainly a favor that was not conferred on any other woman.

The Qur'an does not tell us that Mary was surprised by what she heard, which means that she did not understand what this second choosing exactly meant. When she is later told about her conception of Jesus, she is completely astonished. Earlier in the same chapter, the Qur'an mentions that God had chosen, among others, the family of 'Imrān above all other people:

> Allah chose Adam, Noah, the family of Abraham, and the family of 'Imrān above all nations (3.33) — offspring, one of the other; and Allah hears and knows all things (3.34).

Exegetes have understood the four divine acts of choosing as denoting the distinguished qualities of these two individuals and two families. Adam was chosen to be the first human being. Noah was elected to survive with his followers the deluge and be the one from whom all prophets descended. The family of Abraham was chosen to have a large number of prophets and in a relatively short period of time, through Isaac, and to produce the last Prophet, Muhammad, through Abraham's other son, Ishmael. The family of 'Imrān included the two unique figures of Mary and her son Jesus. However, verse 4.33 seems to suggest that these acts of choosing by God should also be understood in terms of the special offspring that each of these individuals of families was ordained to have and the fact that they all belong to one bloodline. Adam was chosen to be the first human being, and thus the father of the human race, including all prophets. Noah was a great grandfather of Abraham. The family of Abraham was the ancestors of 'Imrān and possibly his wife. This couple was chosen to have the very special daughter Mary, who was in turn given the unique privilege of becoming the mother of Jesus through a unique miracle.

The angels' words "and [has] chosen you above the women of all nations" bear some resemblance to Gabriel's salutation of Mary as "favored one" in Luke (1:28), although the former imply uniqueness in this choosing or favor. This Evangelist also states that after the annunciation Zechariah's wife addressed Mary as "blessed are you among women, and blessed is the child in your womb" (Luke 1:42), which explains that favor. One difference between the angels' words to Mary in the Qur'an and Gabriel's words in Luke is that the latter occur during the annunciation, whereas the angel's words in the Qur'an are uttered in an earlier event. This close similarity between the two texts suggests that this is another contextual displacement.

The next verse reveals the essence of the angels' message to Mary:

> O Mary, be obedient to Your Lord, prostrate yourself, and bow with those who bow [in worship]!" (3.43).

The angels' visits to Mary and their support for her dedication to God were preparing her for the great change to her life and the unique status and role she was destined to have. The absence of any mention of the miraculous conception confirms my view that at this point Mary did not know about her future virginal conception.

In the following verse, which addresses Prophet Muhammad, the Qur'an explains how Zechariah became Mary's guardian, an event that was mentioned in verse 3.37:

> This is part of the tidings of the unseen. We reveal it to you [O Muhammad!]. You were not present with them when they cast lots with their sticks [to decide] who of them should become the guardian of Mary, nor were you present with them when they quarreled [thereupon] (3.44).

Like a number of other verses about the Qur'an's revelation of historical information (see Appendix A), this verse stresses that the Prophet could not have known details of the story of Mary had God not related them to him. The verse suggests that Zechariah and others had a quarrel, probably about who should become Mary's guardian. The dispute was settled by a practice of casting lots in which each of the disputing parties throws his stick. The Qur'an does not give more details about this lottery and how the winner is decided. It implies that Zechariah won the contest and took guardianship of Mary. In verse 3.37, the Qur'an states that it was God who "made Zechariah her guardian," implying that God intervened in some way in the lottery.

This quarrel and the resort to the lottery suggests that Zechariah was not necessarily the nearest of kin to look after the orphan Mary or that there were other equally near relatives, and his religious authority was not universally accepted (pp. 66-67).

The few verses that we studied in this chapter are almost all what the Qur'an says about Mary's birth and her life before the annunciation. There are only two other verses from chapter 19 which also refer to that stage of Mary's life:

> And mention [O Muhammad!] Mary in the Book. When she withdrew from her family to an eastern place (19.16).

Chapter 19 uses the clause *and mention [O Muhammad!] so-and-so in the Book* five times to talk about Mary and Prophets Abraham, Moses, Ishmael, and Idrīs. The verse portrays Mary's withdrawal from her family as her own decision, not simply a decision taken by her mother that she merely had to obey and had a passive role in. Mary did want to dedicate herself to the worship of God.

Exegetes have suggested that the "eastern place" might mean the eastern side of a place of worship. The following verse may indicate that Mary lived in a different place from her family's home, such as the sanctuary that she moved to at some point, or that she lived at the same house, but in isolation:

> She put a veil between herself and them (19.17).

Interestingly, verse 19.16 does not refer to Mary's separation from her "mother," but her "family." The Arabic word that I have translated as "family" is *ahl*. It usually means *parents* or *members of family*, although it can also mean *the people responsible for someone, whether blood relatives or not*. The word can also be used with "places" or "things," referring to the people who own them or are in charge of them. The Qur'an mentions Mary's mother specifically when talking about Mary's birth, so the use of the word *ahl* here may refer to Mary's mother and other family members, such as any sibling she may had, members of her extended family who were looking after her after the death of her mother, or even Zechariah and his wife who might have been the family who were raising her. My choice of the word "family" reflects the uncertainty about the exact meaning of *ahl* here.

3

Prophet Zechariah: Mary's Guardian

As we saw in the previous chapter, Zechariah played an important role in Mary's life — at least in its early stages. It is therefore appropriate to examine the story of this great character in a book about Jesus.

There is no known mention of Zechariah in an independent historical document. The history covered by the Old Testament ends 4 centuries before Jesus, so Zechariah is not mentioned in the Jewish book. We will focus in this chapter on the New Testament, the apocrypha, and the Qur'an.

The Christian sources offer contradictory information about Zechariah and his role in the story of Mary. They might be talking about more than one Zechariah, but even in this case there would be inexplicable inconsistencies. The Qur'an talks about one prophet called Zechariah who became Mary's guardian and later fathered Prophet John, who is clearly John the Baptist of the Christian sources.

3.1. Zechariah in the New Testament

There is considerable confusion in the Christian sources about Zechariah. **First**, it is unclear whether different sources are talking about one Zechariah or two. **Second**, in both cases, different sources give conflicting accounts. Let's start first with the New Testament.

Mark and John, both of which are completely silent on the birth of Jesus, do not mention any Zechariah at all. Matthew has one quick reference to a Zechariah, which we will discuss later. Luke, on the other hand, gives a rather detailed account of Zechariah in the first chapter of his Gospel. The earlier part of this story, which is cited below, has significant similarities and differences with the Qur'an:

> During the reign of Herod king of Judea, there lived a priest named Zechariah who belonged to the priestly division of Abijah, and he had a wife named Elizabeth, who was a descendant of Aaron. They were both righteous in the sight of God, following all the commandments and ordinances of the Lord blamelessly. But they did not have a child, because Elizabeth was barren, and they were both very old.
>
> Now while Zechariah was serving as priest before God when his division was on duty, he was chosen by lot, according to the custom of the priesthood, to enter the holy place of the Lord and burn incense. Now the whole crowd of people were praying outside at the hour of the incense offering. An angel of the Lord, standing on the right side of the altar of incense, appeared to him. And Zechariah, visibly shaken when he saw the angel, was seized with fear. But the angel said to him, "Do not be afraid, Zechariah, for your prayer has been heard, and your wife Elizabeth will bear you a son; you will name him John. Joy and gladness will come to you, and many will rejoice at his birth, for he will

be great in the sight of the Lord. He must never drink wine or strong drink, and he will be filled with the Holy Spirit, even before his birth. He will turn many of the people of Israel to the Lord their God. And he will go as forerunner before the Lord in the spirit and power of Elijah, to turn the hearts of the fathers back to their children and the disobedient to the wisdom of the just, to make ready for the Lord a people prepared for him."

Zechariah said to the angel, "How can I be sure of this? For I am an old man, and my wife is old as well." The angel answered him, "I am Gabriel, who stands in the presence of God, and I was sent to speak to you and to bring you this good news. And now, because you did not believe my words, which will be fulfilled in their time, you will be silent, unable to speak, until the day these things take place."

Now the people were waiting for Zechariah, and they began to wonder why he was delayed in the holy place. When he came out, he was not able to speak to them. They realized that he had seen a vision in the holy place, because he was making signs to them and remained unable to speak. When his time of service was over, he went to his home.

After some time his wife Elizabeth became pregnant, and for five months she kept herself in seclusion. She said, "This is what the Lord has done for me at the time when he has been gracious to me, to take away my disgrace among people." (Luke 1:5-25)

The similarities of this account with the Qur'anic story, which we will cover later in the chapter, leave no doubt that this New Testament character is the same Zechariah of the Qur'an.

Luke mentions another Zechariah once in a sermon in which Jesus attacks the scribes and Pharisees, accusing them of being parties to the killing of prophets and wise men, including a Zechariah: "from the blood of Abel to the blood of Zechariah, who was killed between the altar and the sanctuary. Yes, I tell you, it will be charged against this generation" (Luke 11:51). This is thought to be a reference to Zechariah son of Jehoiada who is mentioned in the Old Testament:

> God's Spirit energized Zechariah son of Jehoiada the priest. He stood up before the people and said to them, "This is what God says: 'Why are you violating the commands of the Lord? You will not be prosperous. Because you have rejected the Lord, he has rejected you!'" They plotted against him and by royal decree stoned him to death in the courtyard of the Lord's temple. King Joash disregarded the loyalty his father Jehoiada had shown him and killed Jehoiada's son. As Zechariah was dying, he said, "May the Lord take notice and seek vengeance!" (2 Chr. 24:20-22)

Joash was the 7th king of Judea who ruled in the 2nd half of the 9th century BCE, so this Zechariah lived over 8 centuries before Zechariah the father of John.

Matthew's equivalent to Luke 11:51 in his version of Jesus' sermon is this: "Zechariah son of Barachiah, whom you murdered between the temple and the altar" (Matt. 23:35). Commentators have suggested that the phrase "son of Barachiah" in Matthew is a mistake. It is thought that Matthew confused Zechariah the son of

Jehoiada with another Old Testament Zechariah, son of Berechiah. The latter, whose story is told in the Book of Zechariah, is said to have received the word of God in the 2nd year of the reign of Persian king Darius (Zech. 1:1), that is in 520 BCE, i.e. over 3 centuries after Zechariah son of Jehoiada. There is no account in the Old Testament of Zechariah son of Berechiah being killed.

3.2. Zechariahs in the Apocrypha

The apocryphal Gospel of the Birth of Mary does not refer to any Zechariah, but a Zechariah who was contemporary to Mary is mentioned in the Infancy Gospel of James. This is the only Zechariah that appears in the story of Mary, and his story has some similarities with that of John's father in Luke, including his temporary loss of the ability to speak. Both accounts must be talking about the same character, but there are considerable differences between the two stories.

Also a priest like the Zechariah of Luke, the Zechariah of the Infancy Gospel of James is the high priest of the temple in which Mary was serving. This is how his name is first mentioned:

> And when she was twelve years of age, the priests met in a council, and said, "Behold, Mary is twelve years of age, what shall we do with her, for fear lest the holy place of the Lord our God should be defiled?" Then replied the priests to Zechariah the high-priest, "do you stand at the altar of the Lord, and enter into the holy place, and make petitions concerning her, and whatsoever the Lord shall manifest to you, that do." Then the high priest entered into the Holy of Holies, and taking away with him the breast-plate of judgment made prayers concerning her. (InJam. 8:3-5)

This gospel then goes on to explain how Zechariah the high priest played a major role in Mary's marriage to Joseph. It states that the high priest later became dumb, although, unlike the story in Luke, no reason is given, and there is no story of Zechariah receiving good news about having a son. Interestingly, shortly after Zechariah's dumbness is mentioned, the Infancy Gospel of James tells us that the angel appeared to Mary and announced her conception of Jesus. The angels also told her:

> And behold your cousin Elizabeth, she also has conceived a son in her old age. And this now is the sixth month with her, who was called barren: for nothing is impossible with God. (InJam. 9:15-16)

These details are similar to what Luke says took place about six months after the dumbness of Zechariah when he was given the good news about John's birth:

> In the sixth month of Elizabeth's pregnancy, the angel Gabriel was sent by God to a town of Galilee called Nazareth, to a virgin engaged to a man whose name was Joseph, a descendant of David, and the virgin's name was Mary. (Luke 1:26-27)

In its last chapter, the apocryphal gospel makes it clear that Zechariah was the husband of Elizabeth and father of John.

Thus, the Infancy Gospel of James and Luke differ substantially in their accounts of the story of Zechariah, John's father. Luke and Matthew also disagree on the identity of a second Zechariah whose death account suggests that he was the "son of Jehoiada" of the Book of 2 Chronicles (24:20) rather than, according to Matthew's misidentification, the "son of Berechiah" of the Book of Zechariah (1:1).

The Infancy Gospel of James seems to further confuse the two different Zechariahs, as it suggests that John's father was also killed in the holy place! This gospel says that Herod, who was looking for John who had escaped his wrath with his mother, pressed Zechariah about the hideout of his son. When Zechariah insisted that he did not know the place, Herod ordered his officers to kill him:

> Zacharias was murdered in the entrance of the temple said altar, and about the partition. But the children of Israel knew not when he want killed. Then at the hour of salutation the priests went into the temple but Zacharias did not according to custom meet them and bless them. Yet they still continued waiting for him to salute them. And when they found he did not in a long time come, one of them ventured into the holy place where the altar was, and he saw blood lying upon the ground congealed. (InJam. 16:16-20)

The author of this gospel seems to have thought that the killed Zechariah was John's father, not "Zechariah son of Jehoiada," as Luke states, or "Zechariah son of Barachiah," as Matthew thinks.

3.3. Prophet Zechariah in the Qur'an

Zechariah, or "Zakariyyāh" as the Qur'an calls him, is the subject of major contextual displacements in Luke and apocryphal sources. As we saw in Chapter 2, the Zechariah of the Qur'an was Mary's guardian, probably her relative, and possibly in charge of the temple where she was living. The Zechariah of Luke is the husband of Mary's relative, but he has no direct involvement in Mary's life. He and his wife were living in a town in Judea in the south (Luke 1:39-40) whereas Mary was living in the northern city of Galilee (Luke 1:26). Zechariah's guardianship of Mary in the Qur'an contradicts Luke. In apocryphal gospels, a Zechariah was involved more in Mary's life, but that is because he was the high priest of the temple where she was living.

Let's look at one particular potential contextual displacement that involves Zechariah. We have seen that verse 3.44 states that Zechariah and others cast lots to decide who should become Mary's guardian (pp. 55-56). Christian writings do not have this event, but the Infancy Gospel of James and Pseudo-Matthew mention the use of "rods" in deciding who should get married to Mary:

And behold the angel of the Lord came to him, and said, "Zechariah, Zechariah, Go forth and call together all the widowers among the people, and let every one of them bring his rod, and he by whom the Lord shall show a sign shall be the husband of Mary." (InJam. 8:6)

The lottery was won by Joseph. From the Qur'anic perspective, this story is unlikely to have happened, as the character Joseph is completely ignored by the Qur'an and might have never existed (§8.2). Here the purpose of the lottery, the identity of its winner, and related details have been displaced by the Christian authors from their original contexts. Instead of being the winner of the lottery, Zechariah becomes the organizer, and Joseph is presented as the winner. The original purpose of the lottery, which is to appoint a guardian for Mary, is changed to choosing a husband for her. Related details have also been displaced from their original contexts.

The Infancy Gospel of James mentions another instance where lots were used under the supervision of Zechariah, when deciding which virgin of the tribe of David would spin the golden thread of the new veil for the temple of the Lord:

And the servants went and brought them into the temple of the Lord, and the high-priest said to them, "Cast lots before me now, who of you shall spin the golden thread, who the blue, who the scarlet, who the fine linen, and who the true purple." (InJam. 9:3)

This story seems to be a contextual displacement of another event reported in the Qur'an in verse 19.17 (p. 91).

The story of Zechariah is related in the Qur'an in chapters 3 and 19. We will analyze first the account in chapter 3, as we have already studied verses 35-37 of this chapter when we examined the birth of Mary (§2.2).

3.3.1. Prophet Zechariah in Chapter 3 (*The Family of 'Imrān*)

Let's recall verse 3.37 before citing verse 3.38 which deals specifically with Zechariah:

Her Lord accepted her with a good acceptance, made her grow a good growth, and made Zechariah her guardian. Whenever Zechariah went into the sanctuary where she was, he found that she had sustenance. He said: "O Mary! How did this [sustenance] come to you?" She answered: "It is from Allah. Allah gives to whom He pleases without measure" (3.37). There did Zechariah pray to his Lord and said: "My Lord! Grant me from You virtuous offspring. You are the Hearer of prayer" (3.38).

Having witnessed and been overwhelmed by the miracle of how Mary was given food, Zechariah asked for a miracle that would grant him offspring. If Mary can have food miraculously, then He could also be given offspring. He asked for a miracle because he was old and his wife was also old as well as barren; it was impossible for her to conceive normally. He wanted to have "virtuous" offspring, like the godly Mary.

The Arabic word translated "offspring" here is *dhurriyya*, which can be used as singular or plural. It is used in the singular here, as Zechariah was asking specifically for a son, as clarified in verse 19.5 which we shall study later.

The translation of verse 3.38 hides a very subtle reference in the original Arabic text. The Arabic phrase translated "from You" is *min ladunka* or "from Your *ladun*." The Arabic word *ladun* is similar to *'inda* which denotes possession, so *min 'indi* means "from the possession of" or simply "from." But *ladun* implies more closeness and intimacy. In all but one of its 18 occurrences in the Qur'an, *ladun* is used with reference to God, i.e. as in from of the *ladun* of God. It denotes things that come directly from Him, as I have explained in detail elsewhere (Fatoohi, 1999). Zechariah's use of *ladun* further emphasizes that he was looking for a miracle, asking God for offspring *from Him*, i.e. by His direct intervention.

Also interesting is the fact that verse 3.38 starts with the word *hunālika* (there). Zechariah was a very pious man who never stopped worshipping God. Clearly, he would have prayed to God so much over many years to have offspring. The use of the word "there" is intended to stress that it was his prayer at that particular instance that God answered, giving him the offspring that he had been asking for.

The verse also shows that the person must never stop praying to God or lose hope, even if His answer took long to come. There is divine wisdom in everything that God does, and much of the time this wisdom remains invisible to the person. What a person asks God for may not be actually good for him at all, not good for him then, or not good for him in that particular form. God can actually help that person by not answering his prayer:

> It may happen that you hate a thing that is good for you, and it may happen that you love a thing that is bad for you. Allah knows, and you know not (2.216).

Additionally, praying is an act of worship, so regardless of whether or not the person's prayer is heard, he would still reap the spiritual benefits of the act of praying itself.

The Qur'an then tells us that as Zechariah stood praying in the sanctuary one day, the angels delivered to him the good news that he was going to have a pious son:

> And the angels called to him as he stood praying in the sanctuary: "Allah gives you the good news of [a son whose name is] John, [who will be] confirming with a Word from Allah, honorable, chaste, and a prophet from among the righteous" (3.39).

The verb *nādā* (called to) suggests that Zechariah did not see the angels, but only heard the voice. This verb is usually used for talking from a distance.

As explained in Appendix A, when relating a particular historical story, the Qur'an highlights only certain significant events, and it does not specify the time between them. Mentioning the speech of the angels after Zechariah's prayer without stating explicitly a passage of time does not necessarily mean that it occurred right after the prayer. However, the use of the word "there" in verse 3.38 suggests that the good news would have been delivered relatively soon, possibly within hours or days, after the prayer.

The angels named Zechariah's son, so the name *Yaḥyā* (John) was also chosen by God. This is in agreement with Luke's account of the angel's words to Zechariah: "Do not be afraid, Zechariah, for your prayer has been heard, and your wife Elizabeth will bear you a son; you will name him John" (Luke 1:13).

Zechariah was also told that his son was going to be godly, as he had asked in his prayers. The elaborate descriptions of John's good qualities suggest that he was even more of a special righteous man than Zechariah had prayed for. For instance, in his prayer, Zechariah did not specifically ask for his son to be of as high a status as a prophet. His patience and persistence on praying to God paid off; he was given even more than he asked for.

Many exegetes understand the Arabic phrase that I have translated as "confirming with a Word from Allah" as meaning "confirming a Word from Allah," taking the "Word" to be the *subject* rather than the *means* of the confirmation. They suggest that the "Word" here denotes Jesus who was created by a Word from God (3.45). This view is based on an incorrect interpretation of the Arabic text. The implication of the difference between this meaning and the one in my interpretation is significant, so it is important to clear up this issue and explain it in some detail.

The Arabic text in question is *muṣaddiqan bi kalimatin*. The words *muṣaddiqan* and *kalimatin* means "confirming" and "word," respectively. There is no ambiguity or disagreement about the literal meanings of these terms. The wrong interpretation of *muṣaddiqan bi kalimatin* as "confirming a Word from God" is the result of overlooking a significant difference between when the word *muṣaddiqan* is followed by the preposition *bi*, as in the unique case of the phrase in question, and when *muṣaddiqan*, or its nominative form *muṣaddiqun*, is followed by *li*, as in another 15 verses. In all of these 15 instances, the combination of *muṣaddiqan* and *li* is used to stress how a prophet was sent or a book was revealed by God to *confirm* the verity of books that He had revealed to previous prophets. The preposition *li* means "for," so the expression *muṣaddiqan li* means providing confirmation for or, more succinctly, confirming. These are example:

> He has sent down to you [O Muhammad!] the Book with truth, confirming that which was revealed before it, and He sent down the Torah and the Injīl (3.3).

> And when a Messenger from Allah came to them confirming that which they have, a party of those who were given the Book threw the Book of Allah behind their backs as if they knew nothing (2.101).

The preposition *bi*, on the other hand, means by or with, hence my translation of the unique expression *muṣaddiqan bi* in verse 3.39 as confirming with. "Conforming a Word" would have been the correct translation had the Arabic phrase been *muṣaddiqan li kalimatin*.

The interpretation "confirming with a Word from Allah" suggests that John was given some form of scriptural revelation. Interestingly, we will find another verse that talks about John and "the Book" when we study the verses of chapter 19 later on.

Back to Zechariah who was stunned by the news about John, his spontaneous response was to mention the fact that he was very old and his wife was barren:

> He said: "My Lord! How can I have a son when I am very old and my wife is barren?" He said: "Thus Allah does what He wills" (3.40).

Although Zechariah never stopped praying to God and never lost hope of His mercy, the news still came as a big pleasant surprise to him. His reactive statement "My Lord! How can I have a son when I am very old and my wife is barren?" does not question God's ability to give him offspring, as he always believed that God can do that, but is a reflection of his happy astonishment at the realization of the miracle he had been praying for. He realized that the voice that he heard was probably angelic and was conveying this news at the command of God, which is why he addressed his reply to God. He knew that the angels were only messengers delivering a message from God to him.

In reply to Zechariah's curious question, the answer came: "Thus Allah does what He wills," emphasizing that God's will is the explanation. These words were probably also uttered by the angels but are attributed to God for the same reason that made Zechariah address his question to God: the angels only spoke what God had ordered them to say. Also, the answer is attributed to God because Zechariah addressed his words to Him.

Zechariah's reference to his old age clearly implies that he understood that the miraculous pregnancy was going to happen after he has had intercourse with his wife. This is a fundamental difference between the conception of John and that of Jesus. In the case of the latter, no sexual intercourse was involved, as we will discuss in detail later.

Upon hearing the reply of the angels, Zechariah went on to ask God to "appoint a sign" for him:

> He said: "My Lord! Appoint a sign for me." He said: "Your sign shall be that you shall not speak to people for three days, except by signs. Remember your Lord much, and praise Him in the early hours of night and morning" (3.41).

Ash-Sha'rāwī (1999: 65) reiterates the view of some exegetes that Zechariah's request was for a sign that would tell him when the pregnancy has happened, but there is no support in the Qur'an for this view. The Qur'an implies that the pregnancy was going to happen when Zechariah has had sexual intercourse with his wife.

Aṭ-Ṭabāṭabā'ī convincingly argues that Zechariah's request reflects an element of uncertainty as to whether the voice that he was hearing was indeed angelic or Satanic. Zechariah was *almost* certain that the voice that he heard was of an angel, but it still occurred to him that Satan may have been trying to trick him with that voice, so he sought reassurance from God. The Qur'an indicates that Satan can interfere not only psychologically but also physically in the lives of people, including prophets. One example is Prophet Job's attribution of the contagious disease that he had, which forced his family away from him, to Satan (21.83-84, 38.41-43).

This interpretation of Zechariah's request for a sign is confirmed by the fact that he was to be temporarily unable to speak *to people only*. Zechariah's ability to speak to God in his prayer is clear from the command to him to remember His Lord and praise Him night and day. Zechariah found himself unable to speak to people, but absolutely normal when praying. This is something that Satan, who does not want man to worship God, could not have worked. It was a clear proof that the voice Zechariah heard was of an angel speaking on behalf of God to him. It was a miracle from God.

Luke's account of the miracle is rather different, claiming that Gabriel told Zechariah: "And now, because you did not believe my words, which will be fulfilled in their time, you will be silent, unable to speak, until the day these things take place" (Luke 1:20). This is an instance of textual corruption in which the change to the text left the miracle serving no purpose; it is mere punishment. The Qur'an does not imply there was any punishment involved, although exegetes, influenced by the Christian story, claim that it was a punishment. It was simply a miracle that confirmed to Zechariah that the news was genuine and the voice was angelic. It was a favor, rather than a punishment. Zechariah asked for a "sign," and he was given one.

Luke's account has another two significant differences with the Qur'an. Interestingly but not surprisingly, the Qur'an's subtle differentiation between Zechariah's inability to speak to people and his ability to pray is completely absent from Luke. Such significant but subtle references are easy to miss, and the writer of Luke or his sources did not notice them in the original source of the story, which could have been the Injīl. Additionally, Luke makes Zechariah's dumbness last until the birth of John, not only for three days.

Verse 41 is the last verse in chapter 3 that talks about Zechariah, as verse 42 (p. 53) picks up the story of Mary. A longer account of Zechariah's story is found in chapter 19, which we shall study next.

3.3.2. Prophet Zechariah in Chapter 19 (*Maryam*)

The 15 verses that detail the story of Zechariah in chapter 19 of the Qur'an start with the following verse about God's mercy to this noble prophet:

> This is the account of the mercy of your Lord [O Muhammad!] to His servant Zechariah (19.2).

Then God starts explaining the nature of this "mercy":

> When he cried to his Lord a cry in secret (19.3).

The meaning of the secrecy of the prayer will become clearer in later verses. The next verse starts recounting Zechariah's prayer:

> He said: "My Lord! My bones have waxed feeble and my head is shining with grey hair, and I have never been deprived in my prayer to You, my Lord (19.4).

After citing his old age, Zechariah moves on to emphasize how God used to generously answer his prayers. The Arabic word *shaqiyyan*, which may be translated as "unanswered" or "deprived," as is the case above, may also mean "evil" or "wretched."

While verse 3.38 used the word "there" to stress that it was the prayer that Zechariah made after talking to Mary that God answered, this verse talks about the nature of Zechariah's prayer in general:

> I fear the inheritors after me, and my wife has been barren, so give me an heir from You (19.5).

The Arabic phrase that is translated "from You" above is *min ladunka* or "from Your *ladun*," which I explained in my comment on verse 3.38 earlier in the chapter. It describes the son that Zechariah prayed to have as being "from Allah's *ladun*" because he could only come by a miracle.

Verses 19.5-6 explain the secrecy of the prayer and tell us more about what kind of son Zechariah was asking for. Old and increasingly isolated, Zechariah was living in a hostile environment. His enemies included relatives, acquaintances, and clerics. The Arabic term *mawālī* which I have translated as "inheritors" may strictly mean "relatives," but I preferred to use the more general and inclusive meaning. The hostility that he faced explains the "quarrel" about the guardianship of Mary that he got involved in:

> This is part of the tidings of the unseen. We reveal it to you [O Muhammad!]. You were not present with them when they cast lots with their sticks [to decide] who of them should become the guardian of Mary, nor were you present with them when they quarreled [thereupon] (3.44).

While still prominent and highly respected by people, Zechariah's authority was being unjustly challenged and undermined by religious clerics who did not have the spiritual status that God conferred on him. He was equally worried because of the relatives who would inherit his position. He was very concerned about what was going to happen after his death to the divine message and mission that he and the preceding prophets brought and which he sincerely honored and protected during his life. Fearing that the religious leadership of the nation would fall in the wrong hands after his death, Zechariah asked God to grant him a pious son who would be seen by people as his legitimate heir, and who would protect that prophetic legacy and offer genuine spiritual leadership:

> Who shall inherit of me and inherit of the house of Jacob, and make him, my Lord, one with whom You are well-pleased" (19.6).

Zechariah's concern was not over worldly matters, but religious and spiritual issues. He could not see in the existing clerics and potential leadership contenders anyone who could take forward the prophetic legacy of Jacob and the prophets who followed him down to Zechariah himself. The description of verse 19.5 of Zechariah's prayer as being "in secret" indicates that he was being intimidated by those who were anxiously waiting for his death. Interestingly, the wording of Zechariah's prayer in verse 3.38 which does not describe the prayer as having been performed "in secret" also does not describe the requested son as being the heir of Zechariah. This indicates that while Zechariah might have been known to have been praying for a son, his wish for that son to become his spiritual heir was something that he kept secret.

Aṭ-Ṭabāṭabā'ī has argued that had Zechariah been asking for a spiritual heir, he would not have necessarily asked for a son, as any pious person could have become his spiritual heir. This argument ignores the difference explained above between the two wordings of Zechariah's prayer, where chapter 19's description of the prayer as being "in secret" and of the son as Zechariah's heir are both missing from chapter 3.

Aṭ-Ṭabāṭabā'ī's argument also ignores the fact that any other genuine religious leader would not have stood a chance of being accepted by those quarreling, powerful priests and leaders. Being the son of and raised by Zechariah would give the new leader a much better chance of being respected and accepted, as Zechariah had commanded over the years great public support and respect, even though others were challenging him. Zechariah's prayer for a son had two dimensions: the natural inclination to have offspring, and his keenness on leaving a genuine spiritual leader behind him.

One difference between Zechariah in the Qur'an and in the New Testament is that while the latter calls him a "priest" (Luke 1:5), the Qur'an describes him, as well as his son John, as a "prophet." The term "prophet" has a very specific meaning in the Qur'an. It signifies a special status of nearness to God which is granted to some individuals only (§15.1.2). The following verse, which belongs to a group of verses that praise a number of prophets, emphasizes the prophethood of Zechariah and John:

> And Zechariah, John, Jesus, and Ilyās, all in the ranks of the righteous (6.85).

Another confirmation that Zechariah and John were prophets occurs in verse 90 of chapter 21. The latter is known as the *Chapter of Prophets*, where a number of prophets and specific events and miracles in their lives are recounted:

> And Zechariah, when he cried to his Lord: "O my Lord, do not leave me alone! And You are the best of inheritors" (21.89). So We responded to him, gave him John, and cured his wife [to bear a child] for him. They used to hasten to do good deeds, and pray to Us with love and reverence, and they were humble before Us (21.90).

After mentioning His favors to a number of His prophets, God goes on to highlight His favor of giving Zechariah a son. Zechariah's description of himself as being "lonely" is in line with my interpretation that he was living in a hostile environment. The second half of Zechariah's prayer, "You are the best of inheritors," stresses the fact that he was seeking an heir, which is also mentioned in verse 19.6. This miracle would have greatly strengthened Zechariah's position not only because he was no more alone with no heir, but because it was clearly a sign that attested to his special spiritual status.

The Qur'an does not give us details about the environment in which Zechariah lived and made him feel this lonely. Luke (1:5) gives information about Zechariah's priesthood, describing him as belonging to "the priestly division of Abijah." The Old Testament states that when the number of priests became very large, King David divided them into 24 groups (1 Chr. 23:1-6), apparently so that one priest at a time would minister the altar. The division of Abijah, to which Zechariah belonged, was the eighth (1 Chr. 24:10). Some may link the hostility that the Qur'an implies Zechariah faced to the Old Testament's description of the division of the priests into courses, so it could be suggested that it was some form of in-fighting between priests. This view ignores the substantial difference between Zechariah's image in the Qur'an and the Bible. As explained above, Zechariah was not simply a priest among many others. The hostility that this prophet experienced did not come from peers, but from religious authorities — say, priests — who did not respect his special status and acted as his rivals.

Back to chapter 19, following Zechariah's prayer for an heir, he is told the good news:

> [It was said to him:] "O Zechariah! We bring to you the good news of [the birth of] a son whose name is John; we have not created someone similar to him before" (19.7).

Unlike verse 3.39 which explicitly states that it was angels who delivered the good news to Zechariah, this verse does not identify the speaker. Clearly, it was the angels who delivered the message, but this verse bypasses the messengers to focus on the message. This reflects the fact that the message was ultimately from God, and that the angels merely spoke to Zechariah on behalf of God.

After confirming that the name of Zechariah's son was chosen by God, the verse goes on to make this statement about John: "We have not created someone similar to him before." Most exegetes — including aṭ-Ṭabarī, aṭ-Ṭabāṭabā'ī, and al-Qummī — understand the passage as meaning "We have not named someone else with this name before." Other exegetes have interpreted the verse in the way I did. The difference in interpretation stems from a difference in understanding the meaning of the Arabic word *samiyyā*. Relating this word to the Arabic word *ism*, which means "name," and noting that it occurs in a verse that talks about the naming of John, exegetes have taken *samiyyā* to mean "of similar name." These exegetes seem to have been influenced by a similar passage in Luke 1:61:

> On the eighth day they came to circumcise the child, and they wanted to name him Zechariah after his father. But his mother replied, "No! He must be named John." They said to her, "But none of your relatives bears this name." (Luke 1:59-61)

Other exegetes have rightly noted that *samiyyā* occurs in another verse in the same chapter where it means "similar" or "equal":

> [He is] the Lord of the heavens and the earth and what is between them, so serve Him and be patient in His service. Do you know any one equal (*samiyyā*) to Him? (19.65).

I think this second occurrence of *samiyyā* clarifies its meaning beyond any doubt, hence my translation above. The meaning of the statement that God had not created someone similar before is clarified in verse 19.15 (p. 81).

The wording of Zechariah's reaction to hearing the good news is very similar to the one reported in verse 3.40:

> He said: "My Lord! How can I have a son when my wife is barren and I have grown very old?" (19.8).

Here and in verses 3.40 and 19.5 Zechariah describes himself as "old" but, notably, calls his wife "barren" rather than "old." It may be suggested that she was not old like him, but that is very unlikely. The Qur'an gives us the impression that Zechariah prayed for a long time for offspring, and that means that he had been married for many years. Even if Zechariah's wife was younger than him, she was probably also old. Zechariah meant that his wife was already barren, that is in addition to her being old. In other words, she could not get pregnant even when she was young, so clearly it is even more supernatural for her to become pregnant having become old also.

Conversely, it may also be thought that Zechariah applied the term "barren" to his wife only because this term is used specifically for females in the Qur'an. But that is not the case, as the following verses show:

> Allah's is the kingdom of the heavens and the earth. He creates what He pleases. He grants to whom He pleases females and grants to whom He pleases males (42.49). Or He bestows both males and females, and He leaves barren whom He will. He is full of Knowledge and Power (42.50).

Zechariah was aware that both the man and the woman had to be fertile for pregnancy to take place, but he also knew that there was a significant difference between his situation and his wife's. His mention of his old age but not barrenness indicates his knowledge that he was not barren and that while it was very difficult for him at that age to impregnate his wife, it was not impossible. His reference to his wife's barrenness, on the other hand, reflects his awareness of the main reason for them not having children.

Zechariah's inquisitive question in verse 19.8 is answered by God in the next verse:

> He said: "So [it will be]. Your Lord said: 'It is easy for Me. I created you before, when you were nothing'" (19.9).

God tells Zechariah that giving him and his old, barren wife a son is an easy feat for Him, reminding him that he also was one day nothing and He created him. The implication here is that whether someone is created naturally or miraculously, that creation can take place *only* by God's intervention. Natural phenomena and events occur as a result of natural laws, but these laws have been created and are maintained by God. The natural laws of physics are not intrinsic to matter, and God can disable or change them as He likes. For instance, when Prophet Abraham's people tried to burn him alive because he believed in the One God, Allah, and abandoned their polytheistic religion and idols, God made the fire lose its *natural* ability to harm Abraham:

> They (Abraham's people) said: "Burn him and stand by your gods; do that" (21.68). We said: "O fire, be coolness and peace for Abraham!" (21.69).

Zechariah then asked God to give him a sign, as explained earlier, to quell an element of doubt inside him that the voice could have been that of Satan trying to seduce him:

> He said: "My Lord! Appoint for me a sign." He said: "Your sign is that you shall not speak to people for three nights" (19.10).

The sign was Zechariah's sudden loss of ability to specifically speak to "people," but not the capability to pray to God. This kind of paranormal feat could not have been caused by Satan who does not want people to worship God.

Having received the good news and had a sign appointed for him, Zechariah came out of the sanctuary where he was praying and spoke to people by signs, instructing them to praise God by night and day:

> Then he came out to his people from the sanctuary, and signaled to them: "Glorify your Lord in the morning and in the evening" (19.11).

Zechariah could not have explained to people then what happened in the sanctuary, but clearly people realized that something momentous took place and that Zechariah was extremely pleased and deeply touched. Luke (1:22) claims that when Zechariah came out of the temple and could not speak to people, they concluded that he must have seen a vision.

Verse 19.11 is the last verse in chapter 19 that speaks about Zechariah specifically, as the following verses talk about his son, John.

Clearly, the Qur'an and Christian sources give very different accounts of Zechariah and his role in Mary's life. The New Testament and apocryphal writings also show confusion about Zechariah's identity and details of his life. One major difference between the Qur'anic Zechariah and the Christian one is that while the latter is merely a "priest," the former is a "prophet" — which is a very special status in the Qur'an that puts him in the same category of great figures such as Moses, Jesus, and Muhammad.

4

Prophet John

The story of John the Baptist is closely tied with Jesus' life in Christian sources. The Gospels present John as the forerunner of the Messiah, but they paint a rather inconsistent picture of his relationship with Jesus and whether he recognized Jesus as the Messiah. Only two of the Gospels claim explicitly that John baptized Jesus.

Of the apocryphal gospels consulted in this book, only the Infancy Gospel of James mentions John. Herod wanted to kill the young boy so John's mother took him to the mountains to hide him. A mountain was divided and received him, and an angel appeared to protect him and his mother. Herod questioned John's father, the priest Zechariah, about the whereabouts of his son, but when Zechariah claimed he did not know, Herod killed him (InJam. 16:3-16).

Unlike Mary and Zechariah, John is also mentioned outside the scripture — although in only one historical source. In *Jewish Antiquities*, the historian Josephus disagrees with the Gospels about the meaning of the baptism that John performed and how he was killed.

John is also mentioned in the Qur'an, but much more briefly. The Qur'an establishes an indirect link between Jesus and John, as John's father was Mary's guardian. John is presented as a prophet, like Jesus.

4.1. John the Baptist in the New Testament

Only Luke among the canonical Gospels talks about John's birth, as it continues its story of Zechariah and how he was given the news about his wife's miraculous conception of a son:

> Now the time came for Elizabeth to have her baby, and she gave birth to a son. Her neighbors and relatives heard that the Lord had shown great mercy to her, and they rejoiced with her.
> On the eighth day they came to circumcise the child, and they wanted to name him Zechariah after his father. But his mother replied, "No! He must be named John." They said to her, "But none of your relatives bears this name." So they made signs to the baby's father, inquiring what he wanted to name his son. He asked for a writing tablet and wrote, "His name is John." And they were all amazed. Immediately Zechariah's mouth was opened and his tongue released, and he spoke, blessing God. (Luke 1:57-64)

Zechariah was filled with the Holy Spirit and prophesied the following about the newborn child:

> And you, child, will be called the prophet of the Most High. For you will go before the Lord to prepare his ways, to give his people knowledge of salvation through the forgiveness of their sins. Because of our God's tender mercy the dawn will break upon us from on high to give light to those who sit in darkness and in the shadow of death, to guide our feet into the way of peace. (Luke 1:76-79)

There is no account given of John's childhood in the canonical Gospels. Luke remarks quickly that after "growing and becoming strong in spirit," John "was in the wilderness until the day he was revealed to Israel" (Luke 1:80). All of the Evangelists talk about an adult John already preaching in the desert when Jesus began his ministry — that is, when Jesus was 30 years old according to Luke (3:23). Luke's account has extra information that may be used for dating the ministry of John:

> In the fifteenth year of the reign of Tiberius Caesar, when Pontius Pilate was governor of Judea, and Herod was tetrarch of Galilee, and his brother Philip was tetrarch of the region of Iturea and Trachonitis, and Lysanias was tetrarch of Abilene, during the high priesthood of Annas and Caiaphas, the word of God came to John the son of Zechariah in the wilderness. (Luke 3:1-2)

This could be any date between January 26 and April 30 CE (p. 191).

It is not clear whether Luke considered the three years in which Tiberius was co-regent with his stepfather Augustus before he became the sole emperor after Augustus' death in 14 CE. Theissen and Merz (1999: 156) cite one study that gives 16 different possible datings of the 15th year of Tiberius, with some datings differing by as much as a few years. Considering different calendars, they conclude that Luke could have meant any date from January 26 to April 30 CE.

According to the Gospels, John called people to repentance. Through baptism by John, God offered forgiveness to people (Matt. 3:1-8; Luke 3:3-7):

> In the wilderness John the baptizer began preaching a baptism of repentance for the forgiveness of sins. People from the whole Judean countryside and all of Jerusalem were going out to him, and he was baptizing them in the Jordan River as they confessed their sins. (Mark 1:4-5)

People had been waiting for the Christ (John 1:19-25), and some thought that John might be the Christ himself (Luke 3:15). John's baptism is also presented by the Gospel of John as paving the way for the coming of the Christ: "I came baptizing with water so that he could be revealed to Israel" (John 1:31). John is shown to be involved in messianic preaching, announcing and preparing for the coming of someone who is *mightier* than and superior to him, who is generally accepted to be Jesus (Matt. 3:11-12, 11:11; Luke 3:16-17; John 1:15, 26-27, 30):

John wore a garment made of camel's hair with a leather belt around his waist, and he ate locusts and wild honey. He proclaimed, "One more powerful than I am is coming after me; I am not worthy to bend down and untie the strap of his sandals. I baptize you with water, but he will baptize you with the Holy Spirit." (Mark 1:6-8)

The Gospels present John as a prophet who was the fulfillment of an Isaiah prophecy (Mark 1:2-3; Matt. 3:3; John 1:23):

A voice cries out, "In the wilderness clear a way for the Lord; construct in the desert a road for our God." (Isa. 40:3)

This prophecy appears in four different versions in the Gospels, and Luke's account is the longest:

The voice of one shouting in the wilderness: "Prepare the way for the Lord, make his paths straight. Every valley will be filled, and every mountain and hill will be brought low, and the crooked will be made straight, and the rough ways will be made smooth, and all humanity will see the salvation of God." (Luke 3:4-6)

Contrary to what the Evangelists say, Isaiah's prophecy actually talks about God, not the Messiah. Committing the same mistake or misunderstanding is one sign that the canonical Gospels are not completely independent of each other.

Mark and, in a slightly more elaborated version, Matthew explicitly state that John baptized Jesus:

Now in those days Jesus came from Nazareth in Galilee and was baptized by John in the Jordan River. And just as Jesus was coming up out of the water, he saw the heavens splitting apart and the Spirit descending on him like a dove. And a voice came from heaven: "You are my one dear Son; in you I take great delight." (Mark 1:9-11)

Then Jesus came from Galilee to John to be baptized by him in the Jordan River. But John tried to prevent him, saying, "I need to be baptized by you, and yet you come to me?" So Jesus replied to him, "Let it happen now, for it is right for us to fulfill all righteousness." Then John yielded to him. After Jesus was baptized, just as he was coming up out of the water, the heavens opened and he saw the Spirit of God descending like a dove and coming on him. And a voice from heaven said, "This is my one dear Son; in him I take great delight." (Matt. 3:13-17)

The Gospel of John, on the other hand, does not state that John baptized Jesus:

On the next day John saw Jesus coming toward him and said, "Look, the Lamb of God who takes away the sin of the world! This is the one about whom I said, 'After me comes a man who is greater than I am, because he existed before me.' I did not recognize him, but I came baptizing with water so that he could be revealed to Israel."

Then John testified, "I saw the Spirit descending like a dove from heaven, and it remained on him. And I did not recognize him, but the one who sent me to baptize with water said to me, 'The one on whom you see the Spirit descending and remaining—this is the one who baptizes with the Holy Spirit.' I have both seen and testified that this man is the Chosen One of God." (John 1:29-34)

Luke has yet another different account that seems to suggest that Jesus was baptized while John was in prison:

And in this way, with many other exhortations, John proclaimed good news to the people. But when John rebuked Herod the tetrarch because of Herodias, his brother's wife, and because of all the evil deeds that he had done, Herod added this to them all: He locked up John in prison.
Now when all the people were baptized, Jesus also was baptized. And while he was praying, the heavens opened, and the Holy Spirit descended on him in bodily form like a dove. And a voice came from heaven, "You are my one dear Son; in you I take great delight." (Luke 3:18-22)

The author might imply that John was imprisoned after baptizing Jesus, as there is no mention of any other person baptizing people.

The four Gospels give contradictory and confused accounts also of what John is supposed to have considered Jesus. None of the Gospels state explicitly that John recognized Jesus as the Messiah. Mark, the oldest Gospel, Matthew, and Luke do not even say explicitly that John realized that Jesus was the man whose coming he had been announcing. Matthew (3:14) states that John recognized Jesus as someone that he should be baptized by, not the other way around. Matthew (3:11-12), Luke (3:16-17), and John (1:26-27) say that John spoke about someone *mightier* than him to come after him, but he did not actually identify Jesus explicitly with that person, although the Evangelists make the context imply that. Yet latter passages in Matthew and Luke contradict these statements, as they show the imprisoned John send two of his disciples to ask Jesus whether he was the one "who is to come" or they should "look for another" (Matt. 11:2-3; Luke 7:19). These passages even suggest that John had never met Jesus, let alone recognized him as the Messiah or the figure he was paving the way for. John's question about Jesus in prison and his earlier recognition of Jesus as the man whose coming he was announcing are irreconcilable. John could not have acted as a forerunner for Jesus and borne witness to him early on, but forget completely about him shortly afterward!

The Gospel of John, on the other hand, states that when John the Baptist saw Jesus he said "This is the one about whom I said, 'After me comes a man who is greater than I am, because he existed before me'" (John 1:30). Here John the Baptist clearly identifies Jesus as the one about whose arrival he was spreading the good news. However, in the following passage John goes on to say that he "did not recognize him," which may mean that he did not recognize Jesus before his baptism. This would imply that John had never met Jesus before, which seems rather strange if we believe Luke who portrays Jesus and John as relatives.

Another, theological problem with John's baptism of Jesus is that baptism was supposedly for forgiving sins, yet Jesus is considered by Christians to have had no sin. Additionally, the image of John baptizing Jesus, in the same way he baptized other ordinary people, seems to contradict the portrayal of Jesus as being superior to John. Some scholars have suggested that the superiority that the Gospels give to Jesus over John, which is repeated in Acts (13:24-25), is nothing more than a response to a rivalry that existed between their followers after the death of the two masters (Miller, 2003: 23-26; Vermes, 2000: 155).

Mark, Matthew, and Luke state that Jesus' miracles made people wonder whether he was the then dead John the Baptist who was performing miracles because he was raised from the dead (Mark 6:14, 8:28; Matt. 14:2; Luke 9:7). These passages suggest that John did not perform miracles, hence those who thought Jesus was John were attributing his *new* miraculous powers to his resurrection. Indeed, the 4th Gospel confirms that "John performed no miraculous sign" (John 10:41).

The Synoptists (Mark 6:17-27; Matt. 14:3-10; Luke 3:19-20, 9:9) state that John was killed by Herod Antipas (d. 39 CE), one of the sons of Herod the Great near the end of whose reign Jesus is believed to have been born. Herod is said to have ordered the imprisonment and then killing of John because the latter objected to his marriage to the wife of his half-brother Philip:

> For Herod himself had sent men, arrested John, and bound him in prison on account of Herodias, his brother Philip's wife, because Herod had married her. For John had repeatedly told Herod, "It is not lawful for you to have your brother's wife." So Herodias nursed a grudge against him and wanted to kill him. But she could not because Herod stood in awe of John and protected him, since he knew that John was a righteous and holy man. When Herod heard him, he was thoroughly baffled, and yet he liked to listen to John.
> But a suitable day came, when Herod gave a banquet on his birthday for his court officials, military commanders, and leaders of Galilee. When his daughter Herodias came in and danced, she pleased Herod and his dinner guests. The king said to the girl, "Ask me for whatever you want and I will give it to you." He swore to her, "Whatever you ask I will give you, up to half my kingdom." So she went out and said to her mother, "What should I ask for?" Her mother said, "The head of John the baptizer." Immediately she hurried back to the king and made her request: "I want the head of John the Baptist on a platter immediately." Although it grieved the king deeply, he did not want to reject her request because of his oath and his guests. So the king sent an executioner at once to bring John's head, and he went and beheaded John in prison. (Mark 6:17-27)

As the Gospels place the execution of John before Jesus' crucifixion, the usual dating of the latter to around 29 CE fixes roughly the date of John's execution.

4.2. John the Baptist in History

The only mention of John the Baptist outside Christian sources occurs in *Jewish Antiquities* of the Jewish historian Joseph ben Matthias, better known with his Roman name Flavius Josephus (37-100 CE). Josephus mentions John the Baptist in a positive tone, describing him as a good man who called on the Jews to be virtuous. He says that John developed loyal followers among the Jews and was accepted as a genuinely righteous man. The Jews even thought that the defeat of Herod's army by the Nabataean king Aretas, whose daughter Antipas had divorced in order to get married to Herodias, was a divine revenge for Herod's murder of John.

Unlike Josephus' reference to Jesus in *Jewish Antiquities* 18.3.3, which is generally accepted to be a Christian forgery (pp. 416-419), Josephus' account of John the Baptist has not been questioned. There is nothing in the text to suggest any Christian influence. In fact, the account differs from what the Gospels say. This is Josephus' full account:

> Now some of the Jews thought that the destruction of Herod's army came from God, and that very justly, as a punishment of what he did against John, that was called the Baptist: for Herod slew him, who was a good man, and commanded the Jews to exercise virtue, both as to righteousness towards one another, and piety towards God, and so to come to baptism; for that the washing [with water] would be acceptable to him, if they made use of it, not in order to the putting away [or the remission] of some sins, but for the purification of the body; supposing still that the soul was thoroughly purified beforehand by righteousness.
>
> Now when [many] others came in crowds about him, for they were very greatly moved [or pleased] by hearing his words, Herod, who feared lest the great influence John had over the people might put it into his power and inclination to raise a rebellion, (for they seemed ready to do anything he should advise,) thought it best, by putting him to death, to prevent any mischief he might cause, and not bring himself into difficulties, by sparing a man who might make him repent of it when it would be too late.
>
> Accordingly he was sent a prisoner, out of Herod's suspicious temper, to Macherus, the castle I before mentioned, and was there put to death. Now the Jews had an opinion that the destruction of this army was sent as a punishment upon Herod, and a mark of God's displeasure to him. (Josephus, *Jewish Antiquities*, 18.5.2)

There is a clear difference between the image of baptism in Christian sources and Josephus. The Gospels present baptism as a sacrament for the forgiveness of sins, whereas Josephus goes out of his way to point out that this is not the case and that it only serves to purify the body. The soul, Josephus stresses, should have already been purified by good deeds. Theissen and Merz (1999: 203) rightly point out that Josephus must have been clearly aware of the sacramental interpretation of baptism, so he rejected it expressly.

Another significant difference between Josephus and the Gospels is that the Jewish historian does not confirm that John preached about the imminent coming of the Messiah, and he does not establish any direct link between John and Jesus, who is mentioned only twice in his writings. Josephus did not believe that Jesus was the Messiah or that a real Messiah appeared around the time when John and Jesus lived. In fact, he condemned all pretending Messiahs in his writings. If he thought that John had preached the imminence coming of the Messiah he would have concluded that John taught a false prophecy and would not have looked favorably at him. If the Jewish historian learned that John declared Jesus as the Messiah, he would have probably considered John a heretic. Similarly, most of the Jews did not believe the messiahship of Jesus or that the Messiah they were waiting for came at the time of John, so Josephus' confirmation that many Jews believed in the virtue of John must mean that he was not associated with prophesying the imminent coming of the Messiah or, even worse, that Jesus was the Messiah.

Josephus confirms the Gospels' claim that John was killed by Herod Antipas, but he gives a different motive. While the Gospels claim that Herod killed John because he opposed his illegal marriage to his half brother's wife, Josephus reports that the execution was the result of Herod's fear that John, with his increasing following, could spark off a rebellion against him. Interestingly, Josephus relates the story of Herod's falling in love with Herodias and consequent marriage to her in the paragraph immediately preceding his account of John's death. Had Josephus believed that Herod's relationship with Herodias had anything to do with John's execution, he would have mentioned it. The fortress of Macherus is near to the east of the Jordan, the area where the Gospels say John baptized people.

Josephus implies that John was murdered before 37 CE, when Aretas defeated Herod. Two years later Antipas was dismissed and sent into exile by the Roman emperor. The fact that people attributed Herod's defeat to his killing of John suggests that the murder happened shortly before the military defeat. This conclusion would place John's death several years after Jesus' crucifixion which is believed to have happened around 29 CE.

4.3. Prophet John in the Qur'an

The Qur'an mentions John only briefly, focusing on his special virtuous attributes. It does not contain any information about John's life, his adulthood, any encounter he may have had with Jesus, or his death. John' story in the Qur'an may be considered as part of the story of Zechariah.

The Qur'an refers to John in 7 verses only, 5 of them in chapter 19. Verses 6.85 and 21.90, which we examined in Chapter 3, mention John only in passing. Verse 6.85 is one of a group of verses in which a number of prophets are mentioned and praised, so this verse confirms John's prophethood:

> And Zechariah, John, Jesus, and Ilyās, all in the ranks of the righteous (6.85).

Verse 90 of chapter 21, which is known as the *Chapter of Prophets*, refers to John's miraculous conception and the righteousness of him and his parents:

> So We responded to him (Zechariah), gave him John, and cured his wife [to bear a child] for him. They used to hasten to do good deeds, and pray to Us with love and reverence, and they were humble before Us (21.90).

The five verses about John in chapter 19 include the following verse which we have already studied in the story of Zechariah:

> It was said to him: "O Zechariah! We bring to you the good news of [the birth of] a son whose name is John; we have not created someone similar to him before" (19.7).

The remaining four verses start with words that God addressed John:

> [It was said to John]: "O John! Take hold of the Book firmly." And we gave him Wisdom while still a child (19.12).

To "take hold of the Book firmly" means to follow and apply it strictly. The Qur'an does not specify the mentioned divine book, but exegetes have suggested that it is the Torah which had been revealed to Moses and which was being followed by people at the time. My view is that it is a book that God revealed to John, as I pointed out in my interpretation of the clause "confirming with a Word from Allah" (p. 63).

When talking about the conferment of divine knowledge on prophets who are known to have received divine books, the Qur'an often mentions both kinds of knowledge, the Book and Wisdom, in succession. This can be seen, for example, in verses 3.164, 3.48, and 2.251, which talk about prophets Muhammad, Jesus, and David, respectively. Verse 19.12 above follows the same pattern of mentioning the Book and Wisdom successively, so the former may well be a book that was revealed to John rather than the Torah of Moses.

Another interesting observation is the suggestion of some that the "Sabaeans," who are mentioned in the Qur'an in three verses alongside three other groups of believers all of whom had divine books, are the "Mandaeans" who are known to venerate John:

Those who believe, the Jews, the Christians, and the Sabaeans — whoever believe in Allah and the Last day and does good — they shall have their reward from their Lord, and there is no fear for them, nor shall they grieve (2.62, 5.69).

Those who believe, the Jews, the Sabaeans, the Christians, the Magians, and those who associate [others with Allah], Allah will decide between them on the Day of Resurrection. Allah is a witness over all things (22.17).

"Those who believe," which is a term that the Qur'an uses for the followers of Prophet Muhammad to emphasize their difference from the polytheists who rejected Islam, have the Qur'an; the Jews had the Torah; and the Christians had the Injīl; so it looks likely that the Qur'an associates the Sabaeans with a Book. The identification of the Sabaeans with the Mandaeans, who are found in Iraq and Iran, is a subject of disagreement, but it is interesting that one of the sacred books of the Mandaeans is called the *Book of John* and reports the activities of John the Baptist, and that they have an elaborate ritual of baptism.

God treated John in a unique way, as He conferred on him the Book and Wisdom while he was still a small child. The term *ṣabiyyā* (child) in verse 19.12 appears only in one other verse in the Qur'an which applies it to the infant Jesus. Although this term is used in Arabic in general for a child who may be as old as, say, 10 years, it's other use in the Qur'an make me inclined to believe that the verse meant that John was a very small child when he received the Book and Wisdom from God.

Other favors that God bestowed on John are mentioned in the next verse:

And compassion from Us, and purity; and he was dutiful (19.13).

The phrase that is translated above as "from Us" is *min ladunka* (p. 62). The listing of the special qualities that God gave to John continues in verse 14:

And [We made him] kind to his parents. And he was not arrogant, disobedient (19.14).

Both of John's parent's were still alive when he had grown up enough to show kindness and obedience to them. God's conferment of "compassion" on John may suggest that he lost one or two of his parents before reaching adulthood. This impressive list of honorable attributes and the brief account of John's story conclude with this verse:

And peace is on him the day he was born, the day he dies, and the day he shall be raised alive (19.15).

This is a unique description that the Qur'an applies to John and later to Jesus. Prophets and righteous people are described in the Qur'an as having *peace on them* (e.g. 37.79, 27.59) which means, among other things, that they would enter paradise on the Day of Resurrection. But no one other than John and Jesus is described as having peace on him at birth, during his life, and in the hereafter. Both John and Jesus were miraculously created, and both received revelation and support from God from their early years. We will see later how God inspired Jesus from the time of his birth and throughout his life (p. 178). God treated John also in a special way from his early years. Verse 19.12 tells us that God gave Wisdom to John when he was still a child and, significantly, mentions even before that God's speech to him to *take firm hold of the Book*. This is very similar to Jesus words when he was still in the cradle: "[He] has given me the Book" (19.30). John and Jesus were worthy of God's peace from birth and throughout their lives, and they will be in peace in the hereafter.

Aṭ-Ṭabāṭabā'ī reckons that this verse identifies three days each of which signals the start of a new phase for the human being: peace upon John the day he is born means that nothing bad would happen to him in the life of this world; peace upon him the day he dies indicates that after death and before resurrection he would be in peace; and peace upon him the day he is resurrected means that he would enter paradise. The verse means that God was going to be satisfied with John throughout his life and will admit him into paradise.

I think the special spiritual status that is associated with John and Jesus only explains God's following words about John: "We have not created someone similar to him before" (19.7). Naturally, the Qur'an does not apply the latter description to Jesus, because God had already created someone with this special gift — that is, John. The word "before" indicates that someone like John was going to be born later.

The Qur'an's account of John is brief, but it is still remarkable that John's practice of baptism and his pronouncement of the coming of the Messiah, which are particularly stressed in the New Testament, are both not mentioned. This does not necessarily mean that the Qur'an denies any of them, but let's examine whether their descriptions in the New Testament are compatible with the Qur'an. Let's start with baptism.

The Qur'an commands Muslims to perform many religious practices and duties — such as praying, fasting, giving alms, and performing pilgrimage — but it does not state that there is any one or one-off religious practice or duty that would certainly grant the person forgiveness. The New Testament's depiction of baptism as a means to attain forgiveness, which is rejected by Josephus, is incompatible with the Qur'an's teachings.

Jesus' baptism of people with the Holy Spirit (Mark 1:8; Matt. 3:11; Luke 3:16; John 1:33), which John's baptism with water is supposed to lead to, is certainly a foreign concept to the Qur'an. A prophet may teach people, guide them to what is good, and influence them spiritually, but that does not involve anything that can be described as *baptism by the Holy Spirit*. Additionally, the Holy Spirit has a completely different meaning in the Qur'an, as we shall see in Chapter 7. The concept of *baptism with the Holy Spirit* does not actually make sense in the Qur'anic thought.

There is only one verse that has been linked by some exegetes to the practice of baptism:

> [This is] the *ṣibgha* of Allah. And who is better than Allah in giving *ṣibgha*! And it is He whom we worship (2.138).

This verse has been associated with baptism for two reasons. **First**, the word *ṣibgha* can mean, among other meanings, "color" and "dye." **Second**, the verse occurs in a group of verses that denounce the Jews and Christians' rejection of Islam and their claim that salvation is confined to them. A number of classical exegetes — including al-Qurṭubī, aṭ-Ṭabarī, and aṭ-Ṭūsī — have mentioned this as a possible interpretation. They claim that it responds to the claim that baptism purifies man and stresses that it is Islam, the religion of God, which is the real purification. I find linking this verse to baptism rather far-fetched. **First**, verse 2.138 is part of a set of verses that reject claims made by both Jews and Christians, yet baptism has become a Christian but not Jewish rite. **Second**, these verses respond to beliefs not rituals. **Third**, even when considering the possible meanings of *ṣibgha* as "color" or "dye," the verse would still not be nearer to baptism. The latter is not really an act of "coloring" or "dyeing," but is performed with clean water, which does not color or dye the body. I think *ṣibgha* here means one of its other reported meanings of "religion" or "belief," and that the verse means that Islam is the religion prescribed by God and that it is the best religion. Note that Islam in the Qur'an does not mean the religion of Prophet Muhammad only, but is a more general term that denotes the one religion of God that was preached by all prophets, including Muhammad and Jesus (§15.1.1).

Like Josephus, the Qur'an is also silent on the New Testament's claim that John foretold the coming of Jesus and acted as his forerunner. Can we conclude that had John foretold the coming of Jesus it would have been mentioned in the Qur'an? Not necessarily. But there are other reasons that make it almost certain that the claim that John's *foretelling* of the coming of Jesus and his description as Jesus' forerunner are both unhistorical. **First**, this New Testament claim is based on its other claim that Jesus' ministry did not begin until he was 30 years old. If Jesus had started teaching earlier in his life, John could not be described as Jesus' forerunner and said to have predicted his coming. According to the Gospels, the miraculously born and famous child, whose birth was predicted by many and whose death was sought by Herod, is supposed to have somehow lived a completely anonymous life, before suddenly appearing to be baptized, start his ministry, and take center stage.

According to the Qur'an, Jesus was a prophet from his very first day. This does not that Jesus became a teacher and preacher while still an infant. This is an unrealistic scenario with nothing to support it. But it is reasonable to conclude that at some point, while probably in his early teens, Jesus started to speak to some people about his mission. This probably continued to be in secret for some time before he went public with his message. We know that, for instance, Prophet Muhammad, whose mission started when he was 40 years old, preached secretly for 3 years before announcing his prophethood publicly. So John could not have been a forerunner for Jesus or predicting his coming, because the latter did not start preaching suddenly, even though he did not speak in public until he was a young man.

Second, even in the case of the unrealistic scenario in which Jesus did not go public with his message until the age of 30 or so, the fact that John was contemporary to Jesus leaves little sense in the suggestions that he *predicted his coming and acted as his forerunner*. The foretelling of the coming of the Messiah by someone who was *contemporary* to him makes it less of a prediction, and takes away much of the power and impact that it is supposed to have. This contemporariness suggests that such *identification* would not have been based on a prediction. The suggestion that John acted as the forerunner for Jesus might be based on the concept that the latter's appearance was the culmination and climax of God's plans — an unauthentic and misguided concept (§15.3).

I take Josephus' statement that many Jews followed John as a righteous man — a description that Josephus also accepts — as evidence that John did not teach publicly about Jesus or claimed that the latter was the Messiah, because the overwhelming majority of the Jews, including Josephus did not believe in Jesus. John might have lived far away from Jesus and did not have any contact with him. He might have been killed before Jesus' reputation grew. As we shall see later, Jesus managed to attract only a small following during his life so he was not the famous figure that the Gospels suggest he was. His following started to grow years after he was gone.

On the other hand, as a prophet with divine knowledge, John must have known that Jesus was the Messiah. The claims of Matthew (11:2-3) and Luke (7:19) that the imprisoned John did not know whether Jesus was the Messiah or not could not be true. John's recognition of Jesus as the Messiah would not have required him to meet Jesus or be his relative. He would have known that from God.

One last point to consider is whether or not Jesus and John were relatives. Only Luke (1:36) of the four Gospels claims that Mary and John's mother were relatives and states that the former visited the latter when the two were pregnant. Another canonical Gospel suggests that, upon seeing Jesus coming to him, John said that he did not recognize him, which means that he had not met him (John 1:30-33), which is quite strange if they were relatives. Moreover, John's pronouncement that Jesus was the Messiah would have been questioned for coming from a relative, which does not seem to have happened, although it may be argued that it did happen but the Gospel simply did not report it.

The Qur'an does not state that Jesus and John were related. Zechariah' guardianship of Mary is the only reference that we can use to form a view. If the guardianship was simply the result of devoting Mary to the temple and the need for someone there to look after her, then it does not imply that Zechariah was related to Mary. But if the guardianship was triggered by Mary's loss of her mother and becoming orphan, which I think is more likely (p. 52), then this means that Zechariah or his wife were related to Mary, which makes John and Jesus relatives, although they might not have met.

5

More Than Annunciation

Of the four Gospels, only Luke recounts the delivery of the news to Mary about her miraculous conception, known as the "annunciation." Apocryphal sources provide more detailed accounts of the annunciation. The Qur'an confirms that Mary conceived Jesus miraculously, but one fundamental difference it has with Christian sources centers on the nature of Gabriel's role in the miracle.

5.1. The Annunciation in the New Testament

This is how Luke starts his account of annunciation:

> In the sixth month of Elizabeth's pregnancy, the angel Gabriel was sent by God to a town of Galilee called Nazareth, to a virgin engaged to a man whose name was Joseph, a descendant of David, and the virgin's name was Mary. The angel came to her and said, "Greetings, favored one, the Lord is with you!" But she was greatly troubled by his words and began to wonder about the meaning of this greeting. So the angel said to her, "Do not be afraid, Mary, for you have found favor with God! Listen: You will become pregnant and give birth to a son, and you will name him Jesus. He will be great, and will be called the Son of the Most High, and the Lord God will give him the throne of his father David. He will reign over the house of Jacob forever, and his kingdom will never end." Mary said to the angel, "How will this be, since I have not had sexual relations with a man?" The angel replied, "The Holy Spirit will come upon you, and the power of the Most High will overshadow you. Therefore the child to be born will be holy; he will be called the Son of God.
>
> "And look, your relative Elizabeth has also become pregnant with a son in her old age — although she was called barren, she is now in her sixth month! For nothing will be impossible with God." So Mary said, "Yes, I am a servant of the Lord; let this happen to me according to your word." Then the angel departed from her. (Luke 1:26-38)

Luke then goes on to talk about Mary's visit to Elizabeth, Zechariah's wife, and later about her journey with Joseph to Judea for the census, which we will discuss in Chapter 10.

Matthew does not talk about the annunciation, but he mentions that Mary "was found to be pregnant through the Holy Spirit" (Matt. 1:18) and that "the child conceived in her is from the Holy Spirit" (Matt. 1:20). He then moves on to speak about Jesus' birth.

5.2. The Annunciation in the Apocrypha

Apocryphal sources have also spoken about Mary's conception of Jesus and emphasized that she conceived him while she was still a virgin. As we saw in §2.1, the Gospel of the Birth of Mary, the Infancy Gospel of James, and the Gospel of Pseudo-Matthew all claim that when Mary approached the age of puberty, the high priest arranged for her to get married and leave the temple where her parents had left her since she was three years old.

According to the Gospel of the Birth of Mary, when Mary became 14 years old, the high priest asked that all unmarried men should bring their rods with them to take part in choosing Mary's husband. Joseph won the lottery and got betrothed to Mary. Then Mary, while still a virgin, conceived Jesus:

> Now at this time of her first coming into Galilee, the angel Gabriel was sent to her from God, to declare to her the conception of our Saviour, and the manner and way of her conceiving him. Accordingly going into her, he filled the chamber where she was with a prodigious light, and in a most courteous manner saluting her, he said, "Hail, Mary! Virgin of the Lord most acceptable! O Virgin full of grace! The Lord is with you. You are blessed above all women, and you are blessed above all men, that have been hitherto born."
>
> But the Virgin, who had before been well acquainted with the countenances of angels, and to whom such light from heaven was no uncommon thing, was neither terrified with the vision of the angel, nor astonished at the greatness of the light, but only troubled about the angel's words, and began to consider what so extraordinary a salutation should mean, what it did portend, or what sort of end it would have.
>
> To this thought the angel, divinely inspired, replies; "Fear not, Mary, as though I intended anything inconsistent with your chastity in this salutation: For you have found favour with the Lord, because you made virginity your choice. Therefore while you are a Virgin, you shall conceive without sin, and bring forth a son." (BirMary. 7:1-10)

Gabriel went on to praise the child, and the account continues as follows:

> To this discourse of the angel the Virgin replied, not, as though she were unbelieving, but willing to know the manner of it. She said, "How can that be? For seeing, according to my vow, I have never known any man, how can I bear a child without the addition of a man's seed?"
>
> To this the angel replied and said, "Think not, Mary, that you shall conceive in the ordinary way. For, without lying with a man, while a Virgin, you shall conceive; while a Virgin, you shall bring forth; and while a Virgin shall give suck. For the Holy Spirit shall come upon you, and the power of the Most High shall overshadow you, without any of the heats of lust. So that which shall be born of you shall be only holy, because it only is conceived without sin, and being born, shall be called the Son of God."
>
> Then Mary stretching forth her hands, and lifting her eyes to heaven, said, "Behold the handmaid of the Lord! Let it be to me according to thy word." (BirMary. 7:15-21)

When Joseph returned from Judea to Galilee intending to get married to Mary, who had been betrothed to him for three months, he noticed that she was pregnant. Disturbed by the discovery, Joseph decided to end their betrothal privately without causing a scandal. Before carrying out his plan, the angel appeared to him in his sleep and explained to him that Mary had not committed any sin, but was made pregnant by a miracle from God.

Joseph then married Mary, but did not have a sexual relationship with her. This gospel ends with a passing mention of Mary giving birth to Jesus.

The Infancy Gospel of James also gives a detailed account of Mary's conception. Having been betrothed to Joseph and left the temple, the virgin was called by the high priest and asked to take part in making a new veil for the temple. When she was back at home she went out to draw water, and she heard a voice saying to her: "Hail you who are full of grace, the Lord is with you; you are blessed among women" (InJam. 9:7). Shaken by the experience, Mary went home and started work on the veil. The gospel then goes on to relate the annunciation:

> And behold the angel of the Lord stood by her, and said, "Fear not, Mary, for you have found favour in the sight of God." Which when she heard, she reasoned with herself what that sort of salutation meant. And the angel said to her, "The Lord is with you, and you shall conceive." To which she replied, "What! Shall I conceive by the living God and bring forth as all other women do?" But the angel returned answer, "Not so, O Mary, but the Holy Spirit shall come upon you, and the power of the Most High shall overshadow you; Wherefore that which shall be born of you shall be holy, and shall be called the Son of the Living God, and you shall call his name Jesus; for he shall save his people from their sins. And behold your cousin Elizabeth, she also has conceived a son in her old age." (InJam. 9:9-15)

Returning from her visit to Elizabeth, and "perceiving herself daily to grow big, and being afraid," Mary "went home, and hid herself from the children of Israel" (InJam. 9:23). When Joseph returned from his work abroad six months later, he noticed Mary's pregnancy and questioned her suspiciously. She protested her innocence but, inexplicably, told him that she did not know how she became pregnant: "Then said Joseph, 'How comes it to pass you are with child?' Mary answered, 'As the Lord my God lives, I know not by what means'" (InJam. 10:11-12). Having decided to part company with Mary privately, Joseph saw an angel in his sleep who instructed him to take Mary and told him that the child she bore was "of the Holy Spirit" (InJam. 10:19).

This gospel then recounts how the news about Mary's pregnancy was leaked to the high priest who accused Joseph and Mary of getting married without announcing their marriage. Although denying this accusation, strangely enough, neither Mary nor Joseph explained to the high priest how the pregnancy came about. Mary told the priest: "As the Lord my God lives, I am innocent in his sight, seeing I know no man", and Joseph said the same: "As the Lord my God lives, I have not been concerned with her." Both of the accused then were tested with the bitter "water of the Lord," which causes the curse, but both remained well, confirming that they did not lie (InJam. 11:11-20).

The book then continues with its account of the events leading to the birth of Jesus.

Another apocryphal source that gives an account of the annunciation that is very similar to the Infancy Gospel of James and the Gospel of the Birth of Mary is the Gospel of Pseudo-Matthew. Having been betrothed to Mary, Joseph took Mary and another five virgins who were with her in the temple to his house. Joseph then left for nine months to his far workplace where he worked as a house building carpenter. Shortly after his departure, the annunciation took place:

> And on the second day, while Mary was at the fountain to fill her pitcher, the angel of the Lord appeared to her, saying: "Blessed you are, Mary; for in your womb you have prepared a habitation for the Lord. For, lo, the light from heaven shall come and dwell in you, and by means of you will shine over the whole world."
>
> Again, on the third day, while she was working at the purple with her fingers, there entered a young man of ineffable beauty. And when Mary saw him, she exceedingly feared and trembled. And he said to her: "Hail, Mary, full of grace; the Lord is with you: blessed you are among women, and blessed is the fruit of your womb." And when she heard these words, she trembled, and was exceedingly afraid. Then the angel of the Lord added: "Fear not, Mary; for you have found favour with God: Behold, you shall conceive in your womb, and shall bring forth a King, who fills not only the earth, but the heaven, and who reigns from generation to generation." (PsMatt. 9)

On his return, Joseph was shocked to find Mary pregnant, but the five virgins explained to him that it was the angel of the Lord who made her pregnant (PsMatt. 10). But Joseph was not reassured until an angel appeared to him in sleep and told him: "receive Mary as your wife, for that which is in her womb is of the Holy Spirit" (PsMatt. 11).

The book also explains how Joseph and Mary were accused of having an illicit relationship by people but were exonerated.

5.3. The Annunciation and the Inducement of the Virginal Conception According to the Qur'an

The account of the annunciation in the Qur'an is found in chapters 19 and 3. In both chapters, Mary's story follows the story of Zechariah and, in the case of chapter 19, his son John. The more detailed account of chapter 19 reveals that Gabriel's role in the virginal conception was more than delivering the good news to Mary.

5.3.1. Gabriel's Visit and the Inducement of the Virginal Conception in Chapter 19

The account in this chapter starts as follows:

> And mention [O Muhammad!] Mary in the Book. When she withdrew from her family to an eastern place (19.16).

We have already studied this verse in our discussion of Mary's life before the annunciation (p. 56). While this verse stresses that Mary lived separately from her family to worship God, it is not clear whether the *eastern place* was part of her family's house, or simply a place of worship, such as the sanctuary that she lived in when Zechariah looked after her.

This is the next verse:

> She put a veil between herself and them. Then We sent to her Our spirit, and he assumed for her the likeness of a human being in all respects (19.17).

The first part of the verse, and specifically the word "veil," seems to reveal another apocryphal contextual displacement, as this word is used in the Infancy Gospel of James in a very different context:

> And it came to pass, in a council of the priests, it was said, "Let us make a new veil for the temple of the Lord." And the high priest said, "Call together to me seven undefiled virgins of the tribe of David." And the servants went and brought them into the temple of the Lord, and the high priest said to them, "Cast lots before me now, who of you shall spin the golden thread, who the blue, who the scarlet, who the fine linen, and who the true purple." Then the high priest knew Mary; that she was of the tribe of David; and he called her, and the true purple fell to her lot to spin, and she went away to her own house. (InJam. 9:1-4)

Then the Infancy Gospel of James tells us that Mary was spinning the purple when the angel appeared to her to give her the good news about Jesus. This account links Mary, the veil, and her being at home. There is a distinct possibility that this story, which is found in another variation in Pseudo-Matthew (8), has developed from a similar story to the one found in the Qur'an.

The Gospel of Pseudo-Matthew describes the angel who appeared to Mary as a "young man of ineffable beauty" (PsMatt. 9). This seems to be a variation of the Qur'anic description of the spirit as having the "likeness of a human being in all respects."

The "spirit" who assumed the likeness of a human being is Gabriel (§7.3.1).

This mysterious being must have had the look of a man, because Mary addressed him in the masculine. Seeing a man appear suddenly in her secluded place, Mary was scared:

> She said: "I seek refuge in God from you, if you are dutiful" (19.18).

Mary's reaction to the sudden appearance of Gabriel indicates that this was the first time she had such an encounter. This suggests that all her previous interactions with angels were via hearing their voices. Indeed, both verses 3.42-43 talk about the angels *speaking* to Mary. They do not state that they appeared to her. Even if they had appeared to her in some form, it must have been a very different experience to what she had with the spirit Gabriel.

Mary was so unfamiliar with that experience that she did not even know whether the man-like being that appeared from nowhere was good or evil. She reminded him that he should fear God and not hurt her. Because God was always first and foremost on Mary's mind, He was the one whom she first mentioned in that disturbing situation.

Gabriel reassured Mary that he was in fact a messenger from God:

> He said: "I am only a messenger of your Lord, that I may bestow on you a pure son" (19.19).

After receiving the news and regaining her composure, Mary asked how she could bear a son when she was not married or involved in illicit relationships:

> She said: "How can I have a son when no man has touched me, neither have I been unchaste?" (19.20).

The Qur'an uses other variations of the Arabic verb for "touch" to mean "have sexual intercourse" (4.43, 5.6, 2.236-237, 33.49, 58.3-4). So Mary here is stressing that she never had a sexual relationship with a man.

Mary knew that Gabriel meant that she was going to become pregnant with a child *immediately*. She understood from his words that he came to *bestow on her a pure son* that she was going to become pregnant there and then. Also, he did not speak about her getting married, but only about her becoming pregnant. We will also see that in the account of chapter 3 of the Qur'an of the meeting that Gabriel told Mary that her son would be called "son of Mary" (3.45), which is a clear reference that her conception of Jesus wound be virginal. Had this not been Mary's understanding, she would have thought that Gabriel meant she would have a child later on after she gets married, and she would not have found the news surprising. It is worth reminding ourselves here that the Qur'an often conveys the gist of an event rather than report a conversation word for word. The reports of the conversation between Gabriel and Mary in both chapters 19 and 3 show clearly that Gabriel talked clearly about a virginal conception and Mary understood that.

There is a significant difference between Gabriel's role in the annunciation story in Christian sources and the Qur'an. In the former, Gabriel only carries the good news to Mary that she was going to become pregnant through the Holy Spirit.

Similarly, Matthew's statements that Mary "was found to be pregnant through the Holy Spirit" (Matt. 1:18) and that "the child conceived in her is from the Holy Spirit" (Matt. 1:20) imply that the messenger, who is an "angel" according to this Evangelist, only delivered the news to Mary. Apocryphal gospels also present Gabriel as a mere messenger: "the Holy Spirit shall come upon you, and the power of the Most High shall overshadow you" (BirMary. 7:19; InJam. 9:13).

Gabriel's words in the Qur'an, on the other hand, mean that he was involved, though in a subtle way, in Mary's pregnancy. Significantly, he is himself described as the "Spirit," so the messenger and the spirit are not two different beings. Gabriel not only informed Mary of the miraculous conception, but his very visit was the cause of that miracle: "I am only a messenger of Your Lord, that I may *bestow on you* a pure son" (19.19). His visit was conducive and essential to the occurrence of that miracle. Gabriel's involvement in Mary's non-sexual conception is confirmed in another two verses which mention that *God breathed into Mary of His spirit* (21.91, 66.12). This is why what happened in that mysterious visit was *more than annunciation; it also included a unique act of impregnation* (pp. 92; 133-134). Limiting Gabriel's role to a messenger in Luke, Matthew, the Gospel of the Birth of Mary, and the Infancy Gospel of James represents a contextual corruption.

Interestingly, in Pseudo-Matthew (10), the virgins who were living with Mary told Joseph that no man had touched Mary and that they think "the angel of the Lord has made her pregnant." The role of the angel here, as in the Qur'an, is one of causing the pregnancy. It must be stressed, however, that the concepts of "Holy Spirit" and "spirit" in Christian literature have different meanings from the Qur'anic term for "spirit," as we shall see in Chapter 7.

Similar to the angel's reply to Zechariah's question about the miracle of having a son, Gabriel replied to Mary that this miracle was an easy thing for God to do, and that it had already been ordained to happen, confirming that her conception was not going to involve a man:

> He said: "Thus Your Lord has said: 'It is easy for Me. And so that We may make of him a sign for people and a mercy from Us, and it is a matter that has been ordained'" (19.21).

Gabriel's words confirm that Mary's conception was going to happen through a miracle and would not involve any sexual relationship. It looks like through Gabriel's presence with Mary, an ovum of hers was fertilized, but there was no sexual contact between the two. Had the man-looking Gabriel needed to have sexual intercourse with Mary, he would not have replied in this way, and from Mary's point of view the whole thing would have looked as normal as any other sexual pregnancy. Gabriel's reply stressed the miraculous nature of the conception. The common description of Mary's encounter with Gabriel as mere "annunciation" is inaccurate.

Further indication to Gabriel's role in Mary's pregnancy comes to light when Gabriel's words to Mary are compared with the angels' words to Zechariah. In the latter case, the angels told Zechariah that they came to *give him the good news of the birth of John* (3.39, 19.7). There is no mention of the angels being involved in *bestowing the child* as in Mary' case. It may be argued that the angels did not say that to Zechariah because it would have been his wife not him to whom the physical act of bestowing a child would be applied. This argument is undermined by Zechariah's reply to the angels in which he mentioned not only his wife's barrenness but also his old age (3.40, 19.8) as natural obstacles for the pregnancy. Zechariah understood the angel's words to mean that his wife's pregnancy was going to happen through him via sexual intercourse. This interpretation is confirmed by the angel's reply that only stressed God's power to do what He likes and did not indicate that Zechariah misunderstood the nature of the miracle.

The spirit told Mary that God wanted to make the miraculous creation of Jesus a sign for people to believe in Him, and that He wanted to make him a mercy to people, guiding them to the straight path. The fact that he was there delivering the message to her, Gabriel said to Mary, means that the matter had already been ordained. God had already decided that this was going to happen. He was there to deliver the good news and cause the miracle to happen.

This verse also suggests that Mary's virginal conception of Jesus was the cause for him becoming a *sign for people*. This expression always refers to miracles, so the passage implicitly refers to a causal relation between Jesus being the fruit of a virginal conception and the miracle worker he came to be. This may be the answer as to why God did the miracle of the virginal conception when no one other than Mary could have known for sure that her conception did not involve a male.

The next verse tells us that Mary did conceive Jesus, and that she "withdrew to a far place":

She conceived him, and she withdrew with him to a far place (19.22).

Since Mary was already living in seclusion even from her family, whether in her family's house or in a sanctuary, her withdrawal to a far place must mean that she left that place and went somewhere else. This is confirmed in a latter verse which states that after giving birth to Jesus, Mary *went back* with her newborn baby to her people (19.27). The Qur'an does not specify the place that Mary went to. Verse 19.22 is reminiscent of the Infancy Gospel of James' statement that, as signs of the pregnancy started to show on her, Mary "went home, and hid herself from the children of Israel" (InJam. 9:23).

The next verses of chapter 19 talk about the birth of Jesus.

5.3.2. Gabriel's Visit and the Annunciation in Chapter 3

Chapter 3 has the other long account of the stories of Zechariah, Mary, and Jesus. It has three verses on the annunciation, starting with the following:

> When the angels said: "O Mary! Allah gives you the good news of a Word from Him, whose name is the Messiah, Jesus son of Mary, who is illustrious in this world and the hereafter, and who is one of those brought near [to Allah] (3.45).

The first thing to notice here is that while verse 19.17 states that the spirit appeared and talked to Mary, the verse above says that angels spoke to Mary. Scholars consider Gabriel, the spirit, to be an angel. Implying that both verses refer to the same event, aṭ-Ṭabāṭabā'ī states that some scholars think that it was actually the spirit, Gabriel, who spoke, but that he is referred to in the plural with the word "angels" as a mark of respect. He also mentions the suggestion that there might have been other angels with Gabriel who took part in speaking to Mary, hence the use of the plural "angels."

Aṭ-Ṭabāṭabā'ī thinks that since Gabriel has a higher status than the other angels, his words can be attributed to lower ranking angels — i.e. although it was Gabriel who spoke, all the angels can be considered to have said the same thing. We will discuss the subject of the spirit and the angels in more detail in §7.3.1, where I conclude that Gabriel is probably a unique angel. This, combined with the fact that angels are always referred to in the plural in the Qur'an, may explain why Gabriel's words are also attributed to the angels. Additionally, the Qur'an depicts all angels as being totally obedient to God, doing whatever they are commanded to do and never do anything that is against God's will. So the action of any one angel or any a number of them may be attributed to the "angels" and vice versa. This is why the term "angels" is used many times in the Qur'an without identifying individual angels or naming them.

Aṭ-Ṭabāṭabā'ī has discussed the view that "Word" in verse 3.45 denotes the prophetic predictions about the Messiah. He rightly points out, however, that since "the Messiah" in this verse identifies the "Word" itself, this "Word" cannot signify prophecies about the Messiah. He also stresses the fact that the Qur'an does not state that Jesus was spoken about by previous prophets, but that he predicted Prophet Muhammad to follow on after him. The meaning of "Word" will become clear when we study verse 3.47 below.

The verse also states that it was God, through the angels, who gave Mary's son the name "Jesus" and the title "Messiah." Matthew (1:21), Luke (1:31), the apocryphal Infancy Gospel of James (9:14) and Pseudo-Matthew (15) also indicate that Jesus had his name chosen for him by the angel. The verse also tells us that Jesus was going to be known as "son of Mary," in reference to the fact that he was going to be conceived without a father.

The voice continued to detail the good news, describing Jesus as a miraculous child who shall be able to speak while still in the cradle, and who will be righteous:

> He shall speak to people in the cradle and when middle-aged, and he shall be one of the righteous (3.46).

As Zechariah did when he heard the news about the birth of John (3.40), Mary addressed God rather than the angel, because she also knew that the voice was only delivering God's message to her:

> She said: "My Lord! How can I have a child when no human being has touched me?" He said: "Thus Allah creates what He wills. When He decrees a matter, He only says to it 'Be!' and it is" (3.47).

This is very similar to verse 19.20. Mary understood that she was going to become pregnant at that time and that her pregnancy would not happen through a sexual relationship. One indication to this was the news that her son would be known as "son of Mary" (ash-Sha'rāwī, 1999: 82).

Replying to Mary's question, the angel stressed that God can do whatever He wishes. He symbolically represented God's power to do anything with ease by the imagery of Him merely uttering the two-letter Arabic imperative verb *kun* (be). This particular symbolic depiction of God's infinite power is repeated in eight verses in the Qur'an (2.117, 3.47, 3.59, 6.73, 16.40, 19.35, 36.82, 40.68), including the following:

> [He is] the Originator of the heavens and the earth! When He decrees a matter, He says to it "Be!" and it is (2.117).

These verses emphasize that God does not need to make things happen in a particular way or through certain means. He can do things with or without their natural causes and means, as it is He who created those causes and means and assigned to them the effects they have. Every natural cause-and-effect relation has been established by God, and He can disable the effect of that cause, produce that effect without its natural cause, and make it happen through different causes. In the Qur'an, natural laws are not inherent in matter, but maintained by God.

The concept of *kun* (be) does not *necessarily* mean that a divine act is instantaneous or that what God wants happens without the use or involvement of any means. It mainly indicates that God can do whatever He wants, even if that act was completely supernatural. It denotes God's unlimited ability to perform miracles and the fact that these miracles may take any shape or form. Let's take the case of Mary's conception. It is described as being the result of the divine *kun* (be) because such a pregnancy is impossible to occur naturally yet it happened because God wanted it. It violated natural biological laws. The fact that God caused the pregnancy by the divine *kun* (be), however, does not mean that Mary became pregnant in no time or without the involvement of anything. In this case, God used Gabriel's visit to Mary to make that miraculous non-sexual pregnancy take place.

Of particular interest is God's description of Jesus in verse 4.171 as "His Word that He sent to Mary":

> O People of the Book! Commit no excesses in your religion or utter anything concerning Allah but the truth. The Messiah, Jesus son of Mary, was only a messenger of Allah, His Word that He sent to Mary, and a Spirit from Him [that He sent] (4.171).

The association of "Word" with the act of "sending" refers to Gabriel's role in the conception, because it was through the sending of Gabriel to Mary that her conception took place. Also, The Spirit Gabriel is mentioned immediately after the Word. This is another confirmation that Gabriel's role in Mary's conception was far more than carrying the good news.

The divine "be" is the "Word" that the angels mentioned in verse 3.45 when they told Mary: "Allah gives you the good news of a Word from Him, whose name is the Messiah, Jesus son of Mary," meaning that God has decreed that she will have Jesus by a great miracle. The role of the word "be" in the creation of Jesus is also found in verse 3.59, which mentions the miracle of the creation of Adam as well:

> The likeness of Jesus in Allah's eye is as the likeness of Adam. He created him of dust, then He said to him "Be!" and he is (3.59).

The term "Word," which stands for the word *kun* (be), denotes a divine command for something to happen. In this case, it was the virginal conception and the birth of a miraculous son.

As I mentioned in my comment on verse 3.39 (p. 63), many exegetes think that "Word" in the description of John as "confirming with a Word from Allah" signifies Jesus. The fact that Jesus is described as a "Word" from God has been seen by these exegetes as supportive of their interpretation. However, I think this interpretation is the result of misunderstanding *muṣaddiqan bi kalimatin* as meaning "confirming a Word" rather than "confirming with a Word," as I have already explained.

The next verses of chapter 3 then start talking about Jesus and his later life.

6

The Virginal Conception

The claim that Mary conceived Jesus without having a sexual relationship with a man, which is stressed in both canonical Gospels and apocryphal sources, is one of the most controversial parts Jesus' story. Unsurprisingly, historical and scientific arguments have been made against the historicity of the virginal conception. What may be surprising to some, however, is that the New Testament itself has also been used to argue that the virginal conception was unhistorical! This scriptural argument is based on major inconsistencies in the New Testament. First, the miraculous nature of Mary's conception of Jesus is confirmed in only two books — Matthew and Luke. Second, there are passages in the New Testament that contradict the virginal conception. Third, the two birth stories that confirm this concept differ fundamentally from each other and, thus, are unreliable. Questioning the virginal conception has, not unexpectedly, led to questioning Jesus' illegitimacy.

The "virginal conception" is often mistakenly referred to as "virgin birth." The latter is a broader Roman Catholic doctrine that incorporates the virginal conception. The virgin birth doctrine states that in addition to conceiving Jesus while a virgin, Mary remained a virgin even after giving birth to him. This is why the Catholic Church describes Mary as the "ever-virgin" (*Aeiparthenos*).

The virginal conception is also at times confused with the "immaculate conception." This is another Catholic doctrine stating that Mary was free from the "original sin" from her conception. The original sin is a state of sinfulness that man is born with because of the sin of Adam and Eve. This is how Pope Pius IX defined the immaculate conception in 1854 when he turned this centuries-old concept into a revealed dogma that all Catholics had to believe in: "The most Blessed Virgin Mary was, from the first moment of her conception, by a singular grace and privilege of almighty God and by virtue of the merits of Jesus Christ, Savior of the human race, preserved immune from all stain of original sin." The immaculate conception was introduced because it was believed that not only Jesus but his mother also had to be free of sin.

Both concepts of the virgin birth and immaculate conception have established themselves in Catholic theology, but they have no foundations in the Qur'an. In fact, the Qur'an's teachings about the noble, yet human, nature of both Mary and Jesus are at odds with these concepts, as well with much of Christian theology. The Qur'an confirms several times, however, that Mary became miraculously pregnant with Jesus while she was a virgin.

6.1. The Virginal Conception in Christian Sources

The conception of Jesus is described in Matthew and Luke in the New Testament and some apocryphal writings, where it is described as miraculously virginal. I have already quoted the relevant passages in Chapter 5, so I will only make quick references to them here.

Matthew makes it clear that Mary conceived a child through the Holy Spirit, without having a sexual relationship with Joseph: "While his mother Mary was engaged to Joseph, but before they came together, she was found to be pregnant through the Holy Spirit". When Joseph became aware of Mary's pregnancy he thought of leaving her, as he was not the father of the child and naturally thought that she must have had an affair with someone else. But then he saw the angel in a dream who reassured him that Mary's pregnancy was "from the Holy Spirit" (Matt. 1:18-20).

Matthew then goes on to say that Jesus' birth would fulfill an Old Testament prophecy of a "virgin" giving birth: "This all happened so that what was spoken by the Lord through the prophet would be fulfilled: 'Look! The virgin will conceive and bear a son, and they will call him Emmanuel,' which means 'God with us'" (Matt. 1:22-23). There is more to say about the word "virgin" and Matthew's quotation of this Old Testament prophecy later in the chapter.

Luke's account of the annunciation is even keener on stressing the virginal conception of Jesus. He first emphasizes that when the angel visited Mary she was a "virgin" (Luke 1:27), although she was betrothed to Joseph. When the angel told Mary that she would conceive and give birth to a child (Luke 1:31), she was astonished and asked the angel how this could happen when she had not known a man. The angel's reply made it clear that Mary's conception was going to be miraculous and involve no man: "The Holy Spirit will come upon you, and the power of the Most High will overshadow you" (Luke 1:35).

The virginal conception is also confirmed in apocryphal writings. The Gospel of the Birth of Mary states that the angel addressed Mary as "Mary! Virgin of the Lord most acceptable! O Virgin full of grace" (BirMary. 7:3). He then went on to tell her: "For you have found favour with the Lord, because you made virginity your choice. Therefore while you are a Virgin, you shall conceive without sin, and bring forth a son" (BirMary. 7:9-10), and then "Think not, Mary, that you shall conceive in the ordinary way. For, without lying with a man, while a Virgin, you shall conceive; while a Virgin, you shall bring forth; and while a Virgin shall give suck. For the Holy Spirit shall come upon you, and the power of the Most High shall overshadow you" (BirMary. 7:17-19).

The Infancy Gospel of James also stresses that Mary was a virgin when she conceived Jesus miraculously. The writer of this gospel has Mary ask the angel who informed her about the conception whether she would conceive naturally like any other women. The angel replied that Mary's conception would not be natural but supernatural: "Not so, O Mary, but the Holy Spirit shall come upon you, and the power of the Most High shall overshadow you" (InJam. 9:13). This gospel also tells us that Joseph wanted to leave Mary when he learned about her pregnancy, but he was instructed in sleep to keep her and was told that the child she bore was "of the Holy Spirit" (InJam. 10:18).

The Gospel of Pseudo-Matthew does not mention the virginal conception explicitly, but it does say that when Joseph had doubts about Mary's pregnancy, the angel appeared to him in his dream, told him to take Mary as his wife, and revealed that the child in her womb was of the Holy Spirit (PsMatt. 11).

6.2. The Arguments Against the Virginal Conception

The virginal conception has been rejected on three main grounds: scriptural, historical, and scientific or rational.

The *scriptural* argument is based on flaws and contradictions in the story of the conception of Jesus in the New Testament. The *historical* objection stems from the resemblance of the scriptural accounts of the virginal conception to historical stories that predate Jesus. The *rational* or *scientific* argument states that a virginal conception is an impossibility, so could not have taken place. We will examine these three arguments in this section.

In my discussion of scriptural and historical rejectionist arguments, I will frequently cite Jocelyn Rhys' comprehensive study *Shaken Creeds: The Virgin Birth Doctrine*, which was originally published in 1922. Rhys' work covers the main arguments against the virginal conception of Jesus.

6.2.1. The Scriptural Arguments

Rejectionists usually ignore the Qur'anic story of Jesus' birth because they do not consider it independent, presuming that it is based on Christian sources. Additionally, the Qur'anic story does not contain any contradictions that can be used to discredit it. Apocryphal writings are also usually given very little attention by critics because what established the belief in the virginal conception is the account in the canonical Gospels, and because of the wider belief that apocryphal books are less original than the canonical ones and have little inherent value. Discrediting the New Testament story of the virginal conception, therefore, is seen as undermining the story in the apocryphal sources also. Thus, it is the New Testament that has been the target of the critics of the virginal conception; and this criticism is not unjustified.

There are three main criticisms of the story of the virginal conception in the New Testament. **First**, it is mentioned in only two of the twenty seven books of the New Testament. Of the four Gospels, the Acts of the Apostles, the twenty one Epistles, and the book of Revelation, only the Gospels of Matthew and Luke talk about the virginal conception. This is taken to mean that there was no knowledge or wide acceptance of the story. **Second**, the books of the New Testament, including Matthew and Luke, contain details that contradict the virginal conception of Jesus. **Third**, the two Gospels that mention Jesus' virginal conception give very different accounts of the events leading to and following his birth. As the birth story is closely tied to that of the conception, serious doubts are raised about the historicity and authenticity of the whole nativity account in the two books. Let's discuss these arguments in more detail.

6.2.1.1. Unknown Story

The Gospels of Mark and John do not contain any information about the birth of Jesus or his childhood. Both start their accounts around the time when Jesus met John the Baptist, which is believed to have happened when Jesus was around 30 years old. It is still very surprising that these two Gospels do not mention even in passing the virginal conception although it is one of the greatest miracles associated with Jesus. It is extremely difficult to accept that Mark and John could not have known of Mary's miraculous conception yet they had good knowledge of Jesus' life. Either they did not know much about Jesus' life, or that they knew about the story of the virginal conception but deliberately ignored it because they did not believe it. They wrote what they knew and believed, so they either did not know the story or did not believe it. Even when John reports how a group of Jews objected to Jesus' claim that he had come down from heaven on the grounds that they knew his mother and father, Jesus does not bother to correct and remind them that Joseph was not his father:

> Then the Jews who were hostile to Jesus began complaining about him because he said, "I am the bread that came down from heaven," and they said, "Isn't this Jesus the son of Joseph, whose father and mother we know? How can he now say, 'I have come down from heaven'?" (John 6:41-42)

It is unlikely that the Evangelists did not believe the story of the virginal conception. After all, they reported many of Jesus' miracles. Also, there is nothing in their theologies that stands against the concept of Jesus' virginal conception.

The fact that the earliest and latest Gospels contain nothing at all about Jesus' early life probably means that the authors had no knowledge of that history. Even if they believed that the most important phase of Jesus' life started at his baptism, his earlier years would surely have merited at least brief coverage and would have been of so much interest to people. Additionally, ancient people had great interest in the birth stories of their heroes. Mark and John did not know anything about Jesus' birth and childhood. If these two Evangelists knew about the virginal conception story but did not believe it, they would have probably written what they knew of Jesus' birth and overlooked or explicitly rejected that story. I am excluding the possibility that the current versions of the Gospels of Mark and John are missing parts as there is no evidence to this effect.

The ignorance of the two Evangelists of that history should not be surprising, as these books were written several decades after the events they describe and in a time where unrecorded history can be as easily lost and forgotten as changed and manipulated. It is still surprising, nevertheless, that the New Testament, which is supposed to be the most authoritative record of Jesus' life and religion, mentions his miraculous birth and his childhood only in 2 of its 27 books.

No matter how this absence of the virginal conception from Mark and John is explained, it represents a major and significant difference between them and Matthew and Luke. Mark's and John's complete silence about Jesus' early history also raises serious questions about the credibility of these two books, but it does not say anything about the credibility of the story of the virginal conception. To say that Jesus' childhood was religiously insignificant undermines the credibility of Matthew and Luke whose accounts are laden with miracles. Suggesting that Jesus' childhood was religiously significant reflects equally as bad on Mark and John.

It may be argued that the infancy story did not need to be reported in all Gospels, and that the four books complement each other. This argument is driven by faith, and it is false. The authors of these books did not sit together and agree who was going to report what, in which case it would have been understandable why the virginal conception, birth, and childhood of Jesus are not reported in all Gospels. Also, there are many events from Jesus' life that are reported in more than one Gospel, and some of them are found in all four Gospels. These books became parts of one scriptural unit centuries after they were written and after the events they describe. There is clear evidence that the Gospels are not completely independent of each other and that they have used earlier sources. There is no evidence that the four Gospels were intended to or do complement each other, and the many contradictions between these books prove the opposite.

The claim that the four Gospels shed light on the same history from different angles is a more general argument whose use is not restricted to explain the absence of Jesus' infancy from two Gospels. This argument is often used to explain why there are four Gospels rather than one and different accounts of the same events. It ignores the fact that there have been many more than four Gospels, and that the canon's embracement of only four of these Gospels and the other New Testament books was the result of a long process that involved many people and much politics.

The Acts of the Apostles, the twenty one Epistles, and Revelation also make no mention of the miracle of Jesus' conception. Even when a reference is made to Jesus' birth, the authors of these books do not make any reference to the virginal conception. For instance, when Paul says "but when the appropriate time had come, God sent out his Son, born of a woman, born under the law" (Gal. 4:4), he seems to either deliberately avoid to mention the virginal conception, or is simply unaware of it. It is not possible that Paul knew and believed in the virginal conception yet did not mention it even when talking specifically about Jesus' birth. As already noted by others, a reference to the miraculous conception would have been as simple as replacing the word "woman" with "virgin" in Paul's words above. After all, from the virginal conception point of view, Jesus' conception was different not because it involved a "woman," but because that woman was a "virgin." It is true that Paul does not mention any of Jesus' miracles, but he clearly believed Jesus did perform and can perform miracles. He prayed to him to heal him (2 Cor. 12:7-9) and claimed to have been converted to Christianity by a major miracle (Acts 9:3-8, 22:6-10, 26:13-18). Paul must have believed that Jesus was conceived naturally. This is confirmed by his tracing of Jesus' genealogy to David, who is Joseph's ancestor, and stressing that Jesus was related though the "flesh" to David: "concerning his Son who was a descendant of David with reference to the flesh" (Rom. 1:3). The Second Epistle to Timothy, whose attribution to Paul is doubtful, also stresses that Jesus descended from David (2 Tim. 2:8). In his letter to the Romans, Paul also emphasizes that Jesus came "by human descent" from the Patriarchs (Rom. 9:5).

This is how the author of *Shaken Creeds: The Virgin Birth Doctrine* summarizes these serious differences and the significance of the chronology of these books:

> Thus neither the authors of the Epistles which are the earliest of our New Testament books, nor the authors of the earliest and the latest of our four Canonical Gospels, make any mention of a Virgin Birth. The Gospels according to St. Matthew and St. Luke are our only authorities for the story, and they, as we have already seen, were not written until about the middle of the first half of the second century. Then for the first time, more than a century after the date assigned to the birth of Jesus, and nearly a century after the date assigned to his death, appears the first mention of the Virgin Birth....
>
> Even if a much earlier date be assigned to the publication of these two Gospels, the argument against the doctrine [of the Virgin Birth] on the score of lateness is not impaired. No scholar, however orthodox, denies that the Epistles are the earliest Christian documents in our Canon, or that the Epistles contain no reference to the Virgin Birth story, or that the Gospels were not written until at least three-quarters of a century after the date assigned to the birth of Jesus. So even the most conservative confess that the story first appears in two comparatively late documents, and that it is peculiar to these two out of all the other New Testament scriptures. Our "witnesses" are two. As we have already seen, neither of them is a first-hand witness. (Rhys 1922: 82-84)

Rhys concludes that the apostles had either never heard of or did not believe in the virginal conception of Jesus. This is the same conclusion that *has* to be reached about Mark's and John's failure to mention the virginal conception, although because these two, like Matthew and Luke, were particularly interested in Jesus' history, it is far more likely that they simply did not know about the virginal conception, as they did not report anything about Jesus' early history, as I explained above.

Even the Qur'an, which does not share the Bible's great interest in historical details and covers Jesus' story only briefly, mentions the virginal conception four times in three different chapters — twice in passing (3.59, 4.171) and twice in more detail (3.45-47, 19.17-22). This further highlights the oddity of the complete silence of all but two of the New Testament books on this unique miracle.

Another group of Qur'anic verses (19.27-33) show Mary's people, expectedly, question Jesus' legitimacy and tell us how the infant Jesus responded on behalf of his mother. In the New Testament, there is no mention that people were aware of Jesus' miraculous virginal conception. This applies even to Matthew's wise men and Luke's shepherds who visited the newborn Jesus. They saw Jesus with Mary and Joseph, and in the absence of any mention of their knowledge of the miracle, the implication is that they thought that Joseph was the baby's father. The presence of Joseph in Mary's life must have had at least some people think that her conception was the result of her relationship with Joseph. This natural conclusion did not escape the author of the Infancy Gospel of James. In one episode of this nativity story, news that Mary was pregnant came to the knowledge of the high priest who accused the couple of getting married secretly. The author solves the problem by having Mary and Joseph pass the test of the "water of the Lord" and thus prove their innocence (InJam. 11). Yet apart from a passing reference in John (8:37-41), we do not read in the New Testament about people suggesting that Jesus was the son of a normal relationship nor any rebuttals for such claims. If this means that people were not aware of the virginal conception then they must have believed that Joseph was Mary's husband, otherwise she would have been accused of adultery and, according to the Jewish law (Lev. 20:10), stoned to death.

Rhys also sets out to prove that the first two chapters in Matthew and Luke, in which the virginal conception is mentioned, were added to their respective books later. He thinks, as many scholars do, that the story of the virginal conception was a relatively late invention that was forced into Matthew and Luke, as well as written in some apocryphal books. One interesting observation is that while Acts and the Gospel of Luke were both written by the same person, the earlier of the two does not mention the virginal conception. It is indeed difficult to understand why the author who was so impressed and fascinated by the virginal conception in his later book did not mention it at all in the first! Is it possible that he learned about it later? Additionally, Acts indicates that Jesus' apostles knew him only from the time of his baptism by John (Acts 1:22).

Scholars have noted that if the first two chapters of Matthew and Luke are ignored, these two Gospels would share with Mark and John the same starting point: Jesus' baptism. The gospel of the Jewish Christian group of the Ebionites (Aramaic: "poor men"), which seems to be a revision of Matthew, also omits the nativity story and starts with the story of John in the wilderness. Irenaeus, the 2nd century bishop of Lyon, pointed out that the Ebionites believed that Jesus was the product of a normal relationship between Mary and Joseph:

> Cerinthus, again, a man who was educated in the wisdom of the Egyptians, taught that the world was not made by the primary God, but by a certain Power far separated from him, and at a distance from that Principality who is supreme over the universe, and ignorant of him who is above all. He represented Jesus as having not been born of a virgin, but as being the son of Joseph and Mary according to the ordinary course of human generation, while he nevertheless was more righteous, prudent, and wise than other men. Moreover, after his baptism, Christ descended upon him in the form of a dove from the Supreme Ruler, and that then he proclaimed the unknown Father, and performed miracles. But at last Christ departed from Jesus, and that then Jesus suffered and rose again, while Christ remained impassable, inasmuch as he was a spiritual being.
>
> Those who are called Ebionites agree that the world was made by God; but their opinions with respect to the Lord are similar to those of Cerinthus and Carpocrates. They use the Gospel according to Matthew only, and repudiate the Apostle Paul, maintaining that he was an apostate from the law. (Irenaeus, *Against Heresies*, 1.26.1-2)

Rhys (1922: 79) also argues that had the virginal conception been true, the baptism and the descent of the Holy Spirit would have be unnecessary, as Jesus is supposed to have received the Holy Spirit in his miraculous birth.

There is another criticism that has been directed at Matthew's use of an Old Testament prophecy to suggest that the virginal conception had been predicted. The Evangelist states that Mary became "pregnant through the Holy Spirit" (Matt. 1:18), and that "the child conceived in her is from the Holy Spirit" (Matt. 1:20). He then has the following quotation from "the prophet": "'Look! The virgin will conceive and bear a son, and they will call him Emmanuel,' which means 'God with us'" (Matt. 1:23). This prophet is Isaiah, and the prophecy Matthew quotes is this: "For this reason the sovereign master himself will give you a confirming sign. Look, this young woman is about to conceive and will give birth to a son. You, young woman, will name him Immanuel" (Isa. 7:14). As is clear from the *New English Translation* of the Bible, which is used in this book, the original Hebrew text of Isaiah 7:14 does not talk about a virgin! It uses the word *'almah*, which means "young woman," who may and may not be virgin. The word *'almah* does not mean virgin inherently. It is the feminine form of the masculine noun *'elem* which is used in 1 Samuel 17:56 and 20:22. In the Greek translation of the Hebrew Bible, the Septuagint, *'almah* is translated into *parthenos*. The latter means "virgin," but it also used in the Septuagint for another two Hebrew words for "girl" and "young woman." Matthew does not quote the original Hebrew Bible which talks about a young woman, but he uses the Greek translation which employs a word that is more suggestive of a virgin.

Bible scholar Robert Miller (2003: 201-206) argues that even if Matthew meant to use "parthenos" to mean "virgin," he would still not necessarily have meant a virginal conception. He might have meant to talk about a lady who was then a virgin and was going to become naturally pregnant later. Miller's argument is derived from his uncommon view that Matthew did not have a virginal conception on his mind when he wrote his Gospel.

That said, since the Hebrew term may still mean "a virgin," a conclusive argument cannot be made for either position.

The real problem in Matthew's use of Isaiah's prophecy is that he takes it completely out of context in order to apply it to Jesus' conception. Around 735 BCE, Rezin, King of Syria, and Pekah, King of the northern kingdom of Israel, formed an alliance against the threat of invasion by the neighboring superpower of Assyria. They wanted Ahaz, King of the southern kingdom of Judea, to join their coalition, but Ahaz was fearful of becoming Assyria's enemy. Rezin and Pekah then sent their armies to depose Ahaz and install a new king who would join their alliance. Ahaz thought of allying himself with Assyria to seek its powerful protection against Rezin and Pekah's advancing armies toward Jerusalem. God sent Prophet Isaiah to ally Ahaz's fears and give him a sign: a young woman will give birth to a boy called Immanuel, and before this boy is old enough to differentiate between right and wrong, the lands of Rezin and Pekah would be destroyed:

> For this reason the sovereign master himself will give you a confirming sign. Look, this young woman is about to conceive and will give birth to a son. You, young woman, will name him Immanuel. He will eat sour milk and honey, which will help him know how to reject evil and choose what is right. Here is why this will be so: Before the child knows how to reject evil and choose what is right, the land whose two kings you fear, will be desolate. (Isa. 7:14-16)

The text goes on to talk about events that would follow.

Matthew has completely misused Isaiah's prophecy in applying it to Jesus' birth. **First**, there was nothing special or miraculous about the conception or birth that Isaiah described. **Second**, the birth was not itself significant, as it was only a sign to Ahaz about future events. **Third**, that birth would be a sign only if it happened during Ahaz's life. **Fourth**, while Isaiah talked about a child called Immanuel (Isa. 7:14, 8:8), Jesus is never actually called "Immanuel" anywhere in the New Testament. The context of Isaiah's prophecy could not be clearer, so Matthew must have consciously decided to take the prophecy out of its context and apply it to Jesus.

This is not the only Old Testament prophecy that Matthew misuses to show that Jesus is the fulfillment of prophecies that he links to the coming of the Messiah, to show that Jesus is the awaited Messiah. The fact that the cited prophecies are forced to seem applicable to their respective parts of the Jesus story makes it highly unlikely that Matthew used those prophecies as a source of inspiration to fabricate the relevant episodes. If Matthew was using his imagination to create history, his keen interest on linking Jesus' life to Old Testament prophecies would have made him come up with events that are much easier to match to those prophecies. Yet almost every time he linked an episode in Jesus' life to a Biblical passage the latter had to be taken out of context, changed, and/or clumsily applied, which means that it is far more likely that the Evangelist was reporting what he believed to be history. He simply used the Old Testament to provide support for the history he had learned about, believed in, and accordingly reported. In the case of the virginal birth, Isaiah 7:14 does not talk about the conception of a virgin but a "young woman" and is not applicable to Jesus' story anyway, so this Biblical passage could not have inspired Matthew with the story. He simply wanted an Old Testament text that he thought he could apply to the story which he already knew to give it Christological dimensions. He reported a story that was already in circulation as part of the tradition of Jesus' birth which he believed. Whether that tradition is historical or not is, of course, a different matter.

Additionally, the suggestion that Matthew made up the events he reported makes the fulfillment argument which he persistently pursued completely meaningless. Matthew must have genuinely believed in the events he reported to diligently seek reference to these events in the Old Testament to prove that Jesus was the Christ (France, 1979: 120).

The fact that other apocryphal gospels misuse prophecies more or less in the same way Matthew does does not necessarily mean that they copied Matthew. It is more likely that these writings, including Matthew, were based on earlier oral or written sources.

6.2.1.2. Contradictory Accounts

The second attack against the authenticity of the Gospel accounts of the virginal conception is that the books of the New Testament, including Matthew and Luke, contain passages that contradict the virginal conception. One contradiction is the repeated reference to Jesus' descent from David, which implies that Joseph was his father, as Mary was probably not Davidic. Rhys links this contradiction to the assumption of the late inclusion of the first two chapters of Matthew and Luke:

> The contradictions involved in a story which frequently refers to Joseph as the father of Jesus, and yet begins by the Virgin Birth episode, can be accounted for only by assuming that the original Gospels did not contain the earlier chapters of our present Gospels, and that when these chapters were

added the editors omitted to make all the alterations in the text of the original chapters which would be necessary to bring these into accordance with the new commencement. Some small modifications seem indeed to have been made, but much remains which is absolutely inconsistent with the Virgin Birth story. (Rhys 1922: 105)

Miller (2003:65) has interestingly pointed out that a number of ancient manuscripts changed the child's "father and mother" in Luke 2:33 to "Joseph and his mother," and Mary's words "your father and I" in Luke 2:48 to "we." Clearly, those ancient copyists recognized that calling Joseph *Jesus' fathers* challenged the story of the virginal conception, so they changed this description. The contradictions and textual variations regarding whether Jesus was the son of David or not, and what this link meant, can be seen also outside the first two chapters of Matthew and Luke. They reflect awareness of the conflict between making Jesus of Davidic descent and his virginal conception. For instance, the clause "the carpenter, the son of Mary" in Mark 6:3 appears in different versions in some copies. In several old manuscripts, including the oldest available manuscript, it reads "the son of the carpenter and Mary," and a few others have it as "son of Mary and Joseph" Miller (2003:213). Matthew also has a different version: "Isn't this the carpenter's son? Isn't his mother named Mary?" (Matt. 13:55). Jesus was repeatedly linked to David not because Joseph was known to be his father, but because the awaited Messiah was believed to be Davidic (p. 234).

Other contradictions that have been identified is that Joseph and Mary "were amazed" at the praise of the child Jesus in the temple (Luke 2:33), and that Jesus' brothers did not believe in him (John 7:5). Mark even suggests that Jesus' brother and mother thought that he was mad (Mark 3:21, 31)! Rhys argues that had Jesus been born of a virginal conception, Mary would not have been "amazed" at the good words that were being said of him. He also contends that Mary would have certainly told Jesus' brother of his miraculous birth, so they would have believed in him. Rhys concludes that these texts show that the Gospels did not contain originally anything about a virginal conception, and that this story was introduced later on.

It is perhaps another sign of the confusing state of the accounts in Matthew and Luke that the basic argument of these texts can be read completely differently by different experts. For example, Miller (2003: 198-206) accepts that Luke's account is clearly suggestive of a virginal conception but raises serious doubts about whether Matthew had a miraculous conception in mind, yet Parrinder (1995: 71-72) concludes almost the opposite, suggesting that it is Matthew's account that is more plainly talking about a virginal conception! Nevertheless, the majority of scholars agree that both Matthew and Luke talk about a virginal conception.

6.2.1.3. Different Infancy Narratives

The third flaw in the New Testament's story of the virginal conception is that the two books that mention the story differ fundamentally in their accounts of Jesus' birth, which is closely tied to the story of his conception, thus raising serious questions about the credibility of the two nativity accounts. There is no disagreement that Mary had a virginal conception. While Luke talks in detail about Gabriel's visit to Mary, Matthew only makes a passing reference to the fact that Mary "was found to be pregnant through the Holy Spirit" (Matt. 1:18) and that "the child conceived in her is from the Holy Spirit" (Matt. 1:20). But the two Gospels give very different accounts of Jesus' birth. I will discuss these differences in more detail when I study Jesus' birth (pp. 168-169), but here I would like to focus on two major differences.

Matthew talks about Herod's massacre of young infants that targeted Jesus' life and forced Joseph to take Mary and little Jesus and escape to Egypt. This major event in the Matthean account is completely missing from Luke. The latter, on the other hand, talks about Joseph and the heavily pregnant Mary traveling from Galilee to Judea to register in a census that was ordered by the Roman empire, yet Matthew makes no mention of this journey. Both Gospels talk about a journey, but each ties its journey to his own version of events. Significantly, both stories of Herod's massacre (§11.3.2) and Roman census (§10.6) have also serious historical problems.

The three arguments above highlight major contradictions and inconsistencies in the New Testament and raise serious questions about the account of the virginal conception. These arguments often lead critics to reject the story of the virginal conception. They conclude that these problems are indicative of the inauthenticity and non-historicity of the story of the virginal conception.

It is undeniable that the story of the virginal conception in the New Testament has real problems. The many contradictions raise serious questions about the credibility of the New Testament authors, not the least the authors of the four Gospels. This does not necessarily mean that the story of the virginal conception, or to that matter other events in Jesus' life that the Gospels mention, did not take place. These flaws and inaccuracies can have an alternative explanation, and the Qur'an offers one.

From the Qur'anic perspective, Biblical textual problems are no surprises. The Qur'an has made it clear that the religious books that the Jews and Christians possess were written and changed by people. Even the Torah and the Injīl were tampered with. There is no reason to believe that the Gospels or other books in the New Testament are more factual or accurate about Jesus' life than other books that were not chosen for canonization. The fact that Luke's and Matthew's infancy narratives look isolated and probably unauthentic undermines the credibility and authenticity of the Gospels not the narratives. Focusing on problems in the two nativity narratives is a red herring, as these problems are not confined to these parts of the New Testament. They are rather a small sample of similar problems permeating many parts and books of the New Testament, and indeed the Old Testament also. They are symptomatic of more fundamental problems with the Bible.

Many scholars believe that the first two chapters of Matthew and Luke — specifically the accounts of the virginal conception — are inauthentic, as they are inconsistent with the rest of the New Testament. The likelihood, however, is that Matthew, Luke, and the other two Evangelists were not as informed and knowledgeable as tradition would have us believe. The contradictory picture of the virginal conception in the New Testament is the result of the confused state of its books not the story's incredibility. This is the Qur'anic perspective.

6.2.2. The Historical Arguments

In his rebuttal of the concept of virginal conception, Rhys compiled ancient stories from various cultures and traditions in which some form of miraculous conception features one way or another. His collection includes many myths and legends from ancient Egypt, Greece, China, India, Asia, Mexico, and North America. Rhys' long list of pre-Christianity characters that traditions claim to have been born by virgin mothers include Pharaoh Amenhotep III (1386-1349), the Phrygian god Attis, the Grecian God Dionysos, Buddha (6th century BCE), the Indian god Rama, and many others.

In his quest to prove that the concept of the virginal conception lived long before Christianity and that the latter copied it from older traditions, Rhys confused this concept, which he inaccurately called the "virgin birth," with "non-sexual, supernatural conception." For instance, Rhys mentions Buddha's mother who is said to have conceived Buddha through a dream. Buddha's mother was actually married, even though she did not conceive Buddha through her husband. The same applies to the mother of the Indian god Rama, Queen Kausalya. She had been married to King Dasarath, but had no children. Dasarath, who was married to other women who also did not have children, performed a special sacrifice at the end of which he was given a divine drink. He gave the drink to his wives who gave birth, with Kausalya giving birth to Rama.

Most of the stories that Rhys cites do not really share anything of significance with Jesus' story. Even when a story does contain some form of virginal conception, the similarity is negligible given the substantial differences between the two stories. Let me give two more ancient examples cited by Rhys, one from Greece and the other from Sicily:

> Dionysos, the Grecian God, was said in one version of the myth concerning him to be the son of Zeus out of the virgin goddess Persephone, and in another version to be the miraculously begotten son of Zeus out of the mortal

woman Semele. He, according to this story, was taken from his mother's womb before the full period of gestation had expired, and completed his embryonic life in Zeus's thigh. Dionysos was thus half human and half divine, born of a woman and also of a god. (Rhys, 1922: 118)

A Sicilian tale, probably very old, tells of a king's daughter who was shut up in a tower which had no aperture through which the sun could shine, as it had been foretold that she would conceive a child by the sun, and her father was anxious to prevent this occurrence. The girl, however, made with a piece of bone a small hole in the wall, and a sunbeam, entering through this hole, impregnated her. (Rhys, 1922: 143)

The attempt to discredit the virginal conception of Jesus because similar stories existed before Jesus is a good example of one of the flaws of the secular approach (§1.1.2). One astonishing aspect of this flaw is that the claimant is not required to prove that the latter story was copied from the earlier one(s), or that all these stories are instances of a literary motif and thus the work of the imagination of man. The mere existence of the two is taken to mean that story copying or creation did take place! The ridiculousness of this conclusion is clear from the fact that it can be applied almost at will, as no evidence is required. For instance, it could be claimed that no story of extraordinary or inexplicable healing, including the miraculous healings performed by Jesus, can be factual, because almost all nations and cultures from ancient times have had such stories in their traditions.

Jesus' virginal conception should be treated as a myth, it is often claimed, because other religious leaders have also been claimed to have been born to virgins. This is how the New Testament story is seen by those critics. This criticism cannot be made of the Old Testament where a number of miraculous conceptions are reported but none is claimed to have been virginal. More significant, the Qur'an also contains a number of stories of miraculous conceptions, but only Jesus is said to have been born of a virgin. Not even Muhammad is described as having been born of a virgin. In fact, the tone of exaggeration that religious books are often accused of engulfing the lives of their leaders with is remarkably missing from the Qur'an's account of Muhammad's life. With respect to the Prophet's birth, we know that he was an orphan (93.6), and there is no claim about him being born by a virginal conception, or that any miracle was involved in his birth. It is interesting to contrast the Qur'an's account with other Islamic literature where the writers associate many miracles with Muhammad from his conception to his birth. This is another example on the fundamental differences between the Qur'an and other writings. Had Muhammad written the Qur'an, you would expect him to have attributed all kinds of miracles and marvels to himself to impress an Arab society that was submerged in myths and legends. It is remarkable and significant that none of this exists in the Qur'an. This adds credibility to the only account of virginal conception in the Qur'an, which is that of Jesus.

By its very nature, a conception can be known to be virginal only by the woman who experiences it. She is the only person who can know whether her pregnancy was indeed miraculous and did not involve a man. Even the presence of the hymen cannot provide conclusive independent evidence that the pregnancy of a woman was not caused by human sperms. This is why we cannot expect of find independent, historical evidence to support the virginal conception of Jesus. This does not mean that history refutes this claim; it simply means that it cannot provide evidence for it.

Aware of the fact that the virginal conception cannot be known or verified by independent evidence, Matthew, the Gospel of the Birth of Mary, and the Infancy Gospel of James have Joseph informed paranormally in a dream that Mary's conception of Jesus was virginal, facilitated by the Holy Spirit. The Infancy Gospel of James (14:18-19) and The Gospel of Pseudo-Matthew (13) address this differently. They have two midwives examine Mary after the birth and find her still a virgin. What they found is actually evidence on a virgin birth not only virginal conception.

In the Qur'an, the supportive evidence from God to Mary's claim to chastity came from her infant son Jesus — the very subject of the accusation — who spoke in the cradle in defense of his mother, as we shall see later in this chapter (also p. 178).

6.2.3. The Scientific Arguments

Science has also been used to reject the virginal conception. This argument appeals to the fact that a human conception happens when a sperm from a male fertilizes an egg from a female. In the virginal conception, there was no male involved, so it is claimed that the pregnancy could not have occurred.

The development of an egg into an individual without fertilization has actually been known to exist in nature since the 18th century. Parthenogenesis, as it is known scientifically, has been observed in lower plants and animals, such as insects. In many social insects, such as the honeybee and the ant, the unfertilized eggs develop into the male drones and the fertilized eggs into the female workers and queens. Recently a captive female hammerhead shark at a zoo in Nebraska made the news when it gave birth without having contact with a male. Scientists confirmed that the young animal possessed no paternal DNA.

Parthenogenesis has also been induced artificially. This was first clearly demonstrated by 1900 by Jacques Loeb, who found that unfertilized frog eggs that he pierced with a needle caused some times normal embryonic development to start. Artificial parthenogenesis has been achieved in almost all major groups of animals and in mammals, although usually resulting in incomplete and abnormal development. What is relevant to the discussion of the virginal conception of Jesus, however, is that there are no reports of successful parthenogenesis involving humans.

The scientific argument has been elaborated further. The nucleus of the human cell contains two sex chromosomes. These are X chromosomes in females, and one X and one Y in males. In a normal fertilization process which involves a sperm and an egg, the fertilized egg would either inherit one X chromosome from the egg and one X chromosome from the sperm and develop into a female, or one X chromosome from the egg and one Y chromosome from the sperm and become a male. As there is no male participation in a virginal conception, no Y chromosome is involved, so the egg would have only X chromosomes and would develop into a female. Since Jesus was a man, he could not have been conceived by virginal conception.

The scientific arguments against the virginal conception are misguided, because Jesus' conception is presented in the scriptures as a miracle — that is, an event that violated natural laws. In fact, the whole point of a miracle is that it is supernatural. Jesus' story in the both the New Testament and the Qur'an contains many miracles, and the virginal conception is only one of those miracles, so the scientific arguments go actually beyond the current discussion of the virginal conception. Science can also be appealed to, for instance, to reject Jesus' miracles of raising the dead. I have already indicated that I will not deal in this book with the question of whether miracles can or cannot happen, as this complex subject is outside the scope of this book. But I have it made clear that, following the Qur'anic approach, I believe that miracle did and can happen.

6.3. The Accusation of the Illegitimacy of Jesus

Unsurprisingly, questioning the virginal conception has led to questioning Mary's chastity. If Mary was unmarried, did not conceive Jesus miraculously, and Joseph was not Jesus' father, then she must have been impregnated by another man. The conclusion is that Mary must have had an illicit relationship that led to her becoming pregnant with Jesus. This is not a new allegation. The Gospel of John seems to include a reference to this accusation being made by Jews in a debate with Jesus:

> I know that you are Abraham's descendants. But you want to kill me, because my teaching makes no progress among you. I am telling you the things I have seen while with the Father; as for you, practice the things you have heard from the Father!" They answered him, "Abraham is our father!" Jesus replied, "If you are Abraham's children, you would be doing the deeds of Abraham. But now you are trying to kill me, a man who has told you the truth I heard from God. Abraham did not do this! You people are doing the deeds of your father." Then they said to Jesus, "We were not born as a result of immorality! We have only one Father, God himself." (John 8:37-41)

Some think that this accusation was probably merely intended as an insult and did not represent a real doubt about Jesus' legitimacy (e.g. Miller, 2003: 214). Strangely, there are no more references to people accusing Jesus of being an illicit son or to rebuttals of this accusation.

One old mention of accusing Jesus of being born of fornication is found in the *Acts of Pilate*, which records Jesus' trial, crucifixion, and resurrection. This work is included in the *Gospel of Nicodemus*, which is believed to have been compiled in the beginning of the 5th century, although it probably used older materials. It is believed that the 2nd century Christian apologist Justin Martyr referred to the Acts of Pilate.

After accusing Jesus, in the presence of Pilate, of breaking the law, the Jewish elders went on to accuse Jesus of being a son of fornication:

> Pilate called Jesus, and said to him: "What is it that these witness against you, and you say nothing to them?" And Jesus answered: "If they had not the power, they would not speak. Everyone has power over his own mouth to say good and evil; let them see to it."
>
> And the elders of the Jews answering, say to Jesus: "What shall we see? First, that you was born of fornication; second, that at your birth in Bethlehem there took place a massacre of infants; third, that your father Joseph and your mother Mary fled into Egypt, because they had no confidence in the people."
>
> Some of the bystanders, kind *men* of the Jews, say: "We say that he was not born of fornication; but we know that Mary was espoused to Joseph, and that he was not born of fornication." Pilate says to the Jews who said that he was of fornication: "This speech of yours is not true, seeing that the betrothal took place, as these of your nation say." Annas and Caiaphas say to Pilate: "We with all the multitude say that he was born of fornication, and that he is a magician; but these are proselytes, and his disciples." And Pilate, calling Annas and Caiaphas, says to them: "What are proselytes?" They say to him: "They have been born sons of the Gentiles, and then have become Jews." Then answered those who testified that Jesus was not born of fornication, Lazarus and Asterius, Antonius and James, Annes and Azaras, Samuel and Isaac, Finees and Crispus, Agrippa and Judas: "We were not born proselytes, but are sons of the Jews, and we speak the truth; for we were present at the betrothal of Mary."
>
> And Pilate, calling to him those twelve men who proved that Jesus had not been born of fornication, said to them: "I adjure you by the health of Caesar, tell me if it is true that Jesus was not born of fornication." They say to Pilate: "We have a law not to swear, because it is a sin; but let them swear by the health of Caesar that it is not as we say, and we are worthy of death." Then said Pilate to Annas and Caiaphas: "Answer you nothing to those things which these testify?" Annas and Caiaphas say to Pilate: "Those twelve believe that he is not born of fornication; we — all the people — cry out that he was born of fornication, and is a magician, and says that he himself is the Son of God and a king, and we are not believed." (Nic. 2)

This piece of text is probably completely forged and does not have much historical value, but what interests us here is its documentation of the fact that there were Jews — possibly many of them — who considered Jesus an illicit son. Equally interesting is the fact that the dispute is not over whether Jesus was conceived miraculously by a virgin or not, but whether he was the legitimate son of Mary and Joseph or the illicit son of Mary and another, unknown man.

Celsus, a staunch 2nd century opponent of Christianity, recounts in his book *The True Doctrine*, which is quoted in Origen's *Against Celsus*, an attack by a Jewish interlocutor on Jesus and the accusation that Jesus fabricated the story of his birth from a virgin:

> He accuses Him of having "invented his birth from a virgin," and upbraids Him with being "born in a certain Jewish village, of a poor woman of the country, who gained her subsistence by spinning, and who was turned out of doors by her husband, a carpenter by trade, because she was convicted of adultery; that after being driven away by her husband, and wandering about for a time, she disgracefully gave birth to Jesus, an illegitimate child, who having hired himself out as a servant in Egypt on account of his poverty, and having there acquired some miraculous powers, on which the Egyptians greatly pride themselves, returned to his own country, highly elated on account of them, and by means of these proclaimed himself a God." (Origen, *Against Celsus*, 1.28)

Other reports have even identified and named the man who is alleged to have fathered Jesus illegitimately. Celsus cites the following claim by a Jew against Mary: "when she was pregnant she was turned out of doors by the carpenter to whom she had been betrothed, as having been guilty of adultery, and that she bore a child to a certain soldier named Panthera" (Origen, *Against Celsus*, 1.32).

The Jewish Talmud also has a few references attributed to rabbis from the early 2nd century that call Jesus "son of Pantera," and appear to treat "Pantera" as a family name. Other Talmudic references call Jesus the "son of Stada." Miller points out that the Rabbis knew that "son of Stada" was not Jesus' real name. He suggests that this seems to have been the name of a Jew who promoted the worship of non-Roman gods and was put to death because of that, so Jewish Rabbis applied it to Jesus because they considered him also to have called to the worship of false gods. In a reference to both "son of Pantera" and "son of Stada," one Rabbi claims that Stada was Mary's husband and Pantera was here paramour (Miller, 2003: 217).

Commenting on linking "son of Stada" to Jesus, France accepts that "it is not unlikely that later Rabbis identified Ben Stada with Jesus," but he voices caution of "assuming that any Ben Stada tradition originated as a historical reminiscence of Jesus" (France, 1999: 38).

One modern variation on these stories which tries to preserve Mary's chastity yet allow for the possibility that Jesus was an illegitimate son is the suggestion that Mary was raped by a Roman soldier. Such a scenario actually requires a considerable amount of creative imagination to stitch together a number of ancient stories of unknown reliability using a good amount of convenient assumptions, as can be seen in Miller's (2003: 220-222) version.

6.4. The Qur'an's Affirmation of the Virginal Conception

It has been claimed by some that the Qur'an does not confirm explicitly the virginal conception of Jesus. Geoffrey Parrinder states that while the Qur'an makes it clear that the conception involved divine intervention, it does not say whether it was natural or not. He also points out that in the past, commentators considered Jesus to have been born without a father, but that some modern Muslim writers deny, on scientific and historical grounds, that the Qur'an teaches the virginal conception (Parrinder, 1995:70-74).

This is probably one of the most obvious misreadings of a Qur'anic text. The Qur'an can hardly be any clearer in stating that Mary conceived Jesus without having a relation with a man. This is clear in the story of annunciation, which we have already studied; the story of the birth of Jesus (§10.4); and some other verses. This is a list of explicit and implicit confirmations in the Qur'an that Mary did not have a sexual relationship and that her conception was caused miraculously:

① After hearing the good news about Jesus, Mary replied to Gabriel: "How can I have a son when no man has touched me, neither have I been unchaste?" (19.20), and "How can I have a child when no human being has touched me?" (3.47). Gabriel did not reply with something such as "yes, but you will get married," but he rather responded with a statement emphasizing that the conception was going to happen miraculously: "Thus Your Lord has said: 'It is easy for Me. And so that We may make of him a sign for people and a mercy from Us, and it is a matter that has been ordained'" (19.21), and, "Thus Allah creates what He wills. When He decrees a matter, He only says to it 'Be!' and it is" (3.47).

② These are two verses that refer to Mary *guarding her private parts*, emphasizing that she was made to conceive miraculously while a virgin: "And [Allah set forth an example] Mary, daughter of 'Imrān, who guarded her private parts, then We breathed therein of Our spirit. And she believed in the words of her Lord and His Book, and was one of the obedient" (66.12), and, "And she who guarded her chastity, so We breathed into her of Our spirit and made her and her son a sign for the peoples" (21.91). The Qur'an keeps stressing Mary's chastity to make it clear that the conception of this *unmarried* woman did not involve a sexual relationship.

③ Gabriel's words to Mary that he was sent to *bestow on her a pure son* mean that he was directly involved in causing the conception of Jesus. This does not mean that Gabriel had a relationship with Mary, because in his reply to her question about how she could get pregnant without having a sexual relationship with a man he still maintained that the pregnancy was going to happen through a miracle. In a subtle way, Gabriel's presence in that room caused Mary's ovum to be fertilized. In another verse, Mary's conception is also described as happening by the breathing of God's Spirit into Mary, confirming Gabriel's involvement and the non-sexual nature of his role: "And she who guarded her chastity, so We breathed into her of Our spirit and made her and her son a sign for the peoples" (21.91).

④ God stresses in another verse that He "made the son of Mary and his mother a sign" (23.50). While Jesus being a "sign" for people may be understood in terms of the many miracles he performed from his birth, calling Mary also a "sign," which is a term associated with miracles in such a context, can only denote her virginal conception of Jesus. There is nothing else in Mary's story to make her a sign for people. The miracle of having food brought to her in the sanctuary was probably witnessed by Zechariah only, as she was living in isolation. This conclusion is also confirmed by the significant observation that the mention of Mary being a sign is made in the context of calling her with her son a sign.

We may also note that the word "sign" is used in the singular, i.e. the speech is not about *two signs* but *one*, so it must be about the virginal conception. Additionally, verses 21.91 and 23.50 talk about making Mary and her son *themselves* a sign, which suggests a miracle that happens to them as opposed to miracles that they perform. Probably even Jesus' ability to perform miracles was related to his paranormal conception.

⑤ Mary's words during the pangs of birth, "I wish I had died before this and had become someone totally forgotten" (19.23) — which reflect distress, despair, a deep sense of shame, and utmost apprehension — indicate that the childbirth was not going to be seen favorably by people, because they would not recognize the legitimacy of the child.

⑥ When Mary went back to her people with baby Jesus they said to her: "O Mary! You have come up with a grave thing. O sister of Aaron! Your father was not a bad man, and your mother was not an unchaste woman" (19.27-28). The accusation means that she was known not to have been married.

⑦ When baby Jesus spoke to defend his mother against her people' accusation, he did not say that he was the legitimate son of Mary and her husband. He spoke instead about his status as a prophet and showed that he was indeed a miraculous boy: "I am Allah's servant. He has given me the Book and has appointed me a prophet. He has made me blessed wherever I may be. He has enjoined upon me prayer and almsgiving so long as I remain alive. And [He has made me] kind to my mother, and has not made me arrogant or wretched" (19.30-32). He is clearly telling people to believe in his miraculous origin on the basis of his miraculous nature.

⑧ In his words above, Jesus states that God made him kind to his mother, but he does not mention his father, because he did not have one.

⑨ The Qur'an calls Jesus "son of Mary" 23 times — 13 times as "Jesus son of Mary," 5 times as "the Messiah son of Mary," 3 times as "the Messiah Jesus son of Mary," and 2 times with no other name or title. Jesus is also referred to once as "her son," i.e. Mary's son (21.91). The title "son of Mary" is clearly intended to emphasize the fact that Jesus had no father. It cannot mean that Jesus had an unknown father, because it is a title that God Himself used for Jesus, not simply one used by people who did not know Jesus' father. God is described as omniscient in the Qur'an, so it cannot be claimed that this title implies that Jesus' father was unknown.

⑩ The Qur'an identifies people after their fathers, so its identification of Jesus after his mother is a unique case. People in general are referred to as "the sons of Adam" (e.g. 7.26, 17.70), the Israelites are called "the Children of Israel" (e.g. 5.72, 20.80), Adam's two sons are called "the sons of Adam" (5.27), and Mary herself is called "the daughter of 'Imrān" (66.12). Note that Mary's father died before her birth (p. 49), but she is still called after him. Even if Jesus' father was no more around after his birth, he would have still been called after his father, had he had one.

I do not think these arguments leave any room to doubt that the Qur'an emphasizes that Mary was virgin when she conceived Jesus and that this conception was not through a sexual relationship with a man. It was a miraculous, virginal conception.

We discussed in the previous section the insinuation that started at least as early as the 2nd century that Jesus was the fruit of an illicit relationship between Mary and someone other than Joseph. We also saw that this defamatory allegation was used by opponents of Christianity, including Jews. The Qur'an also mentions the Jewish accusation to Mary of unchastity. This occurs in the context of criticizing Jews for misbehaviors, including breaking their covenant and killing prophets:

> And because of their disbelief and of their speaking against Mary a tremendous calumny (4.156).

The Qur'an stresses that Mary was virgin when she conceived Jesus miraculously and strongly criticizes those who accused her of unchastity. There is no mention in the Qur'an of Mary's getting married or having other children.

7

The *Rūḥ* (Spirit)

The Hebrew term for "spirit," *ruach*, and its Greek equivalent, *pneuma*, occur hundreds of times in the Old Testament and the New Testament, respectively, where each is given a number of different meanings.

The Arabic term *rūḥ* (spirit) occurs 21 times in the Qur'an, 7 of which in the context of talking about Jesus. Unlike its Biblical equivalents, *rūḥ* has no more than two meanings. In most cases, the term is used to denote the mysterious and shapeless Gabriel, either referring to him as a being or signifying a part of him. In 4 occurrences the term could mean "inspiration," although it may also be a referent to Gabriel.

Studying the concept of *rūḥ* reveals fascinating details about the Qur'anic account of the creation of man.

7.1. The Hebrew *Ruach* in the Old Testament

The Hebrew word *ruach* occurs 389 times in the Old Testament. About two thirds of these occurrences are translated "spirit," but the remaining instances are rendered in more than twenty different ways. Different translations of the Old Testament render the various instances of *ruach* differently. For instance, while the *Authorized Version* (AV) translates 237 occurrences of *ruach* into "spirit" and the remaining 152 instances in 22 different ways, the *Revised Version* (RV) renders *ruach* into "spirit" 224 times, and the remaining 165 are translated differently.

In his study of the term *ruach* in the Old Testament, in an appendix to *The Companion Bible*, Bullinger (1909a: 13) states the following:

> The meaning of the word is to be deduced only from its *usage*. The one root idea running through all the passages is *invisible force*. As this force may be exerted in varying forms, and may be manifested in diverse ways, so various renderings are necessitated, corresponding thereto.
>
> *Ruach*, in whatever sense it is used, always represents that which is *invisible* except by its manifestations. These are seen both externally to man, as well as internally within man.
>
> As coming from God, it is the invisible *origin of life*. All apart from this is death. It comes from God, and returns to God (Ecc. 3:19-20).

Bullinger identifies the following different usages for *ruach*:

① God as being invisible (2 Sam. 23:2).

② The holy spirit or third person of the Trinity (1 Kings 18:12).

③ Invisible divine power manifesting itself in creation (Gen. 1:2); in giving life (Ezek. 37:14); and in executing judgment where it is translated as "blast" (Exo. 15:8), "breath" (2 Sam. 22:16), and "spirit" (Isa. 34:16).

④ Invisible "power from on high," manifesting itself as divine power in giving spiritual gift (Gen. 41:38). In these instances, *ruach* is spoken about as "coming upon," "clothing," "falling on," and "being poured out."

⑤ The invisible part of man which God gives to man at birth, and which returns to God at man's death — translated as "breath" (Gen. 6:17), "spirit" (Gen. 6:3), and "wind" (Ezek. 37:9).

⑥ The invisible characteristics of man, manifesting themselves in states of mind and feeling. These are translated as "mind" (Gen. 26:35), "breath" (Job 19:17), "courage" (Josh. 2:11), "anger" (Judg. 8:3), "blast" (Isa. 25:4), and "spirit" (Gen. 45:27).

⑦ Invisible spirit-beings. These instances are translated as "angels" (Ps. 104:4), "cherubim" (Ezek. 10:15), "neutral spirit-beings" (Job 4:15), and "evil angels" (Judg. 9:23).

⑧ The invisible manifestations of the atmosphere. It is used for "temperature" and translated as "cool" in Gen. 3:8. It is also used for "air" and translated as "wind(s)", "whirlwind" (Ezek. 1:4), "windy" (Ps. 55:8), "spirits" (Zech. 6:5), "air" (Job 41:16), "tempest" (Ps. 11:6), "blast" (Exo. 15:8), "quarters (of the four winds)" (1 Chr. 9:24), and "side(s) (of the four winds)" (Jer. 52:23).

Some of the meanings above appear differently in different translations of the Old Testament, but I am citing them as they appear in Bullinger's study. Obviously this is not a universally agreed listing. For instance, the Jews would not accept that *ruach* occurs in the sense of the "third person of the Trinity," which is a Christian concept. One thing clear from the long list of different translations, meanings, and usages is that the term *ruach* is used very loosely in the Old Testament. When a term is used for this many different meanings, it can be extremely difficult to ascertain its meaning in any specific instance.

Believers in the Old Testament as the literal Word of God would argue that this huge variance in the use of *ruach* underlines some hidden wisdom. Others would see it as a clear indication that the books of the Old Testament were written and edited by different people over a long period of time. Even if these books were based on authentic divine scriptures, their current versions must be the product of considerable editing by man.

7.2. The Greek *Pneuma* in the New Testament

The Greek New Testament term that corresponds to the Hebrew *ruach* is *pneuma*. It occurs about 385 times in the New Testament, according to Bullinger, and 377 times according the *New English Translation* (NET) of the Bible, with just over 100 of them in the canonical Gospels.

In the *King James Version* (KJV), *pneuma* is rendered as "Spirit" 137 times and "spirit(s)" 151 times. The other main translation is "Ghost" in "Holy Ghost," which occurs about 89 times. It is also translated twice as "ghost," and once as "life," "wind," "spirituality," and "spiritual." The term is never rendered "ghost" in the *New International Version* (NIV) and *American Standard Version* (ASV), but translated as "Spirit" 241 and 239 times, respectively. Additionally, the term is rendered between 1-3 times as "breath," "spirituality," "spiritual," "attitude," "demon-possessed," "heart," "mind," and "prophecy." None of these translations is used in the KJV.

In the AV, *pneuma* is given the following meanings: Spirit 111, Holy Ghost 89, Spirit (of God) 13, Spirit (of the Lord) 5, (My) Spirit 3, Spirit (of truth) 3, Spirit (of the Christ) 2, human (spirit) 49, (evil) spirit 47, spirit (general) 26, spirit 8, (Jesus' own) spirit 6, (Jesus' own) ghost 2, and others 21. The NET Bible gives *pneuma* the following meanings: Spirit 334, spirits 33, breath 2, ghost 2, wind 1, enthusiasm 1, resolved 1, spiritual 1, spiritually 1, and life 1. Clearly, different translations have given the term different meanings and have interpreted its instances differently.

Bullinger (1909b: 146-147) notes that *pneuma* was used in the following wide variety of meanings:

① God (John 4:24).
② Christ (1 Cor. 6:17).
③ The Holy Spirit (generally with the article), denoting the Giver.
④ The operations of the Holy Spirit (1 Cor. 12:4-11).
⑤ The new nature in the child of God (John 3:3-7).
⑥ Man (psychologically), where *pneuma* makes man a "living soul."
⑦ Character, as being in itself invisible, and manifested only in one's actions (Rom. 8:15).
⑧ Other invisible characteristics, such as feelings or desires (Matt. 26:41), or that which is supernatural.
⑨ Man (physiologically) (Luke 1:47).
⑩ Adverbially, where it is translated "spiritually" (Rom. 8:6)
⑪ Angels or spirit beings (Acts 8:29).
⑫ Demons or evil spirit beings (Mark 7:25).
⑬ The resurrection body (1 Cor. 15:45).
⑭ Holy spirit (without articles) (Matt. 1:18), denoting the gift.

As we saw with *ruach* in the Old Testament, *pneuma* in the New Testament is a very vague term whose meaning in a passage can be extremely difficult to determine.

7.3. The Arabic *Rūḥ* in the Qur'an

The noun *rūḥ*, which is usually translated as "spirit," occurs 21 times in the Qur'an in 20 verses. Unlike the many meanings of the Biblical *ruach* and *pneuma*, the Qur'anic *rūḥ* has no more than two meanings.

We will start by splitting the Qur'anic verses into three groups each of which may look like employing *rūḥ* in a different way. In the course of examining the second group it will become gradually clear that the first two groups actually use the term in one and the same meaning, denoting Gabriel. We will then examine the third group of 4 verses. Here also *rūḥ* may be seen as signifying Gabriel, although the different, but still related, meaning of "inspiration" is equally applicable to a couple of them.

7.3.1. Gabriel

In at least 10 verses (2.87, 2.253, 4.171, 5.110, 16.102, 19.17, 26.193, 70.4, 78.38, 97.4) *rūḥ* appears as a title for Gabriel. I shall translate these instances as "Spirit" with a capital "S."

The Qur'an describes the messenger who communicated the Qur'an to Prophet Muhammad as the *ar-rūḥ al-amīn* (The Trustworthy Spirit) and the *rūḥ al-Qudus* (The Spirit of Holiness):

> The Trustworthy Spirit has descended with it [the Qur'an] (26.193) upon your [O Muhammad!] heart that you may be of the warners (26.194).
>
> Say [O Muhammad!]: "The Spirit of Holiness has revealed it [the Qur'an] from your Lord with the truth, that it may establish those who believe and as a guidance and good news for the Muslims (16.102).

He is described as "trustworthy" because God has trusted him with delivering His messages to prophets. He is described as being of *al-Qudus*, which I have translated as "Holiness," probably in reference to *al-Quddūs*, which is one of God's "Beautiful Names" (59.23).

We know from another verse that this Spirit is called *Jibrīl* (Gabriel):

> Say [O Muhammad!]: "Whoever is an enemy to Gabriel?" For he sent it (the Qur'an) down on your heart by Allah's permission, confirming that which is before it [of divine Books] and as a guidance and good news for the believers (2.97).

Gabriel also appears in the story of Jesus in the Qur'an as providing support to Jesus (also 2.253 and 5.110):

> And We gave Moses the Book and followed him with a succession of messengers; and We gave Jesus son of Mary clear proofs, and We supported him with the Spirit of

Holiness. Is it that whenever a messenger came to you [O Children of Israel!] with what you do not like you grew arrogant, some you disbelieved and some you killed? (2.87).

The Qur'an does not specify Gabriel's exact role in supporting Jesus, though it may be guessed that he was involved in some of the miracles that Jesus performed. In one verse, God says to Jesus "Remember My favor on you and on your mother, that I have supported you with the Spirit of Holiness, [making you] speak to people in the cradle and when middle-aged" (5.110), before going on to mention other miracles that He granted to Jesus. Aṭ-Ṭabāṭabā'ī has noted that the verse seems to make a direct link between Jesus' ability to speak in the cradle and Gabriel's support.

The Qur'an has two different words for "angel (*malak*)" and its plural "angels (*malā'ika*)". Interestingly, the word *rūḥ* does not have a plural form in the Qur'an, suggesting that, unlike the angels, there is only one *rūḥ*, that is Gabriel. I think the phrase "Our Spirit" (19.17) lends further support to the view that the "Spirit" is one single being.

There is another mysterious being who is only named once in the Qur'an called "Michael (*Mīkāl*)", but there is no indication that he is also a *rūḥ*:

As to anyone who is the enemy of Allah, His angels, His messengers, Gabriel, and Michael, Allah is the enemy of the disbelievers (2.98).

The word *rūḥ* is used for Gabriel also in the following two verses about his visit to Mary:

O People of the Book! Commit no excesses in your religion or utter anything concerning Allah but the truth. The Messiah, Jesus son of Mary, was only a messenger of Allah, His Word that He sent to Mary, and a Spirit from Him [that He sent] (4.171).

She put a veil between herself and them. Then We sent to her Our Spirit, and he assumed for her the likeness of a man in all respects (19.17).

Verse 19.17 tells us that God's Spirit can perfectly take the appearance of a man. The phrase "for her" links Gabriel's appearance as a man to his visit to Mary, implying that he may take other forms in other circumstances.

The canonical Gospels state that after Jesus' baptism, the "Spirit" (Mark 1:10; John 1:32), "Spirit of God" (Matt. 3:16), or "Holy Spirit" (Luke 3:22) descended on him in the form of a "dove." Although this spirit is not taken to mean Gabriel, this New Testament event also indicates that the spirit can assume various forms.

Like the Spirit, the angels also can assume the appearance of human beings:

And they (the disbelievers) say: "Why has not an angel been sent down to him [Muhammad]?" Had We sent down an angel, the matter would have certainly been decided and then they would not have been given a respite (6.8). And if We had made him an angel, We would have made him a man, and We would have confused them as they (the disbelievers) currently are (6.9).

Most Muslim exegetes think that the Spirit is an angel in nature, but one that the Qur'an differentiates from the other angels. As I have already explained (p. 54), the Qur'an always talks about angels in the plural when describing their task of delivering messages. Gabriel, however, is individually identified. Several verses talk about tasks that God specifically assigned to Gabriel. There are angels also who are identified in person, but in contexts other than the delivery of messages. These are the "angel of death," who is mentioned once (32.11), and the angels *Hārūt* and *Mārūt* who taught the Babylonians magic, who are mentioned and named once (2.102). *Mīkāl* (Michael) is also named once (2.98).

There are 3 verses that mention the *rūḥ* and the angels side by side, clearly suggesting that there are differences between them:

> The angels and the Spirit ascend to Him in a day the length of which is fifty thousand years (70.4).
>
> The Day [of Resurrection] on which the Spirit and the angels stand arrayed; they shall not speak except he whom God permits and speaks right (78.38).
>
> The angels and the Spirit descend in it (the Night of Status) by the permission of their Lord for every affair (97.4).

Although it is difficult to talk with confidence about the exact relationship between the Spirit and the angels, the former does look like a unique being — probably a unique angel. This difficulty arises from the fact that these beings are completely different from the forms of life we are familiar with and their true nature is too difficult to comprehend.

The Biblical concept of "holy spirit," which represents one use of the term "spirit" in the Bible (Bullinger, 1909a; 1909b; 1979), is very different from the Qur'an's Gabriel. This is what Vermes has to say about the meaning of "holy spirit" in the Bible:

> In the Bible the spirit of holiness, or holy spirit, symbolizes the power through which God acts in the world. For example the spirit of prophecy inspires the prophets, the spirit of purity cleanses the unclean, and so forth. Likewise in the New Testament, it is through the holy spirit that God causes Mary miraculously to conceive Jesus (Luke 1:35). Jesus speaks of baptizing with fire and the holy spirit (Matt. 3:11). The same holy spirit enables the apostles to converse in tongues on the first day of Pentecost (Acts 2:4). (Vermes, 2000: 49)

Vermes then goes on to explain that John then assigned a personal status to the Holy Spirit, making him the heavenly figure who would continue the work that Jesus did not complete. Jesus was the first paraclete, and the Holy Spirit is the second. The concept of paraclete and John's contribution to it are further discussed in §17.4.

Also, the New Testament's concept of the "Holy Spirit" as the third entity of the Trinity is also refuted by the Qur'an, as the doctrine of Trinity is itself rejected (§14.4).

So the Qur'an uses the term *rūḥ* (Spirit) for Gabriel when mentioning his visit to Mary (4.171, 19.17), his support for Jesus (2.87, 2.253, 5.110), his communication of God's revelation to Muhammad (16.102, 26.193), and tasks that he and the angels are involved in (70.4, 78.38, 97.4).

7.3.2. The Spirit of the Creation of Man

The second meaning of *rūḥ* is probably indicative of its complex nature. This term is used in 5 verses to designate *something* mysterious that God attributes to Himself that He *breathed into* Adam when creating him (also 15.29 and 32.9) and into Mary when creating Jesus (also 21.91):

> When your [O Muhammad!] Lord said to the angels: "I shall create a man from clay (38.71). So when I have fashioned him and breathed into him of My spirit, then fall down before him prostrate" (38.72).

> And [Allah set forth an example] Mary, daughter of ʿImrān, who guarded her private parts, then We breathed therein of Our spirit. And she believed in the words of her Lord and His Book, and was one of the obedient (66.12).

Note that Mary's conception of Jesus involved the *rūḥ* Gabriel, so this second meaning of *rūḥ* is closely related to Gabriel, as we shall see later in the chapter.

The word *rūḥ* in this second and mysterious sense — which I have differentiated from the first meaning by translating it as "spirit," i.e. with a small "s" — appears always in phrases that ascribe it to God only and imply that it is a part not the whole of the *rūḥ*. This last attribute is underlined by the use of the preposition *min* (of) before the word *rūḥ*. The three slightly different phrases in which *rūḥ* is used in this sense are *min rūḥī* (of My spirit) (15.29, 38.72), *min rūḥinā* (of Our spirit) (21.91, 66.12), and *min rūḥih* (of His spirit) (32.9). The *rūḥ* or "spirit" that God breathed into Adam and Mary is related to God, hence the use of the possessive; and it is only part not the whole of the *rūḥ*, hence the use of the preposition "of."

In another verse that can be linked to the verses above, the Qur'an stresses the similarity between the creation of Adam and Jesus:

> The likeness of Jesus in Allah's eye is as the likeness of Adam. He created him of dust, then He said to him "Be!" and he is (3.59).

As discussed earlier, the clause "'Be' and he is" represents God's infinite power and authority. In this particular verse, it highlights the fact that Adam and Jesus were both created by miraculous intervention by God. It looks completely logical to conclude that this divine intervention is represented by the role of the spirit in the creation of Adam and Jesus.

In order to understand more the spirit in this sense and its role in the creation of Jesus, we need to study what the Qur'an says about the creation of Adam and the spirit's role in it.

One essential fact that must be stressed first is that, unlike the Old Testament, the Qur'an does not state that Adam was created *directly or instantly* from dust or clay. The Qur'an makes it clear that the creation of Adam from clay involved a long process, so it was *not instant*; and that the clay was merely the material used in the early stages of the creation, so it was *not direct*:

> [He is the one] who did well everything that He has created, and He *began* the creation of man from clay (32.7). Then He made his progeny from a form of insignificant fluid (32.8). Then He fashioned him and breathed into him of His spirit, and made for you [O people!] the ears, the eyes, and the hearts; little thanks you give! (32.9).

This interpretation is supported by the fact that the Qur'an describes *all human beings, not only Adam*, as having been created from dust or clay:

> It is He who created you [O people!] from clay, then He decreed a term [for your death]; and there is a term [for your resurrection] named with Him, yet you are still in doubt! (6.2).
>
> Then ask [O Muhammad!] them (people) whether they are greater in creation or those [others] whom We have created [the angels, and the jinn who are created of fire]. Surely We created them (people) of sticky clay (37.11).
>
> And Allah created you [O people!] from dust, then from a life-germ, then He made you pairs (35.11).

Further evidence comes from the following verse which describes "water" as the origin of all living creatures:

> Do not those who disbelieve see that the heavens and the earth were jointed together then we separated them, and We made of water every living thing; will they not then believe? (21.30)

Describing the "water" as the origin of all living creatures, and at the same time calling the "dust" and "clay" origins of the human being, can only mean that the creation was not done directly from any of these primitive materials. "Water," "dust," and "clay" are all materials that took part at very early stages of the creation process — a process that lasted for many millions of years. No form of life, whether simple or complex, is ever suggested in the Qur'an to have been created directly or instantly from these original primitive substances. By referring to the latter, God reminds the human beings of their modest origin and nature, and contrasts that with His power and supremacy, thus stressing their duty to worship Him. The Qur'an clearly speaks about a process of evolution, not direct creation.

The mention of "water" in the following passage in the story of creation in the Old Testament might well represent a contextual displacement of the role of water in the process of the *creation of life* as described in the Qur'an:

> In the beginning God created the heavens and the earth. Now the earth was without shape and empty, and darkness was over the surface of the watery deep, but the Spirit of God was moving over the surface of the water (Gen. 1:1-2)

Although both *water* and *God's spirit* are mentioned, they are not linked to the creation of life.

The evolutionary nature of the creation of Adam must mean that he was conceived and given birth to by his mother, like other creatures. The fact that Adam was different, even from his parents, does not mean that he did not have one. He evolved from a hominid species to be the first member of a new species. Scholars have noted that the Qur'an hints that hominids did live before Adam. When God informed the angels about His decision to create a viceroy on earth — that is, Adam — they expected the new race to "make mischief" and "shed blood":

> And when your Lord said to the angels: "I am going to place a viceroy on earth." They said: "What! Will You place in it such as shall make mischief in it and shed blood, while we celebrate Your praise and extol Your holiness?" He said: "I know what you do not know" (2.30).

Exegetes have pointed out that the angels' reply indicates that they must have seen similar species behave in that terrible way, so they could not understand God's decision. What the angels did not realize, however, is that the new creature was destined to be very different from his ancestors. Let's park the conclusion about Adam's origin for a moment to tackle another issue about the spirit.

We have already seen a number of verses that say that *at some point* of God's creation of Adam, He breathed into him *of His spirit* (also 32.9 and 38.72):

> And when your [O Muhammad!] Lord said to the angels: "I shall create a human being out of old clay (15.28). So when I have made him and breathed into him of My spirit, fall down prostrating to him" (15.29).

Significantly, the Qur'an does not state anywhere that God breathes of His spirit into every human beings He created. It says that this happened in the creation of Adam and, later, Jesus. Leaving the creation of Jesus aside for a moment, there are

3 verses about the creation of man that mention the breathing of God's spirit into him. Two of these verses also mention God's command to the angel to prostrate to the new creature:

> So when I have made him and breathed into him of My spirit, fall down [O angels!] prostrating to him (15.29).
>
> So when I have fashioned him and breathed into him of My spirit, then fall down [O angels!] before him prostrate (38.72).

We know from the context of these verses and from other verses that the creature whom the angels were commanded to prostrate to was Adam, as in the following example:

> And when We said to the angels: "Prostrate yourselves before Adam," so they did, except Satan who refused, was arrogant, and was one of the disbelievers (2.34).

The third verse does not name Adam or mention the command to the angels to prostrate to the new creature, but it is still clear that the breathing of spirit is also associated with the creation of the first man, i.e. Adam:

> [He is the one] who did well everything that He has created, and He began the creation of man from clay (32.7). Then He made his progeny from a form of insignificant fluid (32.8). Then He fashioned him and breathed into him of His spirit, and He made for you [O people!] the ears, the eyes, and the hearts; little thanks you give! (32.9).

The observation that only Adam, not all human beings, has spirit breathed into him challenges a common but erroneous assumption. The latter has probably resulted from the equally widespread and false view that it is the "spirit" that gives the human beings, and maybe other creatures, life, and that it is the departure of this spirit from the body that makes a living human being die. There is no Qur'anic verse stating that a "spirit" in the human being is the source of life or that its departure is the cause of death. This is in clear contradiction to the Old Testament which suggests that *life was breathed into Adam*: "The Lord God formed the man from the soil of the ground and breathed into his nostrils the breath of life, and the man became a living being" (Gen. 2:7). In fact, the Qur'an makes it clear that Adam was made or fashioned, i.e. was already physically made or developed to some stage, before the spirit was breathed into him, confirming it is not the source of life:

> So when I have made him and breathed into him of My spirit, fall down [O angels!] prostrating to him (15.29).
>
> So when I have fashioned him and breathed into him of My spirit, then fall down [O angels!] before him prostrate (38.72).

There is another interesting observation that confirms our conclusion that the spirit is not the source of life. One of Jesus' miracles, which we will study in more detail in Chapter 16, was to create birds of clay and then *breathe into them* to turn them into living birds (3.49, 5.110). Significantly, the verses do not state that Jesus *breathed spirit* into the clay birds. The injection of life into clay birds did not require or involve any spirit. Let's also remind ourselves here that the "spirit" is never used by or attributed to other than God in the Qur'an.

We have also already concluded that Adam was not created from water, dust, or clay directly, but was given birth to by his mother like any other child. At the same time, the Qur'an presents Adam as the first human being and the father of the human race. Therefore, the creation of Adam must have represented the emergence of a new species that is very different from the species of his parents. Given that the breathing of spirit into Adam did not give Adam life, it seems very plausible to suggest that the spirit's role was to turn Adam into the new species he came to be. This is also supported by the fact that this breathing of spirit into Adam is described as the miracle of the creation of Adam in verse 3.59: "'Be!' and it is."

Adam was very different from his parents and their species. The supernatural emergence of Adam from his parents' hominid species was immeasurably greater than any natural evolutionary change. The only detail in the story of the creation of Adam in the Qur'an that may be linked to his emergence as a new super species is God's breathing into him of His spirit. This mysterious spirit gave Adam faculties and qualities that made him distinctly different from the hominid species he descended from.

This analysis means that the sudden appearance of this new, super creature who exceeded his ancestors in his abilities could not have happened by natural evolution. It could have occurred only by direct divine intervention. Adam was a unique creature who might be described as half natural and half supernatural. He was not a product of natural evolution only, nor the result of a miraculous instant creation. He emerged through a natural evolutionary process that was guided at some point by a miracle.

This interpretation of the role of the spirit in making Adam a new species finds support in the fact that God ordered the angels to prostrate to Adam *after* He breathes into him of His spirit (15.29, 32.9, 38.72). The injection of the spirit into Adam changed him so much and made him so special that God commanded the angels to prostrate before him. The angel wondered about God's decree to create a viceroy on earth because they did not realize how different this new being was going to be from his savage and bloody ancestors whom they had witnessed cause havoc on the earth. They did not know the role that the spirit would play in the creation of Adam, making him a prophet and the father of a species that would give birth to great spiritual individuals such as Muhammad and Jesus. The angels' prostration was a bow of respect to God's creation of a special species that has the potential and opportunity to lead a life that conforms to God's commandments.

As only Adam had spirit breathed into him to change him to the human being we know, all other human beings must have inherited *from him* the faculties and qualities that characterize the human race, including the potential for *spiritual* development. The spirit changed Adam's genes, and this supernaturally designed genetic code was then passed to his descendants.

This conclusion may seem contestable by the fact that Adam's wife did not have spirit breathed into her, although she obviously was a human being. The Qur'an has the answer to this objection, stating four times that the human beings were created from "one soul" (4.1, 6.98, 7.189, 39.6). Equally significant and interesting is the Qur'an's repeated statement in three of these verses that God created from that soul "its mate":

> O people! Be dutiful toward your Lord who created you from one soul, created its mate from it, and spread from these two many men and women (4.1).
>
> It is He who created you from one soul and made its mate from it (7.189).
>
> He created you from one soul then made its mate from it (39.6).

Some exegetes read these verses as meaning that both mates were created from one soul, i.e. as if that one soul, whatever it is, is something from which both Adam and Eve were created. However, the following three verses, which remind people that God created for them *mates from themselves*, leave no doubt that the *creation of mates from other souls* denotes the marital relationship between man and women, i.e. the creation of man from man:

> And Allah has made for you mates from your souls (16.72).
>
> And one of His signs is that He created for you mates from your souls (30.21).
>
> He made for you mates from your souls (42.11).

Verses 4.1, 7.189, and 39.6 can only mean that every human being, including Eve, was created from Adam. Recalling that Adam grew in a hominid society, he must have fathered Eve with a female from his original species. This explains why the creation of Eve did not involve breathing spirit into her. All human beings are children of Adam and inherited from him the special qualities that God gave him via breathing spirit into him.

The Old Testament also states that Eve was created from Adam, but again the description is different from that in the Qur'an. The Bible's description is in line with its concept of direct and instant creation that the Book of Genesis emphasizes many times:

> So the Lord God caused the man to fall into a deep sleep, and while he was asleep, he took part of the man's side and closed up the place with flesh. Then the Lord God made

a woman from the part he had taken out of the man, and he brought her to the man (Gen. 2:21-22).

This is another context displacement as Eve's creation from Adam is given a different context by the Bible.

Influenced by the Old Testament, many Muslim exegetes have also stated that Eve was created directly from Adam's body and even accepted the Bible's identification of that part of Adam's body as one of his ribs! (The NET Bible translators used "part of the man's side" instead of "on of his ribs" like most translations.) This interpretation is irreconcilable with Qur'anic verses, but many Muslim exegetical works reflect considerable influence by the Old and New Testaments, which undermines their claim to be exegeses of the Qur'an.

Now, if the qualities that make up a human being were being passed from one generation to another by the male, or required both the male and female, then it is clear why the creation of Jesus had to involve the breathing of spirit. As Jesus was not to have a father, spirit had to be involved in his creation in the same way it got involved in the creation of Adam to create the human species.

It may be suggested that the role of the spirit in the creation of Jesus was merely to fertilize the ovum, as there was no sperm involved. Of course, the spirit was God's agent in making Mary pregnant of Jesus without the involvement of a man, as spirit was breathed *into her*:

> And [Allah set forth an example] Mary, daughter of 'Imrān, who guarded her private parts, then we breathed therein something of Our spirit. And she believed in the words of her Lord and His Book, and was one of the obedient (66.12).
>
> And she [Mary] who guarded her chastity, so We breathed into her of Our spirit and made her and her son a sign for the peoples (21.91).

But that was not the only role of the spirit. We know that since the spirit got involved in the creation of Adam *after* he had been fashioned or made, the spirit must have had a role other than creating him physically (15.29, 38.72). Additionally, as Adam was born to parents from another species, the role of the spirit in the miracle of his birth was obviously something other than compensating for the non-involvement of a male in his conception. In this instance of miraculous creation, which God described as one of those paranormal events that are brought about by the divine word "Be," the spirit's role was to give Adam the qualities of the new species. This also, in addition to fertilizing the ovum, was the spirit's role in the creation of Jesus.

There is another observation that supports my conclusion about the role of the spirit in the creation of Adam and Jesus. While John, son of Zechariah, was also created by a miracle, his creation did not involve the breathing of spirit into him or into his mother. The reason is that he inherited the human qualities from his human parents. A miracle to cause his mother to conceive him was brought about in some way unknown to us, but it did not require the intervention of the spirit.

It is revealing to observe that Adam had the spirit breathed *into him* whereas in the case of Jesus it was breathed *into his mother*. Adam formed naturally as a hominid fetus, so the spirit only needed to change him to a human fetus, whereas the spirit was breathed into Mary because its role involved the additional task of fertilizing the ovum.

It is no coincidence that the *rūḥ* (Spirit) Gabriel visited Mary at the annunciation and *rūḥ* (spirit) was *breathed into her*. The breathing of spirit into Mary describes the role of Gabriel in the miracle of the conception of Mary. This strongly indicates that the term *rūḥ* (spirit) might well denote a part of the *rūḥ* (Spirit) Gabriel, in which case the *rūḥ* (spirit) that made Adam a human fetus was also part of Gabriel.

It is clear now why Mary's virginal conception had to be performed by Gabriel. The miracle involved not only fertilizing an ovum, but also giving it the special qualities that the sperm provides in a normal conception.

Thus, the two potential meanings of *rūḥ* that we have examined so far in this chapter turned out to be one and the same: one denotes a mysterious shapeless being, and the other denotes a part of him.

7.3.3. Inspiration

We come now to the third group of verses. There are 4 instances of *rūḥ* which have had exegetes arguing that this term may also mean "revelation" or "inspiration" (40.15, 42.52, 16.2, 58.22). Let's start with 40.15:

> [Allah is] the possessor of the highest ranks, and the Lord of the throne. He throws the *rūḥ* by His command upon whom He pleases of His servants, that he may warn [people] of the Day of Meeting (40.15).

The verb *yulqī* (throws) is used in the Qur'an for physical things, such as human beings (7.120, 28.7, 50.24), "mountains" (15.19), "books" (27.29), the "Torah tablets" (7.150), "gold" (43.53), and "staffs" (7.115). It is also used with non-material things, such as "fear" (8.12), "enmity" and "love" (5.64, 20.39), "peace" (4.94), and "excuses" (75.15). Interestingly, in this category, we find the verb also used with "inspiration," whether divine (28.86, 54.25, 73.5, 77.5) or Satanic (22.52). So it is plausible that *rūḥ* here means "revelation" or "inspiration."

However, *yulqī* can also mean "sends down" and thus the term looks also perfectly consistent with the first sense of this word, i.e. Gabriel — the "Trustworthy Spirit" and "Spirit of Holiness" whom God sent to His messengers to warn people of the Day of Reckoning.

The second verse is 42.52:

> It is not fitting for a man that Allah should speak to him except by inspiration, from behind a veil, or by sending a messenger to reveal, by His permission, what He wills. He is High, Wise (42.51). And thus did We reveal to you [O Muhammad!] a *rūḥ* by Our command. You did not know what the Book was, nor what the faith was, but We made it a light, guiding thereby whom We will of Our servants; and surely you do guide to a straight way (42.52).

If *rūḥ* here means "revelation" or "inspiration," then clearly the pronoun "it" in 42.52 would also refer to it. If it denotes Gabriel, then the pronoun "it" would refer to the "Book" which is described as a "light" in other verses also.

Verse 42.51 lists the three different ways in which God may communicate with a human being: direct inspiration, speaking from behind a veil, or sending a messenger. This is followed immediately by the verse that talks about the *rūḥ* and which starts with "and thus." This phrase links the statement made in verse 42.52 either with the first or third method of communication named in 42.51. The second method of God's communication with human beings from behind a veil, which is how He spoke to Moses, is not how God spoke to Muhammad. I am inclined to think "and thus" refers to the last method, which is listed immediately before it — that is, the sending of a messenger. This means that the *rūḥ* in verse 42.52 is Gabriel. The alternative meaning of "inspiration" is also possible. The expression *revealing a rūḥ* is probably what made exegetes prefer this meaning.

The third verse is this:

> He sends down the angels with/by the *rūḥ* by His command on whom He pleases of His servants, saying: "Give the warning that there is no god but Me, therefore be dutiful toward Me" (16.2).

The preposition *bi* that precedes the word *ar-rūḥ* may either mean "with" or "by." If *bi* is taken to mean the former, then *rūḥ* could either mean "revelation" or denote Gabriel. If the preposition is rather understood to mean "by," then *rūḥ* would refer to Gabriel. It is not clear to me how the angels and Gabriel relate to each other, but I note that when Gabriel was sent to Mary, the angels were also cited speaking to her. This ambiguity is no reason to think that the *rūḥ* here cannot denote Gabriel.

This is the fourth and last verse:

> These are they into whose hearts He has impressed faith, whom He has supported with a *rūḥ* from Him, and whom He will cause to enter gardens beneath which rivers flow, abiding therein. Allah is well pleased with them and they are well pleased with Him. These are Allah's party; surely the party of Allah are the successful ones (58.22).

If *rūḥ* is used here in the sense of "revelation," then the verse would mean that God supports those believers with "inspiration" that strengthens their resolve. But this is not the only possible interpretation. The use of the verb *ayyada* (supported) with *rūḥ* is reminiscent of verses 2.87, 2.253 and 5.110 which also state that God *supported* Jesus with the Spirit of Holiness, i.e. Gabriel. So *rūḥ* could mean Gabriel.

The use of *rūḥ* in the indefinite in verses 42.52 and 58.22 may suggest to some that there are more than one Spirit. Since we have already seen than there is no other being of the kind *rūḥ*, then this rules out the possibility that *rūḥ* here refers to Gabriel. This is a weak argument, however, because the use of *rūḥ* in the indefinite may not necessarily imply that there is more than one *rūḥ*.

In conclusion, in most of its occurrences in the Qur'an, the term *rūḥ* denotes Gabriel. The four verses that we studied in this section may also signify "Gabriel," but they may alternatively mean "inspiration." But even in this case, it is worth noting that the two meanings would still be strongly related, as Gabriel communicated God's revelation to prophets.

Finally, I would like to concede that although this chapter has tried to present a detailed analysis of the term *rūḥ*, it has probably been more successful in showing the complexity of this subject. God has stressed that detailed understanding the *rūḥ* requires special knowledge that is well beyond what people possess:

> And they ask you [O Muhammad!] about the spirit. Say: "The spirit is by command of my Lord, and you have not been given but little knowledge" (17.85).

Nevertheless, the Qur'anic use of the term *rūḥ* is clear, specific, and consistent — something that cannot be said of the Bible's use of the terms *ruach* and *pneuma*.

8

Joseph: Mary's Husband?

Like the question of the virginal conception, the exact nature of Mary's relationship with Joseph and whether she was the mother of those that are described as Jesus' "brothers and sisters" have been debated relentlessly since the early days of Christianity. This debate is extremely unlikely to ever produce a consensus. Nevertheless, no study of the history of Jesus, and indeed Christianity itself as a religion, can afford to ignore any of these questions and their serious implications. We have already addressed the virginal conception, so we will focus here on studying who Joseph was, and deal with the question of Jesus' brothers and sisters in the next chapter. We will also leave that chapter to address the different Christian views on the nature of Joseph's relationship with Mary, as this will be considered in the context of studying the Church's views on what Jesus' brothers and sisters exactly were.

Joseph appears in both Matthew and Luke as Mary's fiancé at the time of the annunciation. He is present in Jesus' childhood, but he is never seen after Jesus starts his ministry. His disappearance is not explained. Joseph also appears in Jesus' story as told by a number of apocryphal gospels.

As we saw in Chapter 6, Matthew and Luke, as well as apocryphal gospels, suggest that Mary's conception of Jesus was virginal, so Joseph was not Jesus' father. Yet each of the two canonical Gospels gives a different genealogy that presents Jesus as Joseph's son! Other references to Joseph as *Jesus' father* add further contradiction to the two Evangelists' accounts about Joseph's relationship with Jesus.

In the Qur'anic story, there is no Joseph in Mary's life. It is clear that at the time of Jesus' birth Mary was alone. Also, while the Qur'an does not state explicitly that Mary never got engaged or married, it does seem to strongly imply that.

8.1. Joseph in Christian Sources

The Gospel of Mark, which does not talk about the birth of Jesus, does not mention Joseph at all. John mentions him only twice in passing as it describes Jesus as "the son of Joseph" (John 1:45, 6:42). The two other canonical Gospels, which show more interest in Jesus' birth, give more prominence to Joseph, as do apocryphal sources.

8.1.1. Joseph and Mary

Matthew recounts how Joseph, who was betrothed to Mary, thought of leaving her when he learned that she had become pregnant. But the angel reassured him of

Mary's chastity and ordered him to stay with her. After the birth of Jesus, Joseph took the newborn and his mother and fled to Egypt to escape from King Herod who wanted to kill the child. Later the angel informed Joseph about Herod's death and ordered him to return home with Jesus and Mary. All of these events are described in the first two chapters of Matthew. Surprisingly, Joseph does not appear at all anywhere later, although he is alluded to once when people describe Jesus as "the carpenter's son" (Matt. 13:55).

In Luke also Joseph is seen only in the early story of the birth of Jesus. The last time we hear about him is when he goes with Mary and Jesus, who was twelve years old at the time, to Jerusalem for the feast of the Passover (Luke 2:41). His name is mentioned later only in passing when Jesus is referred to as "Joseph's son" (Luke 4:22).

The Gospel of the Birth of Mary, the Infancy Gospel of James, and the Gospel of Pseudo-Matthew have more details on Joseph, which we have already touched on in Chapter 2. They talk about how Joseph was betrothed and later got married to Mary and his role before and after Jesus' birth. The Gospel of the Birth of Mary and the Infancy Gospel of James are concerned with the birth of Jesus, so they do not contain anything about Joseph's later role in the life of Jesus and his mother. The Gospel of Pseudo-Matthew covers Jesus' life to at least the age of 8 but no later than 12, and Joseph features prominently throughout.

Betrothal was the first part of the Jewish marriage legal contract after which the woman becomes under the authority of her future husband rather than her father. Usually after 12 months, or 30 days if the groom was a widower or the bride was a widow, the marriage is completed with the woman moving to live with her husband. Betrothed couples were called "husband" and "wife" (e.g. Deut. 28:30). Similarly, Matthew (1:19) and the Infancy Gospel of James (12:3) call Joseph Mary's "husband," and Luke (2:5) and the Gospel of Birth of Mary (8:13) call Mary Joseph's "wife" — although different translations of the Bible may use slightly different words other than "husband" and "wife." A testament to the legal status of betrothal is the fact that it could be dissolved only by a formal divorce. Furthermore, we know from the Mishnah that in 2nd century Judea, unlike in Galilee, betrothed couples were allowed to engage in a sexual relationship, although the applicability of this law to the time of Mary is unknown. In both Judea and Galilee, however, if a child is conceived during the betrothal period, he was considered a legitimate child of the marriage (Miller, 2003: 87-88).

The account of the annunciation in Christian sources indicates that Mary had had no relationship with a man, so clearly she was not expecting a child. When the angel told Mary about her conception of Jesus, her first reaction was one of shock, having known no man:

> Mary said to the angel, "How will this be, since I have not had sexual relations with a man?" (Luke 1:34)

She said, "How can that be? For seeing, according to my vow, I have never known any man, how can I bear a child without the addition of a man's seed?" (BirMary. 7:16)

Mary's replies are difficult to understand, because although she was not married, she was already betrothed to Joseph. This inconsistency has not gone unnoticed by scholars (e.g. Parrinder, 1995: 71-72). This difficulty can be seen clearer when we consider Mary's rather different reaction in the Infancy Gospel of James:

And the angel said to her, "The Lord is with you, and you shall conceive." To which she replied, "What! Shall I conceive by the living God and bring forth as all other women do?" But the angel returned answer, "Not so, O Mary, but the Holy Spirit shall come upon you, and the power of the Most High shall overshadow you." (InJam. 9:11-13)

As she was already betrothed, Mary asked the angel whether he meant that she would get pregnant like other women do, i.e. through her future husband Joseph. This version reflects the writer's realization that Mary must have thought that the angel referred to her future marriage to Joseph, though putting this thought in the less affirmative form of a question was probably influenced by the writer's prior knowledge, which Mary in the story did not possess, that the angel was talking about a miracle. This version of Mary's reaction is more consistent with the presence of Joseph in her life than her reaction in Luke and the Gospel of the Birth of Mary.

8.1.2. Joseph and Jesus

One big controversial issue in the New Testament involves relating Jesus to Joseph's genealogy, as Matthew and Luke also make it clear that Jesus had no biological father. Matthew starts as follows: "This is the record of the genealogy of Jesus Christ, the son of David, the son of Abraham" (Matt. 1:1), and it gives a detailed genealogy that ends with "and Jacob the father of Joseph, the husband of Mary, by whom Jesus was born, who is called Christ" (Matt. 1:16). While also relating Jesus to Joseph, Luke disagrees with Matthew, giving a different genealogy to Joseph (Luke 3:23-38).

It might seem inexplicable that the authors of Matthew and Luke should go out of their way to explicitly link Jesus to a lineage when they stress elsewhere that he had no biological father. Apologists have suggested that the inclusion of the genealogy reflects the fact that Jesus was "legally" considered to be Joseph's son. This actually cannot serve as an explanation, because the detailed listing of Joseph's genealogy would not have supported describing Jesus as Joseph's legal son. Claiming that Jesus was only "legally" the son of Joseph implies that Joseph's ancestry was unrelated to Jesus anyway.

There is a simple and logical explanation for the inclusion of a Jesus genealogy in each of Matthew and Luke. At the time when Jesus was born, the Messiah that the Jews were waiting for was believed to be a "son of David." He was expected to be a new king who would re-establish the kingdom of his great ancestor (pp. 234-235). All Gospel authors stressed that Jesus was a descendant of David, so he can be the Messiah (Mark 12:35; Matt. 22:41; Luke 20:41; John 7:42). Luke (1:32) also claims that the angel of the annunciation said that God was going to give Jesus the throne of "his father David." The Gospels are not the only New Testament books that call Jesus the son of David. Paul also considered Jesus to be a "descendant of David with reference to the flesh" (Rom. 1:3). The Book of Revelation attributes the following to Jesus: "I am the root and the descendant of David" (Rev. 22:16).

Now, there is nothing in Mark and John that contradicts their claim that Jesus descended from David, simply because they do not say anything about Jesus' birth. Because they did not talk about Jesus' ancestry, they did not have anything to explain. The same applies to the Book of Hebrews (7:14) which claims that Jesus descended from Judah, Jacob's son in whose line of blood King David was born. No contradiction here.

The situation is different with Matthew and Luke. These two recounted Jesus' miraculous birth story whereby Jesus had no biological father, and that meant that he had no link to David. This problem was compounded by the fact that Jesus' mother, Mary, was probably of the tribe of Levi, because she was a relative of Elizabeth, Zechariah's wife, who was a Levite (Luke 1:5, 36). David was a descendant of Judah not Levi, who were sons of Jacob. It may be argued that Mary might have had one Levite parent and another Davidic, but had that been the understanding of the Evangelists, they would have certainly linked Jesus' to David through his mother. In order to solve the problem created by the nativity story, Matthew and Luke had to insert those genealogies to connect Jesus explicitly to David. As crude as it may seem to us, the Evangelists were satisfied with this solution. So the common view that Matthew and Luke included Jesus' genealogy to show him to be a descendant of David is inaccurate. They could have simply stated that Jesus was a son of David without having to produce any evidence, which is what Mark and John did. Indeed, they describe Jesus as David's son in more passages than Mark and John do. Matthew and Luke were actually forced to list the genealogy in order to solve the problem that was created by their inclusion of the nativity narrative.

An additional problem comes in the form of references that seem to stress Jesus' blood relation to Joseph. Mary calls Joseph Jesus' "father" (Luke 2:48), and Jesus is called Joseph's "son" (Matt. 13:55; Luke 4:22; John 1:45, 6:42). Another reason to think that relating Jesus to David was not only meant to be symbolic is that Matthew calls him also "son of Abraham" (Matt. 1:1). And just to wrap this whole subject of the relation between Jesus and Joseph in more contradiction, inconsistency, and mystery, three Gospels cite Jesus clearly questioning the Jewish claim that the Messiah descended from David! This is Mark's account, but Matthew (22:41-46) and Luke (20:41-44) have similar versions of the story:

> While Jesus was teaching in the temple courts, he said, "How is it that the experts in the law say that the Christ is David's son? David himself, by the Holy Spirit, said, 'The Lord said to my lord, "Sit at my right hand, until I put your enemies under your feet." 'If David himself calls him 'Lord,' how can he be his son?" And the large crowd was listening to him with delight. (Mark 12:35-37)

The contradictions in the texts that link Jesus to Joseph do not end here. Matthew's and Luke's genealogies also contradict each other! Matthew's 40-name genealogy, which he inaccurately counts as 42 generations (Matt. 1:17), and Luke's 76-name genealogy both list Joseph as Jesus' father, but their disagreements start as early as naming Joseph's father, with Matthew calling him "Jacob" and Luke naming him "Heli." The next two names that appear in both genealogies are "Zorobabel" and his father Salathiel. Between Jacob and Zorobabel, Matthew has 8 names; but between Heli and Zorobabel, Luke has as many as 17. Matthew's 8 names are not a subset of Luke's 17, as the names do not match.

The next agreed ancestor after Salathiel in the two Gospels is King David. While Matthew lists 14 names between Salathiel and David, Luke has 20. Again, Luke's names are different from Matthew's. From David to Abraham both genealogies are in agreement. Matthew's genealogy of Jesus ends with Abraham, but Luke traces his to God, as he lists Adam as "the son of God"! Abraham's genealogy in Luke is very similar to the Old Testament's (1 Chr. 1:1-4, 1:24-17). The only difference is that the name "Cainan" in Luke's list does not appear in the Old Testament.

Table 8.1: Comparison between Jesus' genealogy in Matthew and its counterpart in Luke

Matthew	**Luke**	**Identification**	**Comparison**
Joseph	Joseph	Jesus' father	Same
Jacob	Heli	Joseph's father	Different
8 names	17 names	Joseph's ancestors	All different
Zorobabel	Zorobabel	Joseph's ancestor	Same
Salathiel	Salathiel	Zorobabel's father	Same
14 names	20 names	Zorobabel ancestors	All different
King David	King David	Zorobabel ancestor	Same
12 names	12 names	David's ancestors	Same
Abraham	Abraham	David's ancestor	Same
Unavailable	20 names	Abraham's ancestors	Unavailable
Unavailable	God	God	Unavailable
Total=40	**Total=76**	**Jesus' genealogy**	**Different**

While Zorobabel appears as the son of Salathiel in the Greek version of 1 Chr. 3:19, he is described as the nephew of Salathiel in the Hebrew version. Miller (2003: 74-78) has pointed out other historical problems and contradictions in the two genealogies.

It is interesting that Luke ends his genealogy of Jesus by calling Adam "the son of God": "the son of Enosh, the son of Seth, the son of Adam, the son of God" (Luke 3:38). It is difficult to know what Luke exactly meant by that, but it looks that he felt that a human ancestry that links Jesus to David was not fully in line with the virginal conception, so introducing God in this vague way into Jesus' genealogy would make it more consistent with the fact that Jesus did not have a biological father.

In a nutshell, the Gospels give very confused and contradictory accounts about whether Jesus was or was not related in blood to Joseph. One may accept some accounts and reject the others, but it is impossible to accept all accounts no matter how they are interpreted, unless one empties words of their known meanings. This situation can only attest to the unreliability of the Gospels and indicate that each of these books was probably written and edited by more than one person.

I would like to highlight one other significant difference between three of the canonical Gospels. Matthew tells us that, astonished, but also offended, by Jesus' teaching at the synagogue, people asked with displeasure: "Isn't this the carpenter's son? Isn't his mother named Mary? And aren't his brothers James, Joseph, Simon, and Judas?" (Matt. 13:55). This same event is found in Luke also, where people are reported to have said: "Isn't this Joseph's son?" (Luke 4:22). Mark also has his version of this statement, but in this significantly different wording: "'Isn't this the carpenter, the son of Mary and brother of James, Joses, Judas, and Simon? And aren't his sisters here with us?' And so they took offense at him" (Mark 6:3). What is interesting here is that while Matthew calls Jesus "the carpenter's son" and Luke calls him "Joseph's son," Mark, who never mentions Joseph in his book, refers to Jesus as "the carpenter"! Considering the general consensus that Mark is the earliest of the Gospels, we may conclude that in Matthew and Luke, "the carpenter" was changed to "the carpenter's son" and "Joseph's son," respectively, to stress the role of Joseph — a character that both Matthew and Luke consider Mary's husband but whom Mark is unaware of. The fact that the word "carpenter" in Matthew appears as "Joseph" in Luke is further evidence that this particular word, for some reason, was changed. Whatever the history of the differences between these phrases is, it clearly shows that whether Joseph existed or not and his relation to Jesus were contentious issues among the Evangelists.

Remarkably, in all Christian sources that mention Joseph, he inexplicably disappears from the story with no reference to his death or any other cause. Even when Matthew (12:46-50) and Luke (8:19-21) mention that Jesus was visited by his mother and brothers, Joseph is not mentioned. His disappearance from the later part of Jesus' story is a mystery that Christian writings leave unexplained.

8.2. The Non-historicity of Joseph According to the Qur'an

Contrary to Christian sources, the Qur'an contains no mention of a Joseph who was betrothed to Mary, nor any husband or fiancé of her. It may be suggested that Joseph was ignored due to his minor role, in particular that the Qur'an's account of Jesus' life in general is very concise in comparison with the canonical and apocryphal accounts. This is very unlikely, because the Qur'an is clear in stressing that Mary and Jesus were alone even at times in which, according to the Gospels, Joseph was about, and when his presence would have been important. For instance, the Qur'an tells us that after becoming pregnant of Jesus, Mary "withdrew with him to a far place" (19.22). She did not go with or to a man.

The fact that Mary was alone is confirmed again when the Qur'an tells us that after giving birth, she returned to her people carrying the child — again with no mention of a third person: "Then she brought him to her own folk, carrying him" (19.27). The response of her people to the fact that she had a baby makes it totally clear that she was unmarried: "They said: 'O Mary! You have come up with a grave thing (19.27). O sister of Aaron! Your father was not a bad man, and your mother was not an unchaste woman'" (19.28). Had Mary been married, or even engaged to someone, they would not have rushed to accuse her of having an illegitimate child. Similarly, had they known of any particular person that she might have had an illicit relationship with, they would have said that.

As in Christian sources, Mary was shocked by the angel's news about her conception, as she had not been in a relationship with a man:

> She said: "How can I have a son when no man has touched me, neither have I been unchaste?" (19.20).
>
> She said: "My Lord! How can I have a child when no human being has touched me?" (3.47).

Mary's reaction in the Qur'an is completely consistent with the story in that book. She was not married or engaged when she was told by Gabriel that she was going to give birth. She clearly understood that the pregnancy was imminent, and Gabriel's reply (19.21, 3.47) that the pregnancy was miraculous further confirmed beyond any doubt that no man was to be involved in this pregnancy. The inconsistency between the account of the annunciation and the rest of the story of Mary in Christian sources does not exist in the Qur'an.

The Qur'an implicitly, but clearly, dismisses any blood link between Jesus and a Joseph because it makes it clear that Mary did not get married. It probably also implies that there was never a Joseph in the life of Jesus and his mother, and even in the unlikely situation that there was one, that character would have been just too insignificant to be mentioned; he certainly could not have been her husband. When the infant Jesus spoke in the cradle he said that God had made him *kind to his mother* (19.32). Had there been any other man living with his mother or even only involved in looking after him in the way the father would look after his son or stepson, he would have been included in this mention of Jesus' kindness — in the same way that God described John as being "kind to his parents" (19.14). The Qur'an is absolutely clear that Mary conceived Jesus miraculously without having a relation with a man. There is not a single phrase in the Qur'an that suggests otherwise.

Not surprisingly, the introduction of the mythical character of Joseph into the story of Jesus and Mary has resulted in contextual displacements. The Qur'an states that Zechariah competed with others and won a lottery to become the guardian of Mary. The New Testament has no mention of this event. But the Infancy Gospel of James speaks of a lottery organized by the high priest Zechariah and won by Joseph to become Mary's husband. Instead of being the winner of the lottery, Zechariah is presented as the organizer and Joseph as is its winner. The original purpose of the lottery is also changed from choosing Mary's guardian to her husband. The Gospel of Pseudo-Matthew recounts the same event, but the high priest is here called Abiathar. In this case, the corruption to the original text went further, removing the name of Zechariah altogether.

9

Did Jesus Have Brothers and Sisters?

Another controversial subject that is closely related to the question of Joseph is Jesus' *brothers and sisters*.

Paul has two references to Jesus' "brother" and "brothers," and the four Gospels and Acts mention Jesus' "brothers." Mark and Matthew refer to Jesus' "sisters" also. These rather inconsistent references combined with how Joseph's relationship with Mary is portrayed in Matthew and Luke have led the Catholic, Orthodox, and Protestant Churches to three different views on who Jesus' brothers and sisters actually were.

A prominent early Christian called James, who is mentioned in Paul's letters and Acts, is identified by many with a brother of Jesus that is mentioned in the Gospels and with a James mentioned by the Jewish historian Josephus. However, there are serious problems with this view.

The Qur'an does not suggest, explicitly or implicitly, that Jesus had siblings. But it strongly indicates that Mary never got married, hence my conclusion that the Qur'an implies that Jesus' never had any siblings.

9.1. Paul and Jesus' Brothers

There are two phrases, each appearing once, in Paul's writings that are claimed to refer to Jesus' siblings. The first passage speaks about the "Lord's brothers": "Do we not have the right to the company of a believing wife, like the other apostles and the Lord's brothers and Cephas?" (1 Cor. 9:5). In the second, Paul mentions a James whom he calls the "Lord's brother": "But I saw none of the other apostles except James the Lord's brother" (Gal. 1:19). I will deal with what Paul says about James' alleged blood relation to Jesus in more detail later in the chapter, so I will focus here on his other reference to the Lord's brothers.

Taking this phrase to mean siblings of Jesus is highly controversial and has serious difficulties. **First**, Paul shows almost no interest in Jesus' history, so describing some men as Jesus' blood brothers is not compatible with his writings (pp. 152-153). **Second**, the "Lord's brothers" and *Jesus' brothers* are not necessarily one and the same. Paul does call Jesus at times with his name, and this would have been an ideal place where the name rather than any title should be used, had Paul meant to say *Jesus' siblings*.

Third, I agree with the view of many that the "Lord's brothers" probably denote some form of religious brotherhood rather than a blood relationship. Support for this argument is found in the fact that Paul uses the Greek terms *adelphos* (brothers) and *adelphen* (sisters) to mean brothers and sisters *in the Lord*.

Appending "the Lord" to these terms would not change their meanings, but would further emphasize the nature of the relationship. These are some of the many passages in which Paul calls fellow believers "brothers" and "sisters":

> I urge you, brothers and sisters, by the name of our Lord Jesus Christ, to agree together, to end your divisions, and to be united by the same mind and purpose. (1 Cor. 1:10)

> Then he appeared to more than five hundred of the brothers and sisters at one time, most of whom are still alive, though some have fallen asleep. (1 Cor. 15:6)

> And most of the brothers and sisters, having confidence in the Lord because of my imprisonment, now more than ever dare to speak the word fearlessly. (Phi. 1:14)

The last passage is particularly interesting because it can also be read as "most of the brothers and sisters in the Lord, having confidence...." In another letter, Paul uses the expression "brothers (and sisters) in Christ" (Col. 1:2). Elsewhere, Paul calls a fellow Christian a brother in the Lord (Phm. 1:16). But the most interesting passage is this:

> Because those whom he foreknew he also predestined to be conformed to the image of his Son, that his Son would be the firstborn among many brothers and sisters. (Rom. 8:29)

This represents the strongest indication that Paul used the term "Lord's brothers" to mean *brothers in the Lord*, as he calls fellow Christians here Jesus' brothers and sisters.

I will go into more detail as to why Paul could not have meant that Jesus had siblings when I consider the case of James.

9.2. Jesus' Brothers and Sisters in the Gospels

All four Gospels mention "Jesus' brothers. For instance, John (2:12) says that Jesus "went down to Capernaum with his mother and brothers and his disciples, and they stayed there a few days." One significant event in which Jesus' brothers are mentioned is this:

> Then Jesus' mother and his brothers came. Standing outside, they sent word to him, to summon him. A crowd was sitting around him and they said to him, "Look, your mother and your brothers are outside looking for you." He answered them and said, "Who are my mother and my brothers?" And looking at those who were sitting around him in a circle, he said, "Here are my mother and my brothers! For whoever does the will of God is my brother and sister and mother." (Mark 3:31-35)

The other two Synoptists have their own versions of this event (Matt. 12:46-50; Luke 8:19-21). Jesus' words seem to imply that he did not consider his brothers — or, amazingly, his mother — among those who *do the will of God*. The disbelief of Jesus' brothers is also mentioned by John (7:5) who states that "not even his own brothers believed in him."

Furthermore, Mark (3:21) tells us that Jesus' family, whom he reveals later to be his mother and brothers (Mark 3:31), even thought that Jesus was actually "out of his mind" because of his continuous preaching. This seems to explain why these brothers are mentioned only a few times, and in passing, in the Gospels. They are notably absent at the crucifixion. Mark even states that the crucified Jesus asked his mother to consider one of his disciples as her son and asked that disciple to consider Mary as his mother:

> So when Jesus saw his mother and the disciple whom he loved standing there, he said to his mother, "Woman, look, here is your son!" He then said to his disciple, "Look, here is your mother!" From that very time the disciple took her into his own home. (John 19:26-27)

It has been suggested that Mark's passage about the rejection of Jesus by his family "exemplifies two motifs that figured prominently in the thought of primitive Christianity, namely, the theme of the Messiah's rejection by the Jewish people, and the concept of the Church as the New Israel, transcending all racial and sexual distinctions" (Burkill, 1972: 234-235).

Mark names Jesus' four brothers, and says that Jesus had sisters too. Jesus was once teaching in the synagogue in his hometown when his astonished audience said: "Isn't this the carpenter, the son of Mary and brother of James, Joses, Judas, and Simon? And aren't his sisters here with us?" (Mark 6:3). A similar version of this story, but with "the carpenter" changed to "the carpenter's son" and Joses to Joseph, is found in Matthew: "Isn't this the carpenter's son? Isn't his mother named Mary? And aren't his brothers James, Joseph, Simon, and Judas? And aren't all his sisters here with us? Where did he get all this?" (Matt. 13:55-56). Luke, who places this event earlier in Jesus' life, puts on the mouths of Jesus' Jewish audience significantly different words: "Isn't this Joseph's son?" (Luke 4:22). For some reason, that interesting mention of Jesus' brothers and sisters and the names of the former are missing! The possibilities that Luke removed those references or was unaware of them or that Mark and Matthew added them are equally significant. It looks that the suggestion that Jesus had brothers and sisters, whether these were meant to be siblings or not, was probably a subject of disagreement.

I would like to cite here one argument that is often used to show that Jesus' brothers were not connected to him in blood. The four canonical Gospels talk about the presence of certain women after Jesus' crucifixion, according to Luke, or during it, according to the other three Evangelists:

Mary Magdalene, and Mary the mother of James the younger and of Joses, and Salome. (Mark 15:40)

Mary Magdalene, Mary the mother of James and Joseph, and the mother of the sons of Zebedee. (Matt. 27:56)

Mary Magdalene, Joanna, Mary the mother of James, and the other women with them who told these things to the apostles. (Luke 24:10)

His mother, his mother's sister, Mary the wife of Clopas, and Mary Magdalene. (John 19:25)

It is often claimed that James and Joses/Joseph who are mentioned in the Synoptic accounts are the same James and Joses/Joseph who are named as Jesus' brothers in Mark (6:3) and Matthew (13:55). It is clear that their mother is not Jesus' mother for she is named after them, so they are not Jesus' blood brothers. This other Mary is also equated at times with Mary the wife of Clopas in John's account. Other scholars think that these James and Joses/Joseph are different from their namesakes who are described as Jesus' brothers elsewhere in the New Testament (Witherington III, 2003: 199-202).

The four passages are clearly inconsistent with each other, so they cannot be used to develop a coherent argument. As we will see as we continue our examination of this subject, the New Testament passages on the alleged siblings of Jesus are highly contradictory and confused.

Outside the Gospels and Paul's writings, Jesus' brothers are also mentioned in the New Testament in Acts (1:14), where they appear shortly after his ascension: "All these continued together in prayer with one mind, together with the women, along with Mary the mother of Jesus, and his brothers."

9.3. The Church and Jesus' Brothers and Sisters

The Catholic, Orthodox, and Protestant Churches have different views on the issue of Jesus' brothers and sisters. These disagreements reflect their different readings of Joseph's story and the nature of his relationship with Mary after Jesus' birth, although the three Churches do agree on Mary's virginal conception of Jesus.

The Catholic Church has adopted the view that Mary was perpetually virgin. She was not only virgin when she gave birth to Jesus, but she remained virgin afterward and did not have a marital relationship with Joseph. Furthermore, Mary is also said to have remained physically virgin, i.e. with her hymen intact, even after giving birth to Jesus, as the Infancy Gospel of Pseudo-Matthew explicitly states (13). The Catholic Church does not accept that Mary gave birth to any child other than Jesus.

Mary was not the mother and Joseph was not the father of those brothers and sisters.

The view of the Catholic Church is known as the "Heironymian" view after Jerome, the 4th century father and translator of the Bible into Latin, whose full name was Eusebius Sophronius Hieronymus. The references to Jesus "brother and sisters" are not taken to mean blood brothers and sisters. For instance, it has been stressed that the Greek New Testament word *adelphos* can mean not only blood brothers, but also spiritual brother or fellow countryman. Jerome claimed that these siblings were cousins rather than blood brothers and sisters. Jerome explained his view in *Against Helvidius* (9-17), a work that he wrote around 383 CE to refute Helvidius who, about three years earlier, had published a treatise in which he claimed that Jesus' brother and sisters were his full siblings.

The view of the Orthodox Church, which is also known as the "Epiphanian" view after Epiphanius of Salamis (ca. 315-403 CE), is that Jesus' brothers and sisters were actually Joseph's sons and daughters from an earlier marriage. None of the canonical Gospels suggests that Joseph was married before Mary or denies Mary's motherhood of those four brothers, so this interpretation may be influenced by apocryphal sources, although it is equally possible that the latter reflected an already established view. The Infancy Gospel of James (8:6-8) describes Joseph as a "widower", whereas the Gospel of the Birth of Mary (6:1) portrays him as "very far advanced in years" at the time of his betrothal to Mary. The Arabic Gospel of the Infancy (19:1) explicitly describes James as Joseph's son, and the Gospel of Pseudo-Matthew (8) has Joseph old and had already had children when he was betrothed to Mary. This gospel states that Joseph had two daughters and four sons, called James, Joseph, and Judah, and Simeon (PsMatt. 42), which are the same names found in Matthew (13:55).

The depiction of Joseph as a very old man, to imply he could not have had a sexual relationship with Mary, falls in the contradiction of suggesting that Mary was betrothed to someone who was not qualified to get married. Describing Joseph as a widower, very old, and with children must have been intended to counter any suggestion that Mary had a normal marital relationship with Joseph and gave birth to other than Jesus.

The third major view is that of the Protestant Church and known as the "Helvidian". Helvidius argued that the controversial brothers and sisters were indeed Mary's children from Joseph, i.e. Jesus' half brothers and sisters. Mary and Joseph parented them after they consummated their marriage after Jesus' birth. This view is based on a literal interpretation of the terms brothers and sisters in the Gospels, while accommodating the virginal conception of Mary. Proponents of this interpretation also point out that Matthew's statements that "his mother Mary was engaged to Joseph, but before they came together, she was found to be pregnant through the Holy Spirit" (Matt. 1:18) and Joseph "did not have marital relations with her until she gave birth to a son, whom he named Jesus" (Matt. 1:25) imply that Mary and Joseph did have a normal relationship later on and could have had children. Describing Jesus as Mary's "firstborn" (Matt. 1:25; Luke 2:7) implies that she had more children after him. In his comment on the naming of Jesus' brothers in the Gospel of Mark, Parrinder (1995: 72) notes that "there is no hint that these are other than the children of Joseph and Mary."

A more liberal variation of the Protestant view denies Mary's virginal conception of Jesus also, and concludes that Jesus and his brothers and sisters were all the fruit of a natural marital relationship between Mary and Joseph. We have already examined the arguments of those who reject the virginal conception (§6.2).

It goes without saying that dogmatic differences did and still play a role in dividing the views about the reality of Jesus' alleged brothers and sisters. But we should not underestimate the role played by the confused narratives of the New Testament in creating those differing views. There are certainly passages in the canonical Gospels that suggest that Mary did have a normal relationship with Joseph after the birth of Jesus (Matt. 1:18, 25), and that Jesus was her "firstborn" (Matt. 1:25; Luke 2:7), so she must have given birth to others. On the other hand, the alleged "brothers and sisters" of Jesus do not really behave like his siblings in the Gospels. Those who are supposed to have lived with him under the same roof and known about him more than anyone else did not believe in him (John 7:5), and even accused him of madness (Mark 3:21)! A brother of Jesus would have probably known better than to accuse him of lying or going mad.

We know that in the middle of the 2nd century Hegesippus — as quoted in *Ecclesiastical History* (2.23) by Eusebius (ca. 260 – before 341 CE), bishop of Caesarea in Palestine — argued that James was Jesus' sibling, and later in the same century Tertullian of Carthage (ca. 155- after 220) argued in *Against Marcion* (4.19) that those called Jesus' mother and brothers were biologically so. Nevertheless, these views date to over a century after Jesus' death, and there is no evidence that they represent the view that prevailed at the time of Jesus and shortly after it. I do not believe that early Christians took the references to Jesus' brothers and sisters to mean his siblings.

9.4. James

This particular supposed brother of Jesus deserves a more detailed examination for two reasons. **First**, James is given a special status in Christianity. **Second**, he is the only alleged sibling of Jesus who appears to be mentioned in a non-Christian historical document.

The name James is mentioned over 40 times in the New Testament. It seems to refer to several different people, although some of the apparently different Jameses may denote the same person. The list of Jameses includes the author of the Epistle of James; the brother of the author of the Epistle of Jude; two of the twelve disciples, James son of Zebedee (Mark 3:17; Matt. 10:2) and James son of Alphaeus (Mark 3:18; Matt. 10:3); and the son of an unidentified Mary who is called "James the younger" (or "less" or "lesser") (Mark 15:40). But certainly the most important and controversial James, and the one that interests us here, is the one whom Paul calls "the Lord's brother" (Gal. 1:19) and who is claimed to be the same brother of Jesus who is mentioned in Mark (6:3) and Matthew (13:55).

9.4.1. Paul and James

Paul mentions the name James 4 times in two of his letters. In his letter to the Corinthians, he lists James as one of those to whom Jesus appeared after his ascension to heaven:

> He appeared to Cephas, then to the twelve. Then he appeared to more than five hundred of the brothers and sisters at one time, most of whom are still alive, though some have fallen asleep. Then he appeared to James, then to all the apostles. Last of all, as though to one born at the wrong time, he appeared to me also. (1 Cor. 15:5-8)

He also mentions James 3 times in the Epistle to the Galatians. Three years after his conversion, Paul went to Jerusalem to meet Cephas, who is thought to be Peter. He says that while staying with Peter for 15 days, he "saw none of the other apostles except James the Lord's brother" (Gal. 1:19). This is the only time that Paul describes a James as the "Lord's brother." Paul then mentions twice James whom he met in his 2nd journey to Jerusalem 14 years later:

> When James, Cephas, and John, who had a reputation as pillars, recognized the grace that had been given to me, they gave to Barnabas and me the right hand of fellowship, agreeing that we would go to the Gentiles and they to the circumcised. They requested only that we remember the poor, the very thing I also was eager to do. But when Cephas came to Antioch, I opposed him to his face, because he had clearly done wrong. Until certain people came from James, he had been eating with the Gentiles. But when they arrived, he stopped doing this and separated himself because he was afraid of those who were pro-circumcision. (Gal. 2:9-12)

This meeting is also recorded in much more detail by the author of Acts. According to this book, the trip to Jerusalem was arranged so that Barnabas and Paul, who had been preaching that circumcision is not necessary to be saved, can sort out with "the apostles and elders in Jerusalem" (Acts 15:2) the disagreement that this teaching has created. There was tension and a debate about the observance of the law of Moses which was attended by James. After listening to Paul and Barnabas, James adjudicated that the Gentiles can be exempt from circumcision, and that they should be sent a letter warning them against certain prohibitions (Acts 15:29).

In his third journey to Jerusalem, Paul met James and the elders again (Acts 21:18). The meeting was turbulent because of Paul's reported violation of the Mosaic law. This is the last time we hear about James in Acts. Paul's attitude toward the Mosaic law is discussed in more detail later (pp. 380-382).

I have explained earlier in this chapter that Paul could not have meant "Jesus' siblings" by the term "Lord's brothers," so similarly he could not have meant by his description of James as the *Lord's brother* that he was Jesus' brother in blood. But there are a few more points that I would like to add here.

Paul shows no interest whatsoever in Jesus' earthly life. He is so concerned with the spiritual Christ he is preaching that he does not mention any detail of Jesus' teachings and life. Apart from Jesus' Last Supper with his disciples, which Paul mentions to stress the theological significance of eating the bread and drinking the cup (1 Cor. 11:23-27), the only other events in Jesus' life that concern Paul are his crucifixion and resurrection. For Paul, these events are the culmination of Jesus' mission, and so they are the pillars of the Pauline theology of atonement (§19.4). He shows no interest in Jesus' life before the crucifixion. He is not interested in talking about Jesus' birth, miracles, encounters with the Jewish leaders, arrest, or trial. Even his crucifixion and resurrection are cited mainly in the context of talking about their spiritual significance; their historical details are never addressed. Not even the headlines of the when, where, and how of these most important events are recorded. This over focus on a spiritual Christ and almost complete neglect of the historical Jesus is one of the most striking differences between Paul's writings and the Gospels.

This notable absence of the historical Jesus from Paul's writings and his substitution with a spiritual Christ are so odd that they have been used by a number of scholars in advancing the thesis that Jesus actually never existed (e.g. Doherty, 1999; Wells, 1988)! This highly speculative suggestion fails to explain, among other things, how the unhistorical, spiritual Messiah in Paul's writings can be transformed into a historical one in many other sources. The Gospels were not written to provide history for Paul's spiritual Messiah. They developed from different traditions that were based on real history, and they represent a very different strand of literature.

Paul, who developed his theology and wrote his Epistles in isolation from other Christian thinkers and followers who saw Jesus, did not consider the details of Jesus' earthly life of significance to his own teachings. He probably did not know much about the historical Jesus anyway, because he did not meet him, and did not gain his knowledge of Jesus from others who knew him well. This may be concluded from a statement that he made in his letter to the Galatians in which he makes a virtue of the fact that his understanding of Christianity was developed in isolation of any contact with others. His knowledge was *spiritually* acquired:

> Now I want you to know, brothers and sisters, that the gospel I preached is not of human origin. For I did not receive it or learn it from any human source; instead I received it by a revelation of Jesus Christ. (Gal. 1:11-12)

He then goes on to stress explicitly that he did not acquire his knowledge from any of those who saw or learned from Jesus, and that he started preaching to people immediately after God instructed him to do so:

> For you have heard of my former way of life in Judaism, how I was savagely persecuting the church of God and trying to destroy it. I was advancing in Judaism beyond many of my contemporaries in my nation, and was extremely zealous for the traditions of my ancestors. But when the one who set me apart from birth and called me by his grace was pleased to reveal his Son in me so that I could preach him among the Gentiles, I did not go to ask advice from any human being, nor did I go up to Jerusalem to see those who were apostles before me, but right away I departed to Arabia, and then returned to Damascus.
> Then after three years I went up to Jerusalem to visit Cephas and get information from him, and I stayed with him fifteen days. But I saw none of the other apostles except James the Lord's brother. I assure you that, before God, I am not lying about what I am writing to you! Afterward I went to the regions of Syria and Cilicia. But I was personally unknown to the churches of Judea that are in Christ. They were only hearing, "The one who once persecuted us is now proclaiming the good news of the faith he once tried to destroy." So they glorified God because of me. (Gal. 1:13-24)

Whether Paul was not interested in the historical Christ and focused only on the spiritual one, or whether he also did not have any significant knowledge of Jesus' history, which is the more likely case, he would not have cared to identify a particular believer or a group of believers as being siblings of Jesus. Identifying someone's blood relationship to Jesus is to talk about Jesus' history, which Paul does not show any interest in. The most likely scenario that Paul had no knowledge of Jesus' history undermines the credibility to any supposed historical information about Jesus in his writings.

One may counterargue that Paul identified Jesus' sibling in order to support the points he was making. This argument does not hold water either, because had this been the case, Paul would have used this approach more explicitly and far more than he did. He would have referred to his relationship with James more often, and he would have identified James' blood relationship with Jesus unambiguously. He would have used "Jesus' brother" rather than "the Lord's brother" to identify James, if this is really what he meant.

Guessing why and how Paul's lone identification of James as the "Lord's brother" became seen as meaning "Jesus' brother" is very difficult. It is the outcome of the confused and confusing nature of the early Christian texts and adopted dogmas.

Not all early Christian fathers accepted that James was Jesus' sibling or that Jesus had siblings at all.

9.4.2. James in Other New Testament Books

I have already examined the references to James in the Gospels and apocrypha, but there are other important observations some of which are from other New Testament books:

① Mark (6:3) puts these words of astonishment in people's mouths: "Isn't this the carpenter, the son of Mary and brother of James, Joses, Judas, and Simon? And aren't his sisters here with us?" This passage is also found in Matthew (13:55-56) in a slightly different form. Significantly, Luke (4:22) reduces these words to "Isn't this Joseph's son?" with no mention of James! There is nothing in Luke about a Jesus' sibling called James. It is particularly interesting that the author of Acts also never identifies James as Jesus' brother, because it is generally accepted that Acts was written by the same author of the Gospel of Luke. In addition to linguistic and theological similarities between the two books, the prefaces of both address someone called Theophilus. Also, the author of Acts mentions a book about Jesus' life and teachings that he had already written. Excluding the James who is clearly one of Jesus' 11 disciples (Acts 1:13), in the three times Acts mentions James (Acts 12:17, 15:13, 21:18) the author calls him with his name only and does not give him any title that links him to Jesus, although he uses the expression *Jesus' brothers* once (Acts 1:14).

② Furthermore, according to Acts' history of the early Christians after Jesus, when the disciples first met after Jesus' death, there was no mention of James, although "Mary the mother of Jesus, and his brothers" are mentioned in passing (Acts 1:14). If this phrase meant Jesus' siblings, then clearly James was not prominent enough to be mentioned separately from the rest of Jesus' brothers. Only very late on a quick reference to a James is made (Acts 12:17), before we meet him again even later in a position of authority when he interferes to resolve the conflict that had developed between Peter and Paul (Acts 15:13). There is absolutely nothing about how this James acquired this authority, or who he really was.

③ The New Testament's Epistle of James is claimed by some to have been written by the alleged sibling of Jesus. The author starts his Epistle as follows: "From James, a slave of God and the Lord Jesus Christ, to the twelve tribes dispersed abroad" (Jam. 1:1).

The Epistle of Jude is also claimed to have been written by a sibling of Jesus. This Epistle starts as follows: "From Jude, a slave of Jesus Christ and brother of James, to those who are called, wrapped in the love of God the Father and kept for Jesus Christ" (Jude 1:1). As this James is taken to be the brother of Jesus, Jude is considered to be Jesus' brother who is mentioned with James in Mark (6:3) and Matthew (13:55).

These two attributions are no more reliable than the attributions of the four Gospels to their alleged authors. Also, none of the two Epistles claims to have been written by a brother of Jesus, and nothing in their content suggests that the authors were Jesus' siblings. These unfounded attributions are further undermined by the implication that someone who would like to stress his blood relationship to Jesus would describe himself as Jesus' slave, when the author and his readers would have certainly considered this designation applicable to all Christians! Surely, a sibling of Jesus who wanted to promote the religion of his brother would have gone out of his way to stress his blood relationship with Jesus in order to gain as much readership and lend as much credibility and authority to his writings as possible. Yet the suggestion here is that Jesus' brothers made clear effort to hide their blood relationship! Why? This surely does not make sense.

There is another significant observation about these two Epistles. Had the authors of these letters been written by siblings of Jesus, they would have included some references to personal memories of their brother — things he said or did. Yet the authors are completely silent on Jesus' life. Nothing in these two books suggests that they were written by siblings of Jesus.

The apocryphal Infancy Gospel of James is also attributed to Jesus' supposed brother. All that is to this suggestion is, again, only the fact that the book attributes itself to a James in Jerusalem. At the end of the book, the author says: "I James wrote this History in Jerusalem: and when the disturbance was I retired into a desert place, until the death of Herod, and the disturbances ceased at Jerusalem." Significantly, when introducing himself, the author does not say anything about his relationship with Jesus. Also, it is generally accepted that this gospel must have been composed not earlier than around the end of the first century, whereas James is thought to have died in 62 CE.

④ If the James of Paul and Acts is the same brother of Jesus that is mentioned Mark and Matthew as one of Jesus' accusers of madness, then James' supposed conversion poses a problem. This James did not even bother to attend the crucifixion of his brother. But Paul reports that James saw Jesus after his resurrection, so this must be the miracle that converted him and convinced him of the verity of his brother's religion. But then Jesus performed so many miracles during his life that, according to the Gospels, converted thousands of strangers who had not met him before. Yet we are supposed to believe that James, who seems to have rejected all those numerous miracles, was converted by one miracle!

⑤ Furthermore, this miracle is supposed to have happened after his brother's execution. The brutal crucifixion of his brother would have done nothing other than confirm to him the soundness of his rejection of Jesus' teachings. James' sudden appearance as a convert is inexplicable. The long term rejectionist of the many miracles that were happening all the time during Jesus' life failed mysteriously to question the one-off event that he saw after Jesus' humiliating death! I do not find this suggestion credible.

⑥ There is another equally serious problem if the "Lord's brothers" in Paul (1 Cor. 9:5) are considered to be Jesus' siblings. The Gospels are absolutely clear that Jesus' brothers and sisters did not believe in him, yet these brothers appear suddenly in a Pauline Epistle as believers after his execution. In fact, two of them, James and Jude, are even claimed to have contributed a book each to the canon! While James is supposed to have at least seen a miracle, the other brothers and sisters are not reported to have seen any. Would not the conversion of the other siblings be equally important to mention? And how and why did they convert anyway?

⑦ And the problems do not end here. The Gospels are generally accepted to have been written after Paul's Epistles. It is reasonable to presume that the writers of the Gospels would have been aware of the conversion of any of Jesus' brothers and sisters. Should not we, then, expect the Evangelists to have mentioned this, and not present the siblings only in their earlier state of rejection of Jesus' message? Why would the Evangelists tell us how his brothers and sisters rejected him but not mention that they believed in him later?

It is understandable why people would want to find any historical link to Jesus. It is incredible how little we know of the history of this man. To identify his brothers or sisters, and to know that they were ordinary people that other people met and dealt with, would be a great leap toward a more tangible Jesus. Unfortunately, we can find about the historical Jesus only as much as history has preserved of his story; and that is very little. Yes, we do have various documents that mention Jesus' brothers and sisters, but the credibility and consistency problems in these records are too serious to conclude that Jesus did or did not have siblings. For those who accept that he had siblings, deciding the exact nature of this blood relationship is even more difficult.

9.4.3. James in History

Outside the New Testament and other Christian writings, there is no mention of any of Jesus' brothers and sisters other than James, who appears to be mentioned once in one of Josephus books. Josephus recorded James' death, an event that is not described in the New Testament, and which looks to have taken place in 62 CE. The context of Josephus account is that after the sudden death of Festus, the procurator of Judea, and before the arrival of his successor Albinus, the high priest Ananus took advantage of the ruler's absence to kill James:

> But this younger Ananus, who, as we have told you already, took the high priesthood, was a bold man in his temper, and very insolent; he was also of the sect of the Sadducees, who are very rigid in judging offenders, above all the rest of the Jews, as we have already observed; when, therefore, Ananus was of this disposition, he thought he had now a proper opportunity [to

exercise his authority]. Festus was now dead, and Albinus was but upon the road; so he assembled the Sanhedrin of judges, and brought before them the brother of Jesus, who was called Christ, whose name was James, and some others [or, some of his companions]; and when he had formed an accusation against them as breakers of the law, he delivered them to be stoned: but as for those who seemed the most equitable of the citizens, and such as were the most uneasy at the breach of the laws, they disliked what was done; they also sent to the king [Agrippa], desiring him to send to Ananus that he should act so no more, for that what he had already done was not to be justified; nay, some of them went also to meet Albinus, as he was upon his journey from Alexandria, and informed him that it was not lawful for Ananus to assemble a Sanhedrin without his consent. Whereupon Albinus complied with what they said, and wrote in anger to Ananus, and threatened that he would bring him to punishment for what he had done; on which king Agrippa took the high priesthood from him, when he had ruled but three months, and made Jesus, the son of Damneus, high priest. (Josephus, *Jewish Antiquities*, 20.9.1)

What is particularly interesting here is that Josephus not only mentions James, but also identifies him as Jesus' brother. Josephus' writing survived through Christian copyists, and we know that Christian editors did make changes to Josephus' writings, as we shall see when we study the so called *Testimonium Falvaium* (§18.5). But the James passage is held by many to have been genuinely written by Josephus and to contain no Christian interpolation. The main arguments in favor of the authenticity of this passage are as follows:

① Although the earliest Greek manuscripts of Josephus' *Jewish Antiquities* date to the 10th century, this passage seems to have been mentioned as early as the 3rd century by Origen and later in the 4th century by Eusebius and Jerome, as the three state that Josephus condemned the unfair killing of James, Jesus' brother (France, 1999: 27).

② The text is closely tied to its context, and it does not show particular interest in Jesus. Jesus' name is mentioned only to identify James, and there is no Christian dwelling of any form on Jesus' name.

③ The phrase "who was called Christ" is not a way in which Christians refer to Jesus. Furthermore, it is presumed that Josephus' reference to Jesus' title was to identify him, as the name Jesus was very popular at the time, and a number of people called Jesus were mentioned in Josephus writings. For instance, one Jesus is identified as the "son of Damneus" in the passage.

④ The passage does not attempt, as a Christian editor would have done, to rebuff the charge of breaking the law and exonerate James.

There are other scholars who doubt that Josephus' passage is completely his. The objections have been to the part that interests us — the identification of James with Jesus. These are arguments that neutralize the arguments for the authenticity of the James passage and suggest that the reference to Jesus in this passage is a Christian interpolation:

① There is over two centuries between the writing of the James passage and the first reference to it, which is plenty of time for someone to tamper with it. Furthermore, the Josephus quotes by Origen, Eusebius, and Jerome have serious problems that testify against their authenticity, which we shall discuss in more detail shortly.

② Although the phrase "who was called Christ" is not usually found in Christian writings, it does appear in Matthew (1:16) and John (4:25), so it is perfectly Christian. Additionally, the Greek text "implies neither assent nor doubt" that Jesus was the Christ (Theissen & Merz, 1999: 65), which makes it doubtful that the loyal Jewish historian would have used such an equivocal phrase, and one that is used in two Gospels. The use of this noncommittal language looks even more suspicious if we remember that Josephus' masters, the Romans, are supposed to have crucified Jesus and would have been alarmed by any claim to messiahship, which is linked to the arrival of a new king.

③ Jesus' brief introduction in the passage suggests that he must have already been introduced. There is indeed another mention of Jesus in the same book before the James passage (Josephus, *Jewish Antiquities*, 18.3.3). The problem, however, is that the earlier passage is believed by almost all to be largely or completely a forgery itself (pp. 416-419)! Now, if Josephus did not write the Jesus passage then he could not have referred to him this briefly in the James passage, and the reference to Jesus becomes doubtful.

④ Earl Doherty (1999: 218) points out that the *Jewish Messiah* would not necessarily have been a concept that Josephus' Roman target audience were that familiar with for him to simply mention it in passing as is the case in the James passage. Kirby (2001) notes that Josephus seems to have *deliberately* avoided discussing the concept of the Jewish Messiah in his writings. It is understandable why Josephus would not have wanted to bother his Roman audience with the Jewish concept of Messiah, but this silence makes it difficult to understand how he could introduce Jesus as the Christ. As Doherty says, the natural way to identify Jesus would have been to describe him as "the one who was crucified by Pilate."

⑤ Another argument by Doherty (1999: 217) is that it is difficult to explain why Josephus would have wanted to mention Jesus before the name of James, when the latter is the cause of Ananus' fall. The usual way of introducing James would have been to mention him first, and then to say that he was Jesus' brother. The fact that Jesus is mentioned first suggests that the identification was written by a Christian.

These are the main arguments that have been made in favor of and against the authenticity of the Jesus reference in the James passage. There are more scholars who make the case for authenticity than those who reject it. Doherty's *The Jesus Puzzle* (1999: 205-222) and his undated online article about Josephus (see the References) provide an excellent and comprehensive study of the various arguments for and against the authenticity of the two *Jewish Antiquities* passages that mention Jesus.

In my view, the arguments against the complete authenticity of the passage are far stronger than those in favor of it. However, the main argument that I think all but settles the dispute is that the James passage in its current form contains a major contradiction that Josephus could not have made. If James was really Jesus' brother, then the accusation must have been clearly related to his embracement of the religion of his brother. In fact, introducing Jesus first before James' name, or mentioning Jesus at all, can be seen as implying that James was killed because of following the religion of his brother. Apart from the high priest and the Sanhedrin, Josephus allegedly wrote, the keepers of the religious law whom he describes as the "most equitable of the citizens" and "most uneasy at the breach of the laws" considered the high priest's ruling as "unjustified," which means that they did not view James as a law breaker. Josephus also clearly thought that James was unfairly accused to breaking the law. The contradiction in this combination of statements is that conversion from Judaism to Christianity would have turned any Jew, including James, into a law breaker in the eyes of every Jew, let alone those ardent protectors of the law. Josephus, himself a loyal Jew, would have no doubt considered James a heretic.

This contradiction completely disappears if we simply remove the identification of James as Jesus' brother and the identification of Jesus as an alleged Christ. My view is that Josephus did indeed write most of the James paragraph, but his hands did not write down the two references to Jesus. It is possible that he identified this James differently, and that this identification was changed by a Christian hand, or that he did not identify James at all. This tampering with the passage might have been influenced by the belief in some Christian circles that James was Jesus' blood brother and was unlawfully killed.

Is it a problem that James would be left with no identification? Absolutely not. All that Josephus was interested in is relating how a James and companions of his were wrongly and unlawfully killed by Ananus. He did not care, for instance, to name any of James' companions. He did not even tell us what these wronged people were supposed to have exactly done. None of this was necessary or important for Josephus. Identifying James would not have contributed anything relevant to the aim of the passage, which is to explain how Ananus abused his authority and how he was removed. Josephus may have still identified James, but certainly not the way it is done in the current text. The existing identification of James undermines the very logic of the passage. How could Jewish law keepers not consider Jesus' brother and follower a law breaker? How could the Jewish king punish the high priest for killing a close relative and major follower of Jesus who was himself allegedly executed by the Roman emperor at the behest of the Jews? This does not make sense. What restores sense to the James passage is the removal of the references to Jesus. This leaves the mentioned James with nothing to link him to Jesus or Christianity. Josephus is talking about a Jewish James and companions of his who were not really law breakers, but who were unfairly accused and executed.

Christian authors believed that James, whom they called "the Just," was a major Christian figure — namely, the head of the Jerusalem Church. Had this been true, James would have been an important figure and Josephus would have mentioned that. It is the kind of historical information that we expect Josephus to have been interested in reporting. He has already indicated that James was killed unfairly, so had he known that this James is the so-called "James the Just," he would have probably identified him as such. Josephus, therefore, could not have known that the James he wrote about was supposed to be a major Christian figure. It is likely that he knew nothing at all about this James beyond what he wrote. If Josephus had known that James was Jesus' brother, then surely he would have also known much more interesting things about this relative that would have merited some space in his book.

It may be suggested, in an attempt to resolve this contradiction, that James was indeed Jesus' brother but that his charge was not related to his embracement of Christianity. This, however, would completely undermine James' Christian image, and would bring into question just about everything Christian sources say about him. What's more, this would still not deal with the other problems in the Josephan James passage that I discussed earlier.

Origen in the 3rd century, Eusebius in the 4th century, and Jerome in 392 CE all claimed that Josephus has also said that the unfair murder of James was the cause of the destruction of Jerusalem by the Romans in 70 CE. Origen mentions this reference twice in *Against Celsus* (1.47; 2.13) and a third time in *Commentary on Matthew*, although he makes the Christian point that it was the execution of Jesus, not of his brother, that caused the disaster that befell Jerusalem:

> And to so great a reputation among the people for righteousness did this James rise, that Flavius Josephus, who wrote the "Antiquities of the Jews" in twenty books, when wishing to exhibit the cause why the people suffered so great misfortunes that even the temple was razed to the ground, said, that these things happened to them in accordance with the wrath of God in consequence of the things which they had dared to do against James the brother of Jesus who is called Christ. And the wonderful thing is, that, though he did not accept Jesus as Christ, he yet gave testimony that the righteousness of James was so great; and he says that the people thought

that they had suffered these things because of James. (Origen, *Commentary on Matthew*, 10.17)

Eusebius mentions the same story just before citing Josephus' James passage:

James was so admirable a man and so celebrated among all for his justice, that the more sensible even of the Jews were of the opinion that this was the cause of the siege of Jerusalem, which happened to them immediately after his martyrdom for no other reason than their daring act against him. Josephus, at least, has not hesitated to testify this in his writings, where he says, "These things happened to the Jews to avenge James the Just, who was a brother of Jesus, that is called the Christ. For the Jews slew him, although he was a most just man." (*Ecclesiastical History*, 2.23.19-20)

Over one and a half century after Origen, Jerome also said that Josephus has stated that "Jerusalem was destroyed because of the murder of James the apostle" (*Lives of Illustrious Men*, 13).

Because this claim is not found in the James passage in the available manuscripts of *Jewish Antiquities*, scholars have argued about what passage these early Christian authors are talking about. There are three possibilities, the first of which is that Origen, Eusebius, and Jerome had seen a version of the James passage that is different from the one that survived. Second, they are talking about a different passage altogether which has since been lost. It has been suggested that such a reference was removed by Christian copyists because they thought that the destruction of Jerusalem should have been attributed to the crucifixion of Jesus rather than the killing of James, which is a view expressed by Origen also. The fact that Eusebius cited the James passage in more or less the form it exists in the surviving manuscripts has been taken by some to mean that he must have also referred to a completely different passage that is now lost. Third, Josephus never actually made the statement that links James to the destruction of Jerusalem, and the fathers might have wrongly ascribed it to him.

It is impossible to tell with certainty how these early fathers came to attribute this controversial passage to Josephus. We can say with confidence, however, that Josephus could not have made such a statement — certainly not in the way described by the three fathers. The reason is the same as to why Josephus' surviving James passage must have been at least partly written by Christian scribes. If this James is the alleged brother of Jesus who headed the Jerusalem church after his brother's death, then Josephus would not have said that this Christian leader was just, the Jews were wrong in condemning him, or that they were severely punished by God for his killing. It is impossible that Josephus who did not believe in Jesus could have believed that his Christian brother was a just man for the wrong killing of whom the entire Jewish nation had to suffer!

Other arguments have been made against the suggestion that Josephus could have attributed the destruction of Jerusalem to the killing of James. For instance, it has been pointed out that Josephus attributed the destruction of Jerusalem to revolutionary movements among the Jews against the Romans. Doherty also stresses that the goal of Josephus' writing, which he reveals in the *Jewish War* (3.5.8), to discourage others from revolt, would not have been served at all by claiming that the destruction of Jerusalem was caused by the killing of a righteous man. Josephus was writing under Roman patronage and for the Romans. In fact, he states in *Life* (65) that Emperor Titus himself put his signature to copies of *the Jewish War* and ordered the publication of this work. Josephus' Roman readers would not have liked to see their punishment of the Jewish revolt be attributed to the Jewish God, as if they were mere instruments in the hand of the God of their enemies!

The debate about James and the other alleged brothers and sisters of Jesus which has been going on for centuries was recently given new momentum. In November 2002, the *Biblical Archaeology Review* published a world exclusive about a sensational discovery of an ossuary (a container used in ancient times to bury human bones) with extraordinary inscriptions in Aramaic — the predominant language of the Jews in 1st century Palestine. The ossuary, which was found in Jerusalem and later identified by the renowned French epigrapher André Lemaire, had *Ya'akov bar Yosef achui d'Yeshua* inscribed on one of its sides. In English, the text reads "James, son of Joseph, brother of Jesus." Lemaire had no doubt about which James, Joseph, and Jesus the inscriptions meant. The find immediately caught the imagination of both scholars and the public.

The ossuary passed various tests of forgery, and an increasing number of experts were willing to publicly endorse its authenticity. The find was hailed as one of the greatest discoveries in the history of New Testament archaeology. The enormous excitement that the ossuary generated in scholarly circles and among the public forced the Israel Antiquities Authority (IAA), which is responsible for all archaeological activities in Israel, to move to take a formal position about the discovery. The IAA formed committees of experts to examine all aspects of the ossuary. The finding of the IAA committees was not what many had hoped for or expected: while the ossuary was authentic, the inscription was a modern forgery. The IAA report did not convince everyone, and the debate is still raging. This contentious issue, which developed into a highly acrimonious and disreputable spat, has been consistently and patiently documented in many issues of the *Biblical Archaeology Review*. The level of animosity that has shrouded the question of the authenticity of the ossuary has left very little scholarship in much of what is being said.

Regardless of the status of authenticity of the Josephan James passage and the inscriptions on the ossuary, it is clear that there were — and, of course, still are — people who believed that Jesus had blood brothers and sisters, and others who believed he never had. Christians who believe that James, Jude, and the others were Jesus' siblings often accuse those who deny this claim of being driven by the dogmatic belief that Mary could not have given birth to other than Jesus. The problem, as with many other similar disputes, is that the New Testament contains passages that seem to support both contradictory views.

9.5. The Qur'an's Implicit Rejection of Jesus' Siblings

The Qur'an does not indicate, explicitly or implicitly, that Jesus' had brothers or sisters. But does it rule out the possibility that he had any siblings? We have already seen that the Qur'an makes it clear that Mary conceived Jesus miraculously while still a virgin. It is also clear from the Qur'anic story of the annunciation and birth of Jesus that there was no such a figure as Joseph in the life of Mary, who was dedicated to the worship of God. The Qur'an recounts a few events in Jesus' life as an adult, but there is nothing about Mary. This is unlikely to be due to Mary's early death, but is probably due to the fact that it is Jesus of the two whom the Qur'an mainly focuses on. So, it looks like the Qur'an's account does not rule out the possibility that Mary could have got married some time after giving birth to Jesus.

However, the woman who lived a very unusual life and went through all the difficulties associated with the conception and birth of Jesus unaided by a man is unlikely to have wanted to get married later. The Qur'an tells us that Jesus miraculously spoke in the cradle in support of his mother, and this is sufficient indication that she had a much better life among at least people who knew and believed in her and her son than she had after the annunciation and conception when she needed to hide away.

The Qur'an contains verses that strongly suggest that Mary never got married:

> Allah set forth an example for the disbelievers the wife of Noah and the wife of Lot. They were under two of our righteous servants yet betrayed them, so they (the husbands) did not protect them against Allah, and it was said: "Enter both the Fire with those who enter [it]" (66.10). And Allah set forth an example for the believers the wife of Pharaoh who said: "My Lord! Build for me a home with you in paradise, save me from Pharaoh and his work, and save me from the evil-doing people" (66.11). And Mary, daughter of 'Imrān, who guarded her private parts, then We breathed therein of Our spirit. And she believed in the words of her Lord and His Book, and was one of the obedient (66.12).

These verses look back at four notable women — two notorious disbelievers and two exceptional believers. An observation of interest to our current discussion is that while three of these women are identified by their husbands, Mary is identified by her father: "daughter of 'Imrān." Had Mary been married to a believer, like the wives of Noah and Lot, or to a disbeliever, like the wife of Pharaoh, she would have been identified by her husband and called Mary the wife of so-and-so. In fact, Mary's mother herself was identified in this way in chapter 3:

> When the wife of 'Imrān said: "My Lord! I vow to consecrate to You that which is in my womb, so accept it from me. You are the Hearer, the Knower (3.35).

It may be argued that Mary's was not identified by her husband's name because he was not introduced in the story in the first place, but I find the counter argument much stronger.

Although the Qur'an does not reject explicitly the suggestion that Jesus had brothers or sisters, the discussions in this chapter give me confidence to conclude that Mary never got married and, accordingly, Jesus never had siblings. James could not have been Jesus' brother, and he could not have lived most of his life as a disbeliever just to convert after seeing the resurrected Jesus. That very death is rejected by the Qur'an, as we shall see in Chapter 19, so that supposed miracle could not have happened. If the person named James who rejected Jesus during his life converted at the end to some form of Christianity, then there must have been another reason for his belated faith.

Christian accounts of Jesus' life contain so many claims and counter claims that touch all aspects of his life as a man, and go as far as promoting him to divinity. The question of whether he had siblings or not is no exception. There are at times clear contradictions between the different sources, but also even within the same source; at times there is also as much ambiguity. The accounts are so confused, probably because each is the work of more than one writer and editor, that it is impossible to speculate on how they came into being. Any set of circumstances could have led to the spread of the claim that Mary had children other than Jesus.

10

Jesus' Birth

Mark and John do not say anything about Jesus' birth, whereas Matthew and Luke present very different accounts. Some parts of the two stories may be reconcilable, but there are contradictory details also. Apocryphal gospels also show a lot of interest in Jesus' birth, providing very detailed accounts.

The Qur'an recounts Jesus' birth in 11 verses. The story is substantially different from its Christian counterparts. One detail of the Qur'anic story is that Jesus was born under a palm tree. This seems to have been significantly and differently changed by the editors and copyists of apocryphal gospels. Critiques of the Qur'an claim that it has based this detail of Jesus' birth on ancient sources, but this claim is unfounded and misleading.

The Qur'an does not give any information about the date of Jesus' birth, but Christian sources do. However, this information is highly contradictory, with some of it clearly unhistorical. Using certain details that look more reliable to date Jesus' birth requires discarding many other unhistorical and/or contradictory claims.

10.1 Jesus' Birth in the Canonical Gospels

Matthew only states that Jesus was born in Bethlehem of Judea, and then moves on to talk about the "wise men" who came to visit the newborn and King Herod's concern about what this birth could mean for his reign:

> After Jesus was born in Bethlehem in Judea, in the time of King Herod, wise men from the East came to Jerusalem saying, "Where is the one who is born king of the Jews? For we saw his star when it rose and have come to worship him." When King Herod heard this he was alarmed, and all Jerusalem with him. After assembling all the chief priests and experts in the law, he asked them where the Christ was to be born. "In Bethlehem of Judea," they said, "for it is written this way by the prophet: 'And you, Bethlehem, in the land of Judah, are in no way least among the rulers of Judah, for out of you will come a ruler who will shepherd my people Israel.'" (Matt. 2:1-6)

Herod summoned the wise men and asked them to let him know the birthplace of the newborn when they have found him. But being warned in a dream not to return to Herod, the wise men traveled back to their country without telling Herod where to find the newborn. The king was enraged by the wise men's action and ordered the slaughter of all young children in Bethlehem and its surrounding areas to ensure the death of Jesus.

It is worth noting that, contrary to public belief, Matthew does not say that the wise men were "three." This popular belief seems to have been interpolated from the wise men's offer of "three" gifts to the newborn child, although the Gospel of Pseudo-Matthew (16) states that the magi were three.

One part of Matthew's text that deserves a detailed look here is the scriptural prophecy that the chief priests and scribes revealed to Herod about the birthplace of the Christ: "'In Bethlehem of Judea,' they said, 'for it is written this way by the prophet: And you, Bethlehem, in the land of Judah, are in no way least among the rulers of Judah, for out of you will come a ruler who will shepherd my people Israel'" (Matt. 2:5-6). This is the second of 13 scriptural prophecies that Matthew quotes in his Gospel to show that they were fulfilled by events in Jesus' life (Matt. 1:23, 2:6, 2:15, 2:18, 2:23, 3:3, 4:15-16, 8:17, 12:18-21, 13:14-15, 15:8-9, 21:5, 27:9-10). Five of these are found in the first two chapters which contain the infancy story.

Matthew's fascination with linking events in Jesus' life to alleged Old Testament prophecies aims to show that Jesus was the fulfillment of those prophecies. This link would strengthen the believers' faith and convince others, particularly the Jews, that Jesus is the awaited Messiah and make them follow him. Matthew was so keen on pursuing this endeavor that he often distorted and misused Old Testament passages. He changed them and took them out of context to make them fit his purpose. I have already explained how Matthew (1:23) completely distorted and misused an Isaiah prophecy (7:14) that had absolutely nothing to do with Jesus to make it appear as if it talked about him (pp. 106-107). Let's have a look at the prophecy that Matthew quotes in 2:6; we will examine more of these *Messianic prophecies* in Chapter 11.

The Old Testament prophecy that Matthew cites here is from Micah 5:2: "As for you, Bethlehem Ephrathah, seemingly insignificant among the clans of Judah — from you a king will emerge who will rule over Israel on my behalf." This is not exactly how Matthew quotes it! The Old Testament stresses that Bethlehem was a minor town, whereas Matthew's change confirms the exact opposite, stating that Bethlehem is not the least of Judea's towns. Matthew meant to say that Bethlehem cannot be an insignificant town because the Christ himself came out of it.

There has also been disagreement about whether Micah meant Bethlehem the town or a clan. A more serious problem with linking the messianic "ruler" in Micah with Jesus is that the text that surrounds that passage ascribes to this ruler historical feats that Jesus was never involved in! This is a longer quotation that contains Micah's prophecy:

> But now slash yourself, daughter surrounded by soldiers! We are besieged! With a scepter they strike Israel's ruler on the side of his face. As for you, Bethlehem Ephrathah, seemingly insignificant among the clans of Judah — from you a king will emerge who will rule over Israel on my behalf, one whose origins are in the distant past. So the Lord will hand the people of Israel over to their enemies until the time when the woman in labor gives birth. Then the rest of the king's brothers will return to be reunited with the people of Israel. He will assume his position and shepherd the people

by the Lord's strength, by the sovereign authority of the Lord his God. They will live in peace, for at that time he will be honored even in the distant regions of the earth. He will give us peace. When the Assyrians try to invade our land, and attempt to set foot in our fortresses, we will send against them seven shepherd-rulers, make that eight commanders. They will rule the land of Assyria with the sword, the land of Nimrod with a drawn sword. Our king will rescue us from the Assyrians, when they attempt to invade our land and try to set foot in our territory. (Mic. 5:1-6)

This passage was probably believed by Jews to be talking about the Messiah well before the birth of Jesus, but this interpretation cannot be maintained by anyone who identifies the Messiah with Jesus, simply because the descriptions in this passage do not apply to Jesus. The passage talks about a king who would defeat the Assyrians, which is not something Jesus did. In fact, six centuries before the birth of Jesus, specifically in 612 BCE, the Babylonians defeated the Assyrians and destroyed their capital Nineveh, and within three years Assyria ceased to exist as an independent nation. The story of the seven shepherd-rulers also never took place. If the passage above talks about the Messiah, then Jesus cannot be him. Similarly, if Jesus is the Messiah, then this passage cannot be talking about the Messiah. Matthew not only tampered with Micah's prophecy, but linking it to Jesus is also wrong and misleading.

Luke gives us a significantly different version of the story of birth. After talking about the annunciation of John and Jesus and then the birth of John, this Gospel goes on to say:

Now in those days a decree went out from Caesar Augustus to register all the empire for taxes. This was the first registration, taken when Quirinius was governor of Syria. Everyone went to his own town to be registered. So Joseph also went up from the town of Nazareth in Galilee to Judea, to the city of David called Bethlehem, because he was of the house and family line of David. He went to be registered with Mary, who was promised in marriage to him, and who was expecting a child. While they were there, the time came for her to deliver her child. And she gave birth to her first-born son and wrapped him in strips of cloth and laid him in a manger, because there was no place for them in the inn.

Now there were shepherds nearby living out in the field, keeping guard over their flock at night. An angel of the Lord appeared to them, and the glory of the Lord shone around them, and they were absolutely terrified. But the angel said to them, "Do not be afraid! Listen carefully, for I proclaim to you good news that brings great joy to all the people: Today your Savior is born in the city of David. He is Christ the Lord. This will be a sign for you: You will find a baby wrapped in strips of cloth and lying in a manger." Suddenly a vast, heavenly army appeared with the angel, praising God and saying, "Glory to God in the highest, and on earth peace among people with whom he is pleased!"

When the angels left them and went back to heaven, the shepherds said to one another, "Let us go over to Bethlehem and see this thing that has taken place, that the Lord has made known to us." So they hurried off and located Mary and Joseph, and found the baby lying in a manger. When they saw him, they related what they had been told about this child, and all who heard it were astonished at what the shepherds said. But Mary treasured up all these words, pondering in her heart what they might mean. So the shepherds returned, glorifying and praising God for all they had heard and seen; everything was just as they had been told. (Luke 2:1-20)

Luke then states that Jesus was circumcised on the eighth day, and after Mary's days of purification, she and Joseph took the newborn to Jerusalem to present him to the Lord at the temple.

Jesus' birth is one episode that Luke and Matthew report differently. Others that they cover in their first two chapters, such as the annunciation and events in Jesus' early life, are also presented very differently. In his book *Born Divine*, Robert Miller (2003: 9-12) classified the differences between the two infancy narratives into four groups: **shape**, **atmosphere**, **style**, and **contents**. I will follow this classification in the discussion below.

In terms of **shape**, both narratives progress very differently, giving different beginnings, middles and endings. Matthew's narrative starts with the genealogy of Jesus, and then makes a passing reference to Mary's conception of the Holy Spirit and the angel's revelation to Joseph of that truth. Bypassing Jesus' birth, the narrative then moves to talk about King Herod's concern at the birth of the Christ and his encounter with the wise men from the east. After visiting the child, the wise men avoided going back to Herod to tell him about the birthplace of Jesus. The king then ordered the killing of the infants of Bethlehem, which prompted the holy family's flight to Egypt. They returned after Herod's death and lived in Nazareth, Galilee.

Luke's story starts with the annunciation of the birth of John the Baptist and follows with a more detailed account of the annunciation of Jesus' birth than Matthew's. Mary's visit to Zechariah' house is then related, followed by John's birth, and a quick mention of his moving to the desert where he lived until he became an adult. Next, Luke tells us about a Roman census that forced Joseph and Mary to head to Bethlehem, where Jesus was born. An angel then appeared to shepherds to give them the good news about the birth of a savior, and the shepherds came to visit Jesus. Mary and Joseph then presented Jesus in the temple in Jerusalem, where the little child was recognized to be the Christ by one of the worshippers. The narrative ends with the account of the 12-year-old Jesus astonishing people in the temple with his precocious wisdom.

The infancy narratives in Luke and Matthew have very different, and almost contradictory, **atmospheres**. The atmosphere in Matthew is dominated by anxiety, fear, and sadness, much of which is the result of detailing Herod's attempt to kill Jesus and his heinous murder of the infants. Conversely, Luke's is full of joyful and praising individuals marking a series of delightful events. Miller (2003: 10) notes that "Greek nouns and verbs for joy, glory, praise, blessing, and thanks occur twenty times" in Luke's infancy story.

With respect to **style**, Miller points out five differences between how the infancy story is related in Matthew and Luke. First, the story of John is interwoven with that of Jesus in Luke, whereas John is not mentioned at all by Matthew. Second, Matthew tells the story mainly from Joseph's perspective. Luke makes Mary the central character. Third, Matthew quotes five prophecies of the Old Testament, whereas Luke's usage of the Old Testament is more implicit, citing explicitly only one non-prophetic passage. Four, in Matthew's story, all major events are guided by dreams. Luke's narrative has no dreams, and heavenly messages are delivered by angels. Five, Matthew's account is brief, laconic, and involves little human speech. In Luke, it is human speech that is mainly used for expressing the messages.

Finally, the **contents** of the two Gospels are pronouncedly different. Apart from some similarities between the two scenes of the annunciation of Jesus' birth and some statements of facts — such as Jesus was of Davidic descent and Joseph was not Jesus' father — Matthew and Luke give two completely different accounts. The episodes that form the backbone of each narrative are missing from the other, as shown in table 10.1.

Clearly, the two narratives ignore major events in each other. It may be suggested that the two accounts can still be combined to form one more detailed and cohesive story. But there are also contradictions between the two stories, as pointed out above. Building a mega story that accommodates both narratives in their entirety is not possible. We have already discussed in detail some differences between the two narratives, and we will see more later in the book.

Although Mark and John do not talk about Jesus' birth and childhood, they contain indirect references to his birthplace. Mark (6:1) calls Nazareth Jesus' "hometown," which implies that he was born there. Luke (4:24) also calls Nazareth Jesus' hometown, but he stresses that this was not Jesus' birthplace but the city where he was "brought up" (Luke 4:16). This qualification is missing from Mark. John attributes to a Nathanael the following sarcastic question in reference to Jesus: "Can anything good come out of Nazareth?" (John 1:46). John also makes Pharisees state that "no prophet comes from Galilee!" (John 7:52). Scholars (e.g. Theissen & Merz, 1999: 164) have interpreted these passages to mean that Jesus was born in Nazareth. Indeed, in a third passage, John contrasts Bethlehem, King David's birthplace, with Galilee, thus unambiguously suggesting that the latter, where Nazareth is, is Jesus' birthplace:

> Others said, "This is the Christ!" But still others said, "No, for the Christ doesn't come from Galilee, does he? Don't the scriptures say that the Christ is a descendant of David and comes from Bethlehem, the village where David lived?" (John 7:41-42)

So while Matthew and Luke make Bethlehem Jesus' place of birth, Mark and John suggest that he was born in Nazareth.

Table 10.1: Comparison between the infancy narratives in Matthew and Luke

Matthew	Luke
Starts with a genealogy of Jesus.	Gives a very different genealogy later.
No mention of the annunciation of John.	Detailed account of the annunciation of John.
Passing mention that Mary conceived a child of the Holy Spirit.	Detailed account of Mary's dialog with Gabriel.
Joseph thinks of leaving the pregnant Mary.	No mention of Joseph's doubts about Mary
Jesus was born in Bethlehem, where Mary and Joseph seem to have been living.	Mary and Jesus were living in Nazareth in Galilee, but they went to Bethlehem to register for the census, so Jesus was born there in a manger.
Detailed account of Herod's plot to kill Jesus and his massacre of the innocent children.	No mention of any role for Herod.
Details of the visit of the wise men who were led by the star of Bethlehem.	No mention of the wise men or the star.
No mention of a Roman census. Joseph and Mary were already in Bethlehem.	The Roman census explains why Jesus was born in Bethlehem.
No mention of shepherds.	Shepherds visit the newborn Jesus.
Joseph and Mary had to take Jesus to Egypt to escape Herod's plan to kill the child.	As there is no mention of any role for Herod, there is no flight to Egypt.
The holy family returned from Egypt after Herod's death and went to Nazareth because it was outside the rule of Herod's successor.	Joseph and Mary were already living in Nazareth before Jesus' annunciation.
No mention of any event between the return from Egypt to Jesus' baptism.	Details of the infant Jesus being taken to the temple and how he was recognized there as the Christ.
	The 12-year-old Jesus astonished people in the temple with his knowledge.

10.2. Jesus' Birth in Apocryphal Sources

The Infancy Gospel of James contains a rather long account of Jesus' birth. While Joseph and Mary were on their way to Bethlehem, in response to a taxation decree from Emperor Augustus, Mary felt the pangs of labor. Joseph took her to a cave, and went looking for a midwife from Bethlehem. As he was looking for a midwife, Joseph saw many miraculous signs in the sky and on earth. He found a midwife and brought her to the cave, although the story seems to suggest that Jesus was born without her help. Next, this author gives us another, different version of *the coming of some wise men from the east* and their encounter with Herod (InJam. 15:1).

A very similar account is found in the Arabic Gospel of the Infancy:

> Joseph therefore arose, and with Mary his spouse he went to Jerusalem, and then came to Bethlehem, that he and his family might be taxed in the city of his fathers. And when they came by the cave, Mary confessed to Joseph that her time of bringing forth has come, and she could not go on to the city, and said, Let us go into this cave.
>
> At that time the sun was very near going down. But Joseph hastened away, that he might fetch her a midwife; and when he saw an old Hebrew woman who was of Jerusalem, he said to her, "Pray come hither, good woman, and go into that cave, and you will there see a woman just ready to bring forth."
>
> It was after sunset, when the old woman and Joseph with her reached the cave, and they both went into it. And behold, it was all filled with lights, greater than the light of lamps and candles, and greater than the light of the sun itself. The infant was then wrapped up in swaddling clothes, and sucking the breasts of his mother St. Mary. (AraIn. 1:5-11)

This gospel also contains, among other details, an account of the visit of *wise men from the East* who came to Jerusalem to pay homage to the newborn and offer the three gifts.

The Gospel of Pseudo-Matthew also contains a detailed account of Jesus' birth. It tells us that while Joseph and Mary were on their way to Bethlehem for an enrolment, the time of birth of Jesus came, and Mary gave birth in a cavern.

10.3. The Star of Bethlehem

According to Matthew, the wise men were led to the abode of the child by a star:

> After Jesus was born in Bethlehem in Judea, in the time of King Herod, wise men from the East came to Jerusalem saying, "Where is the one who is born king of the Jews? For we saw his star when it rose and have come to worship him." (Matt. 2:1-2)

> Then Herod privately summoned the wise men and determined from them when the star had appeared. He sent them to Bethlehem and said, "Go and look carefully for the child. When you find him, inform me so that I can go and worship him as well." After listening to the king they left, and once again the star they saw when it rose led them until it stopped above the place where the child was. (Matt. 2:7-9)

This star, which is not found in the Qur'an, features prominently in Christian traditional representations of the birth of Jesus. Matthew is clearly talking about a miraculous rather than natural star, as attested by its supernatural behavior, but still there have been many attempts to associate it with some visible astronomical events from that time, such as the passing of a comet, explosion of a supernova, or stellar conjunction.

Different attempts have been made to discredit and others to confirm the historicity of the star of the Matthean story of birth. Those who discredit it often point out that Matthew was reusing the ages-old motif of the appearance of a new heavenly body when a great man is born or, more generally, an important event takes place. This view finds evidence in what Eusebius, the 4th century bishop of Caesarea, has to say about this star:

> In the case of other remarkable and famous men we know that strange stars have appeared, what some call comets, or meteors, or tails of fire, or similar phenomena that are seen in connection with great unusual events. But what event could be greater or more important for the whole Universe than the spiritual light coming to all men through the Saviour's Advent, bringing to human souls the gift of holiness and true knowledge of God? Wherefore the herald star gave the great sign, telling in symbol that the Christ of God would shine as a great new light on all the world. (Eusebius, *The Proof of the Gospel*, 9.1)

The Infancy Gospel of James, which also has the account of the star, stresses this association between the birth of great figures and the appearance of strange stars. This is what the wise men told Herod when questioned about the sign of the *born king* they saw: "We saw an extraordinary large star shining among the stars of heaven, and so outshined all the other stars, as that they became not visible, and we knew thereby that a great king was born in Israel, and therefore we have come to worship him" (InJam. 15:7). This star is also supposed to have stopped on Jesus' birthplace, which is described as a "cave" in this gospel.

Scholars also cite older stories about the appearance of stars or other omens to mark the births of prominent figures or events associated with them, suggesting that Christian writings developed this story using the same theme. For instance, the Roman writer Cicero (106-43 BCE) claims that a bright star appeared about the time of the birth of Alexander the Great (356-323 BCE) which was noticed by magi (Cicero, *On Divination*, 1.47). One other instance that is often cited is historian Suetonius' (69 - after 122 CE) report of the birth of the Emperor Augustus: "a few months before Augustus was born a portent was generally observed at Rome, which gave warning that nature was pregnant with a king for the Roman people" (Suetonius, *Lives of the Caesars: Augustus*, 94).

Theissen and Merz (1999: 165) have noted that the account of the star was perhaps based on the following Old Testament messianic prediction:

I see him, but not now; I behold him, but not close at hand. A star will march forth out of Jacob, and a scepter will rise out of Israel. He will crush the skulls of Moab, and the heads of all the sons of Sheth. (Num. 24:17)

Details in this and following passages of the prediction do not apply to Jesus, though this would not have necessarily prevented Matthew from linking this prediction to Jesus, as he linked him to other Old Testament passages that are clearly inapplicable to him. But there is no evidence that Matthew meant to use this particular Biblical passage.

Those who think that the story of the star of Jesus' birth is historical, on the other hand, argue that there are independently corroborated records of heavenly phenomena associating the birth of important people, so this association should not be dismissed only because it looks suspicious. In *Epitome of the Philippic History of Pompeius Trogus* (37.2), the 3rd century historian Justin reported that in the years of the birth and accession of King Mithridates of Pontus, who reigned from 120 to 63 BCE, a bright comet appeared for seventy successive days on each occasion that made the sky look to be on fire. He says that the comet, whose rising and setting took four hours, covered a fourth of the sky and obscured the light of the sun. In his defense of the historicity of Matthew's account, Montefiore (1962: 9-10) points out that Justin's record is confirmed independently by three ancient Chinese astronomical records.

One problem that Montefiore and others seem to ignore is that a "star" like that of the birth of Jesus would have been seen by so many people, not only the wise men. A bigger problem that has been pointed out is that no heavenly body can be seen to *stand on one specific house*! This is perhaps why this star came to be known as the "Bethlehem star," although this city related name would make the star rather useless for what the wise men needed it for: pointing precisely to Jesus' birthplace. Identifying the star with an astronomical phenomenon is a rather futile exercise, as no star could have behaved as described by Matthew: leading the wise men to Jesus' place of birth by standing above it.

10.4. Jesus' Birth in the Qur'an

The story of Jesus' birth in the Qur'an is related in 11 verses in chapter 19 starting with verse 23:

> She conceived him, and she withdrew with him to a far place (19.22). And the pangs of childbirth drove her to the trunk of a palm tree. She said: "I wish I had died before this and had become someone totally forgotten!" (19.23).

After conceiving Jesus, Mary went to live away from her family. It seems that she was somewhere outdoors when she went into labor, so she sat under a palm tree. As noted earlier, Mary was clearly alone (§6.4), and the Qur'an does not acknowledge the existence of Joseph or any such male character in Mary's life (§8.2).

Alone, away from her family, in labor in what looks like a public rather than private place, and about to give birth to what people would consider an illicit child, Mary found herself in an extremely distressing situation. The test was so great that her words carried a sense of despair, wishing for a death that would leave no trace of her and make people forget about her. Her prayer reflects the fact that she felt a great sense of shame thinking of what people would accuse her of. This woman who lived all her life in nigh complete solitude worshipping God, and who never committed anything immoral or indecent, found herself facing the unbearable and disgraceful accusation of fornication.

We see in this verse Mary in a moment of weakness that was precipitated by an extraordinary test. All great individuals are subjected to difficult tests, but these ultimately furnish them with more noble qualities and further purify them spiritually. This is how God describes the way He tests even messengers and their followers, taking them to almost the end of their tethers:

> Or do you think that you [O you who believe!] would enter paradise before the like of that which came to those who passed away before you has come to you? Affliction and adversity befell them, and they were shaken so violently that the messenger and those who believed with him said: "When will Allah's help come?" Verily, Allah's help is nigh! (2.214).

The real messenger, the real Mary, and the real believers are not seen in their passing moments of weakness, which are bound to strengthen them, but in the rest of their lives in which they are in a state of obedience and surrender.

Then the beautiful reality of that apparently distressing situation started to emerge as a unique child is sent into this world:

> Then he called her from beneath her: "Do not grieve! Your Lord has placed a rivulet beneath you (19.24).

Almost immediately after Mary gave birth, her newborn miraculously spoke to her. Moreover, the child already knew the psychological state of his mother, so he comforted her by asking her not to grieve and informing her that God has made a stream beneath her so she can drink and wash. Mary was not only in bad need for water, but she was also very hungry or exhausted and in need of energy, so her newborn went on to reveal to her that God has also made food available for her:

> And shake the trunk of the palm tree toward you, and it will let fall fresh dates upon you (19.25).

Jesus told his mother that if she tried to shake the trunk of the palm tree she was laying under, it would drop fresh dates to her. Aṭ-Ṭabāṭabā'ī has suggested that verses 19.23 and 19.25 talk about the "trunk of the palm tree" not simply *palm tree* because the tree was in fact dry, and that it became full of dates by a miracle. The fact that Jesus told his mother about the stream and the dates means that neither was there, otherwise Mary herself would have noticed them. This is also confirmed by the newborn's description of the stream as something that God has placed beneath Mary: "Your Lord has placed a rivulet beneath you." The ability of Mary, who was so weak having just delivered, to shake the trunk of the palm tree must have also been a miracle.

The Qur'an then tells us that Jesus went on to say to his mother:

So eat, drink, and be consoled. If you meet any human being, say: 'I have vowed a fast to God, so I will not speak today to any human being'" (19.26).

Jesus asked his mother to eat, drink, relax, and not worry about what would happen. He asked her to tell any human she meets that she had vowed to God to abstain from speaking to any person. This fast was temporary, as indicated by the word "today," and was intended to spare Mary the trouble of having to argue with her people and to instead leave her miraculous son to speak in her defense.

Mary refrained from speaking to any *insiyyā* or "human being." This excludes the angels, whom she used to speak to. The wording also suggests that Mary might meet non-human beings. The restrictiveness of the fast confirms that it was mainly intended to protect her from the offensive and hostile verbal attacks that people would launch against her. She did not need to defend herself; her son was well placed to fully rebuff those accusations. This fasting has similarity with Zechariah's temporary loss of the ability to speak to human beings, although the latter was forced on Zechariah. None of the two fasts was a punishment, but they were ordained to help Mary and Zechariah, although in different ways.

Now full of trust in God and His favor on her and her son, Mary returned with her newborn to her people, who were shocked to see her with a baby but no husband:

Then she brought him to her people, carrying him. They said: "O Mary! You have come up with a grave thing (19.27).

Clearly, they made a connection between Mary's sudden disappearance and her giving birth to this child. They must have thought that she either fled after becoming illicitly pregnant or became pregnant following her escape. They went on to remind her that she descended from a family that was never involved in immoral behavior:

O sister of Aaron! Your father was not a bad man, and your mother was not an unchaste woman" (19.28).

The descriptions of Mary here as "sister of Aaron" and as "daughter of 'Imrān" in verse 66.12 are often cited by Biblical scholars as evidence that the Qur'an contains corrupt information from the Bible. For instance, pointing out that "Amram" is called the father of "Aaron, Moses, and Miriam their sister" in the Old Testament Book of Numbers (26:60), Tisdall states that "the title 'sister of Aaron' is given to Miriam in Exodus 15:20, and it must be from this passage that Muhammad borrowed the expression." He goes on to explain what he thinks is a mistake in the Qur'an:

> The reason of the mistake which identifies the Mother of our Saviour with a woman who lived about one thousand five hundred and seventy years before His birth is evidently the fact that in Arabic both names, Mary and Miriam, are one and the same in form, *Maryam*. The chronological difficulty of the identification does not seem to have occurred to Muhammad. (Tisdall, 1905:150-151)

Tisdall's explanation contains a contradiction that underlines many similar arguments that accuse Prophet Muhammad of copying inaccurately, deliberately, or unwittingly from the Bible. The problem with this popular approach is that, on the one hand, it claims that Muhammad had access to and detailed knowledge of the Bible and other Jewish and Christian writings, which is reflected in various details in the Qur'an, yet, on the other, he is supposed to have made some clearly wild errors. Tisdall attributes the Qur'an's description of Mary as "sister of Aaron" to Muhammad's knowledge of a *specific* Biblical phrase, yet at the same time accuses him of failing to differentiate between Moses' sister and Jesus' mother — two different characters in two very different stories in completely different books that are just not possible to mix by anyone with the slightest knowledge of the stories let alone the books!

Tisdall's view also represents a misunderstanding of the Qur'anic phrase "sister of Aaron." This phrase does not mean that Mary had a brother called Aaron, but that she *descended* from someone with that name. The Qur'an similarly uses the term "brother" to relate individuals to their peoples, as in verse 46.21 where the prophet of the people 'Ād is called "the brother of 'Ād." There are actually many other verses that call a prophet a "brother" of his people (7.65, 7.73, 7.85, 11.50, 11.61, 11.84, 26.106, 26.124, 26.142, 26.161, 27.45, 29.36). The Aaron that verse 19.28 mentions may be Prophet Aaron, Moses' brother, but he may also be another highly regarded grandfather of Mary.

I should also note that had 'Imrān been Mary's brother, her people would have mentioned Mary's parents first, and they would have probably referred to 'Imrān with *your brother*, as they did with Mary's father and mother, rather than with his name 'Imrān.

As for describing Mary as "daughter of 'Imrān" in verse 66.12, the Qur'an is clear in that this 'Imrān is not Moses' father, who is not actually mentioned directly or indirectly anywhere in the Qur'an, including in Moses' story. The identity of 'Imrān as Mary's father is further stressed in verse 3.35 where Mary's mother is called "wife of 'Imrān." In fact, the name "'Imrān" is mentioned in the Qur'an only in verses 3.35 and 66.12 both of which identify him as Mary's father.

Moreover, chapter 3 is called *the chapter of the family of 'Imrān* because of verse 3.33 which mentions the "family of 'Imrān," which is then followed by the story of Mary, clearly indicating that 'Imrān was Mary's father and that "the family of 'Imrān" is Mary's:

> Allah chose Adam, Noah, the family of Abraham, and the family of 'Imrān above all nations (3.33) — offspring, one of the other; and Allah hears and knows all things (3.34). When the wife of 'Imrān said: "My Lord! I vow to consecrate to You that which is in my womb, so accept it from me. You are the Hearer, the Knower (3.35).

Additionally, the chapter of the family of 'Imrān does not contain any information about Moses and Aaron — another indication that 'Imrān had nothing to do with Moses.

Tisdall's argument is therefore clearly flawed. One last thing to mention is that Tisdall follows the Biblical approach (§1.2). In addition to completely misunderstanding the references to 'Imrān in the Qur'an, his argument is driven by his personal belief in the Bible's assertion that the father of Moses and Aaron was called Amram and their sister was called Miriam. Outside the Bible, these statements have no supportive evidence.

After this analysis of one misunderstanding that is popular among both secular and Biblical critics of the Qur'an, let's get back to our analysis of the Qur'anic text.

Calling Mary "sister of Aaron" was intended to contrast the vice that Mary's people perceived her to have committed with her being a descendant of that highly respected Aaron. They went on to stress this contrast by reminding her of the chastity of her parents.

The response of Mary's people explains why, after becoming pregnant, she had to withdraw "to a far place" (19.22). Mary would have found it almost impossible to convince people of the reality of her pregnancy. It is also likely that by then her guardian and helper, Zechariah, who witnessed some of the miracles that occurred to her had died, and she would have had to face people without the support of a respectable figure who can lend credibility to her account. She might have feared for her life and the life of her child. After giving birth, she must have been commanded by God to go back to her people. This time, the very cause of her accusation was there to defend her:

> Then she pointed to him. They said: "How can we talk to one who is a child in the cradle?" (19.29).

The secret of her fasting is that Jesus was going to speak on her behalf and in her defense. In reply to her people's accusations, Mary only pointed to the baby, suggesting that they should ask him rather than her. Not surprisingly, they found the suggestion rather absurd, as Jesus was still an infant — probably a few days old at most. Surely they would not have even thought of testing her claim and trying to speak to him, which is why, to their astonishment, the little baby started to speak, introducing himself:

> He said: "I am Allah's servant. He has given me the Book and has appointed me a prophet (19.30).

This event is the fulfillment of God's first promise to Mary that the child of her miraculous conception "shall speak to people in the cradle and when middle-aged, and he shall be one of the righteous" (3.46). Jesus did not reply directly to the people's accusations to his mother. He refuted those accusations indirectly by the miracle of speaking in the cradle, and by the nature of what he said. The fact that he could speak in the cradle made it clear to them that this was a miraculous baby, implying that Mary's pregnancy was totally different from what they suspected. Sin could not have produced such an amazing and unique baby; only miracle and virtue could have done that. We do not know if all people believed that Jesus was a legitimate child, but the miracle would have made those who remained suspicious at least hesitate to take any hostile action against Mary, probably also discouraged by those who believed her. The miracle clearly worked in protecting Mary from being stoned to death, which is the Jewish punishment for adultery (Lev. 20:10).

Jesus started speaking by emphasizing his servanthood to God. This was important so that people do not get confused by the unique phenomenon they witnessed and possibly attribute divine qualities to him. Miracles must not make them forget that he was merely one of God's servants, as they were. All those miracles must then be attributed ultimately to God. Jesus' reply might have also fended off the potential accusation that the child and/or his mother were involved in magic or satanic practices.

He, Jesus told people, was a far more complex and miraculous phenomenon than simply a speaking infant. He was an infant who had already been given a divine book and made a prophet. This Book is the "Injīl," which we will talk more about in Chapter 17. What Jesus had to say about himself further confirmed to people that he was a baby who was being raised and protected by God, so he could not have been the son of a sin.

Although the miracle of speaking in the cradle is not mentioned in the canonical Gospels, it is found in the Arabic Gospel of the Infancy: "Jesus spoke even when he was in the cradle, and said to his mother: Mary, I am Jesus the Son of God, that word, which you did bring forth according to the declaration of the angel Gabriel to you, and my father hath sent me for the salvation of the world" (AraIn. 1:2-3). Again, this event has very different contexts in the Qur'an and this gospel. The Qur'an talks about Jesus' speech in the cradle as a miracle that Mary needed to help her convince her people that there was no wrongdoing in her conception of Jesus. The Arabic Gospel of the Infancy does not seem to suggest any particular function that this miracle performed. In fact, Jesus reiterated things that his mother already knew! This poorly edited scene is the result of Christian sources displacing the event from its original context.

There is a significant difference between what Jesus said according to the Qur'an and his words as reported by the Arabic Gospel of the Infancy. Of particular significance is the declaration of the Qur'anic Jesus that he was "a servant of Allah," which contradicts Jesus' assertion in the apocryphal gospel that he was "the Son of God." The author tries hard to stress Jesus' sonship of God, as there are at least two other places where this assertion is made in a context that does not seem to lead to it. For instance, an idol is claimed to have said the following about Jesus: "The unknown God has come here, who is truly God; nor is there any one besides him, who is worthy of divine worship for he is truly the Son of God" (AraIn. 4:11). Also, a priest whose son was cured by Jesus said about him: "perhaps this boy is the son of the living God, who made the heavens and the earth" (AraIn. 4:21). The Qur'an emphasizes that Jesus was a human being who was blessed by God, giving him the power to perform miracles, whereas the Arabic Gospel of the Infancy stresses that those miracles were indicative of Jesus' divine nature, expressed in his sonship of God.

The Qur'an tells us that baby Jesus went on to say to his mother's people:

> He has made me blessed wherever I may be. He has enjoined upon me prayer and almsgiving so long as I remain alive (19.31).

Jesus said that God made him be the source of blessing to people and miracles wherever he went. Like everyone else, he was commanded to worship God and give alms. His words "so long as I remain alive" clearly indicate that he was mortal. The Arabic word which I have translated as "almsgiving" here is *zakāt*. The latter can also mean "purification [of the soul]". I translated it as "almsgiving" because, as noted by aṭ-Ṭabāṭabā'ī, in the over twenty times where the terms *ṣalāt* (prayer) and *zakāt* occur together, the latter signifies "almsgiving."

Jesus went on to mention other noble attributes that God conferred on him. He made him kind to his mother, and He did not make him arrogant or wretched:

> And [has made me] kind to my mother, and has not made me arrogant or wretched (19.32).

Note the absence of any mention of a father.

The last words of baby Jesus that the Qur'an conveys to us are these:

> Peace is on me the day I was born, the day I shall die, and the day I shall be raised alive" (19.33).

We have already discussed the meaning of this verse when we discussed the following very similar verse about John (p. 81): "And peace is on him the day he was born, the day he dies, and the day he shall be raised alive" (19.15). The only difference between the two is that the words in verse 19.15 are uttered by God, whereas those in 19.33 are pronounced by Jesus.

Verses 19.23-33 are the only passages that talk about Jesus' birth. Verse 19.34 then stresses the verity of the information that the Qur'an gives about Jesus and his life:

> Such was Jesus son of Mary: [this is] the statement of the truth which they dispute (19.34).

Verse 19.35 then goes on to deny that God could take a son.

10.5. Birth Under A Palm Tree

The Qur'an states that Jesus was born under a palm tree. It also mentions the miracles of the newborn talking to his mother and the appearance of a rivulet beneath her and dates on the palm tree so Mary can drink and eat. A similar mention of Mary sitting under a palm tree and of a spring of water is found in the apocryphal Gospel of Pseudo-Matthew but, again, in a very different context. On the third day of the journey of Joseph, Mary, and Jesus to Egypt escaping the wrath of Herod, the following happened:

> While they were walking, that the blessed Mary was fatigued by the excessive heat of the sun in the desert; and seeing a palm tree, she said to Joseph: "Let me rest a little under the shade of this tree." Joseph therefore made haste, and led her to the palm, and made her come down from her beast. And as the blessed Mary was sitting there, she looked up to the foliage of the palm, and saw it full of fruit, and said to Joseph: "I wish it were possible to get some of the fruit of this palm." And Joseph said to her: "I wonder that you say this, when you see how high the palm tree is; and that you think of eating of its fruit. I am thinking more of the want of water, because the skins are now empty, and we have none wherewith to refresh ourselves and our cattle."
>
> Then the child Jesus, with a joyful countenance, reposing in the bosom of His mother, said to the palm: "O tree, bend your branches, and refresh my mother with your fruit." And immediately at these words the palm bent its top down to the very feet of the blessed Mary; and they gathered from it fruit, with which they were all refreshed. And

after they had gathered all its fruit, it remained bent down, waiting the order to rise from Him who had commanded it to stoop.

Then Jesus said to it: "Raise yourself, O palm tree, and be strong, and be the companion of my trees, which are in the paradise of my Father; and open from your roots a vein of water which has been hid in the earth, and let the waters flow, so that we may be satisfied from you." And it rose up immediately, and at its root there began to come forth a spring of water exceedingly clear and cool and sparkling. And when they saw the spring of water, they rejoiced with great joy, and were satisfied, themselves and all their cattle and their beasts. Wherefore they gave thanks to God. (PsMatt. 20)

The Arabic Gospel of the Infancy has a different account:

They went on to a city in which were several idols which, as soon as they came near to it, was turned into hills of sand. Hence they went to that sycamore tree, which is now called Matarea. And in Matarea the Lord Jesus caused a well to spring forth, in which St. Mary washed his coat. And a balsam is produced, or grows, in that country from the sweat which ran down there from the Lord Jesus. (AraIn. 8:8-11)

These two accounts represent another contextual difference between the Qur'an and Christian sources. The original account of Jesus' birth under a tree has been changed by the writers or/and copyists of the gospels.

It has been suggested that the Qur'anic account of the birth under the palm tree and the palm tree miracle in the Gospel of Pseudo-Matthew have originated from ancient sources. Let's examine the merits of these claims.

In his book *The Original Sources of Islam*, which was published one century ago, Biblicist William Tisdall speculated that the Qur'anic account of the birth of Jesus under a palm tree was taken from the birth story of Buddha in the *Nidanakatha Jatakam*. According to this story, when Maya was about to give birth to Buddha, she took her husband's permission to return to her father's house to deliver there. On her way to her home town, Maya passed by flowering sal trees. She wanted to enjoy the beauty of the grove, so she stepped down from her palanquin to walk among the trees:

She, having gone to the foot of a well-omened *Sal*-tree, became desirous of grasping a branch of the *Sal*-tree. The *Sal*-tree branch, having bent down like the end of a stick well softened with steam, came within the reach of the princess's hand. She, having stretched out her hand, seized the branch. ... Childbirth came upon her just as she stood, grasping the branch of the *Sal*-tree. (Quoted by Tisdall, 1905: 166)

When he made his claim, Tisdall probably was unaware of Greek sources that could also be claimed to be the origin of the Qur'anic statement that Jesus was born under a palm tree. This other alleged link was examined recently by Suleiman

Mourad in his study *From Hellenism to Christianity and Islam: The Origin of the Palm tree Story concerning Mary and Jesus in the Gospel of Pseudo-Matthew and the Qur'an*. He concludes, as the title of the paper suggests, that early Christians appropriated a Greek story, resulting in the variations of that story in the Qur'an and Pseudo-Matthew. The mythical story in question shows Leto, in desperation and trying to hide herself from the angry queen of Gods Hera, giving birth to Apollo under a palm tree on the Island of Delos. More popular versions of this myth talk about Leto giving birth to the twins Apollo and Artemis. The presence of a palm tree is all that the story of the Gospel of Pseudo-Matthew shares with the Greek myth, but Mourad speculates that this detail in the apocryphal gospel was at some point associated with Jesus' birth, and that it was later changed to be part of Jesus' childhood when the canonical account that Jesus was born in Bethlehem became accepted. He also suggests that the Christian account of the birth under a palm tree is probably the source of the Qur'anic story.

The myth of Leto's birth under a palm tree appears in many versions in Greek folklore as the story developed over the centuries. Mourad (2002: 209-210) has cited a number of versions of this Greek myth, with the following three date back to the 8th century BCE, the 6th-5th century BCE, and around 240 BCE, respectively:

> And as soon as Eilithyia the goddess of sore travail set foot on Delos, the pains of birth seized Leto, and she longed to bring forth; so she cast her arms about a palm tree and kneeled on the soft meadow while the earth laughed for joy beneath. Then the child leaped forth to the light, and all the goddesses raised a cry.

> Lord Phoebus, when the lady Leto gave you birth, gripping the palm-tree with her slender arms, you loveliest of the immortals, by the circle lake, fair Delos was pervaded end to end by an ambrosial fragrance, and the vast earth smiled, and the deep salty white-flecked main rejoiced.

> So didst thou speak, and gladly ceased from her [Leto's] grievous wandering and sat by the stream of Inopus, which the earth sends forth in deepest flood at the season when the Nile comes down in full torrent from the Aethiopian steep. And she loosed her girdle and leaned back her shoulders against the trunk of a palm tree, oppressed by grievous distress, and the sweat poured over her flesh like rain. And she spake in her weakness: "Why, child, dost thou weight down thy mother? There, dear child, is thine island floating on the sea. Be born, be born, my child, and gently issue from the womb."

The speculations that link the Qur'anic story to this Greek myth has a number of serious flaws:

① The underlying assumption of this hypothesis is that *giving birth under a tree*, which happened to be a palm tree in this case, is something that could not have occurred in reality, or at least was extremely rare. This is why the Qur'anic story is said to have been based on the Greek or Buddhist story. This assumption is simply incorrect and even absurd. Giving birth under a tree was a common experience in the past. Pregnant women who suddenly found themselves in labor while in travel or away from home had no other option but to find the nearest place that can provide them with shelter and privacy. This could be a house, cave, the shade of a tree, or any place that keeps away strangers in this very private circumstance.

The story of Jesus' birth in Christian sources also reflects this fact. Matthew implies that Mary was not traveling or away from her house when she gave birth, so there is no mention of the birth happening in an unusual or inconvenient place. He implies that she gave birth at home. Luke has a different story in which Mary found herself about to give birth while traveling. Unable to find a free room in an inn, she seems to have had to give birth in a barn, as Luke states that Mary laid her newborn in a manger. The Infancy Gospel of James and the Arabic Gospel of the Infancy also have Mary giving birth while traveling, but they claim that she had to give birth in a cave. Luke contradicts the two apocryphal gospels in its description of the place in which Jesus was born, but they all reflect a real-life situation which was not uncommon in the past where pregnant women were forced to give birth in very inconvenient places. Interestingly, Mary's laying of little Jesus in a manger is found in the Gospel of James also but the context is hiding Jesus from Herod who was seeking to kill him (InJam. 16:2).

Surely some of the ancient stories about giving birth under trees, such as the mythical Greek story of Leto, are fictional, but even these echoed a common experience in the ancient world. Women did give birth under trees before and after the time of Apollo's and other similar stories. Any attempt to link all such stories to each other is highly misguided and misleading.

In fact, giving birth under a tree is not even something that used to happen only in unusual circumstances. This has been a feature of Apache culture. Furthermore, this experience did not happen in the past only. Even in these days, some women do find themselves in situations where they are forced to give birth under trees. Pregnant women who were made refuges or destitute as a result of wars and disasters, as well as those who live in primitive societies, can find themselves having to give birth in inconvenient places, including under trees. This can be confirmed, for example, by people who had to leave their homes and live in temporary shelters or without shelter. In fact, this simple fact is as easy to confirm as doing a search on the internet for a phrase such as "birth under a tree"! Surely, no reasonable person can suggest that these recent and real stories from around the world of women who gave birth under trees were based on or inspired by a myth from ancient Greece or Nepal!

Significantly, the Qur'an tells us that Mary left her home after becoming pregnant and was alone when she suddenly found herself in labor. These circumstances can lead to giving birth under a tree, if no better place was available at the time:

> She conceived him, and she withdrew with him to a far place (19.22). And the pangs of childbirth drove her to the trunk of a palm tree. She said: "I wish I had died before this and had become something totally forgotten!" (19.23).

② The theme of giving birth under a palm tree is marginal and insignificant in all the stories concerned, so using it to link very dissimilar birth stories from different countries, traditions, and times to each other is speculative in the extreme. This is not really an attempt to understand history as much as create one! We examined earlier the attempt to link different stories to each other because they share the common theme of a virginal conception (§6.2.2). Although I pointed out serious problems with that attempt, its basic assumption is not inherently absurd, because a virginal conception is a genuinely supernatural and, accordingly, rare event. But using the theme of giving birth under a palm tree to do the same is ridiculous, as this is a relatively common and normal event.

Mourad fails to notice that the Qur'an does not present the fact that Mary gave birth under a tree as a miracle or something that distinguishes Jesus' birth from other births — although the tree itself was the subject of two miracles, with dates suddenly appearing on it and Mary being able to shake its trunk. Identifying the tree as palm also does not imply anything uniquely distinctive either. The palm tree is mentioned only twice in the Qur'an — both in the story of Jesus in Chapter 19 — and is not given any special distinction. The birth under a palm tree is not presented in the Qur'an as a special event. This is in line with the fact that having to deliver under a tree, whether palm or something else, is neither a paranormal nor unique experience.

Jesus was conceived miraculously, and immediately after birth he spoke and performed other wonders. These miracles are what distinguished Jesus' birth, not the fact that he was born under a palm tree. The Qur'an cannot be accused of borrowing this detail from any source that talks about a birth under a tree, because this is not considered paranormal or unique and is not given any special significance in the Qur'an. It is presented as a factual description of what happened when Mary found herself going into labor while alone and away from home — as happened and still happens to other women in similar situations. Using Mourad's flawed approach above, any story, Qur'anic or not, could be linked to any number of older stories by simply showing that a minor detail in the more recent story appears in those earlier narratives too!

There is a fundamental difference between linking Jesus' story of birth in the Qur'an to Apollo's and Buddha's stories and linking it to Pseudo-Matthew. The former attempt uses an insignificant and not uncommon detail to link very different stories. Conversely, the latter is very logical as both accounts talk about Jesus and share a lot of details, including specific miracles.

③ The Greek story went through so much change that resulted in many different versions, including the three cited earlier. Significantly, each of these versions has many more fundamental differences with the Qur'anic story than the slight similarity of the birth under a palm tree. The whole context is very different. Some versions have even that lone similarity with the Qur'anic story removed! Some add the olive tree to the palm tree, whereas in others the olive tree replaces the palm tree. Another version of the story reported by Plutarch (46 - after 119 CE) states that Leto delivered her child between two fountains, not two trees. In Egyptian mythology, the birth of Horus, who is identified with the Greek Apollo, does not take place under a tree. The 5th century BCE Greek historian Herodotus talks in *An Account of Egypt* about the story of Apollo where palm trees feature, but only as some of the trees on the island of Chemmis where events took place. The *birth under a palm tree* is not even a theme that is found in all versions of Apollo's story itself.

④ The attempt to link the Qur'anic story to older stories is another example of the second flaw of the secular approach (§1.1.2). Simply put, there is no evidence whatsoever that the Qur'an has borrowed its story from Greek sources. The illiterate Muhammad was accused of appropriating Jewish and Christian sources since his time, as the Qur'an itself states. But adding Greek mythology and Asian tradition to the massive list of sources that he is supposed to have had access to and known well enough to use and abuse to write the Qur'an is, relatively speaking, a modern invention. The following part of Mourad's conclusion shows clearly this flaw in his argument — that there is no evidence on the Qur'an's presumed appropriation of other sources:

> One cannot dismiss altogether the possibility that the version in Pseudo-Matthew was a different, unrelated, appropriation of Apollo's birth story unconnected to the one found in the Qur'an. Yet the assumption that both must have depended upon a common source is more congruent with the evidence in hand, especially due to the major similarity between them — the palm tree miracle — which is not present in any of the known versions of Apollo's myth. Indeed, it seems unlikely that the two versions are unrelated. On the other hand, one cannot point to a precise textual source for the Qur'anic and Pseudo-Matthew versions of the tale; most probably it stems,

like the many other adaptations from the Greco-Roman heritage, from popular lore. (Mourad, 2002: 216)

This is not actually a conclusion, even though it is presented as such. It is the very assumption that Mourad set out to prove. A perfectly valid possibility, which Mourad does not consider, is that the story that links the palm tree to Jesus' birth is actually more historical than the contradictory birth accounts in the canonical Gospels.

The Greek and Asian stories do not need to be linked to each other. Both could have been developed separately. The appearance of the theme of giving birth under a tree in both traditions is simply reflective of the commonality of this experience. Naturally, one would expect stories of births under trees from different locations to report different trees and have different details.

From the Qur'anic perspective, the account in Pseudo-Matthew, which places the palm tree story in Jesus' childhood and includes many other differences with the Qur'anic account, represents an apocryphal contextual displacement of the original, accurate account of this story, which is found in the Qur'an. The Pseudo-Matthew's story could have developed from older Christian sources, and originally the Injīl, that covered Jesus' birth. It is also possible that the Pseudo-Matthew account was developed from the Qur'anic story, as that gospel is believed to have been written one or two centuries after the Qur'an. However, I think this possibility is unlikely. The Arabic Gospel of the Infancy's story of Jesus causing a well to spring is another form of changing the original story.

Finally, I would like to raise a question about whether there is any connection between the fact that Jesus was born under a palm tree and the Christian tradition of using Christmas trees to celebrate Jesus' birth. The modern history of this tradition from the 16th century or so is relatively known. It originated in western Germany and then spread to other Christian countries. But there is almost nothing known about the origin and older history of the Christmas tree. It is tempting to link this tradition and the related practice of placing presents under the tree with the Qur'anic story of the birth of Jesus, but in the absence of any evidence, this remains speculative.

10.6. Jesus' Date of Birth

The Qur'an does not tell us when Jesus was born, but Christian sources contain indirect references to Jesus' date of birth. These can be categorized into two distinct groups each of which implies a different date. At best, one of the two references is correct; at worst, both are wrong. In any case, the exact year of birth cannot be identified with any certainty. We will also look quickly at the end of this section to the role of the "star of Bethlehem" in dating the birth of Jesus.

The **first** group of references links Jesus' birth to King Herod's reign. This is found in Matthew and the apocryphal gospels of the Arabic Gospel of the Infancy, the Infancy Gospel of James, and Pseudo-Matthew. All four books mention Herod's slaughter of infants shortly after Jesus' birth. According to Matthew, in order to ensure Jesus' death, Herod killed all the male children of Bethlehem and it's vicinity who were two years or younger (Matt. 2:16). This implies that Jesus could have been as old as two years when Herod ordered that massacre. Having been warned by an angel of the imminent massacre, Joseph took Jesus and Mary and fled to Egypt before the massacre took place. When Herod died, Joseph, Mary and Jesus returned from Egypt. Before and after his flight to Egypt, Jesus is described as a "young boy" (Matt. 2:14, 2:21).

There is no doubt that the Herod that these sources mention is Herod the Great who ruled Judea and was given the title "King of the Jews" by the Romans. His identity is confirmed in a number of ways, including the names of his sons. After Herod's death, Emperor Augustus divided his kingdom into three parts among his surviving sons, none of whom inherited the royal title. Given larger lands than his brothers, Herod Archelaus was appointed ethnarch of central and southern Palestine — Samaria, Judea, and Idumea — until he was removed by Augustus in 6 CE because of his unpopularity. His brother Herod Antipas was made tetrarch of Galilee and Perea, east of the Jordan River, but was also dismissed and exiled in 39 CE by Emperor Gaius Caesar Caligula. Herod Philip, Herod's third son and Archelaus and Antipas' half brother, was appointed tetrarch of areas to the east and north of Galilee and he remained in this position until he died in 34 CE.

All three sons are mentioned in the Gospels. Matthew (2:22) states that Archelaus ruled Judea after his father. He is also mentioned in apocryphal writings (AraIn 8:15). Antipas appears as "Herod the tetrarch" in Matthew (14:1) and as "tetrarch of Galilee" in Luke (3:1). Philip is mentioned in that same passage by Luke and is introduced as "tetrarch of the region of Iturea and Trachonitis." There is, therefore, no ambiguity about the identity of the king of Judea when Jesus was born.

Herod the Great came to power around 40 BCE, although he did not rule actually until three years later. He died after an illness before the spring of 4 BCE. This means that Jesus must have been born in 4 BCE or before. Given that, according to Matthew, Herod killed infants who were two years or younger, Jesus could have been born as early as around 6 BCE.

Luke states that during Herod's reign, Zechariah was told by an angel about the birth of his son John. The latter was born shortly before Jesus, so Luke also implies that Jesus must have been born in the days of Herod. However, as Luke ignores completely the massacre, Jesus could have been born even earlier than 6 BCE during Herod's rule.

The **second** group of indirect references to Jesus' date of birth links it to a census ordered by Quirinius when he was governor of Syria. This link is found in Luke and, with some variations, in apocryphal sources (AraIn. 1:4-5; InJam. 12:1-5; PsMatt. 13):

> Now in those days a decree went out from Caesar Augustus to register all the empire for taxes. This was the first registration, taken when Quirinius was governor of Syria. Everyone went to his own town to be registered. So Joseph also went up from the town of Nazareth in Galilee to Judea, to the city of David called Bethlehem, because he was of the house and family line of David. He went to be registered with Mary, who was promised in marriage to him, and who was expecting a child. While they were there, the time came for her to deliver her child. And she gave birth to her first-born son and wrapped him in strips of cloth and laid him in a manger, because there was no place for them in the inn. (Luke 2:1-7)

This is how Josephus documented Quirinius' census:

> Now Quirinius, a Roman senator, and one who had gone through other magistracies, and had passed through them till he had been consul, and one who, on other accounts, was of great dignity, came at this time into Syria, with a few others, being sent by Caesar to be a judge of that nation, and to take an account of their substance. Coponius also, a man of the equestrian order, was sent together with him, to have the supreme power over the Jews. Moreover, Quirinius came himself into Judea, which was now added to the province of Syria, to take an account of their substance, and to dispose of Archelaus's money. (Josephus, *Jewish Antiquities*, 18.1.1)

Emperor Augustus ruled from 27 BCE to 14 CE — which includes Herod's last 23 year. So Luke's placing of Jesus' birth during Augustus' reign and Matthew's dating of the birth to Herod's last years are not contradictory. It is a problem, however, to suggest that Jesus was born during the legateship of Publius Sulpicius Quirinius in Syria, as he held office from 6 CE onward. This date cannot be reconciled with the New Testament's other claim that Jesus was born during Herod's reign as the latter died about a decade earlier in 4 BCE. If we take into consideration Matthew's account of the massacre and its implication that Jesus could have been born two years before Herod's death, then the gap between the two suggested dates becomes even wider. Luke, the Arabic Gospel of the Infancy, the Infancy Gospel of James, and Pseudo Matthew all indicate that Jesus was born during Herod's time and at the time of the census — a historical impossibility.

Could Quirinius have governed Syria earlier during Herod's last years or shortly after his death and that Luke is actually talking about that legateship? Josephus allows us to construct the chronology of the legates of Syria from 10 BEC to Quirinius' legateship: M. Titius (ca. 10 BCE), S. Sentius Saturninus (9-6 BCE), Quintilius Varus (6-4 BCE or later), Gaius Caesar (1 BCE – ca. 4 CE), L. Volusius Saturninus (4-5 CE), and Quirinius (6 CE). This chronology seems to allow two possible dates for an earlier governorship by Quirinius, one before Titius, i.e. before 10 BCE, and the other between Varus and Gaius Caesar, i.e. between 1 and 4 BCE. However, Quirinius' tenure is well documented that we can rule both possibilities out with certainty (Brown, 1993: 550).

Placing Jesus' birth during Quirinius' governorship of Syria is irreconcilable with the claim that he was born under Herod's rule, but it has other historical problems:

① There was no levy of taxation that covered "all the world," i.e. the whole empire, in Augustus' time. In his comprehensive analysis of the census story in Luke, Brown has also pointed out that given "the different legal statuses of provinces and client kingdoms, a sweeping universal edict seems most unlikely" (Brown, 1993: 549).

② Brown (1993: 549) notes that Roman taxation censuses did not require sending people back to their place of origin to enroll. The Roman practice was to register people where they lived or in the nearby principal city where the tax would be collected. Theissen and Merz (1999: 154) note that only in Egypt people had to travel to their home towns. They also add that it was not necessary for a woman to appear before officials, as she would be represented by her father or husband. The scene in Luke of a heavily pregnant woman making an 85 mile journey from Nazareth to Bethlehem seems to have been introduced to explain how Jesus was born in Bethlehem (Miller, 2003: 57).

③ While Quirinius conducted a local census in 6-7 CE after the incorporation of Judea into Syria, this census could not have had any effect on those living in Galilee. The latter was a tetrarchy under the rule of Herod Antipas, not under Quirinius' direct supervision. Unlike Judea, Galilee was independent, not a Roman province. Joseph would not have needed to leave Galilee and go to Judea (Brown, 1993: 549-550). Sanders (1995: 87) has noted that as ancient census takers were interested in connecting lands and landowners for tax purposes, it was the census takers not the tax payers who traveled.

Rhys has also this to say about the supposed journey to Bethlehem:

> Such a journey would really be no more necessary than it is now for an English-born Canadian to return to the home of his ancestors whenever a census is taken in England. Joseph would have been under no compulsion, legal or moral, to undertake the journey, and still less so would his future wife in a country and at a time when women counted for nothing. The census was believed to be taken for purposes of taxation (whence the word "tax" in the Gospel), and would therefore be unlikely to attract those who were not compelled to attend. (Rhys, 1922: 95)

Rhys believes that this journey is the equivalent of the journey to Egypt in the Gospel of Matthew.

One way to reconcile the two different datings of Jesus' birth is to suggest that the mention of Quirinius is a mistake and that the Christian writers meant another taxation census that was taken during the reign of Herod the Great. There are at least two problems with this suggestion. **First**, Herod was a client king who collected his taxes with his own tax collectors and paid tribute to Rome. The Romans did not use a census to collect taxes in his kingdom. Quirinius' census took place because Herod's successor on Judea, his son Archelaus, was deposed and Judea was put under direct Roman government and taxation (Brown, 1993: 551). **Second**, the imposition of taxes by Rome on the Jews under Herod would have caused a Jewish revolt, as happened when Quirinius did his census, and there is no record of such a revolt during Herod's reign.

Interestingly, Acts (5:37) mentions a rebellion during a census that is accepted to be the same census of the Gospel of Luke, mainly because Luke and Acts are thought to have been written by the same person. But Luke's mention of the census in Acts has another serious historical problem, as it places a revolt leader called Judas of Galilee after another known as Theudas, when in fact the latter lived 40 years after the former:

> For some time ago Theudas rose up, claiming to be somebody, and about four hundred men joined him. He was killed, and all who followed him were dispersed and nothing came of it. After him Judas the Galilean arose in the days of the census, and incited people to follow him in revolt. He too was killed, and all who followed him were scattered. (Acts 5:36-37)

Luke's dating of the birth of Jesus is not only inconsistent and in contradiction with Matthew's dating of the same event, but his story of the census has a number of historical mistakes.

Tertullian, a 2nd-3rd century Christian writer, wrote in *Against Marcion* (4.19) about a census during the reign of Augustus that was taken in Judea by Sentius Satuninus (9-6 BCE) in which census officials might have enquired about Jesus' ancestry. This has been seen by some as either indicating that Tertullian had a different version of Luke, or that he was correcting Luke. Tertullian's statement lacks evidence, and while it provides another possible dating for Jesus' birth under Herod's rule, it clearly faults Luke. Other historians have rejected the view that Tertullian intended to correct Luke.

In addition to its historical problems, Luke's story of the census has details that confirm that it is fanciful and impossible to have occurred as described. These have been very well expressed by Sanders in his brilliant book *The Historical Figure of Jesus*:

According to Luke's own genealogy (3.23-38), David had lived forty-two generations before Joseph. Why should Joseph have had to register in the town of one of his ancestors forty-two generations earlier? What was Augustus — the most rational of Caesars — thinking of? The entirety of the Roman empire would have been uprooted by such a decree. Besides, how would any given man know where to go? No one could trace his genealogy for forty-two generations, but if he could, he would find that he had millions of ancestors (one million is passed at the twentieth generation). Further, David doubtless had tens of thousands of descendants who were alive at the time. Could they all identify themselves? If so, how would they all register in a little village? (Sanders, 1995: 86)

Many scholars think that Luke introduced the story of census to make sure that Jesus was born in Bethlehem, in order to assert the conviction that he was the descendant of David who was expected to come to save Israel, the Messiah. Luke may have been aware of a census that was taken by Quirinius which he intentionally and crudely confused with his other details about the birth of Jesus.

As I noted earlier, variations of the story of the census appear in a number of different apocryphal gospels. The Arabic Gospel of the Infancy states that Augustus issued a decree demanding that every person should be taxed in their country, and it dates the census to "the three hundred and ninth year of the era of Alexander" (AraIn. 1:4), which is equivalent to 2 BCE. The Infancy Gospel of James claims that the census targeted, inexplicably, all the Jews who came from Bethlehem in Judea (InJam. 12:1). The Gospel of Pseudo-Matthew also states that August published a decree requiring that every person must be enrolled in his native place (PsMatt. 13).

Luke provides us with another two passages that, when considered together, may look usable for dating Jesus' birth. The first is his dating of the appearance of John the Baptist to "the fifteenth year of the reign of Tiberius Caesar, when Pontius Pilate was governor of Judea, and Herod was tetrarch of Galilee, and his brother Philip was tetrarch of the region of Iturea and Trachonitis, and Lysanias was tetrarch of Abilene" (Luke 3:1). In the second, he states that Jesus was "about thirty years old" (Luke 3:23) when he was baptized.

It is not clear whether Luke' first statement considered the three years in which Tiberius was co-regent with his stepfather Augustus before he became the sole emperor after Augustus' death in 14 CE. Theissen and Merz (1999: 156) cite one study that gives 16 different possible datings of the 15th year of Tiberius, with some datings differing by as much as a few years. Considering different calendars, they conclude that Tiberius' 15th year in Luke could mean any date from January 26 to April 30 CE.

The second statement is also imprecise as it talks about Jesus being "about" 30 years old. Theissen and Merz (1999: 156) also note that other Biblical figures are also said to have begun their public work in the age of 30: Joseph attained prominence in Egypt when he was 30 (Gen. 41:46), David was 30 years old when he became king (2 Sam. 5:4), and Ezekiel was also 30 when he started seeing visions (Ezek. 1:1). They wonder whether Luke's mention of the age of 30 is simply influenced by other uses of this age in the Old Testament.

If Jesus was exactly 30 in Tiberius' 15th year then he could have been born between 5 and 1 BCE. Only the first 14 months or so of this range fall during the reign of Herod the Great. If Jesus was over or below 30, then clearly this range would change.

John has also the following passage which, in combination with Luke's reference, could be used to calculate, although even more imprecisely, Jesus' date of birth:

> So then the Jewish leaders responded, "What sign can you show us, since you are doing these things?" Jesus replied, "Destroy this temple and in three days I will raise it up again." Then the Jewish leaders said to him, "This temple has been under construction for forty-six years, and are you going to raise it up in three days?" (John 2:18-20)

In his book *Jewish Antiquities* (15.11.1), the historian Josephus says that Herod began the building of the temple in his 18th year, but in the *Jewish War* (1.21.1) he says that Herod rebuilt the temple in the 15th year of his reign. These two different dates correspond to 20-19 and 23-22 BCE, respectively — counting from the start of Herod's actual reign in 37 BCE. There is little value in a detailed discussion of which date is more accurate or how the two dates may be reconciled. If we presume that Herod built the temple in 20-19 BCE, then this places the Passover in which the exchanges above between Jesus and the Jews leaders took place in the spring of 27 or 28 CE. Now, John indicates that this Passover was shortly after John the Baptist met Jesus, although it is not clear exactly how long after the encounter. If we then link these calculations with Luke's claim that Jesus was 30 when he met John, we can conclude that Jesus was born in 4 or 3 BCE.

Brown has also noted that, leaving aside the question of their historical accuracy, early Church writers placed the date of Jesus' birth before 1 BCE. Tertullian dates it to the 28th year after the death of Cleopatra, that is 2 BCE. Clement of Alexandria's mention of 194 years before the death of the Roman emperor Commodus means 2 BCE. Eusebius says Jesus was born in Augustus' 42nd year, that is 3-1 BCE (Brown, 1993: 548).

The star that allegedly marked Jesus' birth according to Matthew has also been used to date Jesus' birth. This star has been identified with a number of different astronomical phenomena that were visible around the presumed birth of Jesus in the few years before Herod's death. At least as early as the 13th century this star was identified with the triple conjunction of Jupiter and Saturn in Pisces of 7 BCE. The entry for the year 1285 in the Annals of the Abbey of Worcester states the following:

> In the same year, Saturn and Jupiter were in conjunction in Aquarius [sic], which has not happened since the Incarnation, nor, as calculated by the astronomers will it happen again for a long time. (Luard, 1869)

Clark, Parkinson, and Stephenson (1977) have shown that none of the three conjunctions was spectacular and the two planets did not come close enough to form what appears as a single bright object. After scanning records of astronomical observation from the Far East between 10 BCE and 13 CE, these astronomers put forward an alternative possibility. They identified the star of Bethlehem with a Chinese sighting of a supernova in 5 BCE. Another record of a sighting in 4 BCE of what might have been a comet was considered to be unreliable.

To sum up, Christian sources suggest conflicting dates for Jesus' birth. While Matthew states and Luke implies that Jesus was born during Herod's reign, Luke and apocryphal gospels suggest that he was born at the time of Quirinius' census, which took place a decade after Herod's death. Unfortunately, while there is no reason to reject Matthew's claim that Jesus was born during the reign of Herod, his account also suffers from historical mistakes, as we shall see in the next chapter. Jesus was probably born a few years before the start of the first millennium, but any attempt at an exact dating is bound to be highly speculative.

Finally, I should point out that the Christian celebration of Jesus' birth on the 25th of December has nothing to do with Jesus' birthday. In the first two centuries of their history Christians did not celebrate birthdays, not even of martyrs. Their vehement objection can be seen in the critical comments of Church fathers of the pagan custom of celebrating birthdays. The 25th of December was first identified as the birthday of Jesus in as late as 221 CE by the historian Africanus and was being celebrated in Rome by 354 CE. It is commonly believed that the Catholic Church chose this date to celebrate Jesus' birth because it was a day of pagan celebration of the sun god, thus making it easier for pagans to embrace Christianity. The Orthodox Armenian Church is the only ancient Church that continued to celebrate Jesus' birthday on the 6th of January, the celebration date of Epiphany or the manifestation of Jesus' divinity, which occurred at his baptism.

11

Massacre of Truth

Matthew and apocryphal gospels talk about a plot by Herod to kill the newborn Jesus. The attempt at Jesus' life failed, as the he was smuggled out of the country, but other innocent infants were murdered. This massacre, which is missing from Luke's account of Jesus' infancy, is implicitly rejected by the Qur'an.

There are also problems in the Christian account of the massacre that suggest that the alleged massacre never took place. Additionally, there are good reasons to believe that had such a massacre occurred, the Jewish historian Josephus would have reported it in his detailed history of Herod.

The Christian unhistorical accounts of the massacre are likely to have been modeled on Pharaoh's historical massacre of Jewish young boys at the time of Moses' birth.

11.1. Herod's Massacre in Christian Sources

Of the four canonical Gospels, only Matthew mentions the Herodian massacre. This is how these events are described by the Evangelist:

> After Jesus was born in Bethlehem in Judea, in the time of King Herod, wise men from the East came to Jerusalem saying, "Where is the one who is born king of the Jews? For we saw his star when it rose and have come to worship him." When King Herod heard this he was alarmed, and all Jerusalem with him. After assembling all the chief priests and experts in the law, he asked them where the Christ was to be born. "In Bethlehem of Judea," they said, "for it is written this way by the prophet: 'And you, Bethlehem, in the land of Judah, are in no way least among the rulers of Judah, for out of you will come a ruler who will shepherd my people Israel.'"
>
> Then Herod privately summoned the wise men and determined from them when the star had appeared. He sent them to Bethlehem and said, "Go and look carefully for the child. When you find him, inform me so that I can go and worship him as well." After listening to the king they left, and once again the star they saw when it rose led them until it stopped above the place where the child was. When they saw the star they shouted joyfully. As they came into the house and saw the child with Mary his mother, they bowed down and worshiped him. They opened their treasure boxes and gave him gifts of gold, frankincense, and myrrh. After being warned in a dream not to return to Herod, they went back by another route to their own country.
>
> After they had gone, an angel of the Lord appeared to Joseph in a dream and said, "Get up, take the child and his mother and flee to Egypt, and stay there until I tell you, for Herod is going to look for the child to kill him." Then he got up, took the child and his mother during the night, and went to Egypt. He stayed there until Herod died. In this

way what was spoken by the Lord through the prophet was fulfilled: "I called my Son out of Egypt."

When Herod saw that he had been tricked by the wise men, he became enraged. He sent men to kill all the children in Bethlehem and throughout the surrounding region from the age of two and under, according to the time he had learned from the wise men. Then what was spoken by Jeremiah the prophet was fulfilled: "A voice was heard in Ramah, weeping and loud wailing, Rachel weeping for her children, and she did not want to be comforted, because they were gone."

After Herod had died, an angel of the Lord appeared in a dream to Joseph in Egypt saying, "Get up, take the child and his mother, and go to the land of Israel, for those who were seeking the child's life are dead." So he got up and took the child and his mother and returned to the land of Israel. But when he heard that Archelaus was reigning over Judea in place of his father Herod, he was afraid to go there. After being warned in a dream, he went to the regions of Galilee. He came to a town called Nazareth and lived there. Then what had been spoken by the prophets was fulfilled, that Jesus would be called a Nazarene. (Matt. 2:1-23)

Another, very similar account is given in the Gospel of Pseudo-Matthew:

And when the second year was past, Magi came from the east to Jerusalem, bringing great gifts. And they made strict inquiry of the Jews, saying: "Where is the king who has been born to you? For we have seen his star in the east, and have come to worship him." And word of this came to King Herod, and so alarmed him that he called together the scribes and the Pharisees, and the teachers of the people, asking of them where the prophets had foretold that Christ should be born. And they said: "In Bethlehem of Judah. For it is written: 'And you Bethlehem, in the land of Judah, are by no means the least among the princes of Judah; for out of you shall come forth a Leader who shall rule my people Israel.'"

Then King Herod summoned the magi to him, and strictly inquired of them when the star appeared to them. Then, sending them to Bethlehem, he said: "Go and make strict inquiry about the child; and when you have found him, bring me word again, that I may come and worship him also."

And while the magi were going on their way, there appeared to them the star, which was, as it were, a guide to them, going before them until they came to where the child was. And when the magi saw the star, they rejoiced with great joy; and going into the house, they saw the child Jesus sitting in His mother's lap. Then they opened their treasures, and presented great gifts to the blessed Mary and Joseph. And to the child Himself they offered each of them a piece of gold. And likewise one gave gold, another frankincense, and the third myrrh.

And when they were going to return to King Herod, they were warned by an angel in their sleep not to go back to Herod; and they returned to their own country by another road.

And when Herod saw that he had been made sport of by the magi, his heart swelled with rage, and he sent through all the roads, wishing to seize them and put them to death. But when he could not find them at all; he sent anew to Bethlehem and all its borders, and slew all the male children whom he found of two years old and under, according to the time that he had ascertained from the magi.

Now the day before this was done Joseph was warned in his sleep by the angel of the Lord, who said to him: "Take Mary and the child, and go into Egypt by the way of the desert." And Joseph went according to the saying of the angel. (PsMatt. 16-17)

The angel later told Joseph that those who tried to kill Jesus were dead and commanded him to go back to Judea.

In the apocryphal Infancy Gospel of James, Joseph is not warned by an angel to leave to Egypt, but it is Mary who heard about the planned killing of the children:

Then Joseph was preparing to go away, because there arose a great disorder in Bethlehem by the coming of some wise men from the east, who said, "Where is the King of the Jews born? For we have seen his star in the east, and have come to worship him." When Herod heard this, he was exceedingly troubled, and sent messengers to the wise men, and to the priests, and enquired of them in the town-hall, and said to them, "Where have you it written concerning Christ the king, or where should he be born?" Then they say to him, "In Bethlehem of Judea; for thus it is written: 'And you Bethlehem in the land of Judah, are not the least among the princes of Judah, for out of you shall come a ruler, who shall rule my people Israel.'"

And having sent away the chief priests, he enquired of the wise men in the town-hall, and said to them, "What sign was it you saw concerning the king that is born?" They answered him, "We saw an extraordinary large star shining among the stars of heaven, and so outshined all the other stars, as that they became not visible, and we knew thereby that a great king was born in Israel, and therefore we have come to worship him." Then said Herod to them, "Go and make diligent inquiry; and if you find the child, bring me word again, that I may come and worship him also."

So the wise men went forth, and behold, the star which they saw in the east went before them, till it came and stood over the cave where the young child was with Mary his mother. Then they brought forth out of their treasures, and offered to him gold and frankincense, and myrrh. And being warned in a dream by an angel, that they should not return to Herod through Judea, they departed into their own country by another way.

Then Herod perceiving that he was mocked by the wise men, and being very angry, commanded certain men to go and to kill all the children that were in Bethlehem, from two years old and under. But Mary hearing that the children were to be killed, being under much fear, took the child, and wrapped him up in swaddling clothes, and laid him in an ox manger, because there was no room for them in the inn. (InJam. 15:1-16:2)

This is the last passage in the Infancy Gospel of James about Jesus as the rest of chapter 16 focuses on the threat to John the Baptists' life and the killing of his father Zechariah who was accused of hiding his son. Interestingly, this gospel ends with a mention of the appointment of Simeon as Zechariah' successor:

And Simeon and the other priests cast lots, and the lot fell upon Simeon. For he had been assured by the Holy Spirit, that he should not die, till he had seen Christ come in the flesh. (InJam. 16:27-28)

This is the same "righteous and devout" Simeon whom Luke says had been told by the Holy Spirit that he "would not die before he had seen the Lord's Christ," although Luke does not describe him as a priest, but simply a "man in Jerusalem" (Luke 2:25). The Infancy Gospel of James seems to suggest, as Luke does, that there was no flight to Egypt.

The Arabic Gospel of the Infancy also mentions the massacre. Like the other sources, it tells us that Jesus was born in Bethlehem when Herod was king, and that wise men came to worship him and offer to him their gifts (AraIn. 3:1). After giving details about the meeting and the wise men's return journey, this gospel goes on to tell us about what Herod did when he realized that the wise men would not return to him — although it contains no mention of any meeting that Herod had had with the wise men. Here also the massacre is mentioned, although the victims are identified as "infants" only, with no reference to them being two years old and under. These are excerpts relevant to our present subject:

Now Herod perceiving that the wise men did delay and not return to him, called together the priests and wise men, and said, "Tell me in what place the Christ should be born." And when they replied, "In Bethlehem, a city of Judea," he began to contrive in his own mind the death of the Lord Jesus Christ. But an angel of the Lord appeared to Joseph in his sleep, and said, "Arise, take the child and his mother, and go into Egypt as soon as the cock crows." So he arose, and went. (AraIn. 4:1-3)

Now Joseph and Mary when they heard that the idol was fallen down and destroyed were seized with fear and, trembling, and said, "When we were in the land of Israel, Herod, intending to kill Jesus, slew for that purpose all the infants at Bethlehem, and that neighbourhood." (AraIn. 5:1)

At the end of three years he returned out of Egypt, and when he came near to Judea, Joseph was afraid to enter; for hearing that Herod was dead, and that Archelaus his son reigned in his stead, he was afraid. And when he went to Judea, an angel of God appeared to him, and said, "O Joseph go into the city of Nazareth, and abide there." (AraIn. 8:14-16)

The story of Herod's plan and massacre is very similar, and in some parts identical, in Matthew and the three apocryphal gospels.

11.2. The Non-historicity of Herod's Massacre According to the Qur'an

Unlike Christian sources, the Qur'an does not mention any massacre targeting the life of little Jesus. This may be explained by the fact that the Qur'an gives only limited details about Jesus' life, so the massacre is one of those episodes that the Qur'an ignored for one reason or another. A completely different view is that the Qur'an implies that the said massacre never took place. It may be argued that this view is based on the unreliable approach of negative evidence — that is denying the occurrence of an event only because it is not mentioned — but this is not the case. There are very strong arguments supporting the view that had the massacre taken place the Qur'an would have mentioned it:

① The Qur'an talks about a number of favors that God conferred on Jesus, including miracles that are not mentioned in the canonical Gospels, so it sounds natural that the Qur'an would have mentioned the massacre and God's role in protecting Jesus, if it did really happen:

> Lo! When Allah said: "O Jesus son of Mary! Remember My favor on you and on your mother, that I have supported you with the Spirit of Holiness, [making you] speak to people in the cradle and when middle-aged; and that I taught you the Book, Wisdom, the Torah, and the Injīl; and that you create out of clay the figures of birds by My permission, then you breath into them and they become birds by My permission, and heal the blind person and the albino by My permission; and that you raise the dead by My permission; and that I withheld the Children of Israel from you when you came to them with clear proofs, but those who disbelieved among them said: 'This is nothing but clear magic'" (5.110).

There are two particularly interesting observations about this verse. **First**, it lists favors that God granted to Jesus not only in his adulthood, but also when he was an *infant in the cradle*. **Second**, it confirms that God did intervene to *protect the adult miracle performer from the non-believing Israelites* who accused him of practicing magic. If God had intervened to protect Jesus in his infancy against Herod's alleged plot He would have mentioned that. That would have been even a bigger miracle than protecting Jesus when he became a young man. Such a miracle would have merited a mention along with the miracles above.

② The Qur'an does mention more than once that God rescued Moses in his infancy from being killed by Pharaoh:

> And We inspired Moses' mother: "Suckle him, and when you fear for his safety, cast him into the river and fear not nor grieve; We shall bring him back to you and shall make him one of the messengers" (28.7).

And We have [thus] conferred a favor on you [O Moses!] again (20.37). [The first was] when We revealed to your mother that which is revealed (20.38). Saying: "Put him into a coffin, then cast it down into the river, then the river shall throw him onshore; someone who is an enemy to Me and an enemy to him shall take him up"; and I cast down upon you love from Me, and so that you be brought up according to My will (20.39).

The Qur'an's double mention of this event, which is very similar to what Matthew and apocryphal gospels allege to have happened to Jesus, is another confirmation that had Jesus' life come under threat from a Herodian massacre the Qur'an would have mentioned it. As in verses 20.37-39 in which God reminds Moses of His favors to him, in verse 5.110 God reminds Jesus of favors that He conferred on him. Significantly, while the former verses mention how God rescued baby Moses, the favors mentioned in 5.110 do not include the rescuing of little Jesus from a massacre. Why would the Qur'an not mention the alleged massacre of the innocent babies which is supposed to have targeted Jesus' life like it recounts the danger to Moses' life if that was a real event?

The Qur'an also mentions the killing of Israelite males and Pharaoh's intention to kill Moses, both of which happened after God sent Moses to Pharaoh:

And the chiefs of Pharaoh's people said: "Would you leave Moses and his people to cause corruption in the land and forsake you and your gods?" He said: "We will kill their sons and spare their women, and surely we have power over them" (7.127).

So when he [Moses] brought to them [Pharaoh and his people] the truth from Us, they said: "Kill the sons of those who have believed with him and spare their women"; and the scheming of the disbelievers will only be in vain (40.25). And Pharaoh said: "Let me kill Moses and let him call upon his Lord; I fear that he will change your religion or cause corruption in the land" (40.26).

Pharaoh's killing of Israelite males when Moses was an infant and later when he was an adult and his plan to kill Moses himself are all events that the Qur'an considers worth mentioning. Similarly, any attempt to kill Jesus when an infant would have been reported by the Qur'an.

③ The following verses make it clear that the birth of the miraculous baby Jesus became known to people almost immediately after his birth:

Then she brought him to her people, carrying him. They said: "O Mary! You have come up with a grave thing (19.27). O sister of Aaron! Your father was not a bad man, and your mother was not an unchaste woman" (19.28). Then she pointed to him. They said: "How can we talk to one who is a child in the cradle?" (19.29). He said: "I am Allah's servant. He has given me the Book and has appointed me a prophet (19.30). He has made me blessed wherever I may be. He has enjoined upon me prayer and almsgiving so long as I remain alive (19.31). And [has made me] kind to my mother, and has not made me arrogant or wretched (19.32). Peace is on me the day I was born, the day I shall die, and the day I shall be raised alive" (19.33).

If Herod wanted to kill Jesus, he could have identified him very easily, and he would not have needed to kill numerous infants in order to ensure his death. This miraculous baby would have become well known to at least all of the people of his town — something that rejects the implication of the Christian account of the massacre that Herod and his soldiers could not identify Jesus.

These three observations confirm that the absence of any mention in the Qur'an of Herod's alleged attempt to kill Jesus by mass slaughtering of children cannot be due to the Qur'an overlooking this event for one reason or another. They indicate that, contrary to Christian sources, the Qur'an denies the occurrence of this massacre.

11.3. A Massacre That Never Was

In the previous section, we concluded that the Qur'an rejects the claims of Christian sources that Herod committed a massacre of infants in order to kill Jesus. I will now consider other arguments that strongly support the Qur'an's statement on this issue. I will start with arguments based on the New Testament and then consider those based on the writings of Josephus and history.

11.3.1. The Scriptural Arguments

There are three main arguments that undermine the credibility of Matthew's account of the massacre:

① Although the killing of the male infants and the rescue of Jesus would have been major events in his life story, Matthew is the only canonical Gospel that mentions them! With respect to Mark and John, I have already discussed the problems that are represented by their neglect of the whole of Jesus' infancy and childhood and the implications of their specific failure to mention the miracle of the virginal conception (§6.2.1.1). The same arguments can be made about the absence of any mention of Herod's massacre in their Gospels. The two Evangelists either had not heard of this story or did not believe it. These possibilities fault either Mark and John or Matthew, respectively.

The significance of Luke's omission of the massacre cannot be exaggerated, because this particular Evangelist describes in considerable detail the circumstances that surrounded the birth of Jesus and also refers to Herod (Luke 1:5). He mentions, for instance, the census that took place just before Jesus' birth (Luke 2:1-2). Also, Luke stresses in the first passage of his Gospel that he had good knowledge of Jesus' history, yet he makes no mention of the massacre:

> Now many have undertaken to compile an account of the things that have been fulfilled among us, like the accounts passed on to us by those who were eyewitnesses and servants of the word from the beginning. So it seemed good to me as well, because I have followed all things carefully from the beginning, to write an orderly account for you, most excellent Theophilus, so that you may know for certain the things you were taught. (Luke 1:1-4)

The mention of this highly important event by Matthew and its omission by Luke represent an inconsistency between the two books and raise questions about the credibility of at least one of them. Luke either did not know about the massacre or he knew about it but did not find the story credible. Let's discuss these two possibilities, starting with the latter.

It is difficult to understand why Luke, having related miracles and various details about Jesus' life, would consider any reports about the supposed divine rescue of Jesus from Herod's plot lacking in credibility. After all, the event itself stresses Jesus' special status, and it does that in a unique and impressive way. It is true that his infancy narrative is very different from Matthew's, but he could have still accommodated the account of the massacre by changing some details. It sounds far more likely that Luke was simply unaware of this event.

This second possibility can accommodate two different scenarios. **First**, the massacre is historical but Luke had not heard of it. The problem with this explanation, in addition to its conflict with Luke's claim to detailed knowledge of the Jesus' life, is that the killing of all boys younger than two years old in Bethlehem and its vicinity would have been a major catastrophe that would have lived for centuries in people's memory. Additionally, it would have been particularly remembered by someone who was interested in researching and documenting Jesus' life. It is extremely unlikely that the massacre happened yet Luke was unaware of it.

The **second** and by far more likely scenario is that Luke did not know about the massacre because it never took place. Awareness of the occurrence of a major massacre of young boys in Bethlehem and its vicinity would have required only some general knowledge of the history of that region in that period. It would not have required knowledge of the history of the birth of Jesus specifically. This explanation of the absence of the massacre from Luke's Gospel seems very likely, but it clearly discredits Matthew's account. Indeed, Matthew's account itself gives us good reasons to believe that the alleged massacre has no root in history, as explained below.

② As he does in other places in his Gospel, Matthew quotes two alleged Old Testament prophecies in his account of the massacre. But his treatment of these passages is fundamentally flawed, and this undermines the reliability of his account. This is the first instance:

Then he got up, took the child and his mother during the night, and went to Egypt. He stayed there until Herod died. In this way what was spoken by the Lord through the prophet was fulfilled: "I called my Son out of Egypt." (Matt. 2:14-15)

The Old Testament prophet that Matthew mentions is Hosea, and the supposed prophecy is these words that were spoken to him by God: "When Israel was a young man, I loved him like a son, and I summoned my son out of Egypt" (Hos. 11:1). The problem in Matthew is that these words are not a prophecy and they signify a past event that had nothing to do with the Messiah or his birth for Jesus to be claimed to be their fulfillment. The *calling out of Egypt* is something that had happened, not something that the Hosea text was predicting to happen in the future; the passage does not represent a prophecy at all. The term "Israel" denotes the "children of Israel," and the specific event that the passage is talking about is the exodus of the Israelites from Egypt, which happened 12 centuries before the birth of Jesus. In order to use Hosea 11:1 for his purpose, Matthew had to ignore the first part of the passage because it reveals that the "son" denoted Israel the nation, not Jesus or any other individual:

When Israel was a young man, I loved him like a son, and I summoned my son out of Egypt. But the more I summoned them, the farther they departed from me. They sacrificed to the Baal idols and burned incense to images. Yet it was I who led Ephraim, I took them by the arm; but they did not acknowledge that I had healed them. I led them with leather cords, with leather ropes; I lifted the yoke from their neck, and gently fed them. They will return to Egypt! Assyria will rule over them because they refuse to repent! (Hos. 11:1-5)

Furthermore, Hosea 11:1 and the passages that follow it talk about the Israelites' failure to obey God and His consequent anger at them. There is absolutely nothing that links this text to the Messiah, so no wonder these passages are also missing from Mathew's quotation.

Let's examine Matthew's second alleged prophecy:

Then what was spoken by Jeremiah the prophet was fulfilled: "A voice was heard in Ramah, weeping and loud wailing, Rachel weeping for her children, and she did not want to be comforted, because they were gone." (Matt. 2:17-18)

Here also Matthew takes one part of an Old Testament passage completely out of context in order to apply it to Jesus' story. The subject of the passage that Matthew quotes is the exiled Jews in Babylon and their promised return to Palestine:

The Lord says, "A sound is heard in Ramah, a sound of crying in bitter grief. It is the sound of Rachel weeping for her children and refusing to be comforted, because her children are gone." The Lord says to her, "Stop crying and don't shed any more tears. For your continuous mourning will be rewarded. Your children will return from the land of the enemy. I, the Lord, affirm it. Indeed, there is hope for your posterity. Your children will return to their own territory." (Jer. 31:15-17)

The text talks about the deportation of Jews from Palestine. Ramah is the city where captive Jews from the kingdom of Judea were gathered before they were taken into exile to Babylon. Prophet Jeremiah here poetically imagines Rachel, Jacob's wife and the mother of Joseph and Benjamin who are believed to be the fathers of the Israelite population of Judea, lamenting the exile of her descendants. The passage concludes with God announcing that He will return the exiled Jews to Palestine.

Matthew's quote of the Old Testament passage has a number of serious problems. **First**, historically, this passage has no relation to the Messiah. Matthew had to take Jeremiah 31:15 completely out of its context to use it for his story. **Second**, while 31:15 has a sad tone of captivity, it is actually part of a wider hopeful passage about the deliverance and return of the captives. In employing 31:15 in his account of the horrible massacre, Matthew used this passage for the exact opposite of its original hopeful and promising message. **Third**, the part of the passage that Matthew quotes is not a prophecy. It is actually the message of hope in the passage, which Matthew ignores, that is a prophecy. He could have hardly come up with a worse misquotation.

Matthew could not have innocently misunderstood completely the Hosea and Jeremiah passages. The text is as clear as day, and it is blatantly wrong to be used for what Matthew used it for. Matthew selectively quoted and deliberately manipulated the two passages in order to provide Old Testament support for his story of the massacre. This raises very serious doubts about the reliability of Matthew's account in which these two misuses of Old Testament text takes place, although it does not necessarily mean that the alleged massacre never occurred. As I have already pointed out in my comment about Matthew's misuse of another Biblical prophecy in his account of the virginal conception (p. 108), Matthew's poor use of Biblical text to support episodes in his story of Jesus probably means that he *believed* that Jesus story unfolded as he told it, though that does not necessarily mean that his story is historical.

③ Matthew's account of Herod's massacre shows a high level of credulity and contains a number of weaknesses. **First**, Matthew tells us that Herod knew about Jesus' birth through the news about the wise men. Having been told by the chief priests and scribes that the Messiah was to be born in Bethlehem in Judea, instead of sending his own men to locate the exact place of the child, the very concerned Herod, Matthew claims, asked the wise men to bring to him the news about the newborn child — totally relying on them to obey his order willingly!

Second, the text clearly suggests that the wise men visited Jesus shortly after his birth. Herod's order to kill all the young boys who were *two years old or less* means that he waited for a long time before making any move to settle a matter that was of great concern to him! It took Herod about two years to recognize that the wise men had deceived him and to, accordingly, get furious! History speaks of a far less patient Herod than Matthew's account portrays.

This problem in Matthew, the Gospel of the Infancy, and the Infancy Gospel of James is circumvented in the Gospel of Pseudo-Matthew. The latter claims that the wise men came to visit Jesus two years after his birth (PsMatt. 17).

Third, Matthew claims that a star was leading the wise men to Jesus' birthplace, but there is no indication that this star was visible only to the wise men. Herod could have found Jesus as easily as the wise men did, and there is no reason that he had to rely on them. Having said that, the claim that a star could stand over a particular house is clearly impossible.

Matthew's account of the story is completely unrealistic and poorly written. This also applies to the apocryphal accounts.

To sum up, the absence of the massacre from Luke, Matthew's misleading use of Old Testament passages which highlights the unreliability of his story, and other weaknesses in his account suggest that, in all probability, the alleged massacre never took place.

11.3.2. The Historical Arguments

Luke's is not the only significant omission of the massacre. More significant is Josephus' silence on this alleged event. While Roman chroniclers ignored the history of Palestine, the Jewish historian Josephus recorded that history. His detailed account of the history of Herod the Great became the source of all later writings on this king. Josephus' writings show that Herod was an extremely brutal ruler who did not abandon his savagery even in his last days. When he was dying, he gathered the Jewish nobles and locked them up. As he knew his death would be celebrated rather than lamented by his nation, he ordered his sister and her husband to have all the men in custody killed immediately after his death. This was sure to leave the whole nation in genuine mourning when he dies! Fortunately for the prisoners, Herod's sister and her husband released them after Herod's death (Josephus, *Jewish Antiquities*, 17.6.5).

Herod's brutality did not spare even members of his own family. He killed the grandfather and brother of his favored wife, Mariamme. He later killed her also along with their two sons. When he was dying he killed his firstborn, whom he fathered with another wife.

Significantly, while Josephus recorded in detail Herod's brutal actions, he did not mention the massacre of infants that is reported by Matthew and apocryphal sources. Nevertheless, it has been repeatedly suggested that Josephus' records of Herod's brutality show that he could have well committed the massacre (e.g. Montefiore, 1962: 15-16). The problem with this argument is that the question is not *whether Herod could or could not* have perpetrated that massacre, but *whether he did!* The fact that Herod was brutal can be equally used, for instance, to explain why Matthew could have made up the whole story. Herod's brutality may be used *inconclusively* to claim support for the two diametrically opposing arguments. The one indisputable and significant observation from Josephus' writings is that the massacre is not mentioned, even in passing, with Herod's many atrocities. In my view, it is far stronger to argue that had the gruesome massacre really happened and therefore been known to Josephus, it would have merited a mention in this detailed record of Herod's bloody history. Those who take the opposite, hypothetical view would need to explain why Josephus would have chosen not to mention the massacre if it was historical.

Another apologetic argument is that Bethlehem and its surrounding areas had a small population, so the number of murdered infants was small, hence it was not reported by Josephus. One estimate, for instance, puts the whole population of Bethlehem during Herod's reign at about 1,000. It suggests that even considering neighboring areas would mean that no more than 20 boys would have been born in two years, and that many of those infants would have died of natural causes. Accordingly, the argument goes, the killing of the innocents of Bethlehem "scarcely deserves the title massacre" (France, 1979: 114) and would have been "hardly a 'massacre' even by modern standards" (France, 1978: 89).

These figures are hypothetical, particularly given that unidentified surrounding regions were also targeted. But the real problem with this argument is that the killing of infants would have been seen as an extremely and exceptionally brutal act regardless of the number of the victims. It is the very act of intentionally targeting infants, not their number, that would have made this crime particularly heinous and appalling. To suggest that people then or the historian Josephus would not have considered this as a massacre, let alone a unique and particularly cruel one, is a very poor argument indeed. To go even further and suggest that the killing of 20 infants or so was "hardly a 'massacre' even by modern standards" makes that argument so ridiculous. In my view, using the number of victims to suggest that the alleged massacre was not worth mentioning in the records of history is nothing more than a desperate attempt to defend the indefensible Matthean story.

There is another argument that may be raised against drawing this conclusion from Josephus' silence. The massacre implies that Jesus was the Messiah — an implication that the Jews do not accept. Ignoring this event, the argument goes, is only to be expected of a strong defendant of the Jewish faith such as Josephus. This objection is misleading, because accepting the historicity of the massacre and mentioning it would only have confirmed that *Herod believed* that Jesus would pose a future threat to him. It *would not have substantiated that belief.* Additionally, Josephus could have easily made up any cause for the massacre that has nothing to do with Jesus being the Christ.

Another historical reference to what appears to be the same massacre of infants comes from the 4th-5th century Latin writer and philosopher Macrobius. The passage mentions Herod's brutal massacre, which included his son, and Emperor Augustus' reaction: "When he (Augustus) heard that among those male infants about two years old, which Herod the king of the Jews ordered to be slain in Syria, one of his sons was also murdered, he said: 'It is better to be Herod's hog than his son'" (Macrobius, *Saturn*, 2.4.11). As the infants are said to be two years old and the perpetrator of the massacre is Herod, it looks like Macrobius is talking about the same massacre that is mentioned in Christian sources. Macrobius' account was written some 4 centuries after the date of the alleged massacre, so it is almost certain that he relied on Christian sources. This makes Macrobius account worthless in establishing the historicity of the massacre. The credibility of Macrobius' account is also undermined by its confusion of the history of that period. Herod killed his two sons from Mariamme, Alexander and Aristobulus, in 7 BCE — that is three years before his death — and he executed his firstborn, Antipater, five days before his own death. The three sons were young men rather than infants when they were killed, so Macrobius is clearly wrong. Additionally, Josephus explains in detail the historical background of their execution, which has nothing to do with any bigger massacre. It is also unclear why Macrobius thought that the massacre happened in Syria.

It has also been noted that Augustus' comment which Macrobius cites, which is a pun on the similar sounding Greek words for "son" and "pig," relates only to the fate of Herod's sons and has no bearing on the alleged massacre. It has been concluded that the reference to the killing of the two year old boys was added later on to the story that triggered Augustus' sarcastic comment — that is, after the story of the massacre had become established in Christian circles and known to non-Christian writers (France, 1979: 118).

The Qur'an is not the only source that implies that Herod's massacre of the infants of Bethlehem and its vicinity in Matthew and apocryphal gospels never took place. Another major Christian source, the Gospel of Luke, also implicitly rejects the claim of those books. Additionally, history, represented by Josephus' writings, implies that the alleged massacre did not take place.

11.4. The Massacre That Did Happen

We have seen that the Christian story of a massacre committed by Herod which unsuccessfully targeted the infant Jesus is unsupported by the historian of that period, Josephus. We have also noted that the absence of this massacre from the other Gospels implies that it was not known to those writers. This is particularly significant in the case of Luke which shows particular interest in Jesus' infancy and childhood. These, and other arguments we have discussed, lead to one conclusion: the Herodian massacre of the innocent is fictitious.

We also know that the Old Testament has a very similar story about a Pharaonic massacre of Jewish young boys at the time of Moses' birth. The historicity of this massacre is confirmed in the Qur'an, although the latter's account has some differences with the Old Testament's story. So what is the likelihood that the Christian story of the massacre of the infants is modeled on the Old Testament's account? We have already seen how Matthew *manipulated* Old Testament passages in various ways in order to portray Jesus as fulfilling Old Testament prophecies. Similarly, Herod's alleged massacre might be another instance of appropriation and misuse of an Old Testament story, although I think Matthew was not the culprit, but he only reported what he heard. It is perfectly possible that some Christians thought that Jesus must have had a similar miracle like Moses' escape from Pharaoh's massacre. In this section we will examine the assumption that the story of Jesus' miraculous escape from a royal massacre was inspired by Moses' similar story in the Old Testament.

The Old Testament claims that, having noticed the continuous increase of the number of the Israelites in Egypt, Pharaoh feared that one day these slaves might side with one of his enemies in a war in order to earn their freedom. He tried two unsuccessful methods to curtail the increase in the Israelite population before embarking on the most extreme measure of killing all newborn males:

> Then a new king, who did not know Joseph, came to power over Egypt. He said to his people, "Look at the Israelite people, more numerous and stronger than we are! Come, let's deal wisely with them. Otherwise they will continue to multiply, and if a war breaks out, they will ally themselves with our enemies and fight against us and leave the land."
>
> So they put foremen over them to oppress them with hard labor. As a result they built Pithom and Rameses as store cities for Pharaoh. But the more the Egyptians oppressed them, the more they multiplied and spread. As a result the Egyptians loathed the Israelites, and they made the Israelites serve rigorously. So they made their lives bitter by hard service with mortar and bricks and by all kinds of service in the fields. Every kind of service the Israelites were required to give was rigorous.
>
> The king of Egypt said to the Hebrew midwives, one of whom was named Shiphrah, and the other Puah, "When you assist the Hebrew women in childbirth, observe at the delivery: if it is a son, kill him, but if it is a daughter, she may live." But the midwives feared God and did not do what the king of Egypt had told them; they let the boys live.
>
> Then the king of Egypt summoned the midwives and said to them, "Why have you done this and let the boys live?" The midwives said to Pharaoh, "Because the Hebrew women are not like the Egyptian women — for the Hebrew women are vigorous; they give birth before the midwife comes to them!" So God treated the midwives well, and the people multiplied and became very strong. And because the midwives feared God, he made households for them.
>
> Then Pharaoh commanded all his people, "All sons that are born you must throw into the river, but all daughters you may let live." (Exo. 1:8-22)

The Book of Exodus then goes on to recount how Moses was rescued from Pharaoh's massacre:

> A man from the household of Levi married a woman who was a descendant of Levi. The woman became pregnant and gave birth to a son. When she saw that he was a healthy child, she hid him for three months. But when she was no longer able to hide him, she took a papyrus basket for him and sealed it with bitumen and pitch. She put the child in it and set it among the reeds along the edge of the Nile. His sister stationed herself at a distance to find out what would happen to him.
> Then the daughter of Pharaoh came down to wash herself by the Nile, while her attendants were walking alongside the river, and she saw the basket among the reeds. She sent one of her attendants, took it, opened it, and saw the child — a boy, crying! — and she felt compassion for him and said, "This is one of the Hebrews' children."
> Then his sister said to Pharaoh's daughter, "Shall I go and get a nursing woman for you from the Hebrews, so that she may nurse the child for you?" Pharaoh's daughter said to her, "Yes, do so." So the young girl went and got the child's mother. Pharaoh's daughter said to her, "Take this child and nurse him for me, and I will pay your wages." So the woman took the child and nursed him.
> When the child grew older she brought him to Pharaoh's daughter, and he became her son. She called his name Moses, saying, "Because I drew him from the water." (Exo. 2:1-10)

Like the Biblical story, the Qur'an talks of a brutal Pharaoh who oppressed the Israelites and killed their sons but spared their women. It also relates how, instructed by God's inspiration, Moses' mother put him a coffin and let it float on the river when she feared for her son's life. The child was then picked from the river by Pharaoh's wife, who returned him to his mother to raise him for her. The identity of Moses' rescuer, who is Pharaoh's daughter in the Bible, is one of a number of differences between the two accounts. The child was then raised in the castle of Pharaoh who was unaware that he was bringing up and looking after the very person who was going to cause his downfall. These are the verses that mention the massacre and the rescuing of Moses:

> We narrate to you [O Muhammad!] parts of the story of Moses and Pharaoh in Truth, for people who believe (28.3). Pharaoh exalted himself in the earth and made its people into castes — oppressing a sect among them, killing their sons and sparing their women. He was one of the corrupters (28.4). We desired to show favor to those who were oppressed in the earth, and to make them leaders, and to make them the inheritors (28.5). And to establish them in the earth, and to show Pharaoh, Hāmān, and their soldiers from them that which they feared (28.6). And We inspired Moses' mother: "Suckle him, and when you fear for him, cast him into the river; fear not nor grieve; We shall bring him back to you and shall make him one of the messengers" (28.7). Then the people of Pharaoh picked him up [from the river], [It was intended] that he should be to them an enemy and a cause of sorrow; Pharaoh, Hāmān, and their soldiers were sinful

(28.8). The wife of Pharaoh said: "[He will be] delight of the eye for me and you; do not kill him; it maybe that he be of use to us or we adopt him as a son"; and they were unaware [of what was going to happen] (28.9). The heart of Moses' mother became void; she would have revealed it (the secret) had We not strengthened her heart to be of the believers (28.10). She said to his sister: "Trace him"; so she observed him from afar while they (those who had Moses) were unaware (28.11). And We had before forbidden foster mothers for him, so she (his sister) said: "Shall I tell you of a household who could rear him for you and take good care of him?" (28.12). So We returned him to his mother so that she be comforted, does not grieve, and knows that Allah's promise is true, but most of them (people) do not know (28.13). And when he (Moses) attained his full strength and settled, We gave him Wisdom and Knowledge; and thus do We reward the good doers (28.14).

And We have [thus] conferred a favor on you [O Moses!] again (20.37). [The first was] when We revealed to your mother that which is revealed (20.38). Saying: "Put him into a coffin, then cast it down into the river, then the river shall throw him onshore; an enemy to Me and enemy to him shall take him up"; and I cast down upon you love from Me, and that you be brought up according to My will" (20.39).

There are clear similarities and differences between the Old Testament's story of Pharaoh's massacre and the Christian account of Herod's massacre of children. One difference between the two stories that may look to some significant is the goal of the massacre. Pharaoh killed young Israelite boys in order to keep the number of the Israelites under control, whereas Herod killed the young children in order to ensure Jesus' death. This difference does not make it less likely that the Christian story was copied from the Jewish tradition. **First**, Matthew's Gospel has many instances of changing Old Testament passages and taking them out of context in order to make them applicable to Jesus (see the discussions of Matthew 1:23 (pp. 106-107), 2:4-6 (pp. 166-167), 2:15 (p. 202), and 2:18 (pp. 203-204).

Second, there is extra-Biblical Jewish tradition in which "not Israel's phenomenal increase but Pharaoh's fear at the birth of a rival is adduced as the reason for his actions" (Houtman, 1993: 262). This is the same cause of the massacre in the Christian tradition which replaces Pharaoh with Herod and Moses with Jesus. Josephus also states that Pharaoh planned his massacre of all Israelite newborn males after he was told by a sacred scribe of a prediction that this was the time of the birth of "one who would abase the sovereignty of the Egyptians and exalt the Israelites, were he reared to manhood" (Josephus, *Jewish Antiquities*, 2.9.2). As is the case with Christian sources, Jewish extracanonical sources are not necessarily less reliable than canonical writings, and the reason above might well be the reason behind Pharaoh's massacre. Also, the Biblical claim that Pharaoh's massacre aimed at controlling the growth of the Israelite population has many historical problems and inconsistencies which we discuss in detail in the forthcoming revised edition of our book on the exodus of the Israelites from Egypt.

The Qur'an does not state why Pharaoh ordered the massacre. But contrary to the Bible's impossible claim that at the time of their escape from Egypt the Israelites were about 600,000 men (Exo. 12:37), i.e. some 2-3 million including women and children, the Qur'an indicates that the Israelites were a small nation. Its statement of this fact comes in Pharaoh's description of the escaping Israelites as "an isolated group, small in number" (26.54). The massacre, thus, could not have targeted to control the number of the Israelites.

There is a consensus among Muslim scholars that Pharaoh ordered the massacre because he learned of the imminent birth of an Israelite boy who would cause his downfall. It is difficult to know whether this widespread view is authentic or whether it was copied from Jewish sources. Nevertheless, while paranormal in nature, this interpretation is possible, unlike the Bible's which is contradicted by history. As to how Pharaoh came to know about this danger, Muslim exegetes and historians have expressed a number of different views. Some have suggested that Pharaoh had a prognostic dream which was interpreted for him by some priests, some have hypothesized that priests and astrologers informed Pharaoh, whereas others have pointed out that he knew about Moses from old prophecies that specified Moses' place and time of birth.

Another significant difference between the Qur'anic account of Pharaoh's brutality and its Biblical counterpart is that the former states that Pharaoh resorted to killing Israelites males more than once. In addition to his campaign of murder when Moses was an infant, Pharaoh ordered another massacre when Moses, who had escaped Pharaoh's wrath years earlier, returned to Egypt to ask Pharaoh to allow the Israelites to leave Egypt and also to call him to his religion:

> And the chiefs of Pharaoh's people said: "Would you leave Moses and his people to cause corruption in the land and forsake you and your gods?" He said: "We will kill their sons and spare their women, and surely we have power over them" (7.127).
>
> So when he (Moses) brought to them (Pharaoh and his people) the truth from Us, they said: "Kill the sons of those who have believed with him and spare their women"; and the scheming of the disbelievers will only be in vain (40.25). And Pharaoh said: "Let me kill Moses and let him call upon his Lord; I fear that he will change your religion or cause corruption in the land" (40.26).

Significantly, these verses speak about Pharaoh's and his court's perception of the danger of the Israelites to Egypt's established religion, but not to its security due to their increasing number. This is in line with the Qur'an's portrayal of the Israelites as a small minority.

The Christian story of Jesus' birth has other remarkable similarities with the Old Testament's story of Moses' birth:

① The role played by the wise men in the Christian story is very similar to that of the two midwives in Moses'. The Israelite midwives were instructed by Pharaoh to kill the Israelite newborn boys despite the fact that there were themselves Israelite. Similarly, the wise men who came to pay homage to Jesus were commanded by Herod to lead him to his whereabouts. Like the midwives, the wise men did not obey the concerned potentate.

② The Christian image of Herod the Great being in direct contact with the wise men shares with the Old Testament's story of Moses' birth the small scale on which events take place, which has been described as a "village atmosphere" (Houtman, 1993: 188).

③ After taking Jesus out of Egypt, Joseph is told by an angel to "Get up, take the child and his mother, and go to the land of Israel, for those who were seeking the child's life are dead" (Matt. 2:20). This is reminiscent of Moses in Midian being told by the God: "Go back to Egypt, because all the men who were seeking your life are dead" (Exo. 4:19).

But if the Christian account is an appropriation of the Old Testament story then we should expect applying it to Jesus to have introduced contradictions and inconsistencies in the adapted story. Indeed, the story of the Herodian massacre was left with irreconcilable details:

① Pharaoh's knowledge of the imminent birth of an Israelite who would cause his downfall proved to be perfectly true. Moses did indeed bring both Pharaoh's reign and life to an end. Conversely, Matthew's similar claims about Jesus turned out to be untrue. Matthew claimed that the wise me told Herod that Jesus would be "king of the Jews" (Matt. 2:2) and that the chief priests and scribes told the concerned monarch that Jesus would be the "ruler who will shepherd my people Israel," citing an Old Testament prophecy (Mic. 5:2). These two prophecies, which disturbed Herod, turned out to be totally false. Jesus did not become king or any kind of leader of the Jews. In fact, the Gospels, including Matthew, claim that Jesus was humiliated before his death for supposedly claiming to be "the king of the Jews" (Mark 15:2; Matt. 27:11; Luke 23:3). This title, which he never carried, was inscribed on his cross by Roman soldiers to mock him.

It may be argued that the New Testament claims were allegorical, signifying Jesus' spiritual rather than earthly kingship or leadership of the Jews. This explanation is untenable. **First**, Jesus was accepted by only a small minority of the Jews, and this very limited support could not have been called kingship or leadership of the Jews. **Second**, if these descriptions of Jesus were indeed allegorical then they would not have bothered Herod anyway. The high priest or other religious authorities could have seen the appearance of a new spiritual leader a threat, but the emergence of a new religious leader some 20 years or so later would not have concerned Herod a little bit. **Third**, the Jewish were waiting for the

Messiah who would lead and liberate them, so Matthew's wise men's description of Jesus as "the king of the Jews" was literal not metaphorical.

If there were a prophecy that *correctly* predicted the place and time of the Messiah's birth and identified him in person, as portrayed in the story of the wise men, then such a remarkably accurate prophecy would not have wrongly claimed that Jesus was going to be "king of the Jews." Such a precise prophecy would have shown that Jesus would not be a threat to any king, be it Herod or someone else. It would have foretold that God had not destined Jesus to depose any king, lead the Jews in a revolt, or get involved in any form of rebellion against the ruling authorities. It would have left Herod with nothing whatsoever to worry about.

② Any true prophecy about Jesus' future would have been irrelevant to Herod in particular. It would have revealed that Jesus would be doing whatever the prophecy states at a future time that is long after Herod's death. Matthew says that Herod died when Jesus was still a little child. We also know from history that Herod died in March/April 4 BCE, i.e. when Jesus was a small child or even a very young infant. Herod was not destined to live until Jesus had any following. On the contrary, the Qur'an states that Pharaoh was still in power when Moses returned to Egypt and he went on to cause the death of the arrogant Egyptian potentate.

These two arguments show that there could not have been a prophecy that predicted with precision various facts about Jesus yet at the same time claimed, wrongly and misleadingly, that Jesus would become king of the Jews. If that prophecy did not exist, then Herod would have had no reason to think of killing infants. These arguments also show how clumsily Moses' story was applied to Jesus.

③ This argument is based on the Qur'an. This book tells us that baby Jesus was a unique, miraculous child whose reality could not be kept secret. He was created to be known to people and for the news about him as a miraculous child to spread everywhere. He was the child who, among other things, was born without a biological father, was a prophet from the day of his birth, spoke in the cradle, and performed various miracles. These attributes mean that there was no need for indiscriminately murdering all infants of Bethlehem and its vicinity to ensure the death of Jesus. Jesus could have been very easily found and identified if Herod really wanted that. Surely if wise men from another country could find baby Jesus then King Herod also could, even without a mysterious star!

Moses, on the other hand, did not look paranormally different from other children. It is no surprise then that Pharaoh asked for many children to be massacred to ensure that the future leader of his Israelite slaves and danger to his life and rule would also be killed. He had no way of knowing who that child was or how he looked like. In fact, Moses' normal look enabled him to live in the palace of his very enemy, Pharaoh, without causing anyone to doubt that he may have been the child that was supposed to have been killed. The prophecy about Moses is consistent with the rest of his story, whereas the alleged prophecy about Jesus contradicts other details in his story.

The apocryphal Arabic Gospel of the Infancy does has an extra element of contradiction as it states that Jesus was a paranormal child who spoke in the cradle (AraIn. 1:2), yet still claims that Herod had to kill all children to make sure of his death.

All evidence that we have discussed in this section points to one conclusion: the Christian story of Herod's massacre of infants to kill Jesus was based on the Old Testament's story of Moses and that, unlike the latter, is unhistorical. A discussion of the historicity of Moses' story of birth is rather outside the scope of this book, but interested readers may like to consult it in our forthcoming book on the Israelites' exodus from Egypt.

12

Was Jesus A Nazarene From Nazareth?

The Gospels call Jesus a "Nazarene." Matthew explains the title by relating it to the city of "Nazareth" where he thinks Jesus grew up, although the canonical and apocryphal gospels are divided on Jesus' places of birth and youth between Nazareth and Bethlehem. There are several serious problems with Matthew's etymology.

The Qur'an recounts a story that implies that the term "Nazarene" was a title of Jesus' followers, not of him.

12.1. Jesus' Birth and Growing up places

The Qur'an does not specify where Jesus' was born and lived, but the Gospels do, although there are differences between them.

Mark calls Nazareth Jesus' "hometown," implying that he was born there. He also states that when Jesus went to be baptized in the Jordan River, he came from "Nazareth of Galilee" (Mark 1:9), so we know that this is where he also lived.

Matthew (2:1) states in an unambiguous language that "Jesus was born in Bethlehem of Judea" which is situated in the south of Palestine. It does not contain any indication that Jesus and Mary had moved to Bethlehem from another town, so the implication is that Bethlehem was their original living place. This seems to be also implicitly stressed when Matthew says that when Joseph, Mary, and Jesus returned to Palestine after the death of Herod, they were afraid to go back to Judea, so they went to live in the town of Nazareth in the northern province of Galilee: "But when he heard that Archelaus was reigning over Judea in place of his father Herod, he was afraid to go there. After being warned in a dream, he went to the regions of Galilee. He came to a town called Nazareth and lived there. Then what had been spoken by the prophets was fulfilled, that he would be called a Nazarene" (Matt. 2:22-23). The implication here is that Jesus grew up in Nazareth, so he became known as a "Nazarene." Indeed, when Jesus, Joseph, and Mary returned from Egypt and went to Nazareth, Jesus was still a "young child," and the next time that we meet him in this Gospel is when, now a young man, he comes *from Galilee* to the Jordan in Judea to be baptized by John (Matt. 3:13-17). So, according to Matthew, Jesus was born in Judea in the town of Bethlehem, where Mary and Joseph lived, but grew up in Nazareth in Galilee.

Luke has a different story. Here we find Mary living in Nazareth in Galilee when she was visited by the angel Gabriel who told her about her miraculous conception of Jesus (Luke 1:26). A Roman census then stipulated that Joseph and Mary should go to register in Bethlehem, as it is the ancestral city of Joseph. Luke uses this journey to explain Jesus' birth in Bethlehem (Luke 2:1-7). The young child was then taken by Joseph and Mary to Jerusalem to be *presented to the Lord*: "just as it is written in the law of the Lord, 'Every firstborn male will be set apart to the Lord'" (Luke 2:23). Interestingly, the words "will be set apart to the Lord" do not actually exist in the Old Testament. The real literary goal of the visit is to have the devout Simeon and the prophetess Ann, who were present in the temple, see Jesus and announce that he is the savior they were waiting for. After finishing the rituals, Joseph, Mary, and Jesus returned to their "to their own town of Nazareth" in Galilee (Luke 2:39).

The next passage implies that they continued to live there: "And the child grew and became strong, filled with wisdom, and the favor of God was upon him. Now Jesus' parents went to Jerusalem every year for the feast of the Passover" (Luke 2:40-41). When the 12 years old Jesus visited Jerusalem with Joseph and Mary, he stayed there after they left heading home. Inexplicably, after a whole day of travel, Joseph and Mary noticed that Jesus was not with the returning people. They headed back to Jerusalem. Luke then tells us that Mary and Joseph took Jesus back with them to Nazareth — in another confirmation that this is the city where he lived and grew up. Then when Jesus was thirty years old, he went to be baptized by John in the Jordan.

Like Mark, John does not cover Jesus' birth or childhood, so there is no explicit reference to these places. It has two significant passages in which people dismiss Jesus. In the first a Nathanael sarcastically asks: "Can anything good come out of Nazareth?" (John 1:46), and in the second Pharisees declare that "no prophet comes from Galilee!" (John 7:52). These references, which suggest that Jesus was living in Nazareth, have been taken to mean that John makes Nazareth Jesus' place of birth (e.g. Theissen & Merz, 1999: 164). This understanding is confirmed by a third passage that contrasts Bethlehem, King David's birthplace, with Galilee, clearly suggesting that the latter, where Nazareth is, is Jesus' birthplace:

> Others said, "This is the Christ!" But still others said, "No, for the Christ doesn't come from Galilee, does he? Don't the scriptures say that the Christ is a descendant of David and comes from Bethlehem, the village where David lived?" (John 7:41-42)

Apocryphal gospels also mention where Jesus was born and grew up. The Arabic Gospel of the Infancy states that in order to be taxed in their country, Joseph took Mary and went to Jerusalem and then to Bethlehem so that he and his family be taxed in the city of his fathers. It does not tell us where the two had been living. Jesus was then born in Bethlehem (AraIn. 1:4-11). Shortly after Jesus' birth, Mary and Joseph had to take Jesus to Egypt to save him from Herod's massacre. After Herod's death, the three went to Judea, but an angel then instructed Joseph that they should go to Nazareth (AraIn. 8:16). There are then references indicating that Jesus, Mary, and Joseph lived in Bethlehem (AraIn. 9:1, 12:14, 13:10), before they returned to Nazareth (AraIn. 21:27).

The Infancy Gospel of James only tells us that Jesus was born in Bethlehem, which is Joseph's hometown (InJam. 12). The Gospel of the Birth of Mary states that she was born in Nazareth and educated in Jerusalem in the temple (BirMary. 1:1), and that Joseph was from Bethlehem (BirMary. 6:6). It states that Jesus was born in Bethlehem, although clearly indicating that it was not were Joseph and Mary were living (BirMary. 8:15).

The Gospel of Pseudo-Matthew also claims that Joseph and Mary went to Bethlehem because they were originally from there, and that Mary gave birth to Jesus just before entering the town (PsMatt. 13). After returning from Egypt, they went to live in Galilee, but the gospel does not tell us which town they lived in. We know that this happened sometime before Jesus was 4 years old (PsMatt. 26). Jesus was younger than 6 years old when Mary and Joseph took him to Nazareth. Two years later, Jesus went out of Jericho, in the south of Palestine, toward the Jordan (PsMatt. 35). Jesus then lived in Capernaum, in the north in Galilee, before going to Bethlehem (PsMatt. 41).

Table 12.1: Jesus' birthplace and the places where he, Mary, and Joseph lived according to the canonical Gospels and apocryphal sources

Book	Mary	Joseph	Jesus' Birth	Jesus' Youth
Mark	N/A	N/A	Nazareth	Nazareth
Matt.	Lived in Bethlehem	lived in Bethlehem	Bethlehem	Nazareth
Luke	Lived in Nazareth	hometown is Bethlehem	Bethlehem	Nazareth
John	N/A	N/A	Nazareth	Nazareth
AraIn.	N/A	hometown is Bethlehem	Bethlehem	Nazareth/ Bethlehem
InJam.	N/A	hometown is Bethlehem	Bethlehem	N/A
BirMary.	Born in Nazareth and educated in Jerusalem; did not live in Bethlehem	hometown is Bethlehem; did not live in Bethlehem	Bethlehem	N/A
PsMatt.	hometown is Bethlehem	hometown is Bethlehem	Bethlehem	Several cities, including Nazareth and Bethlehem

There are differences and problems in the different accounts that make Bethlehem Jesus' birthplace. For instance, as Luke states that Mary lived in

Nazareth, for Jesus' birth to happen in Bethlehem, he had to introduce the story of the census. Yet this story cannot be historical (pp. 187-190).

Recognizing such problems, noting that Jesus was consistently called "Nazarene," and accepting Matthew's (2:23) explanation that this term means "of Nazareth," many scholars believe that Jesus was actually born in Nazareth rather than Bethlehem. Theissen & Merz (1999: 164) have summarized this view by pointing out that "throughout the Gospel tradition Nazareth is regarded as Jesus' home town. Mark and John implicitly presuppose that Jesus was also born there." Scholars think that the birth was transferred from Nazareth to Bethlehem because of the belief that the Messiah was expected to be born in King David's city (e.g. Miller, 2003: 118-119; Theissen & Merz, 1999: 164-166):

> Our conclusion must be that Jesus came from Nazareth. The shift of his birthplace to Bethlehem is a result of religious fantasy and imagination: because according to scripture the messiah had to be born in Bethlehem, Jesus' birth is transferred there. (Theissen & Merz, 1999: 165)

Matthew's etymology of Nazarene, however, is also problematic; and these problems are the subject of the next section.

12.2. "Nazarene" in the New Testament

One of Jesus' titles in the Greek text of the New Testament is *Nazorios* (Ναζωραῖος) or *Nazarenos* (Ναζαρηνός). Both words, which appear in the four Gospels and Acts, are translated into English as "of Nazareth" or "Nazarene." Only the first form of this epithet is used in Matthew (2:23, 26:71), John (18:5, 18:7, 19:19), and Acts (2:22, 3:6, 4:10, 6:14, 22:8, 24:5, 26:9). Mark (1:24, 10:47, 14:67, 16:6), on the other hand, uses only *Nazarenos*. Luke uses *Nazorios* once (Luke 18:37) and *Nazarenos* twice (Luke 4:34, 24:19). Different manuscripts of some verses replace *Nazarenos* and *Nazorios* with one another, but the statistics in table 12.2 are of the versions that are considered as the most authentic.

Table 12.2: The terms *Nazarenos*, *Nazorios*, and "Nazareth" in the Greek New Testament

Book	Nazorios	Nazarenos	Nazareth	Total
Mark	0	4	1	5
Matthew	2	0	3	5
Luke	1	2	5	8
John	3	0	2	5
Acts	7	0	1	8
Total	13	6	12	31

All occurrences of *Nazorios* and *Nazarenos* in the New Testament are in the singular and refer to Jesus. The only exception is Acts 24:5 where *Nazorios* is used in the plural to denote the Christians. In this passage, we see the orator Tertullus making his case against Paul the Apostle accusing him of being a pestilent fellow and calling him "a ringleader of the sect of the Nazarenes."

According to Matthew (2:23), "Nazarene" is derived from "Nazareth (Ναζαρὲτ or Ναζαρέθ)", the name of the town where Jesus was brought up: "He came to a town called Nazareth and lived there. Then what had been spoken by the prophets was fulfilled, that Jesus would be called a Nazarene." The Matthean etymology has been accepted by scholars (e.g. Pellett, 1962: 525; Davies & Allison, 1988: 281), so the Greek words *Nazarenos* and *Nazorios* are translated as "Nazarene" or "of Nazareth." Nevertheless, a number of problems in Matthew's etymology have been pointed out:

① There is a linguistic problem in this etymology. While *Nazarenos* can be derived from Nazareth without any problem, the same is not true of *Nazorios*, which is the term that Matthew (2:23) uses in explaining his etymology. However, it has been claimed that, though difficult, it is not impossible for *Nazorios* to have come from Nazareth (e.g. Albright, 1946; Davies & Allison, 1988: 281; Moore, 1920: 429). Cullmann has also pointed out that the spelling of the name of Jesus' home town varies in the written tradition so it is not possible to rule out the derivation of *Nazorios* from Nazareth. He, nevertheless, finds it still unexplainable how "in Greek the unusual form *Nazorios* could maintain its position so consistently alongside the simpler form *Nazarenos* which was, after all, available" (Cullmann, 1962: 523). But there are more serious problems with Matthew's etymology.

② The ancient Nazareth is first mentioned in the New Testament, where it appears 12 times in the four Gospels and Acts (Mark 1:9; Matt. 2:23, 4:13, 21:11; Luke 1:26, 2:4, 2:39, 2:51, 4:16; John 1:45-46; Acts 10:38). This town, whose identification with the modern Arabic city of *an-Nāṣirā* is generally accepted, does not appear in any older independent record. It is not mentioned in the Old Testament, the Talmud, the Midrash, or Josephus. The earliest mention of Nazareth outside the New Testament is from the 3rd century Christian historian Julius Africanus as cited by the 4th century bishop and historian Eusebius. This fact has been taken by some to mean that Nazareth may not have existed at the time of Jesus, but it is generally concluded that the absence of Nazareth from ancient historical records indicates that it was a small, insignificant town (e.g. Moore, 1920: 429; Pellett, 1962: 524-525). The population of Nazareth is estimated from archaeological excavations to have been between 50 and 2000 at the time of Jesus (Theissen & Mertz, 1999: 165). The insignificance of Nazareth may also be concluded from this dialog in the Gospel of John:

> Philip found Nathanael and told him, "We have found the one Moses wrote about in the law, and the prophets also wrote about—Jesus of Nazareth, the son of Joseph." Nathanael replied, "Can anything good come out of Nazareth?" Philip replied, "Come and see." (John 1:45-46)

It looks quite possible that Nazareth was indeed an obscure town. But this is where the second problem in the Matthean etymology lies: if Nazareth was a town of no conspicuous note then what sense would it have made to relate Jesus to it? After all, no person is introduced by relating him to a place that is equally unknown!

③ A more fundamental problem lies in the very concept that Jesus could have been given a title after a town at all — even if it was a big and major city. It has been pointed out that it was common custom among Jews to distinguish individuals according to the places of their origin (Davies & Allison, 1988: 281). But then Jesus was by no means an ordinary person for this to apply to him. Jesus could not have been called after the city in which he was brought up or where he became known, because he acquired from the time of his infancy two unique titles: one after his unique, miraculous conception and the other denoting his unique spiritual status. It was inevitable that Jesus was called something that reminded people of his unique birth. This is indeed what the Qur'an tells us happened, calling Jesus *Ibn Maryam* or "the son of Mary." This title signifies one major miracle that identified him uniquely, which is the fact that his mother conceived him virginally.

The fact that Jesus had the very distinguished title of "the son of Mary" since his early days meant that there was no need at any later stage of his life to coin an epithet for him. Even when the news about his miracles started to spread there would have been no reason to give him a new title as his old title already celebrated the greatest miracle in his life. It would have been even more pointless to replace the unique title of "the son of Mary" with a general appellation that merely related Jesus to a certain place. Any person from that city could have been named after it, but only Jesus could have been given a title reflecting the fact that he was conceived without a father. Furthermore, it just does not make any sense to suggest that Jesus' followers in particular could have replaced the meaningful and distinguished title of "the son of Mary" with an unimpressive and undistinguished title that merely related him to a town.

One objection that could be raised is that not everyone believed in or knew of the miracle of the virginal conception, as we have already discussed in Chapter 6. But surely Jesus' followers must have been aware of his virginal conception. Also, there was another equally, if not more important, title that distinguished Jesus from any other person and which no follower of Jesus doubted: the Messiah (Christ). This simple fact cannot be explained away by those who suggest that the epithet Nazarene was used to distinguish Jesus from others. For instance, Moore (1920: 427-428) thinks that the title Nazarene was used to distinguish "the Jesus whom his disciples declared to be the Messiah from other bearers of that common name by designating the place from which he came, in a manner very common among the Jews." In other words, the suggestion is that followers of Jesus who believed that he was the Christ distinguished him from his namesakes by calling him the "Nazarene" instead of calling him "the Christ"! The facts that Christ is the title that survived the time and that Nazarene was almost never used leaves no doubt that the claim that Nazarene was used to distinguish Jesus is false. All of this tells us that the view that Jesus was called after a town is itself incorrect.

There are another two less significant, but still worth mentioning, issues with the suggestion that Jesus and his followers were named after his birthplace. **First**, although names of localities are often used to distinguish persons of similar names, derivatives of such place names are not commonly employed in the direct forms of address. **Second**, in general, a religious movement is unlikely to take its name from the birthplace of its founder — particularly if that place persistently rejected his teachings — so the Christians could not have been called "Nazarenes" because their master was born in Nazareth (Kennard, 1947: 79).

④ The combination of the New Testament's claims that Jesus was known with the title "Nazarene" and the Matthean etymology of this word has yet another insurmountable problem. Acts 24:5, as well as later writings, use the plural word "Nazarenes" for the followers of Jesus. Now, even if we assume that Jesus was called a Nazarene because he lived in Nazareth, it would make no sense to extend this title to his followers who would have come from various places. The followers of a Nazarene, in the Matthean sense of the word, do not become Nazarenes themselves! If Nazarene meant someone from Nazareth, as Matthew has it, then "it would certainly be unusual if [the Christians] were referred to as 'people from Nazareth'" (Cullmann, 1962: 523).

⑤ Let's look at how Matthew derived Nazarene from Nazareth:

> So he got up and took the child and his mother and returned to the land of Israel. But when he heard that Archelaus was reigning over Judea in place of his father Herod, he was afraid to go there. After being warned in a dream, he went to the regions of Galilee. He came to a town called Nazareth and lived there. Then what had been spoken by the prophets was fulfilled, that Jesus would be called a Nazarene. (Matt. 2:21-23)

Like other prophecies cited by Matthew, there is serious a problem with this prophecy: it does not occur anywhere in the Old Testament! This should not be surprising as we have already noted that the name Nazareth first appears in the New Testament.

It has been suggested that the use of "prophets" instead of "prophet" in the passage above is Matthew's way of indicating that he is giving "a paraphrase of the sense of more than one passage rather than a quotation of a specific verse" (Miller, 2003: 115; also Davies & Allison, 1988: 275). There is no evidence that this is the case, as 2:23 is the only prophecy that Matthew attributes to the unidentified "prophets." Of the remaining 12 alleged prophecies that Matthew cites, 6 are attributed to prophet Isaiah, 2 to prophet Jeremiah, and 4 to an unidentified "prophet." It is unclear which "prophets" Matthew meant, but there is no evidence that the use of this plural term indicates that Matthew paraphrased more than one Old Testament passage.

The inexistence of the Matthean prophecy in the Old Testament has not stopped the attempts to find a Biblical passage that Matthew may have used with some liberty. Two theories have been suggested where the word "Nazarene" is assumed to be a play on an Old Testament Hebrew term. I mention these here to show how weak and farfetched they are and that they do not solve the fundamental problem after all.

The first theory states that the word *Nazorios* is a play on the Hebrew word *nazir*, which appears in English as "nazirite" or "nazarite." This Old Testament term signifies someone who consecrated himself or herself to the service of God by taking a special vow. A nazirite did not drink wine, shave, or cut the hair. One famous nazirite is Samson who was the subject of the angel's following words to his mother: "Look, you will conceive and have a son. So now, do not drink wine or beer and do not eat any food that will make you ritually unclean. For the child will be dedicated to God from birth till the day he dies" (Judg. 13:7). This theory first presumes that Matthew was aware that Samson's reference to himself as a "nazir" in the Hebrew version of Judges 16:17 has been translated in Greek into *naziraios* in some versions and into "holy man (*hagios*)" in others. This is taken to mean that *naziraios* and "holy man" are synonymous. Next, it is noted that Jesus himself is called a "holy man" and a *Nazarenos* in Mark 1:24: "Leave us alone, Jesus the Nazarene! Have you come to destroy us? I know who you are — the Holy One of God!" Presuming that Matthew was aware of Mark's passage, he took this to mean that *Nazarenos* and *naziraios* are equivalent. He then concluded that *Nazorios*, which is his preferred version of *Nazarenos*, is also equivalent to *naziraios* and consequently "holy." All that is left now is to find an Old Testament prophecy that contains a suitable reference. One passage that has been chosen to serve this purpose is this: "Those remaining in Zion, those left in Jerusalem, will be called "holy," all in Jerusalem who are destined to live" (Isa. 4:3). In another version, Isaiah 4:3 talks about a single person, so the clause of interest appears as "he will be called 'holy'". Now, since *Nazorios*, is equivalent to "holy," Matthew read Isaiah 4:3 as "he will be called a *Nazorios*," and thus we have the prophecy that he mentions!

The facts that *Nazarenos* does not appear in Matthew, *Nazorios* is not found in Mark, and Mark 1:24 does not link *Nazarenos* to "holy man" are all ignored by this conclusion. Davies and Allison (1988: 277) claim that this reworked version of Isaiah 4:3 is "too close to Matthew's line to be coincidence"! Well, if one sets out to develop at any cost an Old Testament passage similar to Matthew's, then surely getting it would not count as coincidental; would it? Allowed this much freedom, selectivity, and imagination all kinds of links between all kinds of completely unrelated texts may be established.

The second theory considers *Nazorios* a play on the Hebrew word *neṣer* which means "branch" or "bud" and which appears in another Isaiah prophecy: "A shoot will grow out of Jesse's root stock, a bud will sprout from his roots" (Isa. 11:1). This prophecy is taken to mean that the Messiah would be a descendant of King David, the son of Jesse, and it is applied to Jesus to conclude that he was called a "bud" or *neṣer*.

Significantly, Isaiah 4:3 and 11:1 are not the only Biblical passages that have been suggested as the referents of Matthew 2:23 (e.g. Allan, 1983). This is only indicative of the fact that Matthew's quote is not readily traceable to any Old Testament prophecy. All attempts to find this missing link is based on a double act of faith: faith in Matthew's claim that the passage he cites exists in the Old Testament, and faith that the scripture that Matthew refers to is the Old Testament that we have today. A review of more potential candidates for the scriptural reference in Matthew 2:23 would only show how farfetched all such attempts are. Davies and Allison (1988) are one source for reading more about the desperate attempts to reconcile Matthew 2:23 with the Old Testament.

One other serious problem with these attempts to salvage Matthew's credibility by finding the Old Testament text he refers to is that they undermine his etymology of *Nazorios*. If we accept that Matthew replaced "holy" in Isaiah 4:3 with *Nazorios* then this must mean that he equated the two terms. His other claim that *Nazorios* is related to "Nazareth" then becomes meaningless.

Accepting that the prophecy in Matthew 2:23 has no equivalent in the Old Testament does not do the Evangelist's credibility much good, but the alternative suggestion that he deliberately changed an Old Testament passage does not help either. Any attempt to "find" the prophecy of Matthew 2:23 in the Old Testament can only be done at the cost of accusing Matthew of deliberately changing scripture to prove scripture. Does it matter whether he changed an Old Testament passage to create the *Nazorios* prophecy or simply made the latter out of thin air? Not really. Both can only be described as a deliberate falsification.

Matthew 2:23 has five serious problems, and to try to dismiss them all is not only unreasonable but simply impossible. Additionally, this passage is not an isolated case. It is one instance of many problem-riddled passages in that Gospel that use alleged Old Testament prophecies that supposedly show that Jesus was the fulfillment of those Biblical prophecies.

It has been suggested that Matthew introduced that nonexistent Old Testament prophecy in order to rebuff any claim that the Messiah cannot come from the insignificant town of "Nazareth." There is indeed New Testament evidence that people would have resisted the idea that the Christ could come from a small town or Galilee:

Now Philip was from Bethsaida, the town of Andrew and Peter. Philip found Nathanael and told him, "We have found the one Moses wrote about in the law, and the prophets also wrote about — Jesus of Nazareth, the son of Joseph." Nathanael replied, "Can anything good come out of Nazareth?" Philip replied, "Come and see." (John 1:44-46)

Others said, "This is the Christ!" But still others said, "No, for the Christ doesn't come from Galilee, does he? Don't the scriptures say that the Christ is a descendant of David and comes from Bethlehem, the village where David lived?" (John 7:41-42)

Investigate carefully and you will see that no prophet comes from Galilee! (John 7:52)

Some scholars have suggested a *religious* meaning for the word Nazarene, either as an alternative to Matthew's etymology or in addition to it. Moore (1920) has cited a number of such etymologies, including the suggestion by some writers that the term Nazarene is not derived from Nazareth, but from the Hebrew verb *naṣar* which means "protect," "observe," "watch," so can mean "keep (the commandments)". He also mentions the 16th century theologian Faustus Socinus who suggested that Jesus was called Nazarene not only because his home was in Nazareth, but because he was the "Savior" which he derived from *naṣar* which also means "save" (Moore, 1920: 430). Cullmann (1962: 523) has suggested that before it was linked to Nazareth, Nazarene was a name of a Jewish sect or heresy which was derived from the verb for "observe" and meant "observant" or "devotee." Another researcher has rightly noted that "as soon as we leave philology, the evidence seems to preclude connection with Nazareth." He suggests that Nazarene has a "religious rather than a geographical origin" (Kennard, 1947: 79).

The writers of the New Testament are unlikely to have made up the term "Nazarene." Even though Matthew has used this title to emphasize Jesus' status as the fulfillment of an Old Testament prophecy, the writers of the other three Gospels and Acts use this epithet without any implicit or explicit suggestions. "Nazarene" must have been already in circulation when it was used by Mark, the earliest New Testament book in which this term appears. There is no conflict between this and the fact that Matthew's etymology of Nazarene is false. Let's now turn our attention to see what the Qur'an has to say about this intriguing term.

12.3. The Nazarenes of the Qur'an

The plural word *Naṣārā* (Nazarenes) appears 14 times in 13 verses in the Qur'an (2.62, 2.111, 2.113, 2.120, 2.135, 2.140, 5.14, 5.18, 5.51, 5.69, 5.82, 9.30, 22.17). In *all* these verses, the term denotes followers of Jesus, which is why I have translated it as "Christians," as in the following examples:

And the Jews will not be pleased with you [O Muhammad!], nor will the *Naṣārā* (Christians), until you follow their creed. Say: "The guidance of Allah is the real guidance." And if you follow their desires after the knowledge that has come to you, you shall have no guardian or helper from Allah (2.120).

And they [the Jews and Christians] say: "Be Jews or *Naṣārā* (Christians) and then you will be on the right course." Say [O Muhammad!]: "Rather [follow] the religion of Abraham [which is the real guidance], the upright, and he was not one of the polytheists" (2.135).

The singular *Naṣrānī* (Nazarene) appears only once in the Qur'an, also meaning a follower of Jesus or "Christian":

Abraham was not a Jew nor a *Naṣrānī* (Christian) but he was upright, a Muslim (someone who surrendered to God), and he was not one of the polytheists (3.67).

Like other titles and names of individuals and groups, *Naṣrānī* and *Naṣārā* were not introduced into Arabic by the Qur'an at the time of its revelation. They must have been already part of the vocabulary of the Arab population of the Arabian Peninsula who used them for any Christian or group of Christians. Verses 4.14 and 5.82 refer to the Christians as "those who have said 'we are *Naṣārā*,'" clearly indicating that *Naṣrānī* and *Naṣārā* were already in use before the revelation of the Qur'an. These pre-Qur'anic terms must have developed from other languages and made their way into the language of the Arab population of Arabia. They originated in Palestine. The same can be said of the term *yahūd* which is applied to the Jews.

In Hebrew, the adjective *nuṣrī* means "Nazarene"; Jesus is called *Jeshū ha-nuṣrī*. Christians are called *nuṣrīm*. When this word passed into Syriac as an exclusive name for Christians, it became *Naṣraye*. Nazareth in Syriac is *Naṣrat*. It has been suggested that *Naṣārā* was probably developed from the Syriac *Naṣraye* which spread to parts of the Eastern empires (Moore, 1920: 426; Parrinder, 1995: 152-153).

Orientalists often argue that the inclusion of words of non-Arabic origin in the Qur'an contradicts the Qur'an's repeated assertion that it was revealed "in Arabic" (12.2, 13.37, 20.113, 26.195, 39.28, 41.3, 41.44, 42.7, 43.3, 46.12) and "in manifest Arabic" (16.103, 26.195). What this argument fails to consider is that what the Qur'an calls Arabic is simply the language of Muhammad, to whom the Qur'an was revealed, and the Arab population, among whom the Qur'an was revealed. "Arabic" is not a hypothetical language that existed in isolation of people. The fact that the Qur'an was revealed in Arabic is often used by the same book to stress that, unlike other non-Arabic divine books, it is easy to understand by its immediate target audience, so they had no reason not to comprehend and believe in it:

We have sent it down as an Arabic Qur'an that you [O people!] may understand (12.2).

Certainly We know that they (the disbelievers) say: "It is a man that teaches him." The tongue of that to whom they attribute the Qur'an is foreign, and this is clear Arabic tongue (16.103).

Had We made this as a Qur'an in a foreign language, they (the disbelievers) would have said: "Why have its verses not been explained? What! A foreign [book] and an Arab [messenger]?" (41.44).

Calling the Christians *Naṣārā* does not make the Qur'an less Arabic. It is actually what the Qur'an had to call the Christians to be perfectly Arabic. This argument applies to any other names and words in the Qur'an that are thought to be of non-Arabic origin. Any objection to this simple fact is the result of misunderstanding what the Qur'an means by describing itself as being "in manifest Arabic," and is based on the impossible assumption that the language called "Arabic" can be defined in isolation of its speakers. Anything that the Arabs knew and used was Arabic, and anything that they did not know or use was not. This defines what is and what is not Arabic in the Qur'anic terminology.

The fact that the name *Naṣrānī* and its plural *Naṣārā* were adopted from other languages means that they were not derived from an Arabic root. It is possible, of course, to try to relate these terms to an Arabic word — because Hebrew, Syriac, and Arabic are relative languages — but that attempt would be artificial, as these terms were imported into the language of the Arabs. This probably explains the atypical formation of these singular and plural terms. A regular Arabic plural of *Naṣrānī* would have been *Naṣrāniyyūn*.

The non-Arabic origin of *Naṣrānī* and *Naṣārā* and the fact that they were used as names mean that these terms did not have any other meaning. Arabs did not relate them to verbs or nouns in their own language and did not use them to develop new words. Besides being the names of Christians, *Naṣrānī* and *Naṣārā* had no other meaning. The Arabs could not have known how these words came into existence, i.e. what their original meaning was. This meaning, however, is explained in the Qur'an.

The Qur'an does not contain a direct explanation of the meaning of *Naṣrānī* and *Naṣārā* in the same way that Matthew presents the etymology of *Nazorios*. Nevertheless, it contains four verses that combine to explain the meaning of these terms. More specifically, two of these verses — which, interestingly, do not contain the terms *Naṣrānī* or *Naṣārā* — provide the explanation, and the other two confirm that explanation. Let me explain.

Let's look first at the two verses that explain the name given to the Christians (verse 3.52 is further discussed later (p. 437)):

But when Jesus perceived disbelief on their part, he said: "Who are my *anṣār* (supporters) in the cause of Allah?" The companions said: "We are Allah's *anṣār*. We believe in Allah, and do you bear witness that we are Muslims" (3.52).

O you who believe! Be Allah's *anṣār* (supporters), as Jesus son of Mary said to the companions: "Who are my *anṣār* in the cause of Allah?" The companions said: "We are Allah's *anṣār*." Then a party of the Children of Israel believed and a party disbelieved, therefore we aided those who believed against their enemy, so they became the ones that prevailed (61.14).

The plural word *anṣār* means "supporter," "helpers" ...etc. Its singular is *nāṣir* (e.g. 47.13, 72.24) or *nāṣīr* (e.g. 2.107, 22.71). The verb of *anṣār* is *naṣara* which means "supported," aided," helped," sided with" ...etc. The term *anṣār* occurs in other verses in the Qur'an in the sense of "supporters." For instance, the Muslim residents of al-Madīna were called *anṣār* because they offered support and hospitality to and shared their belongings with their immigrant brothers and sisters who had to flee their homes in Mecca because of persecution in the early years of Islam (9.100, 9.117).

Verses 3.52 and 61.14 probably describe an event that happened shortly before an attempt at Jesus' life that was followed by the crucifixion of someone else (p. 437). These verses indicate that the plural word *anṣār* is the Arabic equivalent of *Naṣārā*, and thus reveal its original meaning. These verses also explain the historical event in which this term was coined and its religious significance. The word *anṣār* occurs in the context of calling the Christians the *anṣār* of Jesus on the way to God, which means ultimately the supporters of God to whom Jesus was calling people. It was not a term coined by people to refer to Jesus or relate him to his birthplace, as Matthew claims, but a name that Jesus coined for his followers to underline what he wanted them to be: supporters of God, i.e. supporters of the truth against falsehood. The meaning of *anṣār* in this context, which is what the name "Nazarenes" originally meant, is so praiseworthy and honorific that in verse 61.14 God commands the followers of Prophet Muhammad to become supports of God in the same sense of Jesus' exhortation to his followers to become *anṣār* of God.

Although 3.52 and 61.14 talk about Jesus describing his followers with a term that is very close to the name *Naṣārā*, linking these verses to the term *Naṣārā* may still look questionable or farfetched to some. This is where the other two verses can be called upon to lend support to this interpretation:

> And We made a covenant with those who have said "we are *Naṣārā*," but they forgot a part of what they were reminded of. Therefore We have stirred up enmity and hatred among them till the Day of Resurrection; and Allah will inform them of what they did (5.14).

> You [O Muhammad!] will certainly find the people with most enmity for those who believe to be the Jews and the polytheists. And you will certainly find the nearest in friendship to those who believe to be those who have said "we are *Naṣārā*," because there are among them priests and monks, and because they are not arrogant (5.82).

The expression "those who have said 'we are *Naṣārā*" is unique in the Qur'an. No similar expression is used for the followers of any other religion. For instance, the followers of Moses are not called "those who have said 'we are Jews'" and the followers of Muhammad are not described as "those who have said 'we are Muslims'". Why are the Christians only referred to with this rather unusual expression? The key to understanding this expression is the event described in verses 3.52 and 61.14. God called the Christians "those who have said 'we are *Naṣārā*" in 5.14 and 5.82 after the historical event revealed in verses 3.52 and 61.14. God's description of all Christians, including those who lived after Jesus, as having said "we are *Naṣārā*," indicates that any person who declares himself/herself a *Naṣrānī* or Christian implies by this claim that he or she has taken the same oath taken by Jesus' companions when they declared themselves before him as *anṣār* of God.

It is also possible that in the event described in 3.52 and 61.14 Jesus *did not coin* a new name for his followers but simply *reminded* his companions of the name or description that God had already given to his followers in the book that was revealed to him — the Injīl. In this scenario, it would be God who called the Christians *anṣār* or "Nazarenes," and Jesus' role in the dialog was only to remind his companions of that name and the responsibility it entailed.

There is another very significant observation that confirms the interpretation that links *Naṣārā* or Nazarenes to the historical event of the *anṣār* of Jesus described in verses 5.14 and 5.82. While both words *Naṣrānī* and *Naṣārā* are used for Jesus' followers, they are never applied to the master himself! The Qur'an calls 'Īsā (Jesus) *al-Masīḥ* (the Messiah) and *Ibn Maryam* (son of Mary), describes him as a prophet and messenger, and confers on him a number of superlative descriptions, but it never calls him a *Naṣrānī* or considers him one of the *Naṣārā*. This very specific Qur'anic use of the term Nazarene which excludes Jesus cannot be unintentional or haphazard. It represents a fundamental and significant difference between the use of the terms "Nazarene" and "Nazarenes" in Christian writings and in the Qur'an, reflecting the difference in the meanings of the terms in the two sources.

We discussed in the previous section the serious problems with Matthew's etymology of Nazarene, but let's see if the Qur'anic etymology helps us understand how Matthew could have developed his erroneous view. One problem at the heart of Matthew's etymology is the misconception that Nazarene was a title for Jesus. The Gospels and Acts, where the New Testament uses "Nazarene" as an epithet for Jesus, were written at least several decades after the time of Jesus. Clearly, these authors used Nazarene as a title for Jesus, not only for his followers, because this is how it had come to be used by then. It would be very farfetched to suggest that the New Testament authors introduced this specific use of Nazarene. What seems to have happened is that by the time these books were written, many details and aspects of Jesus' religion, including the book that was revealed to him, had already been lost or become inaccessible to most people. The historical background of the name of Jesus' followers, Nazarene, was one piece of information that had become unavailable to most people, which allowed the development of the misuse of this term as a title for Jesus.

There are two main possibilities as to how Matthew, who was unaware of the real meaning of Nazarene, concluded that this title is derived from the name of the town where Jesus is supposed to have lived. **First**, since Nazareth is not mentioned in any record before the New Testament, it might have come into existence centuries after Jesus, which means that the authors of the New Testament effectively created it. This is in line with the view of some researchers that the silence of ancient writings on Nazareth indicates that this town was only later established. This possibility would mean that it is in fact Nazareth the town which acquired its name from the word "Nazarenes" not the other way around as suggested in Matthew. The problem with this scenario is that it supposes that while Matthew did not know the meaning of Nazarene, he thought, for an unknown reason, that it must have been derived from the place where Jesus lived, so he went ahead and made up Nazareth as the name of that town! This is how one researcher outlined the farfetched nature of this scenario:

> Those who deny Nazareth an existence are constrained to explain its existence in the Gospels as an invention due to a false etymology: *Nazarenos*, *Nazorios*, being mistakenly supposed to be partial adjectives, a "Nazareth" was created to derive them from; then stories were told connecting Jesus with his imaginary home; and finally, in the third or fourth century, when Christians were hunting holy places, the site was discovered, or, more exactly, the name was fastened on an obscure village in Lower Galilee, which has borne it ever since. (Moore, 1920: 429)

The **second**, and more likely, scenario is that there was already a town called Nazareth, and Matthew thought that the similarity between the name of this town and the term Nazarene was too much to be fortuitous. He then surmised that Nazarene must have meant "of Nazareth."

In any case, unlike Matthew, the Qur'an presents a realistic etymology for "Nazarene" which does not have historical or any other problems.

13

The Messiah

Jesus is given a number of titles in the New Testament. Along with "son of God," the "Messiah (Christ)" is the most prominent and used of these titles. The Qur'an also calls Jesus the "Messiah," but Judaism, where the term "Messiah" first appeared, does not accept that Jesus was the Messiah.

In the Old Testament, the title "Messiah" was applied to a number of people who were anointed with oil as a mark of God's support for them. Later in Jewish history this title started to denote a future king who would liberate the Jews from foreign bondage and reinstate the kingdom of Israel.

The New Testament gives the title "Christ" a number of different identities and attributes. He was the son of King David, miracle worker, king of the Jews, founder of the imminent kingdom of God, salvational figure, and virtuous teacher. The "suffering Christ" is a purely Christian image that is not found in Jewish literature.

While the Qur'an confirms that Jesus was the Messiah, the Qur'anic Messiah is very different from the New Testament's.

13.1. The Messiah in the Old Testament

The title "Messiah," which is *Mashiaḥ* in Hebrew and *Meshiḥa* in Aramaic, means the "anointed one." It is derived from the religious practice of anointing with oil, which indicates God's support for and approval of the anointed person. The Old Testament does not apply this term to only one person or role, but to a number of different people and positions. In its 39 occurrences in the Old Testament, the term is applied to people who occupied three different positions: priest, prophet, and king. It is also used for the nation of Israel.

This is one instance where the Old Testament talks about the anointment of priests:

> You are to bring Aaron and his sons to the entrance of the tent of meeting and wash them with water. Then you are to clothe Aaron with the holy garments and anoint him and sanctify him that he may minister as my priest. You are to bring his sons and clothe them with tunics and anoint them just as you anointed their father, that they may minister as my priests; and their anointing will make them a priesthood that will continue throughout their generations. (Exo. 40:12-15)

One example of the anointment of a prophet is Isaiah's:

> The spirit of the sovereign Lord is upon me, because the Lord has anointed me. He has commissioned me to encourage the poor, to help the brokenhearted, to decree the release of captives, and the freeing of prisoners. (Isa. 61:1)

The NET Bible renders the term "chosen," but the original Hebrew word is that for "anointed," so I have used the latter.

The Old Testament says that Prophet Samuel anointed Saul as king (1 Sam. 10:1). After the death of Saul, God commanded Samuel to anoint a new king. Samuel could not recognize in any of Jesse's sons that were presented to him the future king, so he asked Jesse to bring his youngest son — the only one who had not been presented to Samuel:

> So Jesse had him brought in. Now he was ruddy, with attractive eyes and a handsome appearance. The Lord said, "Go and anoint him. This is the one!" So Samuel took the horn full of olive oil and anointed him in the midst of his brothers. The Spirit of the Lord rushed upon David from that day onwards. (1 Sam. 16:12-13)

God's following words to Prophet Elijah give examples of the anointment of both kings and prophets:

> Go back the way you came and then head for the Desert of Damascus. Go and anoint Hazael king over Syria. You must anoint Jehu son of Nimshi king over Israel, and Elisha son of Shaphat from Abel Meholah to take your place as prophet. (1 Kings 19:15-16)

In addition to its application to priests, prophets, and kings, the term "Messiah" is used in the Old Testament as a referent to the entire people of Israel also, in the context of describing God's promise to Abraham (Ps. 105:15):

> Remember continually his covenantal decree, the promise he made to a thousand generations —the promise he made to Abraham, the promise he made by oath to Isaac! He gave it to Jacob as a decree, to Israel as a lasting promise, saying, "To you I will give the land of Canaan as the portion of your inheritance." When they were few in number, just a very few, and foreign residents within it, they wandered from nation to nation, and from one kingdom to another. He let no one oppress them, he disciplined kings for their sake, saying, "Don't touch my anointed ones! Don't harm my prophets!" (1 Chr. 16:15-22)

Furthermore, the Old Testament does not restrict the title "anointed" to Jews. It applies this term to the Persian king Cyrus (580/590-529 BCE) (Isa. 45:1). After defeating the Babylonians in 539 BCE, Cyrus allowed the Jews, who had been taken captive from Jerusalem and forced into exile by the Babylonian king Nebuchadnezzar early in that century, to go back to Palestine.

The term Messiah is applied in the Old Testament to *historical* not *future* figures. According to the *Jewish Encyclopedia*:

> "The Messiah" (with the article and not in opposition with another word) is, however, not an Old Testament expression, but occurs for the first time in apocalyptic literature. Similarly, in all probability, the use of the word "Mashiakh" to denote the Messianic king is not found earlier than the apocalyptic literature.

At the same time, there are Biblical passages that do not use the term Messiah yet are considered to have *messianic expectations* of future figures who would come to rescue Israel and defeat its enemy. These are among the messianic prophecies that do not use the term Messiah (Mic. 5:1; Zech. 9:9):

> For a child has been born to us, a son has been given to us. He shoulders responsibility and is called: Extraordinary Strategist, Mighty God, Everlasting Father, Prince of Peace. His dominion will be vast and he will bring immeasurable prosperity. He will rule on David's throne and over David's kingdom, establishing it and strengthening it by promoting justice and fairness, from this time forward and forevermore. The Lord's intense devotion to his people will accomplish this. (Isa. 9:6-7)

> A shoot will grow out of Jesse's root stock, a bud will sprout from his roots. The Lord's spirit will rest on him — a spirit that gives extraordinary wisdom, a spirit that provides the ability to execute plans, a spirit that produces absolute loyalty to the Lord. He will take delight in obeying the Lord. He will not judge by mere appearances, or make decisions on the basis of hearsay. He will treat the poor fairly, and make right decisions for the downtrodden of the earth. He will strike the earth with the rod of his mouth, and order the wicked to be executed. Justice will be like a belt around his waist, integrity will be like a belt around his hips. A wolf will reside with a lamb, and a leopard will lie down with a young goat; an ox and a young lion will graze together, as a small child leads them along. A cow and a bear will graze together, their young will lie down together. A lion, like an ox, will eat straw. A baby will play over the hole of a snake; over the nest of a serpent an infant will put his hand. They will no longer injure or destroy on my entire royal mountain. For there will be universal submission to the Lord's sovereignty, just as the waters completely cover the sea. At that time a root from Jesse will stand like a signal flag for the nations. Nations will look to him for guidance, and his residence will be majestic. At that time the sovereign master will again lift his hand to reclaim the remnant of his people from Assyria, Egypt, Pathros, Cush, Elam, Shinar, Hamath, and the seacoasts. He will lift a signal flag for the nations; he will gather Israel's dispersed people and assemble Judah's scattered people from the four corners of the earth. (Isa. 11:1-12)

Thus, in the Old Testament the term Messiah and messianic expectations occur in different passages. Those who are called Messiahs are not associated with soteriological expectations, and messianic expectations are not linked to figures called Messiahs.

It is important to realize that messianic passages in the Old Testament were not always understood to be messianic, and that not all Jews agreed on which passages are messianic. These passages were interpreted in different ways by different groups in different periods of Jewish history.

After the overthrowing of the Davidic rulers of Judea by Nebuchadnezzar in 586 BCE, the phrase "the anointed king" started to mean "*the* Messiah" as the final Jewish king who would free them from foreign control, reestablish the Jewish kingdom, and return to Israel its lost glory (Vermes, 2000: 177). Jews started to give more attention to the figure of a Messiah particularly after the fall of the Maccabean dynasty (165-63 BEC), becoming under Roman rule, and the usurping of Judea by Herod the Great (40-4 BCE) and his family who were backed by the heathen Romans. This waiting for the Messiah grew stronger in the years leading to the two Jewish revolts against the Roman in 66-70 and 132-135 CE. But even during these unpleasant periods, the concept of the Messiah and messianic expectation were never central to Jewish theology:

> Christians with no expert knowledge of Jewish religious history tend to conceive of the Messiah as the central figure in the theology of the Jews in the ages of Jesus, a figure dominating every other hope of Judaism. In fact messianic fervour, far from being all-pervasive, was only sporadically attested in Jewish literature, mostly amid the political upheavals of the last two pre-Christian centuries and in the first century AD. The main messianic theme refers to the triumph of the future anointed king of the house of David, who was to restore the sovereignty of the Jewish people after bringing to an end centuries of foreign domination and overthrowing the mighty Roman empire. (Vermes, 2000: 28-29)

Among the many different Messiahs that may be identified in one way or another in the scripture, the one described as the "son of David" became the most prominent:

> This diversity of messianic figures and their function should not obscure the prime importance of the Davidic messiah. Messianic expectation was not universal; both those who chose to speculate in this vein had, in the classical prophetic texts and later apocalyptic interpretations of them, a readily available body of tradition to draw on. The Messiah son of David is the best and most widely attested figure, cutting across sectarian as well as temporal lines. We can trace him from the classical Jewish biblical histories and prophets through the multitudinous intertestamental texts just reviewed on into rabbinic prayers and benedictions. His role in history's final drama was

clear. "See, Lord, and raise up for them their king, the son of David," prayed the author of the pseudonymous Psalms of Solomon sometime in the first century BCE, "at the time that you have knowledge of [i.e., the Endtime], and gird him with strength, so he may smash those who rule without justice" (17:23). Executing Judgment, defeating the enemies of God, reigning over a restored Israel, establishing unending peace, this eschatological prince epitomized the military prowess, valor, and virtues of his royal ancestor, the warrior king David. (Fredriksen, 2001: 124)

The belief that God will send the Messiah, who is a descendant of David, at the end times to effect Israel's redemption was not, however, adopted by all Jews (Fredriksen, 2001: 129).

Professor Sanders draws attention to the fact that pre-Christian sources were not unanimous in their depiction of the awaited royal "son of David" Messiah who would destroy Israel's enemies and restore its glory. He is not presented always as a military leader like his ancestral king. For instance, the Greek Psalms of Solomon, which is probably a translation from the Hebrew, states that the Messiah would subject all nations and establish the rule of God on earth but without resorting to military means, as God will be his source of power:

> For he shall not put his trust in horse and rider and bow,
> Nor shall he multiply for himself gold and silver for war,
> Nor shall he gather confidence from a multitude for the day of battle.
> The Lord Himself is his king, the hope of him that is mighty through his hope in God.
> (PsSol. 17)

While still a military leader, this kingly Messiah does not use the normal military means that his ancestor David used, but he relies on some unclear intervention by God. He is the king, but God is the warrior. David, on the other hand, was a warrior king.

The Dead Sea or Qumran Scrolls — which were written by members of a strict, isolated Jewish sect in the 2nd century BCE that is identified with the Essenes whom Josephus mentions — talk about two awaited Messiahs, one of them descended from David the king, but the other is a descendant of Aaron the priest. It is the priestly Messiah who has the authority. The Davidic Messiah plays no role in the final battle of the Sons of Light against the Sons of Darkness. The priests gather people, but the fighting is done by angels and the final blow is delivered by God himself (Sanders, 1995: 89).

The rather vague and confused concept of the Messiah and messianic expectations in Jewish literature was given yet more ambiguity and contradiction by the authors of the New Testament.

13.2. The Christ in the New Testament

The term "Messiah" appears in the Greek New Testament as many as 571 times — 569 as *Christos* (Χριστός), from which "Christ" is derived, and twice as *Messias* (Μεσσίας) (John 1:41, 4:25). Mark, the oldest of the four Gospels, has the term Christ only 7 times, whereas Matthew uses it 16 times, Luke 11, and John 20. The significantly higher number and frequency in which the term appears in the New Testament than Old Testament shows that the concept of the Messiah plays a substantially bigger role in Christianity. In contrast to its minor role in the Old Testament, the concept of the Messiah takes centre stage in the New Testament. All New Testament writers recognize Jesus as the Christ. Luke (2:11) states that the angel who appeared to the shepherds told them that Jesus is the Christ. Let's examine what Christ meant to the New Testament authors and how this title compares to the Messiahs of the Old Testament.

It would seem logical to start with Paul, mainly because he is the earliest of the New Testament authors, but also because the term "Christ" makes most of its New Testament appearances in his letters. Paul uses the term Christ as a proper name not a title, hence the very common phrase "Jesus Christ" in his writings. He does not explicitly explain his understanding of Christhood. His use of the term Christ seems to suggest that he presumed people understood what Christ meant. Because of this silence, it is difficult to tell with confidence what Paul could have understood Christ to mean. Paul's Jesus is a spiritual figure who came to redeem people, by being crucified and raised. It is possible that this is what Paul took the term Christ to mean. It is not clear where he got this unique understanding from. It is not derived from his Jewish background, nor is it an image that we find in the Gospels to suggest that it was already shared by other early Christians.

Additionally, given Paul's almost complete lack of interest in the historical Jesus, which is partly due to his ignorance of that history, it is reasonable to expect the Evangelists, who recorded Jesus' history, to be more informed on this issue, so we will focus on the Gospels. Over the centuries, most Christians shared Paul's disinterest in the historical Jesus and almost complete concentration on the risen Jesus.

In this section, we will study the various aspects of the Gospels' image of the Messiah, in general, and Jesus' Messiahship, in particular. We should embrace ourselves for some hard work with passages that are not always in harmony and are at times outright contradictory.

13.2.1. Self-proclamation and the Public Acceptance of Jesus' Messiahship

Mark and Luke recount that when Jesus asked his disciples whom they thought he was, Peter replied that Jesus was the Christ. Jesus responded by commanding the disciples not to tell anyone (Mark 8:29-30; Luke 9:20-21). This *implies* that

Jesus accepted that he was the Christ but did not want that to be made public for some reason. Matthew also reports this story, but he changes Jesus' reply to one that is more *explicitly* endorsing of Peter's words: "you are blessed, Simon son of Jonah, because flesh and blood did not reveal this to you, but my Father in heaven!" (Matt. 16:17), and he then reiterates Mark's and Luke's statements that Jesus "instructed his disciples not to tell anyone that he was the Christ" (Matt. 16:20). Luke (4:41) also states that Jesus would not allow demons to reveal that he was the Christ.

John, on the other hand, reports an encounter between Jesus and a Samaritan woman in which he clearly tells the woman that he was the awaited Messiah:

> The woman said to him, "I know that Messiah is coming" (the one called Christ); "whenever he comes, he will tell us everything." Jesus said to her, "I, the one speaking to you, am he." Now at that very moment his disciples came back. They were shocked because he was speaking with a woman. However, no one said, "What do you want?" or "Why are you speaking with her?" Then the woman left her water jar, went off into the town and said to the people, "Come, see a man who told me everything I ever did. Surely he can't be the Messiah, can he?" So they left the town and began coming to him. (John 4:25-30)

Not only ordinary people called Jesus the Christ, but even Pilate described him as the one who is called the Christ (Matt. 27:17, 27:22).

Reports of Jesus' trial contain his most explicit claim to being the Christ. When asked by the high priest if he was the Christ, Jesus told him "you have said it yourself," according to Matthew (26:64), or more emphatically "I am," according to Mark (14:62). The other two Evangelists have a slightly different story. When the Jewish leaders asked Jesus whether he was the Christ, he replied that if he would tell them they would not believe him (Luke 22:67), which must imply that the answer would be yes. According to John's version, Jesus had already told them but they would not believe (John 10:24-25). In Luke (23:2) also, the Jewish elders accuse Jesus of claiming to be the Christ.

Another confirmation that Jesus declared himself as the Christ may also be read in Jesus' following warning to his disciples on the Mount of Olives (also Matt. 24:23-24):

> If anyone says to you, "Look, here is the Christ!" or "Look, there he is!" do not believe him. For false messiahs and false prophets will appear and perform signs and wonders to deceive, if possible, the elect." (Mark 13:21-22)

Mark (13:5-6) and Matthew (24:4-5) report another warning by Jesus that many would claim to be the Christ and would try to mislead people. These passages suggest that there was no shortage of claimants to the role of the Messiah, but they also mean that Jesus considered and declared himself as "the Christ." The emphasis that Jesus is the only Christ may also be seen in his words to people and his disciples: "Nor are you to be called 'teacher,' for you have one teacher, the Christ" (Matt. 23:10).

Some scholars have questioned whether Jesus thought of himself as a Messiah (Sanders, 1995: 241-242), whereas some of those who accepted he did consider himself the Messiah questioned whether he ever called himself so (Parrinder, 1995: 32). The evidence presented above refutes both views. Although there is no Gospel passage in which Jesus goes out of his way to emphasize that he is the Christ or ask people to call him so, there are others in which he clearly claims that he was the Messiah, even if these were in response to a question or statement from someone. If Jesus' reported attempts to limit the use of the title Christ are true, they must reflect his efforts to detach himself from the political and nationalistic expectations that people had attached to this title, which we will consider later. In my view, the Gospels leave no room for questioning the fact that Jesus did believe that he was the Christ and that he did let people know that. Theissen and Merz (1999: 540, 553) also make the point that unlike other qualities that were attached to Jesus and deeds and words that were attributed to him after the Easter experience, which the historical Jesus knew nothing about, the fact that no one would become the Christ after rising from the dead means that this title must have already been assigned to Jesus in his life. It is difficult to see how this title could have spread without at least Jesus' implicit consent.

13.2.2. Faces of the Messiah

The Evangelists presented the Christ through a number of different identities and attributes. Only by considering all these different faces we can see Jesus' complete picture in the Gospels.

13.2.2.1. Son of David

The Synoptics agree that people called Jesus the "son of David" (e.g. Mark 10:48; Matt. 9:27; Luke 18:38), which is one belief about the Messiah that Christians inherited from the Jews. Unable to link Jesus to David through Mary's ancestry, Matthew and Luke used Joseph's genealogy to show that Jesus descended from David. Matthew (1:1) also links this blood relationship with David with the title Christ as he starts his Gospel with what he describes as "the genealogy of Jesus Christ, the son of David, the son of Abraham." This same link is also found in John (7:42) where people are seen asking: "Don't the scriptures say that the Christ is a descendant of David and comes from Bethlehem, the village where David lived?"

Jesus' birthplace and his descent from David have been linked by the Evangelists. Matthew claims that Jewish scholars — or at least those whom Herod consulted — believed that the Christ was to be born in Bethlehem:

> After assembling all the chief priests and experts in the law, he asked them where the Christ was to be born. "In Bethlehem of Judea," they said, "for it is written this way by

the prophet: 'And you, Bethlehem, in the land of Judah, are in no way least among the rulers of Judah, for out of you will come a ruler who will shepherd my people Israel.'" (Matt. 2:4-6)

I have already discussed how Matthew manipulated the prediction in Micah 5:2 and applied it to Jesus (pp. 166-167).

Luke (2:11) states that the angel told the shepherds that the Christ was born in the city of David, which was introduced earlier as Bethlehem (Luke 2:4). The Old Testament already stated that David was from Bethlehem (1 Sam. 16:1). John also states that some rejected that Jesus was the Messiah on the basis that the scripture says that the Christ would not come from Galilee but from Bethlehem (John 7:41-43). John also contains a confusing statement about some people who denied that Jesus was the Christ because they knew where he had come from yet "whenever the Christ comes, no one will know where he comes from" (John 7:27).

Despite the Evangelists' repeated statements, the Synoptics (Matt. 22:41-46; Luke 20:41-44) report an incident in which Jesus clearly objected to the claim that the Christ was the son of David! This is Mark's report:

> While Jesus was teaching in the temple courts, he said, "How is it that the experts in the law say that the Christ is David's son? David himself, by the Holy Spirit, said, 'The Lord said to my lord, "Sit at my right hand, until I put your enemies under your feet."' 'If David himself calls him 'Lord,' how can he be his son?" And the large crowd was listening to him with delight. (Mark 12:35-37)

It may be argued that Jesus was trying to make some theological point here, for instance to emphasize Christ's superiority to David. But if that is the case then Jesus would have at least solved the puzzle for his audience and not left them questioning what is supposed to be one of the basic facts about the Christ: his descent from David. Surely, Jesus could not have helped his audience pick any subtle point he might have wanted to make about the origin of the Christ by presenting his audience with a difficult puzzle that, on the face of it, means that the Messiah could not have been a son of David. In the only instance in which Jesus talks about the Messiah's alleged blood relation to King David, he rejects this link.

13.2.2.2. Miracle Worker

All four Evangelists claim that the Christ was understood to be a miracle worker: "Yet many of the crowd believed in him and said, 'Whenever the Christ comes, he won't perform more miraculous signs than this man did, will he?'" (John 7:31). Luke suggests that Jesus was recognized as the Christ *because he performed miracles*:

> As the sun was setting, all those who had any relatives sick with various diseases brought them to Jesus. He placed his hands on every one of them and healed them. Demons also came out of many, crying out, "You are the Son of God!" But he rebuked

them, and would not allow them to speak, because they knew that he was the Christ. (Luke 4:40-41)

Bringing Lazarus back to life made his sister call Jesus the Christ (John 11:17-27). Elsewhere John states that Jesus' miracles prove that he is the Messiah:

> Now Jesus performed many other miraculous signs in the presence of the disciples, which are not recorded in this book. But these are recorded so that you may believe that Jesus is the Christ, the Son of God, and that by believing you may have life in his name. (John 20:30-31)

Peter acknowledged that Jesus was the Christ after the miracle of feeding 5,000 people (Luke 9:20). John (4:25-29) also tells us that the Samaritan woman who was the subject of one of Jesus' clairvoyance miracles accepted that he was the Messiah.

Matthew (11:2-5) and Luke report another incident in which Jesus clearly stresses to disciples of John the Baptists that his miracles attested to his status as the awaited Messiah, although the term "Messiah" is only implied:

> John's disciples informed him about all these things. So John called two of his disciples and sent them to Jesus to ask, "Are you the one who is to come, or should we look for another?" When the men came to Jesus, they said, "John the Baptist has sent us to you to ask, 'Are you the one who is to come, or should we look for another?' "At that very time Jesus cured many people of diseases, sicknesses, and evil spirits, and granted sight to many who were blind. So he answered them, "Go tell John what you have seen and heard: The blind see, the lame walk, lepers are cleansed, the deaf hear, the dead are raised, the poor have good news proclaimed to them." (Luke 7:18-22)

This passage utilizes an Isaiah (35:4-6) prophecy, which the Dead Sea Scrolls place in the time of the Messiah (Theissen & Merz, 1999: 212), and other Isaiah passages:

> Tell those who panic, "Look, your God comes to avenge! With divine retribution he comes to deliver you." Then blind eyes will open, deaf ears will hear. Then the lame will leap like a deer, the mute tongue will shout for joy; for water will flow in the desert, streams in the wilderness. (Isa. 35:4-6)

> Your dead will come back to life; your corpses will rise up. Wake up and shout joyfully, you who live in the ground! For you will grow like plants drenched with the morning dew, and the earth will bring forth its dead spirits. (Isa. 26:19)

> At that time the deaf will be able to hear words read from a scroll, and the eyes of the blind will be able to see through deep darkness. The downtrodden will again rejoice in

the Lord; the poor among mankind will take delight in the sovereign king of Israel. (Isa. 29:18-19)

The spirit of the sovereign Lord is upon me, because the Lord has chosen me. He has commissioned me to encourage the poor, to help the brokenhearted, to decree the release of captives, and the freeing of prisoners. (Isa. 61:1)

In keeping with his keen interest in representing Jesus' life as the fulfillment of Old Testament prophecies, Matthew reminds his readers that Jesus' miracles fulfilled a specific prophecy in Isaiah:

When it was evening, many demon-possessed people were brought to him. He drove out the spirits with a word, and healed all who were sick. In this way what was spoken by Isaiah the prophet was fulfilled: "He took our weaknesses, and carried our diseases." (Matt. 8:16-17)

The prophecy in question is part of this passage: "But he lifted up our illnesses, he carried our pain; even though we thought he was being punished, attacked by God, and afflicted for something he had done" (Isa. 53:4).

Matthew says that after being physically attacked by the Sanhedrin during his summary trial, Jesus was sarcastically asked by his abusers to "prophesy" who hit him (Matt. 26:68). This also suggests that the Christ was expected to have paranormal powers, including the ability to know the names of people whom he had not met before. The same connection between the Christ and miracles is met in Mark's scene of the crucifixion, when the chief priests and the experts mocked him saying: "Let the Christ, the king of Israel, come down from the cross now, that we may see and believe!" (Mark 15:32).

Matthew reports five different instances in which people called Jesus the "Son of David," meaning the Messiah, because of his miracles (Matt. 9:27, 12:23, 15:22, 20:30, 21:15). One of these incidents (Matt. 20:30) is found in Mark (10:47) and Luke (18:38) also.

Despite what the Gospels say, Jews in the first century, Professor Sanders explains, never linked the title Messiah to performing miracles or sonship of God:

The early Christians thought that Jesus was the Messiah, the Son of God, *and* a miracle-worker. This has led many modern Christians to think that first-century Jews looked for a Messiah who performed miracles, and that Jesus' contemporaries would conclude that a miracle-worker was the Messiah. This view is incorrect. The few references to a coming Messiah in Jewish literature do not depict him as a miracle-worker. There was no expectation of a coming Son of God at all. Like other ancient people, Jews believed in miracles but did not think that the ability to perform them proved exalted status. The combination of the titles "Messiah" and "Son of

God" with the ability to perform miracles is a Christian one, the result of assigning both titles to Jesus, who was known in his day as a miracle-worker. (Sanders, 1995: 132-133)

Even if the Messiah was not expected to perform miracles, Jesus' miracles must have supported his claims, one of which is that he was the Christ. The Gospels' suggestion that Jesus tried to keep some of his miracles secret (e.g. Mark 1:44, 5:43, 7:36; Matt. 8:4, 9:30; Luke 5:14, 8:56) cannot be true. I will deal with this in detail later (§16.2.5).

13.2.2.3. King of the Jews

The Gospels confirm that the Jews were waiting for the appearance of the Messiah who would liberate Israel and bring back its glory. Luke has the following to say about a man who lived during Jesus' childhood:

> Now there was a man in Jerusalem named Simeon who was righteous and devout, looking for the restoration of Israel, and the Holy Spirit was upon him. It had been revealed to him by the Holy Spirit that he would not die before he had seen the Lord's Christ. (Luke 2:25-26)

When Simeon met Jesus in the temple, he took him in his arms and started blessing God:

> Now, according to your word, Sovereign Lord, permit your servant to depart in peace. For my eyes have seen your salvation that you have prepared in the presence of all peoples: a light, for revelation to the Gentiles, and for glory to your people Israel. (Luke 2:29-32)

Given the Messiah's role to liberate Israel and restore its glory, it is no wonder that he was associated with the kingship of the Jews. The Messiah would bring good to the Gentiles also, according to Simeon.

Matthew's account of Jesus' story of birth shows that Herod took the title "king of the Jews" to mean "the Christ." We have already seen in the Old Testament that kings, in addition to priests and prophets, were anointed. In fact, "king of the Jews" is the most emphasized meaning of "the Christ" in the Gospels. Not only Herod, but people in general are shown to have understood "the Christ" in this sense. The term "king of the Jews" is not always explicitly associated with the title "the Christ," but the context makes it clear that Jesus was called king because he was considered to be the Christ. Let's review some of the passages that describe Jesus as a king.

Luke (19:38) tells us that Jesus' disciples praised him as "the king who comes in the name of the Lord." Stunned by what Jesus could know about him, Nathanael called Jesus "the king of Israel" (John 1:49). The same title was applied to Jesus by the crowd who came to meet him on his way to Jerusalem (John 12:13).

Explaining to Pilate Jesus' charges, the Jewish leaders said: "We found this man subverting our nation, forbidding us to pay the tribute tax to Caesar and claiming that he himself is Christ, a king" (Luke 23:2). When they found that Pilate started to sympathize with Jesus and think of releasing him, they used Jesus' supposed claim to kingship, which is what they understood messiahship to mean, to suggest that Jesus was challenging Caesar and that Pilate would not be acting as Caesar's friend if he tolerated that:

> From this point on, Pilate tried to release him. But the Jewish leaders shouted out, "If you release this man, you are no friend of Caesar! Everyone who claims to be a king opposes Caesar!" When Pilate heard these words he brought Jesus outside and sat down on the judgment seat in the place called "The Stone Pavement" (Gabbatha in Aramaic). (Now it was the day of preparation for the Passover, about noon.) Pilate said to the Jewish leaders, "Look, here is your king!" Then they shouted out, "Away with him! Away with him! Crucify him!" Pilate asked, "Shall I crucify your king?" The high priests replied, "We have no king except Caesar!" (John 19:12-15)

The Jewish leaders also mocked Jesus on the cross saying "Let the Christ, the king of Israel, come down from the cross now, that we may see and believe!" (Mark 15:32). The four Evangelists report that during his crucifixion, Jesus was sarcastically referred to as "king of the Jews" (e.g. Mark 15:18; Matt. 27:29; Luke 23:37; John 19:3). The titulus over the cross also called Jesus "king of the Jews" (Mark 15:26; Matt. 27:37; Luke 23:38; John 19:19).

The four Gospels state that Pilate questioned Jesus whether he claimed to be the king of the Jews. The Synoptics agree that Jesus answered "you say so" (Mark 15:2; Matt. 27:11; Luke 23:3). John gives a different, more detailed answer in which Jesus makes the extremely significant declaration that his kingdom was not of this world:

> So Pilate went back into the governor's residence, summoned Jesus, and asked him, "Are you the king of the Jews?" Jesus replied, "Are you saying this on your own initiative, or have others told you about me?" Pilate answered, "I am not a Jew, am I? Your own people and your chief priests handed you over to me. What have you done?" Jesus replied, "My kingdom is not from this world. If my kingdom were from this world, my servants would be fighting to keep me from being handed over to the Jewish authorities. But as it is, my kingdom is not from here." Then Pilate said, "So you are a king!" Jesus replied, "You say that I am a king. For this reason I was born, and for this reason I came into the world — to testify to the truth. Everyone who belongs to the truth listens to my voice." Pilate asked, "What is truth?" When he had said this he went back outside to the Jewish leaders and announced, "I find no basis for an accusation against him." (John 18:33-38)

Jesus here tells Pilate that his kingdom was actually in heaven. The Gospels attribute to Jesus many sayings in which he talks about the "kingdom of heaven." It is a kingdom that can be entered only by those who "turn around and become like little children" (Matt. 18:3; also Mark 10:15 and Luke 18:17). This kingdom, which Jesus also calls "kingdom of God," is clearly a spiritual kingdom. This is how Pilate also understood Jesus and he thus concluded that there was no basis for the charges against him. This is probably also why Pilate, speaking to the Jews, referred to Jesus the "one you call king of the Jews" (Mark 15:12). Indeed, nothing in what the Evangelists recorded of Jesus' sayings or works indicates in any way that he tried to or was interested in establishing an earthly kingdom or had any political ambitions. This is what John says happened after Jesus' miracle of feeding five thousand people:

> Now when the people saw the miraculous sign that Jesus performed, they began to say to one another, "This is certainly the Prophet who is to come into the world." Then Jesus, because he knew they were going to come and seize him by force to make him king, withdrew again up the mountainside alone. (John 6:14-15)

I fully agree with Vermes (2000: 181) that "contrary to the claim of some contemporary New Testament interpreters, the general context of the portrait of Jesus in the Synoptics and in the rest of the New Testament shows that he was not a pretender to the throne of David, or a would-be leader of a revolt against Rome." Even though Luke (1:32) claims that Gabriel told Mary about Jesus that "the Lord God will give him the throne of his father David," Jesus was not only never given that throne, but he never sought it in the first place.

Jewish sources also do not provide any evidence that Jesus claimed to be the king of Jews. The Christian concept of Jesus being a king is clearly inherited from Jewish tradition where the Messiah is an earthly king who would liberate the Israelites and re-establish their lost kingdom. But how and why was this non-political Christ, who appeared in a culture where kings were always earthly and where the awaited Messiah in particular was hoped to become the king who restores the lost earthly glory of Israel, turned into a spiritual king? There are two possible answers.

First, faced with the fact that Jesus' life ended without him establishing the lost and much hoped for kingdom, Christians moved the throne of the Christ from earth to heaven. Jesus' peaceful life did not include any royal achievement, and the way it ended reflected powerlessness of a commoner rather than authority of a royal. In order to salvage the claim that Jesus was the Messiah, this Christ had to be seen as spiritual. On the other hand, the majority who chose to remain faithful to the prevailing Jewish concept of the Messiah had no option but to reject that the powerless Jesus could be the awaited Christ. Even if Jesus tried to re-establish Israel's kingdom, something that is not only unattested but also rejected by the available records, he clearly failed, so he could not have been the Christ. While this version of history is possible, I do not find it likely.

The **second** and most likely scenario is that it was Jesus himself who stressed that he had no interest in earthly matters and that he was a spiritual teacher. The Evangelists' designation of Jesus as a heavenly king was an accurate depiction of how he portrayed himself. In this scenario, the Jews' denial of Jesus being the Christ was a natural result of their rejection of his correction of their definition of "the Messiah" and his failure to live up to their expectations. This version of history convincingly and fully explains how the Christ became a spiritual king. As I have pointed out above, there is nothing in Christian or extra-Christian sources that suggests that Jesus made claim to kingship of the Jews. The Gospels' reports of Jesus trying at times to keep his identity as the Christ secret (Mark 8:29-30; Matt. 16:20; Luke 4:41, 9:20-21), if were authentic, reflect his attempts to reject anything linking him to the concept of the king of the Jews rather than hide his identity as the Christ. The accusation that Jesus sought to become king of the Jews is first met in the Gospels during Jesus' trial whose accounts are full of historical inaccuracies in addition to internal inconsistencies, as we shall see in Chapter 18.

I think Jesus did confirm that he was the Christ, as I explained earlier, but he also disapproved of what the concept of the Christ had become. For him, the Christ was a spiritual prophet and teacher, not someone with a political or earthly agenda. This is probably why only a small minority of the Jews, not many thousands as suggested by the Gospels, believed in him, even though he was a miracle worker.

The Gospels also contain a story that shows Jesus avoid giving any indication that he may represent any political threat to the rulers (also Matt. 22:16-21; Luke 20:22-25):

> When they came they said to him, "Teacher, we know that you are truthful and do not court anyone's favor, because you show no partiality but teach the way of God in accordance with the truth. Is it right to pay taxes to Caesar or not? Should we pay or shouldn't we?" But he saw through their hypocrisy and said to them, "Why are you testing me? Bring me a denarius and let me look at it." So they brought one, and he said to them, "Whose image is this, and whose inscription?" They replied, "Caesar's." Then Jesus said to them, "Give to Caesar the things that are Caesar's, and to God the things that are God's." And they were utterly amazed at him. (Mark 12:14-17)

Jesus' teaching that the Christ was not an earthly king might also be read from his insistence that the Christ could not have been a "son of David" (Mark 12:35-37; Matt. 22:41-46; Luke 20:41-44). While the Synoptists call him the "son of David," in the only time that Jesus himself is cited about this issue he denies it. This contradiction should not surprise us. One striking relevant contradiction that we have already seen is that Matthew and Luke describe Jesus as the "son of David" and provide him with supportive genealogies, yet they claim at the same time that he was born to a virgin. Each Gospel was written to reflect certain traditions and perceptions, and there is no reason to suggest that these different sources and drives were always reconcilable. Clearly, they were not.

John severs another alleged link between Jesus and King David. Both Matthew and Luke claim that Jesus was born in Bethlehem, clearly to link him to David. John's Jesus is a Galilean who has no link with Bethlehem:

> Others said, "This is the Christ!" But still others said, "No, for the Christ doesn't come from Galilee, does he? Don't the scriptures say that the Christ is a descendant of David and comes from Bethlehem, the village where David lived?" So there was a division in the crowd because of Jesus. (John 7:41-43)

Mark also has no reference to Jesus being linked to Bethlehem. Mark (p. 215) and John (p. 216) make Nazareth Jesus' place of birth.

Clearly, it must have been Jesus who promoted the fact that the Messiah was a spiritual not earthly king.

13.2.2.4. Founder of an Imminent Kingdom

Despite the major difference between the Jewish earthly kingdom and the Christian heavenly kingdom of the Messiah, both traditions claimed that the establishment of this kingdom would take place shortly after the appearance of the awaited king. Jewish tradition states the Messiah would come to establish this kingdom. The New Testament authors clearly thought that the heavenly kingdom was imminent. They declared this through John the Baptist (Matt. 3:1-2), and attributed it also to Jesus (Mark 1:15; Matt. 4:17, 10:7). Matthew has Jesus tell his disciples that "there are some standing here who will not experience death before they see the Son of Man coming in his kingdom" (Matt. 16:28). In the earliest known Christian document, Paul wrote to reassure the Christians of Thessalonica in Macedonia as they were confounded by the death of fellow Christians who were expecting to witness the establishment of the kingdom of God in their lifetime:

> Now we do not want you to be uninformed, brothers and sisters, about those who are asleep, so that you will not grieve like the rest who have no hope. For if we believe that Jesus died and rose again, so also we believe that God will bring with him those who have fallen asleep as Christians. For we tell you this by the word of the Lord, that we who are alive, who are left until the coming of the Lord, will surely not go ahead of those who have fallen asleep. For the Lord himself will come down from heaven with a shout of command, with the voice of the archangel, and with the trumpet of God, and the dead in Christ will rise first. Then we who are alive, who are left, will be suddenly caught up together with them in the clouds to meet the Lord in the air. And so we will always be with the Lord. (1 The. 4:13-17)

Many scholars (e.g. Sanders, 1995: 95) think that the imminent arrival of the kingdom of God in the New Testament reflects Jesus' own belief. They think that he believed that God was going to intervene and bring about a radical change to the world. I disagree with this view which I think is a consequence of the wrong assumption that Jesus viewed his messiahship in the same way the Jews had understood it.

The Jews were expecting a military Messiah who would change the world radically during his lifetime, but Jesus saw his messiahship as one of confirming the previous messages that had been sent to people through various prophets. He did not share the view that his time was a climax of universal events. There was never such a culmination of events.

Any Jew who believed that Jesus was the Christ and also thought that he was going to fulfill his message during his lifetime would have believed that the change was imminent. The fact that Jesus had very little impact on the world and the messianic spiritual kingdom never materialized prompted some of Jesus' disappointed followers to create and promote the concept of his second coming, which is supposed to lead to the establishment of the kingdom of God. The imminent kingdom of the Christ is then a reference to Jesus' return.

The concept of the second coming was not created completely out of thin air, but it was based on Jesus' authentic prediction of the coming of Prophet Muhammad (§17.4). In other words, the concept of Jesus' return is a corruption of that prediction. I will discuss the concept of Jesus' second coming in more detail in Chapter 20.

13.2.2.5. Salvational Figure

The Synoptics make it clear that the title "the Christ" was understood to be associated with salvation. According to Luke, the angel told the shepherds: "Today your Savior is born in the city of David. He is Christ the Lord" (Luke 2:11). Similarly, while not using the term Christ, John tells that the Samaritans were convinced that Jesus was really "the Savior of the world" (John 4:42).

The accounts of Jesus' crucifixion contain a number of sarcastic remarks about Jesus being the Christ and saving people but not being able to save himself. Mark (15:31-32) states that the Jewish leaders mocked the crucified Jesus joking that "he saved others, but he cannot save himself! Let the Christ, the king of Israel, come down from the cross now, that we may see and believe!". Almost the same account is also found in Matthew (27:42), although the title Christ is not used: "He saved others, but he cannot save himself! He is the king of Israel! If he comes down now from the cross, we will believe in him!" Luke (23:35) has people who were watching the crucifixion mock Jesus saying: "He saved others. Let him save himself if he is the Christ of God, his chosen one!"

The soldiers told Jesus "if you are the king of the Jews, save yourself!" (Luke 23:37). One of the criminals who were crucified with him also said to Jesus sarcastically: "Aren't you the Christ? Save yourself and us!" (Luke 23:39).

For the Jews, the salvation of the Messiah king was about rescuing them from their heathen rulers and restoring the glory of Israel. For the Christians, whose Messiah described himself as a spiritual leader who was going to realize nothing of the Jewish dream, Jesus' salvation was spiritual. Nevertheless, Luke (24:21) reports that after Jesus' death two of his disciples disappointedly said that they "had hoped that he was the one who was going to redeem Israel."

Paul presented Jesus' salvational role differently, making Jesus save people from sin (§19.4.1).

13.2.2.6. Suffering Messiah

One major difference between the concepts of the Messiah in the New Testament and the Old Testament is that the New Testament's Christ suffered and died. The Gospels claim that Jesus predicted his suffering and death and that he taught that they were inevitable (Mark 8:31, 9:12; Matt. 16:21, 17:12; Luke 9:22, 17:25, 22:15, 24:26, 24:46). As the Evangelists called Jesus the Christ, they believed that the Christ had to suffer and die. One of these accounts directly links the suffering and death of Jesus with his identity as the Christ. Luke here recounts the story of Jesus' appearance to two of his disciples on Easter day:

> Now that very day two of them were on their way to a village called Emmaus, about seven miles from Jerusalem. They were talking to each other about all the things that had happened. While they were talking and debating these things, Jesus himself approached and began to accompany them (but their eyes were kept from recognizing him).
>
> Then he said to them, "What are these matters you are discussing so intently as you walk along?" And they stood still, looking sad. Then one of them, named Cleopas, answered him, "Are you the only visitor to Jerusalem who doesn't know the things that have happened there in these days?" He said to them, "What things?" "The things concerning Jesus the Nazarene," they replied, "a man who, with his powerful deeds and words, proved to be a prophet before God and all the people; and how our chief priests and rulers handed him over to be condemned to death, and crucified him. But we had hoped that he was the one who was going to redeem Israel. Not only this, but it is now the third day since these things happened. Furthermore, some women of our group amazed us. They were at the tomb early this morning, and when they did not find his body, they came back and said they had seen a vision of angels, who said he was alive. Then some of those who were with us went to the tomb, and found it just as the women had said, but they did not see him."
>
> So he said to them, "You foolish people — how slow of heart to believe all that the prophets have spoken! Wasn't it necessary for the Christ to suffer these things and enter into his glory?" Then beginning with Moses and all the prophets, he interpreted to them the things written about himself in all the scriptures. (Luke 24:13-27)

Luke (24:46-47) reinforces this message later by making Jesus say: "Thus it stands written that the Messiah would suffer and would rise from the dead on the third day, and repentance for the forgiveness of sins would be proclaimed in his name to all nations, beginning from Jerusalem." Like other prophecies that Matthew falsely attributes to scripture, this alleged prophecy does not exist in the Old Testament!

Judaism, in fact, never knew of a suffering or resurrected Messiah. The Christ was supposed to come and redeem Israel and reinstate the long-gone kingdom. He was not supposed to be tortured and die on the cross in humiliation. Jesus' crucifixion is a contradiction to the Jewish concept of the Messiah. One passage in John even suggests that the Messiah of the Jewish scripture was supposed to stay forever after he comes, as a crowd told Jesus: "We have heard from the law that the Christ will remain forever. How can you say, 'The Son of Man must be lifted up"? Who is this Son of Man?'" (John 12:34). The New Testament authors repositioned the cross experience and the following resurrection as a fulfillment of messianic expectations (Theissen & Merz, 1999: 553). What was *not supposed to happen* yet did happen to the Messiah was recast to be what *had to happen*. Reality could not be changed or disputed; Jesus did not liberate the Jews or rebuilt their kingdom. His perceived mission, therefore, had to be changed to accommodate and reflect that reality.

As the Jewish concept of the Messiah is not associated with suffering or resurrection, Jesus could not have been declared as the Christ after his alleged suffering or resurrection. He must have been known as the Christ during his life, as the New Testament says.

13.2.2.7. Virtuous Teacher

It is also worth mentioning here that Luke suggests that some people wondered whether John the Baptist was the Christ merely on the basis of his virtuous teachings (Luke 3:15). It is no surprise that people associated the Messiah with calling people to righteous conduct, but it is highly unlikely that the Messiah would have been identified on the basis of moral preaching only.

13.2.3. The Messiah's Entry into Jerusalem

As we have seen in earlier chapters, Matthew claimed that a number of Old Testament prophecies applied to Jesus, to point out that Jesus was the awaited Messiah, although most of the alleged prophecies had nothing to do with the Messiah! I have already discussed some of these prophecies and will discuss others later. It is appropriate to discuss here the prophecy that Matthew links to Jesus' entry into Jerusalem:

> Now when they approached Jerusalem and came to Bethphage, at the Mount of Olives, Jesus sent two disciples, telling them, "Go to the village ahead of you. Right away you will find a donkey tied there, and a colt with her. Untie them and bring them to me. If anyone says anything to you, you are to say, 'The Lord needs them,' and he will send them at once." This took place to fulfill what was spoken by the prophet: "Tell the people of Zion, 'Look, your king is coming to you, unassuming and seated on a donkey, and on a colt, the foal of a donkey.'"
> So the disciples went and did as Jesus had instructed them. They brought the donkey and the colt and placed their cloaks on them, and he sat on them. A very large crowd

spread their cloaks on the road. Others cut branches from the trees and spread them on the road. The crowds that went ahead of him and those following kept shouting, "Hosanna to the Son of David! Blessed is the one who comes in the name of the Lord! Hosanna in the highest!" As he entered Jerusalem the whole city was thrown into an uproar, saying, "Who is this?" And the crowds were saying, "This is the prophet Jesus, from Nazareth in Galilee." (Matt. 21:1-11)

This story is found also in very similar versions in Mark (11:1-11) and Luke (19:29-41), but John's version (12:12-15) is quite different.

One particularly interesting detail in this story is the proclamation of the crowd. Mark makes the crowd shout "Hosanna! Blessed is the one who comes in the name of the Lord! Blessed is the coming kingdom of our father David! Hosanna in the highest!" Luke has them praise: "Blessed is the king who comes in the name of the Lord! Peace in heaven and glory in the highest!" and John "Hosanna! Blessed is the one who comes in the name of the Lord! Blessed is the king of Israel!" Mark, Luke, and John clearly make the crowd recognize Jesus as the king of Israel. Matthew does that in a more implicit way by having them call Jesus the "Son of David." But the really interesting difference between Matthew and the other three Evangelists is that none of the latter has the prophecy.

The prophet that Matthew mentions is Zechariah:

> Rejoice greatly, daughter of Zion! Shout, daughter of Jerusalem! Look! Your king is coming to you: he is legitimate and victorious, humble and riding on a donkey — on a young donkey, the foal of a female donkey. (Zech. 9:9)

The Hebrew text of this Old Testament prophecy talks about one animal which is described twice, but its Greek translation uses "and," and thus mentions two animals. Matthew relied on the Greek translation of the Old Testament, the Septuagint, so he made Jesus ride on two animals. He, therefore, had to change the earlier part of the story to make Jesus order his two disciples to bring a donkey and a colt. The versions of this story in the other three Gospels, which are not influenced by the Zechariah prophecy, state that Jesus wanted a colt and rode only a colt. This is yet another example on how Matthew fine-tuned his Gospel to fulfill Old Testament prophecies. The fact that Jesus could not have ridden on two animals at the same time did not bother Matthew.

Matthew believed that Jesus was the Messiah, so he tried to apply Old Testament prophecies, or what he considered as prophecies, to him:

> Matthew and his audience already believe that Jesus is the messiah. They also believe that God must have been dropping hints about the messiah in the scriptures, especially in the books of the prophets. So Matthew goes back to the scriptures and studies them carefully, looking for clues about Jesus the messiah. For Matthew, the recognition of Jesus as the messiah is the newly

revealed key that can unlock the hidden meaning of prophecy. When Matthew finds a prophetic statement that *could* be about Jesus, he tries to match it up with something he already knows — or believes — about Jesus' life. (Miller, 2003: 171-172)

The significance of this observation, Miller stresses, is that "the belief that Jesus was the messiah was the basis for the belief that he was the fulfillment of prophecy. It was not the case that people noticed that Jesus had fulfilled a series of prophecies and so concluded that he must be the messiah." He considers this to be the real reason why Jews who were contemporary to Matthew did not find the proof from prophecy credible: "Matthew's use of prophecy has no persuasive power, and can even look like a deliberate distortion of the scriptures aimed at deceiving those who are uninformed and easily impressed" (Miller, 2003: 172). I agree with Miller's analysis which is in line with my observation that only a small minority of the Jews believed in Jesus.

Having examined the different aspects of Jesus' messiahship in the New Testament, let's see how the Qur'an presents his Christhood.

13.3. *Al-Masīḥ* in the Qur'an

Jesus is called *al-Masīḥ* (the Messiah) 11 times in the Qur'an. It occurs 3 times alone (4.172, 5.72, 9.30), 3 times in the phrase "the Messiah, Jesus son of Mary" (3.45, 4.157, 4.171), and 5 times in "the Messiah son of Mary" (5.17, 5.72, 5.75, 9.31).

The Qur'an does not explain the meaning of the term *al-Masīḥ*. The prefix *al* is the Arabic definite article. This means that *al-Masīḥ* is a title. One verse states that when the angels brought to Mary the news about the miracle of her virginal conception, they told her that miraculous son would be known as "the Messiah," "Jesus," and "son of Mary":

> When the angels said: "O Mary! Allah gives you the good news of a Word from Him, whose name is the Messiah, Jesus son of Mary, who is illustrious in this world and the hereafter, and who is one of those brought near [to Allah] (3.45).

Muslims exegetes have different opinions about the etymology and meaning of the word *Masīḥ*. In his commentary on verse 2.40, al-Qurṭubī mentions the view of some that the term is a name which is not derived from another word. Later in his comments on verse 3.45, he cites the view that *Masīḥ* means "truthful," but he also gives several different views on the origin of this term, relating it to the root *masḥ* and its different meanings in different contexts:

- Wonder: he was a wonderer who never settled in one place.

- Rub: whenever he rubbed on a disable person the disability was cured.
- Anoint: he was anointed with the good smelling oil of blessedness with which prophets were anointed. This refers to Jesus' saying about himself: "He has made me blessed wherever I may be" (19.31).
- Flat: he had flat feet.
- Clean: he was cleaned of sins and was purified.
- Give good looking: he was given good looking.

This list still does not include all meanings that have been associated with the word *Masīḥ*. Aṭ-Ṭabāṭabā'ī, for instance, who mentions some of the meanings above, gives other meanings that link the word with the verb *masaḥa* or "rub": Gabriel "rubbed" Jesus at his birth with his wings to protect him from Satan; Jesus used to "rub" on the heads of orphans; and Jesus used to "rub" on the eye of the blind so that he can see. As-Sha'rāwī (1999: 9-14) cites 23 meanings of *Masīḥ* that al-Qurṭubī attributes to various exegetes, as well as other meanings suggested by other scholars.

The title Messiah does not look like being used in verses that talk about specific issues, so it does not look possible to try to study the Qur'anic meaning of Messiah by studying its contexts.

The use of definite article in the *al-Masīḥ* may suggest that the Qur'an implies that there was only one Messiah. Indeed, nowhere does the Qur'an mention any other Messiah, whether past or future. Even through the term "Messiah" was used in Judaism for different individuals, the Qur'an acknowledges only one Messiah: Jesus.

The Qur'an does not use the title "Christ" to call Jesus' followers "Christians." Christians in the Qur'an are not named after the title "Messiah" but are called *Naṣārā* or "Nazarenes." This Qur'anic title, however, does not presume that Jesus was a Nazarene, but it is derived from a particular historical event that involved Jesus and his companions (pp. 226-228).

Like the Qur'an, and probably contrary to what many think, the term *Christianos* (Χριστιανός) or "Christian" is never used in the Gospels. Furthermore, it appears only three times in the New Testament — twice in Acts and once in the Epistle of 1 Peter. The first mention in Acts is particularly significant: "So for a whole year Barnabas and Saul met with the church and taught a significant number of people. Now it was in Antioch that the disciples were first called Christians" (Acts 11:26). This suggests that it was well after Jesus had gone that *his disciples* or any of his followers started to be known as "Christians."

The term is then used twice to refer to *any follower of the Christ*, which is what it ultimately came to mean. In its second occurrence in Acts (26:28), King Agrippa II argues with Paul for trying to convert him to a "Christian." In the third and last appearance of the term in the New Testament the follower of the Christ is reminded not to be ashamed of suffering as a "Christian" and to glorify God for bearing such a name (1 Peter 4:16).

It may be suggested that it was Paul and Barnabas who introduced this term in Antioch. One argument against this view is that Paul never uses the term in his letters, preferring to call fellow Christians *adelphos* (brothers) and *adelphen* (sisters). This may suggest that the term was introduced by non-Christians, which could explain Acts' anonymous attribution of the coining of the term. If that is the case, it is doubtful that the term was first applied to Christ's disciples and then to all his followers, as non-Christians would not have differentiated between the two.

The Qur'an agrees with some but rejects many of the New Testament's claims about the Messiah:

① **Jesus' public claim to messiahship**: In the Qur'an, Jesus is called the Messiah by the angels (3.45), his followers (9.30), and God (4.171). Those who rejected him, including the Jews, also called him the Messiah (4.157), but that is to identify him rather than to accept his messiahship. Jesus is not cited as calling himself the Messiah, but that is because there are only a few statements attributed to Jesus, and even fewer in which he talks about himself. Jesus clearly told people that he was a prophet who was given wisdom, the Injīl, and knowledge of the Torah, and had the authority to perform miracles (19.30, 61.6, 3.49). It is unjustified to presume that Jesus who told people all of this hid the fact that he was the Messiah. He must have announced publicly his messiahship. Nevertheless, it is not unreasonable to suggest that at times, probably near the end of his mission, Jesus had to be rather reticent about the title Messiah because of its *Jewish* political connotations.

② **Miracle worker**: The Qur'an describes Jesus as an exceptional miracle worker. While these miracles would have attested to his claims, including being the Messiah, there is no claim that miracles in general or those specific miracles characterized the Messiah in particular. Miracles in the Qur'an are attributed to a number of prophets. We shall discuss Jesus' miracles in more detail in Chapter 16.

③ **Sonship of David**: Jesus of the Qur'an has no father and, logically, is not linked to any ancestry. He is specifically called "son of Mary," which is probably what people called him at the time to stress his unique, miraculous origin. The Qur'an thus rejects describing Jesus as a "son of David." The Qur'anic concept of Messiah cannot have any link to any ancestry.

④ **Kingship of the Jews**: Jesus never claimed or wanted to be a king of the Jews or any other people. His mission was spiritual and similar to that of the prophets who came before him. Messengers in the Qur'an do not have political ambitions, although becoming political or military figures may be required for the fulfillment of their messages. The Jewish image of the Messiah as someone who was expected to re-establish the glory of Israel is incompatible with the function of messengers in the Qur'an. Messengers may be sent to a particular nation to guide them to the right path, but they are never sent to exalt an ethnic nation over others or lead them to earthly glory.

The New Testament also suggests that Jesus called himself the Christ but was at the same cautious of people calling him so. This could be due to the fact that the concept of the Christ had been distorted by the waiting Jews, who gave it a political dimension. In order to avoid any possible misunderstanding of his mission by the authorities, Jesus may have had to start showing more caution about using the title of "Messiah" and focus more on his equally significant titles of God's "messenger" and "prophet."

⑤ **Founding an imminent kingdom**: It entails from the point above that Jesus was not commissioned by God to establish an earthly kingdom at that time or later. The concept of a *spiritual or heavenly kingdom* that is specific to Jesus is also absent from the Qur'an. Jesus was sent to call people to follow God and be prepared for the Day of Resurrection. This is basically what other messengers of God said to people. As we will see in Chapter 15, the Messiah of the Qur'an does not represent a culmination of the earlier divine messages. He was surely one of the greatest messengers, but he delivered the same message that those before him brought and the one after him, Muhammad, did. He was not commissioned to establish any special kingdom. He worked hard to bring people into the one and same kingdom of God that all messengers of God worked for.

⑥ **Jewish and Christian salvations**: The Messiah's mission was never to restore Israel's glory and make it prevail over the nations of the earth. This Jewish concept of salvation is not supported by the Qur'an. Similarly, Paul's view that Jesus came to save people from the original sin is rejected by the Qur'an (§19.4.2). The only salvational role that any prophet can have is to show people the right path of God and help them follow it. By doing this, he helps them attain salvation. This is a purely spiritual rather than earthly salvation.

⑦ **Suffering Messiah**: The concept of a suffering Messiah was a novelty that Christian writers introduced. It never existed in Judaism. The Qur'an also rejects this concept, because the Qur'anic Messiah never suffered the Passion. This subject is dealt with in more detail in Chapter 19.

⑧ **Virtuous teacher**: Jesus, like any other prophet, was surely a virtuous teacher who called people to the path of righteousness.

⑨ **The Messiah's Entry into Jerusalem**: The New Testament scene of Jesus entering Jerusalem is clearly political, and is linked to the wrong portrayal of him as a political, as well as spiritual, leader. The Qur'anic Jesus had no political mission or ambition.

⑩ **Prophecies about the Messiah**: Jesus' entry into Jerusalem, which is found in different versions in the four Gospels, is linked in Matthew to an Old Testament prophecy, which he changes to fit his story. The Qur'an does not mention any prophecies about the coming of the Messiah. Even when the angels bring to Mary the good news about her giving birth to the Messiah, there is no hint in what they say that this Messiah was being particularly expected and waited for. The Messiah of the Qur'an was not a figure whose coming was to signal the end of times, represent the culmination of history, or anything of such universal scale. This means that most of the prophecies and expectations that were linked to Jesus were false. There might well have been a prophecy or more by previous prophets about the coming of a great messenger who would perform miracles and guide people, but citing these prophecies in the Qur'an over 6 centuries after Jesus and at the time of a new Prophet, Muhammad, would not have served any purpose. Yet the Qur'an cites a Jesus prophecy about Muhammad because it is a reminder to those who believed in Jesus to believe in Muhammad. I will discuss this further in §15.3.

So while the Qur'an and the New Testament agree that Jesus was the Messiah, there are major differences between the meanings of "Messiah" in the two sources.

14

The Divine Son of God That Jesus Never Was

The New Testament stresses that there is a son-father relationship between Jesus and God. Jesus is called the "son of God," and God is described as his "father." The concept of "sonship of God" is found in the Old Testament and is applied to a number of human and non-human beings. The Jewish concept of "son of God" does not imply that a son is divine, as Judaism restricted divinity to God.

This is the main difference that the Jewish concept has with how Christianity applied it to Jesus. Jesus' *unique* sonship of God has become an expression of his divinity. The different New Testament authors had different views about when Jesus became the son of God. Paul links Jesus' unique sonship of God to his resurrection. Mark and Luke suggest that Jesus became the son of God at his baptism. Matthew thinks this happened at the time of the conception of Jesus, and John believes that Jesus was the unique son of God from eternity.

These authors differed also about the nature of Jesus' sonship of God, with John in particular describing Jesus in terms that make him much closer to being God than a man and all but remove any difference between the son and the father. In early Christianity, different groups saw Jesus differently with the deification of Jesus likely to have started after he was gone. The prevailing of the Johannine theology meant that Jesus became to be conceived as divine by most believers. The history of the development of the doctrine of the Trinity shows that Jesus' divinity was gradually enforced until it became accepted by most Christians.

Jesus never claimed to be divine, and his frequent use of the expression "son of man" was one way of stressing his human nature. But this title was eclipsed by the epithet "son of God" that early Christian theologians conferred on Jesus.

The Qur'an's rejection of the concept of "sonship of God" will be discussed in Chapter 15.

14.1. The Jewish "Sonship of God"

The title "son of God" is used in the Old Testament in four distinct ways:

① It is used for unidentified non-human beings:

> When mankind began to multiply on the face of the earth, and daughters were born to them, the sons of God saw that the daughters of mankind were beautiful. Thus they took wives for themselves from any they chose. So the Lord said, "My spirit will not remain in mankind indefinitely since they are mortal. They will remain for one hundred and twenty more years." The Nephilim were on the earth in those days (and also after this) when the sons of God were having sexual relations with the daughters of mankind, who

gave birth to their children. They were the mighty heroes of old, the famous men. (Gen. 6:1-4)

In the book of Job (2:1, 38:7) the same Hebrew expression, *beney ha'elohim*, is used for Angels, suggesting that they are the unidentified non-human creatures of Genesis:

> Now the day came when the sons of God came to present themselves before the Lord — and Satan also came among them. (Job 1:6)

A very similar Hebrew expression with the same meaning, *beney 'elim*, in the book of Psalms (29:1, 89:6) also denotes angelic beings.

② King David is described as the "son of God" and God is called his father. Speaking to the Prophet Nathan, God said about David: "I will become his father and he will become my son" (2 Sam. 7:14). In one of the Psalms, the king says: "I will tell you what the Lord decreed. He said to me 'You are my son! This very day I have become your father!'" (Ps. 2:7).

③ All of Israel is described as God's son (Hos. 11:1). This is part of God's instructions to Moses:

> You must say to Pharaoh, "Thus says the Lord, 'Israel is my son, my firstborn, and I said to you, "Let my son go that he may serve me," but since you have refused to let him go, I will surely kill your son, your firstborn!'" (Exo. 4:22-23)

④ In post-Biblical periods the title "son of God" started to be applied only to pious Jews, as in the following passage from the apocryphal Book of Jubilees, which is dated to the middle of the 2nd century BCE:

> And the Lord said to Moses: "I know their contrariness and their thoughts and their stiffneckedness, and they will not be obedient till they confess their own sin and the sin of their fathers. And after this they will turn to Me in all uprightness and with all (their) heart and with all (their) soul, and I will circumcise the foreskin of their heart and the foreskin of the heart of their seed, and I will create in them a holy spirit, and I will cleanse them so that they shall not turn away from Me from that day unto eternity. And their souls will cleave to Me and to all My commandments, and they will fulfill My commandments, and I will be their Father and they shall be My children. And they all shall be called children of the living God, and every angel and every spirit shall know, yes, they shall know that these are My children, and that I am their Father in uprightness and righteousness, and that I love them." (Jub. 1:21-24)

According to the 1st century BCE book of the Psalms of Solomon, the Messiah will purify the Jews, who will then become "sons of their God":

> And he shall gather together a holy people, whom he shall lead in righteousness,

And he shall judge the tribes of the people that has been sanctified by the Lord his God.
And he shall not suffer unrighteousness to lodge any more in their midst,
Nor shall there dwell with them any man that knows wickedness,
For he shall know them, that they are all sons of their God.
And he shall divide them according to their tribes upon the land,
And neither sojourner nor alien shall sojourn with them anymore. (PsSol. 17)

Vermes (2000: 32) suggests that in the 2nd century BCE, the title "son of God" started to be applied to the awaited royal Messiah, but other scholars contend that this was never a title of the Messiah (Miller, 2003: 224).

In all four Jewish uses, the title "son of God" is always used as a figure of speech. A son of God is someone who is close to God, but he does not share the divinity of God. Sonship of God does not mean that the person is divine. The Talmud states that Jewish miracle workers Honi and Hanina ben Dosa were both called sons of God. In one of his prayers in which he calls himself God's son, Honi calls the Jews God's children (Ta'an. 23a, p. 314). A divine voice used to call Hanina "My son" (Bera. 17b; Ta'an. 24b, p. 317). This sonship of God did not mean that Honi or Hanina had any divine attributes or were more than human beings. They were merely closer to God than most people. Unlike in Roman polytheistic religion where a son of God was divine, Judaism restricted divinity to God. This is the main difference between the Jewish use of the title "son of God" and its use in Christianity.

14.2. The Christian "Sonship of God"

The title "son of God" is applied to Jesus not only in the canon, but in apocryphal sources also. For instance, in the Arabic Gospel of the Infancy idols are made to tell Egyptian priests that Jesus was the son of God (AraIn. 4:11). Studying the use of this term in apocryphal writings, however, adds almost nothing to what we can already learn from the New Testament, so we will focus on the latter.

Jesus is called the "son of God" numerous times in the New Testament, but the authors used this term in a number of different ways and gave it various connotations and meanings. Before we study the different usages, we need to be aware of evidence that suggests that this significant title was at times added by the Evangelists. More specifically, the title "son of God" appears in Matthew's version of some events but is absent from Mark's account of the same events (e.g. Mark 6:47-51; Matt. 14:24-33). In one example Mark (8:29) makes Peter say that people thought that Jesus was "the Christ" but in Matthew's (16:16) account Peter's words have an interesting addition: "the Christ, the Son of the living God." Given that it is generally accepted that Mark's Gospel is older than Matthew's and Luke's and that these two were partly based on the former, we should conclude that in such instances Matthew has discretionally added the title "Son of God" to the original text.

Comparing texts of the same event in different Gospels can reveal such significant changes and additions. But unfortunately straightforward comparisons are not always possible, and it is often difficult to identify changes to the text. This caveat should be kept in mind as we look into the different meanings of the title "son of God" in the Gospels, although this warning applies to the study of the New Testament in general.

14.2.1. Sonship of God, Messiahship, and Miracle Working

The title "son of God" has been linked with another two of Jesus' titles: Christ and king of the Jews. The association with the latter is seen when one enthusiastic believer hails Jesus saying: "Rabbi, you are the Son of God; you are the king of Israel!" (John 1:49).

The Gospels associate the title "son of God" with the "Christ" in four passages. In one passage John tells his readers that he recorded Jesus' miracles so that they believe "that Jesus is the Christ, the Son of God" (John 20:31). Mark (1:1) starts his Gospel with: "The beginning of the gospel of Jesus Christ, the Son of God." When Jesus asks Lazarus' sister whether she believed that the one who believes in him will live even if he dies and that the one who lives and believes in him will never die, she replies "Yes, Lord, I believe that you are the Christ, the Son of God who comes into the world" (John 11:27). This link between the titles Christ and son of God is also clear in the high priest's accusation of Jesus: "I charge you under oath by the living God, tell us if you are the Christ, the Son of God" (Matt. 26:63).

The Gospels contain also a number of passages that indicate that the son of God was perceived to be a miracle performer. For instance, reminding Jesus that he was the son of God, the Devil tempted him to turn stones into bread (Matt. 4:3; Luke 4:3). The Devil also tempted Jesus to throw himself from the highest point of the temple and rely on his sonship of God to be saved (Matt. 4:6; Luke 4:9). A demon-possessed man (Mark 5:7; Luke 8:28), who appears as two possessed men in Matthew 8:29, Jesus' disciple who had just witnessed him walk him on the water and still the wind (Matt. 14:33), unclean spirits who saw him (Mark 3:11), and demons that came out of people (Luke 4:41) called Jesus the "Son of God."

When Jesus stopped the wind, people proclaimed that he was the son of God (Matt. 14:33). Lazarus' sister believed that Jesus could have prevented the death of her brother because he was the son of God (John 11:27). Indeed, Jesus went on to bring her Lazarus back to life. Jesus had already revealed that Lazarus' sickness "will not lead to death, but to God's glory, so that the Son of God may be glorified through it" (John 11:4).

Because the son of God must have miraculous power, Jesus was sarcastically challenged to prove his sonship of God by coming down from the cross (Matt.

27:40). When the Roman centurion saw the miracles that occurred immediately after Jesus' death, he proclaimed that "Truly this man was God's Son!" (Mark 15:39; Matt. 27:54).

Even Paul started to teach that Jesus was the son of God after his vision was miraculously restored by one of Jesus' disciples, Ananias (Acts 9:20). John also states that Jesus' miracles proved that he was the Christ and son of God:

> Now Jesus performed many other miraculous signs in the presence of the disciples, which are not recorded in this book. But these are recorded so that you may believe that Jesus is the Christ, the Son of God, and that by believing you may have life in his name. (John 20:30-31)

The Epistle of 1 John goes as far as stating that the son of God came to destroy the works of the Devil:

> The one who practices sin is of the devil, because the devil has been sinning from the beginning. For this purpose the Son of God was revealed: to destroy the works of the devil. (1 John 3:8)

The implication that performing miracles indicates that the person was the son of God is found in apocryphal gospels also. When a man found out that his possessed son was cured by touching the swaddling clothes of the infant Jesus, he concluded that "perhaps this boy is the son of the living God" (AraIn. 4:21).

As pointed out earlier (p. 241), the link between the title Messiah, sonship of God, and performing miracles is a 1st century Christian invention that had no origin in Judaism. It is the result of calling Jesus "son of God" and at the same time portraying him as a miracle worker (Sanders, 1995: 132-133, 160-162).

14.2.2. Sonship of God and Blasphemy

All four Evangelists agree that Jesus' claim to the sonship of God was considered blasphemous by the Jewish authorities (Matt. 26:63-65; Luke 22:70-71; John 10:32-36, 5:16-18):

> But he was silent and did not answer. Again the high priest questioned him, "Are you the Christ, the Son of the Blessed One?" "I am," said Jesus, "and you will see the Son of Man sitting at the right hand of the Power and coming with the clouds of heaven." Then the high priest tore his clothes and said, "Why do we still need witnesses? You have heard the blasphemy! What is your verdict?" They all condemned him as deserving death. (Mark 14:61-64)

> The Jewish leaders replied, "We have a law, and according to our law he ought to die, because he claimed to be the Son of God!" (John 19:7)

The rending of one's garment is a Jewish legal requirement for hearing the name of God blasphemed directly or for hearing the blasphemy from the person who heard it first (Sanh. 60a).

One serious historical problem with these passages is that the title "son of God" was not considered to be blasphemous in Judaism (Theissen & Merz, 1999: 464; Vermes, 2005: 29, 101-103). It was not an act of blasphemy or a religious crime to claim to be a son of God. This proclamation could not have been considered a capital offense. This title is used in the Old Testament itself for various people. Pronouncing the four-letter divine name YHVH or speaking disrespectfully about God is blasphemous. This is an instance of pronouncing and abusing the sacrosanct Tetragram from the time of Moses:

> Now an Israelite woman's son whose father was an Egyptian went out among the Israelites, and the Israelite woman's son and an Israelite man had a fight in the camp. The Israelite woman's son misused the Name and cursed, so they brought him to Moses. Now the name of his mother was Shelomith daughter of Dibri, of the tribe of Dan. So they placed him in custody until they were able to make a clear legal decision for themselves based on words from the mouth of the Lord. Then the Lord spoke to Moses: "Bring the one who cursed outside the camp, and all who heard him are to lay their hands on his head, and the whole congregation is to stone him. Moreover, you are to tell the Israelites, 'If any man curses his God he will bear responsibility for his sin, and one who misuses the name of the Lord must surely be put to death. The whole congregation must surely stone him, whether he is a foreigner or a native citizen; when he misuses the Name he must be put to death.'" (Lev. 24:10-16)

According to Vermes (2005: 101), by the start of the 1st century CE blasphemy became specifically linked to pronouncing the divine name YHVH. Rabbinic literature states categorically that "the blasphemer is punished only if he utters [the divine] name" (Sanh. 55b, 56a).

Interestingly, John tells us that Jesus did indeed contest the accusation of blasphemy, although not on the basis of the fact that was known to all that the claim to sonship of God was not blasphemous, but by pointing out that the Jewish scripture used the term "gods" itself for people:

> Jesus said to them, "I have shown you many good deeds from the Father. For which one of them are you going to stone me?" The Jewish leaders replied, "We are not going to stone you for a good deed but for blasphemy, because you, a man, are claiming to be God." Jesus answered, "Is it not written in your law, 'I said, you are gods'? If those people to whom the word of God came were called 'gods' (and the scripture cannot be broken), do you say about the one whom the Father set apart and sent into the world, 'You are blaspheming,' because I said, 'I am the Son of God'?" (John 10:32-36)

Jesus argues that as the term "gods" is used figuratively in the scripture, and hence does not break the law, the title "son of God" is similarly metaphorical and cannot be considered blasphemous.

The Old Testament referent in question seems to be Psalms 82:7, which appears to call some gods and sons of God:

> God stands in the assembly of El; in the midst of the gods he renders judgment. He says, "How long will you make unjust legal decisions and show favoritism to the wicked? (Selah) Defend the cause of the poor and the fatherless! Vindicate the oppressed and suffering! Rescue the poor and needy! Deliver them from the power of the wicked! They neither know nor understand. They stumble around in the dark, while all the foundations of the earth crumble. I thought, 'You are gods; all of you are sons of the Most High.' Yet you will die like mortals; you will fall like all the other rulers." (Ps. 82:1-7)

The Evangelists mistakenly believed that the Jews considered the claim to sonship of God blasphemous. Accordingly, when objecting to the Jewish accusation, Jesus is also seen unaware of the non-historicity of this claim, so he is made to use a different argument to defend himself.

14.2.3. Christian Sons of God

The term "son of God" was not applied to Jesus only in the New Testament. Jesus himself used the phrase "your father" in reference to God around 20 times in his sermons. In the majority of these instances (e.g. Mark 11:25; Luke 6:35; John 20:17), he was addressing his disciples, i.e. he called them *sons of God*:

> Let your light shine before people, so that they can see your good deeds and give honor to your Father in heaven. (Matt. 5:16)

> Do not be afraid, little flock, for your Father is well pleased to give you the kingdom. (Luke 12:32)

Paul also applies the term *sons of God* to all Israelites as he describes them as "to them belong the adoption as sons" (Rom. 9:4). Luke (3:38) calls Adam also the son of God.

In a confused account in John in which Jesus argues with people who are described as "had believed him" (John 8:31) and who call God their father (John 8:41), Jesus accuses them of not accepting his teachings and goes on to label them as *sons of the devil* (John 8:42-44). This suggests that that Jesus called God the father of the believers only. The following passage, in which Jesus addresses his disciples, seems to suggest that only those who do good works would be sons of God:

> Love your enemies, and do good, and lend, expecting nothing back. Then your reward will be great, and you will be sons of the Most High, because he is kind to ungrateful and evil people. Be merciful, just as your Father is merciful. (Luke 6:35-36)

The Epistle of 1 John also contains passages that seem to restrict the sonship of God to the righteous (also 1 John 5:1, 5:18):

> If you know that he is righteous, you also know that everyone who practices righteousness has been fathered by him. (1 John 2:29)

> Everyone who has been fathered by God does not practice sin, because God's seed resides in him, and thus he is not able to sin, because he has been fathered by God. (1 John 3:9)

This restrictive use of the term is similar to how its exclusive application in post-Biblical times to pious Jews (p. 258).

Jesus' application of the sonship of God to the righteous and not only himself is in line with the historical fact that this was never considered blasphemous, yet it further highlights the non-historicity of the Jewish leaders' accusation of Jesus of blasphemy for claiming to be the son of God.

14.2.4. The *Unique* Son of God

While Jesus called others also sons of God, the following peculiar Johannine passages state that the title "son of God" was actually Jesus' only:

> For this is the way God loved the world: He gave his one and only Son, so that everyone who believes in him will not perish but have eternal life. (John 3:16)

> The one who believes in him is not condemned. The one who does not believe has been condemned already, because he has not believed in the name of the one and only Son of God. (John 3:18)

> By this the love of God is revealed in us: that God has sent his one and only Son into the world so that we may live through him. (1 John 4:9)

Reconciling these with passages in which the title "son of God" is applied to others also would require assuming that Jesus was considered a *special and unique son of God*. While believers are sons of God, Jesus is *The Son of God*. This could then explain the title "the Son," which appears once in each of the Synoptics (Mark 13:32; Matt. 11:27; Luke 10:22) and a number of times in the Gospel of John and the Epistle of 1 John. Jesus is also called God's "one dear son" (Mark 1:11, 9:7; Matt. 3:17, 17:5; Luke 3:22) and the *chosen son* (Luke 9:35). It may then be assumed that this specific sense of "son of God" is what the Jewish leaders objected to and led them to accuse Jesus of blasphemy and ask for his death. This would solve the problem of this unhistorical claim, but this assumption has no supportive evidence. The Jewish leaders seem to be angry simply at the claim to sonship of God.

In the following passage, John states that Jesus' claim to the sonship of God was considered blasphemous because it was understood to have made him equal to God:

> Now because Jesus was doing these things on the Sabbath, the Jewish leaders began persecuting him. So he told them, "My Father is working until now, and I too am working." For this reason the Jewish leaders were trying even harder to kill him, because not only was he breaking the Sabbath, but he was also calling God his own Father, thus making himself equal with God. (John 5:16-18)

There is actually nothing in what Jesus said and did here that would justify the Jewish leaders' conclusion that he was claiming equality with God. It looks like John believed that this equality with the Divine is what made the law experts charge Jesus with blasphemy so he decided to introduce it here even though the context does not justify it.

Indeed, among the over 40 Gospel passages in which Jesus uses the term "my father" and others in which he talks about "the father" there are some that reflect a special intimacy and unique relationship between the son and his father. The question is then whether some of them express the uniqueness of Jesus' sonship of God in terms that could be interpreted as blasphemous.

The writer of the Epistle of 1 John links the son of God to eternal life, as it is through the belief in the son of God eternal life is earned: "God has given us eternal life, and this life is in his Son. The one who has the Son has this eternal life; the one who does not have the Son of God does not have this eternal life. I have written these things to you who believe in the name of the Son of God so that you may know that you have eternal life" (1 John 5:11-13). In the following two passages, the Evangelists state that the father gave his son Jesus the special authority to acknowledge or deny people before God, and made him the only way to the father:

> Whoever, then, acknowledges me before people, I will acknowledge before my Father in heaven. But whoever denies me before people, I will deny him also before my Father in heaven. (Matt. 10:32-33)

> Jesus replied, "I am the way, and the truth, and the life. No one comes to the Father except through me." (John 14:6)

This unique son has been handed everything that the father has, and he is a mystery that no one knows other than his father (Luke 10:22):

> Everything that the Father has is mine. (John 16:15)

All things have been handed over to me by my Father. No one knows the Son except the Father, and no one knows the Father except the Son and anyone to whom the Son decides to reveal him. (Matt. 11:27)

It is the Evangelist John who stresses in the most striking way the uniqueness of Jesus' sonship of God, stretching its meaning far beyond what the other Evangelists ever thought, and making it confer on Jesus the God-like status that has become accepted by most Christians. John's descriptions of this special son of God blur the differences between him and his father. Among what the father has handed to his unique son, according to John, is the ability to lay down his life and take it back:

This is why the Father loves me — because I lay down my life, so that I may take it back again. No one takes it away from me, but I lay it down of my own free will. I have the authority to lay it down, and I have the authority to take it back again. This commandment I received from my Father. (John 10:17-18)

God has even given his special son the authority to raise people from the dead on the Day of Resurrection:

For this is the will of my Father — for everyone who looks on the Son and believes in him to have eternal life, and I will raise him up at the last day. (John 6:40)

This ability to raise the dead is stressed in another Johannine passage which goes even further as it lists the powers that this son has from his father:

For just as the Father raises the dead and gives them life, so also the Son gives life to whomever he wishes. Furthermore, the Father does not judge anyone, but has assigned all judgment to the Son, so that all people will honor the Son just as they honor the Father. The one who does not honor the Son does not honor the Father who sent him. "I tell you the solemn truth, the one who hears my message and believes the one who sent me has eternal life and will not be condemned, but has crossed over from death to life. I tell you the solemn truth, a time is coming — and is now here — when the dead will hear the voice of the Son of God, and those who hear will live. For just as the Father has life in himself, thus he has granted the Son to have life in himself, and he has granted the Son authority to execute judgment, because he is the Son of Man. "Do not be amazed at this, because a time is coming when all who are in the tombs will hear his voice and will come out — the ones who have done what is good to the resurrection resulting in life, and the ones who have done what is evil to the resurrection resulting in condemnation. I can do nothing on my own initiative. Just as I hear, I judge, and my judgment is just, because I do not seek my own will, but the will of the one who sent me. (John 5:21-30)

Like many other New Testament passages, this pericope promotes the father and the son as two distinct beings, but it does that in a strange way, as the more John tells us about the specialness and uniqueness of this son the less clear becomes the difference between the son and his father. This Evangelist makes his Jesus say that seeing him is seeing the father, and that he is in the father and the father is in him (John 10:38):

> If you have known me, you will know my Father too. And from now on you do know him and have seen him. Philip said, "Lord, show us the Father, and we will be content." Jesus replied, "Have I been with you for so long, and you have not known me, Philip? The person who has seen me has seen the Father! How can you say, 'Show us the Father'? Do you not believe that I am in the Father, and the Father is in me? The words that I say to you, I do not speak on my own initiative, but the Father residing in me performs his miraculous deeds. Believe me that I am in the Father, and the Father is in me, but if you do not believe me, believe because of the miraculous deeds themselves." (John 14:7-11)

Any meaningful distinction between the son and father is explicitly denied when John makes Jesus tell Jewish leaders: "The Father and I are one" (John 10:30)! This relationship of oneness is encountered again in Jesus' prayer to the father:

> I am no longer in the world, but they are in the world, and I am coming to you. Holy Father, keep them safe in your name that you have given me, so that they may be one just as we are one. (John 17:11)

John goes on to spell out what this unity between the son and the father exactly means in an equally stark fashion in a dialog between the resurrected Jesus and Thomas in which the disciple declares unequivocally that Jesus is God:

> Then he said to Thomas, "Put your finger here, and examine my hands. Extend your hand and put it into my side. Do not continue in your unbelief, but believe." Thomas replied to him, "My Lord and my God!" (John 20:27-28)

In summary, while the Synoptists described Jesus as a special and unique son of God, John took this concept well beyond what the other Evangelists thought. He gave the concept of "son of God," albeit a *special* sonship, dimensions that it never knew in the history of the monotheistic Judaism.

Paul, the earliest of the New Testament authors, also believed that Jesus was divine. He says that "by human descent, came the Christ, who is God over all" (Rom. 9:5), and this descent of the divine as a human being is what Paul means when he describes Jesus as a "descendant of David with reference to the flesh" (Rom. 1:3). Unlike Adam who was "made of dust," Paul's Jesus came "from heaven" (1 Cor. 15:47).

14.2.5. The *Eternal* Son of John

The way in which John reconciled talking about Jesus and God as two distinct beings with making them also one and the same further underlines the fundamental difference between his theology and the theologies of the Synoptists. John claimed that although Jesus was born and sent at some point in time, which is how he is distinct from the eternal father, he was actually an embodiment of the Word, which existed from eternity. John starts his Gospel as follows:

> In the beginning was the Word, and the Word was with God, and the Word was fully God. The Word was with God in the beginning. (John 1:1-2)

He later tells us that this Word took the form of a human being, Jesus, and came to live with people on earth:

> Now the Word became flesh and took up residence among us. We saw his glory — the glory of the one and only, full of grace and truth, who came from the Father. (John 1:14)

The Evangelist also has John the Baptist declare that Jesus existed before him, implying again that Jesus' existence predates his physical appearance in this world:

> John testified about him and shouted out, "This one was the one about whom I said, 'He who comes after me is greater than I am, because he existed before me.'" (John 1:15)

John also described Jesus as primordial light:

> The true light, who gives light to everyone, was coming into the world. He was in the world, and the world was created by him, but the world did not recognize him. He came to what was his own, but his own people did not receive him. (John 1:9-11)

Jesus' preexistence and coexistence with God are also clearly stressed in his following words:

> I glorified you on earth by completing the work you gave me to do. And now, Father, glorify me at your side with the glory I had with you before the world was created. (John 17:4-5)

John stresses a number of times in his Gospel that Jesus came from God and returned to Him:

> Just before the Passover feast, Jesus knew that his time had come to depart from this world to the Father. Having loved his own who were in the world, he now loved them to the very end. The evening meal was in progress, and the devil had already put into the

heart of Judas Iscariot, Simon's son, that he should betray Jesus. Because Jesus knew that the Father had handed all things over to him, and that he had come from God and was going back to God. (John 13:1-3)

For the Father himself loves you, because you have loved me and have believed that I came from God. I came from the Father and entered into the world, but in turn, I am leaving the world and going back to the Father. (John 16:27-28)

John's Jesus was with God from eternity, became flesh and came to live with people, and then left them and went back to where he originally came from: God. John's Jesus is clearly divine.

John still has passages that portray Jesus as having a lower status than the father. For instance, Jesus proclaims that he was sent by the father (John 20:21), the father is greater than him (John 14:28), and he is under the command of the father (John 12:49, 14:31). There is clear inconsistency in John's portrayal of the divine Jesus and his relationship with God. As has been rightly pointed out, with his "plain affirmation of the pre-eminence of the Father contradicting all the metaphors which suggest equality, John created a doctrinal problem the resolution of which kept the church, the councils, the bishops, and the theologians fully occupied for several centuries" (Vermes, 2000: 48).

John's doctrine of the Word, or *Logos* in Greek, is believed to have been inspired by the Alexandrian Jewish philosopher Philo (ca. 15 BCE – ca. 45 CE) who taught that the Logos was the intermediary between God and the cosmos, as it is God's tool of creation and the agent through which the human mind can apprehend and comprehend God. The idea of the Logos actually dates back to the 6th century BC Greek philosopher Heraclitus who believed that the cosmic processes have a logos, or reason, similar to the reasoning power in man, and was developed by other Greek philosophers. Vermes suggests that John's Logos doctrine was also influenced by Hermetism. According to this 1st century CE pagan Hellenistic mysticism, deification of man is achieved through knowledge, and the Logos is referred to as the "son of God" (Vermes, 2000: 51).

I should point out that the Qur'anic concept of the divine word *kun* (be), which we discussed earlier (pp. 96-97), is completely different from the concept of the Logos. The former is not something that can take a form of or be represented by a being, and it has nothing to do with man's ability or, more accurately, the lack of it to comprehend God. Philo's idea that the Logos is God's agent of creation might seem closer to the Qur'anic concept of *kun* (be), but that is not the case. The latter is merely a symbolic expression of God's limitless power and His ability to do whatever He wants whenever He likes.

14.2.6. When Did Jesus' Sonship of God become Special?

For John, Jesus existed and was divine from eternity, which is what made him a special son of God. But Paul and the Synoptists favored different versions of an alternative doctrine which came to be known as "adoptionism." This doctrine was widespread in the first three centuries of Christianity before its opponents succeeded in suppressing it and turned it into a heresy. It states that Jesus was adopted at some point by God as his special son.

Although Paul believed that Jesus was a human incarnation of God, he also believed that Jesus became *the* son of God by virtue of his resurrection:

> Concerning his Son who was a descendant of David with reference to the flesh, who was appointed the Son-of-God-in-power according to the Holy Spirit by the resurrection from the dead, Jesus Christ our Lord. (Rom. 1:3-4)

> You should have the same attitude toward one another that Christ Jesus had, who though he existed in the form of God did not regard equality with God as something to be grasped, but emptied himself by taking on the form of a slave, by looking like other men, and by sharing in human nature. He humbled himself, by becoming obedient to the point of death — even death on a cross! As a result God exalted him and gave him the name that is above every name, so that at the name of Jesus every knee will bow — in heaven and on earth and under the earth — and every tongue confess that Jesus Christ is Lord to the glory of God the Father. (Phi. 2:5-11)

In another passage that Acts attributes to Paul, the apostle is quoted as saying: "That this promise God has fulfilled to us, their children, by raising Jesus, as also it is written in the second psalm, 'You are my Son; today I have fathered you'" (Acts 13:33). Here also God's fatherhood of Jesus is said to have happened after he was raised. Paul is quoting from the Book of Psalms in which David says that when God made him king He told him: "You are my son! This very day I have become your father!" (Ps. 2:7).

Paul's passages above talk about Jesus being son of God but not necessarily a *unique* or *only* son. But since Paul believed that Jesus was already a human incarnation of God (Rom. 9:5, 1:3; 1 Cor. 15.47), he must have meant that the crucifixion and resurrection made Jesus a *special* son of God.

Mark identifies a different transformation point that made Jesus the special son of God: his baptism. When Jesus was baptized by John, and as he was coming out of the water, he saw "the heavens splitting apart and the Spirit descending on him like a dove." He then heard a voice from heaven say: "You are my one dear Son; in you I take great delight" (Mark 1:10-11).

As Mark's Gospel starts with Jesus' encounter with John, there is no earlier event that signifies Jesus' special status as God's only son.

Mark mentions another event in which Jesus' special status as *the* son of God is stressed, which is Jesus' transfiguration:

Six days later Jesus took with him Peter, James, and John and led them alone up a high mountain privately. And he was transfigured before them, and his clothes became radiantly white, more so than any launderer in the world could bleach them. Then Elijah appeared before them along with Moses, and they were talking with Jesus. So Peter said to Jesus, "Rabbi, it is good for us to be here. Let us make three shelters — one for you, one for Moses, and one for Elijah." (For they were afraid, and he did not know what to say.) Then a cloud overshadowed them, and a voice came from the cloud, "This is my one dear Son. Listen to him!" Suddenly when they looked around, they saw no one with them any more except Jesus. (Mark 9:2-8)

It is speculative to suggest that the transfiguration represents another level of exaltation of Jesus' status, because the voice from the cloud did not add anything new to the words of the heavenly voice after the baptism.

Luke, who in Acts (10:37-38) links God's anointment of Jesus with the Holy Spirit to his baptism, reproduces in his Gospel almost exactly Mark's count of what happened after Jesus' baptism. He changes Mark's account slightly, making the Holy Spirit descend on Jesus while he was praying, not as he was coming out of the water (Luke 3:21-22).

There is an interesting textual variation in one early Greek and several later Latin manuscripts of Luke. Most manuscript copy Mark in stating that after Jesus' baptism, a voice from heaven said "you are my one dear Son; in you I take great delight" (Luke 3:22). Yet the other manuscripts have instead this variant of the text: "You are my son; today I have begotten you." Ehrman (2007: 158-160) argues that this is what Luke originally wrote and that the text was later changed by copies who did not believe that Jesus became God's son at baptism.

Unlike Mark, Luke has the story of the virginal conception, in which he tells us that Gabriel told Mary that her son Jesus "will be great, and will be called the Son of the Most High" (Luke 1:32), and that he "will be holy; he will be called the Son of God" (Luke 1:35). Gabriel's words may be taken to mean that Jesus was the special son of God from the time of his conception, but a more plausible reading is that Luke meant that the angel was mainly conveying future news, and the realization of the special descriptions of Jesus happened after his baptism.

Matthew's nativity story makes Jesus special from the time he was miraculously conceived. This Evangelist states that Mary became "pregnant through the Holy Spirit" (Matt. 1:18), and that "the child conceived in her is from the Holy Spirit" (Matt. 1:20). This surely makes Jesus a special son of God. But it probably also elevates him to divinity in Matthew's eyes. He states that the fruit of this miraculous, virginal conception will be called "Emmanuel," which he translates as "God with us" (Matt. 1:23). As we have already seen (pp. 106-107), in Isaiah's (7:14) prophecy which Matthew quotes here completely out of context, the name Emmanuel was that of an ordinary, human child whose name stressed God's imminent help in destroying Judea's enemies. This child was not divine. Nevertheless, the way Matthew used Isaiah's prophecy suggests that he believed the child Jesus to be divine. This is in line with his claim that the wise men who came to visit the new born Jesus "worshiped him" (Matt. 2:11). It should be noted, however, that Matthew's account of Jesus' life does not contain any of John's extravagant claims about Jesus' divine attributes. In Matthew's out-of-context application of the Old Testament passage "I called my Son out of Egypt" to Jesus (p. 202), the latter is already a special son of God.

Matthew (3:17) introduces a small change to Mark's story of the baptism of Jesus, making the heavenly voice speak *about* Jesus rather than *to* him: "This is my one dear Son; in him I take great delight." The Evangelist (17:1-5) also reproduces Mark's account of the transfiguration which, as pointed out above, does not seem to be particularly significant in stressing Jesus' special status, as this had been established earlier. While the baptism story means that Matthew believed that some kind of elevation to Jesus' status happened then, earlier details in his Gospel clearly shows that he considered Jesus to have been special from birth.

So to sum up, Paul thought that Jesus became *the* son of God after his resurrection, Mark believed that this happened after Jesus' baptism, and Matthew reckoned that it happened as early as the time of the conception of Jesus. Luke may have shared Matthew's view, but he is more likely to have adopted Mark's belief. The fundamentally different John believed that Jesus was the special son of God from eternity, although this should not surprise us, as he went as far as deifying Jesus and making him and God almost one.

Theissen and Merz (1999: 554-555) suggest that Jesus became the *only* son of God after the Easter experience. This is clear in the case of Paul. Whether the Evangelists, having accepted that Jesus was *the* son of God, simply reworked when this transformation happened, is difficult to tell.

Paul, Mark, Matthew, Luke, and John have different views about when Jesus became the son of God and the nature of this sonship. In fact, even within the same book it is possible to find passages different enough as to paint a discrepant picture of this relationship and what the author really wanted to say, raising questions about whether he himself had a clear idea about these elusive theological issues.

14.3. The Prevailing of the Johannine Theology

The Johannine image of the divine Jesus is not found in the other three Gospels. None of the latter describes Jesus as an incarnate of the Word, portrays him as the primordial light, suggests that he always existed, states that Jesus and the father are in each other, makes them one and the same, or calls Jesus God. None of this is found in the Synoptics. The Johannine deification of Jesus would have appalled any Jew as blasphemy, and would have been seen so even by Mark, Matthew, and Luke also. Although these authors took Jesus' special sonship of God to reflect a more intimate relationship with God that may imply giving Jesus some divinity, John's divine Jesus remains alien to them.

Despite its major difference from the Synoptics, John's Gospel succeeded in making its unique theology central to Christian belief. The divine image of Jesus is mainly drawn by the Johannine writings, but its seeds can be found in Paul's letters. The Gospel of John was written as late as the 2nd century CE, so it must have been influenced by earlier oral and written traditions that have been completely lost. Had the Gospel of John failed to make it into the canon, the Jesus that Christianity knows today would have been completely different indeed. The deification of Jesus, which probably started after him, led ultimately to the doctrine of the Trinity — the most influential doctrine in Christianity besides Paul's atonement.

Christianity gave the Jewish title "son of God" a strong divine connotation that was never part of its original Jewish meaning. Christianity used the title "son of God" as another way of saying "God." If the earliest Christian writers remained faithful to Jewish monotheism, Jesus would not have become divine, but their influence by Roman polytheism and possibly other factors made them turn the historical human Jesus into an unhistorical divine being. The concept of *son of a god* was well-known and accepted in the Hellenistic culture. The unique and supernatural qualities of heroes and their extraordinary lives were explained in terms of divinity, and this divinity usually came in the form of sonship of a god. Gods often physically fathered those heroes. Most heroes had a divine father and a human mother, but there were exceptions where the mother was a goddess and the father a man. Ancient Greek sons of gods include the athlete Theagenes, whose father, the god Heracles, appeared to Theagenes' mother in the form of her husband and impregnated her; the 6th century BCE philosopher Pythagoras who was fathered by Apollo; the 5th-4th century BEC philosopher Plato whose father was the god Phoebus; Alexander the Great who was fathered by a god who took the form of a snake and slept with his mother; the sage Apollonius of Tyana whose father was Zeus; and Emperor Augustus whose mother is said to have claimed that he was fathered by the god Apollo (for more details, see Miller, 2003: 133-153). The Christian divine son of God was clearly influenced by the same concept that was part of the Hellenistic culture.

Miller thinks that Jesus, like the previous sons of gods, was considered a divine son of God in order to explain his extraordinary life. However, while the Jews at the time of Jesus were influenced by the Hellenistic culture, they were certainly under much bigger influence from their own cultural heritage. Jesus' sonship of God cannot be explained as being *mainly* the result of the influence of the Hellenistic culture. For instance, both the Old and New Testaments have stories of prominent holy figures whose lives were clearly extraordinary and supernatural, yet they were not called sons of God, and certainly not considered divine — for example, Abraham in the Old Testament and Zechariah in the New Testament.

It is difficult to see how Jesus' Jewish followers could have started the move to deify him and his mother. Judaism is a strictly monotheistic religion, so even if someone wanted to promote Jesus' divinity, he would have met very little acceptance. On the other hand, the deification of Jesus and his mother would have been seen completely logical and natural for pagan converts. I am therefore inclined to think that the deification of Jesus started by Paul, the apostle who never knew Jesus, who focused his missionary efforts on pagan people. These people accepted Jesus' divine image very easily, and might have even needed it to believe in him. The Gospel of John is a later document which relied on earlier sources, but the source of the concept of Jesus' divinity must have come from Paul and his communities of heathen converts. The deification of Jesus is yet another one of Paul's successes in shaping Christianity the way he wanted.

Miller also believes that the story of Mary's virginal conception of Jesus was made up because it was required by the title "son of God." This suggestion also ignores completely the Jewish influence on the authors of the Gospels and tries to explain parts of their reports as if they were written in complete isolation from their main culture. **First**, the concept of miraculous conception and birth is applied in both the Old and New Testament to human beings who were not called sons of God, although none of these was conceived without a father. For instance, the Old Testament talks about the miraculous conception of Isaac, and the New Testament has the story of John the Baptist. Neither of these two was called a son of God, so the story of their miraculous conceptions could not have been inspired by this title. **Second**, the Old Testament contains stories of holy figures who lived extraordinary lives, and the Jewish title son of God was thus applicable to them, yet they were conceived and born naturally, without any miracle. One instance is King David.

It is interesting to note the different positions of the main Christian sources and the Qur'an about Jesus' virginal conception and sonship of God: Matthew and Luke mention both the virginal conception and the sonship of God; Paul, Mark, and John talk only about Jesus' sonship of God; whereas the Qur'an talks about the virginal conception but rejects the sonship of God. The Qur'an's rejection of Jesus' sonship of God reflects a fundamental difference between its theology and Christian theologies, as we shall discuss in more detail in Chapter 15.

Jesus, who stressed the importance of the law and confirmed the message of Moses, had nothing to do with this fundamental transformation of his image from man to god. We do not have a detailed history of this transformation, as we do not have earlier documents that can help us trace the changes. Putting aside Paul's writings, which did not touch on Jesus' life, when we compare the Johannine later writings with the earlier writings of Mark, Matthew, and Luke, we can see clearly such changes. It is generally accepted that John wrote his Gospel to assert the divinity of Jesus — a highly contentious view in early Christianity.

It was early Christian theologians, not Jesus, who developed his divine image, and this happened through a process that involved so much politics and authoritarianism. If there is any doubt about this, a quick read of the history of the conflict between competing concepts, doctrines, and theologies in early Christianity should put any doubt to rest. The Trinity is a good example. A detailed study of this doctrine and its history is outside the scope of the book, but because it is mentioned in the Qur'an we need to have a quick look at it. Our main interest is to learn about what it came to be, rather than the history of its early development, as its final form is what the Qur'an deals with.

14.4. The Trinity

The New Testament, as well as other early Christian writings, contains passages that promote monotheism and others that ascribe to Jesus divine attributes, and passages that stress the distinctness of the Father and the Son and others that fuse the two. These contradictory writings served as a fertile environment for the development of a number of conflicting doctrines. This confused theological language reflects the authors' influence by the Roman understanding of divinity, which was not in line with the Jewish monotheism. Even if only the Gospel of John is considered and all other canonical and apocryphal Christian books are ignored, this single book would still provide too many discrepant, confusing, and vague statements to allow a harmonious and coherent picture of Jesus.

Probably as soon as Jesus was gone, some Christians started to debate whether he was a mere human being, with some ascribing to the man divine attributes and others making him essentially a god. These heated debates resulted in the development of a number of concepts and doctrines. Adoptionism, for instance, stated that the Son joined the Father in divinity at some point. Docetism claimed that Jesus had only an appearance and did not have a physical body. Theologians interested in Jesus' divinity tackled issues such as whether the Son and the Holy Spirit were always present with the Father, the nature of the relationship between the three, and whether they were equal. Ultimately, the majority of Christians accepted the answers to these questions that the doctrine of the Trinity provided. However, this doctrine was developed over centuries of controversies, and different theologians have understood and explained it differently.

Tertullian, who introduced the term "trinity" from the Latin "trinitas," taught the concept of one God in three persons: the Father, the Son, and the Holy Spirit. These three are distinct, but not separate. Because these three persons are not separate or divided, God is one, not three. Tertullian's Trinity is therefore a form of monotheism not tritheism.

Another form of the Trinity, which Tertullian considered heresy is known as "Sabellianism," after the 3rd century theologian Sabellius. "Modalism," as it is also known, states that God is one in three aspects. In this version, the Father, the Son, and the Holy Spirit are not distinct persons but different manifestations of the Godhead. Accordingly, it was God who suffered on the cross, hence this view is also called "patripassionism," which is derived from the Latin words for "father" and "suffer." Like Tertullian's version, this form of the Trinity equally claims to promote the oneness of God.

In the 4th century a major controversy broke out between Bishop Alexander of Alexandria, Egypt, and the Alexandrian priest and theologian Arius. The former believed that the Father and the Son were both eternal and of equal status. Arius believed the Son was not eternal and was inferior to the father. The Arians, while still advocating the divinity of the Son, insisted that there is substantial difference between the Father and the Son.

The spread of this controversy prompted Emperor Constantine to arrange and oversee the first Ecumenical Council, which was held in Nicea in 325 CE. The convening bishops, whose number has been put by different sources between 250 and 318, released the first decree that addressed the status of the Father and the Son and their relationship, but it only affirmed the belief in the Holy Spirit. This decree was not the result of as much consensus as Constantine's influence and pressure. Having been given the choice of signing to the decree or being sent into exile, Arius and his allies chose the latter. The wording of the decree was vague and open to different interpretations, but it was still clear enough to reject Arianism:

> We believe in one God, the Father, almighty,
> maker of all things visible and invisible;
> And in one Lord Jesus Christ, the Son of God,
> begotten from the Father, only-begotten, that is,
> from the substance of the Father, God from God,
> light from light, true God from true God,
> begotten not made, of one substance with the Father,
> through whom all things came into being,
> things in heaven and things on earth,
> Who because of us men and because of our salvation
> came down and became incarnate, becoming man,
> suffered and rose again on the third day, ascended to the heavens,
> will come to judge the living and the dead;
> And in the Holy Spirit.
> But as for those who say, there was when He was not,
> and, before being born He was not,
> and that He came into existence out of nothing,
> or who assert that the Son of God is of a different
> hypostasis or substance, or is subject to alteration or
> change — these the Catholic and apostolic Church anathematises. (Kelly, 1999: 215-216)

In the following half a century the debates and disagreements continued unabated, and when the second Ecumenical Council was convened in

Constantinople in 381, the convening 150 bishops revised the creed and gave it its final shape, which now addressed the status of the Holy Spirit also and, thus, the doctrine of the Trinity:

> We believe in one God, the Father, almighty,
> maker **of heaven and earth**, of all things visible and invisible;
> And in one Lord Jesus Christ, the **only-begotten** Son of God,
> begotten from the Father **before all ages**, light from light,
> true God from true God, begotten not made,
> of one substance with the Father, through whom all things came into existence,
> Who because of us men and because of our salvation came down from heaven,
> and was incarnate **from the Holy Spirit and the Virgin Mary** and became man,
> **and was crucified for us under Pontius Pilate,**
> and suffered **and was buried**, and rose again on the third day
> **according to the Scriptures** and ascended to heaven,
> **and sits on the right hand of the Father,**
> and will come again with glory to judge living and dead,
> **of whose kingdom there will be no end;**
> **And in the Holy Spirit, the Lord and life-giver,**
> **who proceeds from the Father, who with the Father and the Son is together worshipped and together glorified, who spoke through the prophets;**
> **in one holy Catholic and apostolic Church.**
> **We confess one baptism to the remission of sins; we look forward to the resurrection of the dead and the life of the world to come.** Amen. (Kelly, 1999: 297-298)

The deletions from the Nicean formulary and the additions, which are highlighted in bold above, are instructive in understanding issues that were at the center of the debates between Christian theologians.

Some doubts have been raised about whether this revision was made in the 381 council (Kelly, 1999: 305-331). It is first mentioned as an official formulary in the Chalcedon council in 451 where the convening bishops clearly believed that the creed had been composed and ratified in Constantinople.

The Niceno-Constantinopolitan Creed, as it has become known, was accepted by both the Eastern and Western Churches. The history leading to the formulation of this authoritative formulary, however, was full of controversy, and the consensus that was finally achieved conceals many bitter battles and much struggle between opposing views by prominent Churchmen. For a detailed study of the history of the development of this creed, the reader may like to see *Early Christian Creeds* (Kelly, 1999).

Jesus was not the only holy figure that Christianity deified. His mother Mary was also later transformed into an object of worship in a doctrine known as Mariolatry or the "worship of Mary," even though there is nothing to support this exaltation of Mary's status in the New Testament. Among the titles Christians conferred on Mary are "Mother of God" and "Queen of Heaven." Mariolatry led to the introduction of dogmas such as the "immaculate conception," by Pope Pius IX in 1854, which states that Mary was free of the original sin from birth, and "assumption of Mary," by Pope Pius XII in 1950, which teaches that after her death, Mary's soul and body were taken to heaven.

The Qur'an's position on the Trinity and Mariolatry will be discussed in the next chapter.

14.5. Son of Man

In the Gospels Jesus frequently refers to himself as the "son of Man." We will see in this section how this expression, which sets a marked contrast with the title "son of God," is another indication that Jesus rejected the attempts to deify him.

The term "son of man" translates the Aramaic *bar nasha* or *bar nash* and the Hebrew *ben 'adam* (literally, "son of Adam"). In the Old Testament, it is found once in Job, twice in Daniel, and over 90 times in Ezekiel. In the Gospels this expression occurs at a much higher frequency — 82 times in that much smaller text. It occurs 14 times in Mark, 30 in Matthew, 25 in Luke, and 13 in John. In the rest of the New Testament it is found only twice in Revelation in quotations from the Old Testament, once in Acts, and once in Hebrews.

Scholars have been arguing about the exact meaning of "son of Man." More specifically, some have maintained that it was a pre-Christian Jewish title that denoted the eschatological figure of the Messiah, and this is how they understand Jesus' natural and repeated use of the term. The majority of scholars reject this view. Those who take "son of Man" to be a Jewish designation for the Messiah cite three main textual sources in support of their theory: 1 Enoch 37-71, 4 Ezra 13, and Daniel 7:13.

1 Enoch ascribes itself to the 7th patriarch in Genesis, but it is considered as a pseudepigraphical work whose author is unknown. Its complete version survives in an Ethiopic translation which is believed to have been made as late as the 6th century CE, but its earliest extant manuscript comes from as late as the 16th century. The book is a conglomeration of a number of works of different origins, and it has been rated by some scholars as one of the hundred worst books (Campbell, 1947: 148). The chapters that interest us here are 37-71 or the *Parables* or *Similitudes*. They talk about an eschatological figure who is described as "the righteous one," "the elect one" and "the Messiah." He is linked to Jesus because he

is also called "the son of man." Nevertheless, the *Parables* cannot be proved to be pre-Christian. In fact, many scholars believe that it was written by Christians, probably around the end of the 1st century or in the 2nd, so it does not reflect pre-Christian Jewish beliefs (Longenecker, 1969: 152-153; Sanders, 1995: 246, 308).

The second source, 4 Ezra 13, survives in a number of translations of the Greek version. The latter and its Semitic source have both been lost. This source does not actually use the term "son of man," but it talks about an eschatological *man* who comes from the sea and with the clouds of heaven. He destroys the multitudes that start a war against him. Like 1 Enoch 37-71, this book is also believed to have been written late in the first century (Longenecker, 1969: 153).

Unlike the first two sources, the Old Testament Book of Daniel is certainly pre-Christian. This is how Prophet Daniel describes what he saw in one of his visionary dreams:

> I was watching in the night visions, "And with the clouds of the sky there was coming one *like a son of man*. He approached the Ancient of Days and was escorted before him. To him was given ruling authority, honor, and sovereignty. All peoples, nations, and language groups were serving him. His authority is eternal and will not pass away. His kingdom will not be destroyed. (Dan. 7:13-14)

The son of man in this passage has been taken to signify an eschatological individual, giving the term a titular function. It was interpreted as a reference to *the Messiah*. I find this interpretation of Daniel's "son of man" misguided. **First**, this is the only instance of its 96 appearances in the Old Testament where the term is supposed to be used as a title and to have messianic eschatological connotations. **Second**, this expression appears again in the next chapter in Daniel in an angel's speech to the prophet where it simply means "human" or "mortal" (Dan. 8:17). **Third**, Daniel 7:13 does not actually describe the heavenly figure as "a son of man." To the contrary, by describing him as being "like a son of man" the author is pointing out that he is *not* a son of man (Campbell, 1947: 148). Daniel meant that although the supernatural figure he saw looked like a son of man, he knew that he was not. That figure was not a human being, so he could not have been the Messiah.

So there is no textual evidence on the existence of the concept of the "son of man" as an apocalyptic figure in pre-Christian Jewish thought. The expression "son of man" does not appear as a title in Daniel, the Parables, or 4 Ezra 13 (Bock, 1991: 111; Campbell, 1947; Longenecker, 1969, 1975). This is how the Christian professor Frederick Bruce puts it:

> "[T]he Son of man" was not a current title, whether for the Messiah or for any other eschatological figure. When Jewish thinkers devised a title for the figure who is brought to the Ancient of Days, it was not the Son of man but Anani (the "cloud-man"). There does not appear to have been any existing

concept of "the Son of man" which Jesus could have taken over and used either to identify himself or to denote a being distinct from himself. (Bruce, 1982: 60)

Researchers who insist that "son of man" existed as a title in pre-Christian Judaism have had to assume that the three texts above use "son of man" as a title and then conclude that the existence of this titular use means that the expression must have been established before Jesus (e.g. Horbury, 1985). This is actually more of a clever wording of the assumption than an argument based on evidence.

The Jewish history from the fall of Palestine to the Roman general Pompey in 63 BCE to the 2nd failed Jewish revolt against Rome (132-135 CE) was very turbulent. During this period, the Jews and their kingdom became Roman subjects, and this led to a growing interest among the Jews in the concept of the Messiah and an increasing tendency to reinterpret texts in messianic terms. This, in my view, is what forced the emergence of that Christological misinterpretation of Daniel 7:13. Although Daniel 7:13 actually denies that this eschatological figure was a "son of man," its use of the term was misunderstood and linked to the Messiah.

The New Testament, which was written in this period, must have been influenced by this atmosphere. Indeed, there are passages that have been clearly modeled on Daniel 7:13, showing the son of man coming with or on the clouds from heaven (also Mark 13:26; Matt. 26:64; Luke 21:27):

> And you will see the Son of Man sitting at the right hand of the Power and coming with the clouds of heaven. (Mark 14:62)

> Then the sign of the Son of Man will appear in heaven, and all the tribes of the earth will mourn. They will see the Son of Man arriving on the clouds of heaven with power and great glory. (Matt. 24:30)

> Then I looked, and a white cloud appeared, and seated on the cloud was one like a son of man! He had a golden crown on his head and a sharp sickle in his hand. (Rev. 14:14)

Note Revelation's use of "like a son of man" like Daniel does.

There are other appearances of the term "son of man" in the Gospels that *may* be taken to reflect the Evangelists' association of this term with the Messiah. For instance, these passages present the "son of man" as a victorious eschatological heavenly figure who commands the angels (also Matt. 16:27, 25:31; Luke 9:26, 12:8):

> For if anyone is ashamed of me and my words in this adulterous and sinful generation, the Son of Man will also be ashamed of him when he comes in the glory of his Father with the holy angels. (Mark 8:38)

The Son of Man will send his angels, and they will gather from his kingdom everything that causes sin as well as all lawbreakers. (Matt. 13:41)

I tell all of you the solemn truth — you will see heaven opened and the angels of God ascending and descending on the Son of Man. (John 1:51)

The son of man is also associated with the forgiving of sins and healing (e.g. Matt. 9:6; Luke 5:24):

"But so that you may know that the Son of Man has authority on earth to forgive sins," — he said to the paralytic — "I tell you, stand up, take your stretcher, and go home." And immediately the man stood up, took his stretcher, and went out in front of them all. They were all amazed and glorified God, saying, "We have never seen anything like this!" (Mark 2:10-12)

John applies many of the attributes of his special son of God to the son of man. The son of man came from God and returned to Him: "No one has ascended into heaven except the one who descended from heaven — the Son of Man" (John 3:13). He also has Jesus say to his disciples: "Then what if you see the Son of Man ascending where he was before?" (John 6:62). The son of man has authority to judge, and believing in him gives eternal life (also John 6:27):

For just as the Father has life in himself, thus he has granted the Son to have life in himself, and he has granted the Son authority to execute judgment, because he is the Son of Man. (John 5:26-27).

"Just as Moses lifted up the serpent in the wilderness, so must the Son of Man be lifted up, so that everyone who believes in him may have eternal life." For this is the way God loved the world: He gave his one and only Son, so that everyone who believes in him will not perish but have eternal life. (John 3:14-16)

If the Gospel authors or their sources did mean *at times* to use "son of man" as a *title* for the Messiah, which is far from clear, then I think that would have been the result of the combination of the facts that Jesus used this term frequently to refer to himself, the Evangelists' belief that Jesus was he Messiah, and their influence by a certain interpretation of Daniel 7:13. What is clear, however, is that most of the time the expression did not have any Messianic function, as it was not a Jewish designation for the Messiah. In explaining the titular, religious use of the expression "son of man" in the Gospel of John, Vermes notes the following about the religious use of this phrase in Jewish literature:

From the completion of the Book of Daniel in the 160s BC to the time of the destruction of Jerusalem in AD 70 there is no attestation in extant Jewish literature of the use of "son of Man" as describing a religious function.

> However, in the decades following the first Jewish war against Rome which ended in AD 70, that is during the period of the composition of the Gospels, we possess independent literary evidence in which such a man-like figure is portrayed as a heavenly Messiah (4 Ezra 13), or a superterrestrial final Judge (Parables of Enoch, or 1 Enoch 37-71). (Vermes, 2000: 39)

There are other facts and arguments that support our earlier conclusion, which Vermes confirms, that there is no evidence that the expression "son of man" was a recognized title for the Messiah before Jesus. **First**, neither before nor after Jesus did the term "son of man" ever gain popularity as a designation for the Messiah, despite the fact that Jesus applies it to himself in the Gospels over 80 times and more explicitly and directly than any other title, including the Christ. It is almost completely absent in Acts and the Epistles. Furthermore, its possible use as a title for an eschatological figure remained limited to a very small number of sources.

Second, unlike the title "son of God" which occurs on the lips of a number of different people and spiritual beings, almost all occurrences of "son of man" in the Gospels are found in sayings of Jesus. The only exception is John 12:34, but even here people mention it in the context of asking Jesus about what he meant by saying that the "son of man" would be lifted up. Had "son of man" been an established title before Jesus we would have seen it in the Gospels used by people to refer to Jesus, not only used by him. **Third**, hearing this expression did not have any unusual effect on people. Had it been a special title of some prominence, let alone an epithet of the Messiah, it would have invoked certain reactions. Nothing of the sort is reported.

But is it possible that it was Jesus who introduced "son of man" as a special title? The answer is no, because there is no indication anywhere in the Gospels that people needed Jesus to explain to them the term "son of man." At no point were Jesus' hearers puzzled by the expression or could not understand it. Had Jesus introduced the expression as a special appellation he would have needed to explain it to people and they would have asked him about it.

So what was the meaning of "son of man" which was clear enough not to require explaining by Jesus or enquiring by people? This is what Vermes — who shares the scholarly consensus that Jesus' main language was Aramaic, like the Jews of Palestine — has to say:

> Outside the New Testament, "son of man" is most commonly employed in the Aramaic language by Jews either as a noun ("a man/the man"), or as the indefinite pronoun ("one/someone"), but neither of these usages is applicable to the Synoptic Gospels. Furthermore, in the Galilean dialect of Aramaic spoken by Jesus, "son of man" sometimes appears in a monologue or dialogue as a circumlocutional reference to the speaker himself. It is not unlike the English figure of speech, "yours truly," used in place of "I." For

example, "Who is the author of this splendid piece?" or "Who is responsible for this horror?" may produce the modest or shamefaced reply, "Yours truly." The purpose of such a periphrastic style was to camouflage something fatal dreaded by the speaker or something that would sound boastful if directly asserted. So one would say in Aramaic, *the son of man* is going to die, or *the son of man* is about to become king, rather than *I* will die, or *I* will be proclaimed king. (Vermes, 2000: 38-39)

While Vermes notes that unlike the Synoptics which use "son of man" for "I," John combines this circumlocutional use with a titular one. This should not surprise us, as John is far more focused on theology than the Synoptic Gospels. John was also developed later than the other Gospels and is thus more distant from Jesus, so we can safely conclude that Jesus used the expression "son of man" in the sense of "I." Also, as this term was not connected to any particular imagery in the minds of Jesus' audiences, they must have simply taken it to mean "I," i.e. as a reference to Jesus himself.

This is one example in which Jesus clearly uses in the same passage "son of man" for the personal pronoun "I":

> For if anyone is ashamed of me and my words in this adulterous and sinful generation, the Son of Man will also be ashamed of him when he comes in the glory of his Father with the holy angels. (Mark 8:38)

Matthew's wording of a passage that is found also in Mark and Luke is particularly instructive of how the Evangelists understood "son of man":

> Then Jesus and his disciples went to the villages of Caesarea Philippi. On the way he asked his disciples, "Who do people say that I am?" (Mark 8:27)

> Once when Jesus was praying by himself, and his disciples were nearby, he asked them, "Who do the crowds say that I am?" (Luke 9:18)

> When Jesus came to the area of Caesarea Philippi, he asked his disciples, "Who do people say that the Son of Man is?" (Matt. 16:13)

Matthew has replaced the "I" in Mark with "son of man," whereas Luke left the original. This is another example where the term "Son of Man" in Luke appears as "I" in Matthew:

> Whoever, then, acknowledges me before people, I will acknowledge before my Father in heaven. (Matt. 10:32)

I tell you, whoever acknowledges me before men, the Son of Man will also acknowledge before God's angels. (Luke 12:8)

These examples show that the Evangelists treated the expression "son of man" as a circumlocution for "I" (compare also Mark 8:38, Matt. 10:33, & Luke 9:26; and Mark 10:45, Matt. 20:28, & Luke 22:27).

Theissen and Merz would object to this conclusion, pointing out that the association of the expression "son of man" with Jesus could not have been derived from everyday language only. They ask: "Why should an expression which in principle everyone could use and which could mean anyone be so closely associated with Jesus that it was retained even after Easter, when for Christians Jesus had already long since been more than a man?" They argue that Jesus must have persistently used the everyday term to turn it into a title for himself, with one possible reason being Jesus' attempt to counteract specific expectations that were being associated with him:

> Jesus must have used the everyday expression emphatically so that it could become his "title" — say by using it to correct excessive expectations; other people might expect miracles of him, other people might hope that he was the stronger one expected since John the Baptist, others might throng after him — but as a correction of such expectations he emphasized his human status as "son of man" (Mark 2:10; Matt. 11:18, 8:20). So among other things the expression became a christological title because Jesus opposed it to christological expectations and thus made it a mysterious honorific title first for his followers. In the Gospel texts after they have been subjected to redaction, this corrective function of the term "Son of Man" can still be detected: Peter confesses Jesus as the Messiah, but Jesus answers by prophesying the suffering of the Son of Man (Mark 8:29). Jesus is asked about his messiahship before the Sanhedrin, but replies with a saying about the Son of Man (14:61.) (Theissen & Merz, 1999: 550)

I completely agree that it must have been Jesus who used the expression "son of man," and I also accept that Jesus did so in order to countervail excessive beliefs about him. I do not agree, however, that the target of his action was Christological or miracle expectations:

① The phrase "son of man" does nothing other than emphasize the human nature of Jesus, yet the Messiah was expected to be a human being anyway, albeit with special authority and powers. Those powers were not linked to any superhuman origin, so they could not be offset by reminding people that the Christ was human.

② Jesus did proclaim to be the Messiah, but he set the right expectations by stressing what his messiahship meant. In the simplest terms, it was a call for people to obey God. He clearly and robustly rejected any attempt by people to assign to his messianic role any political function, as in his rebuke to his testers to "give to Caesar the things that are Caesar's, and to God the things that are God's" (Mark 12:17; Matt. 22:21; Luke 20:25).

③ The expectations of miracles from him could not have been the target of his persistent use of the expression "son of man," because he did perform miracles.

The expression "son of man," which emphasized Jesus' human nature, could have had only one target to counteract: claims or expectations of Jesus' divinity. By frequently using this phrase periphrastically, Jesus stressed his human nature and rejected claims about his divinity that had either already started to circulate or, more likely, he expected to appear at some point after him. As has been pointed out, this expression "could not be understood in the Greek world otherwise than as referring simply to the humanity of Jesus." Furthermore, the early Church fathers saw in this title a reference to the human nature of Jesus' descent. So "from the Apostolic Fathers to the present, the title has come to be regarded in the dogmatic theology of the Church as but the converse of the title Son of God. But in the early Church it was not so" (Longenecker, 1969: 157). So even those who recognized and promoted Jesus' divinity accepted that the title "son of man" denoted his humanity.

The tension between the terms "son of man" and "son of God" may be seen in Matthew's adaptation of one of Mark's passages:

> Then Jesus and his disciples went to the villages of Caesarea Philippi. On the way he asked his disciples, "Who do people say that I am?" They said, "John the Baptist, others say Elijah, and still others, one of the prophets." He asked them, "But who do you say that I am?" Peter answered him, "You are the Christ." (Mark 8:27-29)

> When Jesus came to the area of Caesarea Philippi, he asked his disciples, "Who do people say that the Son of Man is?" They answered, "Some say John the Baptist, others Elijah, and others Jeremiah or one of the prophets." He said to them, "But who do you say that I am?" Simon Peter answered, "You are the Christ, the Son of the living God." (Matt. 16:13-16)

Significantly, the replacement of "I" with the expression "Son of Man" is followed by the addition of the epithet "Son of the living God." This suggests that the author was aware of what "Son of Man" meant to people so he went out of his way to stress Jesus' sonship of God also.

The relentless attempts to change Jesus' status from man to God after he had gone, which succeeded at the end, fully justified every action that Jesus took to stress his human nature. The determination to promote Jesus' divinity was so strong that, ironically, the refutative expression "son of man" was itself used, as in

John, to ascribe divine attributes to Jesus! The circumlocutional expression "son of man" was turned into a title and used at times exactly like the epithet "son of God" which was applied to Jesus in a special way. Jesus could not have replaced the term "God" in "son of God" with "man" to coin a new appellation and then used both titles interchangeably!

Of course, not all "son of man" sayings are authentic. Probably many of them were made up and others changed to convey whatever messages the Evangelists wanted to pass to their readers. For instance, I do not believe that Jesus talked about coming back to this world after departing it, be it on the clouds or in any other way. (I will discuss the subject of Jesus' second coming further in Chapter 20.) Also, any use of "son of man" in other than its periphrastic function is inauthentic. What makes me believe that Jesus did indeed use the expression "son of man" is its frequent use in many of his reported sayings, its use exclusively by him, and its particular suitability for averting and rejecting his deification.

I should also mention that the Gospels, including John, state that Jesus called himself a prophet (Mark 6:4; Matt. 13:57; Luke 4:24; John 4:44). Prophets in the Old Testament are human beings, so Jesus must have used this title, like the expression "son of man," to stress his human nature, although there is more to this title, as we shall see in the next chapter. Other people also described Jesus as a "prophet" (Mark 6:15; Matt. 21:11, 21:46; Luke 7:16, 24:19; John 4:19, 6:14, 7:40, 9:17), which is another confirmation that had "son of man" been a recognized title like "prophet" the Gospels would have shown people not only Jesus use it.

Given that Jesus frequently called himself the "son of man" to reject and/or preempt any attempt to ascribe divine attributes to him, how likely is it that Jesus could have referred to God as *his father*, thus calling himself indirectly "son of God"? Since at the time of Jesus the Jewish concept of "sonship of God" had no divine connotation, it may be argued that Jesus could have called God his father. But the counter, and probably stronger, argument is that given that Jesus realized that he was going to be deified, he would have recognized that a claim to sonship of God might be used as a vehicle to suggest he was divine, so it is unlikely that he called God his father. Interestingly, while all instances of "son of man" occur in sayings of Jesus, the title "son of God" is applied to Jesus only by others in the Synoptics; only John puts it on Jesus' lips (e.g. John 10:36)!

I should finally mention that my conclusions above clearly refute the suggestion of some Muslim scholars that "son of man" was a title that Jesus used for Prophet Muhammad (Dawud, 1994: 223-263).

15

The Human Jesus

Judaism, unlike Christianity and Islam, does not accept that Jesus was a man of God like Abraham, Moses, and other Old Testament figures. Both Christianity and Islam venerate Jesus, accept that he was commissioned by God, and attribute to him many miracles. But the two religions have fundamental differences about the person of Jesus, his message, and the nature of his relationship with God. The main difference between the reverences of these great religions for Jesus can be summed up by the fact that the Christian Jesus is both man and God whereas the Muslim Jesus is only a man.

The Qur'anic Jesus is a human prophet and messenger of God who never claimed to be divine. He was also the forerunner of Prophet Muhammad, having predicted his coming. The Qur'an stresses the oneness of God, confirms that He has no offspring, and denounces the doctrine of the Trinity.

15.1. Muslim Messenger and Prophet

Jesus in the Qur'an is portrayed as a prophet of Islam. This description may sound rather odd to those who are not familiar with the Qur'anic meaning of Islam and think that Islam is the religion that is associated with Prophet Muhammad only. We need first to look at the concept of "Islam" in the Qur'an before discussing the image of Jesus as a Muslim Prophet and Messenger.

15.1.1. Islam

The Arabic verb *yuslim* means "to surrender" or "to submit." It is used in a special way in the Qur'an to mean *to surrender (one's self) to God*. The derived Qur'anic noun *Islām*, therefore, means *surrender or submission to God* whom the Qur'an calls Allah. To be a Muslim is to believe in God as the One Lord, submit to His will, and carry out His commandments.

Contrary to the common misconception that it is the religion that was revealed to Prophet Muhammad only, Islam is a universal term that describes the one religion that God commanded, through His various messengers, all people to embrace.

The Qur'an also tells us that the name "Muslim" was in fact coined by God who used it long before Prophet Muhammad and the Qur'an:

> And do *jihād* [O you who believe!] in the way of Allah the kind of *jihad* that is due to Him. He has chosen you and has not laid upon you a hardship in religion; it is the faith of your father Abraham. He [Allah] has named you Muslims earlier and in this [the Qur'an], so that the Messenger be a witness over you, and you be witnesses over the

people. Therefore keep up prayer, pay the obligatory alms, and hold fast to Allah; He is your Master; so how excellent a Master and how excellent a Supporter! (22.78).

This verse tells us that God has named the followers of His religion "Muslims" not only in the Qur'an but also in books that He revealed to previous prophets, such as the Torah of Moses and the Injīl of Jesus. The following verse states that Prophet Noah, who lived long before Prophet Abraham, told his people that God ordered him to be "one of the Muslims":

But if you [O people!] turn away [from my call], I have not asked you for any reward; my reward is only with Allah, and I have been commanded to be one of the Muslims (10.72).

Thus, previous divine books and prophets used terms equivalent to "Islam" and "Muslim" in their respective languages.

Islam is the name of the one religion that Allah, the One and only God, revealed to every prophet He sent to people since the time of the first man and Prophet, Adam. For instance, all of the following prophets were Muslims who taught Islam to people: Noah, Abraham, Ishmael, Isaac, Jacob, Joseph, Moses, Aaron, David, Solomon, Zechariah, John, and Jesus. The following verse describes Israelite prophets as "Muslims":

Surely We revealed the Torah in which there was guidance and light; with it, the prophets who became Muslims guided the Jews (5.44).

These are other verses about prophets Abraham and his sons and grandsons:

And who turns away from the religion of Abraham but he who makes himself a fool; and surely We chose him [Abraham] in this world, and in the hereafter he is surely among the righteous (2.130). When his Lord said to him: "Be a Muslim"; he said: "I have become a Muslim (I have submitted) to the Lord of the people" (2.131). And Abraham enjoined the same on his sons, and so did Jacob (Abraham's grandson): "O my sons! Surely Allah has chosen for you the [true] religion, therefore die not except as Muslims" (2.132). Or were you [O People of the Book!] witnesses when death visited Jacob, when he said to his sons: "What will you worship after me?" They said: "We shall worship your God and the God of your fathers, Abraham, Ishmael, and Isaac, one God, and to Him we are Muslims (submit)" (2.133).

The commissioning of Muhammad was not an unprecedented event. It was another instance of God sending a prophet, which is how He communicated with people:

Say [O Muhammad!]: "I am not a novelty among the messengers, nor do I know what will be done with me or with you. I only follow that which is revealed to me; I am but a manifest warner [of hell]" (46.9).

The revelation that Muhammad received came from the same source of the earlier divine revelations:

> We have revealed to you [O Muhammad!] as we revealed to Noah and the prophets after him; and as We revealed to Abraham, Ishmael, Isaac, Jacob, the children of Jacob, Jesus, Job, Jonah, Aaron, and Solomon. And We gave David a Book (4.163). And [We gave Books] to other messengers whom We have mentioned to you before and other messengers whom We have not mentioned to you. And Allah spoke to Moses — certainly spoke to him (4.164).

> He has ordained for you [O you who believe!] the religion that He enjoined on Noah; that which We revealed to you [O Muhammad!]; and that which We enjoined on Abraham, Moses, and Jesus: "Establish the religion, and make no divisions therein." What you call the polytheists to is hard for them. Allah chooses for Himself whom He wills, and guides to Him who turns to Him (42.13).

Muhammad's message was a continuation of the previous messages, in the same way that Jesus' message continued Moses', Moses' message continued Joseph's, Joseph's continued Jacob's, and so on. What distinguishes Prophet Muhammad from other Muslim prophets is that he is the *last prophet* of Islam, which means that the Qur'an is the last divine Book:

> [O people!] Muhammad is not the father of any of your men, but he is the Messenger of Allah and the last of the prophets; and Allah is aware of everything (33.40).

In addition to the belief in the oneness of God, the hereafter, and the angels, the Qur'an requires the Muslim to believe in all previous messengers and the books and messages that God revealed to them. This is consistent with the Qur'an's affirmation that all messengers taught the same religion and were sent by the one and same God. The Muslim is commanded to hold all prophets in high esteem and reverence. The failure to believe in any prophet is a failure to believe in all prophets, and a failure to be a Muslim:

> The Messenger [Muhammad] believes in that which has been revealed to him from his Lord, and so do the believers; they all believe in Allah, His angels, His Books, and His messengers; [they say] we do not discriminate between any of His messengers; and they say: "We hear and obey [Allah's commandments]; grant us Your forgiveness, our Lord. And to You is the eventual course" (2.285).

This brief introduction should help in understanding the Qur'anic description of Jesus as a Muslim prophet.

15.1.2. Messenger and Prophet

The Arabic word for "prophet" is *nabī*, whose root is *naba'*, which means "news" or "tidings." The word for "prophecy" is *nubū'a* and shares the same root. A "prophet" in the Qur'an is a human being to whom God revealed tidings of the Day of Resurrection and teachings about the true religion. The prophet is charged with communicating this knowledge to people so that they may know the purpose of their creation and act as God wants them to do. As we have already seen, Biblical figures such as Adam, Solomon, David, Moses, Zechariah, John, and many others were all prophets.

The prophets in the Old Testament are also human beings. Interestingly, in the New Testament Jesus is called a prophet (Mark 6:15; Matt. 21:11, 21:46; Luke 7:16, 24:19; John 4:19, 6:14, 7:40, 9:17) and he calls himself so (Mark 6:4; Matt. 13:57; Luke 4:24; John 4:44). Surely, if Jesus was divine, he would not have called himself a prophet.

Another Qur'anic term that is related to "prophet" is "messenger." The latter has a rather broader sense, denoting anyone that God sends on a mission, such as delivering a message or performing a particular task. Another difference between prophet and messenger is that the former is used only for human beings, whereas a messenger may or may not be a human being — for instance, he may be an angel.

As a prophet is sent by God to deliver a message to people, every prophet is a messenger. The opposite, however, is not true. Not every messenger is a prophet, because not every messenger receives from God the kind of knowledge that characterizes prophets — that is, knowledge of religion and the Day of Judgment — or is charged with the responsibility of acting as a religious teacher to people.

Some exegetes take the opposite view, thinking that messengers are a special group of prophets whose messages are targeted at many more people than the target audience of ordinary prophets. There are observations from the Qur'an that refute this view. **First**, the Qur'an uses the title "messenger" for some prophets, such as Hūd (7.67), whose preaching activities were limited in place and time and could not be compared to the activities of other prophets, such as Moses and Jesus, whose messages spread far and survived well beyond their times. **Second**, the angels, who are spiritual beings, and who are never called "prophets," are called "messengers," because they are "sent" by God to people on specific missions:

> Praise be to Allah, who has created the heavens and the earth, and who has made the angels messengers (35.1).

The angels who were sent to prophets Abraham and Lot (11.69-83, 15.51-74, 29.31-34), those who attend the dying person (6.61, 7.37), and those who record what people say and do (43.80) are all called "messengers," but not prophets.

Third, the Qur'an uses the title "messenger" several times to denote *any* human spiritual guide inspired and sent to people by God, without any other specific attributes, such as targeting a larger number of people:

> We did not send any messenger but that he should be obeyed by Allah's permission (4.64).

Four, the following verse indicates that prophets were all human beings, so the term "messenger," which is applied to the angels also, cannot include the term "prophet":

> And We have not sent [prophets] before you [O Muhammad!] but men to whom We gave revelations, [who were] from the people of the towns (12.109).

Jesus, the Qur'an tells us, was a prophet (also 4.163):

> He [Jesus] said: "I am Allah's servant. He has given me the Book and has appointed me a prophet" (19.30).
>
> And when We took a covenant from the prophets; and from you [O Muhammad!]; and from Noah, Abraham, Moses, and Jesus son of Mary. We took from them a solemn covenant (33.7).

The following verses also confirm the prophethood of Jesus, but in the context of reminding the Jews, Christians, and Muslims that they must believe in all prophets and honor them equally (also 3.84):

> Say [O you who believe!]: "We believe in Allah; and in that which has been sent down to us; and in that which was sent down to Abraham, Ishmael, Isaac, Jacob, and the children of Jacob; and in that which was given to Moses and Jesus; and in that which was given to the prophets from their Lord. We do not discriminate between any of them, and to Him we are Muslims (we submit)" (2.136).

Being a prophet, Jesus is naturally described as a "messenger" also (also 2.87, 3.49):

> The Messiah son of Mary was no other than a messenger before whom [similar] messengers passed away (5.75).
>
> Then We made Our messengers to follow in their (Noah and Abraham) footsteps, and followed them up with Jesus son of Mary (57.27).

As all prophets were Muslims and taught Islam, their true followers were also called Muslims. These two verses show that Jesus' companions called themselves Muslims (more on Jesus' companions in §21.2.1):

But when Jesus perceived disbelief on their part, he said: "Who are my supporters in the cause of Allah?" The companions said: "We are Allah's supporters. We believe in Allah, and do you bear witness that we are Muslims" (3.52).

Lo! When I inspired the companions: "Believe in Me and in My messenger [Jesus]". They said: "We believe. Bear witness that we are Muslims" (5.111).

Jesus was one of the prophets and messengers, but he was also distinguished. He was actually unique. He is the only prophet who did not have a biological father. Probably related to his unique miraculous conception is his other distinctive quality that he became a prophet while still in his mother's womb or almost immediately after his birth. These are the words of the infant Jesus to his mother's people in defense of their questioning of her chastity: "I am Allah's servant. He has given me the Book and has appointed me a prophet" (19.30). Jesus' unique conception and the fact that, unlike other prophets, he was made a prophet almost immediately after, or even before, his birth must have distinguished him with special spiritual qualities.

Believing in every prophet is an essential requirement of Islam, because all prophets had one and the same message. This duty does not mean that all prophets have the same spiritual status. God mentions in a number of verses that He made some prophets better than others. For instance, some prophets were given more knowledge, others were given scriptures, and so on:

And your Lord [O Muhammad!] best knows those who are in the heavens and the earth. And We conferred on some prophets more favor than on others, and We gave a Book to David (17.55).

In another verse which states that God endowed some prophets with more gifts than others, Jesus is singled out as one of those specially favored prophets:

Those are the messengers. We conferred on some more favor than on others. Among them there are some to whom Allah spoke, while some of them He exalted [above others] in degree; and We gave Jesus son of Mary clear proofs and supported him with the Spirit of Holiness (Gabriel) (2.253).

God here emphasize two major favors that He bestowed on Jesus but not on many other prophets: the ability to perform miracles and the support with Gabriel. Although Gabriel delivered the Qur'an to Prophet Muhammad and probably communicated with other prophets, only Jesus is described as having been "supported" by Gabriel — probably hinting at a unique role that Gabriel played in Jesus' life. This should not be surprising given that, according to the Qur'an, Gabriel was also involved in the miraculous conception of Jesus, not only conveyed the news about it (pp. 92; 133-134).

With respect to miracles, the Qur'an tells us that other prophets were also given the gift of performing miracles. The verse above contrasts Jesus with other prophets who did not work wonders, but it may also imply that Jesus performed more miracles than the prophets who performed them. This may also be concluded from the mention of Jesus' miracles in some detail in a number of verses. We will study Jesus' miracles in Chapter 16.

15.2. Human Servant of God

The Qur'an stresses in many verses that all prophets were human beings. This is not meant to confirm that prophets were not divine, as this was never in doubt, but to emphasize that they were not supernatural being with unusual powers, such as the angels. The polytheistic population of Arabia, and many other peoples and cultures, believed that any individual that God or a god sends must be divine in some way. The Qur'an cites a number of specific prophets — including Noah (11.27, 23.24), Ṣāliḥ (26.154, 54.24), Shu'aib (26.186), Moses and Aaron (23.47), and Muhammad (17.94, 21.3) — who had to defend themselves against the claim that since they were human beings, they could not have been God's messengers. In the following verses, God explains that messengers who were sent to teach human beings religion had to be humans themselves, and that had the population of the earth been angels, His messengers to them would have also been angels:

> And nothing prevented people from believing when the guidance came to them except that they said: "What! Has Allah sent a human being to be a messenger?" (17.94). Say [O Muhammad!]: "Had there been on earth angels walking about feeling secure, We would certainly have sent down to them from the heaven an angel as a messenger" (17.95).

For instance, when prophet Ṣāliḥ was sent to his people, they rejected him, with one reason being that they could not believe that, being a human being like them, he could have received revelation from God. Even if they could accept that God may have chosen a human being as a messenger, they could not believe that it could have been Ṣāliḥ:

> The [people of] Thamūd rejected their warnings (54.23). They said: "A human being from among ourselves that we are to follow? In that case we would be in delusion and madness (54.24). Has the Remembrance been sent down to him from among us? He must be an insolent liar" (54.25).

The following verses show a typical exchange between messengers and their disbelieving people where the former argue that they could not come up with miracles at will, to satisfy their doubting people, as they were no more than human beings who could perform miracles only when God allows them to do that:

Their messengers said: "Is there a doubt about Allah, the Creator of the heavens and the earth? It is He who invites you, in order that He may forgive you your sins and give you respite until an appointed term." They said: "You are no more than human beings, like us! You wish to turn us away from what our fathers used to worship; bring us then some clear authority" (14.10). Their messengers said to them: "True, we are human beings like you, but Allah confers His favor on such of his servants as He pleases. It is not for us to bring you an authority except as Allah permits. And on Allah let all believers rely" (14.11).

Like all other prophets, Jesus was a human being. The Qur'an tells us that Jesus stressed his human nature in his teachings and that his deification was the result of changes made to his original message by some of his followers later on. Jesus told people that he was God's servant and prophet, and that he also had to worship God like he was calling people to do:

I am Allah's servant. He has given me the Book and has appointed me a prophet (19.30). He has made me blessed wherever I may be. He has enjoined upon me prayer and almsgiving so long as I remain alive (19.31).

The New Testament also describes Jesus as a "servant," although only once in the Gospels (Matt. 12:18) and three times in Acts (3:13, 4:27, 4:30). But the New Testament also promotes Jesus' divinity. In the Qur'an, servanthood is a description of the created, whereas lordship and divinity are exclusive descriptions of the Creator. The Qur'anic term *'abd* (servant) does not apply to Jesus only, but to all created beings. Describing Jesus as both "servant" and "divine" is another aspect of Jesus' confused nature in New Testament.

Jesus asked people to obey him, because he was a trustworthy messenger of God — his and everyone else's Lord:

Keep your duty to Allah, and obey me (43.63). Allah is my Lord and your Lord. So worship Him. This is a straight way (43.64).

The Qur'an stresses that Jesus' unique, miraculous conception did not mean that he was not a human being. He was a miraculously created human being like the first human being:

The likeness of Jesus in Allah's eye is as the likeness of Adam. He created him of dust, then He said to him "Be!" and he is (3.59).

Note also the emphasis in this verse that Jesus was created of dust like all human beings (22.5, 30.20). I have already discussed in detail the nature of the miraculous creation of Jesus as a human being (§7.3.2).

In the New Testament, Paul makes a direct link between Jesus and Adam. He explains that because Adam sinned, all his descendants inherited this sin which causes death. Through his resurrection, Jesus can free people from their sins and give them eternal life (Rom. 3:21-26, 5:6-21). These statements reflect Paul's doctrine of atonement, which we will study in more detail later (§19.4.1). This comparison between Jesus and Adam, and the whole doctrine itself, is not the only thing that the Qur'an rejects in what Paul had to say about these two prophets. Paul also claimed that Jesus and Adam were of completely different nature. After describing Jesus as a second Adam who gives life, Paul goes on to talk about the creation of the two:

> So also it is written, "The first man, Adam, became a living person"; the last Adam became a life-giving spirit. However, the spiritual did not come first, but the natural, and then the spiritual. The first man is from the earth, made of dust; the second man is from heaven. Like the one made of dust, so too are those made of dust, and like the one from heaven, so too those who are heavenly. And just as we have borne the image of the man of dust, let us also bear the image of the man of heaven. Now this is what I am saying, brothers and sisters: Flesh and blood cannot inherit the kingdom of God, nor does the perishable inherit the imperishable. (1 Cor. 15:45-50)

What Paul says here is the exact opposite to the Qur'an's statement which stresses the similarity between the creation of Adam and Jesus as being both from dust. Paul has stated in another Epistle that Jesus was a "descendant of David with reference to the flesh" (Rom. 1:3), clearly indicating that Jesus had another, deeper reality than his human body suggests.

15.3. Forerunner of Prophet Muhammad

One important difference between the image of Jesus in the New Testament and its counterpart in the Qur'an is that the latter does not present Jesus as the culmination of the divine messages (pp. 254, 255). His appearance was not a unique event in the history of God's messengers to people or its climax. He was very much part of that history in the same way that every other prophet was. Every messenger carried the same message and confirmed the messages of those who were sent before him. Similarly, Jesus was sent to confirm the verity of the Torah and to modify some of the legal aspects of that law:

> I have come to confirm that which was revealed before me of the Torah, and to make lawful some of that which was forbidden to you. I have come to you with a sign from your Lord, so keep your duty to Allah and obey me (3.50).

Matthew also confirms that Jesus' message was a continuation of the law (Matt. 5:17-48). Jesus' position toward the law will be discussed in more detail later (§17.5.1).

One indication that Jesus' appearance was not a climax in the history of God's messages is that he spoke about another prophet to come after him:

> And when Jesus son of Mary said: "O Children of Israel! I am a messenger of Allah to you, confirming that which was revealed before me of the Torah, and bringing good news about a messenger who will come after me, whose name is Aḥmad." But when he came to them with clear proofs, they said: "This is clear magic" (61.6).

This Prophet, Muhammad, whom Jesus described as being greater than him (p. 367), was mentioned in the both the Torah of Moses and the Injīl of Jesus:

> Those (the believers) who follow the Messenger, the unlettered Prophet, whom they find mentioned in the Torah and the Injīl which they have: He will enjoin on them that which is right and forbid them that which is evil; he will make lawful for them all good things and prohibit for them only the foul; and he will relieve them of their burden and the yokes that are upon them. Those who believe in him, honor him, help him, and follow the light which is sent down with him — those are the successful (7.157).

As Jesus lived about 6 centuries before Prophet Muhammad (570-632 CE), his foretelling of the coming of Muhammad and confirmation of his prophethood were particularly important for two main reasons. **First**, by the time Prophet Muhammad appeared, there were many millions of Christians in various countries, including a small minority in the Arabian Peninsula. Jesus had to tell those Christians to accept the new prophet whose message continued his. Some Christians followed the new prophet, but most did not. Obeying Jesus' command by most or many of his followers would have resulted in a very different history from the one we know today — the history that should have been, rather than the history that is.

Second, the Qur'an tells us that every prophet testified to the verity of the prophets who preceded him and confirmed their messages. For instance, Muhammad confirmed the messages of Jesus, Moses, Aaron, and the other prophets who had come before him; Jesus confirmed the messages of Moses, Aaron, and the earlier prophets; and so on. However, Muhammad was destined to be the last of God's prophets:

> Muhammad is not the father of any of your men, but he is the Messenger of Allah and the Last of the prophets; and Allah has full knowledge of all things (33.40).

Muhammad's prophethood was not going to be confirmed by a later prophet, so it was confirmed *in advance* by the prophet who came before him, Jesus, as well as by other earlier prophets.

An interesting difference between the New Testament and the Qur'an is that while the former claims that many Old Testament prophecies spoke about Jesus, the Qur'an records Jesus' pronouncement of Muhammad's prophethood in one verse only. As we have already seen, almost all of the messianic prophecies that the Evangelists attribute to the Old Testament are false and have nothing to do with Jesus or the Messiah.

We will discuss in more detail Jesus' prediction of the coming of Prophet Muhammad when we study the meaning of the term "Injīl" (p. 367).

15.4. The Exclusiveness of Divinity

As we saw in the previous chapter, the Jesus of the New Testament is no normal human being. He is essentially divine. Paul and John state this clearly, Matthew seems to suggest it, whereas Mark and Luke are rather ambivalent. Jesus' divinity seems to be the essence of his *unique* sonship of God, even when not spelt out explicitly. This dogma has been central to the Christian faith, yet it is completely rejected by the Qur'an.

Before we study what the Qur'an says about the deification of Jesus, we will discuss its concept of the oneness of God and take a look at how it dealt with Arabia's polytheism.

15.4.1. The Oneness of God

Unlike the God of the New Testament, the image of God in Islam is very clear, and it can be described in a number of simple statements. **First**, He is the only god: "There is not god save Allah" (47.19). **Second**, He is the "creator of everything" (6.102). **Third**, before starting the creation, God was alone; eternity is strictly God's: "He is the first and the last" (57.3). **Fourth**, as the supreme ruler of the universe, "Allah is able to do all things" (5.17), and "Allah does what He wishes" (2.253). **Fifth**, God is unique and dissimilar to anything: "There is nothing like Him" (42.11). **Sixth**, he is subtle and out of the reach of anyone's senses: "Vision cannot grasp Him, but He grasps all vision; and He is the Subtle, the Aware" (6.103). **Seventh**, everything and everyone is in submission to Him, whether by choice or by force: "To Him submits whoever is in the heavens and the earth, willingly or unwillingly" (3.83).

Almost all these statements are found in one form or another in the Bible. But the New Testament has other affirmations that blur the meanings of those fundamental statements, or even contradict them. One distinguishing feature of the Qur'an is the absence of such contradictory statements. For instance, while emphasizing that only God is eternal, the Qur'an does not go on elsewhere to qualify this statement by describing someone else as eternal. Similarly, there is a clear-cut ontological separation between God and His creation. No earthly or heavenly being is a god, part of God, or related to God in any form. There is one God, and everyone and everything else is created by Him.

The Qur'an considers any alleged god other than God false. It condemns in the strongest terms polytheism, i.e. associating gods with God. It states more than once that assigning partners to God is the gravest sin and the one sin that may not be forgiven (also 4.116):

> Allah does not forgive that anything should be associated with Him, but He forgives anything other than this to whomsoever He pleases; and whoever associates anything with Allah, he devises indeed a great sin (4.48).

One important difference between the image of God in the Qur'an and that of the New Testament, at least according to the most popular understanding of the latter, is that God of the Qur'an is *one* whereas God of the New Testament is *a unity*. Allah is not a number of persons in one, one person in multiple manifestations, one being in different aspects, or any such designations that developed in Christianity. All that can be said about Him is that He is one. His oneness cannot be broken down into any smaller units or different aspects. In his effort to show that the Qur'an does not actually contravene Christian theology, Parrinder (1995: 137) claims that the Qur'an affirms the unity of God. This suggestion is completely untrue. Under pressure to reconcile contradictory statements in the New Testament, Christian theologians work hard to stress that the concepts of divine oneness and unity are one and the same. The Qur'an, as logic does, rejects this equation. The God of the Qur'an is *one, not united*.

According to the Qur'an, God's divinity cannot be shared or divided. Everything and everyone other than God are merely His creation and servants. Spiritual development brings the servant closer to God, but it does not get him close to divinity. It actually confirms his servanthood. Being nearer to God means being closer to becoming the perfect Muslim, and the latter is one who has attained complete surrender and submission to God. This is the state in which the individual is no more a servant by compulsion only, but by will also. This means, for instance, that as Jesus was developing spiritually, he was getting closer and closer to attaining the state of perfect servanthood, not divinity.

The Qur'an ascribes to God what it calls *al-Asmā' al-Ḥunsā* (the Beautiful Names) (7.180, 17.110, 59.24): "Allah, there is no god but Him; His are the Beautiful Names" (20.8). These are different attributes that reflect God's actions, including names such as "The Merciful," "The Majestic," and "The Creator." Verses 59.22-24 list a number of these divine names. Many other verses end with a pair of Beautiful Names, such as verse 6.103 above. Most scholars count 99 Beautiful Names. In some polytheistic religions, the actions associated with these different names may be assigned to or shared by different gods.

15.4.2. No Offspring of God

The Qur'an's strict monotheism was revealed in the highly polytheistic society of Arabia. The Arabs believed in God, but they also believed in other deities (e.g. 13.33, 14.30). They considered God to be the chief God and believed in other, lower deities whom they saw as intermediaries who would bring them closer to God:

> It is We who have sent down to you [O Muhammad!] the Book with the truth, therefore worship Allah, making religion pure for Him (39.2). Pure religion is surely for Allah only, and as for those who take guardians besides Him, [saying] "we do not worship them save that they may bring us nearer to Allah," surely Allah will judge between them about that in which they differ; surely Allah does not guide aright one who is a liar, disbeliever (39.3).

The Arabs also considered these idols God's offspring (also 18.4-5, 23.84-92):

> And they (the disbelievers) say: "Allah has taken offspring [to Himself]". Glory be to Him; rather, whatever is in the heavens and the earth is His; all are subservient to Him (2.116).

> They (the disbelievers) say: "Allah has taken offspring [to Himself]". Glory be to Him. He is the Self-sufficient. His is all that is in the heavens and all that is in the earth. You have no authority for this [claim]; do you say about Allah what you do not know? (10.68).

These gods were also believed to be females, so they were described as *God's daughters*. Interestingly, the polytheistic society of Arabia considered the female inferior to the male, and the practice of female infanticide was widespread among them until it was prohibited and stopped by Islam (81.8-9). Despite this poor view of females, the Arabs were quite comfortable with making God's offspring females. This contradiction was one argument that the Qur'an used to expose the falsehood of assigning daughters to God, as it ridiculed the polytheists for wanting males for themselves yet assigning females to God:

> And they (the disbelievers) assign daughters to Allah, glory be to Him, and for themselves what they desire (16.57). And when one of them is given the news of the birth of a female, his face darkens, and he becomes filled with anger (16.58). He hides himself from people because of the evil of that which is announced to him. Shall he keep it with disgrace or bury it [alive] in the dust? Surely evil is what they judge (16.59).

> Or has He taken [to Himself] daughters out of what He creates and preferred you [O you who disbelieve!] with sons? (43.16). And when one of them is given the news of the birth of what he links to God, his face darkens, and he becomes filled with anger (43.17).

> Or has He daughters whereas you have sons? (52.39).

The Qur'an names three of the Arab's female idols, in the context of sarcastically contrasting the miracles that God showed to Prophet Muhammad with the fact that these goddesses could not show anything to their believers:

> He [Prophet Muhammad] has seen of His Lord's greatest sings (53.18). Have you [O you who disbelieve!] seen the Lāt and the 'Ūzzā? (53.19). And Manāt, the third, the other one? (53.20). So the male is for you and the female is for Him? (53.21). This is an unfair division! (53.22).

The Qur'an then continues its sarcastic tone to remind the Arabs that it is unfair of them to attribute to God females and take to themselves males!

The polytheists of Arabia did not restrict the daughtership of God to idols. They believed that the angels, whom they claimed to be females, were also His daughters. The Qur'an rejects that the angels were females and that they were God's daughters:

> Those who do not believe in the hereafter call the angels with female names (53.27). They have no knowledge of it; they follow nothing but conjecture, and surely conjecture can never take the place of the truth (53.28).
>
> Has Your Lord [O you who disbelieve!] then preferred for you males and taken [to Himself] females from among the angels? Most surely you utter a grievous saying (17.40).
>
> And they (the disbelievers) make the angels, who are servants of God, females. Have they witnessed their creation? Their testimony shall be written down and they shall be questioned (43.19). And they say: "Had God willed, we would not have worshipped them." They have no knowledge of this; they only lie (43.20).

The idolatrous Arabs also believed that the jinn, whom God created of fire (15.27, 55.15, 7.12, 38.76), have some form of kinship with Him:

> So ask them [O Muhammad!]: "Has your Lord daughters whereas they have sons?" (37.149). Or did We create the angels females while they were witnesses? (37.150). It is from their falsehood that they say (37.151). "Allah has begotten"; and most surely they are liars (37.152). Has He chosen daughters in preference to sons? (37.153). What is the matter with you? How do you judge [so wrongly]? (37.154). Will you not then reflect? (37.155). Or have you a clear authority? (37.156). Then bring your book, if you are truthful (37.157). And they claim a kinship between Him and the jinn, whereas the jinn know well that they will be brought before Him [on the Day of Resurrection] (37.158).

Not surprising, the people of Arabia worshipped the jinn:

> And on the Day [of resurrection] when He will gather them all together, He will say to the angels: "Did these (the disbelievers) worship you?" (34.40). They shall say: "Glory

be to You! You are our Guardian, not they. No; they worshipped the jinn; most of them believed in them" (34.41).

We have already quoted verses in which the Qur'an says that the polytheists believed that the angels were God's daughters. One interpretation that at-Ṭabarī mentions is that the disbelievers used to see jinn and worship them, and they mistook them for angels. So the angels' reply to God clarifies that the jinn were actively promoting this partnership with God, perhaps through shamans and mediums, whereas the angels never did anything to invite or encourage the polytheists to treat them as divine and worship them. We will later see a similar denial by Jesus when God asks him a similar question.

In another verse which also denounces the deification of the jinn, the Qur'an argues that the polytheistic claim that some deities were God's offspring, as opposed to being unrelated deities or having any other relationship with Him, can only imply that God fathered them through a relationship with a consort. The concept of *God's offspring* conjures up an image of a god that is very similar to the human being and other creatures:

> And they make the jinn partners with Allah, while He created them; and they attribute to Him sons and daughters, without knowledge; glory be to Him, and highly exalted is He above what they describe (6.100). He is the Originator of the heavens and the earth! How could He have offspring when He has no consort, and He created everything? And He is the knower of all things (6.101).

The Qur'an rejects the suggestion that God has a consort, and this rejection is repeated in another verse in words attributed to some Muslim jinn:

> And that exalted be the majesty of our Lord, He has not taken [to Himself] a consort or offspring (72.3).

Another Qur'anic argument against the claim that God had offspring is that had God had offspring, Prophet Muhammad himself would have been commanded to worship them, yet Muhammad was sent to call to the worship of the one and only God:

> Say [O Muhammad!]: "If God had offspring, I would be the first worshipper" (43.81). Glory be to the Lord of the heavens and the earth, the Lord of Throne, above what they describe (43.82).

The Qur'an also uses the concept of *offspring of God* to reject the divinity of anyone other than God:

> Had Allah wanted to take offspring [to Himself], He would have chosen as He liked from what He has created. Glory be to Him; He is Allah, the One, the Subduer (39.4).

This verse argues that even if God had wanted to take offspring to Himself, He would have chosen them from His creation. The verse does not mean that it is possible that God could take offspring, but it stresses rhetorically that even in this impossible case God would not have created divine beings, and that such choosing would not have made the chosen creatures divine.

In the same way it stresses that the jinn are a mere creation of God, the Qur'an also clarifies that the angels, whom the polytheists called God's offspring, are no more than pious servants:

> And all creatures in the heavens and in the earth and the angels prostrate themselves to Allah, and they do not show pride (16.49).
>
> And they (the disbelievers) say: "God has taken offspring [to Himself]". Glory be to Him. They are rather honored servants (21.26). They do not precede Him in speech, and they act by His command (21.27). He knows what is before them and what is behind them; and they do not intercede except for him whom He approves, and they are wary because of their fear of Him (21.28). And should any of them say: "I am a god besides Him," such a one We reward with hell; thus do We reward the wrongdoers (21.29).

The Qur'an did not reject the concept of offspring of God only as it was understood by the polytheists of Arabia. It's rejection of this concept is absolute and without any qualification, reservation, or exception (also 18.4, 17.111):

> He to whom belongs the kingdom of the heavens and the earth; and who did not take offspring [to Himself], who has no partner in the sovereignty, and who created everything and ordained for it a measure (25.2).
>
> And they (the disbelievers) say: "God has taken offspring [to Himself]" (19.88). You [O you who disbelieve!] have made an abominable assertion (19.89) whereby the heavens may almost be rent, the earth cleave asunder, and the mountains fall down in utter ruin (19.90), that they ascribe offspring to God (19.91). And it is not fit for God to take offspring [to Himself] (19.92). There is no one in the heavens and the earth but will come to God as a servant (19.93).
>
> Say [O Muhammad!]: "He, Allah, is One (112.1). Allah, on whom all depend (112.2). He has not begotten, nor was he begotten (112.3). And none is comparable to Him" (112.4).

Not surprisingly, therefore, Christianity's claim that Jesus was God's son is as strongly and comprehensively rebutted.

15.4.3. False Sonship of God

Jesus' sonship of God in Christianity is no different from the concept of offspring of God of the polytheists of Arabia:

> He [Jesus] said: "I am Allah's servant. He has given me the Book and has appointed me a prophet (19.30). He has made me blessed wherever I may be. He has enjoined upon me prayer and almsgiving so long as I remain alive (19.31). And [He has made me] kind to my mother and has not made me arrogant or wretched (19.32). Peace is on me the day I was born, the day I shall die, and the day I shall be raised alive" (19.33). Such was Jesus son of Mary: this is the statement of the truth which they (the Christians) dispute (19.34). Allah would never take offspring [to Himself]. Far exalted is He above this. When He decrees a matter, He says to it only "Be!" and it is (19.35).

Verses 19.34-35 make it clear that Jesus' alleged sonship of God is as false as any claim of offspring of God. It is the concept that God could have offspring that the Qur'an unreservedly rejects, not the identification of particular beings as God's offspring. Another indirect rebuttal of Jesus', as well as the angel's, divinity is made in this verse:

> And neither would he command you that you should take the angels and the prophets for lords. Would he command you to disbelieve after you have become Muslims? (3.80).

The Arabs were aware of the Christians' claim of Jesus' sonship of God, so when they saw Jesus being mentioned and praised in the same book that rejected their daughters of God they argued that Jesus was also considered a son of God:

> And when the son of Mary was quoted as an example, your people [O Muhammad!] turned away from him (43.57). They said: "Are our gods better, or is he?" They raise this only by way of disputation; they are merely a contentious people (43.58). He is only a servant on whom We bestowed favor and whom We made an example for the Children of Israel (43.59).

The Qur'an rejects this argument, because Jesus is not considered a son of God in the Qur'an. On the contrary, it refutes this Christian claim. The Qur'an also stresses that the polytheists knew all too well what the Qur'an says about Jesus, so their argument was not genuine, but contentious.

Contrary to what the New Testaments states, it was not Jesus who claimed to be the son of God. Jesus' sonship of God is very much seen by most Christians as a form of divinity, yet Jesus never claimed to be divine. He stressed that he was human, and that he was sent by God to deliver a message. His followers later split into different factions and distorted his teachings, and his original message was lost:

When Jesus came with clear proofs, he said: "I have come to you with Wisdom, and to make plain some of what you have disagreed on. So keep your duty to Allah, and obey me (43.63). Allah is my Lord and your Lord. So worship Him. This is a straight way" (43.64). But factions from among them differed. Woe to those who do wrong from the torment of a painful day (43.65).

It is rather irrelevant, according to the Qur'an, what terminology is used to express Jesus' divinity and his relationship to God. This terminology, the discussion of which occupied Christian theologians since the early days of Christianity, would not change the fact that the very claim that Jesus is divine removes the distinction between him and God. In Qur'anic theology, divinity sums up the difference between God, on the one hand, and everything and everyone else, on the other. To say that someone is divine yet try to differentiate him from God is a meaningless exercise. Indeed, no matter how theologians express Jesus' divinity, he and God end up being treated equally and interchangeably. Any prayer that can be made to God can be equally addressed to Jesus. To attribute divinity to Jesus, therefore, is to make him equal to God:

> They have indeed disbelieved those who say: "Allah is the Messiah son of Mary." Say [O Muhammad!]: "Who then can do anything against Allah if He had willed to destroy the Messiah son of Mary, his mother, and everyone on earth?" Allah's is the kingdom of the heavens and the earth and all that is between them. He creates what He wills. Allah is able to do all things (5.17). And the Jews and the Christians say: "We are the sons of Allah and His beloved ones." Say [O Muhammad!]: "Why does He then chastise you for your faults? No, you are human beings from among those whom He has created; He forgives whom He pleases and chastises whom He pleases." And Allah's is the kingdom of the heavens and the earth and what is between them, and to Him is the eventual coming (5.18).

Some Christian scholars have wrongly claimed that the Qur'an rejects the concept of sonship of God because it implies procreation. What the Qur'an therefore actually denies, they suggest, is a corrupt interpretation of the New Testament's concept of Jesus' sonship of God that does not imply any act of procreation (Cragg, 1999: 189-207; Parrinder, 1995: 136-137). It is common among critics of the Qur'an to claim that its rejection of certain concepts and practices represents a response to particular groups that held a corrupt understanding of the Jewish and/or Christian scriptures, or reflects a misunderstanding by the author of the Qur'an, who is supposed to be Muhammad, of what the scriptures say.

The Qur'an rejects that God was involved in any procreation but, as I have already explained in detail, it is the divinity of Jesus that the Qur'an rejects, regardless of how this divinity is explained — whether it implies procreation or not. Interestingly, none of the verses (6.101, 72.3, 37.152, 112.3) that deny that God had a consort or begot offspring occurs in the context of talking about Jesus' sonship of

God. The Qur'an's rejection is not directed at an outlandish interpretation of the Christian scriptures or derives from a misunderstanding of these writings. Christian writings present Jesus' sonship of God as a mark or divinity, and this is why this sonship is rejected by the Qur'an. Verse 5.18 above sheds clear light on this issue.

The Qur'an mentions the historical fact, which we discussed in Chapter 14, that the Jews, and later the Christians, called themselves sons of God. Significantly, the Qur'an differentiates between this *mass* sonship of God and Jesus' *unique* sonship of the Divine. While the latter sonship is condemned as imbuing Jesus with divinity, the former is not considered blasphemous. The Qur'an recognizes that the Jews' and Christians' claims to sonship of God are not a claim to any form of divinity, and that they only signify close servanthood to God. So its rejection of these claims is only directed at their implication that God treats the Jews and Christians preferentially. The Qur'an refutes this implication by pointing out that the followers of these religions are treated in the same way others are treated. Should a Jew or Christian fail in his duty toward God, this believer would be punished accordingly, and the "son of God" tag would do nothing to protect him from that punishment. The verse then reminds all that the Jews and Christians are merely human beings created by God, and that what applies to humans in general applies to the followers of these religions.

This condemnation of the claim that the Jews and Christians are the sons of God is reminiscent of other verses that criticize the Jews' and Christians' self-image as the chosen people of God:

> And they [the People of the Book] say: "No one shall enter paradise except those who are Jews or Christians." These are [merely] their desires. Say [O Muhammad!]: "Produce your proof if you are truthful" (2.111). Yes, whoever becomes a Muslim (surrenders himself) to Allah and is a doer of good, his reward is with his Lord, and there is no fear for them nor shall they grieve (2.112).

The Qur'an states that people are not judged by how they label themselves or are labeled by others, but by their beliefs and deeds:

> Those who believe, the Jews, the Christians, and the Sabaeans — whoever believe in Allah and the Last day and does good — they shall have their reward from their Lord, and there is no fear for them, nor shall they grieve (2.62, 5.69).

In another verse that condemns describing Jesus as the son of God, the Qur'an also anathematizes the claim by some Jews that a "'Uzayr" was the son of God:

> The Jews say: "'Uzayr is the son of Allah", and the Christians say: "The Messiah is the son of Allah". That is a saying from their mouths, imitating the saying of the disbelievers of old. May Allah fight them! How deluded they are! (9.30). They have taken their rabbis

and monks as lords besides Allah, and so they treated the Messiah son of Mary, although they were not commanded to worship other than One God; there is no God save Him. Far exalted is He above their attribution of partners to Him! (9.31).

The name 'Uzayr is usually translated as "Ezra" and identified by exegetes with the Prophet Ezra of the Old Testament. This is a possible identification, but there is no evidence to support it. Verse 9.30 does not accuse *all Jews* of considering 'Uzayr the son of God. The Qur'an uses the definite name of a group to refer to some of them. For instance, "the Qur'an states that "the Jews," meaning *some Jews*, killed prophets and tampered with God's word. Similarly, "the people" is used to mean "some people" (e.g. 2.13), and so on. So "the Jews" in verse 9.30 means *some Jews*. As we have already seen in Chapter 14, Judaism did not use the title son of God to imply divinity. Verse 9.30 makes it clear that 'Uzayr's sonship of God was taken to mean that he was divine, as it was the case with Jesus, so clearly the reference is to a heterodox belief among a small Jewish group or cult, which perhaps lived in Arabia at the time of Prophet Muhammad. The older disbelievers that the verse mentions are people who lived before the Jews and the Christians and believed, as the latter later did, in forms of sonship of God.

The reference to the Jews and Christians taking their rabbis and monks, respectively, as lords besides God does not mean that they considered them divine. It rather highlights the unconditional surrender to what these clerics taught, even when their teachings went against God's. It is reported that Prophet Muhammad was asked about this verse by a Christian who pointed out that the Christians did not worship their monks. The Prophet replied that the Christians followed their monks who permitted things that God had declared unlawful and prohibited things that God had made lawful, and this was the equivalent of worshiping them, because they were allowed to overrule God's law.

The Qur'an separates the condemnation of the claims of 'Uzayr's and Jesus' sonship of God from its indictment of treating the rabbis and monks as lords. Also, verse 9.31 mentions the treatment of the rabbis and monks as lords separately from the fact that Jesus was also treated so. Jesus' lordship is derived from the belief in his divinity, whereas treating rabbis and monks as lords only referred to the fact that people followed them blindly. Indeed, two verses later in the same chapter the Qur'an exposes the fact that many rabbis and monks had conned people and turned them away from the right path:

> O you who believe! Many of the rabbis and monks eat away the property of people falsely and turn [people] away from Allah's way; and [as for] those who hoard up gold and silver and do not spend it in Allah's way, to them give [O Muhammad!] tidings of a painful chastisement [on the Day of Judgment] (9.34).

The Qur'an makes is clear that it does not reject the lordship of the rabbis and monks just to replace it with lordship of Muhammad. No human being should treat another as a lord, as God is the only Lord:

> Say [O Muhammad!]: "O People of the Book! Come to an equitable agreement between us and you: we shall not serve any other than Allah, we shall not associate anything with Him, and we shall not take from among each other lords besides Allah." But if they turn away, then say: "Bear witness that we are Muslims" (3.64).

Another misconception advocated by some Christian scholars, such as the Methodist minister Geoffrey Parrinder (1995: 137), is that the Qur'an does not rejects Jesus' sonship of God absolutely, but only denies adoptionism, i.e. the belief that God adopted Jesus at some point as His son (§14.2.6). Bishop Kenneth Cragg shares this view, and he argues that the Qur'an's rebuttal of adoptionism is no indication of its rejection of the doctrine of Incarnation, i.e. that God took a human form in the person of Jesus:

> Where the Qur'an remonstrates against Christian faith in Jesus' Incarnation, what it in fact accuses is not Incarnation but adoptionism, itself a heresy. However, it serves little purpose for Christians to "exploit" this and argue from it that the Qur'an mistakes what it is rejecting and, therefore, might be claimed not to reject what Christians believe. This would be both barren and contentious, a disservice both to fact and to right intention. The operative term is *ittikhāth* (cf. 17.111, 19.35, 19.92, 39.4). "God's not taking to himself a son" is a conviction Christians share. The phrase does not describe, and so does not in itself deny, what the Gospel means by "the Word made flesh" and the Creed by "the only begotten Son." (Cragg, 1999: 38-39)

I have already presented substantial evidence that what the Qur'an rejects is Jesus' divinity, whether this is presented as procreation, adoptionism, incarnation, or any other form. I would like to add two more points here about Cragg's wrong link of the Arabic verb *yattakhith* (takes to himself) to Adoptionism. **First**, the Qur'an's rejection of Jesus' sonship of God is not always associated with the use of the verb *yattakhith* or God's *taking of a son to Himself*. We have already seen verses where this sonship is denied without any qualification and where there is no room to suggest that what is being rejected is one particular form of divinity but not another. **Second**, scholars such as Cragg ignore the fact that *yattakhith* is used with many nouns, not only "son," that its general meaning is "considers" or "treats as," and that it has no explicit or implicit emphasis on the time of occurrence of the action it refers to. There are numerous verses to show this (e.g. 2.67, 2.80, 3.28, 4.89). One example is the Qur'an's statement that "Allah took (*ittakhatha*) Abraham as a close friend" (4.125). The verb clearly does not imply any act of adoption of Abraham by God.

Furthermore, the Qur'an uses the verb *ittakhatha* with the rejection of the concept of offspring of God, not only the Jesus' sonship. The verses that are particularly interesting here are those where the verb *yattakhith* is used specifically when talking about the taking of alleged gods other than Jesus. When referring to the sin of the Jews who disobeyed Moses and worshipped a calf, the Qur'an uses the verb *yattakhith* to mean "take as a god" (2.92, 4.153, 7.148, 7.152). The verb *yattakhith* here cannot mean "adopt." The same applies to these verses (also 19.81, 21.21, 21.24):

> And Allah has said: "Do not take (*tattakhithū*) two gods; He is only one God; so be fearful of Me" (16.51).
>
> These, our people, have taken (*ittakhathū*) gods besides Him; why do they not produce a clear authority in their support? Who is then more wrong than he who forges a lie against Allah? (18.15).

In each and every one of these verses, the verb *yattakhith* is used to mean "take" and appears in the context of rejecting the taking of something or someone as a god. No sense of "adopt" is implied or even possible. Moreover, in verse 5.116 the verb *yattakhith* is used in the context of denying the divinity of not only Jesus, but also his mother Mary, so clearly it cannot mean "adopt":

> And when Allah said: "O Jesus son of Mary! Did you say to people: 'Take me (*ittakhithūnī*) and my mother for two gods besides Allah?'" He said: "Glory be to You! I could never say what I have no right to say. If I have said it, then You know it. You know what is in my mind, but I do not know what is in Your mind. You know all unseen things (5.116). I never said to them anything other than what You commanded me: 'worship Allah, my and your Lord.' I was a witness over them while I was among them, and when You took me You were the watcher over them. You are a witness over all things (5.117). If You punish them, then they are Your servants; and if You forgive them, then You are the Invincible, the Wise" (5.118).

This dialog happened after God took Jesus to live in a heavenly place, as we shall study in more detail later (§19.3). Jesus lived until his *middle age*. The Arabic term in verses 3.46 and 5.110 that I have translated as "middle-aged" is *kahl*. This term is taken by exegetes and linguists to denote the period after youth and before old age, with almost all identifying it as covering the late thirties and forties and when the person has grown grey hair. According to the highly regarded lexicon *al-Qāmūs al-Muḥīṭ* of the well-known linguist al-Fayrūz Ābādī, *kahl* means "someone with grey hair and a respectable appearance, or someone who is over thirty or thirty four up to fifty one." I am inclined to think that Jesus was still a young man when he left the earth, so he might have lived some 20-30 years in the new, non-earthly place before he died. This dialog, therefore, does not mean that Jesus and his mother were already being treated as divine before he was taken to heaven. It is far more likely that the distortion of Jesus' teachings began when he was no more around to confirm his real message and counter the attempts to turn him and his mother into gods. It was probably Paul who sowed the seeds of the deification of Jesus and it was among his communities of pagan converts that this distorted teaching gained momentum and flourished and ultimately influenced even Jewish converts (p. 273).

Verse 5.116 gives another clear confirmation that Jesus never claimed to be divine, which means he never claimed to be the son of God. The verse also mentions the fact that many Christians turned Mary also into an object of worship, i.e. made her divine like her son. The worship of Mary or "Mariolatry" is also a concept that is foreign to Jesus' teachings. In verse 5.116 Jesus stresses that he never commanded people to consider him or his mother divine. Jesus tells God that he only taught what God ordered him to teach, which is to worship God, who is his and everyone's Lord.

The Qur'an also stresses Jesus' human nature through the metronymic title "son of Mary." Semitic people are called after their fathers, so in addition to emphasizing the fact that Jesus had no father, this metronymic is intended to deny any suggestion that he was a son of God. This description of Jesus occurs 23 times in the Qur'an. Only the name Jesus occurs more — 25 times. Interestingly, Jesus is only once called "son of Mary" in the whole of the New Testament: "Isn't this the carpenter, the son of Mary and brother of James, Joses, Judas, and Simon? And aren't his sisters here with us? And so they took offense at him" (Mark 6:3). However, the New Testament uses frequently the significant title "son of man." I have already indicated that it is likely that Jesus used this title to stress his human nature and rebuff the suggestion that he was the son of God or any attribution of divinity to him (pp. 284-286).

There is no reason to suggest that the title "son of man" is directly linked to the metronymic "son of Mary." The latter is always used by God in the Qur'an. There is no instance of Jesus referring to himself as "son of Mary." It is difficult to think of a suitable use by Jesus of this title anyway. On the other hand, almost all occurrences of "son of man" in the New Testament are found in sayings of Jesus. My conclusion is that God, as well as people, called Jesus after his mother, "son of Mary," and that Jesus used the periphrastic expression "son of man" to refer to himself. Both are intended to stress Jesus' human nature and refute claims that he his divinity.

15.4.4. The Fallacy of the Trinity

Unsurprisingly, the Qur'an also denounces explicitly the Trinity doctrine:

> O People of the Book! Commit no excesses in your religion or utter anything concerning Allah but the truth. The Messiah, Jesus son of Mary, was only a messenger

of Allah, His Word that He sent to Mary, and a Spirit from Him [that He sent]. So believe in Allah and His messengers, and do not say "Three." Desist, it is better for you! Allah is one God. Far exalted is He above having offspring. His is all that is in the heavens and all that is in the earth. Allah is sufficient a disposer of affairs (4.171). The Messiah would never scorn to be a servant to Allah, nor would the angels who are nearest to Allah. As for those who scorn His service and are arrogantly proud, He shall gather them all to Himself to answer (4.172).

The Trinity is presented as being contrary to Jesus' servanthood to God. The New Testament portrays Jesus as being both divine and a servant of the Divine. The Qur'an's argument rejects this duality as an impossibility. Verse 4.171 also clearly considers the Trinity as a form of tritheism not monotheism. Put differently, the concept that God is a unity is not the same as God is one. The next verse then stresses that Jesus and the nearest angels have completely accepted their servanthood to God.

The second rejection of the doctrine of Trinity occurs in this set of verses:

Surely they disbelieve those who say: "Allah is the Messiah son of Mary." The Messiah himself said: "O Children of Israel! Worship Allah, my Lord and your Lord. Whoever joins other gods with Allah, for him Allah has forbidden paradise. His abode is the Fire. The evildoers shall have no helpers" (5.72). Surely they disbelieve those who say: "Allah is one of three." There is only one God. If they will not desist from what they say, a painful torment shall befall the disbelievers among them (5.73). Will they not rather repent to Allah and seek His forgiveness? Allah is forgiving, merciful (5.74). The Messiah son of Mary was no other than a messenger before whom similar messengers passed away, and his mother was a saintly woman. They used to eat food. See how We make the revelations clear to them, and see how they are deluded! (5.75). Say [O Muhammad!]: "Will you worship besides Allah that which has no power to harm or benefit you?" Allah is the Hearer, the Knower (5.76). Say: "O People of the Book! Commit no excesses of falsehood in your religion, and do not follow the vain desires of folk who erred of old, led many astray, and strayed from the even path (5.77). Those who disbelieved from among the Children of Israel were cursed by the tongue of David and of Jesus son of Mary. That was because they disobeyed and used to transgress (5.78).

After rejecting the Trinity, the Qur'an goes on in verse 5.75 to stress that Jesus was only a messenger like many others who lived and died in the past, so Jesus was no special case. It also emphasizes that Mary was merely a righteous woman, in clear reference to her elevation by many Christians to a divine or semi divine status.

Some scholars have suggested that the Qur'an mistakenly takes the Trinity to be the Father, the Mother, and the Son, or the divine family. This conclusion is probably influenced by the fact that in verses 5.72-75 the denouncement of deification of Mary, as well as that of Jesus, occurs after the rejection of the Trinity. I agree with Parrinder (1995: 135) that there is actually nothing in the Qur'an to suggest this interpretation. The weakness of the conclusion above becomes clear when we observe that the rejection of the Trinity in verses 4.171 is followed in verses 4.172 by the confirmation that the Messiah and the nearest angels would not scorn to be servants to God. The Qur'an could not have defined the Trinity in one verse as being God, the Messiah, and the nearest angels, and in another as God, Jesus, and Mary. The names mentioned after the Trinity are not meant to be its members.

Additionally, I think that the Qur'an deliberately ignores naming the members of the Trinity. Verse 4.171 rejects the concept of "three" and verse 5.73 describes that concept as the belief that "Allah is one of three." What is being rejected, therefore, is not the unity of a particular group of three, but the very concept of threesome — that God is three beings, aspects, manifestations, or whatever. The Qur'an focuses on rejecting the concept of the unity of three rather than who those three are. As I have already said, the Qur'an considers the Trinity a form of tritheism, and no playing with words can make the Trinity a form of monotheism.

Verse 5.75 makes the interesting observation that both Jesus and his mother ate food, which is a sign of being human. Having to eat food in order to live is used elsewhere in the Qur'an as a sign that the messengers were normal human beings:

> And We did not send before you [O Muhammad!] other than men to whom We gave revelation, so ask the people of the remembrance if you do not know (21.7). And We did not make them bodies that do not eat food, and they were not immortal (21.8).
>
> And they (the disbelievers) say: "What is the matter with this Messenger (Muhammad) that he eats food and walks in the markets? why has not an angel been sent down to him, so that he should have been a warner with him?" (25.7).
>
> And We have not sent before you [O Muhammad!] any messengers but they ate food and walked in the markets. And We have made some of you a test for others: will you have patience? And your Lord is ever Seeing (25.20).

I should stress another important point. A common mistake in studying the Qur'an's discussion of Christian beliefs, including the doctrine of the Trinity, is to think that the Qur'an talks only about the New Testament, or simply misunderstands it. The Qur'an rejects particular Christian beliefs, regardless of whether they are found in the New Testament or not. For instance, the Qur'an rejects the worship of Mary, even though Mariolatry is not a New Testament doctrine. The New Testament does not have any special scriptural value outside mainstream Christianity, which was itself defined in the first few centuries after Jesus. The Qur'an is interested in clarifying its positions on doctrines that Christians hold, regardless of the origin of those doctrines.

To sum up, the Qur'an absolutely rejects the suggestions that Jesus was God's son, God ever had offspring, or there is anyone divine other than God. The nature of Jesus' or anyone else's alleged divinity is irrelevant, as the divinity of other than God is rejected without any qualification.

16

Miracles

Modern scholars usually dismiss miracles as pure fantasy, the products of natural causes, or symbolic narratives. In religious scriptures, however, miracles are portrayed as real, albeit uncommon, supernatural events.

The Gospels attribute to Jesus healings, exorcisms, resurrections of dead people, clairvoyance, prophecies, and other miracles involving nature, but there are significant differences between the miracle accounts found in the four Gospels. Jesus' miracles played a major role in attracting people to him and having them to accept that he was the Messiah. According to the Gospels, Jesus taught that miracles depend on the faith of the miracle worker, but may also depend on the faith of the subjects.

Understandably, Jesus sought to publicize his miracles. Some of his miracles are said to have been performed in front of thousands of people. Yet the Gospels also claim that at times Jesus, inexplicably, shrouded his miracles in secrecy. These few reports are unlikely to be authentic, as they contradict the accounts of the majority of Jesus' miracles which show him actively seeking to publicize his wonders to attract more followers.

The apocryphal gospels ascribe to Jesus many miracles that are not found in the canonical Gospels. Some of these wonders, which Jesus performed in his childhood, were rather sinister. They involved harming people who annoyed him or even causing their death.

The Qur'an confirms that Jesus performed impressive miracles. Some of these, such as curing blindness, are similar to miracles found in the Gospels, whereas others, such as speaking in the cradle, are found in the apocryphal gospels.

Apart from these religious sources, Jesus' miracles are mentioned only in one passage in *Jewish Antiquities* in which Josephus calls Jesus a "doer of wonderful works" (18.3.3). This lone passage, however, is almost certainly, at least partly, the work of Christian editors.

This chapter will focus on miracles that Jesus himself performed. Other miracles which were associated with him but in which he was a passive player, such as the miracles that surrounded his birth, will not be covered in this chapter, as they have already been examined in previous chapters.

16.1. Wonder Workers at the Time of Jesus

The Jews and the Greeks both believed in a world in which the natural and supernatural happily coexisted. The Jews believed that God can interfere in nature and change its course and laws, and the Greeks believed the same about their gods.

God or gods were not the only source of supernatural power. Other supernatural beings, such as demons, were also seen as capable of interfering in the affairs of the world. A supernatural intervention was labeled as good or evil depending on people's perception of its source and purpose. What was a good, divine miracle for some might well be seen as evil, black magic by others. Jesus' miracles were no different. The Gospels claim that thousands of people witnessed his wonders and believed in them as divinely aided miracles, but his enemies were always ready to accuse him of using demonic powers to perform his wonders.

People believed that God could interfere directly, but he could also act through agents. These could be human beings who are spiritually close to God, like the prophets of the Old Testament. A human being can also act as an agent for evil paranormal powers. In Greek mythology, a human being can become divine, and can himself be the source of paranormal feats. This, in brief, is how the Jews and Romans viewed miracles.

There is no information about the names of Jewish wonder workers who were active during Jesus' lifetime, but we know of a few who lived before or after him. One of them, Honi, who lived around the middle of the 1st century BCE, developed fame for successfully praying for rain by drawing a magical circle:

> Once it happened that the greater part of the month of Adar had gone and yet no rain had fallen. The people sent a message to Honi the Circle Drawer, "Pray that rain may fall." He prayed and no rain fell. He thereupon drew a circle and stood within it in the same way as the Prophet Habakuk had done, as it is said, "I will stand upon my watch, and set upon me the tower etc." He exclaimed [before God], "Master of the Universe, Thy children have turned to me because [they believe] me to be a member of Thy house. I swear by Thy great name that I will not move from here until you have mercy upon Thy children!" Rain began to drip and his disciples said to him, "We look to you to save us from death; we believe that this rain came down merely to release you from your oath." Thereupon he exclaimed: "It is not for this that I have prayed, but for rain [to fill] cisterns, ditches, and caves." The rain then began to come down with great force, every drop being as big as the opening of a barrel and the Sages estimated that no one drop was less than a log.
>
> His disciples then said to him: "Master, we look to you to save us from death, we believe that the rain came down to destroy the world." Thereupon he exclaimed before [God], "It is not for this that I have prayed, but for rain of benevolence, blessing, and bounty." The rain fell normally until the Israelites [in Jerusalem] were compelled to go up [for shelter] to the Temple Mount because of the rain. [His disciples] then said to him, "Master, in the same way as you have prayed for the rain to fall pray for the rain to cease." He replied: "I have it as a tradition that we may not pray on an account of an excess of good. Despite this, bring unto me a bullock for a thanksgiving-

offering." They brought unto him a bullock for a thanksgiving-offering and he laid his hands upon it and said, "Master of the Universe, Thy people Israel whom Thou hast brought out of Egypt cannot endure an excess of good nor an excess of punishment; when Thou wast angry with them, they could not endure it; when Thou didst shower upon them an excess of good they could not endure it; may it be Thy will that the rain may cease and that there be relief for the world." Immediately the wind began to blow and the clouds were dispersed and the sun shone and the people went out into the fields and gathered for themselves mushrooms and truffles.

Thereupon Shimon b. Shetah sent this message to him, "Were you not that you are Honi I would have placed you under the ban; for were the years like the years [of famine in the time] of Elijah (in whose hands are the keys of rain) would not the name of Heaven be profaned through you? But what shall I do unto you who acts petulantly before the Omnipresent yet He grants your desire, as a son who acts petulantly before his father and he grants his desires; thus he says to him, 'Father, take me to bathe in warm water, wash me in cold water, give me nuts, almonds, peaches, and pomegranates and he gives them unto him.' Of you Scripture says, 'Let thy father and thy mother be glad and let her that bore thee rejoice.'" (Ta'an. 23a).

Although the historian Josephus was extremely suspicious about those who claimed to be miracle workers and called them cheats, he accepted that Honi ("Onias" in Greek) was genuinely capable of praying successfully for rain, and he described him as a "righteous man:

Now there was one, whose name was Onias, a righteous man he was, and beloved of God, who, in a certain drought, had prayed to God to put an end to the intense heat, and whose prayers God had heard, and had sent them rain. This man had hid himself, because he saw that this sedition would last a great while. However, they brought him to the Jewish camp, and desired, that as by his prayers he had once put an end to the drought, so he would in like manner make imprecations on Aristobulus and those of his faction.

And when, upon his refusal, and the excuses that he made, he was still by the multitude compelled to speak, he stood up in the midst of them, and said, "O God, the King of the whole world! Since those that stand now with me are thy people, and those that are besieged are also thy priests, I beseech thee, that thou wilt neither hearken to the prayers of those against these, nor bring to effect what these pray against those." Whereupon such wicked Jews as stood about him, as soon as he had made this prayer, stoned him to death. (Josephus, *Jewish Antiquities*, 14.2.1)

During the civil war between brothers and Jewish princes Hyrcanus and Aristobulus, Honi was captured by supports of the former who, believing in his gift, ordered him to curse Aristobulus. As Josephus tells us, Honi's refusal led to his death.

A more interesting miracle wonder is the healer Hanina ben Dosa who lived in the 1st century CE, about one generation after Jesus. Hanina is reported to have performed many miracles, some similar to Jesus' miracles — a point that I will discuss later. Let's examine some of Hanina's miracles in the Babylonian Talmud, starting with these two:

> Our Rabbis taught: Once the son of R. Gamaliel fell ill. He sent two scholars to R. Hanina b. Dosa to ask him to pray for him. When he saw them he went up to an upper chamber and prayed for him. When he came down he said to them: Go, the fever has left him; they said to him: Are you a prophet? He replied: I am neither a prophet nor the son of a prophet, but I learnt this from experience. If my prayer is fluent in my mouth, I know that he is accepted: but if not, I know that he is rejected. They sat down and made a note of the exact moment. When they came to R. Gamaliel, he said to them: By the temple service! You have not been a moment too soon or too late, but so it happened: at that very moment the fever left him and he asked for water to drink.
>
> On another occasion it happened that R. Hanina b. Dosa went to study Torah with R. Johanan ben Zakkai. The son of R. Johanan ben Zakkai fell ill. He said to him: Hanina my son, pray for him that he may live. He put his head between his knees and prayed for him and he lived. Said R. Johanan ben Zakkai: If Ben Zakkai had stuck his head between his knees for the whole day, no notice would have been taken of him. Said his wife to him: Is Hanina greater than you are? He replied to her: No; but he is like a servant before the king, and I am like a nobleman before a king. (Bera. 34b)

The first healing incident is particularly interesting because it has strong resemblance to Jesus' distant healing of the centurion's sick servant (Matt. 8:5-13; Luke 7:2-10). In another incident, a poisonous lizard died after biting Hanina:

> Our Rabbis taught: In a certain place there was once a lizard which used to injure people. They came and told R. Hanina b. Dosa. He said to them: Show me its hole. They showed him its hole, and he put his heel over the hole, and the lizard came out and bit him, and it died. He put it on his shoulder and brought it to the Beth ha-Midrash and said to them: See, my sons, it is not the lizard that kills, it is sin that kills! On that occasion they said: Woe to the man whom a lizard meets, but woe to the lizard which R. Hanina b. Dosa meets! (Bera. 33a)

Hanina is also credited with clairvoyance:

> Our Rabbis taught: It once happened that the daughter of Nehonia the well-digger fell into a large cistern, and people went and reported [the accident] to R. Hanina b. Dosa. During the first hour he said to them, "All is well." In the second hour he again said, "All is well." In the third he said to them, "She is saved." "My daughter," he asked her, "who saved you?" — "A ram came to my help with an aged man leading it." "Are you," the people asked him, "a prophet?" — "I am," he replied, "neither prophet nor the Son of a prophet." (Yeba. 121b)

Miracles used to happen to Hanina's wife also because of him:

> Rab Judah said in the name of Rab: Every day a Heavenly Voice is heard declaring, the whole world draws its sustenance because [of the merit] of Hanina my son, and Hanina my son suffices himself with a kab of carobs from one Sabbath eve to another. Every Friday his wife would light the oven and throw twigs into it so as not to be put to shame. She had a bad neighbor who said, I know that these people have nothing, what then is the meaning of all this [smoke]? She went and knocked at the door. [The wife of R. Hanina] feeling humiliated [at this] retired into a room. A miracle happened and [her neighbor] saw the oven filled with loaves of bread and the kneading trough full of dough; she called out to her: "You, you, bring your shovel, for your bread is getting charred"; and she replied, I just went to fetch it. A Tanna [author of the Mishnah] taught: She actually had gone to fetch the shovel because she was accustomed to miracles.
>
> Once his wife said to him: "How long shall we go on suffering so much?" He replied: "What shall we do?" — "Pray that something may be given to you," [she replied]. He prayed, and there emerged the figure of a hand reaching out to him a leg of a golden table. Thereupon he saw in a dream that the pious would one day eat at a three-legged golden table but he would eat at a two-legged table. Her husband said to her: "Are you content that everybody shall eat at a perfect table and we at an imperfect table?" She replied: "What then shall we do?" — "Pray that the leg should be taken away from you," [she replied]. He prayed and it was taken away. A Tanna taught: The latter miracle was greater than the former; for there is a tradition that a thing may be given but once, it is never taken away again (24b-25a). (Ta'an. 24b-25a)

Again, there is clear similarity between the bread miracle and Jesus' miraculous multiplication of bread (Mark 6:35-44, 8:1-9; Matt. 14:15-21, 15:32-38; Luke 9:12-17; John 6:5-13).

Hanina's prayer caused goats to develop horns with bears impaled on them:

> R. Hanina b. Dosa had goats. On being told that they were doing damage he exclaimed, "If they indeed do damage may bears devour them, but if not may they each of them at evening time bring home a bear on their horns. In the evening each of them brought home a bear on their horns. (Ta'an. 25a)

Another miracle attributed to Hanina which has very close similarity with others attributed to Jesus, although in the apocryphal gospels (AraIn. 16:2, 16:14; InThom. 13; PsMatt. 37), is causing beams to get longer by merely praying:

> Once a woman neighbour of R. Hanina was building a house but the beams would not reach the walls. She thereupon came to him and said: "I have built a house but the beams will not reach the walls." He asked her: "What is your name?" She replied: "Aiku." He thereupon exclaimed: "Aiku, may your beams reach [the walls]." A Tanna taught: "They projected one cubit on either side." Some say, "New pieces joined themselves [miraculously] to the beams." It has been taught: Polemo says: "I saw that house and its beams projected one cubit on either side, and people told me: 'This is the house which R. Hanina b. Dosa covered with beams, through his prayer.'" (Ta'an. 25a)

Hanina is also said to have had power over evil spirits:

> "And do not go out alone at night," for it was taught: One should not go out alone at night, i.e. on the nights of Wednesdays nor Sabbaths, because Igrath the daughter of Mahalath, she and 180,000 destroying angels go forth, and each has permission to wreak destruction independently. Originally they were about all day. On one occasion she met R. Hanina b. Dosa [and] said to him: "Had they not made an announcement concerning you in Heaven, 'Take head of Hanina and his learning,' I would have put you in danger." "If I am of account in Heaven," replied he, "I order you never to pass through settled regions." "I beg you," she pleaded, "leave me a little room." So he left her the nights of Sabbaths and night of Wednesdays. (Pesa. 112b)

This is another miracle that bears close resemblance to the miracles of Jesus, who practiced exorcism and had control over demons.

These wonders did not make people consider Honi or Hanina exalted in a way that would make them less human and more divine. Both were seen as merely good servants whose prayers God answered. We saw that when Hanina was asked after one of his wonders whether he was a prophet, which is the most that people could have thought about him, he replied "I am neither a prophet nor the son of a prophet, but I learnt this from experience. If my prayer is fluent in my mouth, I know that he is accepted: but if not, I know that he is rejected." Hanina attributed the wonder to God, as he believed that it was performed by God who accepted his prayer.

The tradition about Honi and Hanina was written long time after them, so its historicity and accuracy are questionable. Furthermore, the Talmud was written much later than the time of Jesus and even the Gospels, so what it says about Honi and Hanina might have well been influenced by Jesus' story. The resemblance of some of Hanina's wonders to Jesus' miracles is remarkable. One New Testament professor notes:

> The accuracy of their [Talmudic writings'] representation of Honi or Hanina is thus even more questionable from a historical perspective than the New Testament's representation of Jesus. The earliest references to Honi and Hanina, furthermore, do not present them as miracle workers but as righteous men whose prayers were answered by God. And Josephus (writing in the first century AD.) locates Honi in Jerusalem, not Galilee. The suspicion of many historians, then, is that legends about these men grew over time, possibly in response to the stories Christians told about Jesus. The late traditions regarding Honi and Hanina contains accounts similar to those in the Gospels precisely because Jewish writers wanted to create Galilean holy men of their own who would be on a par with Jesus. (Powell, 2000:63-64)

Josephus has an interesting report of another Jew whom he witnessed drive out demons:

> I have seen a certain man of my own country, whose name was Eleazar, releasing people that were demoniacal in the presence of Vespasian, and his sons, and his captains, and the whole multitude of his soldiers. The manner of the cure was this: He put a ring that had a Foot of one of those sorts mentioned by Solomon to the nostrils of the demoniac, after which he drew out the demon through his nostrils; and when the man fell down immediately, he abjured him to return into him no more, making still mention of Solomon, and reciting the incantations which he composed. And when Eleazar would persuade and demonstrate to the spectators that he had such a power, he set a little way off a cup or basin full of water, and commanded the demon, as he went out of the man, to overturn it, and thereby to let the spectators know that he had left the man; and when this was done, the skill and wisdom of Solomon was shown very manifestly: for which reason it is, that all men may know the vastness of Solomon's abilities, and how he was beloved of God, and that the extraordinary virtues of every

kind with which this king was endowed may not be unknown to any people under the sun for this reason, I say, it is that we have proceeded to speak so largely of these matters. (Josephus, *Jewish Antiquities*, 8.2.5)

This account shows that belief in possession, the practice of driving out demons, and belief in the existence of individuals who were capable of doing it were well established. Matthew (12:27) and Luke (11:19) both report an incident in which Jesus mentions others who were practicing the expulsion of demons.

One important difference between Jesus and Honi and Hanina ben Dosa is that the two Jewish wonder workers performed their wonders through prayer and/or certain rituals, whereas Jesus' miracles did not involve him offering prayers. He had the authority to perform them, and they happened instantly.

One last alleged wonder worker that is worth mentioning here is the Greek Apollonius of Tyana (south of Turkey) who died at the end of the 1st century. Portrayed as a superhuman with various miraculous powers, Apollonius, like Jesus, is credited with prophecy, exorcisms, healings, and raising the dead:

> Here too is a miracle which Apollonius worked: A girl had died just in the hour of her marriage, and the bridegroom was following her bier lamenting as was natural his marriage left unfulfilled, and the whole of Rome was mourning with him, for the maiden belonged to a consular family. Apollonius then witnessing their grief, said: "Put down the bier, for I will stay the tears that you are shedding for this maiden." And withal he asked what was her name. The crowd accordingly thought that he was about to deliver such an oration as is commonly delivered as much to grace the funeral as to stir up lamentation; but he did nothing of the kind, but merely touching her and whispering in secret some spell over her, at once woke up the maiden from her seeming death; and the girl spoke out loud, and returned to her father's house, just as Alcestis did when she was brought back to life by Hercules. And the relations of the maiden wanted to present him with the sum of 150,000 sesterces, but he said that he would freely present the money to the young lady by way of a dowry. Now whether he detected some spark of life in her, which those who were nursing her had not noticed — for it is said that although it was raining at the time, a vapour went up from her face — or whether life was really extinct, and he restored it by the warmth of his touch is a mysterious problem which neither I myself nor those who were present could decide. (Philostratus, *The Life of Apollonius*, 4.45)

There is probably little history in what is reported about Apollonius. Note only his biography was written over a century after his death, but it is believed that

Empress Julia Domna commissioned the Athenian writer Philostratus to write it specifically to neutralize the effect of the Christians' biography of their master.

Finally, Josephus mentions a number of pseudo 1st century prophets who promised the Jews to perform impressive miracles. Around 36 CE a Samaritan convinced people to get together on Mount Gerizim and promised them that he would show them the vanished temple sacred vessels. But Pilate prevented them and killed many of them, although the Samaritan fled (Josephus, *Jewish Antiquities*, 18.4.1).

Shortly after 44 CE, Theudas, whom Josephus describes as a "magician," persuaded a large number of people that he was going to divide the Jordan River and afford them an easy passage over it. Fadus, the procurator of Judea, was not very impressed by this claimant, so he killed many of Theudas' followers, captured many others, and had Theudas also captured and beheaded (Josephus, *Jewish Antiquities*, 20.5.1). The Book of Acts also mentions Theudas and his doomed fate, without specifying whether he claimed to be a miracle worker: "Theudas rose up, claiming to be somebody, and about four hundred men joined him. He was killed, and all who followed him were dispersed and nothing came of it" (Acts 5:36).

During the procuratorship of Felix (52-60 CE), some imposters persuaded multitudes of people to follow them to the wilderness where they claimed they would exhibit wonders and signs, but Felix punished them. Another Egyptian who came to Jerusalem and also claimed to be a prophet led his followers to the Mount of Olive and promised to show them from there how the walls of Jerusalem would fall at his command and that he would enter with them the city through those walls. Felix killed hundreds of them, captured hundreds others, and the Egyptian imposter fled (Josephus, *Jewish Antiquities*, 20.8.6).

After this brief introduction to how miracles and miracle workers were seen at the time of Jesus, we will now study Jesus' miracles.

16.2. Jesus' Miracles in the New Testament

Outside the Gospels, there are no reports in the New Testament of specific miracles that Jesus performed during his life, although there are general references to Jesus' miracles, such as Peter's description of Jesus in his address to the men of Israel in Acts (2:22) as "a man clearly attested to you by God with powerful deeds, wonders, and miraculous signs." Paul does not mention any of Jesus' miracles, but he attributes his conversion to Christianity to a miracle by Jesus. He claims that Jesus appeared to him while he was on his way to Damascus, caused him to lose his sight temporarily, and then led someone to heal him (Acts 9:3-8, 22:6-10, 26:13-18).

Paul also prayed to Jesus, although unsuccessfully, to heal him from a disease that had afflicted him, so he must have believed that Jesus performed miracles:

Therefore, so that I would not become arrogant, a thorn in the flesh was given to me, a messenger of Satan to trouble me — so that I would not become arrogant. I asked the Lord three times about this, that it would depart from me. But he said to me, "My grace is enough for you, for my power is made perfect in weakness." So then, I will boast most gladly about my weaknesses, so that the power of Christ may reside in me. (2 Cor. 12:7-9)

The absence of any reference to Jesus' miracles in any of Paul's writings is not particularly remarkable. As already pointed out, Paul has either deliberately attempted to ignore the virginal conception or, more likely, was unaware of this miracle (Rom. 1:3, 9:5; Gal. 4:4; 2 Tim. 2:8). The almost complete absence of the historical Jesus from Paul's Epistles suggests that the apostle did not know much about that history and was not in a position to talk about it with authority, particularly as other followers who lived with Jesus were still around. Paul did not have firsthand knowledge of Jesus' life. He knew Jesus only through revelation.

Additionally, there are reports, mainly in Acts but in Paul's Epistles also, of miracles that Jesus' disciples and apostles, including Paul, performed in his name (Acts 2:43, 3:1-9, 5:12, 5:16, 6:8, 8:6, 9:32-34, 9:36-40, 13:11, 14:8-10, 16:16-18, 19:6, 19:11-12, 20:9-12; 1 Cor. 12:9-10, 12:28-29; 2 Cor. 12:12; Gal. 3:5). These point indirectly to the fact that Jesus was a miracle worker.

Apart from the miracles that preceded and followed Jesus' birth, which only Matthew and Luke relate, all four Gospels attribute to Jesus a number of different paranormal feats. John (15:24) claims that Jesus said that he performed "miraculous deeds that no one else did." Mark (2:12) and Matthew (9:33) have witnesses of Jesus' wonders declare that they had never seen anything like this.

Comparisons with the Old Testament are at times easy to make. While Prophet Elisha miraculously fed a hundred men with only twenty loaves of bread and fresh ears of grain (2 Kings 4:42-44), Jesus once fed over 5,000 people with five loaves and two fish (Mark 6:35-44) and in another instance 4,000 people with seven loaves and a few small fish (Mark 8:1-9).

In this section, we will first study what miracles the Gospels attributes to Jesus and then examine how, according to the Evangelists, these miracles were portrayed by Jesus and how they were understood by his disciples and people in general.

16.2.1. The Categories of Jesus' Miracles

Jesus' miracles may be divided into four categories: **healings**, **nature** miracles, **prophecies**, and **clairvoyance** miracles. Studies of Jesus' miracles usually do not consider Jesus' prophecies and clairvoyance. In the context of the Gospels, and indeed in the Bible in general, these paranormal feats are as significant and impressive as any of healing or nature miracle, which is why I am including them here.

In the listings of miracles in this section, I have mentioned first the miracles that appear in Mark and in the order in which they appear in that Gospel. Miracles that appear in Matthew but not Mark are then listed, followed by those that are found in Luke but not in Mark or Matthew, and finally the exclusively Johannine.

16.2.1.1. Healing Miracles

The most reported type of miracles in the Gospels is healing. These miracles may be subdivided into **healings of diseases**, **exorcisms of devils**, and **resurrections of dead people**. Let's look at these subgroups separately, starting with the former.

The Gospels record Jesus' healings of the following illnesses and disabilities: seizures, paralysis, lameness, crippled limbs, leprosy, hemorrhage, withered hands, dumbness, fever, deafness, dropsy, coma, and blindness, including blindness from birth. Most of the miracle accounts talk about certain individuals being healed of specific conditions, but the Gospels also make general references to Jesus healing diseases and disabilities (e.g. Matt. 4:23):

Table 16.1: Jesus' healing miracles in the Gospels

Subject of Healing	Mark	Matthew	Luke	John
Peter's mother-in-law with a fever	1:29-31	8:14-15	4:38-39	N/A
Many sick and demon possessed people	1:32-34	8:16	4:40	N/A
Leper	1:40-42	8:2-3	5:12-13	N/A
Paralytic	2:10-12	9:6-7	5:24-25	N/A
Man with a withered hand	3:1-5	12:10-13	6:6-10	N/A
Many sick people	3:10	N/A	N/A	N/A
Woman with hemorrhage	5:25-29	9:20-22	8:43-44	N/A
Synagogue ruler's, Jairus, daughter in a coma	5:22-42	9:18-25	8:41-55	N/A
Few sick people	6:5	N/A	N/A	N/A
Many sick people	6:56	14:35-36	N/A	N/A
Deaf and mute man	7:32-35	N/A	N/A	N/A
Blind man	8:22-25	N/A	N/A	N/A
Demon-possessed Man who had seizures	9:17-26	17:14-18	9:38-42	N/A
Blind man (two men in Matthew) in Jericho	10:46-52	20:29-34	18:35-42	N/A
People with all kinds of diseases, including seizures and paralysis	N/A	4:23-24	N/A	N/A
Paralyzed/sick centurion servant	N/A	8:5-13	7:2-10	N/A
Two blind men	N/A	9:27-30	N/A	N/A
Mute, demon-possessed man	N/A	9:32-33	N/A	N/A
People with every kind of disease and	N/A	9:35	N/A	N/A

sickness				
mute and blind (only mute in Luke) demon-possessed man	N/A	12:22	11:14	N/A
The lame, blind, crippled, mute, and many others	N/A	15:30	N/A	N/A
Blind and lame people	N/A	21:14	N/A	N/A
Disabled women	N/A	N/A	8:2	N/A
Woman disabled by a spirit	N/A	N/A	13:11-13	N/A
Man with dropsy	N/A	N/A	14:2-4	N/A
Ten lepers	N/A	N/A	17:12-14	N/A
Man with a cut off ear	N/A	N/A	22:50-51	N/A
Sick son of a royal official	N/A	N/A	N/A	4:46-53
Disabled man	N/A	N/A	N/A	5:5-9
Sick people	N/A	N/A	N/A	6:2
Man blind from birth	N/A	N/A	N/A	9:1-7
Total	**14**	**18**	**16**	**4**

The differences in the reported miracles, their chronological orders, and their contexts in the various Gospels are reflective of the broader fact that the Evangelists give different accounts of Jesus' life. Some episodes appear in one Gospel but not another, and others are given different orders by different authors.

Some miracles that are reported separately here may have been meant to denote one and the same event, but the significant differences between the different accounts have made me treat them as different miracles. Similarly, I may have lumped together accounts that the Evangelists intended to report as different miracles. For instance, the miracle of restoring the sight of two blind men in Jericho in Matthew (20:29-34) is very similar to the healing of one blind man in the same city in Mark (10:46-52) and Luke (18:35-42). The differences between the Gospels' accounts of Jesus' miracles are discussed later (§16.2.2).

Disease healings and exorcisms at times overlap, as possession by demons was believed to be a source of disease. I have included in Table 16.1 above healings by driving out demons when the illness is identified. Table 16.2 is restricted to healings of possessed individuals where no specific illness is reported.

Jesus healed sick and demon-possessed people face to face. He performed most healings by touching the person by his hand (e.g. Mark 6:5; Matt. 8:3). But in some instances he commanded the ill person to be healed (e.g. Mark 2:10-12) or the demon to leave the possessed person (e.g. Mark 1:25-26), and in one occasion he healed a blind person by his saliva (John 9:6-7). People were also healed when they touched his cloak (e.g. Mark 6:56; Matt. 14:36). So at times he healed by touch and at others by word only.

Table 16.2: Jesus' exorcisms in the Gospels

Subject of Exorcism	Mark	Matthew	Luke	John
A man with an unclean spirit	1:23-26	N/A	4:33-35	N/A
Many demon-possessed people	1:32-34	8:16	4:41	N/A
Demon-possessed people	1:39	N/A	N/A	N/A
one (two in Matthew) violent demon-possessed man	5:1-13	8:28-32	8:27-33	N/A
Demon-possessed girl	7:24-30	15:21-28	N/A	N/A
Demon-possessed people	N/A	4:24	N/A	N/A
Women with evil spirits	N/A	N/A	8:2	N/A
Total	5	4	4	0

John does not contain any exorcism, and the exorcisms in the Synoptics stop early in the three books. Theissen and Merz (1999: 298-299) take this to mean that "this part of Jesus' activities caused difficulties and is historical." They think that it reflects the belief that Jesus' victory over Satan was achieved not through miracles, but through his death on the cross and resurrection. These scholars conclude from textual analysis of the Gospels that although Jesus' healings and exorcisms have been enriched by popular tradition and motifs, they are essentially historical, whereas the other miracles have been attributed to Jesus later on after the Easter experience (Theissen & Merz, 1999: 301-304).

In addition to these instances of *close healing*, Jesus also performed *distant healing* (e.g. John 4:46-53). For example, he healed the paralyzed servant of a Roman centurion remotely without going to see the patient (Matt. 8:5-13).

The last subcategory of healing miracles is raising dead people:

Table 16.3: Jesus' raisings of dead persons in the Gospels

Dead Person	Mark	Matthew	Luke	John
Son of a widow	N/A	N/A	7:12-15	N/A
Lazarus	N/A	N/A	N/A	11:38-44

Interestingly, only two resurrections are reported — one in Luke and the other in John. Neither Mark nor Matthew reports such miracles.

16.2.1.2. Nature Miracles

In the second major category of Jesus' miracles we see him exercising paranormal power over natural things and phenomena. I have considered the "Transfiguration," in which Jesus' face and clothes temporarily changed, as a nature miracle:

Table 16.4: Jesus' nature miracles in the Gospels

Nature Miracle	Mark	Matthew	Luke	John
Stilling the winds	4:35-39	8:23-26	8:22-24	N/A
Feeding five thousand men with five loaves and two fish	6:35-44	14:15-21	9:12-17	6:5-13
Walking on the water	6:47-51	14:24-31	N/A	6:18-21
Feeding four thousand men with seven loaves and a few small fish	8:1-9	15:32-38	N/A	N/A
Jesus' Transfiguration	9:2-3	17:1-2	9:28-29	N/A
Withering the fig tree	11:12-21	21:18-19	N/A	N/A
Causing many fish to be caught after a drought	N/A	N/A	5:2-7	N/A
Turning water into wine	N/A	N/A	N/A	2:1-10
Causing many fish to be caught after a drought	N/A	N/A	N/A	21:3-7
Total	**6**	**6**	**4**	**4**

16.2.1.3. Prophecies

The Gospels contain a number of Jesus' prophecies about the future that, according to the same sources, were fulfilled. All these prophecies relate to his death and resurrection:

Table 16.5: Jesus' prophecies in the Gospels

Prophecy	Mark	Matthew	Luke	John
Jesus' death and resurrection	8:31	16:21	9:20-22	N/A
	10:32-35	20:17-19	18:31-33	N/A
	14:6-8	N/A	N/A	N/A
	N/A	26:2	N/A	N/A
Jesus' betrayal by one of the disciples	14:18	26:21	22:21	N/A
The disciples' desertion of Jesus	14:27	26:31	N/A	N/A
Jesus' reunion with His disciples in Galilee after the resurrection	14:28	26:32	N/A	N/A
Peter's denial of Jesus three times	14:29-31	26:33-35	22:31-34	N/A
Total	**5**	**5**	**3**	**0**

There are other Jesus' sayings that *may* be interpreted as referring to his death and resurrection. I have not included these with the unambiguous prophecies in the table.

Like healings by exorcism, Jesus' miracles of fulfilled prophecies are not found in John.

16.2.1.4. Clairvoyance

The last and fourth category of Jesus' miracles is instances of **clairvoyance**.

Table 16.6: Jesus' miracles of clairvoyance in the Gospels

Subject of Clairvoyance	Mark	Matthew	Luke	John
Ruler's daughter was in a coma not dead	5:22-42	9:18-25	8:41-55	N/A
Four drachma coin hidden in the fish mouth	N/A	17:24-27	N/A	N/A
The Samaritan woman with five husbands and a lover	N/A	N/A	N/A	4:7-29

While prophecies are predictions of future events, clairvoyance miracles are expressions of knowledge of things in the present that are not possible to know by normal means. In order to clarify the difference between prophesying and clairvoyance, let's look at one of the three instances of clairvoyance in table 16.6:

> He said to her, "Go call your husband and come back here." The woman replied, "I have no husband." Jesus said to her, "Right you are when you said, 'I have no husband,' for you have had five husbands, and the man you are living with now is not your husband. This you said truthfully!" The woman said to him, "Sir, I see that you are a prophet." (John 4:16-19)

This is clearly different from, for instance, Jesus' prediction that Peter was going to deny knowing him three times one night before a rooster crows. In the other two instances of clairvoyance, Jesus knew that the ruler's daughter was in a coma and not dead even before seeing her, and he told Peter to go to the lake for fishing and predicted that the first fish that Peter would catch would have a four drachma coin hidden in its mouth.

16.2.2. Different Gospel Accounts

The four Gospels report different numbers of Jesus' miracles, as shown in Table 16.7, which is a summary of tables 16.1-6. Any reference to an unspecified number of healings appears as one miracle in this table. For instance, Mark's (3:10) remark that Jesus healed "many sick people" is reported as one miracle in table 16.1 and accordingly so in table 16.7.

The miracle accounts in the four Gospels are significantly different. **First**, with the exception of the miracle of feeding 5000 people, which is found in all four Gospels, every other miracle is missing from at least one Gospel. For instance, John in particular contains only a few miracles, and he does not report any instance of exorcism. He, however, says that "Jesus performed many other miraculous signs in the presence of the disciples, which are not recorded in this book" (John 20:30), and he reiterates in the very last passage of his Gospel that "there are many other things that Jesus did. If every one of them were written down, I suppose the whole world would not have room for the books that would be written" (John 21:25). This may explain why John did not mention some of the miracles or sayings that the other Evangelists reported, but it does not explain why he did not report a single exorcism or prophecy although both are popular miracles in the Synoptics and very familiar paranormal feats in Jewish tradition. Also, none of the Synoptists makes a similar statement about not reporting all of Jesus' miracles.

Table 16.7: The number of Jesus' miracles in each Gospel

Miracle Category		Mark	Matthew	Luke	John
Healing	Diseases	14	18	16	4
	Exorcisms	5	4	4	0
	resurrections	0	0	1	1
	Total	19	22	21	5
Nature		6	6	4	4
Prophecies		5	5	3	0
Clairvoyance		1	2	1	1
Total		**31**	**35**	**29**	**10**

The appearance of a unique type of miracles in only one Gospel is particularly significant. For instance, the miracle of turning water into wine is mentioned only by John. The other Evangelists did not mind repeating many healing miracles and the miracle of feeding thousands of people from little food, yet for some reason they are completely silent on the unique miracle of turning the water into wine. John (2:11) described this miracle as follows: "Jesus did this as the first of his miraculous signs, in Cana of Galilee. In this way he revealed his glory, and his disciples believed in him." It is difficult to reconcile the importance of this miracle and its uniqueness with the fact that it is completely ignored by the Synoptists. Either the latter did not know about this miracle or did not believe it happened. Interestingly, the miracle of curing the sick son of a royal official, which John (4:54) introduces as Jesus' "second miraculous sign," is also nowhere to be found in the Synoptics.

The same applies to the resurrection miracles. There are only two such miracles in the Gospels, each of which is mentioned by one Evangelist. Given the

Evangelists' interest in reporting Jesus' miracles, and given that raising a dead person is certainly as impressive as a miracle can get, one has to ask why Mark and Matthew do not mention any of the two resurrection miracles in Luke and John, and why the latter do not confirm the report of each other.

In our discussion of Jesus' virginal conception we concluded that the silence of Mark and John on this event reflects either their denial or, far more likely, ignorance of it (pp. 102-103). A similar conclusion can be drawn from the presence of unique or particularly impressive miracles in one Gospel but not the others. In the case of the resurrection miracles, for instance, either Mark and Matthew did not know of these miracles, or they did not believe those reports. Similarly, either Luke was not aware of Lazarus' story, or he simply did not find it credible. Likewise, John must have either been unaware of the miracle of resurrecting the widow's son, or rejected the authenticity of this story. But there is no reason to believe that any of the Evangelists rejected certain miracles. After all, they were all keen on reporting Jesus' wonders, and more miracles would have been more testimonies to his status. Also, they clearly believed that he could have performed such marvelous deeds. I therefore think that the different reports in the Gospels reflect the different traditions, both oral and written, that the Evangelists used to write their accounts.

This conclusion is further confirmed by our **second** observation that some miracles are reported differently by the different Evangelists. For instance, the one violent demon-possessed man in Mark (5:1-13) and Luke (8:27-33) appears as two in Matthew (8:28-32). Similarly, the one blind man in Mark (10:46-52) and Luke (18:35-42) is doubled by Matthew (20:29-34):

> They came to Jericho. As Jesus and his disciples and a large crowd were leaving Jericho, Bartimaeus the son of Timaeus, a blind beggar, was sitting by the road. When he heard that it was Jesus the Nazarene, he began to shout, "Jesus, Son of David, have mercy on me!" Many scolded him to get him to be quiet, but he shouted all the more, "Son of David, have mercy on me!" Jesus stopped and said, "Call him." So they called the blind man and said to him, "Have courage! Get up! He is calling you." He threw off his cloak, jumped up, and came to Jesus. Then Jesus said to him, "What do you want me to do for you?" The blind man replied, "Rabbi, let me see again." Jesus said to him, "Go, your faith has healed you." Immediately he regained his sight and followed him on the road. (Mark 10:46-52)

> As they were leaving Jericho, a large crowd followed them. Two blind men were sitting by the road. When they heard that Jesus was passing by, they shouted, "Have mercy on us, Lord, Son of David!" The crowd scolded them to get them to be quiet. But they shouted even more loudly, "Lord, have mercy on us, Son of David!" Jesus stopped, called them, and said, "What do you want me to do for you?" They said to him, "Lord, let our eyes be opened." Moved with compassion, Jesus touched their eyes. Immediately they received their sight and followed him. (Matt. 20:29-34)

It is also not uncommon for a miracle to appear in different contexts in different Gospels, and for miracles to be given different chorological orders by different Evangelists.

The miracle categories tables in the previous section should make comparing the miracle accounts in the different Gospels rather easy. The result of such comparison does not reflect well on the accuracy and credibility of the four books.

16.2.3. The Significance and Purpose of Miracles

Miracles have always played an important role in religions across the world, being portrayed and seen as proofs on the verity of those religions and divine support to their leaders and main figures. Judaism is no different, with the Old Testament talking about many miracles by Jewish prophets and righteous people. Among the most famous Old Testament miracles are those attributed to Moses, such as the ten plagues which he inflicted on the Egyptians and the splitting of the sea. One particular Old Testament miracle that the Jews cited when challenging Jesus about his miracles (John 6:31) is God's sending of the "manna" from heaven for them to eat when they were in the wilderness (Exo. 16:11-35). Jesus (Luke 4:25-27) himself mentioned how Elijah was sent to a widow, in reference to how that prophet's prayer healed the widow's son (1 Kings 17:17-24), and Prophet Elisha's healing of the Syrian commander Naaman who had a skin disease (2 Kings 5:1-14).

Miracles serve the same function in the Gospels, which is to attest to the authenticity of the religious teachings and status of the miracle worker. Jesus is said to have told a royal official in Capernaum in Galilee: "unless you people see signs and wonders you will never believe!" (John 4:48). Indeed, when people witnessed Jesus' miracles "they were afraid and honored God who had given such authority to men" (Matt. 9:8). Miracles are performed to make people believe (also Luke 10:13; John 12:9-11):

> Then many of the people, who had come with Mary and had seen the things Jesus did, believed in him. But some of them went to the Pharisees and reported to them what Jesus had done. So the chief priests and the Pharisees called the council together and said, "What are we doing? For this man is performing many miraculous signs. If we allow him to go on in this way, everyone will believe in him, and the Romans will come and take away our sanctuary and our nation." (John 11:45-48)

Miracles are also powerful tools in driving people to repent:

> Then Jesus began to criticize openly the cities in which he had done many of his miracles, because they did not repent. "Woe to you, Chorazin! Woe to you, Bethsaida! If the miracles done in you had been done in Tyre and Sidon, they would have repented long ago in sackcloth and ashes. But I tell you, it will be more bearable for Tyre and Sidon on the day of judgment than for you! And you, Capernaum, will you be exalted to heaven? No, you will be thrown down to Hades! For if the miracles done among you

had been done in Sodom, it would have continued to this day. But I tell you, it will be more bearable for the region of Sodom on the day of judgment than for you!" (Matt. 11:20-24)

The Gospels contain many references to how people were amazed, impressed, and moved by Jesus' miracles (e.g. Mark 5:20, 5:42, 7:37; Matt. 15:31). The fact that miracles were seen as proofs on the authenticity of the teachings of the miracle worker are clearly illustrated by the fact that Jesus' miracles made people confer various honorific titles on him. Jesus' miracles are said to have led people to accept that he was the awaited Messiah (§13.2.2.2), which is how he also portrayed his miracles (Matt. 11:2-5; Luke 7:18-22), and also prompted them to call him the "Son of God" (§14.2.1). Sanders (1995:132-133, 160-162) has pointed out that neither the title "Messiah" nor "Son of God" was associated with performing miracles in Judaism, and that this link is Christian in origin.

Another title people applied to Jesus because of his miracles is "prophet." This title is associated with miracles in the Old Testament, and it was used for Jesus after he raised a dead person (Luke 7:16), showed paranormal knowledge of the Samaritan woman's private life (John 4:19), and healed a blind person (John 9:17). After his miracle of feeding 5,000 people, they called him "the Prophet who is to come into the world" (John 6:14), in another reference to the Messiah. Jesus was also recognized as "the Holy One of God" by a man with an unclean spirit (Mark 1:24; Luke 4:34).

At the time of Jesus, the Jews consisted of two main groups: the Pharisees and the Sadducees. The latter did not believe in the resurrection of the dead, so Jesus' miracle of bringing the dead back to life might have served the purpose of refuting the Sadducees' belief and emphasizing the verity of the resurrection.

People are also reported to have been uncertain about what to make of Jesus and his miracles, with some thinking he was John the Baptist having risen from the dead, the Old Testament's Elijah, or one of the old prophets having come back from death (Mark 8:28; Luke 9:7-8). After another miracle of healing a man with an unclean spirit people were too uncertain even to suggest who this honorable man might be (Mark 1:27; Luke 4:36). In another incident in which Jesus stilled the wind in the sea even his disciple are said to have wondered "Who then is this? Even the wind and sea obey him!" (Mark 4:41). Strangely, the disciples had already seen many healing miracles by Jesus by this point! Even stranger is Matthew's assertion, which is found in Luke (8:22-25) also, that the disciples had almost exactly the same reaction to the even later miracle of calming down a storm in the sea: "What sort of person is this? Even the winds and the sea obey him!" (Matt. 8:27)! We will revisit this point later in the chapter.

Yet Jesus' miracles were not always met with positive reaction. For instance, when Jesus drove demons out of one possessed man (Mark 5:1-17), or two possessed men according to Matthew (8:28-34), and into a herd of pigs, the frightened people asked him to leave their town. Luke's story has a better ending. After Jesus was asked by the people of the Gerasenes and the surrounding region to leave them alone, because they were seized by fear, he asked the healed man to go back to the town and talk to people about what Jesus had done to him. When next time Jesus comes back to the town, he is welcomed.

Jesus' miracles, according to Mark (11:28), made the chief priests, the experts in the law, and the elders express doubts about their source. The people of Nazareth had similar doubts (also Matt. 13:54-57):

> Now Jesus left that place and came to his hometown, and his disciples followed him. When the Sabbath came, he began to teach in the synagogue. Many who heard him were astonished, saying, "Where did he get these ideas? And what is this wisdom that has been given to him? What are these miracles that are done through his hands? Isn't this the carpenter, the son of Mary and brother of James, Joses, Judas, and Simon? And aren't his sisters here with us?" And so they took offense at him. (Mark 6:1-3)

When one day Jesus was teaching people in the temple courts, the chief priests and experts in the law questioned him: "By what authority are you doing these things? Or who it is who gave you this authority?" (Luke 20:2). More seriously, the Pharisees (Matt. 9:34, 12:24), experts in the law (Mark 3:22), and some people (Luke 11:15) accused him of performing his miracles by the power of Beelzebul, the chief of demons. The exorcist and subduer of demons cleverly pointed out a contradiction in their accusation:

> How can Satan cast out Satan? If a kingdom is divided against itself, that kingdom will not be able to stand. If a house is divided against itself, that house will not be able to stand. And if Satan rises against himself and is divided, he is not able to stand and his end has come. (Mark 3:23-26)

Having criticized the religious authorities for their improper practice and hijacking of religion, Jesus was, understandably, highly unpopular among the religious establishment. Provocative corrective actions, such as driving out traders from the temple courts and turning the tables of the money exchangers (Matt. 21:12-13), would have enraged the religious authorities who were in charge of the temple and had condoned trading in its courts. Like any charismatic religious leader, Jesus posed an obvious threat to the status, power, and influence of the religious elite. He also seems to have deliberately targeted the priests with his teachings, trying to have them to change and ultimately follow him. On two separate occasions he commanded lepers he healed to show themselves to the priests (Mark 1:44; Luke 17:14). It is no surprise that hearing Jesus being called the "Son of David" made the chief priests indignant (Matt. 21:15). They were so angry at his rising star that they even thought of killing Lazarus, whom Jesus had raised from the dead, because he was one reason why many Jews from Jerusalem were believing in Jesus (John 12:10-11).

Jesus also clashed with the religious authorities over his interpretations of the law, and his miracles were at the center one of those major differences. Jesus insisted on healing on the Sabbath even when the experts in the law told him that he must not do that. Jesus refuted their arguments and insisted that it was right to help people even on the Sabbath (Mark 3:1-6; Matt. 12:10-13; Luke 6:1-11, 13:10-16; John 5:16-17). Jewish leaders considered Jesus a sinner because of his failure to observe the Sabbath (John 9:16). Jesus' attitude toward the law will be discussed later (§17.5.1).

Another action that incensed the Jewish religious authorities is Jesus' suggestion that telling a paralytic to stand up and walk is more difficult than telling him that his sins are forgiven, thus implying that he can forgive sins. For the experts in the law, any suggestion that someone other than God can forgive sins is blasphemous (Mark 2:3-12; Matt. 9:2-8; Luke 5:17-26). This link between healing and the forgiveness of sins stems from the belief that disease is the result of being in a state of sin and that it is some form of divine punishment. However, Jesus is also portrayed in another incident as rejecting this connection. When he was asked whether a certain man was blind from birth because of sins committed by him or by his parents, Jesus rejected this causal relationship between disease and sin stressing that "neither this man nor his parents sinned, but he was born blind so that the acts of God may be revealed through what happens to him." The Jewish leaders had described this blind man as having been born "completely in sinfulness" (John 9:1-34).

It is interesting that the chief priests and law experts did not deny Jesus' miracles but chose to attribute them to demonic power. They could not accuse Jesus of fraud because he had performed so many miracles in front of so many witnesses. Any attempt to deny the occurrence of those miracles would have found little credibility in the eyes of people. In fact, Pharisees and law experts had themselves witnessed some of Jesus' miracles and had to confess that what they saw was "incredible" (Luke 5:26). Their only option was to claim that Jesus' power was demonic. But even this view was far from being easy to support. Some of the Pharisees themselves questioned the suggestion that a sinner can "perform such miraculous signs" (John 9:16). One blind man whom Jesus healed told the Pharisees who were questioning him about Jesus: "We know that God doesn't listen to sinners, but if anyone is devout and does his will, God listens to him. Never before has anyone heard of someone causing a man born blind to see. If this man were not from God, he could do nothing" (John 9:31-33).

Despite Jesus' emphasis and the perception of people in general that miracles can only be performed by divine support, Jesus warned his disciples that at the end of time "false messiahs and false prophets will appear and perform signs and wonders to deceive, if possible, the elect" (Mark 13:22; also Matt. 24:24). It is not clear whether this implies that wonders could be performed by sinners also, and that the difference between miracles like Jesus' and wonders of sinners is the more impressive nature of the former. Jesus did say that "no one else" performed his "miraculous deeds" (John 15:24). We have already seen that healing a man who was blind from birth was an unheard of miracle.

Despite the negative reaction that Jesus' miracles drew from some, they played a major role in attracting people to him and having them to accept him as a special man of God and the Messiah.

16.2.4. Miracles and Faith

The Gospels make an interesting link between miracles and faith — both the faith of the miracle worker and the faith of the subject of the miracle. Let's start with the former.

The ability to perform miracles is supposed to reflect one's faith. When Jesus made a fig tree wither, he told his amazed disciples: "if you have faith and do not doubt, not only will you do what was done to the fig tree, but even if you say to this mountain, 'Be lifted up and thrown into the sea,' it will happen. And whatever you ask in prayer, if you believe, you will receive" (Matt. 21:18-22; also Mark 11:20-25).

This relationship between faith and the ability to work miracles is further discussed in the context of detailing the attempts of Jesus' disciples to perform miracles. Jesus was not only able to work wonders, but was also capable of giving other people the authority to do the same. Jesus "gave them authority over the unclean spirits" and they successfully "cast out many demons and anointed many sick people with oil and healed them" (Mark 6:7-13; see also Luke 9:1-2). In Matthew's account, the miraculous power that Jesus assigned to the disciples allowed them even to raise the dead: "heal the sick, raise the dead, cleanse lepers, cast out demons" (Matt. 10:8). Luke also states that, on another occasion, Jesus sent another 72 to every town and place he was about to go to, giving them the authority to "heal the sick," although on their return they reported success even in having demons submit to them in Jesus' name (Luke 10:1-17). Mark (9:38-40) and Luke (9:49-50) also say that the disciples came across someone who was casting demons in Jesus' name. Healing in the name of Jesus continues to be an established practice in many Christian Churches to our day.

Acts (2:43, 5:12) and Paul's Epistles record many miracles that Jesus' disciples and apostles performed after him. For instance, Peter healed a person who was lame from birth (Acts 3:1-9), a man who had been paralyzed for eight years (Acts 9:32-34), and many others (Acts 5:16). He even raised the disciple Tabitha from death (Acts 9:36-40). Stephen (Acts 6:8) and Philip (Acts 8:6) both performed various miracles. Paul made a magician blind (Acts 13:11), drove a spirit out of a girl (Acts 16:16-18), caused people to speak in tongues and to prophesy (Acts 19:6), made a person who was crippled from birth walk (Acts 14:8-10), and quickened a dead person (Acts 20:9-12). He performed other miracles, and even handkerchiefs or aprons that had touched his body healed the sick and drove out evil spirits (Acts 19:11-12). Paul also mentions a number of times the gift of miracles that God gave to the disciples and Christians (1 Cor. 12:9-10, 12:28-29; Gal. 3:5), including himself (2 Cor. 12:12).

The disciples were not always successful in their attempts to perform miracles. Mark (9:18), Matthew (17:16), and Luke (9:40) have the story of a demon-possessed boy whom the disciples failed to heal. When Jesus heard from the boy's father about his disciples' failure, he started talking about an *unbelieving generation.* He then went on to complain about how much longer he had to stay with that generation and endure it, which suggests that he meant his disciples by his words about the lack of faith. Jesus then healed the boy. According to Luke, the disciples were "astonished at the mighty power of God," and the story ends there. Mark and Matthew each has a longer account, as the disciples are said to have asked their master why they could not cast out the demon. The two Evangelists, however, attribute different answers to Jesus.

Mark (9:29) states that Jesus explained to his disciples that they could not drive the demon out because this kind of demons "can come out only by prayer." The implication here is that they used the standard method for driving this demon out, which did not work. This is a different explanation from Jesus' earliest angry words about the "unbelieving generation." It may be argued that the two answers can be reconciled by suggesting that the disciples' little faith meant that they did not know how to drive the demon out. This reconciliatory explanation is rather far-fetched though, and certainly not what Matthew had in mind.

Matthew seems to have recognized the tension in Mark, so he did away with the mention of the special method for casting out those demons and replaced it with a reference to the disciples' "little faith," which fits well with Jesus' complaint about the unbelief of the generation. He then went on to stress that faith can allow the person to work impressive wonders: "I tell you the truth, if you have faith the size of a mustard seed, you will say to this mountain, 'Move from here to there,' and it will move; nothing will be impossible for you" (Matt. 17:14-20). Interestingly, this saying appears also in another event cited by both Mark (11:23) and Matthew (21:21), which suggests that Matthew used it in his redactional attempt to remove the contradiction from Mark. Luke's solution to this contradiction was simply to do away with the disciples' question.

In another incident, when Peter saw someone claiming to be Jesus walking on the water, he said to him: "Lord, if it is you, order me to come to you on the water." Jesus called Peter who then left the boat and started to walk on the water toward his master: "But when he saw the strong wind he became afraid. And starting to sink, he cried out, 'Lord, save me!' Immediately Jesus reached out his hand and caught him, saying to him, 'You of little faith, why did you doubt?'" (Matt. 14:24-31). Mark's (6:47-51) and

John's (6:18-21) accounts of Jesus walking on the water do not include the incident about Peter.

In addition to questioning the disciples' ability to understand their master and at times portraying them as dimwits who could not understand plain language (e.g. Mark 9:31-32; Luke 18:34; John 10:6, 12:16), the Gospels call into question the disciples' faith a number of times, even as late as before Jesus' arrest and crucifixion. Their reaction of astonishment at miracles and their fear in danger even when Jesus was with them are other signs of the uncertainty of their faith (Mark 4:35-41, 6:47-51; Matt. 8:23-27, 21:18-22; Luke 8:22-25, 24:36-42), despite the fact that they had believed in Jesus as early as seeing the miracle of turning water into wine, which John calls Jesus' first miraculous sign (John 2:11).

Jesus taught that miracles depend on the faith of their subjects also, not only the faith of the miracle worker. He told a woman who had been suffering from a hemorrhage for twelve years and who touched his clock seeking cure from her disease that *her faith made her well* (Matt. 9:18-26). The accounts of Mark (5:25-34) and Luke (8:43-48) of this story are particularly interesting because they claim that the woman was healed even though Jesus was not aware of the miracle taking place. He felt that "power had gone out" from him, and that is when he realized what had happened.

In another instance, Jesus told a synagogue ruler whose daughter was in a coma: "Do not be afraid; just believe, and she will be healed" (Luke 8:50). Mark (5:35) does not have "and she will be healed," whereas Matthew (9:18-25) does not attribute to Jesus any saying about the faith of the ruler.

In a different story, a blind man asked Jesus to let him see again. As soon as Jesus replied "your faith has healed you," the man regained his sight (Mark 10:46-52; Luke 18:35-43). Again, Matthew's (20:29-34) account of this miracle, which talks about two blind men instead of one, does not contain an equivalent statement from Jesus about faith. However, this Evangelist has another miracle involving two blind men, which is not found in any of the other Gospels, in which Jesus touches the eyes of the two men saying "let it be done for you according to your faith," and both had their eyes opened (Matt. 9:27-30).

Matthew (15:21-28) also reports about a woman who asked Jesus to heal her demon-possessed daughter. He told her: "woman, your faith is great! Let what you want be done for you," and her daughter was healed immediately.

There is also a unique account in Luke about Jesus' healing of ten lepers, which is worth citing in full:

> Now on the way to Jerusalem, Jesus was passing along between Samaria and Galilee. As he was entering a village, ten men with leprosy met him. They stood at a distance, raised their voices and said, "Jesus, Master, have mercy on us." When he saw them he said, "Go and show yourselves to the priests." And as they went along, they were cleansed. Then one of them, when he saw he was healed, turned back, praising God

with a loud voice. He fell with his face to the ground at Jesus' feet and thanked him. (Now he was a Samaritan.) Then Jesus said, "Were not ten cleansed? Where are the other nine? Was no one found to turn back and give praise to God except this foreigner?" Then he said to the man, "Get up and go your way. Your faith has made you well." (Luke 17:11-19)

Here also Jesus tells someone he healed that his faith made him well. What is different is that the other nine lepers do not seem to deserve to be described as having faith, or at least not like the repentant leper whose faith made him well, yet they were equally healed.

A unique but very interesting account in Mark states that Jesus himself was at some point unable to perform miracles in his hometown:

Then Jesus said to them, "A prophet is not without honor except in his hometown, and among his relatives, and in his own house." He was not able to do a miracle there, except to lay his hands on a few sick people and heal them. And he was amazed because of their unbelief. Then he went around among the villages and taught. (Mark 6:4-6)

Mark indicates that people's disbelief prevented even Jesus himself from performing miracles. Given that Jesus was a perfect believer, this situation would suggest that the subject of the miracle must have a minimum degree of faith for a miracle to take place. In the case of the people of Nazareth, only a few of their sick had the threshold of faith that would allow Jesus to heal them. In his account of this incident, Matthew (13:58) states that Jesus "did not do many miracles there because of their unbelief," but this is more ambiguous, as it is not clear whether Jesus *did not want* to perform miracles because of this unbelief or whether he simply *could not* perform them.

The requirement of faith may be the reason why Matthew says that Jesus did not want to heal non-Jews. The Gentiles did not have faith in the God that Jesus, the prophets of Israel, and the Jews believed in. He told a Canaanite woman who wanted him to heal her demon-possessed daughter that he "was sent only to the lost sheep of the house of Israel" (Matt. 15:24). But when he saw the woman's faith, he granted her wish and healed her daughter. Mark, who is the only other Evangelist to report this story, does not have the statement about Jesus being sent exclusively to the Jews, which seems to be a Matthean addition. He only said "let the children be satisfied first, for it is not right to take the children's bread and to throw it to the dogs," which indicates that he considered the Jews, whom he describes as "children," to have priority over others, whom he describes as "dogs" (Mark 7:27).

Matthew tells us that when Jesus gave his twelve disciples the power to heal, he told them: "Do not go to Gentile regions and do not enter any Samaritan town. Go instead to the lost sheep of the house of Israel" (Matt. 10:5-6). Interestingly, Mark's (6:7-13) and Luke's (9:1-5) accounts of this incident do not contain the instruction to the disciples to go to the Jews only. Matthew (8:5-13) and Luke (7:2-10) also include a story about Jesus healing the servant of a centurion without suggesting that Jesus did that reluctantly. In fact, both Evangelists state that Jesus said that he had not found in all of Israel the kind of faith that the Roman army officer had. Matthew was keen on stressing that Jesus was sent to the Jews only.

In conclusion, while the Gospels at times suggest that the faith of the miracle worker is all that is needed, at others the faith of the subject of the miracle is considered to be at least as important. It looks like whether the subject of a miracle was a Jew or not, the only relevant issue is whether he had faith in Jesus or not.

16.2.5. Miracles between Publicity and Secrecy

As we have already seen, Jesus used miracles to attract people to his teachings. Sanders (1995: 154) stresses that "initially Jesus' *fame* came as the result of healing, especially exorcism. This is an important corrective to the common view, that Jesus was essentially a teacher. He was also, and for some people primarily, a miracle-worker." This is not an unlikely possibility given the nature of Jesus' impressive miracles.

Jesus did not target individuals only, but he also performed miracles in front of large numbers of people. The largest reported number of witnesses of one of Jesus' miracles is 5,000 men (Mark 6:44; Luke 9:14; John 6:10), in addition to an unspecified number of women and children according to Matthew (14:21). The second largest group of people who witnessed a miracle, which was also a feeding miracle, is 4,000 men (Mark 8:9), to which Matthew (15:38) again adds an unspecified number of women and children. There are other miracles that were also witnessed by large crowds (e.g. Mark 1:33; Matt. 8:1, 12:15, 14:14; Luke 18:36; John 12:17).

Unsurprisingly, then, the news about Jesus' miracles reached many places (e.g. Mark 1:45, 7:36; Matt. 9:26; Luke 4:37, 5:15, 8:39). The news spread "throughout all the region around Galilee" (Mark 1:28), reaching Herod in Judea (Mark 6:14), and "throughout Syria" (Matt. 4:24). Luke (23:8) claims that "when Herod saw Jesus, he was very glad, for he had long desired to see him, because he had heard about him and was hoping to see him perform some miraculous sign." This publicity was greatly helped by the fact that Jesus performed miracles in various towns and villages and the countryside (Mark 1:38-39, 6:56; Matt. 9:35, 11:21-23).

Furthermore, Jesus did ask people to publicize his miracles. When a man he healed wanted to go with him he ordered him to go home and tell people how he drove a demon out of him (Mark 5:18-20; Luke 8:39). When Pharisees warned Jesus that he should disappear because Herod wanted to kill him, he told them to go and tell Herod that he was "casting out demons and performing healings" (Luke 13:31-32).

Yet this understandable image of Jesus seeking and achieving publicity using his miracles is completely contradicted by a number of passages in the Gospels that claim that Jesus tried to keep secret a number of his wonders. He is supposed to have commanded two blind men (Matt. 9:30) and a deaf man (Mark 7:36) not to tell others that they were healed by him. He told a leper not to speak about his healing to anyone but to only show himself to the priest (Mark 1:44; Luke 5:14). This story has another problem in Matthew (8:4), because this Evangelist claims that there were already large crowds following Jesus (Matt. 8:1), so asking the leper to keep the miracle secret does not make much sense.

The story of the miracle of the girl in a coma has the same problem. Both Mark (5:43) and Luke (8:56) claim that after awakening the girl Jesus commanded her parents not to disclose the miracle to anyone. Yet both authors also state that many people, who had thought the girl was dead, were present at the house when the miracle took place. Asking the parents to keep the miracle secret would not have made it so. Interestingly, Matthew's account (9:18-25) of this miracle does not contain an order from Jesus to anyone to keep it secret.

Another inexplicable call for secrecy is found in the accounts of the Transfiguration. Mark (9:2) and Matthew (17:9) state that Jesus took Peter, James, and John the brother of James "privately" up a high mountain where they later witnessed the transformation of his appearance. In keeping with this secrecy, Jesus is supposed to have commanded the three disciples not to tell anyone about what they saw until he was raised from the dead (Mark 9:9; Matt. 17:9). Luke (9:28) confirms that Jesus took with him the same three disciples only, but he does not state that this election was done privately. Luke's story also does not show Jesus commanding the disciples not to talk about the miracle, but the Evangelist only tells us that they decided to keep silent and tell no one at that time (Luke 9:36).

Mark states that Jesus drove out many demons but that he "would not permit the demons to speak, because they knew him" (Mark 1:34). This Evangelist also claims that whenever the unclean spirits saw Jesus "they fell down before him and cried out, 'You are the Son of God'", and that he "sternly ordered them not to make him known" (Mark 3:11-12).

John has yet another story that is full of contradictions about Jesus' alleged attempts to shroud his miracles in secrecy. He has Jesus' brothers tell him: "Leave here and go to Judea so your disciples may see your miracles that you are performing. For no one who seeks to make a reputation for himself does anything in secret. If you are doing these things, show yourself to the world" (John 7:3-4). Jesus replied: "My time has not yet arrived, but you are ready at any opportunity! The world cannot hate you, but it hates me, because I am testifying about it that its deeds are evil. You go up to the feast yourselves. I am not going up to this feast because my time has not yet fully arrived" (John 7:6-8). One problem with this account is that by the time Jesus' brothers gave him this advice, he had already performed in public most of the miracles that John reports! The Jewish leaders were looking for him at the feast, and "There was a lot of grumbling about him among the crowds. Some were saying, 'He is a good man,' but others, 'He deceives the common people'" (John 7:11-12). In fact, the Jewish leaders were seeking his death (John 7:1). Clearly, Jesus was already well known after all. Further contradiction in the story comes from the fact that, despite what he told his brothers, Jesus went to Jerusalem "in secret" (John 7:10), and taught in the temple openly (John 7:14), albeit without revealing his identity!

The passages that talk about Jesus being secretive about his miracles are irreconcilable with the much larger number of passages that stress that he was keen on publicizing his miracles and bringing them to the notice of as many people as possible. While the secrecy passages are not found very late in Jesus' ministry, their use does overlap with the use of the opposite passages, so the contradiction cannot be solved by claiming that Jesus was first secretive about his miracles and then went public.

Sanders thinks that the contradictory reports about the publicity and secrecy of Jesus' miracles might reflect a tension between actual history and how the Evangelists reported it. More specifically, he points out that Jesus had actually a small number of followers, yet the many reported miracles and their many thousands of witnesses suggest that he had a large following. Sanders (1995:123-127) argues that Jesus had twelve "disciples," and a larger number of "followers" and "sympathizers." He thinks that the "more than five hundred of the brothers and sisters" that Paul (1 Cor. 15:6) claims Jesus appeared to after his resurrection were more or less all his followers and sympathizers. This scholar suggests that this small number of followers indicates that Jesus probably performed a much smaller number of miracles, yet the Evangelists enhanced Jesus' miracles to make them more impressive. They had to account for the miracles' limited efficacy in attracting followers by claiming that Jesus kept some of them secret (Sanders, 1995: 157).

I agree with Sanders that Jesus had only a small following — an assumption that is necessary to explain various aspects of his life and the history of Christianity. I also find it perfectly logical to expect Jesus' followers to have exaggerated his miracles and their impact. But I do not think that the limited number of Jesus' followers led the Evangelists to suggest that he kept some of his miracles secret. After all, the Gospels also show Jesus performing many miracles happily in public and attribute to him actions and behaviors that are sure to attract publicity. My view is that the inclusion in the Gospels of those odd reports of Jesus' alleged attempts to keep *some* miracles secret is the result of the fact that each Gospel is the outcome of putting together different traditions from various sources. This fact explains the numerous contradictions and inconsistencies in each Gospel. I do not believe that Jesus tried or even thought of keeping his miracles secret. That would have been against the purpose of performing them in the first place. Jesus used his miracles to convince people of the verity of his message, and that meant performing them publicly.

Another claim that cannot be reconciled with Jesus' real attitude toward his miracles is that he did not perform a miracle when he was challenged to do so:

So then the Jewish leaders responded, "What sign can you show us, since you are doing these things?" Jesus replied, "Destroy this temple and in three days I will raise it up again." Then the Jewish leaders said to him, "This temple has been under construction for forty-six years, and are you going to raise it up in three days?" But Jesus was speaking about the temple of his body. So after he was raised from the dead, his disciples remembered that he had said this, and they believed the scripture and the saying that Jesus had spoken. (John 2:18-22)

One problem with this account is that it would have made no sense for Jesus to respond to this straightforward challenge with a statement about the miracle of his resurrection. If Jesus really meant his resurrection, as John thinks, then his words were hardly an answer to the challenge. People wanted to see a miracle performed by him, not on him, and there and then, not at some unknown future point. Anyone can promise a miracle in the future! Jesus' reported words would not have been an answer that made much sense, let alone satisfy those who challenged him.

Furthermore, to use the temple as a reference to his body made for a reply that could not have been made more cryptic. Surely, no one would have even thought that Jesus meant his body by the temple. Even the disciples did not understand what Jesus' reply allegedly meant, yet those words were supposed to respond to the challenge of the Jewish leaders! It is difficult to understand why Jesus would not give these leaders a sign, having already performed numerous miracles in front of many thousands of people in various places throughout his ministry. The answer attributed to him is yet another problem.

Interestingly, Mark (14:57-58) and Matthew (26:61) mention Jesus' words about the temple as one of the accusations against him when he was being questioned by the high priest. They do not tell us when Jesus said those words, nor do they link the temple allegorically to his body. They clearly understood the temple to be the physical temple of the Jews in Jerusalem.

Another incident in which Jesus failed to respond to a challenge to perform a miracle is given by Matthew:

Then some of the experts in the law along with some Pharisees answered him, "Teacher, we want to see a sign from you." But he answered them, "An evil and adulterous generation asks for a sign, but no sign will be given to it except the sign of the prophet Jonah. For just as Jonah was in the belly of the huge fish for three days and three nights, so the Son of Man will be in the heart of the earth for three days and three nights. The people of Nineveh will stand up at the judgment with this generation and condemn it, because they repented when Jonah preached to them — and now, something greater than Jonah is here! The queen of the South will rise up at the judgment with this generation and condemn it, because she came from the ends of the earth to hear the wisdom of Solomon — and now, something greater than Solomon is here!" (Matt. 12:38-42)

Luke's version of the incident restricts Jesus' comment about Jonah's sign to: "as Jonah became a sign to the people of Nineveh, so the Son of Man will be a sign to this generation" (Luke 11:30). Luke does not elaborate as Matthew does.

In another incident reported by Matthew (16:4), Jesus' reply to the Pharisees and Sadducees who asked him to show them a sign is far briefer and vague: "a wicked and adulterous generation asks for a sign, but no sign will be given to it except the sign of Jonah."

Again, promising people a miracle after one's death is surely no reply to the challenge. However, there are other serious problems in likening Jonah's miraculous escape from the belly of the whale to Jesus' death and resurrection, but I will address these elsewhere (pp. 399-400).

Mark (8:11-12), Luke (11:16-20), and John (6:28-33) report other instances where Jesus declined the challenge to give a sign. These accounts, which we will get back to later in this chapter, and the passages cited earlier clearly contradict Jesus' systematic use of miracles to impress and attract people to his teachings.

16.3. Jesus' Miracles in Apocryphal Writings

Apocryphal gospels attribute a large number of miracles to Jesus. Many of these wonders are not mentioned in the canonical Gospels, as they are supposed to have occurred in Jesus' childhood — a period that the canonical Gospels completely ignore. The Arabic Gospel of the Infancy states that "Jesus did very many miracles, in Egypt, which are neither to be found in Gospel of the Infancy nor in the Gospel of Perfection" (AraIn. 8:13). It is not clear which gospel of infancy is meant here, whereas the Gospel of Perfection has been lost.

Apocryphal gospels portray Jesus as a miracle worker from his early years. There is little value in surveying many sources to compile a long list of Jesus' miracles, so we will focus our attention on two apocryphal gospels that we have been considering in this book, the Arabic Gospel of Infancy and the Gospel of Pseudo-Matthew, and a third source known as the Infancy Gospel of Thomas. These books give considerable details about Jesus' miracles.

We classified Jesus' miracles in the canonical Gospels into four major categories — healings, nature miracles, prophecies, and clairvoyance miracles — and subdivided the healing miracles into healings of diseases, exorcisms, and resurrections of dead people. The apocryphal gospels contain some miracles that do not fit in any of these groups. One major difference between Jesus' miracles in the canonical Gospels and those of the apocryphal writings is that the latter include paranormal feats in which Jesus causes harm to people and even kills them. The child Jesus is shown at times to have a sinister mood which makes him react at times extremely violently to children or adults who annoy him. These wonders may be seen as the opposite of the healing miracles; I will refer to them **harm miracles**. There are also what may be called **precociousness miracles** in which Jesus shows knowledge of astronomy, physics, and other sciences that he could not have acquired normally. Again, there is at times overlap between the different categories, with some miracles belonging to more than one category.

Jesus is reported to have performed a number of **healing miracles**. He healed dumbness (AraIn. 6:5-7), leprosy (AraIn. 6:16-17, 6:25-34, 12:5-6, 12:9-20), impotence (AraIn. 7:2-3), venomous viper bites (AraIn. 18:14-17, 19:2-3; InThom. 16; PsMatt. 41), badly injured foot (InThom. 10), loss of consciousness (InThom. 15), and other unspecified diseases (AraIn. 9:2-5, 9:8-10, 10:3). In one particularly spectacular miracles, Jesus returned a man who had been bewitched into a mule to his human shape (AraIn. 7:13-26).

Objects that had touched Jesus' body acquired healing powers. Two boys with unspecified diseases were healed when they were sprinkled with the water with which the infant Jesus was washed (AraIn. 9:2-5, 9:8-10). Another boy was cured after he was made to wear a coat made of Jesus' swaddling clothes (AraIn. 10:3). This blessed dress also protected the child from burning when he was put in a hot oven (AraIn. 10:6-7) and from drowning when he was thrown into a well (AraIn. 10:9-10).

The dumbness and impotence mentioned earlier are said to have been caused by sorcery. But there are instances of **exorcisms** where no disease is mentioned and Jesus is only said to have driven out demons from possessed people (AraIn. 4:15-16, 6:11-14, 13:17-19). In two cases the demons were expelled when the possessed person was covered by Jesus clothes (AraIn. 4:15-16, 13:17-19), and in another a possessed woman was healed immediately after carrying the infant Jesus (AraIn. 6:11-14).

Apocryphal gospels attribute to Jesus **resurrection miracles** also (AraIn. 19:6-11; InThom. 9, 17, 18; PsMatt. 32, 40). Some of the resurrected individuals were people that had been caused to die by Jesus himself (PsMatt. 26, 29). One child was brought back to life when he was covered with Jesus' clothes (AraIn. 11:5-6). The Arabic Gospel of Infancy claims that this is the same child who "in the Gospel is called Bartholomew" (AraIn. 11:8), but neither this miracle nor this name is mentioned in the canonical Gospels, so the author must be referring to another gospel.

The opposite of these philanthropic miracles are a number of wonders in which the little child Jesus caused harm or death to people who displeased him. In those punitive **harm miracles**, Jesus punished the subjects of the miracles, most of them where children, severely for petty offences. On a number of occasions children destroyed the water pools that Jesus had prepared, so he cursed them, causing them to drop dead immediately (AraIn. 19:20-21; PsMatt. 26, 28). Another running child who collided with Jesus and threw him down was cursed so he died on the spot (AraIn. 19:22-24; InThom. 3, 4). When the parents of one of the children that Jesus paranormally killed complained to Joseph that Jesus was killing children, Jesus cursed them too, making them blind (InThom. 5). There are only two miracles in the canonical Gospel that come any close to these pernicious paranormal feats, although none involves human victims. In one instance Jesus made a fig tree wither because he did not find any fruit on it (Mark 11:13-20; Matt. 21:19), and in another he sent demons into a herd of pigs who threw themselves in a lake and drowned (Mark 5:9-13; Matt. 8:31-32; Luke 8:30-33).

Jesus' teachers did not have a better luck with him. One teacher who raised his hand to hit Jesus had it withered and he died (AraIn. 20:15-16). Another who struck Jesus and was cursed by the pupil fainted and fell to the ground on his face (InThom. 14). Jesus developed some considerable notoriety for killing those who displeased him that Joseph thought the only way to stop those deaths was to prevent Jesus from leaving the house (AraIn. 20:15-16). People were afraid of angering Jesus that he may cause them to be maimed (InThom. 8).

In school, Jesus showed **precociousness miracles**. He knew more than the teacher (AraIn. 20:11). When Rabbis examined him, he showed knowledge of the religious law, astronomy, mathematics, physic, natural philosophy, metaphysics, and medicine (AraIn. 21:5-21).

In one **prophecy**, the three year old Jesus prophesied that the Jews would crucify him after 30 years, and he recognized two thieves as those who would be with him on the cross (AraIn. 8:6-7).

When it comes to **nature miracles**, apocryphal gospels have many of them. We have already seen that Jesus' clothes were immune to fire (AraIn. 10:6-7). Jesus was able to help Joseph in his carpentry work by paranormally making logs of woods longer or shorter (AraIn. 16:2, 16:16-14; InThom. 13; PsMatt. 37). He could change the colors of clothes to any colors he wished (AraIn. 15:13-14). He could carry water with his cloak (InThom. 11; PsMatt. 33). A little wheat that Jesus sowed produced as much as 300 gallons (1.3 cubic meters) (PsMatt. 34). In another version, Jesus sowed only one grain of wheat which yielded 100 large bushels (InThom. 12).

When one day Jesus crossed the Jordan, the water of the river split on the right and left (PsMatt. 36) — a miracle that is reminiscent of Moses' dividing of the sea. Jesus caused a well to spring forth for his mother to wash his coat (AraIn. 8:10). A palm tree obeyed Jesus' order and bent its top down so that he, Mary, and Joseph could eat from it. It stayed bent down until Jesus ordered it to rise again. He also caused a spring of water to appear at its root (PsMatt. 20).

Jesus performed a number of miracles involving animals. He had control over even the most dangerous beasts. One day he called a serpent and made it submit to him. He then cursed it, causing it to die (AraIn. 18:14-17). Lions and panthers worshiped and obeyed him (PsMatt. 19, 36). The Gospel of Pseudo-Matthew (14) states that an ox and an ass worshiped Jesus, and claims that this fulfilled one of Isaiah's prophecies: "An ox recognizes its owner, a donkey recognizes where its owner puts its food; but Israel does not recognize me, my people do not understand" (Isa. 1:3). According to the Arabic Gospel of Infancy, one day the seven-year-old Jesus made clay into shapes of a number of different animals and made them move forward and backward at his command. He also made the figures of birds and sparrows out of clay and made them fly, drink, and eat:

> And when the Lord Jesus was seven years of age, he was on a certain day with other boys his companions about the same age; who, when they were at play, made clay into several shapes, namely asses, oxen, birds, and other figures; each boasting of his work, and endeavouring to exceed the rest. Then the Lord Jesus said to the boys, "I will command these figures which I have made to walk." And immediately they moved, and when he commanded them to return, they returned. He had also made the figures of birds and sparrows, which, when he commanded to fly, did fly, and when he commanded to stand still, did stand still; and if he gave them meat and drink, they did eat and drink. (AraIn. 15:1-6)

In another instance Jesus created 12 sparrows of clay and at the clap of his hands made them fly and chirp (AraIn. 19:16-19; InThom. 2; PsMatt. 27).

Jesus' miracles included turning boys into kids (AraIn. 17:10), shortening the way of a 30-day journey and making take one day only (PsMatt. 22), and speaking while still an infant in the cradle (AraIn. 1:2-3).

Unsurprisingly, the writers of the apocryphal gospels use Jesus' miracles to glorify him and testify to his status. They make people react to his miracles the kind of reaction they would like the reader to have — which is a method used by the authors of the canonical Gospels also. For instance, when Jesus impressed his teacher with his knowledge, the latter was left declaring: "I think that he lived before the flood, and was born before the deluge. For what womb bore him? Or what mother brought him forth? Or what breasts gave him suck?" (PsMatt. 31).

The miracles in the apocryphal gospels may, at first sight, look more fantastic, hence less credible, than their counterparts in the canonical Gospels. But a closer look and comparison should dispel this impression, although it is true that the apocryphal gospels contain *different* miracles from those found in the canonical Gospels. Some of Jesus' miracles in the canonical Gospels are as sophisticated and fantastic as any miracle in the apocryphal gospels. Both canonical and apocryphal gospels contain narratives of wonders that can be accepted only if the concept that natural laws can be violated is entertained.

I should point out, again, that the fact that the canonical Gospels ended up being the Gospels of choice for the Church does not mean that the accounts in those Gospels, including the miracle stories, are more factual or accurate than the apocryphal gospels. Both types of writings are as likely to have true and false accounts. All of these books were written by people who had very little knowledge of Jesus, who lived long after him, and who used their books to convey to their readers their own image of Jesus and their own version of his life and teachings.

16.4. Jesus' Miracles in the Qur'an

Five Qur'anic verses (2.87, 2.253, 5.110, 43.63, and 61.6) state that Jesus was sent with *bayyināt*:

> And We gave Moses the Book and followed him with a succession of messengers; and We gave Jesus son of Mary clear proofs (*bayyināt*), and We supported him with the Spirit of Holiness (2.87).

> Those are the messengers. We conferred on some more favor than on others. Among them there are some to whom Allah spoke, while some of them He exalted [above others] in degree; and We gave Jesus son of Mary clear proofs (*bayyināt*) and supported him with the Spirit of Holiness (2.253).

When used as a noun, which is how *bayyināt* appears in those five verses, this term means "clear proofs" *on or signs of the truth*. Being sent with *bayyināt* is a description that the Qur'an applies to God's messengers in general, not only Jesus. The Qur'anic verses (e.g. 2.185), verses of other divine books (e.g. 2.159), and messages of messengers in general (e.g. 57.25) are all called *bayyināt*, because they are clear proofs on and signs of the divine truth. This means that Jesus' "clear proofs" may be the Injīl which God revealed to him or his teachings in general. However, these "clear proofs" may also signify "miracles":

> And when Jesus son of Mary said: "O Children of Israel! I am a messenger of Allah to you, confirming that which was revealed before me of the Torah, and bringing good news about a messenger who will come after me, whose name is Aḥmad". But when he came to them with clear proofs, they said: "This is clear magic" (61.6).

The Jews' description of Jesus' "clear proofs" as "magic" suggests that the referent here is Jesus' miracles. The labeling of Jesus' "clear proofs" as "magic" is mentioned in another verse which clearly talks about Jesus' miracles, so in this verse the clear proofs undoubtedly denote miracles:

> Lo! When Allah said: "O Jesus son of Mary! Remember My favor on you and on your mother, that I have supported you with the Spirit of Holiness, [making you] speak to people in the cradle and when middle-aged; and that I taught you the Book, Wisdom, the Torah, and the Injīl; and that you create out of clay the figures of birds by My permission, then you breath into them and they become birds by My permission, and heal the blind person and the albino by My permission; and that you raise the dead by My permission; and that I withheld the Children of Israel from you when you came to them with clear proofs, but those who disbelieved among them said: 'This is nothing but clear magic'" (5.110).

So the Qur'an mentions Jesus' miracles both explicitly and implicitly.

As we mentioned earlier (p. 124), while the Qur'an does not tell us exactly the nature of God's support for Jesus through Gabriel, it seems to suggest a direct link between that support and at least Jesus' miraculous ability to speak in the cradle. There are another two verses (2.87, 2.253) that mention the support of Spirit of Holiness for Jesus. This association of Gabriel's support with Jesus specifically suggests that Jesus' ability to perform miracles might have something to do with that support.

Jesus' miracles are mentioned in three sets of verses in chapters 3, 5, and 19, with a number of these miracles appearing in both of chapters 3 and 5. Unlike the Gospels, and in line with its succinct style, the Qur'an does not recount in detail the stories of most of those miracles. For instance, it states that Jesus healed blind people, but it does not tell us how and when Jesus did that or who those people were. The encounters between Jesus and the subjects of his miracles are not related in the Qur'an. The exceptions are Jesus' first miracles, which are mentioned in chapter 19, and the miracle of the *feast from heaven* which is described in some detail in chapter 5.

We will look first at the verses of chapter 3 and leave those of chapter 5 last. The verses of chapter 19 will cited as we examine chapter 3:

> When the angels said: "O Mary! Allah gives you the good news of a Word from Him, whose name is the Messiah, Jesus son of Mary, who is illustrious in this world and the hereafter, and who is one of those brought near [to Allah] (3.45). He shall speak to people in the cradle and when middle-aged, and he shall be one of the righteous (3.46). She said: "My Lord! How can I have a child when no human being has touched me?" He said: "Thus Allah creates what He wills. When He decrees a matter, He only says to it 'Be!', and it is (3.47). And He shall teach him the Book, Wisdom, the Torah, and the Injīl (3.48).

Verse 3.46 tells us that Jesus started performing miracles when he was still in the cradle. His first reported miracle is his reassuring speech to his upset mother immediately after his birth:

> And the pangs of childbirth drove her to the trunk of a palm tree. She said: "I wish I had died before this and had become someone totally forgotten!" (19.23). Then he called her from beneath her: "Do not grieve! Your Lord has placed a rivulet beneath you (19.24). And shake the trunk of the palm tree toward you, and it will let fall fresh dates upon you (19.25). So eat, drink, and be consoled. If you meet any human being, say: 'I have vowed a fast to God, so I will not speak today to any person'" (19.26).

By having his mother to fast from speaking to people, Jesus protected her from getting involved in arguments with her people and having to defend her chastity. Jesus was going to do the job for his mother. He was going to respond to her accusers and attackers and silence them by revealing his miraculous nature. When

Mary went back to her people carrying her son, they accused her of giving birth to an illicit child:

> Then she brought him to her people, carrying him. They said: "O Mary! You have come up with a grave thing (19.27). O sister of Aaron! Your father was not a bad man, and your mother was not an unchaste woman" (19.28). Then she pointed to him. They said: "How can we talk to one who is a child in the cradle?" (19.29).

At this point the infant leaped to his mother's defense, stunning her attackers as he miraculously spoke about his unique nature:

> He said: "I am Allah's servant. He has given me the Book and has appointed me a prophet (19.30). He has made me blessed wherever I may be. He has enjoined upon me prayer and almsgiving so long as I remain alive (19.31). And [He has made me] kind to my mother and has not made me arrogant or wretched (19.32). Peace is on me the day I was born, the day I shall die, and the day I shall be raised alive" (19.33).

Jesus' miracle and his words can only mean that he could not have been the son of sin; he must have been the product of divine intervention. Before Jesus spoke, Mary's people did not know what had exactly happened, but they could not accept that a miracle of some form had taken place. In order for the audience not to attribute to him divine qualities and mistake him for anything other than a human being, the wonderful infant affirmed his servanthood to God. He was a servant, although a very special one; actually, he was unique. The infant had already been made a prophet and a book had already been revealed to him.

This miracle is not only about the infant Jesus having the ability to speak, but it is equally about the nature of his speech. Jesus spoke with the kind of wisdom, knowledge, and logic that can only be expected from well educated adults. He astonished people by both speaking in the cradle and what he had to say, i.e. his precociousness. These are two miracles, not one.

Jesus' speaking while still an infant is not mentioned in the canonical Gospels. Interestingly, Matthew and Luke contain no alternative incident or explanation as to why people did not think that Jesus was an illicit child, which would have led them to subject Mary to the Jewish capital punishment of stoning.

But this miracle is found in the apocrypha:

> Jesus spoke even when he was in the cradle, and said to his mother: "Mary, I am Jesus the Son of God, that word, which you did bring forth according to the declaration of the angel Gabriel to you, and my father has sent me for the salvation of the world." (AraIn. 1:2-3)

The context of this miracle is different from the Qur'an's. In the latter Jesus spoke immediately after his birth to his mother to console her, mention the miraculous appearance of food and drink, and ask her not to talk to people. He then spoke in the cradle to his mother's people to defend her against their accusations. So the miracle is placed in a logical and understandable context. In the Arabic Gospel of the Infancy, Jesus is shown telling his mother things she was already aware of and without any reason for him to say them. The miracle is poorly weaved into the fabric of the story. This is another example of a miracle that the apocryphal writer, or his source, was aware of but did not know correctly its context so the report is poorly integrated into the story. It is a contextual displacement. The Injīl, which God revealed to Jesus, is certain to have included a lot of details about Jesus' life and miracles. The miracle of speaking in the cradle to defend his mother was one of them.

Another very significant difference between Jesus' words in the two accounts is that the Qur'an's "servant of Allah" appears as "Son of God" in the apocryphal gospel. The gospel's author went out of his way to stress that Jesus was the son of God, in the same way that he did in another two instances. In the first instance, he made the idols say the following about Jesus: "The unknown God has come here, who is truly God; nor is there any one besides him, who is worthy of divine worship for he is truly the Son of God" (AraIn. 4:11). In the second, a priest, whose son was cured by Jesus, is made to declare that: "perhaps this boy is the son of the living God, who made the heavens and the earth" (AraIn. 4:21).

Jesus' words that God had made him blessed wherever he is probably mean that he was going to be a source of blesses for people, and that he was going to perform miracles wherever he went.

After mentioning Jesus' miracle of speaking in the cradle, chapter 3 goes on to name, citing Jesus' words to the Jews, more of his miracles and stress their significance:

> And [He shall make him] a messenger to the Children of Israel, saying: 'I have come to you with a sign from your Lord. I create for you out of clay the figures of birds, then I breathe into it [the clay], and it becomes birds by Allah's permission. I heal the blind person and the albino; I raise the dead, by Allah's permission. And I tell you what you eat and what you store in your houses. Herein verily is a sign for you, if you are to be believers (3.49).

The miracle of creating figures of birds from clay and then breathing life into them is missing from the canonical Gospels, but the apocryphal gospels have a number of different and more detailed versions of this miracle. The Arabic Gospel of Infancy (15:2-4) talks about Jesus making clay into shapes of asses, oxen, birds, and other figures, and making them move forward and backward at his command. It also states that Jesus made the figures of birds and sparrows out of clay, and made them fly, drink, and eat (AraIn. 15:6). This gospel (19:16-19), the Infancy Gospel of Thomas (2), and the Gospel of Pseudo-Matthew (27) report another miracle in which Jesus created 12 sparrows of clay and at the clap of his hands he made them fly and chirp.

The healing of blindness is also mentioned in the canonical Gospels (Mark 8:22-25, 10:46-52; Matt. 9:27-30, 12:22, 15:30, 20:29-34, 21:14; Luke 18:35-42), including an instance of blindness from birth (John 9:1-7). Curing albinism is not mentioned in the Gospels, but healing leprosy is (Mark 1:40-42; Matt. 8:2-3; Luke 5:12-13, 17:12-14).

Theissen and Merz (1999: 311) make the following interesting observation about the exact definition of some of Jesus' miracles in the Gospels:

> When there is mention of leprosy, blindness, or possession in the New Testament, we must not simply think of modern leprosy, blindness, or psychoses. Rather, sicknesses are defined differently in every society, and narratives about sickness and healing are stylized accordingly. In the New Testament "leprosy" probably covered every possible kind of skin disease and blindness any impairment of sight.

The question is then whether this applies to the Qur'an's use of the Arabic terms *akmah* and *abraṣ*, which are translated here as "blind person" and "albino," respectively. Was each of these terms used by the Arabs to mean more than one disease or disability? What makes this question particularly uneasy to answer is that these two terms appear only in those two verses about Jesus' miracles, so their meanings cannot be clarified by studying their use in other contexts in the Qur'an.

Exegetes and linguists are not in complete agreement about the meaning of *akmah*. In his classical exegesis of the Qur'an, aṭ-Ṭabarī says that exegetes have suggested four meanings for this term. It has been claimed that the term denotes a person who is blind, is born blind, is born blind with closed eyes, or has night blindness. Given the impressive nature of the rest of Jesus' miracles, we can discount the latter meaning, as night blindness is not as serious a form of blindness. Interestingly, there is another word in the Qur'an, *a'mā* (e.g. 24.61, 80.2), which all agree means "blind." This may suggest that the term *akmah* signifies a certain kind of blindness. However, the term *a'mā* is used by the Qur'an not only for the physically blind, but also allegorically for the person who cannot see the truth (e.g. 13.19, 17.72), so it could be suggested that the term *akmah* denotes the physically blind person. Because of this uncertainty, I have chosen to translate *akmah* as "blind person."

Exegetes and Linguists have explained *abraṣ* as someone with a skin disease that turns it white, which is suggestive of "albinism" or "vitiligo." Translators of the Qur'an, on the other hand, have consistently translated *abraṣ* into "leper." This translation is undoubtedly influenced by the Gospels stories of Jesus' healings of lepers. Arabic has different terms for "leper," *ajtham* or *majthūm*, which are derived from *juthām* (leprosy). The seriousness of blindness as a disability and the impressive nature of the other miracles suggest to me that *abraṣ* is probably used in the Qur'an for a person with a serious disease, which is likely to be skin-related. Like *akmah* which probably signified more than one kind of blindness, *abraṣ* is likely to have denoted more one type of serious skin disease.

The next miracle that verse 3.49 mentions is Jesus' ability to raise the dead. There are two instances of raising a dead person in the canonical Gospels. Luke (7:12-15) has a story about Jesus bringing back to life the son of a widow, and John (11:38-44) mentions the raising of Lazarus from the dead.

Jesus then reminds his people that he was able to know what they ate and stored in the privacy of their homes. The canonical Gospels attribute to Jesus three instances of clairvoyance, but they do not include this specific one.

Having described his miracles as a "sign" in verse 3.49, Jesus goes on in the next verse to describe further his mission and stress again that he has brought a sign to people, meaning a sign that he was indeed sent by God:

> [I have come] to confirm that which was revealed before me of the Torah, and to make lawful some of that which was forbidden to you. I have come to you with a sign from your Lord, so keep your duty to Allah and obey me (3.50)

Jesus then stresses that despite his very special spiritual status and the privileges that God has given him, he was a mere servant in the same way that everyone is a servant of God:

> Allah is my Lord and your Lord, so worship Him. That is a straight path'" (3.51).

Let's study now the verses of chapter 5, starting with verse 110:

> Lo! When Allah said: "O Jesus son of Mary! Remember My favor on you and on your mother, that I have supported you with the Spirit of Holiness, [making you] speak to people in the cradle and when of old age; and that I taught you the Book, Wisdom, the Torah, and the Injīl; and that you create out of clay the figures of birds by My permission, then you breath into them and they become birds by My permission, and heal the blind person and the albino by My permission; and that you raise the dead by My permission; and that I withheld the Children of Israel from you when you came to them with clear proofs, but those who disbelieved among them said: 'This is nothing but clear magic'" (5.110).

Unlike the verses of chapter 3, this verse does not list Jesus' miracles in the context of citing what Jesus told people, but as a direct speech from God to Jesus. The miracles are listed in the same order in which they appear in chapter 3. Verse 5.110 does not contain the clairvoyance miracle of verse 3.49, but it mentions another miracle. God's reminder to Jesus of how He protected him against Jewish attempts to hurt him in the context of talking about miracles suggests that this protection was miraculous, i.e. involved direct intervention from God. This protection is not described as one of Jesus' miracles, i.e. not as something that Jesus did, but as help that God gave to Jesus.

It is worth noting that in this one verse God stresses four times that Jesus performed miracles *by His permission*. Like verse 3.51, this is intended to emphasize the fact that although Jesus was chosen by God, he was no more than a human being who could not have done anything without God's permission. It was God who granted Jesus, and his mother, favors: supporting him with Gabriel; teaching him the Book, Wisdom, the Torah, and the Injīl; giving him the power to perform various wonders; and protecting him against the scheme of his enemies. The Qur'an stresses several times that no prophet can show a sign or miracle without God's permission (e.g. 40.78):

> It is not in the power of a messenger to bring a sign except by Allah's permission (13.38).
>
> Their (the disbelievers') messengers said to them: "True, we are humans like yourselves, but Allah confers His favor on such of his servants as He pleases. It is not for us to bring you an authority except as Allah permits. And on Allah let all believers rely" (14.11).

Like verses 3.49-50 that describe Jesus' miracles as a "sign," verse 5.110 describes them as "clear proofs."

Both chapters 3 and 5 talk about creating live "birds" and raising "the dead," i.e. in the plural. Arabic has a special form for the dual, so the use of the plural form means that at least three birds and three dead people were involved in those miracles. It is not clear whether the Arabic terms for the blind person and for the albino are in the plural or singular, but since they are both preceded by the definite article then they are used in the plural sense. Additionally, the verbs that describe the miracles occur in the present tense, which indicates continuity, i.e. repeated performance of these miracles.

Chapter 5 then goes on to describe in some detail a very interesting miracle performed by Jesus:

> Lo! When I inspired the companions: "Believe in Me and in My messenger." They said: "We believe. Bear witness that we are Muslims" (5.111). Lo! When the companions said: "O Jesus son of Mary! Can your Lord send down for us a table of food from heaven?" He said: "Observe your duty to Allah, if you are true believers" (5.112). They said: "We wish to eat of it, have our hearts be at ease, know that you have spoken the truth to us, and be witnesses to it (the table)" (5.113). Jesus son of Mary said: "O Allah our Lord! Send down for us from heaven a table of food, that it may be a feast for the first and the last of us, and a sign from You. Give us sustenance; You are the best of Sustainers" (5.114). Allah said: "I shall send it down for you, so whoever of you disbelieves afterward I will

punish him with a torment wherewith I do not inflict on anyone among all the nations" (5.115).

I use in verse 5.112 and other places the term "companions" rather than "disciples" for those special followers of Jesus because there is little information that justifies equating them with the disciples of the Christian writings (p. 498).

Some exegetes have suggested that after hearing Jesus' criticism, the companions withdrew their request so no miracle took place. This unsupported view has been proposed to exonerate the companions of the apparent guilt implied in that request, yet God's words "I shall send it down for you" leave no doubt that the table was sent down. It is also worth nothing that chapter 5 is called *the Chapter of the table of food* after the miracle it mentions.

Jesus' request that the table of food "may be a feast for the first and the last of us" is taken by most scholars to mean that he asked for that miracle to become an event that Christians continue to celebrate. The term "first" would then mean the early Christians, including those who were with Jesus, and "last" would denote the Christians of later times. One difficulty with this interpretation is that it is the "table" not the "miracle" that Jesus wanted to be a feast for the first and last. Also, taking the rather intimate pronoun "us" to mean *all Christians* does not sound right. I prefer instead the much less popular interpretation that Jesus meant that the table would feed all of those who were with him. The expression "the first and the last of us" then indicates that there was a relatively large number of people. It is not clear whether all of these people were the group of followers that the Qur'an calls "companions" or whether they included other followers of Jesus.

While the companions asked for a table of food from heaven to eat from, Jesus request for it to be a *īdan* (feast) means that he asked for plenty of food, as during feasts people eat a lot of food. If we also consider the possibility that, while the companions asked for a table of feed that *they* can eat from, Jesus prayed for one that would feed *all of the present people*, it becomes clear that the miracle that Jesus performed was even greater than what the companions wanted to see.

Given that the companions were close followers of Jesus, they must have already seen many of his miracles. This is confirmed by the fact that Jesus first censured them before granting them their request. So why would they ask him for yet another miracle then? They wanted to see one specific miracle that Jesus had not performed before: bringing down from heaven a table of food. But why this particular miracle? The companions wanted to make sure that Jesus can bring for them food from heaven in the same way that God sent down manna and quails from heaven to the Israelites in the desert of Sinai after fleeing Egypt with Moses — a miracle recorded in both the Qur'an (also 7.160, 20.80) and the Old Testament:

> And We made the clouds to give shade over you [O Children of Israel!], and We sent to you manna and quails [saying]: "Eat of the good things that We have given you"; and

they did not do Us any harm [by their disobedience], but they did wrong themselves (2.57).

> Then the Lord spoke to Moses: "I have heard the murmurings of the Israelites. Tell them, 'During the evening you will eat flesh, and in the morning you will be satisfied with bread, so that you may know that I am the Lord your God." And in the evening the quail came up and covered the camp; and in the morning a layer of dew was all around the camp. When the layer of dew had evaporated, there were small round things on the surface of the desert, small like the frost on the earth. When the Israelites saw it, they said to one another, "What is it?" because they did not know what it was. And Moses said to them, "It is the bread that the Lord has given you for food." (Exo. 16:11-15)

Making their request for a miracle from *Jesus' Lord* and then linking it to them believing that *Jesus had spoken the truth to them*, the companions were clearly thinking of God's miracle to the Israelites in the desert. They meant to say that if your Lord can bring for us food from heaven like God did for the Israelites who were with Moses, then we would believe your claim that the Lord who sent you is the same Lord who sent Moses. My interpretation that the request of Jesus' companions is linked to God's miracle to the early Israelites is confirmed by the following passage in John:

> So then they said to him, "What must we do to accomplish the deeds God requires?" Jesus replied, "This is the deed God requires — to believe in the one whom he sent." So they said to him, "Then what miraculous sign will you perform, so that we may see it and believe you? What will you do? Our ancestors ate the manna in the wilderness, just as it is written, 'He gave them bread from heaven to eat.'" Then Jesus told them, "I tell you the solemn truth, it is not Moses who has given you the bread from heaven, but my Father is giving you the true bread from heaven. For the bread of God is the one who comes down from heaven and gives life to the world." (John 6:28-33)

This account clearly refers to the same event reported in the Qur'an, with the most noticeable difference being the fact that the Jesus of John declines to perform the required miracle, whereas the Jesus of the Qur'an does it. Mark and Luke also have a passage each about Jesus being asked to produce a miracle from heaven — also with him refusing to deliver the miracle:

> Then the Pharisees came and began to argue with Jesus, asking for a sign from heaven to test him. Sighing deeply in his spirit he said, "Why does this generation look for a sign? I tell you the truth, no sign will be given to this generation." (Mark 8:11-12)

> Now he was casting out a demon that was mute. When the demon had gone out, the man who had been mute began to speak, and the crowds were amazed. But some of them said, "By the power of Beelzebul, the ruler of demons, he casts out demons." Others, to test him, began asking for a sign from heaven. But Jesus, realizing their

thoughts, said to them, "Every kingdom divided against itself is destroyed, and a divided household falls. So if Satan too is divided against himself, how will his kingdom stand? I ask you this because you claim that I cast out demons by Beelzebul. Now if I cast out demons by Beelzebul, by whom do your sons cast them out? Therefore they will be your judges. But if I cast out demons by the finger of God, then the kingdom of God has already overtaken you. (Luke 11:14-20)

Matthew has an account of Jesus refusing to show a miracle from heaven, although in this case he is said to have mentioned the sign of Jonah, despite the fact that the latter is not a sign from heaven in the sense meant by those who wanted the miracle:

Now when the Pharisees and Sadducees came to test Jesus, they asked him to show them a sign from heaven. He said, "When evening comes you say, 'It will be fair weather, because the sky is red,' and in the morning, 'It will be stormy today, because the sky is red and darkening.' You know how to judge correctly the appearance of the sky, but you cannot evaluate the signs of the times. A wicked and adulterous generation asks for a sign, but no sign will be given to it except the sign of Jonah." Then he left them and went away. (Matt. 16:1-4)

We discussed earlier (pp. 340-342) other New Testament passages in which Jesus was asked to perform a miracle but he rejected the request (Matt. 12:38-42, 16:4; Luke 11:30; John 2:18-22). The difference between those passages and the ones cited above is that the latter talk specifically about a sign from heaven.

Significantly, the four Gospels (Mark 14:16-26; Matt. 26:18-30; Luke 22:10-38; John 13:1-17:26) contain a story of Jesus having a supper with his companions around a table on the eve of his arrest. It appears that the story of the Last Supper, which Paul (1 Cor. 11:23-25) also refers to, and the story of the challenge to Jesus to show a sign from heaven — which, according to John (6:28-33), was about bringing food from heaven — are corrupted versions of the real event of the miracle of the table of food from heaven that the Qur'an recounts. The Gospel accounts represent substantial contextual displacements of this miracle. This miracle is certain to have been reported in the Injīl — the very original source of the corrupted Christian texts.

Interestingly, the miracle of the table of food from heaven is recounted immediately before a dialog between God and Jesus that took place after Jesus left the earth (p. 449). Also, Jesus' censure of the companions for their request for this miracle suggests that they had been with him for some time and had already seen many of his miracles. It is therefore likely that this miracle happened late in Jesus' life on earth — possibly shortly before he was lifted up by God. This would then represent another similarity between the Qur'anic miracle and the Last Supper which the Evangelists place at the end of Jesus' ministry.

The fact that the Qur'anic account talks about a miracle of feeding a lot of people might also indicate that this miracle is the original source of the two Gospel miracles of the multiplication of food and feeding of large crowds. But Jesus did not have that many followers for this miracle to have involved thousands of people as the Evangelists claim.

To recap, the Qur'an attributes the following miracles to Jesus:

① Speaking in the cradle.
② Showing paranormal precociousness — having deep knowledge and wisdom while still an infant.
③ Creating figures of birds from clay and then giving them life.
④ Healing blindness.
⑤ Healing albinism or serious skin diseases.
⑥ Raising the dead.
⑦ Knowing what people ate and stored in the privacy of their homes.
⑧ Bringing down from heaven a table of food.

It is notable that the Qur'an does not attribute to Jesus one of the most common miracles in the Gospels: exorcisms. In fact, no miracle of exorcism is mentioned anywhere in the Qur'an.

Apart from the unique miracle of the heavenly feast, each of the other miracles was performed a number of unspecified times, but not less than three. It looks that the Qur'an implies that these were all of Jesus' miracles.

The Qur'an confirms that Jesus worked impressive miracles, but it names a smaller number of miracles than those found in the canonical and apocryphal sources, as well as different ones. It also reveals contextual differences in the Christian accounts.

17

The *Injīl* (Gospel)

The New Testament's use of "gospel" distinguishes this term from its use in the Hebrew and Greek Old Testaments where it has no religious connotation. The authors of the New Testament have given "gospel" a number of different, albeit related, meanings. It is used to mean Jesus' message, the news about his message, and the act of proclaiming the message.

Jesus' sayings in which this term appears have known problems. For instance, some of these passages are reproduced by other Evangelists with the term "gospel" missing. This has prompted some scholars to question whether Jesus used that term at all.

Scholars agree that "gospel" is never used in the New Testament to mean a written document. It is thought that this the term, which never appears in the New Testament in the plural, started to be used in this sense in the 2nd century, when it was used for a particular genre of writings — narratives recounting the life and death of Jesus. However, in the first passage of his Gospel, Mark might have meant by the term a *written account*.

The Qur'an's equivalent of "gospel" is "Injīl," which has one specific meaning: the name of the book that God revealed to Jesus. God called Jesus' book "Injīl" because it contained the good news about the future coming of Prophet Muhammad. The Gospel of John states that Jesus spoke about a mysterious being who would come sometime after he had gone called *parakletos*. This Greek term, which is also mentioned in the First Epistle of John, is probably a corruption of the term *periklytos*, which differs only in three vowels. The latter has exactly the same meaning as "Muhammad" or "highly praised."

The Injīl confirmed the message the Torah. It did not contain a new law, but it complemented the Torah, modifying some aspects of its law. The Qur'an rejects the common Christian view that Jesus abrogated the law or taught that it can be transgressed. The New Testament has nothing to support this view. The successful demotion of the law in Christianity is the work of Paul who stressed instead the role of grace in salvation, thus making it easier for non-Jews to convert to the new religion.

17.1. The Term "Gospel" Before and After Christianity

The English noun "gospel" comes from the Anglo-Saxon word god-spell, which means a story from or about a god. It is popularly understood to mean "good news." This term is an accurate rendering of the Greek adjectival noun *euangelion* (εὐαγγέλιου). It is found 77 times in 74 passages in the New Testament. In the

Gospels, the terms occurs 8 times in Mark (1:1, 1:14, 1:15, 8:35, 10:29, 13:10, 14:9, 16:15), 4 in Matthew (4:23, 9:35, 24:14, 26:13), but none in Luke or John. It occurs around 60 times in Paul's Epistles, including 8 in the Deutero-Pauline Epistles (Colossians, Ephesians, and 2 Thessalonians) and 4 in the Pastoral Epistles (1 & 2 Timothy and Titus).

The verb *euangelizo* (εὐαγγελίζω), which means "bring good news" or "proclaim glad tidings," is found 61 times in 52 New Testament passages. It occurs only once in Matthew (11:5), 12 times in Luke, but none in Mark or John. The book of Acts, which is attributed to the same author of Luke, uses the verb as many as 16 times. Paul uses the verb 27 times in his letters, including the Deutero-Pauline Epistles.

Table 17.1: The number occurrences of the Greek noun *euangelion* and verb *euangelizo* in the New Testament books

Book	euangelion	euangelizo	Book	euangelion	euangelizo
Matt.	4	1	1 Tim.	1	0
Mark	8	0	2 Tim.	3	0
Luke	0	12	Titus	0	0
John	0	0	Phm.	1	0
Acts	2	16	Heb.	0	2
Rom.	10	4	James	0	0
1 Cor.	8	7	1 Peter	1	3
2 Cor.	8	2	2 Peter	0	0
Gal.	7	8	1 John	0	0
Eph.	4	2	2 John	0	0
Phi.	9	0	3 John	0	0
Col.	2	0	Jude	0	0
1 The.	6	2	Rev.	1	2
2 The.	2	0	**Total**	**77**	**61**

Among the Greeks, *euangelion* was used to mean "good news" or "reward for good news." It is used as a technical term for "news of victory" in battle (Friedrich, 1971: 722). In a decree in 9 BCE that honored Augustus by making his birthday on the 23rd of September the beginning of the civil year, the Greeks of the province of Asia described the birth of the emperor-god Augustus as good news (*euangel*). The Jewish historian Philo does not use *euangelion*, but he uses the verb *euangelizo*. The noun is found in Josephus.

In the Greek translation of the Old Testament, the noun is used far less than the verb — occurring only 6 times, all of which in the plural *euangelia* (εὐαγγέλια). It is used once, although sarcastically, to mean "reward for good news" (2 Sam. 4:10). King David killed the person who brought to him the supposedly good tidings about the death of his enemy Saul, and he described the killing as "the good news I gave to him!" In the remaining 5 instances, *euangelia* means "good news" (2 Sam. 18:20, 18:22, 18:25, 18:27; 2 Kings 7:9). This distinction between "good news" and "reward for good news" is not found outside the Septuagint.

Based on a linguistic analysis of the interrelations between the verb and noun, the *Theological Dictionary of the New Testament* traces the use of the term *euangelion* in the New Testament to the Jewish not the Greek world (Friedrich, 1971: 726). However, it was not derived from the Septuagint, where the term has no religious use. Additionally, the New Testament does not have the sense of "reward for good news" (Friedrich, 1971: 725), using the term to mean "good news" only. The *Exegetical Dictionary of the New Testament* notes that the difference between the use of *euangelion* in the Old Testament and the New Testament is considerable, particularly because the Hebrew and Greek nouns do not appear in the Hebrew and the Greek Old Testaments to have a theological meaning. It still claims that the primary basis of the use of this term in the New Testament is probably found in the circle of the Hellenistic ruler cult (Strecker, 1991: 71).

Contrary to the Septuagint, the New Testament never uses *euangelion* or gospel in the plural. It is used both absolutely and with further qualification. Mark uses the term absolutely, but Matthew use gospel mainly with qualification, calling it "the gospel of the kingdom" (4:23, 9:35) or "this gospel of the kingdom" (24:14).

"Gospel" is used in the New Testament in a number of related meanings at the center of all is Jesus. It can mean Jesus' message (e.g. Mark 1:15), and in Paul's writings it also means the very act of proclaiming and executing this message. It is the proclamation of the message that turns it into reality. Paul's influence on Christianity has also meant that "gospel" has become inseparable from the concept of salvation through Jesus. The term, then, is taken to mean the good news that God has acted to redeem people from sin, through the incarnation, crucifixion, and resurrection of His son Jesus. Becker (1976: 110) thinks that there is good reason to believe that it was Paul who established the use of "gospel" in the vocabulary of the New Testament. But Paul was not the first to use it for Jesus' message, as he assumes that the term, which he uses absolutely, was known to churches that he founded and other churches (Strecker, 1991: 71).

Jesus' use of the term in the Gospels is also usually linked to Old Testament prophecies that are associated with the coming of the Messiah (e.g. Isa. 40:9, 52:7). In this sense, "gospel" is the good news about something that was about to happen — not something that had already happened, which is the non-Biblical use of the term.

There is clearly tension in the Christian use of "gospel" to mean *the news about a message, the message itself,* and *the act of proclaiming that news or message*. This tension is circumvented by the use of loose theological language.

Out of the 12 instances of "gospel" in the Gospels, 8 appear in sayings attributed to Jesus (Mark 1:15, 8:35, 10:29, 13:10, 14:9, 16:15; Matt. 24:14, 26:13). This suggests that it was Jesus himself who introduced this term with the message he preached. However, there are problems in these passages. Three of Mark's 6 sayings of Jesus that contain "gospel" are reported by the other two Synoptists with that particular term missing:

> He said, "The time is fulfilled and the kingdom of God is near. Repent and believe the gospel!" (Mark 1:15)
> From that time Jesus began to preach this message: "Repent, for the kingdom of heaven is near." (Matt. 4:17)

> For whoever wants to save his life will lose it, but whoever loses his life for my sake and for the gospel will save it. (Mark 8:35)
> For whoever wants to save his life will lose it, but whoever loses his life for my sake will find it. (Matt. 16:25)
> Whoever finds his life will lose it, and whoever loses his life because of me will find it. (Matt. 10:39)
> For whoever wants to save his life will lose it, but whoever loses his life for my sake will save it. (Luke 9:24)

> Jesus said, "I tell you the truth, there is no one who has left home or brothers or sisters or mother or father or children or fields for my sake and for the sake of the gospel who will not receive in this age a hundred times as much — homes, brothers, sisters, mothers, children, fields, all with persecutions — and in the age to come, eternal life." (Mark 10:29-30)
> And whoever has left houses or brothers or sisters or father or mother or children or fields for my sake will receive a hundred times as much and will inherit eternal life. (Matt. 19:29)
> Then Jesus said to them, "I tell you the truth, there is no one who has left home or wife or brothers or parents or children for the sake of God's kingdom who will not receive many times more in this age — and in the age to come, eternal life." (Luke 18:29-30)

Although Mark is the oldest of the four Gospels, the missing of "gospel" is taken to mean that this term was not present in the original text of the three passages and that it appeared as a result of later redaction.

Mark's remaining three passages have a different problem. In these passages, two of which correspond to passages in Matthew, Mark states that Jesus commanded the disciples to preach the gospel to the whole world:

> First the gospel must be preached to all nations. (Mark 13:10)
> And this gospel of the kingdom will be preached throughout the whole inhabited earth as a testimony to all the nations, and then the end will come. (Matt. 24:14)

> I tell you the truth, wherever the gospel is proclaimed in the whole world, what she has done will also be told in memory of her. (Mark 14:9; Matt. 26:13)

Go into all the world and preach the gospel to every creature. (Mark 16:15)

The problem here is that these conflict with other passages in both Mark and Matthew that clearly state that Jesus restricted the preaching to the Jews only:

The woman was a Greek, of Syrophoenician origin. She asked him to cast the demon out of her daughter. He said to her, "Let the children be satisfied first, for it is not right to take the children's bread and to throw it to the dogs." (Mark 7:26-27)

So he answered, "I was sent only to the lost sheep of the house of Israel." But she came and bowed down before him and said, "Lord, help me!" "It is not right to take the children's bread and throw it to the dogs," he said. (Matt. 15:24-26)

Jesus sent out these twelve, instructing them as follows: "Do not go to Gentile regions and do not enter any Samaritan town. Go instead to the lost sheep of the house of Israel." (Matt. 10:5-6)

The problems with the passages that suggest that Jesus used the term "gospel" are one reason why scholars often questioned whether Jesus actually used that term. Another reason is the fact that Gospels are not a stenographic reproduction of Jesus' preaching or an official record of his activity as a teacher, as they were originally oral tradition. According to one scholar, the question of whether Jesus used the term "gospel" or not cannot be decided by textual criticism, so the useful question is whether he could have used it. He concludes that this is down to whether Jesus was aware of his messianic mission, so if he was, he would have used it (Friedrich, 1971: 727-728).

It has also been suggested that Jesus used the Hebrew or Aramaic verb when talking about his saving message which he called "the word" or "the word of God." The Greek speaking Church then used the equivalent Greek verb, which was part of the religious vocabulary of the time, to coin the term *euangelion*, and endowed it with the characteristics of "the word" (Piper, 1992: 444). In support of this view it is pointed out that all the verbs used in connection with "gospel" — such as "proclaim," "obey," "announce," and "hear" — are also applied to "word" (Piper, 1992: 443).

Although "gospel" has become widely used for particular writings, there is consensus among scholars that the term originally signified oral tradition and was never applied to a written document. It is agreed that nowhere in the New Testament is "gospel" used to denote a written document (Becker, 1976: 113; Friedrich, 1971: 735; Hartman, 1967: 635; Ryan, 1979: 1528). It is believed that the use of gospel to mean written documents started in the 2nd century (Becker, 1976: 113; Piper, 1992: 444). This is when the term was used for a particular genre of writings — a practice that became established by the 4th century (Vorster, 1992: 1077). Only after the term was used for a written document that it started to appear in the plural, designating that group of written documents. In the light of the commonly accepted meaning of "gospel" in the New Testament, the plural "gospels" is seen as a "contradiction of its nature" (Becker, 1976: 113).

The term *euangelistes* or "evangelist" appears three times in the New Testament:

> On the next day we left and came to Caesarea, and entered the house of Philip the evangelist, who was one of the seven, and stayed with him. (Acts 21:8)

> It was he who gave some as apostles, some as prophets, some as evangelists, and some as pastors and teachers. (Eph. 4:11)

> You, however, be self-controlled in all things, endure hardship, do an evangelist's work, fulfill your ministry. (2 Tim. 4:5)

"Evangelist" looks to denote the person who proclaims the gospel. The use of this term for the author of a gospel is not found before the time when "gospel" appears as the designation of a book and the plural "gospels" is in circulation (Becker, 1976: 114).

The first passage in Mark is particularly interesting in its use of "gospel": "The beginning of the gospel of Jesus Christ, the Son of God." At first sight, this passage seems to suggest that Mark meant to describe his book as "gospel," but most scholars argue against this interpretation. Mark's use is taken by some to indicate that, at that time, this term was used in some circles for the whole public ministry of Jesus, not only for the message brought by him (Piper, 1992: 444). It is also suggested that it was Mark's association of "gospel" with stories about Jesus that ultimately led in the 2nd century to "gospel" becoming a name for a book in which his biography is described (Becker, 1976: 113). Attention is usually drawn to the fact that Luke does not use the term gospel in the passage in which he describes his book: "Now many have undertaken to compile an account of the things that have been fulfilled among us" (Luke 1:1). It is interesting to note what the NET Bible has to say about the term in Luke 1:1 it translates as "account":

> This is sometimes translated "narrative," but the term itself can refer to an oral or written account. It is the verb "undertaken" which suggests a written account, since it literally is "to set one's hand" to something. "Narrative" is too specific, denoting a particular genre of work for the accounts that existed in the earlier tradition. Not all of that material would have been narrative.

The NET Bible also points out that "things" in Luke 1:1 may be translated as "events." This suggests that Luke might have used the term "account" in the same sense of the term "gospel" in Mark 1:1, which in turn can mean that Mark used "gospel" to mean his written account of Jesus.

Regardless of what explanation is given to the supposed development of the meaning of "gospel" from oral tradition to a written document, it is difficult to accept that if it was the name of Jesus' message, which means it would have been fully understood and in popular circulation among all Christians, it could have been ended up being used for written documents. One would expect Christians to coin a completely new term, or at least derive a new one from "gospel," but certainly not use one of the most important terms of their religion in a very different meaning. Let's remember also that it was not only used to denote the four canonical Gospels, but also the many apocryphal books about Jesus' life.

In the apocryphal sources that we considered in this book, "gospel" appears only in the *Arabic Gospel of the Infancy*. This late source uses this term to mean a written document about Jesus' life as it mentions a number of gospels (AraIn. 8:13, 11:8, 18:19).

17.2. The Injīl: Jesus' Divine Book

Unlike "gospel" in Christian sources, the Qur'an uses its equivalent term "Injīl" in one specific meaning: the name of a book that God revealed to Jesus. The term "Injīl" occurs 12 times in 12 different verses. Eight of these appearances are in the phrase "the Torah and the Injīl." In the course of studying the meaning of "Injīl," we will examine all 12 verses.

The Injīl was revealed to Jesus in the same way that the Torah was revealed to Moses, the Qur'an was revealed to Muhammad, and the other books were revealed to their respective prophets:

> Then We made Our messengers to follow in their (Noah and Abraham) footsteps, and followed them up with Jesus son of Mary, and We gave him the Injīl (57.27).

Each divine book is a manifestation of the Qur'anic concept of "Book." The latter signifies a special kind of knowledge that God reveals to some messengers in the form of specific books in different languages. For instance, the Qur'an is an "Arabic" manifestation of the divine Book:

> It [the Qur'an] is a revelation from Allah, the Merciful (41.2). A Book whose verses have been detailed as an Arabic Qur'an for a people of knowledge (41.3).

Naturally, as all these divine books derive from the same divine source and convey the same core message, they attest to the verity of each other. Each book is considered as a confirmation of the books that were sent before it:

> He has sent down to you [O Muhammad!] the Book with truth, confirming that which was revealed before it, and He sent down the Torah and the Injīl (3.3) before it; and He sent down the criterion [of judgment between right and wrong] (3.4).

One unique aspect of the revelation of the Book to Jesus is that it happened when he was only a few days old; it could have even started when he was still in his mother's womb. When Mary took her newborn baby to her people he said to them: "I am Allah's servant. He has given me the Book and has appointed me a prophet" (19.30).

In addition to revealing to Jesus the Injīl, which is a form of the Book, God also endowed him with the right understanding of the book of Moses and with Wisdom (5.110):

And He shall teach him (Jesus) the Book, Wisdom, The Torah, and the Injīl (3.48).

The Injīl that the Qur'an talks about is clearly completely different from the books that have come to be called Gospels. The Torah and the Injīl were both still available in their original form to their believers in Arabia at the time of the revelation of the Qur'an. Nevertheless, the attempts to change the text and teachings of the Injīl had started centuries ago, shortly after Jesus. By the time of the Qur'an, the four Gospels had long been canonized and many other books had appeared (§1.2.3).

17.3. The Meaning of "Injīl"

The first question that we need to consider is the language of the Injīl.

In the 7th and 6th centuries BCE Aramaic, which probably first appeared among the Aramaeans late in the 11th century BCE, gradually replaced Akkadian as the lingua franca of the Middle East. Long before Jesus' time Aramaic had supplanted Hebrew as the main language of the Jews, as a result of the destruction of their kingdom by the Assyrians in 721 BCE and the Babylonians early in the 6th century BCE. As Aramaic was the main language of the Jews in 1st century Palestine, the scholarly consensus is that Jesus taught in this language. Evidence that Jesus used Aramaic exists in the form of Aramaic quotes of his words in the Greek Gospels. For instance, this is how Mark (5:41) describes Jesus' healing of the synagogue rule's daughter who was in a coma: "Then, gently taking the child by the hand, he said to her, 'Talitha koum,' which means, 'Little girl, I say to you, get up.'" There are other instances in which Jesus' is quoted in Aramaic and his words are translated into Greek by the Evangelists (Mark 7:34, 14:36, 15:34; Matt. 27:46).

But Jesus actually lived in a multi-cultural, multi-lingual region. For instance, the people of Sepphoris, the largest city in Galilee, were pagans who spoke Greek. Again, the Gospels contain references that suggest that Jesus spoke Greek, such as his dialog with a Roman centurion (Matt. 8:5-13). Jewish traders are also likely to have spoken Greek for business needs.

As for Hebrew, it remained the language of literary and the scriptures. The Dead Sea Scrolls, which date from the 3rd century BCE to the 1st century CE, were also mainly written in Hebrew. Jesus' interest in religion and the scripture means that he must have known Hebrew also. So Jesus was probably trilingual, speaking Aramaic, Greek, and Hebrew. But can we determine the language of the Injīl?

The term Injīl is derived from the Greek *euangelion*, so the name of Jesus' book means "good news." This may suggest that the Injīl was in Greek, but it may be also argued that the Greek term *euangelion* was itself a translation of an Aramaic word. Another potentially interesting observation is the fact that all Gospels, which inherited the name of Jesus' divine book, are written in Greek. Were they written in Greek because the Injīl was in Greek? While I see this as a distinct possibility, the question of the language of Jesus' book cannot be answered with any certainty.

We have seen how the term *euangelion* is understood in Christianity, but the Qur'an does not share those interpretations, some of which are based on concepts that the Qur'an rejects, such as the concept of salvation through Jesus.

Significantly, the Qur'an describes all prophets, not only Jesus, as *mubashshirīn* or "bearers of good news" in several verses. Every prophet brings the good news about how to earn God's satisfaction and, thus, avoid the eternal torment of hell and live in paradise forever. He brings the good news that should people accept his message, God will reward them generously. In fact, the very coming of every prophet is good news, because it is another divine favor and opportunity for people to attain salvation, although this salvation is achieved through following the divine instructions that the prophet conveys, not through the prophet himself.

Similarly, every prophet is described as a "warner" in the Qur'an, because he warns people of the forthcoming Day of Resurrection when everyone is judged. The very reason for sending a prophet is to act as a "bearer of good news" and a "warner." This is one verse that calls all prophets "bearers of good news" and "warners," and another that talks about Prophet Muhammad specifically:

> And We do not send the messengers but as bearers of good news and warners. Then those who believe and do good deeds, they shall have no fear, nor shall they grieve (6.48).
>
> And We have not sent you [O Muhammad!] but as a bearer of good news and a warner (25.56).

Additionally, the Qur'an describes itself with the singular word *bushrā*, which means "good news," because it is good news for the believers (also 2.97, 16.89, 16.102, 27.2):

> And before it (the Qur'an), [We sent down] the book of Moses as a guide and a mercy, and this is a confirming book, in the Arabic language, to warn the wrongdoers and good news (46.12).

Because the book of any prophet contains his message, it is also described as "good news" and a "warner." Such good news is in each and every book that God revealed, and is the essence of the message of every prophet he sent. Why, then, has God called Jesus' book "Injīl"? The Qur'an does not explain explicitly the meaning of "Injīl," but I will show how it explains the name indirectly.

In looking for a clue in the Qur'an to the meaning of "Injīl," we need to look for a reference to "good news" specifically in association with the story of Jesus. There are indeed two instances where the verb *yubashshir* (brings good news) and the active participle *mubashshran* (bringing good news) occur in verses that recount the story of Jesus.

Historically, the first instance in which the verbal form *yubashshir* appears is when the angels tell the virgin Mary that they have come to bring to her the good news from God about a Word. This Word, as we saw earlier (pp. 96-97), denotes the divine command for the virginal conception and the birth of Jesus to take place:

> When the angels said: "O Mary! Allah gives you the good news of a Word from Him, whose name is the Messiah, Jesus son of Mary, who is illustrious in this world and the hereafter, and who is one of those brought near [to Allah] (3.45). He shall speak to people in the cradle and when middle-aged, and he shall be one of the righteous" (3.46).

Deriving Injīl from this instance of good news is doubtful. **First**, Mary's conception of Jesus is not the only miraculous conception or birth that the Qur'an describes as good news. The births of prophets Isaac and John to very old parents are both called "good news":

> And his (Abraham's) wife was standing there; she laughed, and we gave her the good news of [the birth of] Isaac and after him Jacob (11.71). She said: "What! Shall I bear a son when I am an old woman and this, my husband, is an old man? Surely this is an astonishing thing" (11.72).
>
> [It was said to him:] "O Zechariah! We bring to you the good news of [the birth of] a son whose name is John; we have not created someone similar to him before" (19.7).

Also, the term "good news" in verse 11.71 is applied to an instance of normal birth, which is that of Jacob, in addition to Isaac's miraculous birth. The fact that the term "good news" can be used for any birth, because the birth of any child is a happy event, is shown in the following verse which describes the negative attitude of Arabs before Islam to the birth of female children:

> And if one of them is given the good news of [the birth of] a female, his face would darken and he would be filled with suppressed anger (16.58).

So it is very unlikely that the Qur'an called Jesus' book "Injīl" after the "good news" of his conception and birth. The fact that God described Jesus' conception as "good news" had nothing to do with its miraculous nature. If Jesus' conception was going to be normal, the divine messenger who was sent to inform Mary of that conception would have still described his task as delivering "good news."

Second, there is no logic in naming Jesus' book after a description of his conception and birth. Jesus' conception and birth, albeit miraculous, were not related to his book or to him receiving a divine book. Other prophets received books without being conceived by miracles. Also, the Injīl is a book that carried a message to people, so calling it after the good news of the conception and birth of the messenger would have had nothing to do with the function of the book. Bringing the good news to Mary about Jesus was a single past event that using it as the name for Jesus' book would have made little sense.

We are, then, left with the only other mention of good news in the story of Jesus in the Qur'an. In this instance, the active participle *mubashshran* (bringing good news) is used:

> And when Jesus son of Mary said: "O Children of Israel! I am a messenger of Allah to you, confirming that which was revealed before me of the Torah, and bringing good news about a messenger who will come after me, whose name is Aḥmad." But when he (Jesus) came to them with clear proofs, they said: "This is clear magic" (61.6).

Jesus told the Jews that his message was about confirming the verity of the Torah and delivering the good news about the coming of a future messenger called "Aḥmad." This word shares the root *ḥamd* (praise) with the name "Muḥammad." Muḥammad means "highly praised" or "highly celebrated." Aḥmad is a comparative which some suggest means "more praised" and others "more praising." In the latter case it is taken to mean "more praising of God." In the other four times in which the name of the Prophet is mentioned in the Qur'an (3.144, 33.40, 47.2, 48.29) it appears as "Muḥammad," so why is it "Aḥmad" in Jesus' prophecy? All four mentions of Muḥammad occur in words attributed to God, whereas Aḥmad appears on Jesus' lips. The fact that Jesus' uses the *comparative* Aḥmad as the name of the future Messenger *after* mentioning his own message suggests that he wanted to say that the future Messenger is even *greater* than him. Jesus must have used for the name of that Prophet an equivalent word for Aḥmad in the language of the people he was speaking to.

Confirming the truth of the Torah was done mainly through the book that was revealed to Jesus. The *giving of good news about the future prophet* was part of Jesus' message, so it must have also been contained in that book. It is logical for this book then to derive its name from that part of the message. There is indeed another verse that states that Prophet Muhammad is mentioned in both the Torah and the Injīl:

> Those (the believers) who follow the Messenger, the unlettered Prophet, whom they find mentioned in the Torah and the Injīl which they have: He will enjoin on them that which is right and forbid them that which is evil; he will make lawful for them all good

things and prohibit for them only the foul; and he will relieve them of their burden and the yokes that are upon them. Those who believe in him, honor him, help him, and follow the light which is sent down with him — those are the successful (7.157).

The fact that Muhammad is mentioned in the Torah of Moses also confirms the special and unique status of this Prophet and the explanation above of Jesus' naming of Muḥammad as "Aḥmad." This Prophet is called "highly praised" in the Injīl and Torah, but Jesus called him "more praised" when talking to people to emphasize his superiority and adjure people to follow that Prophet and not accept Jesus' prophethood only.

It was so clear to the Jews and the Christians, who had the Torah and the Injīl, that Muhammad was the Prophet they were promised and commanded to follow that they could recognize him as they recognize their offspring:

> Those to whom We have given the Book recognize him as they recognize their sons, and a party of them conceal the truth which they themselves know (2.146).

The pronoun which I translated as "him" above is translated as "it" by those who take it to mean the Qur'an not the Prophet of the Qur'an. While the latter translation is linguistically possible, likening the People of the Book's recognition of the object of the verse to their recognition of their sons strongly indicates that the referent is a human being, i.e. Muhammad not the book that was sent with him.

The following verse states that the likeness of Prophet Muhammad and his followers are mentioned in the Torah and the Injīl:

> Muhammad is the Messenger of Allah. And those with him are hard against the disbelievers but merciful among themselves. You see them bowing and falling prostrate in worship, seeking favor from Allah and His acceptance. Their marks are on their faces from the traces of prostration. Such is their likeness in the Torah and their likeness in the Injīl: like a seed which sent forth its blade, and then strengthened it; then it became thick, then it stood firm on its stalk, delighting the sowers, to enrage the disbelievers with them. Allah has promised those of them who believe and do good deeds forgiveness and great reward (48.29).

This verse is reminiscent of the following passage in Mark:

> He [Jesus] also said, "The kingdom of God is like someone who spreads seed on the ground. He goes to sleep and gets up, night and day, and the seed sprouts and grows, though he does not know how. By itself the soil produces a crop, first the stalk, then the head, then the full grain in the head. And when the grain is ripe, he sends in the sickle because the harvest has come." (Mark 4:26-29)

The clear similarities between the two passages suggest that the passage in Mark is based on the original passage in the Injīl that verse 48.29 mentions. Another important difference between the Injīl's passage and Mark's is that the former, by definition, is God's words, in the same way that verse 48.29 is the words of God, whereas Mark presents it as a saying of Jesus. This is another instance of contextual displacement.

We have covered so far 11 out of the 12 verses that mention the Injīl. For completeness, this is the remaining verse:

> O People of the Book! Why do you argue about Abraham, when the Torah and the Injīl were not sent down till after him? Have you no sense? (3.65).

This verse mentions the Injīl in the context of stressing that Abraham could not been considered as a Jew or Christian as both the Torah and Injīl were revealed after his.

My conclusion is that God called Jesus' book "Injīl" because it contained the good news about the future coming of Prophet Muhammad.

17.4. The Paraclete

Muslim scholars have identified a term in the New Testament that they think denotes Prophet Muhammad and is therefore linked to Jesus' prophecy in verse 61.6: "bringing good news about a messenger who will come after me, whose name is Aḥmad." The term in question appears in the Greek New Testament as *parakletos* (παράκλητος). Let's first look at the occurrences of this term in the New Testament, and then see how it is linked to the name of Prophet Muhammad and ultimately Jesus' prophecy of verse 61.6.

While not found in the Septuagint, *parakletos* is found outside and earlier than the New Testament. According to the *Theological Dictionary of the New Testament*, the use of *parakletos* as a noun is attested in secular Greek from the 4th century BCE. where it appears in the sense of a "person called in to help" or "summoned to give assistance," giving the meaning of "helper in court" (Behm, 1970: 801). Behm concludes that "the history of the term in the whole sphere of known Greek and Hellenistic usage outside the NT yields the clear picture of a legal adviser or helper or advocate in the relevant court" (Behm, 1970: 803).

This term, which is anglicized as "paraclete," is said to have a wide range of meanings, including "intercessor," "counselor," and "helper." There is no equivalent English word that provides all the nuances of the meanings of "paraclete," hence the use of different words by different translators of the New Testament. For instance, the *International Standard Version, New American Standard , English Standard Version,* and *New King James Version* translate the term as "helper; the *American Standard Version* and *King James Version* render it as "comforter"; the *New International Version* uses "counselor"; and the *New English Translation (NET)* has it as "advocate." This is how the translators of the NET Bible, which is used in this book, explain their decision to choose "advocate":

"Advocate," the word chosen for this translation, has more forensic overtones than the Greek word does, although in John 16:5-11 a forensic context is certainly present. Because an "advocate" is someone who "advocates" or supports a position or viewpoint and since this is what the Paraclete will do for the preaching of the disciples, it was selected in spite of the drawbacks.

"Paraclete" is found 5 times in the New Testament — 4 times in the Gospel of John in Jesus' sermon to his disciples after the Last Supper and once in the First Epistle of John. This term, whose origin is the subject of much debate (Porsch, 1993: 29), is introduced without any explanation:

Then I will ask the Father, and he will give you another Advocate to be with you forever. (John 14:16)

But the Advocate, the Holy Spirit, whom the Father will send in my name, will teach you everything, and will cause you to remember everything I said to you. (John 14:26)

When the Advocate comes, whom I will send you from the Father — the Spirit of truth who goes out from the Father — he will testify about me. (John 15:26)

But I tell you the truth, it is to your advantage that I am going away. For if I do not go away, the Advocate will not come to you, but if I go, I will send him to you. (John 16:7)

(My little children, I am writing these things to you so that you may not sin.) But if anyone does sin, we have an advocate with the Father, Jesus Christ the righteous One. (1 John 2:1)

Apart from the *New International Version* all of the Bible translations mentioned earlier use "advocate" for 1 John 2:1. This version still translates the term as meaning someone who speaks in defense of others, which also means "advocate." This agreement is reflects the fact that the passage is very suggestive of an advocate of the sinning Christians, whereas the disagreement on the translation of the Gospel four passages is the result of the unclear nature of how the term is used.

We should point out first that there are fundamental differences between how the term paraclete is used by in the Gospel and how it is used in the Epistle. The latter uses the term unambiguously to denote Jesus, where he is said to intercede on behalf of people with God, so Jesus and the paraclete are one and the same. The Gospel, on the other hand, is equally unambiguous but in making the exact opposite assertion that the paraclete is not Jesus. All four Gospel passages stress that the paraclete is distinct from Jesus. The paraclete would come only after Jesus had left (John 16:7), and the "very fact that they [the "paraclete" passages] appear as part of Jesus' farewell to his disciples reinforces the connection between Jesus' departure and the coming of the paraclete" (Brown, 1970: 1136). Also, unlike Jesus, he would stay with them "forever" (John 14:16). One passage identifies the paraclete with the "Holy Spirit" (John 14:26) and another with the "Spirit of truth" (John 15:26).

Although the First Epistle of John is usually attributed to the author of the Gospel of John, the two sources use the term "paraclete" clearly differently. This is what the *Theological Dictionary of the New Testament* has to say about the inconsistent use of the term paraclete in the two sources:

> The use of the term παράκλητος in the NT, though restricted to the Johannine writings, does not make any consistent impression, nor does it fit smoothly into the history of the word as described [earlier]. In 1 John 2:1, where Jesus Christ is called the παράκλητος of sinning Christians before the Father, the meaning is obviously "advocate," and the image of a trial before God's court determines the meaning. In John 16:7-11 (cf. 15:26) we again find the idea of a trial in which the Paraclete, the Spirit, appears (16:8-11). The Spirit, however, is not the defender of the disciples before God — nor the advocate of God or Christ before men, which involves an unwarranted shift of thought — but their counsel in relation to the world. Nor is the legal metaphor adhered to strictly. What is said about the sending, activity and nature of this paraclete (16:7, 16:13-15, 15:26, 14:14 f, 14:26) belongs to a very different sphere, and here (cf. Jesus in 14:16) παράκλητος seems to have the broad and general sense of "helper." The only thing one can say for certain is that the sense of "comforter" .... does not fit any of the NT passages. Neither Jesus nor the Spirit is described as "comforter." (Behm, 1970: 803-804)

The Gospel's identification of the paraclete with the Holy Spirit has faced a number of objections. **First**, it has been pointed out by those who link the paraclete to Prophet Muhammad is that John speaks about the paraclete as if he is a person — a description that does not apply to the Holy Spirit (Bucaille, 1995: 102-106). Indeed, it is generally accepted that "the paraclete is more clearly personal than is the Holy Spirit in many TN passages" (Brown, 1970: 1139). But expectedly, Christian scholars look at this issue differently. They consider John's personal presentation of the Holy Spirit as an extension to, rather than a contradiction with, its image outside that Gospel. This is what the *Interpreter's Dictionary of the Bible* has to say about this issue:

> The use of masculine pronouns and adjectives (John 14:16: "another"; 14:26: "he"; 16:13: "he") shows that the Spirit is regarded as fully personal; indeed, the "paraclete" passages of the Fourth Gospel mark the most highly

developed thought in the NT in respect of the personality of the Spirit of God. (Lampe, 1962: 654)

But the French researcher Maurice Bucaille adds that the descriptions given to the paraclete matches those of Prophet Muhammad:

> According to the rules of logic therefore, one is brought to see in John's Paraclete a human being like Jesus, possessing the faculties of hearing and speech formally implied in John's Greek text. Jesus therefore predicts that God will later send a human being to Earth to take up the role defined by John, i.e. to be a prophet who hears God's word and repeats his message to man. This is the logical interpretation of John's texts arrived at if one attributes to the words their proper meaning.
>
> The presence of the term "Holy Spirit" in today's text could easily have come from a later addition made quite deliberately. It may have been intended to change the original meaning which predicted the advent of a prophet subsequent to Jesus and was therefore in contradiction with the teachings of the Christian churches at the time of their formation; these teachings maintain that Jesus was the last of the prophets. (Bucaille, 1995: 106)

Second, it has also been noted that in a 4th or 5th century Syriac manuscript of the Gospel of John passage 14:26 omits the word "Holy" in the only passage that identifies the paraclete with the Holy Spirit, thus talking about "the Advocate, the Spirit, whom the Father...." This is taken to mean that the identification of the paraclete with the Holy Spirit was contentious and might not have been in John's original manuscripts. This objection is usually rejected by pointing out that John wrote originally in Greek and that all Greek manuscripts have the word "Holy," so the variation in the Syriac manuscript was introduced by the process of translation.

Third, Islamic commentators have noted that the paraclete designates a *future human being* who would come after Jesus and deliver a message similar to his, so the paraclete could not be the Holy Spirit. The Holy Spirit was already with the believers (Al-Kadhi, 1996). A number of New Testament scholars have also pointed out that the paraclete was originally identified with a *future figure of salvation* and that its confusion with the Holy Spirit happened later. This is what the highly regarded scholarly Biblical commentary series *The Anchor Bible* has to say:

> The word paraklētos is peculiar in the NT to the Johannine literature. In 1 John 2:1 Jesus is a paraklētos (not a title), serving as a heavenly intercessor with the Father. In five passages in John (14:15-16, 14:26, 15:26-27, 16:7-11, 16:12-14) the title paraklētos is given to someone who is not Jesus, nor an intercessor, nor in heaven. Christian tradition has identified this figure as

the Holy Spirit, but scholars like Spitta, Delafosse, Windisch, Sasse, Bultmann, and Betz have doubted whether this identification is true to the original picture and have suggested that the Paraclete was once an independent salvific figure, later confused with the Holy Spirit. (Brown, 1970: 1135)

Indeed, it is this understanding of the paraclete that made some individuals claim to be the paraclete mentioned by Jesus. Montanus, who founded the Christian movement Montanism in the 2nd century, and the Persian preacher Mani (216–274? CE), the founder of the religion of Manichaeism, both claimed to be the paraclete. The eminent Church leader Tertullian, who introduced the terms *trinitas* (trinity) and *novum testamentum* (New Testament), defected at some point from Catholicism to Montanism.

The translation of paraclete as "comforter" or "consoler" has also been particularly criticized as being contradictory to Christian thought:

① The belief that the death of Jesus upon the Cross redeemed the believers from the curse of original sin, and that his spirit, grace, and presence in the Eucharist would be forever with them, left them in need of no consolation nor of the coming of a consoler at all. On the other hand, if they needed such a comforter, then all the Christian presumptions and pretentions concerning the sacrifice of Calvary fall to the ground....

② Consolation can never make restitution of the loss. To console a man who has lost his sight, wealth, son, or situation, cannot restore any of those losses. The promise that a consoler would be sent by God after Jesus had gone would indicate the total collapse of all hope in the triumph of the Kingdom of God. The promise of a consoler indicates mourning and lamentation and would naturally drive the Apostles into disappointment if not into despair. They needed, not a consoler in their distress and afflictions, but a victorious warrior to crush the Devil and his power, one who would put an end to their troubles and persecutions. (Dawud, 1994: 212)

The use of the term "paraclete" in the Johannine writings is clearly inconsistent and highly ambiguous. It looks as if John was aware of the term but was not sure about what it stood for so every time he mentioned it he gave it a meaning, but these meanings are inconsistent. John knew that his readers were not familiar with the term "paraclete" which is why he identifies it three times for his audience — once with someone who shared with Jesus some things (John 14:16), in another with the "Spirit of truth" (John 15:26), and in a third passage with the "the Spirit of truth" (John 15:26). One scholar notes that the Evangelist must have been aware that this title was not self-explanatory as he accompanies each mention of the term with an account of the paraclete's function (Lindars, 1981: 63). The author of 1

John 2:1 also felt the need for identification, so he told his readers that the paraclete is Jesus himself.

The discussion above clearly supports the efforts for a different identification of the paraclete. But what evidence is there for identifying the paraclete with Prophet Muhammad?

This controversial identification was made at least as early as the 8th century by Ibn Isḥāq (ca. 704 - 767) in his history of Islam and Prophet Muhammad, and it has been the focus of an ongoing argument between Muslims and non-Muslims ever since. We do not have Ibn Isḥāq's original writings, but Ibn Hishām's (died 833 CE) famous biography of the Prophet is a freely edited version of Ibn Isḥāq's work. This biography is the main source of other biographies of the Prophet. This is the passage of interest in Ibn Hishām's book:

> Ibn Isḥāq said: "Among the things that have reached me of what Jesus son of Mary had stated in the Injīl — which was revealed to him by Allah for the people of the Injīl — about the signs of the Messenger of Allah, which was set down by John the disciple for the people of the Injīl, when he wrote for them the Injīl about the covenant of Jesus son of Mary with them regarding the Messenger of Allah that he said: 'He who hates me, hates the Lord. Had I not performed in front of them works that no one before me had done, they would not have had any sin. But they showed conceit and thought that they would overpower me and the Lord. But the word of the Law has to be fulfilled: 'they hated me for no reason', i.e. unjustly. And when the *munhamanna* who is sent by Allah to you comes, and the holy spirit that is with the Lord comes out, he will testify to me, and so you. Because you had been with me from the beginning. I said to you: 'so that you do not complain'".
>
> The *munhamanna* in Syriac means "Muhammad" (highly praised), and in Greek it is "faraklete."

It is unclear whether the last sentence is Ibn Hishām's or part of his quote of Ibn Isḥāq's, but I have left it outside the quotation.

Ibn Isḥāq's quote from John is clearly related to the following passage from that Gospel:

> The one who hates me hates my Father too. If I had not performed among them the miraculous deeds that no one else did, they would not be guilty of sin. But now they have seen the deeds and have hated both me and my Father. Now this happened to fulfill the word that is written in their law, 'They hated me without reason.' When the Advocate comes, whom I will send you from the Father — the Spirit of truth who goes out from the Father — he will testify about me, and you also will testify, because you have been with me from the beginning (John 15:23-27).

The term "faraklete" in Ibn Hishām's text is an arabicization of *parakletos* in John's Greek text; it is not uncommon for the letter "p" to be changed to "f" when a non-Arabic word is arabicized.

It is not clear whether Ibn Isḥāq was aware of or neglected other Johannine passages that mention paraclete, or whether he used a manuscript in which paraclete is mentioned only once. In a comment on the passage above in his translation of Ibn Hishām's work, Guillaume suggests that Ibn Isḥāq's citation comes from the Palestinian Syriac Lectionary and not from the ordinary Bible of the Syriac-speaking Churches (Guillaume, 1955: 104). Ibn Isḥāq's citation of the Syriac term *munhamanna* suggests that he had access to a Syriac version, although it is not clear whether his citation of its Greek equivalent comes from a Greek version of the Gospel of John or a Greek lexicon.

I should note that Guillaume's translation of Ibn Isḥāq's passage, which is used by most commentators who cannot use the Arabic origin, is rather misleading, as it is influenced by his preconception of what Ibn Isḥāq *should have said*. Guillaume translates the first occurrence of the Syriac *munhamanna* in Ibn Isḥāq's passage as "Comforter." This is what Guillaume thinks the term should mean, not what Ibn Isḥāq meant to say, as the latter believed that the term meant "highly praised."

Knowing that early Muslim writers said that the Gospel of John contains a term, pronounced in Greek as "faraklete," that meant "highly praised" and which described a future messenger, later Muslim scholars concluded that the term *parakletos* that exists in the available Greek versions of the Gospel of John must mean "highly praised," and is the term that describes the Prophet Muhammad. The problem with this conclusion is that *parakletos* does not mean "highly praised." The logical conclusion, as identified by Professor Abdu Allah Dawud — a Roman Catholic priest who converted to Islam early in the 20th century — is that *parakletos* (παράκλητος) is actually a corrupted form of the completely different Greek word *periklytos* (περικλυτός). The Greek spellings of these two words differ in three vowels. It is *periklytos* that has exactly the same meaning as "Muhammad" or "highly praised" and which was the original term in the text (Dawud, 1994: 198-223). In other words, Dawud points out that early Muslim scholars talked about a different word from the one found in the surviving manuscripts of John.

Significantly, all the four instances of *parakletos* in the Gospel of John occur on Jesus' lips, which is exactly how the name "Aḥmad," which is derived from the name Muhammad or *periklytos* in the Injīl, appears in the Qur'an:

> And when Jesus son of Mary said: "O Children of Israel! I am a messenger of Allah to you, confirming that which was revealed before me of the Torah, and bringing good news about a messenger who will come after me, whose name is Aḥmad." But when he (Jesus) came to them with clear proofs, they said: "This is clear magic" (61.6).

Dawud also questions the accepted translation of *parakletos* as "comforter:

The "Paraclete" does not signify either "consoler" or "advocate"; in truth, it is not a classical word at all. The Greek orthography of the word is Paraklytos which in ecclesiastical literature is made to mean "one called to aid, advocate, intercessor" (Dict. Grec.-Francais, by Alexandre). One need not profess to be a Greek scholar to know that the Greek word for "comforter or consoler" is not "Paraclytos" but "Paracalon." I have no Greek version of the Septuagint with me, but I remember perfectly well that the Hebrew word for "comforter" ("mnāḥem") in the Lamentations of Jeremiah (i. 2, 9, 16, 17, 21, etc.) is translated into Parakaloon, from the verb Parakaloo, which means to call to, invite, exhort, console, pray, invoke. It should be noticed that there is a long alpha vowel after the consonant kappa in the "Paracalon" which does not exist in the "Paraclytos." In the phrase ("He who consoles us in all our afflictions") "paracalon" and not "paraclytos" is used. ("I exhort, or *invite, thee to work*"). Many other examples can be cited here.

There is another Greek word for comforter and consoler, i.e. "Parygorytys" from "I console."

As to the other meaning of "intercessor or advocate" which is given in the ecclesiastical word "Paraclete," I again insist that "Paracalon" and not "Paraclytos" can convey in itself a similar sense. The proper Greek term for "advocate" is *Sunegorus* and for "intercessor" or "mediator" *Meditéa*. (Dawud, 1994: 208-209)

The Islamic interpretation that the paraclete is Prophet Muhammad assumes that *parakletos* in the surviving manuscripts of Johannine writings is a corrupted form of *periklytos*. There is no direct evidence that earlier versions of the Johannine writings used the term *periklytos*, but if Ibn Isḥāq was not mistaken, then his words may be seen as indirect evidence. This assumption is perfectly possible, as the New Testament books went through far more substantial changes than this rather minor one. Another possibility is that the term was originally wrongly copied by the author(s) of the Gospel of John and the First Epistle of John from its source.

However, there is strong circumstantial evidence that supports the Islamic identification of *parakletos* with Prophet Muhammad. Even if the New Testament had used a Greek term that was not easily related to the name "Muhammad," there would have still been good reasons to think that it referred to the Prophet who was going to come after Jesus. The fact that this Prophet is identified with a term that is so close to another word that means "Muhammad" makes it very likely that the current term is a corrupted form of a term that originally referred to Prophet Muhammad.

Unsurprisingly, some scholars have also tried to show that the current paraclete passages apply to Prophet Muhammad. For instance, one commentator notes that the paraclete would be with the believers forever (John 14:16), and Muhammad is the last prophet whose law will stay forever (As-Saqqā, 1972: 53); and the paraclete would testify about Jesus (John 15:26), and Muhammad testified to the verity of the message of Jesus (As-Saqqā, 1972: 57-58). The latter point is logical, but the former is not as strong as the alternative view that the concept of staying forever with the believers is a *corruption* of the fact that Muhammad is the last Prophet. As a general observation, however, it would require too much stretching of the Johannine text to make it *all* applicable to Prophet Muhammad. It is only logical to expect that much more details than the term *periklytos* have been tampered with or completely made up by the authors of those passages. So while it is legitimate to try and see how some passages can be related to Prophet Muhammad, this cannot be done to the whole text in its current form.

To sum up, the Islamic position that Jesus spread the good news about Muhammad stems from the Qur'an's statement that Jesus told people about the forthcoming mission of Prophet Muhammad and that the latter was mentioned in both the Torah and Injīl. But there is also strong independent circumstantial evidence that the *parakletos* passages in the New Testament are based on Jesus' original good news about the coming of Prophet Muhammad.

17.5. The Injīl and the Law

The Qur'an states that Jesus was commanded to legalize some things that had been unlawful to the Jews in their law. Before we study the Injīl's modification of the law, we first need to study what the New Testament says about Jesus' attitude toward the law.

17.5.1. Jesus and the Law in the New Testament

Jesus' attitude to the law has been a hotly debated subject among theologians and historians. The main disagreements stem from differences about: i) the interpretation of the Jewish law; ii) the authenticity of New Testament pericopes that discuss Jesus' position from the law; and iii) the meanings of these passages. A detailed discussion of this major topic is outside the scope of the current book, so I will restrict myself to a concise review that provides enough information to understand the differences and similarities between Jesus' attitude toward the law in the New Testament and its equivalent in the Qur'an.

That Jesus objected to parts of the law has been the view of many New Testament scholars. It is usually claimed that Jesus *intensified the moral norm* and *relaxed the ritual norm*. The classical example that is often used to show that Jesus accentuated the moral law is the "antitheses" in his sermon to his disciples on the mountain:

> You have heard that it was said to an older generation, 'Do not murder,' and 'whoever murders will be subjected to judgment.' But I say to you that anyone who is angry with a brother will be subjected to judgment....
>
> You have heard that it was said, 'Do not commit adultery.' But I say to you that whoever looks at a woman to desire her has already committed adultery with her in his heart....
>
> It was said, 'Whoever divorces his wife must give her a legal document.' But I say to you that everyone who divorces his wife, except for immorality, makes her commit adultery, and whoever marries a divorced woman commits adultery.
>
> Again, you have heard that it was said to an older generation, 'Do not break an oath, but fulfill your vows to the Lord.' But I say to you, do not take oaths at all — not by heaven, because it is the throne of God....
>
> You have heard that it was said, 'An eye for an eye and a tooth for a tooth.' But I say to you, do not resist the evildoer. But whoever strikes you on the right cheek, turn the other to him as well....
>
> You have heard that it was said, 'Love your neighbor' and 'hate your enemy.' But I say to you, love your enemy and pray for those who persecute you. (Matt. 5:21-44)

Jesus here is not calling for the transgression of the law or replacing those six commandments with others he introduced, but he is intensifying and accentuating those laws. As noted by Sanders (1995: 210), "no one who observed the admonitions of Matthew 5 would transgress the law, and Jesus does not propose that any part of the Mosaic law should be repealed." The fact that Jesus meant to heighten rather than oppose the law is clearly seen in his words that precede the six antitheses:

> Do not think that I have come to abolish the law or the prophets. I have not come to abolish these things but to fulfill them. I tell you the truth, until heaven and earth pass away not the smallest letter or stroke of a letter will pass from the law until everything takes place. So anyone who breaks one of the least of these commands and teaches others to do so will be called least in the kingdom of heaven, but whoever obeys them and teaches others to do so will be called great in the kingdom of heaven. For I tell you, unless your righteousness goes beyond that of the experts in the law and the Pharisees, you will never enter the kingdom of heaven. (Matt. 5:17-20)

Observing the Sabbath and eating clean food only are the two main legal requirements that Jesus' is said to have called to be relaxed. The controversial text about the cleanness of food is found in Mark. In this passage, some Pharisees and experts in the law criticized Jesus' disciples because they ate without washing their hands. The Evangelist explains that "the Pharisees and all the Jews do not eat unless they perform a ritual washing, holding fast to the tradition of the elders" (Mark 7:3). This statement is historically inaccurate. Not all Jews washed their hands before eating. This was only a Pharisaic tradition — but one that even some Pharisees considered optional. Jesus replied by scolding the Pharisees for their transgression of the law, then he called a crowd and told them: "There is nothing outside of a person that can defile him by going into him. Rather, it is what comes out of a person that defiles him." When he was alone with his disciples they asked him about the meaning of this parable, and he answered: "Don't you understand that whatever goes into a person from outside cannot defile him? For it does not enter his heart but his stomach, and then goes out into the sewer." The Evangelist follows Jesus' reply by an explanatory comment of his own stating that "this means all foods are clean" (Mark 7:15-19).

Mark is certain about what Jesus meant, but Matthew undermines this certainty as he gives us a significantly different version of the same incident:

> Then he called the crowd to him and said, "Listen and understand. What defiles a person is not what goes into the mouth; it is what comes out of the mouth that defiles a person." Then the disciples came to him and said, "Do you know that when the Pharisees heard this saying they were offended?" And he replied, "Every plant that my heavenly Father did not plant will be uprooted. Leave them! They are blind guides. If someone who is blind leads another who is blind, both will fall into a pit." But Peter said to him, "Explain this parable to us." Jesus said, "Even after all this, are you still so foolish? Don't you understand that whatever goes into the mouth enters the stomach and then passes out into the sewer? But the things that come out of the mouth come from the heart, and these things defile a person. For out of the heart come evil ideas, murder, adultery, sexual immorality, theft, false testimony, slander. These are the things that defile a person; it is not eating with unwashed hands that defiles a person." (Matt. 15:10-20)

One difference is the absence of a statement equivalent to Mark's emphatic words that "nothing outside of a person that can defile him by going into him." Matthew also, significantly, does not have the Markan pronouncement that "all foods are clean." Finally, Matthew suggests that the defiling that Jesus' denied was the supposed result of eating without washing the hands, not eating unclean foods.

The fact that Jesus did not declare that all food is legal to eat can also be read in the report of a vision that the disciple Peter saw some time after Jesus' resurrection:

> He saw heaven opened and an object something like a large sheet descending, being let down to earth by its four corners. In it were all kinds of four-footed animals and reptiles of the earth and wild birds. Then a voice said to him, "Get up, Peter; slaughter and eat!" But Peter said, "Certainly not, Lord, for I have never eaten anything defiled and ritually unclean!" The voice spoke to him again, a second time, "What God has made clean, you must not consider ritually unclean!" This happened three times, and immediately the object was taken up into heaven. (Acts 10:11-16)

Had Peter heard Jesus say that all food was clean, this vision would have been meaningless and Peter's reaction would have made no sense.

The Gospels carry reports of Jews accusing Jesus of violating the Sabbath (John 9:16). In one incident condemned by Jesus' enemies, he defended his hungry disciples who, on a Sabbath, picked heads of wheat in a field and ate them (Mark 2:23-27; Matt. 12:1-4; Luke 6:1:4). He was also strongly criticized for healing on the Sabbath (Mark 3:2-5; Matt. 12:10-13; Luke 6:7-10, 13:10-14, 14:3-4; John 5:5-10). Jesus defended himself against the accusation that these actions broke the Sabbath. He never encouraged or authorized violating the Sabbath or any other parts of the law. Jesus' positive view of his actions aside, his behaviors have been seen by scholars also to be open to different interpretations some of which do not attribute to him opposing any law. For a concise and informative discussion of Jesus' attitude toward the Sabbath and other legal issues the reader may consult Sanders (1995: 205-237) and Theissen and Merz (1999: 357-372).

Acts and Paul's letters recount sharp disputes that Paul had with prominent early Christians because of his abolishment of certain legal requirements. He dropped circumcision as a requirement from Gentiles who convert to Christianity (e.g. Rom. 2:25-29, 3:29-30; 1 Cor. 7:18-19). Paul and Barnabas, who had been preaching the Gentiles that circumcision is not necessary to be saved, traveled from Antioch to Jerusalem to sort out with the apostles and elders the disagreement that this teaching has created. This was about 17 years after Paul's conversion. There was a heated debate about the observance of Moses' law at the end of which James decided that the Gentiles can be exempted from circumcision. James also said that the Gentiles should be sent a letter telling them that they should simply "abstain from meat that has been sacrificed to idols and from blood and from what has been strangled and from sexual immorality." If the Gentile converts avoided these four, the letter stated, they would be fine (Acts 15:29).

It is difficult to know what to make of this amazing reduction of the law to four prohibitions. Not even the rest of the Ten Commandments are listed in the letter. On the one hand, Paul's mere exemption of the Gentile converts from circumcision started an uneasy debate between the early Christian teachers; on the other, the Gentiles were allowed to get away with a very watered down version of the law! Something seems to be wrong or missing. Paul succeeded in differentiating between himself as the apostle to the Gentiles and Peter and others as apostles to the Jews. He did not want the Mosaic law to apply to the Gentile converts, and he surely got his way:

> When James, Cephas, and John, who had a reputation as pillars, recognized the grace that had been given to me, they gave to Barnabas and me the right hand of fellowship, agreeing that we would go to the Gentiles and they to the circumcised. They requested only that we remember the poor, the very thing I also was eager to do. (Gal. 2:9-10)

In the following passage from the same letter, Paul tells us about another conflict that he had with Peter and Barnabas about another law which prevented the Jews from eating with the Gentiles:

> But when Cephas came to Antioch, I opposed him to his face, because he had clearly done wrong. Until certain people came from James, he had been eating with the Gentiles. But when they arrived, he stopped doing this and separated himself because he was afraid of those who were pro-circumcision. And the rest of the Jews also joined with him in this hypocrisy, so that even Barnabas was led astray with them by their hypocrisy. But when I saw that they were not behaving consistently with the truth of the gospel, I said to Cephas in front of them all, "If you, although you are a Jew, live like a Gentile and not like a Jew, how can you try to force the Gentiles to live like Jews?" We are Jews by birth and not Gentile sinners. (Gal. 2:11-15)

Paul also sharply criticized those who stressed that all must observe "religious days and months and seasons and years" (Gal. 4:10), which probably include the Sabbath. Paul saw a conflict between accepting the law as the path to obedience and salvation and the role of Jesus, which is the reason behind his unrelenting insistence on demoting the law: "I do not set aside God's grace, because if righteousness could come through the law, then Christ died for nothing" (Gal. 2:21).

Paul also did not believe that the food laws were of any significance, and he did not think that they played any role in people's nearness to or remoteness from God. He preached that "the one who eats everything must not despise the one who does not, and the one who abstains must not judge the one who eats everything, for God has accepted him" (Rom. 14:3).

The disputes about the law between those early Christians show that Jesus had not taught the abolishment of any of those contentious laws. Had Jesus himself abrogated certain laws or taught that they can be transgressed, his immediate followers and later Christians would not have found themselves quarreling about these issues. Also significant is the fact that when any dilution of a law was introduced, Jesus was never quoted in support of the change. Even on the food law, which touches everyone's daily life, Jesus is not cited. Mark, for instance, could not ascribe the conclusion that "all foods are clean" — which is not justified by his own text and is, rightly and significantly, missing from Matthew's version — to Jesus. Paul also never claimed that the views he advocated on the law were Jesus'. Christianity's low view of the law has nothing to do with Jesus. One individual that has particularly influenced the development of this view is the apostle Paul.

The Gospels attribute to Jesus an ambivalent attitude toward the Jewish law. But this is not how Jesus viewed the law. His attitude toward the law is yet another victim of the confusion and contradiction in which the New Testament engulfs just about every aspect of his life and teachings. This ambivalence is created by the myriad of differing and inconsistent passages and stories. By the time the Gospels were written, various views had spread about what Jesus is supposed to have taught about the law. These views were more reflective of the thinking of those emerging communities than of Jesus' original teachings.

This is what one prominent scholar on the historical Jesus concludes:

> Jesus did not teach his disciples that they could break either the sabbath or the food laws. Had he gone around Galilee, teaching people that it was all right to work on the sabbath and to eat pork, there would have been an enormous outcry. A man who claimed to speak for God, but who taught that significant parts of God's law were not valid? Horrendous! Nowadays, non-Jewish readers may not see how terrible this would have been. Since sometime in the last half of the first century, most Christians have been Gentile. The mostly Gentile Christian church has been accepting parts of the Jewish law but not other parts for more than 1,900 years. Consequently, people today do not feel the shock that this position first occasioned when it surfaced, probably in the fifties, in Paul's debates with other Jewish Christians. Paul thought that Gentiles could become "children of Abraham" without being circumcised. The fight over this was bitter. Pious Jews — and most Jews were pious — thought that there really was a God, that he had given his law to Moses, that it was recorded in the scriptures, and that it should be obeyed. How in the world could anyone say that *parts* of it were invalid? Either all or nothing. If God gave it, it should be kept. If he did not, or if there was no God, then there was no point in keeping any of it. The difference between Paul's letters to the Galatians and the Romans, on the one hand, and Mark, on the other, is enormous. Mark calmly tosses in the sentence, "He declared all foods clean." Paul's letters crackle with the rage and hostility that *his* position on circumcision and food laws occasioned. Paul experienced the debate about the law firsthand. Mark (a second-generation Christian) did not, since it was largely over, nor did Jesus, since it had not yet arisen. The gospels do not contain the kind of material that would have been generated had Jesus taught his followers that they could disregard part of God's law. (Sanders, 1995: 220-221)

I fully agree with Sanders that the position of the law was gradually eroded in Christianity. But, following the Qur'an, I disagree with two fundamental statements he makes. **First**, the definition of the law is more flexible than the rigid picture Sanders paints. The law can be changed by its legislator, that is God. **Second**, Jesus was commanded by God to change certain flexible aspects of the law. I will discuss now how the Qur'an addresses both of these points.

17.5.2. The Injīl's Modification of the Law

The law in the Qur'an may be divided into two parts that may be described as *doctrinal* and *behavioral*. The doctrinal law covers various fundamental beliefs, such as the oneness of God, worship worthiness of God only, and necessity of the belief in all of His messengers. This part of the law never changed. At no point in history, for instance, God ordered some people to worship other than or others besides Him (e.g. 2.133, 14.52), or allowed people to believe in the message of one prophet but not another (2.4). All prophets received revelation of the same doctrinal law, which is why the Qur'an presents the messages or all of them as one and the same and describes each one of them as confirming the message of those who preceded him (e.g. 2.89, 3.50).

The behavioral part of the law covers various practices, rituals, and codes of conduct. It sets rules for daily life behaviors — such as marriage, inheritance, and foods — as well as behaviors that express doctrinal laws — such fasting and praying. Unlike doctrinal laws, behavioral laws — both religious and social — can change. For example, while the doctrinal law that one must worship God does not change, the way this commitment is expressed and practiced may change. For instance, the way one prays to God is not the same in all religions.

Let's look, for example, at some of the verses that talk about what the Qur'an says about food laws. The following two verses contrast the lawful and unlawful foods of the followers of Prophet Muhammad with those of the Jews (see also 2.173, 5.96, 6.118-121, 16.115, 22.30):

> Say [O Muhammad!]: "I do not find in that which has been revealed to me anything forbidden to be eaten by one who wishes to eat it, unless it is a dead animal, [poured] blood, the flesh of swine — for these are abomination — or impurity which is slaughtered as a sacrifice for other than Allah." But whosoever is forced by necessity, without exceeding the limit or transgressing, [for him] your Lord is forgiving, merciful (6.145). And for the Jews We forbade every animal with claws (undivided hoof), and We forbade them the fat of the cows and the sheep except what adheres to their backs or their entrails or what is mixed up with a bone. Thus We recompensed them for their rebellion. And We are Truthful (6.146).

A longer list of foods that are prohibited for Muslims is given in the following verse:

> It has been made forbidden to you [the following for food]: the dead animal, blood; the flesh of swine; that which is slaughtered as a sacrifice for other than Allah; that which is killed by strangling, by a violent blow, by a headlong fall, or by the goring of horns; that which has been [partly] eaten by a wild animal, unless you are able to slaughter it [before its death]; and that which is slaughtered [as a sacrifice] on stone altars.... But as for him who is forced [to eat any such meat] by severe hunger, with no inclination to sin, then surely Allah is forgiving, merciful (5.3).

The Qur'an then goes on to tell the followers of Prophet Muhammad: "The food of the People of the Book is lawful to you and your food is lawful to them" (5.5).

Verses 6.145-146 clearly state that the food laws of the Muslims and Jews differed. Verse 5.5, which includes the Christians also, implies the same. The ruling in verse 5.5 may also imply that the food that was made lawful to the Jews and Christians did not contain any of the foods that were made unlawful to Muslims. In other words, the Jews and Christian had been given stricter food laws. The Qur'an has also relaxed the laws of the Jews and Christians, making the food of the Muslims — which, for instance, includes fat of the cows and sheep — lawful to them.

Not only different religions may be given different food laws, but even the same religion may have its food laws changed. Verse 6.146 points out that some foods were forbidden for the Jews as some form of punishment, which means that they had been permissible before then. The fact that some of the unlawful foods were at some point lawful is highlighted more explicitly in this verse:

> Because of the wrongdoing of the Jews We made unlawful to them good things which had been made lawful for them, and because of their hindering many [people] from Allah's way (4.160).

In another verse, the Qur'an tells us that before the revelation of the Torah, all food was lawful for the Israelites except the foods that Jacob considered unlawful:

> All food was lawful to the Children of Israel except that which Israel had forbidden to himself, before the Torah was revealed. Say [O Muhammad!]: "Bring then the Torah and read it, if you are truthful" (3.93).

These verses leave no doubt that the laws on food, as well as on many laws on various practices and behaviors, change from time to time in different ways and for different reasons. But did Jesus bring any changes to the law?

Like the Torah, in which the Jewish law was revealed, the Injīl contained some form of a law the transgression of which is a sin:

> If they (the People of the Book) had observed the Torah, the Injīl, and that which was sent down to them from their Lord, they would have been nourished from above them and from beneath their feet. There is a moderate nation among them, but many of them follow an evil course (5.66).
>
> Say [O Muhammad!]: "O People of the Book! You follow no good till you observe the Torah, the Injīl, and that which was sent down to you from your Lord." That which was sent down to you [O Muhammad!] from your Lord is certain to increase many of them in contumacy and disbelief. But do not grieve for the disbelieving people (5.68).

The nature of the law of the Injīl and its relation to the law of the Torah is made clearer in another verse that states that part of Jesus' mission was to make lawful some of the things that God had made unlawful to the Jews in the Torah:

[I have come] to confirm that which was revealed before me of the Torah, and to make lawful some of that which was forbidden to you. I have come to you with a sign from your Lord, so keep your duty to Allah and obey me (3.50).

This verse, which gives another example of how behavioral laws may change, does not state explicitly that these abrogations were delivered specifically through the Injīl, and it may be suggested that they could have been communicated orally by Jesus. However, as the Injīl contained Jesus' message, I am inclined to believe that these changes were mentioned in that book. In the same way that the Jewish law was recorded in the Torah, the abrogations of parts of that law are almost certain to have also been revealed in a book. The Injīl, then, contained some legal commandments.

As noted by aṭ-Ṭabāṭabā'ī, this description of the Injīl's legal role also implies that, contrary to the common view among exegetes, the Injīl was sent to act as a *complement not a replacement* to the Torah. The Injīl did not contain a complete, new law that targeted followers of the new religion. Christians and Jews were commanded to continue to follow the law of Torah but with the modifications introduced in the Injīl.

This complementary, rather than substitutionary, relation of the Injīl with the Torah can also be concluded from these verses:

And We caused Jesus, son of Mary, to follow in their (the prophets') footsteps, confirming that which was revealed before him in the Torah, and We bestowed on him the Injīl wherein is guidance and a light, confirming that which was revealed before it in the Torah, and as a guidance and an admonition to the Allah-fearing (5.46). Let the People of the Injīl judge by that which Allah has sent down therein. Whoever does not judge by that which Allah has sent down, these are the transgressors (5.47).

The term "People of the Injīl" does not designate Christians only, as if the Jews were the "People of the Torah." Otherwise, the Injīl would have been a completely different law whose followers would have needed to abandon the Torah and follow the law in the new book. The "People of the Injīl" here means the people to whom the Injīl was sent, and that includes the followers of the Torah, because the Injīl was sent to all, and because it modified the law of the Torah. The "People of the Injīl" means the *people of the Torah and the Injīl* because the latter is based on and modifies the former. Significantly, later in the same chapter verses 5.66 and 5.68 call on the "People of the book" to observe *both* the "Torah" and the "Injīl." The "transgressors" in verse 5.47 denotes mainly the Jews who rejected the Injīl as a follow-up to the Torah.

It is clear that the Injīl, which was available to the Jews and Christians in Arabia at the time of the revelation of the Qur'an, is completely different from any Christian scriptures that exist today. While there are hints in the New Testament that Jesus relaxed and intensified some Jewish laws, the accounts are too confusing and contradictory to be certain of what Jesus is exactly supposed to have said and done. More important, the New Testament does not present clear modifications of the Jewish law. It attributes to Jesus vague and contradictory behaviors, and this could not have been how changes to a law that had been practiced for hundreds of year were communicated.

Parrinder (1995: 145) is completely wrong when he claims that "there is no suggestion in the Qur'an that the Gospel given to Jesus was different from the canonical Gospels held by Christians." The Qur'an's descriptions of the Injīl mean that it is a completely different book from the New Testament. The same applies to the original Torah, which is very different from the Old Testament, including the so-called Moses five books, which the Jews call "Torah."

Verse 3.50 does not detail what unlawful things Jesus made lawful. These most probably included foods, but they are also likely to have included other things. Had it been food or any one type of things only, the verse would have named that thing. The wording of the verse suggests that Jesus was commanded to relax the law of the Torah on a number of different things.

There is a critical point that I need to stress. The Qur'an's revelation that Jesus' relaxed parts of the Jewish law must not make us speculate on the nature of these laws and the level of relaxation by studying the law that Christianity adopted. Acts and the Pauline Epistles show that Paul played a major role in changing the law as he thought would better serve his purposes, with no reference to Jesus' teachings. For instance, we do not know what Jesus taught about the law on circumcision, but we know that Paul did not find it helpful in his efforts to convert Gentiles into Christianity, so he did away with it and managed to have other prominent early Christians to agree with him. All that we know from the Gospels about circumcision is that John the Baptists (Luke 1:59) and Jesus (2:21) were both circumcised on the eighth day, in compliance with the Jewish law, and that Jesus mentioned it in passing in one of his debates with people but without any indication that he opposed it or thought that it was not essential (John 7:22-23). The reason that circumcision is not an obligatory practice in Christianity is Paul, not Jesus. Paul demoted the law in Christianity by stressing the role of grace in salvation (e.g. Gal. 2:21, 5:4; Eph. 2:5-15). This is not to suggest that Paul advocated a complete abolishment of the law, as his statements on the law involved considerable inconsistency, but the outcome of his words and actions has been the demotion of the law to a great extent. Someone who declares that Jesus "nullified in his flesh the law of commandments in decrees" (Eph. 2:15) is surely much closer to abolishing the law than enforcing it. The very loose sense of the law and weak attachment to it that Christians have had must be credited to Paul, although later Christians, following in his footpath, have also contributed to the establishment of this attitude. Jesus was sent to confirm the Torah and modify some aspects of its law, but he did not abolish that law.

I would like to mention briefly the Qur'an's reference to the Sabbath, which is one of the laws at the center of the debate on Jesus' attitude toward the law in the Gospels. The Qur'an mentions the *sabt* (Sabbath) five times, but not in connection with Jesus. The term is read by some as meaning *Saturday* or the *law of the Sabbath*. Three of these verses talk about those who transgressed the Sabbath and were punished (2.65, 4.47, 7.163); one states that God commanded the Jews not to transgress the Sabbath (4.154); and the fifth — which clearly uses the term *sabt* to mean the *law of the Sabbath*, hence this is my preferred reading of the term in the other verses also — states the following:

> The Sabbath was only decreed for those who differed concerning it, and verily your Lord will judge between them on the Day of Resurrection about that wherein they used to differ (16.124).

This verse suggests that the Sabbath was introduced at some point, so it is one of those changeable laws. The Qur'an does not give many details about what the Sabbath was, and verse 7.163 suggests that it had something to do with relinquishing certain works on a particular day. This image is reconcilable with the Jewish description of the law of the Sabbath, but it does not mean that the Qur'an endorses the Old Testament's detailed description of this law. Indeed, verse 16.124 indicates that were differences among the Jews about this law. Also, the Sabbath in the Qur'an has nothing to do with the Old Testament's claim that it relates to God's day of rest after finishing the creation in six days (Gen. 2:2-3). One Qur'anic verse explicitly rebuffs the suggestion that God could need rest:

> And We created the heavens, the earth, and what is between them in six Days and no weariness touched Us (50.38).

So the Qur'an confirms that at some point God introduced a Sabbath law, but this law must not be equated to the Jewish Sabbath, and the Qur'an does not mention whether the Injīl contained any changes to that law.

In contrast to the Injīl, the Qur'an is a completely new law. It is not revealed to complement or change the Torah or both the Torah and Injīl, but it is a different law that sets anew what is lawful and what is unlawful. Furthermore, this law was sent to supersede the previous law, i.e. that of the Torah and the Injīl, as the Qur'an targeted with its legislations the people of the Torah and Injīl also:

> He (Prophet Muhammad) will enjoin on them (the People of the Torah and the Injīl) that which is right and forbid them that which is evil; he will make lawful for them all good things and prohibit for them only the foul; and he will relieve them of their burden and the yokes that are upon them. Those who believe in him, honor him, help him, and follow the light which is sent down with him — those are the successful (7.157).

The difference between how the Qur'an relates to the Torah and the Injīl and how the Injīl relates to Torah can also be seen in this verse:

> And We have revealed to you [O Muhammad!] the Book with the truth, confirming that which is before it of the Book, and having authority over it. Therefore, judge between them by what Allah has revealed, and do not follow their low desires instead of the truth that has come to you. For every one of you did We appoint a law and a way, and had Allah wished, He would have made you all a single nation, but that He might try you in what He gave you. Therefore, race with one another to good deeds. To Allah is your return, all of you, so He will let you know about that in which you differed (5.48).

The Qur'an confirmed the Torah and the Injīl, as the Injīl did to the Torah. While the Injīl confirmed most of the law of the Torah and changed only some parts of it, the Qur'an is described as having authority over the previous books. It is a new law that supersedes the previous law.

The picture that the Qur'an draws of the Injīl and, consequently, the law of the Christians is very different from how Christianity sees the law. The Christian view is essentially that of one man who succeeded in imposing it. This man was not Jesus, but Paul.

18

The Crucifixion in the New Testament and Historical Sources

Jesus' crucifixion is recounted in detail in the four canonical Gospels. In summary, just before the Passover feast, Jesus, who had earlier predicted his arrest and death, was betrayed by one of his disciples, Judas Iscariot. The latter handed his master over to the chief Jewish priests. After being arrested and interrogated by Jewish religious leaders, Jesus was found guilty of a number of charges, including blasphemy. The Jewish leaders took Jesus to Pontius Pilate, the Roman governor, to try and get him sentenced to death.

Pilate was particularly interested in questioning Jesus about the politically sensitive charge of claiming to be the king of the Jews. The Roman governor was not convinced that Jesus was guilty of anything and wanted to release him. The Jewish leaders and people insisted that Pilate should crucify Jesus, and Pilate at the end bowed to their pressure and ordered the execution of the innocent man. Jesus was crucified on a Friday, but he was raised two days later. After his resurrection on Sunday, he appeared a number of times to his followers.

This brief summary is shared by the Gospels but it hides substantial differences between the stories of Jesus' crucifixion in the four books. It has been known for a long time that the Gospels give highly confused and contradictory accounts of this event. For instance, the 3rd century Neoplatonist Greek philosopher Porphyry (*Against the Christians*, 2.12) noted that "the evangelists were inventors not historians of the events concerning Jesus. For each of them wrote an account, especially of the passion, which was not in harmony with other respective account."

Increasing understanding of 1st century Judaism and Palestine in recent years has also exposed historically wrong information and impossible claims in the Gospel accounts of Jesus' death. The reports that propagated the alleged events of Jesus' crucifixion and resurrection and turned them into history in the minds of billions of unsuspecting people over two millenniums are highly unreliable and cannot be considered historical.

It is often suggested that the crucifixion is attested in independent historical sources also, not only in the New Testament. The fact is that history does not provide any witnesses evidence or report from that time, and none of the late 1st or 2nd century references to the crucifixion is likely to be independent of Christian sources. In the next chapter we shall study in detail the Qur'an's rejection of Jesus' crucifixion.

Many scholars who accept Jesus' crucifixion still refuse to accept his resurrection as a paranormal event. This view has resulted in a number of theories about how the body of the crucified Jesus might have disappeared from the tomb.

Because of the impreciseness and contradictions of the Gospel accounts of Jesus' birth date and how long he lived, it can only be concluded that the Evangelists imply that Jesus was killed during Pilate's governorship — that is, sometime between 26 and 36 CE.

18.1. Inconsistencies in the New Testament Accounts of the Crucifixion

There are considerable similarities between the accounts of the four Gospels of the arrest, conviction, crucifixion, and resurrection of Jesus. There are also details that are found in one Gospel but not the other. It is difficult to understand why one Evangelist would ignore events reported by another one, again, unless he was either unaware of them, or simply did not accept them as authentic. It may still be argued that these extra details do not constitute a problem as long as they remain compatible with the other parts of the story. What cannot be dismissed, however, are serious contradictions between the four narratives. Matthew and Mark have fewer contradictions between them than they have with Luke or, even more so, with John. Acts also has differences with the Gospels. Historical problems in the Gospel accounts will be discussed in the next section.

A simple comparison between what each Gospel says about any episode of the story of the crucifixion reveals clear differences and contradictions. We will not concern ourselves with listing all those many inconsistencies, but we will focus on particularly significant contradictions. We will list them in their chronological order in the story:

① **Arrested on or before the Passover?** The contradictions between the Gospels' accounts of the crucifixion start as early as their specification of the date on which Jesus was arrested. All four Gospels state that Jesus was crucified on a Friday (Mark 15:42; Matt. 27:62; Luke 23:54; John 19:31), although some interpret John as meaning that Jesus was crucified on a Wednesday. John disagrees with the Synoptic assertion that this Friday was the first day of the Jewish festival of the Passover, suggesting that it was the day of rest of the Passover, i.e. one day earlier.

According to Jewish law, the lamb of the Passover is slaughtered in the evening of the 14th of Nisan, which is the first month in the Jewish calendar, and it is then eaten on that night (Exo. 12:1-8). As the Jewish day is reckoned from sunset to sunset, this night represents the start of the 15th of Nisan. The Synoptics claim that after having the Passover meal with his disciples, Jesus was arrested later in the night, i.e. the night of the first day of the Passover (Mark 14:12-46; Matt. 26:19-50; Luke 22:7-54), and was crucified in the morning, that is on the morning of 15th Nisan.

John states that after being arrested and questioned by the high priest, Jesus was taken to Pontius Pilate very early in the morning on the day of rest of the Passover, clearly implying that he was arrested on the previous night (John 18:28). The crucifixion that happened hours later must have thus taken place on the 14th of Nisan. So John contradicts the Synoptic Gospels, placing the arrest and crucifixion one day earlier. According to John, the Friday of the crucifixion was the day of the rest of the Passover, whereas the other three Evangelists make it the first day of the feast. So the agreement of the four that it was on a Friday hides a disagreement on when that Friday was.

John's timeline of the crucifixion makes Jesus die at the same time of the slaughter of the Passover lambs. This works very well for his description of Jesus as "the Lamb of God" in the opening chapter of his Gospel (John 1:29, 1:36). As we shall see later in more detail, John also applies to Jesus' crucifixion (John 19:36), in the form of a prophecy, a description that the Old Testament applies to the Passover lamb, thus suggesting that in his crucifixion Jesus played the role of the true Passover lamb. The fact that John's dating of the crucifixion is in such agreement with his theology has made some scholars reject the historicity of his dating and favor the Synoptic date (Sanders, 1995: 72).

Interestingly, while Mark makes it clear that Jesus was crucified on the first day of the Passover, it also states earlier that when, two days before the Passover, the chief priests and the experts in the law were conspiring to kill Jesus they did not want to kill him "during the feast, so there won't be a riot among the people" (Mark 14:2). This passage may belong to a different tradition which is in line with the Johannine chronology of the crucifixion.

Not surprising, there have been attempts to harmonize the contradictory Gospel accounts about the date of the crucifixion. One popular attempt suggests that John used a different calendar from that used by the other three Evangelists. There is no evidence to support this suggestion, and there are strong arguments against it (Theissen & Merz, 1999: 159; also Vermes, 2005: 97-98). The one day difference between John and the other three Gospels has historical implications, as we shall see later.

② **One or Three Passovers?** The Synoptic Gospels mention only one Passover, which is the one in which Jesus was crucified. Their accounts suggest that Jesus' public ministry lasted for no longer than a year. John disagrees, as he mentions two other Passovers (John 2:13, 2:23, 6:3) before the one of the crucifixion.

③ **Nocturnal or morning trial?** Mark (14:30-53) and Matthew (26:31-57) state that Jesus was arrested and tried by the Jewish leaders in the night. John also implies the same, as he states that after the arrest and interrogation, Jesus was taken to the Roman governor "very early in the morning" (John 18:28). While Luke agrees that Jesus was arrested at night, he claims that the trial was in the morning (Luke 22:66).

④ **Questioned by the Sanhedrin or high priest?** There is confusion as to whether Jesus was questioned by the high priest or the Sanhedrin. The latter was a Jewish judicial body of 71 members, headed by the high priest, which settled religious and legal matters. According to Mark (14:53-55, 15:1) and Matthew (26:57-59), the Sanhedrin tried Jesus in the house of the high priest, whom Matthew names as Caiaphas. Luke states that after his arrest, Jesus was taken to Caiaphas' house, and in morning he was tried by "the council of the elders of the people... both the chief priests and the experts in the law" (Luke 22:66). We can safely presume that he meant the Sanhedrin even though he did not use that term.

John, on the other hand, claims that after his arrest, Jesus was taken to the house of Annas, the father-in-law of Caiaphas who is introduced as the "high priest that year" (John 18:12-13). However, during Annas' questioning of Jesus, the former is repeatedly described as the "high priest" (John 18:15-22). When Annas finished the interrogation, he sent Jesus to Caiaphas, who is also described as the "high priest" (John 18:24)! Surprisingly, there is no account of another interrogation by Caiaphas.

Thus, the Sanhedrin is completely missing from John's account, although he earlier indicates that the Sanhedrin, led by Caiaphas, had been planning to kill Jesus (John 11:47-53). This Evangelist also confusingly suggests in one passage that Caiaphas was the high priest and describes Annas as his father-in-law but then calls the latter in several passages the high priest. One way of harmonizing this apparent contradiction is to suggest that while Caiaphas was the high priest that year, Annas was the high priest before, which is why he retained the title. This suggestion has historical problems, which we will discuss later in the chapter.

⑤ **What charges before the Jews?** According to Mark (14:53-65), many testified against Jesus before the Sanhedrin, but their testimonies disagreed. Some falsely accused him of saying "I will destroy this temple made with hands and in three days build another not made with hands." When questioned about this charge, Jesus inexplicably remained silent. The high priest, persecuting on behalf of the Sanhedrin, then went on to question Jesus about whether he claimed to be "the Christ, the Son of the Blessed One" (Mark 14:61). Jesus' answer "I am, and you will see the Son of Man sitting at the right hand of the Power and coming with the clouds of heaven" led to the high priest accusing him of blasphemy.

The trial in Matthew is very similar to Mark's. Jesus was accused of claiming to be able to destroy the temple and rebuild it in three days (Matt. 26:61) — a charge that he met with silence. The high priest then asked Jesus if he was "the Christ, the son of God" (Matt. 26:63). When Jesus replied "You have said it yourself. But I tell you, from now on you will see the Son of Man sitting at the right hand of the Power and coming on the clouds of heaven," the high priest accused him of blasphemy (Matt. 24:64-65) and declared that no more witnesses were required. One difference between Mark and Matthew is that the latter states that two witnesses testified that Jesus had made the claim about the temple (Matt. 26:60) whereas Mark says that witnesses disagreed about this accusation.

This charge is mentioned again in Acts, when a Christian called Stephen was put on trial by people from the Synagogue:

Then they secretly instigated some men to say, "We have heard this man speaking blasphemous words against Moses and God." They incited the people, the elders, and the experts in the law; then they approached Stephen, seized him, and brought him before the council. They brought forward false witnesses who said, "This man does not stop saying things against this holy place and the law. For we have heard him saying that Jesus the Nazarene will destroy this place and change the customs that Moses handed down to us." (Acts 6:11-14)

The accusation about the temple relates to a Jesus prophecy that is reported in the three Synoptics (also Matt. 24:1-2; Luke 21:5-6):

Now as Jesus was going out of the temple courts, one of his disciples said to him, "Teacher, look at these tremendous stones and buildings!" Jesus said to him, "Do you see these great buildings? Not one stone will be left on another. All will be torn down!" (Mark 13:1-2)

Jesus did not actually say that he would destroy the building, so the implication must be that the charge was false. He only pronounced a prophecy.

It is often claimed that Jesus' prophecy was fulfilled when the Romans destroyed the temple in 70 CE after the revolt of the Jews that started in 66 CE. If the walls that presently surround the Islamic site of *al-Ḥaram ash-Sharif* are those of the ancient temple, which means that thousands of stones were left intact in their position, then clearly the alleged prophecy was not exactly fulfilled. But let's leave the subject of the temple aside, and get back to our main subject.

In the shorter account of the trial in Luke (22:66-71), the prophecy of destroying and rebuilding the temple is not mentioned as a charge. There is no mention of witnesses either. Jesus was asked whether he was the Christ. His unclear answer triggered a question about whether he was "the son of God." Jesus' second vague answer, "you say that I am," made the prosecutors conclude that they have got the evidence they needed. It looks that this evidence was not only Jesus' claim that he was "son of God," but also his other claim that he was the Christ.

In John also the accusation about the temple is missing, as John has what looks like a very different version of the same event that the Synoptics report:

So then the Jewish leaders responded, "What sign can you show us, since you are doing these things?" Jesus replied, "Destroy this temple and in three days I will raise it up again." Then the Jewish leaders said to him, "This temple has been under construction for forty-six years, and are you going to raise it up in three days?" But Jesus was speaking about the temple of his body. So after he was raised from the dead, his disciples remembered that he had said this, and they believed the scripture and the saying that Jesus had spoken. (John 2:18-22)

But even in John's version, Jesus does not talk about him destroying and rebuilding the temple. A different problem in this passage is that Jesus' words do not actually answer the Jews' challenge (p. 340).

In this Gospel, Annas questions Jesus about "his disciples and about his teaching" (John 18:19), but no explicit or specific charges are made. When Jesus was brought before Pilate, Jewish leaders told the Roman governor that according to their law Jesus had to die because he "claimed to be the Son of God" (John 19:7). Earlier that Gospel states that Caiaphas sought Jesus' death at any cost to repel what he perceived as danger of Roman aggression against the Jewish nation:

> So the chief priests and the Pharisees called the council together and said, "What are we doing? For this man is performing many miraculous signs. If we allow him to go on in this way, everyone will believe in him, and the Romans will come and take away our sanctuary and our nation."
> Then one of them, Caiaphas, who was high priest that year, said, "You know nothing at all! You do not realize that it is more to your advantage to have one man die for the people than for the whole nation to perish." (Now he did not say this on his own, but because he was high priest that year, he prophesied that Jesus was going to die for the Jewish nation, and not for the Jewish nation only, but to gather together into one the children of God who are scattered.) So from that day they planned together to kill him. (John 11:47-53)

The Gospels give confusing and contradictory accounts of Jesus' charges.

⑥ **Was he tried or interrogated by the Jews?** Another disagreement between the Gospels is whether the Sanhedrin and high priest subjected Jesus to a trial or an interrogation (Theissen & Merz, 1999: 443). Both Mark (14:64) and Matthew (26:65-66) report a trial that ends with finding Jesus guilty of blasphemy and condemns him to death.

The Gospel of Luke describes more of an interrogation than a trial, although it ends with the Sanhedrin getting the evidence they wanted (Luke 22:71), which implies that they found him guilty. No sentencing is mentioned. But this is contradicted later when the Gospel states that "chief priests and rulers handed him over to be condemned to death, and crucified him" (Luke 24:20). In Acts, the same author has the following to say about the Sanhedrin's questioning of Jesus: "For the people who live in Jerusalem and their rulers did not recognize him, and they fulfilled the sayings of the prophets that are read every Sabbath by condemning him. Though they found no basis for a death sentence, they asked Pilate to have him executed" (Acts 13:27-28). These contradictory statements by the same author have made some researchers wonder whether "Luke wanted to depict the interrogation as a trial" or it is "a sign that the Lukan interrogation scene goes back to a pre-Lukan tradition which contradicts Luke's view elsewhere" (Theissen & Merz, 1999: 450). The fact that Luke's account concludes with the council finding the evidence they were after seems to imply that the Evangelist may have still thought of it as a trial, although no sentence is passed.

John's account is one of interrogation rather than trial. The questioning was conducted by Annas; no witnesses were called, no evidence was obtained, no verdict was reached, and no sentence was passed (John 18:19-24). Annas then transferred Jesus to Caiaphas, the other high priest, but the Evangelist seems to imply that Caiaphas did nothing other than send Jesus to Pilate (John 18:24-28). Jesus was never brought before the Sanhedrin, although John had told us earlier that the high priest and the Sanhedrin were seeking Jesus' death well before his arrest (John 11:49-53).

⑦ **Were the Jews competent to sentence to death?** Mark and Matthew clearly indicate that the Sanhedrin had the power to pass the death penalty, as the Jewish body condemned Jesus to death at the end of his trial. Luke makes the same claim (Acts 13:27; Luke 24:20), although he seems to contradict that elsewhere in his Gospel where no verdict is passed. John contradicts Mark, Matthew, and Acts, but agrees with Luke as it claims that the Jewish leaders did not have the legal power to put someone to death: "Pilate told them, 'Take him yourselves and pass judgment on him according to your own law!' The Jewish leaders replied, 'We cannot legally put anyone to death'" (John 18:31). Amazingly, the Roman prefect, who had been governing the Jews for at least 3-4 years at the time of Jesus' supposed crucifixion, is portrayed as being ignorant of the fact that the Sanhedrin did not have the power to impose capital punishment.

⑧ **What charges before Pilate?** All four Gospels agree that after his trial or interrogation by the Sanhedrin and high priest Jesus was brought before Pilate to be punished. According to Mark and Matthew, Pilate asked Jesus whether he was the king of Jews, to which Jesus answered vaguely "you say so" (Mark 15:2; Matt. 27:11). Pilate's question implies that the Jewish leaders accused Jesus of claiming to be the king of the Jews — a highly charged political accusation which was bound to raise the interest of the Roman governor. This seems to be what mattered to Pilate of the original charge of claiming to be the Messiah. The chief priests and the elders then brought many unspecified charges against Jesus, but he did not respond to any of them.

Luke has a different story in which the claim to messiahship is only mentioned third, preceded by one religious charge and another political: "We found this man subverting our nation, forbidding us to pay the tribute tax to Caesar and claiming that he himself is Christ, a king" (Luke 23:2). At this point, Luke reports the same question and answer between Pilate and Jesus about the kingship of the Jews that Mark and Matthew have. Later passages assert that Jesus was accused of "inciting the people" (Luke 23:5) and "misleading the people" (Luke 23:14).

John's account differs yet further. When Pilate asks the people about Jesus' charge, their reply was simply to stress his guilt: "If this man were not a criminal, we would not have handed him over to you" (John. 18:30). Upon the Jews' insistence that

Jesus must be killed, Pilate asked him whether he was the king of the Jews. Unlike in the Synoptics, Jesus replies by explaining that his kingdom is heavenly and not from this world (John 18:36). This should have allied Pilate's concerns. John also states that the Jews told Pilate that Jesus had to die because of his claim to the sonship of God (John 19:7).

Despite their differences about what charges were brought against Jesus before Pilate, all four Gospels agree that at the crucifixion Jesus was mocked by having a titulus with the inscription "the king of the Jews" put on his cross. This agreement highlights the charge that was of significance for the Roman governor, which is the claim to kingship. Since the Jews believed that the Christ would become their king, this mocking of Jesus ridiculed his claim to messiahship.

The titulus incident is one instance that shows that even when the Gospels are consistent, they do not actually completely agree with each other. The inscription according to Mark is "The king of the Jews" (Mark 15:26), in Matthew it is "This is Jesus, the king of the Jews" (Matt. 27:37), but Luke has "This is the king of the Jews" (Luke 23:38), and John has yet a fourth variation, "Jesus the Nazarene, the king of the Jews" (John 19:19).

⑨ **Was there a trial by Herod Antipas?** Mark, Matthew, and John state that Jesus was tried by Pontius Pilate. Luke adds to the story a trial by Herod also. He claims that after questioning Jesus, Pilate learned that he was from Galilee, which was under Herod's jurisdiction, so he sent him to the later. Herod mocked and humiliated Jesus and sent him back to Pilate (Luke 23:6-12). This whole episode is missing from the other three Gospels.

⑩ **What was the timeline of the crucifixion?** The day of the ancient Jewish lunar calendar was reckoned from sunset to sunset. The night and the daytime consisted of 12 hours each, with the 1st hour of the night starting at around 6 pm and the first hour of the daytime at around 6 am. John (11:9) says that in one of Jesus' dialogs with his disciples he said: "Are there not twelve hours in a day?"

According to Mark, Jesus was crucified at the 3rd hour in daytime (15:25), and at the 6th hour the land was covered with darkness which lasted until the 9th hour (15:33), at which point Jesus died (15:34-37). These times correspond to 9 am, 12 am, and 3 pm, respectively. Both Matthew (27:45-50) and Luke (23:44-46) reiterate Mark's statement that the darkness lasted from the 6th to the 9th hour and that Jesus died at the 9th hour.

John (19:14-16) disagrees with the Synoptists, claiming that it was the 6th hour in daytime, or 12 o'clock, when Pilate handed over Jesus to be crucified. It is not clear whether John agrees with the Synoptics that Jesus' ordeal lasted for 6 hours, in which case his death would have been at 6 pm.

To resolve the conflict between John and the Synoptists about the time when Jesus' crucifixion started, it has been suggested that John reckoned the time from midnight. However, it is far more likely that John reckoned the time the Jewish way because that would make the crucifixion coincide with the slaughter of the

Passover lambs — something that reflects his description of Jesus as "the Lamb of God" (John 1:29, 1:36) and works well for his theology.

⑪ How did Judas die? All four Gospels state that Jesus was betrayed by one of his twelve disciples, Judas Iscariot, who handed him over to the Jewish leaders for money (Mark 14:43-46; Matt. 26:47-50; Luke 22:47-54; John 18:2-12). Matthew (26:15) also tells us that Judas was paid 30 silver coins to betray his master, and that he then regretted what he did and committed suicide:

> Now when Judas, who had betrayed him, saw that Jesus had been condemned, he regretted what he had done and returned the thirty silver coins to the chief priests and the elders, saying, "I have sinned by betraying innocent blood!" But they said, "What is that to us? You take care of it yourself!" So Judas threw the silver coins into the temple and left. Then he went out and hanged himself. The chief priests took the silver and said, "It is not lawful to put this into the temple treasury, since it is blood money." After consulting together they bought the Potter's Field with it, as a burial place for foreigners. For this reason that field has been called the "Field of Blood" to this day. Then what was spoken by Jeremiah the prophet was fulfilled: "They took the thirty silver coins, the price of the one whose price had been set by the people of Israel, and they gave them for the potter's field, as the Lord commanded me." (Matt. 27:3-10)

The alleged Jeremiah prophecy that Matthew cites does not exist. If Matthew has not completely made it up, then it could be a very garbled mixture of passages from Zechariah (11:12-13) and Jeremiah (18:2-3), as explained later in more detail.

None of the other three Gospels mentions Judas' suicide, but Acts does, although it gives different details about Judas' suicide:

> (Now this man Judas acquired a field with the reward of his unjust deed, and falling headfirst he burst open in the middle and all his intestines gushed out. This became known to all who lived in Jerusalem, so that in their own language they called that field Hakeldama, that is, "Field of Blood.") "For it is written in the book of Psalms, 'Let his house become deserted, and let there be no one to live in it,' and 'Let another take his position of responsibility.'" (Acts 1:18-20)

This account contradicts Matthew's.

⑫ How did the robbers speak? Mark and Matthew briefly state that the two robbers who were crucified with Jesus "spoke abusively to him" (Mark 15:32; Matt. 27:44). It is quite a claim that someone who is about to be put through the unimaginable horror of crucifixion should be engaged in abusing another person who is about to suffer the same ordeal!

Luke has the following, very different account:

> One of the criminals who was hanging there railed at him, saying, "Aren't you the Christ? Save yourself and us!" But the other rebuked him, saying, "Don't you fear God, since you are under the same sentence of condemnation? And we rightly so, for we are

getting what we deserve for what we did, but this man has done nothing wrong." Then he said, "Jesus, remember me when you come in your kingdom." And Jesus said to him, "I tell you the truth, today you will be with me in paradise." (Luke 23:39-43)

John (19:18) does not have anything to say about any exchanges between Jesus and his crucifixion mates whom he mentions only in passing.

⑬ **Who and where were the women at the crucifixion?** The four Gospels name different women who were present during or after the crucifixion and place them at different locations. The woman supporters who were watching the crucifixion *from a distance* included "Mary Magdalene, and Mary the mother of James the younger and of Joses, and Salome" according to Mark (15:40), or "Mary Magdalene, Mary the mother of James and Joseph, and the mother of the sons of Zebedee" according to Matthew (27:56). While Luke does not name any woman, he says that some were witnessing *from a distance*: "And all those who knew Jesus stood at a distance, and the women who had followed him from Galilee saw these things" (Luke 23:49).

John clearly disagrees with the Synoptic Evangelists as he reports that Jesus' "mother, his mother's sister, Mary the wife of Clopas, and Mary Magdalene" were actually "standing beside Jesus' cross" (John 19:25). They were so close that Jesus spoke to his mother (John 19:26).

⑭ **Were the disciples present at the crucifixion?** By mentioning only the women, Mark and Matthew imply that none of Jesus' disciples witnessed the crucifixion. This is in line with Jesus' prediction in Mark (14:27) that his disciples would scatter at the time of the crucifixion.

Luke (23:49) seems to contradict this when he suggests that "all those who knew Jesus," which must include the disciples, were watching, although from a distance. John (19:26) has a third version in which one particular disciple, whom he describes as the one whom Jesus loved, was present so close to Jesus that the latter spoke to him.

Interestingly, the four Gospels agree that when faced with the accusation of being one of Jesus' followers, the disciple Peter denied any relation with Jesus (Mark 14:66-71; Matt. 26:69-74; Luke 22:54-60; John 18:16-17, 18:25-27). John states that another, unnamed disciple was with Peter. Peter's denial and the fact that three of the Evangelists claim that Peter followed Jesus "at a distance" (Mark 14:54; Matt. 26:58; Luke 22:54) suggest that Jesus' disciples could have been prosecuted and had to go into hiding. This is in line with John's claim that Annas questioned Jesus about his disciples (John 18:19), so the appearance of one of Jesus' disciples near the crucified Jesus in John looks rather contradictory. One explanation is that this disciple was the unnamed disciple who appears with Peter in John, as that disciple is claimed to have been acquainted with the high priest (John 18:15).

⑮ **Who buried Jesus?** The four Gospels claim that a good man called Joseph of Arimathea buried Jesus (Mark 15:42-46; Matt. 27:57-60; Luke 23:50-53; John

19:38-42). Acts states that it was the people of Jerusalem, whom it blames for the killing of Jesus, who "took him down from the cross and placed him in a tomb" (Acts 13:29). Luke's (23:51) description of Arimathea as a "Judean town" suggests that it was not in Jerusalem.

⑯ **What was the sign of Jonah?** The Old Testament contains a story of a Jonah who was commissioned by God to go to preach in Nineveh. Jonah disobeyed the divine order and, traveling by sea, tried to escape from God and the mission. While in the sea, a powerful wind started to shake the boat dangerously. Jonah confessed to the sailors that this was the result of God's wrath at him, and suggested a solution: "Pick me up and throw me into the sea to make the sea quiet down, because I know it's my fault you are in this severe storm" (Jonah 1:12). After he was thrown in the sea, "The Lord sent a huge fish to swallow Jonah, and Jonah was in the stomach of the fish three days and three nights" (Jonah 1:17). Having repented and prayed to God from inside the whale, "the Lord commanded the fish and it disgorged Jonah on dry land" (Jonah 2:10).

Matthew includes a prediction by Jesus in which he likens his burial and resurrection to what happened to Jonah:

> Then some of the experts in the law along with some Pharisees answered him, "Teacher, we want to see a sign from you." But he answered them, "An evil and adulterous generation asks for a sign, but no sign will be given to it except the sign of the prophet Jonah. For just as Jonah was in the belly of the huge fish for three days and three nights, so the Son of Man will be in the heart of the earth for three days and three nights." (Matt. 12:38-40)

There is actually hardly any similarity between the two events, yet there are clear and fundamental differences. Indeed, drawing similarity between the two disappearances is meaningless:

(i) Jesus here is not simply likening his burial to the disappearance of Jonah in the belly of the whale, but he is also emphasizing the duration of his death, making it clear that it is three days and three nights, like Johan's. The problem is that Jesus did not actually stay that long in the tomb. The Synoptists agree that he died just after 3 pm (Mark 15:33-37; Matt. 27:45-50; Luke 23:44-46). John does not tell us when Jesus died on the cross, but it must have happened after he was handed over at noon to be executed. All four Gospels also agree that Jesus had already risen from the dead in the early morning of the Sunday that followed the Friday of the crucifixion (Mark 16:1; Matt. 28:1; Luke 24:1; John 20:1). This means that Jesus remained buried for only one day and two nights, contradicting the prediction in Matthew.

Luke perhaps realized this contradiction so his account of Jesus' prophecy — which, unlike Matthew's, is placed after the Transfiguration — makes no mention of the time, despite the fact that without close resemblance between the time in both cases the comparison would make little sense:

> As the crowds were increasing, Jesus began to say, "This generation is a wicked generation; it looks for a sign, but no sign will be given to it except the sign of Jonah. For just as Jonah became a sign to the people of Nineveh, so the Son of Man will be a sign to this generation." (Luke 11:29-30)

The apologetic argument that Jesus' mention of the three days and nights was not intended to refer to an exact period of time is inadmissible, as it makes the reference to that specific, or in fact any, timeframe meaningless.

(ii) Jesus' alleged miracle was his resurrection from death. This miracle would not become more impressive if Jesus had stayed, say, 10 days in the tomb or less impressive if he had spent only one night. The reported miracle is simply one of *resurrection from death.* Conversely, the miraculous aspect of Jonah's experience is his *survival inside the whale for three days and nights.* Inside the tomb Jesus did not experience any miracle; he was dead like all the dead.

(iii) Jonah's ordeal was a punishment for his failure to obey God. Jesus' was to fulfill a divine plan that reflected Jesus' special status in God' eye.

(iv) Matthew reports a second incident in which Jesus was asked to show a sign, which he refused to do, and pointed to Jonah's miracle:

> Now when the Pharisees and Sadducees came to test Jesus, they asked him to show them a sign from heaven. He said, "When evening comes you say, 'It will be fair weather, because the sky is red,' and in the morning, 'It will be stormy today, because the sky is red and darkening.' You know how to judge correctly the appearance of the sky, but you cannot evaluate the signs of the times. A wicked and adulterous generation asks for a sign, but no sign will be given to it except the sign of Jonah." Then he left them and went away. (Matt. 16:1-4)

The Pharisees and Sadducees' demand for a sign has been completely misunderstood by Matthew, as shown in the irrelevant reply that he attributes to Jesus, and was actually taken from a different context, which is the story of the miracle of the food from heaven (pp. 353-355).

⑰ **To whom did Jesus appear first?** Mark says that "at sunrise" of the Sunday that followed Jesus' crucifixion on Friday "Mary Magdalene, Mary the mother of James, and Salome" (Mark 16:1) — the same women who watched the crucifixion at a distance (Mark 15:40) — went to the tomb to anoint the body. In the longer ending of Mark, which is not found in some manuscripts, it is stated that Jesus appeared first to *Mary Magdalene* (Mark 16:9). Mark also says that a "young man" who appeared to the women at the tomb and told them that Jesus had risen also said that Jesus was going to appear to the disciples, as he had promised them, in Galilee (Mark 16:7), but this appearance is not mentioned later in that Gospel.

According to Matthew, the women who went to the tomb "at down" on Sunday were "Mary Magdalene and the other Mary." It is not clear which other Mary Matthew meant, but he had already said that the women who witnessed the crucifixion at a distance included "Mary Magdalene, Mary the mother of James and Joseph, and the mother of the sons of Zebedee" (Matt. 27:56), so it could be one of those two other women. When Mary Magdalene and the other Mary arrived to the tomb an "angel" told them that Jesus had already been raised. Jesus then made his first appearance after his resurrection to *these two women* (Matt. 28:1-10).

Luke's version is different. He talks about "women" visiting the tomb "at early dawn" on Sunday, but he does not report any appearance of Jesus there (Luke 24:1-12). They were told by "two men" that Jesus had been raised. Luke states that Jesus appeared first to *two of his disciples, Cleopas and an unnamed one*, while they were heading to Emmaus, a village that is seven miles from Jerusalem (Luke 24:13-16).

John has yet another different version in which Mary Magdalene, Peter, and another disciple went to the tomb when "it was still dark" on Sunday. They were told by "two angels" about Jesus' resurrection. When the two disciples left, Jesus appeared to *Mary Magdalene* (John 20:14).

In addition to their differences about who saw Jesus first and who told the visitors to the tomb about his resurrection, the Evangelists have disagreements about other appearances of Jesus to his disciples, including the places of those appearances.

Paul contradicts the Gospels when listing the people Jesus appeared to:

> And that he was buried, and that he was raised on the third day according to the scriptures, and that he appeared to Cephas, then to the twelve. Then he appeared to more than five hundred of the brothers and sisters at one time, most of whom are still alive, though some have fallen asleep. Then he appeared to James, then to all the apostles. Last of all, as though to one born at the wrong time, he appeared to me also. (1 Cor. 15:4-8)

The notable absence of women in Paul's account has been attributed to the fact that women were not fully qualified as witnesses in Jewish law (Theissen & Merz, 1999: 497).

⑱ **When was the ascension?** Mark states that after appearing to his eleven disciples while they were eating, Jesus "was taken up into heaven and sat down at the right hand of God" (Mark 16:19). No date is given.

Matthew ends with Jesus' appearance to his disciples in Galilee (Matt. 28:16-20). It has no mention of Jesus' ascension to heaven. John also does not make any mention of the ascension, closing his Gospel with Jesus' appearance to his disciples by the Sea of Tiberias (John 21:1-25).

Luke mentions Jesus' ascension, which occurred after he appeared to his disciples, but he gives more details: "Then Jesus led them out as far as Bethany, and lifting up his hands, he blessed them. Now during the blessing he departed and was taken up into heaven" (Luke 24:50-51). It is clear in Luke that this appearance happened on the same day of resurrection (Luke 24:1, 24:13, 24:21-22).

Acts, on the other hand, states that the ascension happened actually forty days after the resurrection:

> I wrote the former account, Theophilus, about all that Jesus began to do and teach until the day he was taken up to heaven, after he had given orders by the Holy Spirit to the apostles he had chosen. To the same apostles also, after his suffering, he presented himself alive with many convincing proofs. He was seen by them over a forty-day period and spoke about matters concerning the kingdom of God. (Acts 1:1-3)

These accounts are inconsistent.

⑲ Were there prophecies? The problems in the arrest, crucifixion, and resurrection narratives of the Gospels are not restricted to inconsistencies within individual Gospels and contradictions with each other. The Gospels cite a number of alleged scriptural prophecies about the Messiah that are related to these episodes of Jesus' life. The problem is that these prophecies are either inexistent, taken out of their original Old Testament context, or not prophecies and have nothing to do with the Messiah. Let's look at those six prophecies:

(i) Matthew states that Judas regretted handing Jesus over, returned the money that he was paid for the treason, which was used to buy the Potter's field, and hanged himself. Then — in keeping with his use of false Old Testament prophecies, some of which we have already studied — the Evangelist goes on to say:

> Then what was spoken by Jeremiah the prophet was fulfilled: "They took the thirty silver coins, the price of the one whose price had been set by the people of Israel, and they gave them for the potter's field, as the Lord commanded me." (Matt. 27:9-10)

There is actually no match for this passage in Jeremiah! All that can be found in that book is a reference to the prophet being commanded to visit a potter (Jer. 18:2-3) and elsewhere to him buying a field from his cousin (Jer. 32:7-9).

The closest passage to this text is found in Zechariah, but the context is completely different and has no relation to the Messiah, as the Prophet Zechariah here recounts a vision he had:

> Then I said to them, "If it seems good to you, pay me my wages, but if not, forget it." So they weighed out my payment—thirty pieces of silver. The Lord then said to me, "Throw to the potter that exorbitant sum at which they valued me!" So I took the thirty pieces of silver and threw them to the potter at the temple of the Lord. (Zech. 11:12-13)

The erroneous attribution to Jeremiah has resulted in some scribes changing "Jeremiah" to "Zechariah" in some manuscripts, or omitting the name of the prophet altogether in others!

(ii) Mark states that Jesus cited an Old Testament prediction to declare that his disciples will scatter after his crucifixion: "I will strike the shepherd, and the sheep will be scattered" (Mark 14:27). The Biblical prophecy that this passage talks about is Zechariah 13:7. However, the Old Testament prophecy uses the term "sheep" to denote the disobedient Israelites and the "shepherd" for their unbelieving kings! Surely the negative term "shepherd" could have signified the Messiah.

(iii) In Luke, Jesus tells his disciples: "For I tell you that this scripture must be fulfilled in me, 'And he was counted with the transgressors.' For what is written about me is being fulfilled" (Luke 22:37). Jesus here cites Isaiah 53:12, but the Old Testament prophecy talks about Israel not the Messiah.

(iv) John has this passage:

> Now when the soldiers crucified Jesus, they took his clothes and made four shares, one for each soldier, and the tunic remained. (Now the tunic was seamless, woven from top to bottom as a single piece.) So the soldiers said to one another, "Let's not tear it, but throw dice to see who will get it." This took place to fulfill the scripture that says, "They divided my garments among them, and for my clothing they threw dice." So the soldiers did these things. (John 19:23-24)

Psalms 22:18, which this passage references, is not actually a prophecy, but a prayer in which King David complains to God about his enemies.

(v) John has also this passage about another alleged scriptural prophecy:

> After this Jesus, realizing that by this time everything was completed, said (in order to fulfill the scripture), "I am thirsty!" A jar full of sour wine was there, so they put a sponge soaked in sour wine on a branch of hyssop and lifted it to his mouth. (John 19:28-29)

This passage seems to cite Psalms 69:21 or 22:15, neither of which is a prophecy nor related to the Messiah.

(vi) John relates the following events that that took place after Jesus' crucifixion:

> Then, because it was the day of preparation, so that the bodies should not stay on the crosses on the Sabbath (for that Sabbath was an especially important one), the Jewish leaders asked Pilate to have the victims' legs broken and the bodies taken down. So the soldiers came and broke the legs of the two men who had been crucified with Jesus, first the one and then the other. But when they came to Jesus and saw that he was already dead, they did not break his legs. But one of the soldiers pierced his side with a spear, and blood and water flowed out immediately. And the person who saw it has testified (and his testimony is true, and he knows that he is telling the truth), so that you also may believe. For these things happened so that the scripture would be fulfilled, "Not a

bone of his will be broken." And again another scripture says, "They will look on the one whom they have pierced." (John 19:31-37)

The first passage seems to refer to Exodus 12:46 and Numbers 9:12 in which God states that the Passover lamb must not have any of its bones broken. An unlikely referent is Psalms 34:20 which talks about God's protection of the believer's bones so that no one of them is broken. John is probably linking Jesus' crucifixion to the Passover lamb, as in this Gospel Jesus is crucified at the same time of the slaughter of the Passover lamb. The original text is clearly not a prophecy.

The second prophecy seems to be a clause from this passage:

> I will pour out upon the kingship of David and the population of Jerusalem a spirit of grace and supplication so that they will look to me, the one they have pierced. They will lament for him as one laments for an only son, and there will be a bitter cry for him like the bitter cry for a firstborn. (Zech. 12:10)

Like the passage about the unbroken bones, this passage has been taken completely out of context. It occurs in the Old Testament in the context of describing a war against Israel that ends with the victory of Israel (Zech. 12:1-9). Then the piercing of someone is mentioned, and that is followed by great lamentation by Israel. In addition to the fact that the Old Testament passage does not talk about the Messiah, the circumstances of the death of Jesus bear no resemblance whatsoever to the descriptions given, and the Jews certainly did not cry over Jesus, according to John.

This section has shown that the New Testament narratives about the events surrounding Jesus' crucifixion and resurrection are highly contradictory and inconsistent, yet the discussion can be extended further to cover other discrepancies and more details of the story. It is virtually impossible to reconcile all the different accounts and come up with one version of the story that accommodates all differences and details in all of the Gospels. The Gospels also contain incorrect information, as in the case of the prophecies.

This is how the Gospels judge each other's account of Jesus' crucifixion and resurrection; but what does history say about those narratives?

18.2. Historical Problems in the New Testament Accounts of the Crucifixion

There are equally significant historical problems in the New Testament accounts of the trial, crucifixion, and resurrection of Jesus.

A number of historically erroneous statements can be identified by comparing the Gospel narratives of Jesus' trial with the Jewish law of trials according to the

Mishnah (Theissen & Merz, 1999: 461). Commenting on the problems in Matthew, Mark, and Luke in particular, Vermes (2000: 169) has summarized the situation as follows: "practically every detail of the Synoptic account conflicts both procedurally and substantively with any known Jewish law."

This is part of what the Mishnah says about trials involving capital sentence:

> Civil suits are tried by day, and concluded at night. But capital charges must be tried by day and concluded by day. Civil suits can be concluded on the same day, whether for acquittal or condemnation; capital charges may be concluded on the same day with a favourable verdict, but only on the morrow with an unfavourable verdict. Therefore trials are not held on the eve of a sabbath or festival. In civil suits, and in cases of cleanness and uncleanness, we begin with [the opinion of] the most eminent [of the judges]; whereas in capital charges, we commence with [the opinion of] those on the side [benches.] (Sanh. 32a)

Given that Jesus' hearing involved a capital charge, the following details in the Gospel narratives show ignorance of the Jewish legal system:

① Mark (14:30-53), Matthew (26:31-57), and John (18:28) claim that Jesus' trial was nocturnal, which could not be true.

② Mark and Matthew have the trial conducted and concluded with the guilty verdict on the same day, which contradicts the Mishnah. Luke's account is a mix or interrogation and trial, and John talks about an interrogation, so it may be argued that these two accounts do not contradict Jewish law. In the Synoptics, Jesus' trial/interrogation was not only concluded on the same day, but lasted one session only. Only John seems to suggest that more than one session took place, as after questioning Jesus, Annas sent him to the high priest Caiaphas, although there is no report of another interrogation. But John still suggests that all sessions happened on the same day.

③ Mark and Matthew state that Jesus was tried by the Sanhedrin on the Passover night and Luke makes it on the Passover morning, i.e. during a festival when trials cannot actually be held. Some scholars have argued against using the Mishnah for assessing Jesus' trial because of its late redaction date of around 200 CE. But there are other 1st century sources, such as Philo and the Dead Sea Scrolls, that confirm that it was illegal to hold trials on the Sabbaths and festivals (Vermes, 2005: 100).

④ The Mishnah makes the admission of guilt invalid without confirmation by witnesses. Yet Mark states that after listening to what he considered a confession by Jesus, the high priest declared that *no witnesses were needed*, and turning to the Sanhedrin members he demanded a guilty verdict: "You have heard the blasphemy! What is your verdict?" They all obliged and "condemned him as deserving death" (Mark

14:63-64). The witnesses spoke *before the alleged confession*, and they also disagreed with each other (Mark 14:56-58). In Matthew also false witnesses are called at the beginning of the trial (Matt. 26:59-61), and Jesus is convicted on the basis of his confession, with no witnesses called to confirm the admission of guilt. Luke's does not contain a clear verdict, but the implication is that what Jesus said, again without support from witnesses, proved the case against him. If the Mishnah law on the need for witnesses was in force in Jesus' days, then Jesus' confession could not have been sufficient to convict him.

⑤ As well as giving a detailed process for examining witnesses and ensuring that the court is satisfied with their testimony, which is missing from the Gospels accounts, the Mishnah also states that each judge had to cast his vote for the verdict he reached individually, one judge after another. Announcing a capital sentence by common proclamation, as we see in the Gospels, is unhistorical (Vermes, 2005: 23).

⑥ The Gospels state that Jesus was tried in the house of the high priest, but the usual place of assembly is the hall of cut stone within the temple (Theissen & Merz, 1999: 461; Vermes, 2005: 22). The template gates were closed at night.

⑦ Mark, Matthew, and Luke in Acts, but not in his Gospel, claim that the Sanhedrin had the power to impose the death penalty. John, on the other hand, states that when Pilate told the Jews to take Jesus and sentence him according to their law, the Jewish leaders, who were seeking the death of Jesus, told the Roman governor: "We cannot legally put anyone to death" (John 18:31). Whether or not the Jews at around 30 CE were competent to carry out capital punishment is an area of disagreement between scholars (Theissen & Merz, 1999: 455-456). Vermes (2005, 103-108) gives a very good summary of the two positions, and I find the argument made in favor of the Jews being able to execute capital punishments strong. Interestingly, John who denies in one place that the Jews could carry out capital sentence has the Jewish leaders tell Jesus elsewhere "We are not going to stone you for a good deed but for blasphemy, because you, a man, are claiming to be God" (John 10:33), implying that the Jews had the power to carry out executions. Anyway, Mark and Matthew are at odds with John, and even if Mark and Matthew are historically correct, John would be wrong, and vice versa.

⑧ Mark and Matthew talk about one high priest, Caiaphas. Luke, however, dates God's revelation to John the Baptism to a period "during the high priesthood of Annas and Caiaphas" (Luke 3:2). This implies that the office of the high priest was jointly held. Later in the story the high priest is mentioned indirectly and only twice. When they came to arrest Jesus, one of Jesus' disciples struck with his sword "the high priest's slave" (Luke 22:50), and after the arrest, Jesus was brought to the "high priest's house" (Luke 22:54). The implication seems to be that there was only one high priest.

John also calls both Annas and Caiaphas high priests. In addition to calling Caiaphas "high priest" (John 18:24, 18:26), John describes Caiaphas three times as the "high priest that year" (John 11:49, 11:51, 18:13), implying that this position was rotated annually. He also calls Annas, Caiaphas' father-in-law, directly and indirectly, the high priest (John 18:15-16, 18:19). Annas was appointed as the high priest in 6 CE by Quirinius the governor of Syria, but he remained an influential figure even after his removal in 15 CE by Valerius Gratus the new Roman prefect of Judea. He managed to have his son-in-law (Caiaphas), five of his sons, and one of his grandsons appointed to the high priesthood in succession (Vermes, 2005: 98-99). Acts reports that Annas the high priest was involved with Caiaphas and other members of the high priest's family in the Sanhedrin's investigation of Peter and John in Jerusalem (Acts 4:6). This continuing influence could explain why Annas got involved in interrogating Jesus even though Caiaphas was the high priest at the time. However, the Gospels still contain two historical mistakes. **First**, the Old Testament, the writings of Josephus and Philo, and rabbinic literature unanimously testify that the office of high priest can be occupied by one person only. The claim that Annas and Caiaphas held the high priesthood jointly is therefore unhistorical. **Second**, John's claim that the high priesthood was rotated annually is untrue (Vermes, 2005: 43).

⑨ The Gospels state that Jesus was accused of claiming to be the Christ and son of God and was therefore accused of blasphemy (also Matt. 26:63-65; Luke 22:70-71; John 19:7):

> But he was silent and did not answer. Again the high priest questioned him, "Are you the Christ, the Son of the Blessed One?" "I am," said Jesus, "and you will see the Son of Man sitting at the right hand of the Power and coming with the clouds of heaven." Then the high priest tore his clothes and said, "Why do we still need witnesses? You have heard the blasphemy! What is your verdict?" They all condemned him as deserving death. (Mark 14:61-64)

While claiming divine dignity was blasphemous, the claim to messiahship and/or sonship of God was neither a crime nor blasphemy (pp. 262-263). Writing decades after Jesus when Christians had already developed the term "son of God" to involve the sharing of divine attributes, the four Evangelists attributed to Jesus' Jewish accusers their own, late understanding of "son of God" — a meaning that the Jews of the time of Jesus, like those who lived long before him, had never known. These are anachronous mistakes by the Evangelists (Vermes, 2005: 103).

⑩ Mark and Matthew included in their charges of Jesus his prophecy to destroy the temple and rebuild it in three days. Critics of the temple did attract hostility, but not the death penalty. Most of those who criticized the temple survived (Theissen & Merz, 1999: 463).

⑪ Mark (15:6), Matthew (27:15), and John (18:39) claim that it was a custom during the feast for one prisoner to be released to the people. Luke (23:18) also hints at this practice. Mark is unclear as to whose custom the Passover amnesty was, Matthew makes it Roman, and John have Pilate clearly state that is was Jewish! This alleged custom has no historical basis (Theissen & Merz, 1999: 465; Vermes, 2005: 95). Josephus reports that when the new Roman procurator of Judea Albinus came to Jerusalem, the high priest requested him to release ten prisoners, which was the price that was asked for the freedom of his kidnapped son (Josephus, *Jewish Antiquities*, 20.9.3). Albinus granted the high priest his wish, but that was a one-off event and not a custom in any way.

Additionally, Mark (15:7), Luke (23:25), and (John 18:40) state that the freed prisoner, Barabbas, had been imprisoned for involvement in an insurrection — an extremely serious crime to which Mark and Luke add murder. The claim that this dangerous, political prisoner was freed, when there must have been many other prisoners with less serious crimes and danger to the state, further confirms that the story of the Passover amnesty is unhistorical.

Clearly, the Gospel narratives do not only contradict each other, but they are also in contradiction with known historical facts.

The problems in the Gospels that we have highlighted in this and the previous section seem to be the result of the limited knowledge of their authors and the attempt of each of them to present Jesus' story in a way that reflected his belief. There is an element of relating the story as the Gospel author thought it *must have happened* rather than in a way reflecting knowledge of *what really happened*:

> The survey of the redactional tendencies in the Easter stories shows that each Gospel has reshaped the Easter stories with motifs from its own theology. These stories comprise not just an account of the Easter experience but also further experiences of Easter down to the time of the evangelists. (Theissen & Merz, 1999: 495)

The role of the Romans in the Gospel stories of the crucifixion also creates a major historical problem for this account. Although the Roman governor is supposed to have ordered the execution of Jesus, he does not seem to have been bothered by the news about Jesus' apparent avoidance of death. Surely, Pilate would not have believed that Jesus was risen from death or taken to heaven, and would have done everything in his power to get to the bottom of this Christian rumor and make sure that his act has not resulted in the trouble maker attaining further exaltation. Pilate would have either thought that Jesus' body was stolen and that all stories about his rising from death were fabrication by his followers, or that Jesus simply did not die and was rescued from the tomb later. In the former case, Pilate would have certainly sent his soldiers to investigate the matter, capture the body thieves, and expose the sham. Note that the body in the tomb was supposed to have been guarded, so Pilate was clearly keen on the body not being taken away. If, according to the second possibility, Pilate thought that the execution was not fatal, he would have had his soldiers look for the rescued half dead, capture him, and have him killed for sure this time. There is no indication whatsoever in the Gospels that anything of this happened. The Romans are treated like complete idiots who did not know about or bother to investigate the amazing miracle that involved someone that they had just executed.

But let's look in more detail into the Gospels' identification of Jesus' killers.

18.3. Who Killed Jesus?

The Gospels differ on what the high priest and Jewish leaders charged Jesus with, and they also give contradictory accounts on the other, different charges that were examined by Pilate, as we have already seen. However, the Evangelists agree on the identity of Jesus' killer, making the Jewish leaders and crowds responsible for his execution, and more or less exonerate the Roman governor. The Jews, the Gospels stress, indicted Jesus, wanted him killed, and asked Pontius Pilate to do the dirty job for them. Although not convinced by the case against Jesus and not believing that he deserved death, the Roman governor is said to have bowed to pressure from the Jews and granted them their wish, crucifying Jesus. It was leaders of the Jews who initiated Jesus' prosecution, but it ended up a popular cause that involved the Jewish public in general. This has made many accuse the Gospels of anti-Semitism.

According to Mark (15:10), Pilate knew that the Jewish chief priests handed Jesus over to him because of envy. After questioning the accused, Pilate said to the crowd who were demanding Jesus' crucifixion that he did not know what wrong Jesus had done. But because he wanted to satisfy the crowd, he handed him over to be crucified (Mark 15:14-15).

Matthew develops this story further to emphasize Pilate's innocence and the Jews' complete responsibility for the crucifixion. He introduces Pilate's wife in the plot to stress her husbands' innocence, but, more importantly, he makes Pilate declare that he is innocent of Jesus' blood and makes *the Jews* accept *with their children* the responsibility for his execution:

> So after they had assembled, Pilate said to them, "Whom do you want me to release for you, Jesus Barabbas or Jesus who is called the Christ?" (For he knew that they had handed him over because of envy.) As he was sitting on the judgment seat, his wife sent a message to him: "Have nothing to do with that innocent man; I have suffered greatly as a result of a dream about him today." But the chief priests and the elders persuaded the crowds to ask for Barabbas and to have Jesus killed. The governor asked them, "Which of the two do you want me to release for you?" And they said, "Barabbas!" Pilate said to them, "Then what should I do with Jesus who is called the Christ?" They all said, "Crucify him!" He asked, "Why? What wrong has he done?" But they shouted more insistently, "Crucify him!" When Pilate saw that he could do nothing, but that instead a riot was starting, he took some water, washed his hands before the crowd and

said, "I am innocent of this man's blood. You take care of it yourselves!" In reply all the people said, "Let his blood be on us and on our children!" Then he released Barabbas for them. But after he had Jesus flogged, he handed him over to be crucified. (Matt. 27:17-26)

This version of Pilate's trial of Jesus has made Matthew in particular accused of anti-Semitism.

Luke (23:4) also has Pilate say that he could "find no basis for an accusation against this man." In order to avoid getting involved in killing Jesus, Pilate even sent Jesus to Herod Antipas, on the basis that the accused was Galilean and the case therefore fell under Herod's jurisdiction. Luke then goes on to exonerate Herod also, thus laying the blame completely on the Jews:

> Then Pilate called together the chief priests, the rulers, and the people, and said to them, "When I examined him before you, I did not find this man guilty of anything you accused him of doing. Neither did Herod, for he sent him back to us. Look, he has done nothing deserving death. I will therefore have him flogged and release him." But they all shouted out together, "Take this man away! Release Barabbas for us!" (This was a man who had been thrown into prison for an insurrection started in the city, and for murder.) Pilate addressed them once again because he wanted to release Jesus. But they kept on shouting, "Crucify, crucify him!" A third time he said to them, "Why? What wrong has he done? I have found him guilty of no crime deserving death. I will therefore flog him and release him." But they were insistent, demanding with loud shouts that he be crucified. And their shouts prevailed. So Pilate decided that their demand should be granted. (Luke 23:13-24)

Luke stresses Pilate's innocence of Jesus' blood by having him declare three times his belief that Jesus was innocent. This Evangelist later makes two of Jesus' disciples say that their "chief priests and rulers handed him over to be condemned to death, and crucified him" (Luke 24:20).

The same picture is found in John also. Pilate told the Jews that he could "find no basis for an accusation against him" (John 18:38). John's account then goes on as follows:

> Again Pilate went out and said to the Jewish leaders, "Look, I am bringing him out to you, so that you may know that I find no reason for an accusation against him." So Jesus came outside, wearing the crown of thorns and the purple robe. Pilate said to them, "Look, here is the man!" When the chief priests and their officers saw him, they shouted out, "Crucify him! Crucify him!" Pilate said, "You take him and crucify him! Certainly I find no reason for an accusation against him!" The Jewish leaders replied, "We have a law, and according to our law he ought to die, because he claimed to be the Son of God!" When Pilate heard what they said, he was more afraid than ever, and he went back into the governor's residence and said to Jesus, "Where do you come from?" But Jesus gave him no answer. So Pilate said, "Do you refuse to speak to me? Don't

you know I have the authority to release you, and to crucify you?" Jesus replied, "You would have no authority over me at all, unless it was given to you from above. Therefore the one who handed me over to you is guilty of greater sin." From this point on, Pilate tried to release him. But the Jewish leaders shouted out, "If you release this man, you are no friend of Caesar! Everyone who claims to be a king opposes Caesar!" When Pilate heard these words he brought Jesus outside and sat down on the judgment seat in the place called "The Stone Pavement" (Gabbatha in Aramaic). (Now it was the day of preparation for the Passover, about noon.) Pilate said to the Jewish leaders, "Look, here is your king!" Then they shouted out, "Away with him! Away with him! Crucify him!" Pilate asked, "Shall I crucify your king?" The high priests replied, "We have no king except Caesar!" Then Pilate handed him over to them to be crucified. (John 19:4-16)

John (19:11) makes Jesus also declare that those who handed him to Pilate, i.e. the Jews, were the main perpetrators of this crime.

This canonical image of Pilate's innocence and the Jews' guilt is found in apocryphal writings also. For instance, in the Gospel of Peter, Pilate says "I do not have the blood of the son of God on my hands. This was all your doing" (GoPeter 11:4). The rather lengthy Acts of Pilate, which is part of the Gospel of Nicodemus, shows Pilate trying over and over to convince the Jews that Jesus had not done anything wrong and that he should not be killed.

For many centuries, Christians accepted this image of Pilate as an unwilling participant in the execution of Jesus and the Jews as Jesus' real killers and the ones who deserved the full blame for what happened to him. However, this image gradually came under questioning, and modern scholars have identified serious problems with it:

① The whole story of the arrest, trial, and execution of Jesus reflects an inexplicable, sudden, and fundamental change to Jesus' image, from a popular healer and teacher to a much detested blasphemer and a hate figure that the mobs were adamant he should be killed. The people who loved Jesus so much are suddenly asking for his head:

> The Gospel account of Jesus' first two or three days in Jerusalem further attests indirectly that large groups were listening to his teaching in the Temple and that his patent popularity is given as the cause of why the priestly authorities abstained from immediately taking steps against him. In short, until his arrest Jesus seems to have been the darling of the Galilean country folk and even warmly welcomed by the Jewish crowd in Jerusalem.
>
> Yet, if we are to believe the same evangelists, on the last day of the life of Jesus a sea-change suddenly occurred. Jesus became the object of hatred not only for the leaders of Judaism, the chief priests and the Sanhedrin, but also for the Jewish people at large. No one had a good word to say in his favour.

Many witnesses testified against him, but none for him. The crowd abominated him. All the people, "the Jews," asked for his death and egged on the Roman governor to crucify him. Luke, it is true, attempts to diminish the contrast by reporting that the previously hostile crowd present at the crucifixion beat their breasts after the death of Jesus, but this mitigating circumstance seems to be of the evangelist's own making, unsupported by Mark, Matthew or John. (Vermes, 2005: 7)

Before Jesus' arrest, the Jewish leaders were even hesitant to do so because they feared that the crowds would turn against them (Matt. 26:5).

② Crucifixion was a Roman not Jewish punishment. It was used for several centuries until it was abolished in 337 by the first Christian emperor Constantine in veneration of Jesus. Capital penalty in Jewish law was performed by one of four ways. The Old Testament mentions stoning (e.g. Deut. 17:5) and burning (e.g. Lev. 20:14), and the Mishnah adds slaying by the sword and strangulation (Sanh. 49b). Crucifixion is mentioned in the Old Testament as it states that stoning to death is followed by hanging the executed person on a tree (Deut. 21:21-23). So it was a way of displaying the corpse of the executed person, not a method of execution as the Romans used it. Killing by crucifixion is rare in Jewish history. One notable instance, which is reported by Josephus (*Jewish Antiquities*, 13.14.2), is when the Maccabean king and high priest Alexander Janneus (103-76 BCE) crucified 800 rebellious Pharisees while they were alive and had the throats of their wives and children cut before their eyes. Vermes (2005, 26) also notes that crucifixion "was no longer attested as part of Jewish legal practice in the Herodian age, that is, from 37 BC onwards."

③ Two ancient non-Christian sources (Tacitus, *Annals*, 15.44; Josephus, *Jewish Antiquities*, 18.3.3) incriminate Pilate in Jesus' death, although the authenticity and accuracy of these sources are questionable, as we shall see later.

④ The titulus was written from a Roman not Jewish perspective (Theissen & Merz, 1999: 458). It read "king of the Jews" (e.g. Mark 15:26), whereas the Jews would speak of the "king of Israel" (Mark 15:32).

⑤ The suggestion that the Roman governor executed Jesus because of the pressure of Jewish mobs is absurd. It must have been his own decision.

The incrimination of Christian sources of the Jews and exculpation of Pilate of Jesus' crucifixion are believed to have fueled Christian anti-Judaism for a long time. It has been suggested that this Christian portrayal aimed at absolving the Roman governor and blaming the Jews who, at the time of the writing of the Gospels, had become very unpopular with the Romans (Vermes, 2005: 121), having had their first war with the Romans in 66-70 CE. It helped to show that Christianity was not incompatible with the Roman Empire. The validity of this interpretation is rather questionable as it was supposedly the Romans who killed Jesus anyway.

The Gospel accounts may be read to conclude that the Evangelists wanted to blame the Jews for something that the Romans did. Yet they may be similarly seen as trying to implicate the Romans in something that the Jews did because the authors thought that the Jews did not have the power to kill Jesus. Actually, the Gospel accounts are so confused and contradictory that they can be used to lend some support to completely different theories.

But what is the significance of the contradictory story of the responsibility for killing Jesus for the subject of this chapter? It exposes more fundamental problems in the story of Jesus' arrest, trial, and execution, thus further undermining the reliability and historical value of this story.

So were the Romans involved in any attempt at Jesus' life? The Gospels give two reasons as to why the Romans were. **First**, perceiving Jesus as a pretender to the kingship of the Jews, the Romans would have seen him as a danger. It is believed that people's reception of Jesus as a king when he entered Jerusalem contributed to seeing him as a threat (Mark 11:9; Matt. 21:9; Luke 19:38). This political threat is what many modern scholars accept as the reason for Pilate's killing of Jesus, and it is used to shift the blame for Jesus' death from the Jews to the Romans. The problem with this suggestion is that Jesus had no political ambitions (pp. 243-246). He was the Messiah, but not the military Messiah that the Jews were expecting. He was a spiritual Messiah who resisted any attempt to drag him into secular politics. He did not give the Romans any reason to perceive him as a threat. He advocated giving to "Caesar the things that are Caesar's, and to God the things that are God's."

It may be counterargued that what Jesus actually did and say is not what mattered, but what Jewish leaders told Pilate about him. If Pilate accepted any fake political accusation that the Jews leveled at Jesus, then that would have been a sufficient reason for him to eliminate Jesus. Indeed, the fact that, according to the Gospels, the Jews had to alert Pilate to Jesus' danger is in line with the fact that Jesus did not do anything to draw the attention of the Roman authorities; Pilate entered the story of Jesus only after the Jews contacted him. But this solution itself has a problem.

Christians were allowed to continue to practice their religion for decades after the execution of their master. Acts reports Jewish but no Roman persecution of Christians after Jesus. Contrary to common belief, it was not illegal to be Christian, to worship the Jewish God or Jesus, or even to try to convert others to Christianity (Ehrman, 2007: 196). The earliest documented case of official Roman persecution of Christians is linked to the Roman emperor Nero (54-68 CE) who accused Christians of the great fire that he started to burn Rome. Early Roman persecution of Christians was sporadic and localized, rather than organized and driven by Rome. That did not change until 250 CE, when Emperor Decius made the persecution of Christianity an imperial policy. Now, if the Romans had though that Jesus was a danger and killed him, as the Gospels claim, his religion and followers would have been immediately persecuted, which does not seem to have happened.

An answer to this argument is that as Christians were a very small sect, Pilate thought that killing their leader was enough to destroy the sect. He and later Roman governors did not need to launch a persecution campaign against the Christians.

The **second** reason that Pilate got involved in killing Jesus, according to the Gospels, is the immense pressure that the Jews put on him. That the powerful Roman governor of Judea could have been manipulated by a Jewish mob that he treated with utter contempt is too absurd to take seriously. However, if we remove that element of absurdity from the Gospels version of events then it can be reconciled with the argument made earlier about the Jews misleading Pilate about Jesus' real intent. In this revised version, Jewish leaders *petitioned rather than pressurized* Pilate to take out Jesus. He obliged because of the reason they gave him, which could be the accusation that Jesus was a potential insurgent.

In conclusion, if Pilate was indeed involved in killing Jesus, then that would have happened only because the Jews convinced him to do that. Without them, the Roman governor of Judea would not have had anything to do with Jesus — that is if he were to hear of him at all. According to this reconstruction of history, Jewish leaders were the instigators and Pilate was the executioner of Jesus' crucifixion.

Most scholars (e.g. Sanders, 1995: 265) think that the immediate cause for Jesus' death was his prediction about the destruction of the temple (Mark 13:1-2; Matt. 24:1-2; Luke 21:5-6) which was one of the charges leveled at him during his trial (Mark 14:58; Matt. 26:61). This view makes the Jewish leaders even more responsible for his death at the hand of the Romans than the suggestion that he was a political threat, which would have bothered the Romans more.

I cannot see how even a very liberal and selective reading of the Gospels can fail to implicate the Jews in Jesus' death and present them as a non-player. It looks to me that the modern attempts to exonerate the Jews and lay the complete responsibility for Jesus' death on Roman shoulders are influenced by an element of political correctness and resentment to the centuries-long Christian persecution of the Jews because of their role in the alleged crucifixion of Jesus.

18.4. The Crucifixion in History

Christian sources are of very limited historical value. But what do early non-Christian sources say about Jesus' crucifixion?

Although Jesus is supposed to have been crucified by the Romans, there is no Roman record of his trial and death. It may be argued that Jesus was not a significant figure for his execution to make it into the record of the empire, or that the record of his execution has been lost. It may be similarly argued that the silence of the official Roman record reflects the fact that the supposed killing of Jesus by the Romans never took place. What no one argues about is the fact that the alleged crucifixion is not attested in extant Roman records.

The execution of Jesus is supposed to have been mentioned by a number of ancient writers who were not themselves Christian so their statements could not have been influenced by faith. In order for any ancient source to be considered reliable for studying the historicity of any detail of Jesus' life it has to meet three conditions: *independence of Christian sources, authenticity,* and *accuracy.* Let's discuss the significance of these three requirements.

First, clearly a document has to be independent of Christian sources to be reliable as a *historical* source about Jesus' life. This does not mean that anything written by a Christian is unhistorical, but that it is very likely to have been influenced by the writer's beliefs and not written to impartially report what happened.

Second, if there is doubt about the authenticity of a source, i.e. a possibility that it might have been written by someone unknown other than the person it is attributed to, then this means that the source could be of little historical value. For instance, the real author may have been a Christian, someone who was influenced by Christian beliefs, or someone who lived long after the events. Each of these significantly reduces the source's historical value.

Third, if the historical accuracy of a source is questionable, then any statement about Jesus' life would be equally open to question.

If a source does not meet any of these three conditions, then it is unreliable and has a very limited value, if any, for studying Jesus' history. This is why we need to examine every source against these three requirements.

There is one other dimension to any source that can greatly influence its reliability, and that is how early it was written. Any source that was written long after the time of Jesus cannot be used to establish the historicity of the crucifixion, or to that matter any detail of Jesus' life, because it is likely to be inaccurate and to have been influenced by Christian or other sources that might be unreliable. The more distant the date of an account from Jesus' time the less likely that it is accurate and free from Christian influence.

The most valuable sources are those that provide firsthand accounts. Unfortunately, no Christian or non-Christian firsthand accounts of Jesus' life exists. The Gospels were written decades after Jesus, and the many problems in these reports clearly show that they were not written by people who knew Jesus. The earliest non-Christian biographical information about Jesus is even later. This greatly reduces the value of those potentially independent sources. Nevertheless, we shall still review the oldest sources — and there are only a handful of them in the first two centuries — and see how they fare against the three requirements of independence of Christian sources, authenticity, and accuracy:

① **Flavius Josephus (37-100 CE)**: The Jewish historian Josephus mentions Jesus in a very famous and highly controversial passage known as the *Testimonium Flavianum*:

> Now there was about this time Jesus, a wise man, if it be lawful to call him a man; for he was a doer of wonderful works, a teacher of such men as receive the truth with pleasure. He drew over to him both many of the Jews and many of the Gentiles. He was [the] Christ. And when Pilate, at the suggestion of the principal men amongst us, had condemned him to the cross, those that loved him at the first did not forsake him; for he appeared to them alive again the third day; as the divine prophets had foretold these and ten thousand other wonderful things concerning him. And the tribe of Christians, so named from him, are not extinct at this day. (Josephus, *Jewish Antiquities*, 18.3.3)

Suspicions about the authenticity of this passage were first voiced in the 16th century. Today it is almost universally accepted that this passage is either a complete forgery that was introduced in its entirety into Joseph's work by a Christian or a major Christian reworking of a very different passage that Josephus wrote. The defense of the authenticity of the Testimonium has been based on a number of arguments that I list below along with counter arguments:

(i) *The passage was cited as early as the early 4th century by Eusebius of Caesarea (The Proof of the Gospel, 3.5.124)*. This is hardly a convincing argument; two centuries is plenty of time to tamper with the original text. Additionally, the fact that the passage is not cited until the 4th century is actually more of a problem for the authenticity claim, as explained later below in the discussion of the counter arguments.

(ii) *It seems to be written from a Jewish rather than Christian perspective, describing the Christians in a demeaning way as a tribe*. This could be easily explained to have been indicative of deft forgery. Alternatively, if the passage was only embellished by a Christian hand, then it would naturally contain both Josephus' Jewish tone and a Christian one.

(iii) *Unlike the Christian sources that blame mainly the Jewish authorities for condemning Jesus to death and portray Pilate as being put under pressure by them to execute him, the passage restricts the guilt of the Jewish leaders to advising Pilate and portrays the latter as the executioner*. The passage does not exonerate the Jews but shows more knowledge of the legal system in Judea in which the Jews had no executive power. That writer could be Josephus, but it could also be a Christian who knew better about what roles Pilate and the Jews could have played. If the Jews had the power of execution, then the passage could not have been written by Josephus who would have known that.

(iv) *Josephus' passing mention of "Jesus" later in Jewish Antiquities (20.9.1) when talking about James* — *"the brother of Jesus, who was called Christ"* — *indicates that he must have introduced this name earlier, and that must be in passage 18.3.3. Additionally, Josephus mentions the term "Christ" only in these two passages. Given that Josephus' Gentile readers would not have understood the meaning of this term, its brief mention in 20.9.1 indicates that it was mentioned in more detail earlier, that is in 18.3.3.* This argument only means that Josephus mentioned "Jesus" and called him the "Christ" before his reference to him in the context of talking about James; it does not mean that the content of the Testimonium is accurate or authentic. Additionally, there is circular logic in operation here, as the two passages are cited to support each other. Finally, I have already shown that the James passage itself could not have been written by Josephus (pp. 158-162).

(v) *The style is that of Josephus.* This argument is equally inconclusive, as it has been pointed out that Josephus' style was not impossible to imitate.

These arguments are hardly accepted anymore as sufficient for establishing the authenticity of the contentious passage, not only because of the weaknesses explained above, but also because any power they may have is greatly outweighed by counter arguments that suggest that the passage is substantially, if not completely, the work of a Christian:

(i) None of the apologetic fathers of the church of the 2nd and 3rd century mentions the Testimonium, despite the fact that they quote Josephus about the interpretation of the Old Testament. Had they known of its existence, they would have certainly used it in their debates with Jews. Even Origen who cited in the 3rd century Josephus' another alleged, less important reference to Jesus in the James passage does not mention the Testimonium. This does not necessarily exclude the possibility that the Testimonium existed in a form that did not contain Christian interpolations, as it would not have served any Christian debating purpose.

(ii) The early Christian theologian Origen (ca. 185 – ca. 254 CE) explicitly stated twice that Josephus did not believe that Jesus was the Christ (*Against Celsus*, 1.47; *Commentary on Matthew*, 10.17) while at the same time quoting freely from *Jewish Antiquities* to argue in support Christianity. When Jerome (*Lives of Illustrious Men*, 13) quoted the Testimonium in 392 CE he changed the clause "He was [the] Christ" to "[he] was believed to be Christ," which suggests that he also believed that the passage was tampered with by Christians. An 18th century translator of Josephus' complete works put forward the bizarre argument that Josephus was an Ebionite Christian who believed that Jesus was the Christ but did not believe in his divinity (Whiston, 1998: 985-986), but this apologetic hypothesis has no support in the writing of Josephus, Christians, or non-Christians.

(iii) In addition to its proclamation of Jesus' messiahship, the passage promotes the Christian beliefs that Jesus was more than a man, performed miracles, appeared on the third day after his crucifixion to his disciples, and that these things had been predicted by prophets. All of these make the passage too Christian to have been written by a non-Christian, let alone a faithful Jew. These Christian statements are *impossible* to reconcile with Josephus' Jewish beliefs.

Leaving Josephus' belief aside, the fact that this Jewish historian was working for the Romans — Jesus' alleged killers — means that he could not have proclaimed that Jesus was the Messiah. Additionally, Josephus condemned all pretending Messiahs and popular leaders that the Romans opposed or killed, so it is not possible that he would have exempted Jesus from his typical pouring of scorn on such figures (Doherty, 1999: 210-211). We are asked to accept that Josephus even went out of his way to praise this particular executed rebel!

(iv) Even the claim that Pilate killed Jesus at the suggestion of Jewish leaders is problematic. Stating that Pilate executed a wise man because Jewish leaders requested him to do so, Earl Doherty explains, portrays the Roman governor as a bit of an idiot. Writing for the Romans and under their patronage, Josephus could not have said that.

(v) The passage breaks the continuity of a narrative text that details a series of riots. It has nothing to do with the paragraphs that precede and follow it. There are two answers to this argument. First, although Josephus, like other ancient authors, wrote annalistically, he did at times interrupt the recounting of a certain chain of events to mention a different incident that took place at the same time. Second, footnotes and similar techniques that are used today for inserting intractable material that would otherwise break the main discussion were not known to ancient authors. This forced them at times to resort to digression (Smallwood, 1981: 20-21).

(vi) Josephus recounts the same disturbances elsewhere but with no mention of Jesus.

(vii) A different version of the Testimonium has been cited by the 10th century Arab Melkite bishop of Hierapolis Agapius in his work called *Book of the Title*. Interestingly, some of the Christian claims have been removed, and what is left has been toned down, making Josephus only report what Christians claimed:

> Similarly Josephus, the Hebrew. For he says in the treatises that he was written on the governance of the Jews: 'At this time there was a wise man who was called Jesus. His conduct was good, and he was known to be virtuous. And many people from among the Jews and the other nations became his disciples. Pilate condemned him to be crucified and to die. But those who had become his disciples did not abandon his discipleship. They reported that he had appeared to them three days after his crucifixion, and that he was alive; accordingly he was perhaps the Messiah, concerning whom the prophets have recounted wonders'.

(viii) The view of the majority that the James passage in *Jewish Antiquities* is genuine creates two other problems for the Testimonium. Let's remind ourselves of the James passage:

> Festus was now dead, and Albinus was but upon the road; so he [the high priest Ananus] assembled the Sanhedrin of judges, and brought before them the brother of Jesus, who was called Christ, whose name was James, and some others [or, some of his companions]; and when he had formed an accusation against them as breakers of the law, he delivered them to be stoned. (Josephus, *Jewish Antiquities*, 20.9.1)

There are significant differences between the two passages. **First**, Josephus shows no interest here in Jesus other than to identify James, who is the subject of the passage. His identification of Jesus as he "who was called Christ," as the name Jesus was widely used then, clearly suggests that he did not share the belief that Jesus was the Christ. He does not bother to mention anything about Jesus, let alone laud him as a miracle performer and someone who was more than a man. The contrast between how Josephus speaks about Jesus in the two passages is remarkable.

Second, the James passage talks about how he was tried and executed by the Sanhedrin, something that is strikingly similar to what is supposed to have happened to his brother Jesus. According to the Gospels, Jesus was tried by the same Jewish court and handed over to Pontius Pilate to be executed. Yet although Josephus mentions Jesus to identify James — implying that Jesus was more famous than his brother — he inexplicably passes over the clear opportunity to stress the similarity between the fates of the two brothers. If James' trial and execution were worth mentioning, then surely the trial and execution of his brother, because of whom James was supposedly ultimately killed, would have been at least equally interesting to mention — that is, if the author believed that Jesus was executed.

The contrast between the James passage and the Testimonium represents serious problems for attributing them both to one author, let alone Josephus.

These are the main arguments against the authenticity of the Testimonium.

Some scholars have suggested that Eusebius himself forged, totally or in part, the Testimonium (Feldman, 1965: 49). It has also been suggested that similarities between the Testimonium and the so-called Emmaus passage in Luke (24:13-27), which recounts the appearance of Jesus after his resurrection to two of his disciples, indicate that both had a common Christian source.

Testimonium Flavianum is not the only passage in a Josephus work that has been written or edited by a Christian hand. The Slavonic version of *The Jewish War* contains longer sections about John the Baptist and Jesus which do not exist in the

Greek version. Except rare exceptions, such as Williamson (1974: 396-397), scholars agree that these additions are Christian forgeries and that Josephus could never have written them.

It should not surprise us, therefore, to find that the relatively short Testimonium has been completely written, or at least heavily edited, by a Christian hand. It is likely that Josephus made a mention of Jesus and it was substantially changed by Christians to promote their image of Jesus. It is not possible to completely rule out the possibility that the Testimonium is in its entirety a Christian forgery. The Testimonium fails the test of authenticity and, consequently, the test of independence.

A fuller discussion of various arguments that have been made against and in support of the Testimonium can be found in Kirby (2001).

② **Cornelius Tacitus (56 – ca. 120 CE):** Jesus was mentioned by a number of Roman writers, including Tacitus who mentions also his death. This aristocrat occupied a number of important positions among them the Proconsul of Asia. He wrote a number of books, including his *Annals* of the Roman empire from its birth to the death of Emperor Nero (54-68 CE). It is in this work, which was written around 117 CE, that Tacitus mentions Jesus' death. He tells us that in order to scotch the rumor that the great fire that engulfed Rome in 64 CE was ordered by him, Nero accused the Christians of arson and inflicted on them the worse of punishment:

> Nero substituted as culprits, and punished with the utmost refinements of cruelty, a class of men, loathed for their vices, whom the crowd styled Christians. Christus, the founder of the name, had undergone the death penalty in the reign of Tiberius, by sentence of the procurator Pontius Pilatus, and the pernicious superstition was checked for a moment, only to break out once more, not merely in Judea, the home of the disease, but in the capital itself, where all things horrible or shameful in the world collect and find a vogue. First, then, the confessed members of the sect were arrested; next, on their disclosures, vast numbers were convicted, not so much on the count of arson as for hatred of the human race. And derision accompanied their end: they were covered with wild beasts' skins and torn to death by dogs; or they were fastened on crosses, and when daylight failed were burned to serve as lamps by night. Nero had offered his Gardens for the spectacle, and gave an exhibition in his Circus, mixing with the crown in the habit of a charioteer, or mounted on his car. Hence, in spite of a guilt which had earned the most exemplary punishment, there arose a sentiment of pity, due to the impression that they were being sacrificed not for the welfare of the state but to the ferocity of a single man. (Tacitus, *Annals*, 15.44)

The authenticity of this passage has been questioned by a minority on the basis that it is not mentioned by any of the early fathers of the church, but the text is generally accepted to be authentic.

If Tacitus' passage relied on official Roman documents, it must be considered independent of Christian sources. But it looks unlikely that Tacitus used official records. **First**, he would not have made the mistake of calling Pilate (26-36 CE) a procurator, when in fact he was a prefect (Theissen & Merz, 1999: 83). Among the differences between these two titles is that the latter was a military position, whereas the former was a civilian, financial administrator. Judea was ruled by a prefect from the removal of Herod Archelaus in 6 CE until probably after the death of Herod Agrippa in 44 CE when the governor became a procurator. There is also a Roman inscription that describes Pilate as the "prefect of Judea."

Second, Roman imperial documents could not have referred to Jesus with his Christian title, Christus or Christ. As pointed out rather sarcastically Tacitus "could hardly have found in archives a statement such as 'the Messiah was executed this morning'" (Wells, 1988: 16-17).

The fact that Tacitus did not rely on official Roman documents does not necessarily mean that his information is of Christian origin. However, as Tacitus does not tell us where he got his information from, we cannot say with certainty that his passage did not rely on Christian sources. Some scholars have pointed out that it is possible that Tacitus' reference to Jesus' death was based on what he learned from Christians (France, 1999: 23; Sanders, 1995: 50; Wells, 1988: 17). Tacitus' passage shows clearly that there was a significant Christian community in Rome, something that makes it more likely that Christians were his sources.

The mistake about the title of Pilate may also be seen as casting some doubt on the accuracy of Tacitus' passage, even though Tacitus' reliability is generally accepted. This reliability, however, becomes a moot point if all that he did is to *faithfully* report what Christians believed had happened to their master.

Finally, the account was written almost nine decades after Jesus' supposed death, which makes it very likely that it is not independent.

③ **Lucian of Samosata (120 – after 180 CE)**: This Greek satirist wrote a piece about a philosopher who becomes a leader of the Christians to take advantage of their gullibility:

> They revered him as a god, made use of him as a lawgiver, and set him down as a protector, next after that other, to be sure, whom they still worship, the man who was crucified in Palestine because he introduced this new cult into the world.....
>
> Furthermore, their first lawgiver persuaded them that they are all brothers of one another after they have transgressed once, for all by denying the Greek gods and by worshipping that crucified sophist himself and living under his laws. (Lucian, *The Passing of Peregrinus*)

There are no doubts about the authenticity of this passage. The satiric nature of the Lucian's work, however, has made some question whether he gave real attention to historical accuracy. Additionally, the late date of this source makes it highly likely that the author simply accepted the Christian belief about the fate of their master rather than relied on an independent source.

④ **Mara Bar Serapion (ca. 73 CE)**: An alleged mention of Jesus has been noted in a letter written from a Roman prison by this Syrian pagan Stoic. Writing to his son about how even wise men can be persecuted, Serapion goes on to say:

> What advantage did the Athenians gain from putting Socrates to death? Famine and plague came upon them as a judgment for their crime. What advantage did the men of Samos gain from burning Pythagoras? In a moment their land was covered with sand. What advantage did the Jews gain from executing their wise King? It was just after that their Kingdom was abolished.
>
> God justly avenged these three wise men: the Athenians died of hunger; the Samians were overwhelmed by the sea; the Jews, ruined and driven from their land, live in complete dispersion.
>
> But Socrates did not die for good; he lived on in the teaching of Plato. Pythagoras did not die for good; he lived on in the statue of Hera. Nor did the wise King die for good; He lived on in the teaching which He had given. (Bruce, 2003: 117)

One obvious problem with this passage is that while it talks about a "wise king" of the Jews, it does not actually mention Jesus by name. Also, the Jews never accepted Jesus as their king anyway. There is a good deal of speculation in suggesting that the author is talking about Jesus. Additionally, Pythagoras and Socrates lived in the 6th and 5th centuries BCE, respectively, so the wise king of the Jews could refer to someone who lived at any time in a period of several entries. The fact that there are serious questions about whether the passage is talking about Jesus at all rules it out as a reliable source of information on Jesus' death. The passage might well be completely irrelevant to Jesus' life.

Even if we consider the unproven assumption that Serapion's passage talks about Jesus, the historical value of this passage is undermined by its wrong descriptions of what happened to Pythagoras, the Athenians, and the people of Samos. What Serapion says happened to the wise king could be equally wrong. The passage fails the accuracy test.

With the passage being historically inaccurate, the question of whether Serapion meant Jesus or someone else by the "wise king" of the Jews becomes irrelevant. However, it has also been rightly pointed out that Serapion's view of the destruction of Jerusalem as a punishment for the Jews for their killing of their king sounds very much like a Christian argument against the Jews (France, 1999: 24) — something that undermines the possible independence of the passage.

Whether Serapion wrote really shortly after the destruction of temple in 70 CE has also been questioned. Some have suggested that it is not possible to rule out the possibility that he could have written as late as a century after the destruction (France, 1999: 24).

⑤ **Thallus (date?)**: Writing about 221 CE, the Christian chronographer Julius Africanus (ca. 180 – ca. 250 CE) quoted the historian Thallus about the darkness that, according to the Synoptics (Mark 15:33; Matt. 27:45; Luke 23:44), befell the earth from noon until 3 during Jesus' crucifixion. This is what the Christian historian says:

> As to His works severally, and His cures effected upon body and soul, and the mysteries of His doctrine, and the resurrection from the dead, these have been most authoritatively set forth by His disciples and apostles before us. On the whole world there pressed a most fearful darkness; and the rocks were rent by an earthquake, and many places in Judea and other districts were thrown down. This darkness Thallus, in the third book of his History, calls, as appears to me without reason, an eclipse of the sun. For the Hebrews celebrate the Passover on the 14th day according to the moon, and the passion of our Saviour fails on the day before the Passover; but an eclipse of the sun takes place only when the moon comes under the sun. And it cannot happen at any other time but in the interval between the first day of the new moon and the last of the old, that is, at their junction: how then should an eclipse be supposed to happen when the moon is almost diametrically opposite the sun? (Africanus, *Chronograph*, 18)

We do not have direct access to the text about the eclipse that Africanus mentions. Thallus' three-volume history of the world has been lost. There are no grounds to doubt the authenticity of the quote from Thallus, as there is nothing to suggest that the vague reference to an eclipse could have been written by someone else. There is also no reason to doubt the accuracy of the information.

Significantly, there is nothing in Africanus' passage to suggest that he meant to say that Thallus linked the eclipse to Jesus in anyway! Indeed, Africanus has himself rightly pointed out that an eclipse of the Sun occurs at the time of new moon not full moon, which is when the Passover is celebrated. We also know today that a total eclipse of the Sun cannot last for more than a few minutes. It is perfectly possible to read Africanus' passage to mean that he found Thallus talk about an eclipse that the Christian historian associated with the darkness that the Gospels say took place during Jesus' crucifixion. This raises serious questions about the relevance of Thallus' eclipse record to the historicity of Jesus' death.

In fact, Africanus' claim that Thallus talked about the crucifixion eclipse of around 30 CE might well be in conflict with a reference by Eusebius to a brief compendium by Thallus that covers the years from the fall of Troy in 1184 BCE to the 167th Olympiad of 109 BCE. The end date of this chronology might suggest that Thallus actually lived well before Jesus and so he could not have said anything about the alleged eclipse that happened over a century after him. This has prompted many modern scholars to claim that 167 must have been a corruption of the original figure, suggesting instead an Olympiad that took place after the date of the eclipse.

If Thallus' reference to the eclipse has nothing to do with the crucifixion darkness, which is far more likely than the opposite assumption, then there is no reason to rule out the possibility that Thallus lived well before Jesus. It is also possible that he lived as late as the 2nd half of the 2nd century, as the earliest reference to Thallus we have is from about 180 CE. This late date also completely undermines the historical value of Thallus' alleged reference to the crucifixion eclipse, as it makes it almost certain that the reference cannot be considered independent.

I have cited Africanus' reference to Thallus in this section because it is often mentioned in the context of examining the early non-Christian sources on Jesus. This very vague, probably irrelevant, secondhand source has no historical value for studying the historicity of Jesus' crucifixion.

⑥ **Jewish Sources**: The earliest rabbinic literature, the Mishnah, which was compiled over 2 centuries by many scholars and put in its final form early in the 3rd century, contains no mention of Jesus. A later collection of rabbinic teachings, the Talmud, mentions Jesus several times. The Talmud — which contains the Mishnah, commentary on and interpretation of the Mishnah called "Gemara," and certain auxiliary materials — was transmitted orally for several centuries before it was written around 5th century. It contains passages that accuse Jesus' mother of unchastity, calling Jesus "son of Pantera" and "son of Stada" (p. 116). One text is particularly relevant to our current discussion because it mentions the death of Yeshu — the name with which Jesus is known in other Talmudic passages. Theissen and Merz (1999: 75) have suggested that this text may have come from the early 2nd century:

> On the eve of the Passover Yeshu was hanged. For forty days before the execution took place, a herald went forth and cried, "He is going forth to be stoned because he has practised sorcery and enticed Israel to apostasy. Any one who can say anything in his favour, let him come forward and plead on his behalf." But since nothing was brought forward in his favour he was hanged on the eve of the Passover! — 'Ulla retorted: "Do you suppose that he was one for whom a defence could be made? Was he not a Mesith [enticer], concerning whom Scripture says, 'Neither shalt thou spare, neither shalt

thou conceal him?' With Yeshu however it was different, for he was connected with the government [or royalty, i.e., influential]."

Our Rabbis taught: Yeshu had five disciples, Matthai, Nakai, Nezer, Buni and Todah. When Matthai was brought [before the court] he said to them [the judges], "Shall Matthai be executed? Is it not written, 'Matthai [when] shall I come and appear before God?'" Thereupon they retorted; "Yes, Matthai shall be executed, since it is written, 'When Matthai [when] shall [he] die and his name perish.'" When Nakai was brought in he said to them: "Shall Nakai be executed? It is not written, 'Naki [the innocent] and the righteous slay thou not?'" "Yes," was the answer, "Nakai shall be executed, since it is written, 'In secret places does Naki [the innocent] slay.'" When Nezer was brought in, he said: "Shall Nezer be executed? Is it not written, 'And Nezer [a twig] shall grow forth out of his roots.'" "Yes," they said, "Nezer shall be executed, since it is written, 'But thou art cast forth away from thy grave like Nezer [an abhorred offshoot].'" When Buni was brought in, he said: "Shall Buni be executed? Is it not written, 'Beni [my son], my first born?'" "Yes," they said, "Buni shall be executed, since it is written, 'Behold I will slay Bine-ka [thy son] thy first born.'" And when Todah was brought in, he said to them: "Shall Todah be executed? Is it not written, 'A psalm for Todah [thanksgiving]?'" "Yes," they answered, "Todah shall be executed, since it is written, 'Whoso offereth the sacrifice of Todah [thanksgiving] honoured me.'" (Sanh. 43a)

This text contradicts the Synoptic Gospels but agrees with John in placing the killing of Jesus on the eve of the Passover. It also, surprisingly, talks about Jesus having 5 disciples. Additionally, apart from Matthai whose name may be linked to Matthew, none of the names of the other four can be linked to any of Jesus' disciples in the New Testament.

The very late dates of the Jewish sources that mention Jesus make them highly unreliable. They are also clearly influenced by anti-Christian religious beliefs, as they are used as polemic tools. Their statements about Jesus have no historical value.

I have mentioned in this section all the known references to Jesus' death in early non-Christian sources. Let's summarize our conclusion about these sources:

① **Flavius Josephus**: The Testimonium fails the authenticity and independence tests.

② **Cornelius Tacitus**: describing Pilate mistakenly as a procurator instead of prefect and calling Jesus with his Christian title indicate that Tacitus did not copy this information from official Roman records. The late date of around 117 CE of his statement also suggests that it is unlikely to be independent.

③ **Lucian of Samosata**: There are doubts about the reliability of Lucian's passage. Its satiric nature means that it might not be accurate. While we cannot prove conclusively that it fails the independence test, it is highly likely this late account from the 2nd half of the 2nd century CE relied on Christian sources.

④ **Mara Bar Serapion**: This account fails the accuracy test, and it is likely that it does not refer to Jesus anyway. Additionally, the passage seems to have been written from a Christian point of view, so its independence is also highly questionable. It has also been suggested that Serapion may have written his passage as late as the 2nd half of the 2nd century CE.

⑤ **Thallus**: There is no evidence that Thallus' reference to an eclipse had anything to do with Jesus. There is also a possibility that his passage about that eclipse was too late to be likely to have been independent — that is, if it has any relevance to Jesus to start with.

⑥ **Jewish Sources**: These fail both tests of independence and accuracy.

Most of these sources clearly fail at least one of the independence, authenticity, and accuracy tests. None of them is likely to be independent. Crucially, we do not have firsthand accounts. We do not have testimonies by people who were witnesses, or even contemporary, to Jesus' alleged death and had direct knowledge of it. At best, our sources copied from older oral and written sources. Although ostensibly non-Christian, these sources are as lacking historical reliability as their Christian counterparts. In fact, they might well be based on Christian sources. According to one notable professor, "Roman sources that mention [Jesus] are all dependent on Christian reports" (Sanders, 1995: 49). This is how another Christian New Testament scholar, Professor Richard France, assesses the available sources:

> The first thing to be said about non-Christian historical evidence for Jesus is that there is not much of it, at least from a period close enough to the events to be of any value as an independent witness to Jesus as seen through non-Christian eyes. (France, 1999: 19)

One suggested explanation for the almost complete absence of any independent references to Jesus is that, unlike the very prominent character he later came to be, he was not an important figure during his life. He became important only after his religion started to spread, and that was after he was no more. My reading of the various sources, including the Qur'an, on Jesus' life and how his religion developed after him leads me also to conclude that Jesus had a low-key life. Another explanation is that the sources in which he was mentioned have been simply lost (France, 1999: 19-20; Sanders, 1995: 49). These two explanations are not mutually exclusive.

Regardless of the historical value of these sources, and assuming, for the sake of argument, that some of these sources are genuinely non-Christian and were written by their alleged authors, it is clear that these authors share with the Evangelists their belief that Jesus was executed by the Romans. So what we have here is an agreement between Christian and non-Christian sources, all of which written at least several decades after Jesus, that he was given the death penalty by the Romans. We can reject the historical value of these sources, but we have to accept that the belief that Jesus was executed by the Romans was widespread a few decades after Jesus. To put it differently, *there is no evidence that Jesus was executed, but there is evidence that, decades after Jesus, many people believed that he was killed by the Romans*. There is no evidence to confirm or reject Jesus' alleged execution, but there is evidence that a perception that he was killed had developed by the time the first Gospel was written, that is some 30-40 years after Jesus. This is the only logical conclusion that can be inferred from early Christian and allegedly independent sources.

Geoffrey Parrinder claims that "secular historians also accept the crucifixion as a fact. No serious modern historian doubts that Jesus was a historical figure and that he was crucified, whatever he may think of the faith in the resurrection" (Parrinder, 1995: 116). This statement is misleading. It is true that most modern historians accept that Jesus was crucified, but no historian can claim that this view is based on *conclusive* historical evidence. At best, it is based on a balance of probabilities. With the acknowledged unreliability of the non-Christian sources on the crucifixion, it is Christian sources that have played the main role in asserting the crucifixion account. But the New Testament books are anything but reliable historical sources. Parrinder argues that whether the crucifixion occurred or not "has a vital bearing on the understanding of the life of Jesus, and on the reliability of the Gospel and all the New Testament" (Parrinder, 1995: 117). This is exactly the problem. The Gospels are the main source of the belief — and it is a belief — in the crucifixion, yet these books, and the New Testament in general, have so many historical problems, so their reports of any single event or set of events cannot be relied upon.

Contrary to Parrinder's attempt to portray the crucifixion as an independent historical event which the Gospels simply reported, these books have actually given this alleged event its prominent place in people's minds and history. If the historically highly unreliable Gospels had remained silent on the fate of Jesus, and if Paul, who never knew Jesus, had not placed Jesus' alleged crucifixion at the heart of his theology, any suggestion that Jesus was crucified, if that would have been made in the first place, would not have gained any acceptance as a historical event. While the New Testament is no more seen as the infallible book that it was believed to be for many centuries, it still has, albeit totally unjustifiably, a great influence on people's understanding and perception of the history of Jesus. The belief among many in the crucifixion is a lingering effect of the once indisputable acceptance of the New Testament as a book of truth and nothing but the truth. The absence of historical sources on the life of Jesus combined with an enormous interest in his history have more or less forced many to accept the New Testament's version of history, even if this position can be sustained only through a cherry picking attitude when dealing with the Gospels. There is an element of desperation in the interest of both scholars and lay people in what the New Testament says about Jesus. People desperately need to know about how he lived, what he said and did, and how he died, and the New Testament books are unjustifiably seen as the only sources to satisfy this need.

Parrinder's affirmation above is not only misleading because there is no evidence on the historicity of the crucifixion, but also because there is no alleged detail of Jesus' life that is beyond doubt! This is why there are scholars, though a very small minority, who have gone as far as advocating the fantastic theory that Jesus never existed (e.g. Doherty, 1999; Wells, 1988)! We have to accept that almost all of what we know about Jesus comes from religion, not history, and this applies to his alleged execution. Equally interesting is the fact that there is actually more than one biography for Jesus. His life is described differently not only in Islam and Christianity, but also within Christian tradition. This does not mean that *all* those religious biographies are *necessarily* wrong or inaccurate, but of course conflicting accounts cannot all be correct.

A religious account may be perfectly based on real history, but in the absence of independent historical evidence, we have to accept and make it clear that these accounts are not attested independently. Even when we conclude that a religious account of a particular detail in Jesus' life is not incompatible with established history, this can only mean that, from an independent historical point of view, this detail is possible and cannot be ruled out. It is an *act of faith* to accept absolutely such a detail.

Christian scholars have successfully popularized the view that the New Testament is more historical than the Qur'an. Unsuspecting people who have not studied closely the sources on Jesus are often mislead into thinking that there is an independent version of Jesus' history and that the New Testament is, if not completely then at least largely, in agreement with that history. Sources that disagree with the New Testament, such as the Qur'an, are then positioned as *unhistorical* and *inaccurate*. The reality is that there is cyclical logic in operation here: the history of Jesus' life that the New Testament has *created* is often cited as independent historical evidence on the Gospel accounts! Sources that disagree with the New Testament are, expectedly, discredited as historically unreliable. This is a real crucifixion of truth which is attested by history.

18.5. Alternative Scenarios

While the crucifixion and the resurrection of Jesus are both unattested by independent historical sources, there is still a significant difference between the two events from the point of view of the independent historian. Execution is a *normal* event that happened to countless people throughout history, so its historicity may be entertained without subscription to any paranormal beliefs, whether Christian or not. Indeed, there are historians who would not describe themselves as Christians or believers in the paranormal who think that Jesus was executed.

Conversely, the resurrection is a supernatural event whose historicity can be seriously considered only by people who believe in the paranormal and, more specifically, accept a Christian version of the paranormal. A person who does not believe in the paranormal cannot accept the rising from the dead of Jesus, because such an event is a natural impossibility. A non-Christian believer in the supernatural would consider this event possible, but he would probably find it more likely to belong to Christian theology than history. Only a Christian, who by definition believes in the paranormal, can accept that this paranormal event could have happened and did happen.

A third event that sits between the crucifixion and the resurrection in Jesus' story in the Gospels, the empty tomb, is amenable to both normal and paranormal explanations. The same applies to Jesus' appearances after his alleged resurrection.

Unsurprisingly, the historicity of the resurrection has been rejected by non-Christian scholars. The rejection has not been based only on the paranormal nature of the event, but also on the fact that its reports in the Gospels are shrouded in contradiction and confusion. One widely held view is that the resurrection account is a late editorial addition to the story. This is how Professor Vermes — a Jew by birth who was baptized and became a Catholic priest before reverting to Judaism — convincingly explains it:

> It seems clear that the disciples did not entertain any hope of any impending resurrection, judging from their behaviour after Jesus' arrest — they all fled — and their original disbelief on Easter day. Neither did the women who set out for the tomb to anoint the body of Jesus. But this lack of expectation potently conflicts with the claim repeated no less than five times in the Synoptic Gospels that Jesus distinctly predicted not only his death, but also his resurrection on precisely the third day (Mark 8:31, 9:9, 9:31, 10:33-34, 14:28). This most significant prophecy of Jesus appears to have fallen on deaf ears or to have sunk straight into oblivion, with not a single apostle or disciple recalling it during the crucial hours between Friday and Sunday, or even later when the resurrection became the central topic of the preaching of the primitive church. Luke alone realized this internal contradiction and tried to overcome it by suggesting that the women were reminded of Jesus' prediction by the two men they had met in the empty tomb (Luke 24:7-8). If all his close companions had known exactly what was going to happen, despite their instinctive anxiety they would have comforted themselves with the thought that on the third day all would be well. As this manifestly was

not the case, one is inclined to conclude that the announcements concerning the resurrection of Jesus are later editorial interpolations. They are often accompanied by clumsy explanations, namely that Peter was unwilling to believe the words of Jesus and began to rebuke him (Mark 8:32-33; Matt. 16:22-23), and that the apostles were dim-witted and could not comprehend what resurrection from the dead meant (Mark 9:10, 9:32; Matt. 17:23; Luke 18:34). (Vermes, 2000: 171-172)

This should not be surprising if we remember that:

> Neither the authors of the Old Testament nor post-biblical Jewish writers inferred that either the death or resurrection of Israel's Messiah was expected in any way. This means that Jesus and his disciples were not preconditioned by tradition or education to look forward to a risen Christ; so the first narrators of the Jesus story had no pattern to follow when they tried to explain what happened to their deceased and buried teacher. (Vermes, 2000: 171)

Like other episodes of Jesus' life, the resurrection and related events were introduced by Christian authors to serve theological purposes.

As a result of the view that the account of the resurrection is nothing more than an editorial creation by the Gospel authors and their sources, a number of rational alternatives to the Gospel versions of events have been developed. According to these alternative scenarios, which accommodate the normal crucifixion, the paranormal resurrection is rejected, and the empty tomb and the appearances are either rejected as never happened, or explained in normal terms.

In addition to those that reject the historicity of these events, these are the main normal alternative hypotheses that have been put forward (see also Theissen & Merz, 1999: 476-482):

① **The stolen body hypothesis**: Jesus died and was never raised from the dead. The tomb was found empty because Jesus' disciples stole his body from the tomb. This version of the story, which was put forward by the German professor Hermann Samuel Reimarus (1694-1768), makes use of the charge in a Matthean passage that explains what happened to the guards of the tomb after seeing the angel and discovering that Jesus' body had disappeared:

> Some of the guard went into the city and told the chief priests everything that had happened. After they had assembled with the elders and formed a plan, they gave a large sum of money to the soldiers, telling them, "You are to say, 'His disciples came at night and stole his body while we were asleep.' If this matter is heard before the governor, we will satisfy him and keep you out of trouble." So they took the money and

did as they were instructed. And this story is told among the Jews to this day. (Matt. 28:11-15)

Reimarus, who considered Jesus an unsuccessful political claimant, believed that this charge, which is presented as fake in Matthew, is what actually happened.

② **The second tomb hypothesis**: Joseph of Arimathea who, the Gospels say, buried Jesus on Friday, later moved Jesus' body to another tomb, hence his original tomb was found to be empty on Sunday. This version was first suggested anonymously in 1799.

③ **The subjective appearances hypothesis**: Jesus did not appear in reality to anyone after his death, but those who claimed to have seen him only imagined that they did. It was some form of hallucination. This interpretation was put forward by D. F. Strauss in the first half of the 19th century.

④ **The non-fatal crucifixion hypothesis**: One other fundamental hypothesis that explains in normal terms the empty tomb and the appearances claims that Jesus did not die when he was crucified. Advocates of this theory often cite a report by Josephus about someone who survived crucifixion as proof that this extremely cruel method of execution did not always lead to death:

> And when I was sent by Titus Caesar with Cerealins, and a thousand horsemen, to a certain village called Thecoa, in order to know whether it were a place fit for a camp, as I came back, I saw many captives crucified, and remembered three of them as my former acquaintance. I was very sorry at this in my mind, and went with tears in my eyes to Titus, and told him of them; so he immediately commanded them to be taken down, and to have the greatest care taken of them, in order to their recovery; yet two of them died under the physician's hands, while the third recovered. (Josephus, *Life*, 75)

There have been a number of various versions of this hypothesis. It has been suggested that Jesus survived the crucifixion after falling in a deep swoon on the cross, pretending to have died, or putting himself in a state of self-hypnosis. It is claimed that he was treated in the tomb, or that he managed to use up whatever energy he had after the ordeal of the crucifixion to escape the tomb. Surviving the crucifixion has been then used to explain Jesus' appearances to his disciples. These alternative versions usually accept some parts of the Gospel accounts, often with some modifications, and reject others.

Some writers have suggested that Jesus went on to live for long and away from his homeland. For instance, according to Mirza Ghulam Ahmad (ca. 1839 - 1908), the founder of a small Muslim sect called the Ahmadiyya, after surviving the crucifixion and receiving medical treatment in the tomb, Jesus journeyed as far as India (Ahmad, 2004).

All these alternative histories of Jesus lack evidence. But it should be remembered that the Gospel versions of the story are equally unsupported by any evidence. The only real difference between the Gospel accounts and those alternative hypotheses is that the former are far more popular.

18.6. The Date of the Crucifixion

The four Gospels agree that Jesus was crucified by Pontius Pilate. This dates Jesus' death to sometime between 26 and 36 CE when Pilate was prefect of Judea. Matthew and John state that Caiaphas was the high priest at the time, which is in line with these dates as Caiaphas was in office from 18 to 37 CE. But this information does not help in narrowing down the possible period of 26-36 CE.

The other priest that John mentions, Annas, was the high priest from 6 to 15 CE, but these dates are rather irrelevant.

Of course, if we know Jesus' date of birth and how long he lived, we can work out the year of his death. But neither of these is explicitly given in the Gospels, leaving aside the unreliability of these books and their inclusion of incorrect historical information. As we concluded earlier (§10.6), the Gospels are not only imprecise but also contradictory in their indirect specification of Jesus' date of birth. There is no need to repeat our discussion of the problem of the date of birth of Jesus again here, but I would only like to add one point.

Luke (3:23) states that Jesus was "about thirty years old" when he was baptized by John and started his public ministry. The account in Luke also suggests that Jesus' public ministry lasted for around one year before he was crucified. There is, for example, one Passover mentioned in that Gospel. So Luke implies that Jesus was about 31 years old when he was executed. The other two Synoptics do not specify Jesus' age, but they also talk about one Passover and imply that Jesus preached for one year or so.

John, however, talks about three Passovers. Scholars differ as to whether Jesus' ministry lasted less than one year, as suggested by the Synoptists, or around three, as John claims. One prominent authority on Jesus thinks that John might have extended Jesus' public ministry to "accommodate his numerous and lengthy, almost certainly fictional speeches" (Vermes, 2005: 15).

But a more interesting reference in John is found in a heated debate between Jesus and Judeans in which the latter tell him "You are not yet fifty years old! Have you seen Abraham?" (John 8:57), implying that Jesus was in his late forties! A similar, interesting claim is made by the 2nd century bishop of Lyon Irenaeus who claimed that Jesus lived past his fifties and that one of his disciples was in Asia:

> They, however, that they may establish their false opinion regarding that which is written, "to proclaim the acceptable year of the Lord," maintain that

He preached for one year only, and then suffered in the twelfth month. [In speaking thus], they are forgetful to their own disadvantage, destroying His whole work, and robbing Him of that age which is both more necessary and more honourable than any other; that more advanced age, I mean, during which also as a teacher He excelled all others. For how could He have had disciples, if He did not teach? And how could He have taught, unless He had reached the age of a Master? For when He came to be baptized, He had not yet completed His thirtieth year, but was beginning to be about thirty years of age (for thus Luke, who has mentioned His years, has expressed it: "Now Jesus was, as it were, beginning to be thirty years old," when He came to receive baptism); and, [according to these men,] He preached only one year reckoning from His baptism. On completing His thirtieth year He suffered, being in fact still a young man, and who had by no means attained to advanced age. Now, that the first stage of early life embraces thirty years, and that this extends onwards to the fortieth year, everyone will admit; but from the fortieth and fiftieth year a man begins to decline towards old age, which our Lord possessed while He still fulfilled the office of a Teacher, even as the Gospel and all the elders testify; those who were conversant in Asia with John, the disciple of the Lord, [affirming] that John conveyed to them that information. And he remained among them up to the times of Trajan. Some of them, moreover, saw not only John, but the other apostles also, and heard the very same account from them, and bear testimony as to the [validity of] the statement. Whom then should we rather believe? Whether such men as these, or Ptolemaeus, who never saw the apostles, and who never even in his dreams attained to the slightest trace of an apostle? (Irenaeus, *Against Heresies*, 2.22.5)

The statement that the apostles confirmed is that Jesus lived to beyond the age of fifty; there is no ambiguity about Irenaeus' point.

The Gospels are so imprecise, contradictory, and inconsistent about Jesus' birth date and how long he lived. They cannot be used to add any precision to their implication that he was killed sometime between 26 and 36 CE, which is when Pilate was prefect of Judea.

19

The Qur'an and the Cross Fiction

The event in Jesus' life that has had the greatest role in defining Christianity is the crucifixion and the subsequent resurrection. This extremely violent death is presented as the climax and ultimate goal of Jesus' life which brought salvation to people. Yet rejecting that this event ever took place is one of the major differences between Jesus' story in the Qur'an and its Christian counterparts. According to the Qur'an, the crucifixion of Jesus is fiction that gained popularity like many other myths. It states that someone else was crucified instead of Jesus. There are apocryphal gospels that suggest the same. According the Qur'an, sometime after the crucifixion, Jesus was taken by God to an unidentified place in heaven where he stayed until he died.

The Qur'an does not only deny the historicity of the crucifixion, but it also rejects its theological significance. Paul developed and popularized the doctrine of atonement which claims that the death and resurrection of Jesus brought about the reconciliation between God and man. Significantly, the Gospel authors show complete unawareness of the doctrine that Paul managed to turn into the foundation of Christian theology. The theology of the cross is incompatible with the teachings of the Qur'an. The latter rejects the claim that sins are inherited or that salvation can be secured by someone on behalf of someone else.

19.1. The Fiction of Jesus' Crucifixion

The Qur'an challenges the Christian belief that Jesus was killed on the cross. This striking rejection is made as clear it can be in the following verses:

> And because of their saying: "We killed the Messiah, Jesus son of Mary, Allah's messenger." They did not kill or crucify him, but it was made to appear so to them. Those who disagree concerning it are in doubt thereof; they have no knowledge thereof, but a conjecture they follow; they did not kill him for certain (4.157). Allah rather raised him up to Himself. Allah is invincible, wise (4.158).

It is not clear whether the expression "Allah's messenger" is the words of God or part of the words of the Jews, as in my translation above. In the latter case, the expression is clearly used derisively, like the word "Messiah." The Jews' use of the title "Messiah" possibly contrasts their perception that they killed Jesus with their belief that the awaited Messiah was going to be a powerful and victorious military leader. Again, an element of derision is implied.

These verses follow ones that criticize the Jews for their failure to obey Moses, their disobedience to God, their unlawful killing of prophets, and their calumny against Mary. The rejection of the claim that the Jews killed Jesus is further emphasized by its occurrence after the confirmation that they had indeed killed prophets in the past, as if God is stressing that although the Jews did kill prophets before, they did not kill Jesus. The pronoun "it" in "concerning it" may also be read as "him" in reference to Jesus, but I think the context is clear in talking about the crucifixion, hence my translation as "it."

Verse 4.157 does not exonerate the Jews from the intention or attempt to kill Jesus. It rather stresses that they boasted that they killed Jesus, but it denies that their claim was true. This does not mean that the Jews lied, but that they *mistakenly thought* that they killed Jesus, because "it was made to appear so to them." The verse emphasizes that the Jews' claim is not based on real knowledge and certainty, but is mere conjecture. They did try to kill Jesus, but they failed.

Unlike the New Testament, the Qur'an does not mention a Roman role in the attempt to kill Jesus. There are three reasons for this:

① While the local Roman governor would have likely been involved and ordered the crucifixion, it would have been the Jewish authorities who asked him to do so. Pilate would not have thought of killing the peaceful Jesus, nor would have even heard of him, had the Jewish leaders not petitioned him to do so. Jesus was a spiritual teacher who had no political agenda (pp. 243-246).

② The Romans, as polytheists, were naturally not anticipated to embrace Jesus' religion. But the Jews were expecting the Messiah and had been ordered to follow him. Jesus appeared in a Jewish environment and targeted mainly Jews not Romans with his teachings. The opposition to Jesus and attempts to kill him would have been Jewish.

③ Even in the Gospels, the Romans' involvement in the crucifixion was restricted to Pilate and a few individuals who acted on his orders. There was no Roman popular interest in Jesus, nor was he known to them. The Jews, on the other hand, came in large numbers against Jesus.

The crucifixion is probably one of the Jewish attempts at Jesus' life which God protected him against and which He referred to with other miracles in the following verse:

> Lo! When Allah said: "O Jesus son of Mary! Remember My favor on you and on your mother, that I have supported you with the Spirit of Holiness, [making you] speak to people in the cradle and when middle-aged; and that I taught you the Book, Wisdom, the Torah, and the Injīl; and that you create out of clay the figures of birds by My permission, then you breath into them and they become birds by My permission, and heal the blind person and the albino by My permission; and that you raise the dead by My permission; and that I withheld the Children of Israel from you when you came to them with clear proofs, but those who disbelieved among them said: 'This is nothing but clear magic'" (5.110).

The mention of God's protection of Jesus in the context of talking about various miracles that He granted to him suggests that this protection was miraculous. This probably includes Jesus' escape from the attempt to crucify him.

The Jew's attempt to kill Jesus and his miraculous escape are further alluded to in these verses:

> But when Jesus perceived disbelief on their (the Children of Israel's) part, he said: "Who are my supporters in the cause of Allah?" The companions said: "We are Allah's supporters. We believe in Allah, and do you bear witness that we are Muslims (3.52). Our Lord! We believe in that which You have sent down, and we follow the messenger, so write us down among those who bear witness [to the truth]" (3.53). And they (the Children of Israel) schemed, and Allah schemed; and Allah is the best of those who scheme (3.54). Lo! When Allah said: "O Jesus! I am taking you (*mutawaffika*), raising you up to Me, and cleansing you of those who disbelieve, and setting those who follow you above those who disbelieve until the Day of Resurrection. Then to Me you shall all return, and I shall judge between you concerning what you differed on" (3.55).

There is more than one reason for taking the pronoun "they" in verse 3.54 to refer to the *Children of Israel*. First, the disbelievers of verse 3.54 are the same of verse 3.52, and the latter are the Jews, as verses 3.49-51 clearly show. Second, this interpretation is confirmed by comparing verses 3.52-54 with verse 61.14. The latter also talks about the same event of the companions declaring their support for Jesus, and then follows that with a criticism of those who disbelieved, who are explicitly identified as some of the Children of Israel:

> O you who believe! Be Allah's supporters, as Jesus son of Mary said to the companions: "Who are my supporters in the cause of Allah?" The companions said: "We are Allah's supporters." Then a party of the Children of Israel believed and a party disbelieved, therefore we aided those who believed against their enemy, so they became the ones that prevailed (61.14).

The disbelief of the Jews was not the mere rejection of Jesus' message. This kind of disbelief would have been clear to all, including Jesus. The verse talks about something more *subtle* that Jesus "perceived." The wording is suggestive of a secret plot against Jesus. This understanding of the term "disbelief" is in line with Jesus' call for the *support* of his followers. But the direct confirmation that what Jesus perceived was a secret attempt to kill him comes in verse 3.53 where the Qur'an states that the Israelites "schemed," before it goes on to say that God foiled their plan by His counter scheme. The divine scheme rescued Jesus, as God raised him up to Him. This divine intervention to rescue Jesus confirms that he was under threat and that the Jews' disbelief in verse 3.52 denoted their attempt to kill him.

Verses 3.53-55 are preceded by ones that talk about Jesus' miracles. Interestingly, verse 5.110 which mentions almost the same miracles of Jesus does not talk about God's rescue of Jesus but mentions God's protection of Jesus against the Children of Israel. So by comparison we can infer that both references mean the same thing. Verses 3.53-55, thus, signify a Jewish conspiracy to kill Jesus which God thwarted.

The Qur'an is emphatic in denying both the killing and crucifixion of Jesus. Denying the killing only could have still left the possibility that Jesus was crucified but not fatally, which is indeed one of the alternative scenarios that have been suggested by scholars (§18.5). Verse 4.157 makes it clear that this was not the case.

Despite these clear-cut statements, there have been a few attempts to suggest that the Qur'an confirms the crucifixion of Jesus! This bizarre argument is advanced, for instance, by Geoffrey Parrinder (1995: 120), who claims that verse 4.157 means that it was not the Jews who crucified Jesus, but it was God who did! He likens this verse to verse 8.17 in which God tells Prophet Muhammad "and you did not throw but it was Allah who threw." This verse, which is thought to refer to the Prophet's symbolic throwing of a fistful of gravels in the direction of the enemy in the battle of Badr, stresses that it is God who was the real doer and giver of victory, not the Prophet. Parrinder suggests that, similarly, verse 4.157 is meant to attribute the crucifixion of Jesus to God not to the Jews, meaning that the latter were simply an instrument that carried out God's plan. Parrinder's argument is not based on the wording of the Qur'anic verse, but it reflects his eagerness to show that the Qur'an is closer to the Gospels than generally believed.

There are a number of clear faults in Parrinder's and similar interpretations:

① God explicitly attributes to the Jews in verse 4.155 the killing of other prophets, so clearly the statement in 4.157 cannot be referring to the *always true* fact that God is the ultimate doer of everything. It cannot be claimed that God ascribes to the Jews their killing of prophets but attributes to Himself their killing of Jesus.

② God mentions the Jews' killing of prophets in a number of verses (e.g. 3.181 and 2.183) in order to remind them of sins they committed, but never to suggest that it was Him who committed that evil!

③ If Parrinder's reading was correct, God would have refuted the Jews' claim that they crucified and killed Jesus by saying something along the lines that it was Him who "crucified and killed Jesus," not by revealing that the reality of what happened is that He "raised him up to Himself." The Jews did not kill Jesus, the Qur'an tells us, not because it was God who killed him, but because they only thought they killed Jesus when in fact Allah raised him up to Him.

④ Describing the Jews' belief that they killed Jesus as a "conjecture" and confirming that this did not happen "for certain" further stress that what is being refuted is the Jewish belief that Jesus was killed, not their mistaken belief that it was them rather than God who was Jesus' killer.

⑤ The alleged crucifixion has no theological value whatsoever in the Qur'an for God to claim it for Himself. In fact, the very Christian concept of redemption, which is what the crucifixion represents in Christian theology, is explicitly rejected by the Qur'an, as we shall see later in the chapter.

Suggesting that the Qur'an does not deny Jesus' crucifixion is simply preposterous.

What the Qur'an says in the verses above about the alleged crucifixion of Jesus mirrors what we concluded in the previous chapter: *the existence of the perception that Jesus was crucified, but the absence of historical evidence to confirm that his perception reflects a real historical event.*

The fact that the alleged crucifixion has been considered to be one of the main, or even the most important, event in the life of Jesus must not be seen as lending more credibility to this particular event. Throughout history, religious followers have had the histories of their leaders mixed with myths and legends to the point that separating between them is at times impossible. The strength of popular belief in a concept or claim or is no guarantee that this concept or claim is more likely to be real.

But was there any crucifixion? What did exactly happen?

19.2. The Crucifixion of Jesus' Substitute

The Qur'anic statement that the Jews "did not kill or crucify him" (4.157) does not necessarily mean that the Jews sought to kill Jesus by crucifixion. It may be argued that the crucifixion is specifically denied in the verse because this is how the Christians claim the Jews killed Jesus. If the attempt at Jesus' life was a Jewish act in which the Romans did not play any part at all, then it would be unlikely that it was a crucifixion, as the latter is not a Jewish but Roman method of punishment. However, we have already discussed how the Romans might have got involved, in which case the attempt would be crucifixion (p. 412).

The Qur'an's statement that *it was made to appear to the Jews that they crucified and killed Jesus* can have one of two meanings. The first is that the Jews experienced some kind of a collective illusion thinking that they crucified Jesus, when in fact no crucifixion happened. This purely supernatural interpretation has no supportive evidence and I find it very unlikely. The second, natural, and far more likely reading is that the Jews crucified someone else thinking that he was Jesus. It is not clear whether God's elevation of Jesus occurred before or after this mistaken crucifixion.

In their interpretation of verse 4.157, Muslim exegetes agree that it was another person who was mistaken for Jesus and killed in his stead. A number of them have even tried to identify the crucified person. One popular view is that it was one of Jesus' disciples who was made to look like Jesus and ended up being crucified instead of him. One variation of this story is that when the Jews were on their way to arrest Jesus, he asked for a volunteer among his disciple who would be made to look like him and be killed instead of him, and one of them came forward. In another version of the story all of Jesus' disciples became looking exactly like him, so the Jews could not know which one was Jesus and ended up killing the wrong man. Others identified Judas Iscariot as the one who, involuntarily, became Jesus' lookalike and was crucified. There are other versions of these stories.

While verse 4.157 can only mean that someone else was mistaken for Jesus and killed, there is actually nothing in this verse or anywhere in the Qur'an that supports or justifies any attempt to identify that person. Nevertheless, classic exegetical works of the Qur'an, such as that of aṭ-Ṭabarī (840-922 CE), are full of quotations of scholars who have made claims about the identity of the killed. Aṭ-Ṭabāṭabā'ī's (1892-1981) more careful and disciplined interpretation does not make any claim about the identity of the executed person.

The Qur'an does not state that the person who was crucified was made to look like Jesus. A misidentification could have happened even without this specific kind of miraculous intervention. Two thousand years ago, when identity verification was very basic and totally relied on people who knew the person, misidentification was much more likely and frequent than today.

According to the Gospels, Jesus' arrest and crucifixion did not happen where he lived most of his life but in Jerusalem — a city he went to on short visits and where fewer people knew him. Additionally, as we have already pointed out, Jesus did not have a large following anyway, so the number of people who knew him was small, and the number of Jerusalemites who could recognize him must have been even much smaller. It is plausible, then, that those who came to arrest Jesus did not know how he looked like. Interestingly, this is exactly what the Gospels suggest was the case. Accordingly to the Synoptists, Judas Iscariot led the guards to Jesus' place and *identified* him from among his disciples by kissing him (also Matt. 26:47-50; Luke 22:47-48):

> Right away, while Jesus was still speaking, Judas, one of the twelve, arrived. With him came a crowd armed with swords and clubs, sent by the chief priests and experts in the law and elders. (Now the betrayer had given them a sign, saying, "The one I kiss is the man. Arrest him and lead him away under guard.") When Judas arrived, he went up to Jesus immediately and said, "Rabbi!" and kissed him. Then they took hold of him and arrested him. (Mark 14:43-46)

John's story differs from the Synoptics, but it still shows that those who came to arrest Jesus could not recognize him. They had to rely on him to identify himself:

> So Judas obtained a squad of soldiers and some officers of the chief priests and Pharisees. They came to the orchard with lanterns and torches and weapons. Then Jesus, because he knew everything that was going to happen to him, came and asked them,

"Who are you looking for?" They replied, "Jesus the Nazarene." He told them, "I am he." (Now Judas, the one who betrayed him, was standing there with them.) So when Jesus said to them, "I am he," they retreated and fell to the ground. Then Jesus asked them again, "Who are you looking for?" And they said, "Jesus the Nazarene." Jesus replied, "I told you that I am he. If you are looking for me, let these men go." He said this to fulfill the word he had spoken, "I have not lost a single one of those whom you gave me." (John 18:3-9)

As Jesus was unknown to the authorities, it was perfectly possible for a misidentification to take place. The fact that the crucifixion was hastily carried out — as the Gospels suggest that it took place less than 24 hours after the arrest — would have made it less likely for the authorities to discover that they had the wrong person before it was too late.

This argument shows that Jesus' evasion of arrest could be explained in *normal* terms, but it does not exclude the possibility that a miracle was involved. I have pointed out that referring to God's protection of Jesus in the context of mentioning his miracles in verse 5.110 indicates that this protection involved an element of paranormality, and that it could include the failed attempt to crucify Jesus. The point I am making above, however, is that a miracle is *not necessary* to explain how the wrong person was caught and crucified.

The suggestion that someone else was executed instead of Jesus is not found only or first in the Qur'an. The "substitute" theory, as it is known, was adopted throughout history by various *heretical* Christian groups that refused to accept that Jesus, as a divine being and Son of God, could die (Parrinder, 1995: 109-110). This theory, however, lived outside mainstream Christianity. Let's review some of the early Christian sources that cited this theory.

In his letter (2.1) to the Christians of Smyrna (today's Izmir in Turkey), Bishop Ignatius of Antioch, Syria, spoke of "unbelievers" who claimed that Jesus "only *seemed* to suffer." The exact date of this letter is unknown, but Eusebius states that Ignatius was martyred during the reign of the Roman emperor Trajan, so that must have happened before the emperor's death in 117. Ignatius' statement targeted the Docetists who believed that Jesus did not have a physical body, so his sufferings and death were apparent, not real.

According to Irenaeus, the 2nd century Egyptian gnostic Christian Basilides taught that the Jews crucified a Simon of Cyrene instead of Jesus and that Jesus ascended to God. Writing around 185, the orthodox bishop Irenaeus has the following to report about Basilides' heretical beliefs about the alleged crucifixion of Jesus:

> ...he did not himself suffer death, but Simon, a certain man of Cyrene, being compelled, bore the cross in his stead; so that this latter being transfigured by him, that he might be thought to be Jesus, was crucified,

through ignorance and error, while Jesus himself received the form of Simon, and, standing by, laughed at them. For since he was an incorporeal power, and the Nous (mind) of the unborn father, he transfigured himself as he pleased, and thus ascended to him who had sent him, deriding them, inasmuch as he could not be laid hold of, and was invisible to all. Those, then, who know these things have been freed from the principalities who formed the world; so that it is not incumbent on us to confess him who was crucified, but him who came in the form of a man, and was thought to be crucified, and was called Jesus, and was sent by the father, that by this dispensation he might destroy the works of the makers of the world. If any one, therefore, he declares, confesses the crucified, that man is still a slave, and under the power of those who formed our bodies; but he who denies him has been freed from these beings, and is acquainted with the dispensation of the unborn father. (Irenaeus, *Against Heresies*, 1.24.3)

The theologian Clement of Alexandria, writing early in the 3rd century, contradicted Irenaeus as he suggested that Basilides rejected that Simon was crucified instead of Jesus. What Basilides exactly believed is not the main point of interest here, but Irenaeus' report clearly suggests that the substitute theory was well known and accepted by some as early as the 2nd century.

Another two early sources that advance the substitute version of events come from a collection of 13 codices of mostly gnostic texts which were discovered at Nag Hammadi in Egypt in 1945. The first is the *Apocalypse of Peter*, which is dated to the 2nd or 3rd century. It contains the accounts of visions that were seen by the apostle Peter and interpreted by Jesus. In the second visionary scenes, Jesus explains to Peter that the physical body of the crucified person had nothing to do with the living Jesus. While someone who looked like Jesus was being crucified, the real Jesus was watching the events in derision from above a tree. The observer was invisible to the executioners:

When he had said those things, I saw him seemingly being seized by them. And I said, "What do I see, 0 Lord, that it is you yourself whom they take, and that you are grasping me? Or who is this one, glad and laughing on the tree? And is it another one whose feet and hands they are striking?"

The Savior said to me, "He whom you saw on the tree, glad and laughing, this is the living Jesus. But this one into whose hands and feet they drive the nails is his fleshly part, which is the substitute being put to shame, the one who came into being in his likeness. But look at him and me."

But I, when I had looked, said, "Lord, no one is looking at you. Let us flee this place."

But he said to me, "I have told you, Leave the blind alone! And you, see how they do not know what they are saying. For the son of their glory instead of my servant they have put to shame."

And I saw someone about to approach us resembling him, even him who was laughing on the tree. And he was (filled) with a Holy Spirit, and he is the Savior. And there was a great, ineffable light around them, and the multitude of ineffable and invisible angels blessing them. And when 1 looked at him, the one who gives praise was revealed.

And he said to me, "Be strong, for you are the one to whom these mysteries have been given, to know them through revelation, that he whom they crucified is the first-born, and the home of demons, and the stony vessel (?) in which they dwell, of Elohim, of the cross which is under the Law. But he who stands near him is the living Savior, the first in him, whom they seized and released, who stands joyfully looking at those who did him violence, while they are divided among themselves. Therefore he laughs at their lack of perception, knowing that they are born blind. So then the one susceptible to suffering shall come, since the body is the substitute. But what they released was my incorporeal body. But I am the intellectual Spirit filled with radiant light. He whom you saw coming to me is our intellectual Pleroma, which unites the perfect light with my Holy Spirit.

The second Nag Hammadi scroll that shares a similar view is the *Second Treatise of the Great Seth*, which is supposed to be a revelation from Jesus to an audience of agnostic believers. Like the view that Irenaeus attributes to Basilides, this text claims that a Simon of Cyrene was crucified instead of the laughing Jesus:

And the plan which they devised about me to release their Error and their senselessness — I did not succumb to them as they had planned. But I was not afflicted at all. Those who were there punished me. And I did not die in reality but in appearance, lest I be put to shame by them because these are my kinsfolk. I removed the shame from me and I did not become fainthearted in the face of what happened to me at their hands. I was about to succumb to fear, and I <suffered> according to their sight and thought, in order that they may never find any word to speak about them. For my death which they think happened, (happened) to them in their error and blindness, since they nailed their man unto their death. For their Ennoias did not see me, for they were deaf and blind. But in doing these things, they condemn themselves. Yes, they saw me; they punished me. It was another, their father, who drank the gall and the vinegar; it was not I. They struck me with the reed; it was another, Simon, who bore the cross on his shoulder. I was another upon whom they placed the crown of thorns. But I was rejoicing in the height over all the wealth of the archons and the offspring of their error, of their empty glory. And I was laughing at their ignorance.

And I subjected all their powers. For as I came downward no one saw me. For I was altering my shapes, changing from form to form. And therefore, when I was at their gates I assumed their likeness. For I passed them by quietly, and I was viewing the places, and I was not afraid nor ashamed, for I was undefiled. And I was speaking with them, mingling with them through those who are mine, and trampling on those who are harsh to them with zeal, and quenching the flame. And I was doing all these things because of my desire to accomplish what I desired by the will of the Father above.

Another interesting source that advocates the substitute theory is an apocryphal document known as the *Gospel of Barnabas*. Mention of a book under this name is found as early as the 6th century, but the earliest surviving manuscripts date to the 16th century. Some Muslim scholars attribute this gospel to the apostle Barnabas (e.g. 'Ata ur-Rahim, 1991: 39-44; Durrani, 1998; al-Kadhi, 1996), but scholars in general consider it to be a forgery. While containing an account of Jesus' life that shares a lot with the canonical versions, the book also promotes various Islamic beliefs. For instance, after his creation, Adam is said to have seen the Islamic declaration of faith, "There is only one God, and Muhammad is the Messenger of God," written in the air (Bar. 37). If the relatively recent manuscripts of this gospel are not the original gospel that is mentioned in the 6th century, the clearly they are of little value. With this in mind, let's look into this gospel's version of the substitute theory.

According to this gospel, before Judas Iscariot betrayed Jesus to the authorities, angels took Jesus to the third heaven. God then made Judas look and speak like Jesus, thus causing him to be arrested instead of Jesus:

> Judas entered impetuously before all into the chamber whence Jesus had been taken up. And the disciples were sleeping. Whereupon the wonderful God acted wonderfully, insomuch that Judas was so changed in speech and in face to be like Jesus that we believed him to be Jesus. And he, having awakened us, was seeking where the Master was. Whereupon we marvelled, and answered: "You, Lord, are our master; have you now forgotten us?"
>
> And he, smiling, said: "Now are you foolish, that know not me to be Judas Iscariot!" And as he was saying this the soldiery entered, and laid their hands upon Judas, because he was in every way like to Jesus....
>
> The soldiers took Judas and bound him, not without derision. For he truthfully denied that he was Jesus; and the soldiers, mocking him, said: "Sir, fear not, for we have come to make you king of Israel, and we have bound you because we know that you do refuse the kingdom." Judas answered: "Now have you lost your senses! You have come to take Jesus of Nazareth; with arms and lanterns as [against] a robber; and you have bound me that have guided you, to make me king."…. (Bar. 216-217)

Not only the soldiers and the disciples, but all those who knew Jesus closely, including his mother, mistook Judas for Jesus:

> When it was morning there assembled the great council of scribes and elders of the people; and the high priest with the Pharisees sought false witness against Judas, believing him to be Jesus: and they found not that which they sought. And why say I that the chief priests believed Judas to be Jesus? No, all the disciples, with him who writes, believed it; and more, the poor virgin mother of Jesus, with his kinsfolk and friends, believed it, insomuch that the sorrow of every one was incredible. (Bar. 217)

Judas was ultimately crucified instead of Jesus:

So they led him to Mount Calvary, where they used to hang malefactors, and there they crucified him naked, for the greater ignominy. Judas truly did nothing else but cry out: "God, why have you forsaken me, seeing the malefactor has escaped and I die unjustly?" Verily I say that the voice, the face, and the person of Judas were so like to Jesus, that his disciples and believers entirely believed that he was Jesus; wherefore some departed from the doctrine of Jesus, believing that Jesus had been a false prophet, and that by art magic he had done the miracles which he did: for Jesus had said that he should not die till near the end of the world; for that at that time he should be taken away from the world. (Bar. 217)

These and other ancient sources show that the "substitute" theory was adopted by some Christian individuals and circles, although there is no evidence that it was ever popular.

If Jesus had to avoid the authorities who were after him, then he must have been forced into hiding when they started looking for him. Indeed, the Gospel accounts of Jesus' appearances after the crucifixion are all suggestive of someone in hiding, appearing only briefly to a certain people and then disappearing again.

But if Jesus was not crucified, what exactly happened to him?

19.3. After the Crucifixion

We have already seen in verse 4.157 that God *raised Jesus up to Him*. Jesus is not the only righteous person that the Qur'an tells us God *raised up* to a particular place. Prophet Idrīs is also described as having been *raised* to a lofty place:

And mention [O Muhammad!] Idrīs in the Book. He was a truthful man, and a prophet (19.56). And We raised him up to a high place (19.57).

The Qur'an also contains a story of a people who rejected three messengers that Allah sent. One man who believed in the messengers was taken to a place described as being a "paradise." That this location is somewhere in heaven is confirmed by God's description of the hosts that he sent to destroy that city as being "from heaven":

[The believer said to the messengers]: "I have believed in your Lord, so hear me" (36.25). It was said [to him]: "Enter paradise." He said: "Only if my people know (36.26). How my Lord has forgiven me and made me one of the honored" (36.27). And We did not send down upon his people after him any hosts from heaven, and We were not going to (36.28). It was only one blast, and lo! They became extinct (36.29).

The Qur'an also states that those who are killed in the cause of God continue to live in the presence of their Lord (2.154, 3.169), that is somewhere other than the earth.

So the Qur'an states explicitly and implicitly that the earth is not the only place where human beings can live. Some individuals who were born and lived on this planet were taken, for different reasons, to live elsewhere. Jesus was one of those individuals. His transfer was related to the risk to his life.

There are Qur'anic verses other than 4.157 that shed further light on God's elevation of Jesus and His protection of this noble prophet after Jews set out to kill him. Let's study first this verse, giving special attention to the Arabic word *mutawaffika*, which I have translated as "taking you":

> Lo! When Allah said: "O Jesus! I am taking you (*mutawaffika*), raising you up to Me, and cleansing you of those who disbelieve, and setting those who follow you above those who disbelieve until the Day of Resurrection. Then to Me you shall all return, and I shall judge between you concerning what you differed on" (3.55).

The active participle *mutawaffika* is derived from the verb *tawaffa*. In the Qur'an, only God and the angels appear as the subject of this verb, and people appear only as the object. The verb is used in at least two *related* meanings. **First**, it is used to mean "cause to die" (also 2.234, 2.240, 10.46, 13.40, 40.77):

> It is He who created you from dust, then from a small life germ, then from a clot, then He brings you forth as a child, then that you may attain your full strength, then that you may be old — and some of you are caused to die (*yatawaffa*) earlier — and that you may reach an appointed term, and that you may understand (40.67).

Other verses in which *tawaffa* is used in association with death talk about God or the angels taking the person at the time of death, so translating the verb as "took" is more appropriate (also 6.61):

> As for those of your women who are guilty of lewdness, call to witness four of you against them. And if they testify [to the truth of the allegation] then confine them to the houses until death (*mawt*) takes them (*yatawaffahunna*) or [until] Allah opens some way for them (4.15).

> Say [O Muhammad!]: "The angel of death who is given charge of you [O people!] shall take you (*yatawaffakum*), then to your Lord you shall be brought back" (32.11).

In its **second** usage, *tawaffa* signifies something that happens when the person falls asleep, as seen in the first occurrence of this verb in the following verse:

> And it is He who takes you (*yatawaffakum*) at night [in sleep] and knows what you acquire in the day, then He resurrects you therein so that an appointed term may be fulfilled; then to Him is your return, then He will inform you of what you were doing (6.60). And He is the Supreme above His servants, and He sends keepers over you; until when death comes to one of you, Our messengers take him (*tawaffathu*), and they never fail in their duty (6.61).

The two usages of *tawaffā* are related, as each talks about a state of unconsciousness, albeit the two states are biologically very different and one lasts much longer than the other. I did not describe death as being *permanent* and sleep as *temporary* because, as noted by the great exegete aṭ-Ṭabāṭabā'ī, the Qur'an considers death as the end of the person's life in this world only. In this sense, death also is a temporary loss of unconsciousness.

Some Exegetes, such as aj-Jalālayn and aṭ-Ṭabarī, have pointed out that *tawaffā* may also have the third meaning of *taking the person* without causing him to die or lose consciousness. The only verses that may be claimed to use *tawaffā* in this sense are 3.55 and 5.117 in which the verb is applied to Jesus, as the other occurrences support the other two meanings. As there is no other verse in the Qur'an that explains the exact state of Jesus when he was "taken" by God, these two verses cannot be used as evidence that God's taking of Jesus did not involve making him lose consciousness. In other words, assigning this third meaning to *tawaffā* is the result of making a particular assumption about Jesus' state of consciousness. There is no evidence then to support this sense of *tawaffā*, so we will ignore it.

The verses that say God *tawaffā* Jesus can either mean that God caused Jesus to die, or that He caused him to enter in a state of unconsciousness. As rightly pointed out by aṭ-Ṭabāṭabā'ī in his commentary on verse 3.55, we cannot know the exact state of unconsciousness that God put Jesus through — sleep, coma, or any other state of unconsciousness. Nevertheless, as God later restored Jesus' consciousness, as we shall see shortly, I am inclined to think that this state is different from death. Death is something that Jesus experienced later. Translating *tawaffā* as "took" is one way of bypassing the uncertainty about the exact meaning of the verb. It should be noted that the Qur'an (18.9-22) has a story of seven young believing men and their dog whom God put to some form of sleep for 309 years and then awakened them. The duration of their sleep is mentioned because it is one important dimension of the miracle. Jesus' loss of consciousness probably lasted only for the short period of time that his transfer from the earth to heaven took.

The Qur'an also tells us that Jesus continued to live in the place where he was lifted up to — which must mean that his consciousness was restored. There are at least six references in five different places in the Qur'an that lead to this conclusion:

① The first pointer is found in verses 4.157-158:

> And because of their saying: "We killed the Messiah, Jesus son of Mary, Allah's messenger." They did not kill or crucify him, but it was made to appear so to them. Those who disagree concerning it are in doubt thereof; they have no knowledge thereof, but a conjecture they follow; they did not kill him for certain (4.157). Allah rather raised him up to Himself. Allah is invincible, wise (4.158).

The use of the Arabic word *bal*, which is translated as "rather" in "Allah rather raised him up to Himself," leaves no doubt that the elevation is presented as the reality of what happened *as opposed* to the deluded belief of the crucifixion and killing. God's counter reply was not that it was rather Him who caused Jesus to die, but He rebuffed the untrue allegation by saying that Jesus was actually *elevated* by Him. This lifting up meant that Jesus continued to live elsewhere.

② Verse 3.55 states that after God took Jesus He raised him up. Now, if that act of taking Jesus meant causing him to die like all people die and not come back to life until the Day of Resurrection, it would be difficult to understand why God would elevate Jesus' corpse. The elevation took place because God wanted to restore Jesus' consciousness.

③ This verse then goes on to say that by lifting Jesus up from the earth, *God cleansed him of the disbelievers*. This can only mean that Jesus continued to live, as this spiritual cleansing makes sense only to the living. Also, the use of this verb suggests that Jesus' new living place did not contain disbelievers. This could be the place where those who are martyrs continue to live (2.154, 3.169).

④ Aṭ-Ṭabāṭabā'ī has cleverly noticed that while the Qur'an uses the term *mawt* (death) to talk about the end of man's life on earth, it uses *tawaffā* when it emphasizes not only the end of that life but also God's preservation of man's soul, or whatever one calls that part of the human being that is not destroyed by death. Verse 5.117, which we will study shortly, and verse 3.55, both of which talk about God's raising of Jesus, use the term *tawaffā* rather than "caused to die." Significantly, the latter is used instead when Jesus refers to his normal death: "Peace is on me the day I was born, the day I shall die, and the day I shall be raised alive."

⑤ The fifth hint, in verse 3.46, is more subtle. The angels told Mary that the son she was going to give birth to would speak to people while still an infant and when he is in his middle age: "He shall speak to people in the cradle and when middle-aged, and he shall be one of the righteous" (3.46). The angels informed Mary that her son would speak in the cradle because this is a miracle, as infants are unable to speak. But why did they mention in the same context that Jesus would also speak to people in his middle age when this is natural and normal? They must have meant that a miracle was involved in this also. The fact that Jesus' speaking in old age was a miracle is also confirmed in another verse which lists it with other miracles that God granted to Jesus:

> Lo! When Allah said: "O Jesus son of Mary! Remember My favor on you and on your mother, that I have supported you with the Spirit of Holiness, [making you] speak to people in the cradle and when middle-aged; and that I taught you the Book, Wisdom, the Torah, and the Injīl; and that you create out of clay the figures of birds by My permission, then you breath into them and they become birds by My permission, and heal the blind person and the albino by My permission; and that you raise the dead by My permission; and that I withheld the Children of Israel from you when you came to

them with clear proofs, but those who disbelieved among them said: 'This is nothing but clear magic'" (5.110).

The Jewish threat to Jesus' life probably made his public mission very short. He was a very young man when God took him, so he was able to speak to people in his middle age *only* because God miraculously saved him from the Jews by elevating him. Jesus lived until he became middle-aged, and so he spoke to people at that age, by a miracle in the same way that his speech in the cradle was a miracle. I will discuss later what "people" are meant here.

⑥ That Jesus lived after his elevation can be inferred from this set of verses, although the argument from these verses might not be as conclusive as the earlier five arguments:

> And when Allah said: "O Jesus son of Mary! Did you say to people: 'Take me and my mother for two gods besides Allah?'" He said: "Glory be to You! I could never say what I have no right to say. If I have said it, then You know it. You know what is in my mind, but I do not know what is in Your mind. You know all unseen things (5.116). I never said to them anything other than what You commanded me: 'worship Allah, my and your Lord.' I was a witness over them while I was among them, and when You took me (*tawaffaytanī*) You were the watcher over them. You are a witness over all things (5.117). If You punish them, then they are Your servants; and if You forgive them, then You are the Invincible, the Wise" (5.118). Allah said: "This is a day on which the truthful will benefit from their truthfulness; they shall have gardens beneath which rivers flow in which they will abide for ever: Allah is well pleased with them and they are well pleased with Allah; this is the great triumph" (5.119).

In this dialog with God, Jesus uses that special term *tawaffaytanī* for the state that God put him in before lifting him up. As I have already noted, the use of *tawaffaytanī* instead of the verb that is associated with normal death indicates that this state of unconsciousness was not death. But leaving aside this argument, which we covered earlier, the very fact that Jesus spoke to God after his elevation means that he continued to live somewhere, unless the dialog is one that will occur on the Day of Resurrection. There are a number of reasons to believe that the latter is not the case:

(i) Jesus' linking of being *no longer* able to watch his followers' behavior and beliefs to being taken by God Jesus implies that the dialog was about followers that he was living with and could have influenced had he not been separated from them. Jesus could not have cited God's taking of him as a cause for not watching his followers if God was asking him about all billions who followed him and who lived from his time to the Day of Resurrection! A question about Jesus' observation of those countless people would not have made any sense. The fact that God asked

Jesus about those people means that He was talking about people that Jesus knew and could have influenced their beliefs and behaviors.

(ii) The dialog in this verse is mentioned immediately after the miracle of the feast from heaven, which itself occurred shortly before Jesus was lifted up, suggesting that the dialog occurred then.

(iii) Aṭ-Ṭabarī notes that the word *ith* (when) with which the account of the dialog starts is used in the Qur'an mainly to cite past events.

(iv) Aṭ-Ṭabarī also draws attention to the fact that Jesus knew all too well that dying while believing in the divinity of other than Allah, which includes associating other gods with Him, is the one sin that will not be forgiven by God (4.48, 4.116). So his words "if You forgive them" cannot refer to dead people. This in turn means that Jesus' dialog with God is not one that will take place on the Day of Resurrection.

The reason that many scholars believe that the dialog in verses 5.116-118 is to happen on the Day of Resurrection and not one that happened after Jesus was lifted up is verse 5.119. God's words in the latter are clearly about the Day of Resurrection. Because it occurs after the dialog with Jesus, this verse is taken to be a continuation of that dialog. One possible alternative interpretation can be seen when looking at verse 5.119 in the wider context of a larger number of verses, starting with verse 5.109: "On the Day when Allah will assemble the messengers then say: 'What answer were you given [to your calls to people to worship me]?' They shall say: 'We have no knowledge; You are the Knower of the unseen'". This verse reports a dialog between God and His messengers on the Day of Resurrection, and verse 5.119 can perfectly be seen as a continuation for this verse, i.e. containing God's comment on the messengers' reply to his question. But what about the 9 verses between 5.109 and 5.119?

Using one verse or more parenthetically in the middle of a discourse is very common in the Qur'an (e.g. 2.62, 75.16-19), so the question is whether it is possible to see those 9 verses as parenthetical. This group of verses consists of one verse (5.110) that mentions Jesus' miracles, five verses (5.111-115) that recount the miracle of the feast from heaven, and three verses (5.116-118) that contain the dialog between God and Jesus. The fact that all 9 verses are about Jesus and that at least the first six (5.110-115) talk about his life on earth and have nothing to do with the Day of Resurrection suggest that they should be seen as parenthetical, separating two verses (5.109 and 5.119) that describe a dialog between God and the messengers on the Day of Resurrection. One possible reason for the inclusion of verses about Jesus in the middle of the dialog about how the messengers' calls to God were answered by their people is that Jesus' message suffered probably the biggest distortion. Also, the dialog between God and Jesus in 5.116-118 carries resemblance to His dialog with the messengers on the Day of Resurrection in 5.109. So to recap, verse 5.109 reports a dialog between God and the messengers on the Day of Resurrection, verses 110-118 interrupt the recounting of this dialog as they relate certain episodes from Jesus' life, and then verse 110.119 resumes the thread started by verse 5.109.

While I accept that the sixth argument may not be conclusive, I think the earlier five arguments prove that the Qur'an states, although indirectly, that Jesus continued to live in the place where he was lifted to.

Note that verse 5.117 confirms that Jesus' deification started after he had gone. This is in line with our conclusion that Paul played a major role in promoting Jesus' divinity as he preached his version of Christianity among his followers of pagan converts. Jesus was not around when Paul started his missionary work.

The angels' good news to Mary about her son's ability to speak to people mentioned two miracles — one she understood and another she did not. Although Mary did not realize that Jesus would speak in his old age because of a miracle, she used to draw reassurance from this promise about her young son's safety as his life was coming increasingly under threat. This news about Jesus' future had a similar function to the promise that God gave to Moses' mother, having ordered her to cast baby Moses in the river, that He would return her infant to her and make him grow up to become a messenger:

> And We inspired Moses' mother: "Suckle him, and when you fear for his safety, cast him into the river and fear not nor grieve; We shall bring him back to you and shall make him one of the messengers" (28.7).

We have already seen that the Gospels are inconsistent about Jesus' age at his crucifixion, with Luke implying that he was about 31 years old, John suggesting over 50, and the other two being noncommittal (§18.6). The Qur'an does not tell us explicitly how old Jesus was when he was lifted up, but probably he was not old yet.

That God lifted Jesus up from the earth and made him continue to live in his new place is the only explanation that accommodates all the information in the relevant verses. There is only one other verse, 4.159, that I have left out of this discussion, which I will consider in Chapter 20.

It is not clear whether the "people" Jesus spoke to in his middle age were earthly people — in which case probably including some of his followers to whom he appeared — or other people whom he met in the place he was raised up to. What is clear, however, is that he lived in that place long enough to become middle-aged. The implication of specifying that he would reach middle age is that this is when he would die like all human beings.

If Jesus did indeed appear *physically* after his supposed crucifixion, as the New Testament claims, then the Qur'anic story allows for two different, though not mutually exclusive, interpretations for the appearance. The first is that these appearances happened after the crucifixion of Jesus' substitute, but before his elevation from the earth. Jesus was still on earth, probably in hiding, so he was able to appear to his followers. The other interpretation is that Jesus' appearances happened after he was transported from the earth, which means that he was able to revisit the earth. This is reminiscent of Prophet Muhammad's visit to heaven, which is known as the *Mi'rāj* (ascension). The latter, which seems to be alluded to in the Qur'an (53.1-18) but is mentioned in fanciful details in many alleged Prophetic sayings, is said to have followed his *Isrā'* (night journey) from Mecca to the *al-Ḥaram ash-Sharif* in Palestine which is explicitly mentioned in the Qur'an (17.1). Interestingly, according to Prophetic sayings Muhammad is said to have been accompanied in both the night journey and ascension by Gabriel whom the Qur'an describes as someone who supported Jesus (2.87, 2.253, 5.110). If Gabriel did indeed help Prophet Muhammad in his short visit to heaven, then the suggestion that he might have also helped Jesus visit the earth after leaving it would look more plausible. Gabriel's role in any of these events, however, remains speculative.

As the two possible interpretations are not mutually exclusive, both could have happened. Jesus' reply to God in their dialog after his elevation strongly indicates that he had no access to his followers after he was lifted up: "I was a witness over them while I was among them, and when You took me (*tawaffaytani*) You were the watcher over them" (5.117). It may still be suggested that Jesus was talking about his followers in general, not the few that he appeared to, but I do not favor this suggestion.

It is fascinating that the death, resurrection, and ascension to heaven in the New Testament's story of Jesus may be all present in the Qur'anic story but in a very different context and order. The Gospels talk about a death caused by Jews, resurrection on earth, and then ascension to heaven. If the taking of Jesus by God in the Qur'an meant some form of loss of consciousness that required some kind of awakening, then we have a death-like state, followed by an ascension to heaven, then a resurrection from that state of unconsciousness, and ultimately a natural death. Here again we have an instance of contextual displacement where the authors of the New Testament and other Christian sources placed events in wrong contexts.

We have studied how the story of Jesus' crucifixion developed. The belief that he died prevailed over the alternative possibility that he escaped death, because the death of someone thought to be Jesus was witnessed by people and because Jesus was not seen after that in public — at least not by strangers. The story of his resurrection came about as the result of one or both of two causes. **First**, he was seen after the crucifixion by some, so people concluded that he must have been raised from death. **Second**, the Messiah was expected to achieve much more than Jesus he did, and the low-key nature of his life was highlighted and stressed in the most emphatic way by his most humiliating death, so the concept of resurrection provided a solution for this dilemma. The resurrection meant that he would come back and establish the heavenly kingdom that he was expected to found in his first coming. Paul provided the theological foundations for the Messiah's supposed Easter experience.

19.4. The Theology of the Crucifixion

The Qur'an's refutation of the New Testament's repeated claims that Jesus was crucified and raised from the dead is more than a difference about the historicity of these events. It is also a rejection of the central doctrine of "atonement" that Paul developed on and around these events. Paul considered this doctrine so fundamental to Christianity that he told fellow Christians: "if Christ has not been raised, your faith is useless; you are still in your sins" (1 Cor. 15:17). The Qur'an's alternative history is a rejection of the theological significance that Christianity, through Paul, has given to the crucifixion. In this section, we will study first the theology of the crucifixion in the New Testament and then examine it in the light of the Qur'an.

19.4.1. The New Testament and Theology of the Cross

In brief, the atonement denotes the reconciliation between God and man that is brought about by the death and resurrection of Jesus. Adam sinned, and all people inherited his sin. Sin means death, and in order to save people from perishing for good after death and give them eternal life, God made his son, Jesus, die and rise from the dead. Jesus' resurrection signifies the hope to be freed from sin and to attain eternal life: "For just as in Adam all die, so also in Christ all will be made alive" (1 Cor. 15:22). Those who believed in Jesus as their savior would be rewarded with salvation. In these lengthy quotations from his letter to the Romans, Paul explains the theological significance of the Easter experience and its role in the salvation of man:

> But now apart from the law the righteousness of God (which is attested by the law and the prophets) has been disclosed — namely, the righteousness of God through the faithfulness of Jesus Christ for all who believe. For there is no distinction, for all have sinned and fall short of the glory of God. But they are justified freely by his grace through the redemption that is in Christ Jesus. God publicly displayed him at his death as the mercy seat accessible through faith. This was to demonstrate his righteousness, because God in his forbearance had passed over the sins previously committed. This was also to demonstrate his righteousness in the present time, so that he would be just and the justifier of the one who lives because of Jesus' faithfulness. (Rom. 3:21-26)

> For while we were still helpless, at the right time Christ died for the ungodly. (For rarely will anyone die for a righteous person, though for a good person perhaps someone might possibly dare to die.) But God demonstrates his own love for us, in that while we were still sinners, Christ died for us. Much more then, because we have now been declared righteous by his blood, we will be saved through him from God's wrath. For if while we were enemies we were reconciled to God through the death of his Son, how much more, since we have been reconciled, will we be saved by his life? Not only this, but we also rejoice in God through our Lord Jesus Christ, through whom we have now received this reconciliation.

So then, just as sin entered the world through one man and death through sin, and so death spread to all people because all sinned — for before the law was given, sin was in the world, but there is no accounting for sin when there is no law. Yet death reigned from Adam until Moses even over those who did not sin in the same way that Adam (who is a type of the coming one) transgressed. But the gracious gift is not like the transgression. For if the many died through the transgression of the one man, how much more did the grace of God and the gift by the grace of the one man Jesus Christ multiply to the many! And the gift is not like the one who sinned. For judgment, resulting from the one transgression, led to condemnation, but the gracious gift from the many failures led to justification. For if, by the transgression of the one man, death reigned through the one, how much more will those who receive the abundance of grace and of the gift of righteousness reign in life through the one, Jesus Christ!

Consequently, just as condemnation for all people came through one transgression, so too through the one righteous act came righteousness leading to life for all people. For just as through the disobedience of the one man many were made sinners, so also through the obedience of one man many will be made righteous. Now the law came in so that the transgression may increase, but where sin increased, grace multiplied all the more, so that just as sin reigned in death, so also grace will reign through righteousness to eternal life through Jesus Christ our Lord. (Rom. 5:6-21)

Indeed, he who did not spare his own Son, but gave him up for us all — how will he not also, along with him, freely give us all things? (Rom. 8:32).

Because of Jesus' sacrifice, following the law is no more necessary for attaining salvation. Paul says that Jesus' death and resurrection "nullified" the law (Eph. 2:15), although he does not advocate a complete abolishment of the law.

Paul's understanding of Jesus' death and resurrection as an act of atonement might have been inspired by the Old Testament practice of animal sacrifice to atone for one's sins:

Moses then said to Aaron, "Approach the altar and make your sin offering and your burnt offering, and make atonement on behalf of yourself and on behalf of the people; and also make the people's offering and make atonement on behalf of them just as the Lord has commanded." (Lev. 9:7)

Indeed, in one of his letter, Paul likens Jesus' crucifixion to the sacrifice of the Passover lamb:

Clean out the old yeast so that you may be a new batch of dough — you are, in fact, without yeast. For Christ, our Passover lamb, has been sacrificed. (1 Cor. 5:7)

Unlike the Old Testament's atonement ritual of sacrificing animals, Paul's new atonement was accomplished not only by Jesus' death but ultimately by his subsequent resurrection.

Atonement is very much a Pauline doctrine. It was Paul who introduced and stressed in his writings this theology of the cross. Significantly, Jesus of the Evangelists does not seem to have been aware of the Pauline concept of atonement. There is *only one* Jesus saying, found in Mark and Matthew (20:25-28) only, that *may* be seen as referring to the atonement:

> Now when the other ten heard this, they became angry with James and John. Jesus called them and said to them, "You know that those who are recognized as rulers of the Gentiles lord it over them, and those in high positions use their authority over them. But it is not this way among you. Instead whoever wants to be great among you must be your servant, and whoever wants to be first among you must be the slave of all. For even the Son of Man did not come to be served but to serve, and to give his life as a ransom for many." (Mark 10:41-45)

Jesus' words that he came to offer his life "as a ransom for many" could be seen as an allusion to the atonement. But it is the only phrase in the four Gospels that may refer to Jesus' vicarious sacrifice. There is no elaboration of any form or shape, and the reference remains hidden in those two passages in Mark and Matthew.

Significantly, Luke's report of the same event above has this lone reference missing:

> A dispute also started among them over which of them was to be regarded as the greatest. So Jesus said to them, "The kings of the Gentiles lord it over them, and those in authority over them are called 'benefactors.' Not so with you; instead the one who is greatest among you must become like the youngest, and the leader like the one who serves. For who is greater, the one who is seated at the table, or the one who serves? Is it not the one who is seated at the table? But I am among you as one who serves." (Luke 22:24-27)

Even if Mark's and Matthew's passages are more authentic than Luke's, the absence of that particular phrase from Luke's account means that it could not have signified a fundamental and important doctrine such as the atonement, whether Luke dropped it deliberately or did not realize its supposed meaning. Ehrman notes that in Acts also the same author recounts a number of apostolic speeches that stress the importance of Jesus' death as a means to drive people to repent and seek forgiveness from God, but nowhere he considers Jesus' death as atonement for sins. Ehrman also makes the interesting observation that in some manuscripts of Luke, Jesus' speech during the Last Supper misses the following words about his body which may be seen as a reference to the atonement: "which is given for you" (Luke 22:19). Ehrman concludes that these were later added by copyists (Ehrman, 2007: 166-167).

Another passage that is often cited by the believers in the atonement is found in John (3:16): "For this is the way God loved the world: He gave his one and only Son, so that everyone who believes in him will not perish but have eternal life." This, like other Johannine passages (e.g. John 6:40; 1 John 5:12-13), does not actually teach the atonement of Paul. They merely state that those who believe in Jesus will have eternal life. Trading Jesus' life for the lives of the believers is a different, Pauline concept.

Similarly, non-Pauline passages in the New Testament stating that Jesus will save people from their sins (e.g. Matt. 1:21; John 1:29) should not be confused with the doctrine of atonement. Any spiritual guide may be described as being commissioned to save people by making them rid of their sins. Let's read, for instance, in the Old Testament what the Prophet Malachi was told by God about Levi's guidance of people to forgiveness:

> Then you will know that I sent this commandment to you so that my covenant may continue to be with Levi," says the sovereign Lord. "My covenant with him was designed to bring life and peace. I gave its statutes to him to fill him with awe, and he indeed revered me and stood in awe before me. He taught what was true; sinful words were not found on his lips. He walked with me in peace and integrity, and he turned many people away from sin. For the lips of a priest should preserve knowledge of sacred things, and people should seek instruction from him because he is the messenger of the sovereign Lord." (Mal. 2:4-7)

God describes the righteous Levi as someone who "turned many people away from sin." Note also how the covenant with Levi was "designed to bring life and peace." Paul's doctrine of atonement is different, because it establishes a direct and essential link between Jesus' death and resurrection and the forgiveness of the sins of people.

John describes Jesus as the "lamb of God" (John 1:29, 1:36) and manipulates the date of the crucifixion to suggest that Jesus died at the time of the slaughter of the Passover lamb. This is taken by some to be a subtle reference to the atonement. Even though John likens Jesus to a sacrificial lamb, he actually does not say explicitly that Jesus died to save the sinful or that his death was necessary to give life to others. John, who shows much more interest in theology at the cost of history than the Synoptics, could not have meant this yet stopped short of spelling it out.

Significantly, even when the Gospels talk about Jesus telling his disciples about the suffering he was expecting, he never says a single word indicating that this suffering has a vicarious function (Mark 8:31, 9:12; Matt. 16:21, 17:12; Luke 9:22, 17:25, 22:15, 24:26, 24:46)! Jesus said, the Synoptics claim, that he "had" to suffer and die, yet he does not explain why that "had" to happen, nor do his disciples show any interest in learning why. Even when Luke talks about Jesus' death and rise and the forgiveness of sins in his name, he fails to make a direct, causal connection: "Thus it stands written that the Messiah would suffer and would rise from the dead on the third day, and repentance for the forgiveness of sins would be proclaimed in his name to all nations, beginning from Jerusalem" (Luke 24:46-47). To claim that Jesus kept secret the purpose of his suffering and death, as explained by the theology of redemption, hardly makes any sense.

Equally significant is the fact that Jesus linked his miraculous healing to forgiving sins (Mark 2:3-12; Matt. 9:2-8; Luke 5:17-26), and was even accused of blasphemy because of that, yet he never attempted to link his death to the forgiveness of sins.

As I have already pointed out (p. 249), the concept of a suffering Messiah never existed in Judaism. This concept was developed to reconcile the beliefs that Jesus was the Messiah and that he suffered and died. This suffering was then given a theological dimension.

It is incomprehensible that Jesus would have mentioned only once, and in passing, what is arguably one of the most, if not the most, important doctrine in Christianity. The Gospels describe in detail Jesus' death and resurrection, yet they are completely silent on the alleged role of these events in the salvation of man. They cite in detail what they claim to be Jesus' teachings, yet the master is nowhere heard telling his followers anything about the central doctrine that Paul, who never met Jesus and converted to Christianity a few years after the master had gone, was going to reveal over two decades later in his letters.

If Jesus taught redemption, which he did not, then the Evangelists' ignorance of this central doctrine does not do their credibility any good. It is equally a problem if they were aware of this theological concept but decided against mentioning it. It can only mean that they did not believe it to be part of Jesus' genuine teachings. All evidence suggests that Paul is the author of the theology of the cross. He turned Christianity into some kind of Cross-ism, effectively reducing the life and teachings of Jesus to one alleged episode.

The Gospels portray Jesus as a teacher who educated his followers about the godly behavior that would bring them near to God and take them into the kingdom of heaven. Paul moved the focus from the teachings to the teacher. Jesus, according to Paul, did not come to deliver a message, but to redeem people, all of whom are sinful, by becoming a substitutionary sacrifice. He was the message. According to the Gospels, Christianity it is what Jesus did during his life — that is, before his crucifixion. In Paul's theology, it is Jesus' death and resurrection that sum up Jesus' mission and religion. The fact that the atonement became one of the most central doctrines in Christianity is a testimony to Paul's much greater role than Jesus of the Gospels in defining this religion.

We should not be surprised that the doctrine of atonement is not part of the Gospels. Paul was completely open about the fact that his teachings had not come from the historical Jesus or those who were close to him. He was proud that his knowledge came through direct revelation from the spiritual Jesus: "Now I want you to know, brothers and sisters, that the gospel I preached is not of human origin. For I did not receive it or learn it from any human source; instead I received it by a revelation of

Jesus Christ" (Gal. 1:11). This is why he uses the term "my gospel" (Rom. 2:16, 16:25; Phi. 4:15; 2 Tim. 2:8) — the only New Testament author to do so. Having hardly any knowledge of the teachings and history of his religious master yet managing to become the most influential Christian theologian, Paul represents a truly unique phenomenon in the history of religion. While the Evangelists do not show any knowledge of Paul's teachings, the author of the Second Epistle of Peter describes Paul's Epistles as "scriptures" (2 Peter 3:16). In the rest of the New Testament, as in later Christian writings, the term "scripture" is reserved for the Old Testament only.

Paul managed to exert the most influence on Christianity and develop it to what it came to be. The revelation of Jesus that Paul claims to have experienced has modified and changed the understanding of even God's revelation to Jesus. If Paul's claim to his miraculous conversion is set aside and his writings are seen as any other pious texts, the Christianity that would emerge from the remaining scriptures would be completely different. Christianity is not simply based on faith in the Christ or Scripture, but first and most on faith in Paul. No Christian can doubt Paul's credibility without having to fundamentally change his understanding of Christianity.

Significantly, we know from Paul himself that *his Jesus* was not the same the Jesus that was being preached by other *distinguished apostles*. This is what he wrote in his second letter to the Corinthians:

> For I am jealous for you with godly jealousy, because I promised you in marriage to one husband, to present you as a pure virgin to Christ. But I am afraid that just as the serpent deceived Eve by his treachery, your minds may be led astray from a sincere and pure devotion to Christ. For if someone comes and proclaims another Jesus different from the one we proclaimed, or if you receive a different spirit than the one you received, or a different gospel than the one you accepted, you put up with it well enough! For I consider myself not at all inferior to those "super-apostles." And even if I am unskilled in speaking, yet I am certainly not so in knowledge. Indeed, we have made this plain to you in everything in every way. (2 Cor. 11:2-6)

Paul's words that other apostles proclaimed a "different gospel than the one you accepted" are another confirmation that the Jesus that he preached was very different from the Jesus preached by his competitors. Unfortunately, he does not explain the differences between his teachings and the others'.

Equally significant is Paul's description of his adversaries as "super-apostles." He goes on to tell his audience how he matched certain qualifications of those apostles:

> But whatever anyone else dares to boast about (I am speaking foolishly), I also dare to boast about the same thing. Are they Hebrews? So am I. Are they Israelites? So am I. Are they descendants of Abraham? So am I. Are they servants of Christ? (I am talking

like I am out of my mind!) I am even more so: with much greater labors, with far more imprisonments, with more severe beatings, facing death many times. (2 Cor. 11:21-23)

Interestingly, Paul does not mention what attribute gave the super status to the other apostles. This superiority can only mean that these apostles, unlike him, had direct knowledge of Jesus and might have even been followers who saw, listened to, and lived with their master. The special status of those apostles did not stop Paul from vilifying them completely:

And what I am doing I will continue to do, so that I may eliminate any opportunity for those who want a chance to be regarded as our equals in the things they boast about. For such people are false apostles, deceitful workers, disguising themselves as apostles of Christ. And no wonder, for even Satan disguises himself as an angel of light. (2 Cor. 11:12-14)

The writers of the four Gospels, or more accurately their sources, as reporters of what they believed Jesus said and did, have played a significant role in how Jesus and his religion are seen. But it is Paul, who claimed to have received direct revelations from Jesus, who became the most influential individual in shaping how Christianity and its founder came to be understood.

Paul's theology of the cross is foreign not only to the teachings of the Gospels, but also to the teachings of the Old Testament. The latter does not know of the concept of salvation of man through the death of one person acting as a vicarious sacrifice. In the many centuries that the Old Testament spans, neither God nor any of the individuals He instructed to guide people taught them that their sins would be erased only if they believed that forgiveness can be brought about only by the death and resurrection of someone who was going to come to the world many centuries later. Unsurprisingly, there have been attempts to suggest that some words here and there in the Old Testament may have alluded to the concept of atonement, but certainly no one can claim that many Israelites or other nations of the Old Testament had a clue about Paul's concept of redemptive salvation. It is absurd to suggest that redemption through Jesus was a genuine divine doctrine when prominent figures such as Abraham, Jacob, Moses, as well as the numerous people who followed them over the centuries, show no sign of knowledge of it. The alternative suggestion that some of these spiritual guides knew that salvation can only happen through Jesus but left their followers in the dark is equally ridiculous.

The fact that the atonement is purely Paul's handwork is far from being the only insurmountable problem of the theology of the cross, as the Qur'an shows.

19.4.2. The Qur'an's Rejection of the Theology of the Cross

The Qur'an portrays Jesus as a prophet. Every prophet guided people to God, but without the involvement of any form of redemption. The role of the prophet in the

Qur'an has a lot of similarity with how the Gospels, not Paul's letters, describe Jesus' life and his efforts to guide people to salvation. A prophet is a messenger whose duty is to deliver God's instructions about belief and behavior. People have to believe that the prophet was sent by God, but the prophet himself is not the focus of the message. There was nothing that a prophet could do that would save people in the same way the crucifixion and resurrection of Jesus are supposed to do.

According to the Qur'an, all prophets, including Jesus, delivered the same message. Jesus worked hard to guide people to the righteous way, and so did every other prophet. While the Gospels have lots of differences with the Qur'an, they do share with it this view of Jesus' life. Paul discarded this view of Jesus' message to create for him a different and unique role.

The Qur'an rejects Paul's claim that Jesus' coming to the world changed the meaning and method of salvation. The salvation of the people who lived before Jesus was no different from that of those who lived after him. Each and every people were commanded to believe in the same doctrinal laws, as well as any behavioral laws they were given specifically to them. This is one verse in which God explains the basic message of salvation which all His messengers delivered to people:

> Those who believe, the Jews, the Christians, and the Sabaeans — whoever believe in Allah and the Last day and does good — they shall have their reward from their Lord, and there is no fear for them, nor shall they grieve (2.62, 5.69).

Salvation means avoiding the eternal life in hell and winning eternal life in paradise. It requires having true beliefs and doing good works. The Jews who followed Moses and the prophets after him and behaved properly, and the Muslims who followed Muhammad and acted righteously, are as worthy of salvation as the Christians who believed in God, the prophethood of Jesus, and acted properly. The Jews who lived before Jesus did not lose out nor their salvation was not as complete as that of the Christians. Similarly, the Muslims who lived after the commissioning of Prophet Muhammad have not been given a preferential treatment.

Another fundamental difference between the Qur'an and the concept of atonement concerns the relation between individual responsibility and sin. The theology of the cross is based on the concept of the *original sin*, which states that Adam committed a sin which all his descendants were made to inherit and thus be born in a state of sinfulness. The other fundamental assumption of Paul's atonement is that Jesus, who was born free of the original sin, came to this world to pay the price for that sin. In other words, the first assumption is about someone committing a sin and someone else inheriting it, and the second is about someone having a sin and someone else paying for it. Both of these assumptions are totally rejected by the Qur'an.

According to the Qur'an, every individual takes full responsibility for his own actions, whether good or bad. He is the only one who suffers the consequences of the sins he commits, and he is the only one who benefits from his obedience and good works. An individual may help others, but only as far as teaching them about sound beliefs and righteous actions. He cannot believe or act on their behalf. These are some of the verses that stress these fundamental principles (see also 39.7, 53.38-39):

> Say [O Muhammad!]: "Shall I seek other than Allah for Lord, when He is the Lord of all things?" No soul shall earn anything [evil] but against itself, and no bearer of burden shall bear the burden of another; and to your Lord is your return, so He will inform you about that in which you differed (6.164).

> Whoever goes aright, he does so for his own benefit; and whoever goes astray, he does so to his own detriment. No bearer of burden shall bear the burden of another. We would not punish until We have sent a messenger (17.15).

> No bearer of burden shall bear the burden of another, and if one heavily laden calls for [help with] his load, none of it will be lifted even though he [to whom he calls] be of kin. You [O Muhammad!] warn only those who fear their Lord, who is unseen, and keep up prayer. And whoever purifies himself, he does so only for his own benefit; and to Allah is the eventual coming (35.18).

Sins are acquired, not inherited, by the individual who commits them; and sins are forgiven by God if the sinful person repents and behaves righteously, not through the sacrifice of another person. Contrary to Paul's teachings, no man would answer for Adam's sin, and no sin of any man can be redeemed by a sacrifice offered by Jesus.

These Qur'anic principles are also found in the Old Testament, as shown, for example, in the following extended passage that Prophet Ezekiel attributes to God:

> Suppose a man is righteous. He promotes what is just and right, does not eat pagan sacrifices on the mountains or pray to the idols of the house of Israel, does not defile his neighbor's wife, does not have sexual relations with a woman while she is having her period, does not oppress anyone, but gives the debtor back his pledge, does not commit robbery, but gives his bread to the hungry and clothes the naked, does not engage in usury or charge interest, but refrains from wrongdoing, promotes true justice between men, obeys my statutes and guards my laws by being trustworthy. That man is righteous; he will certainly live, declares the Sovereign Lord.
>
> Suppose such a man has a violent son who sheds blood and does the aforementioned things (though the father did not do any of them). He eats pagan sacrifices on the mountains, defiles his neighbor's wife, oppresses the poor and the needy, commits robbery, does not give back a pledge, prays to idols, performs abominable acts, engages in usury and charges interest. Will he live? He will not! Because he has done all these

abominable deeds he will certainly die. He will bear the responsibility for his own death.

But suppose he in turn has a son who observes all the sins his father commits and does not follow his father's example. He does not eat pagan sacrifices on the mountains, does not pray to the idols of the house of Israel, does not defile his neighbor's wife, does not oppress or keep what has been given as a pledge, does not commit robbery, gives his food to the hungry, and clothes the naked, refrains from iniquity, does not engage in usury or charge interest, carries out my laws and obeys my statutes. He will not die because of his father's sin; he will surely live. As for his father, because he practices extortion, robs his brother, and does what is not good among his people, he will die for his sin.

Yet you say, 'Why should the son not suffer his father's punishment?' When the son does what is just and right, and keeps all my statutes and obeys them, he will surely live. The person who sins is the one who will die. A son will not suffer his father's punishment, and a father will not suffer his son's punishment; the righteous person will be judged according to his righteousness, and the wicked person according to his wickedness. (Ezek. 18:5-20)

What is also interesting in this passage is its description of sin as the equivalent of death. However it offers this description, which is how Paul also sees sin, while denying the concept of original sin and making no reference to the need for any savior to remove the sin. It clearly states that it is the person himself who can earn or repent from a sin. The relation between life and sin are also different from what we find in Paul's writing and John 3:16 where eternal life is attained by believing in Jesus.

Some have argued that, despite the verses cited above, the Qur'an contains passages that accommodate the inheritability and transferability of sins. These verses may be split into three categories. The **first** category includes verses in which God accuses people of being participants in sins committed by their ancestors. For instance, Jews at the time of Prophet Muhammad are accused of being party to the killing of previous prophets:

> And We gave Moses the Book and followed him with a succession of messengers; and We gave Jesus son of Mary clear proofs, and We supported him with the Spirit of Holiness. Is it that whenever a messenger came to you [O Children of Israel!] with what you do not like you grew arrogant, some you disbelieved and some you killed? (2.87).
>
> And when it is said to them (the Children of Israel): "Believe in what Allah has revealed," they say: "We believe in that which was revealed to us," and they deny that which came after it, though it is the truth, confirming that which they already have. Say [O Muhammad!]: "Why then did you kill Allah's prophets before if you were indeed believers?" (2.91).

The accusations to those Jews do not imply that they *inherited* the sins of their ancestors. They simply tell those Jews that they are as sinful as their fathers who killed the prophets and, therefore, had they lived then they would have taken part in the killing of the prophets. This is particularly clear in the following verses which condemn some Jews as participants in the killing of prophets centuries earlier, and praise others for obeying God:

> Abasement has been imposed on them wherever they are found, except under a covenant with Allah and a covenant with men, and they have become deserving of wrath from Allah, and humiliation is made to cleave to them. This is because they disbelieved in the verses of Allah and slew the prophets unjustly; this is because they disobeyed and exceeded the limits (3.112). They are not all alike; among the People of the Book there is an upright party; they recite Allah's verses in the nighttime, falling prostrate (3.113). They believe in Allah and the Last Day, they enjoin what is right and forbid what is wrong, and they hasten to good works, and those are among the righteous (3.114). And whatever good they do, they shall not be denied it, and Allah knows the dutiful [toward Him] (3.115).

Neither the good Jews inherited their piety from their good ancestors, nor did the evil ones inherit their disobedience from their prophet killing ancestors. Both parties earned their descriptions by their own works.

Likening people who lived centuries apart reflects the similarity of their intentions and deeds:

> And those who have no knowledge say: "Why does not Allah speak to us or a sign come to us?" Those before them said the like of what they say. Their hearts are all alike. We have explained the verses for a people of certainty [of faith] (2.118).

The following verse takes the allegory even further, suggesting that the behaviors of the disbelievers down the centuries were so similar as if they have passed them to each other:

> Similarly, no messenger came to those before them but they said: "[He is] a magician or a mad man" (51.52). Have they handed it (the attitude) down as an heirloom to one another? No, they are a transgressing people (51.53).

The **second** category includes one verse that is claimed to suggest that sins may be borne by someone other than the sinner:

> That they may bear their burdens in full on the Day of Resurrection and also of the burdens of those whom they lead astray without knowledge; surely evil is what they bear (16.25).

This verse does not talk about someone completely innocent bearing responsibility for someone else's sin, like the concept of original sin. Neither it says that someone's sins can be borne by another person, leaving the former free of sin.

It only says that, as those who guide people to the right path get rewarded for their guidance in addition to being rewarded for being on the right path themselves, those who lead people astray bear not only the burden of misleading themselves, but also that of misguiding others. The misled person takes responsibility for going astray, while the misleading person takes responsibility for misleading himself as well as the other person. His responsibility for misleading others does not mean that the latter would not be responsible for being astray. This distinction is made clearer in the following verses:

> And those who disbelieve say to those who believe: "Follow our path and we will bear your sins." But they shall not be bearers of any of their sins; they are liars (29.12). Most certainly they shall carry their own burdens, and other burdens with their own burdens, and most certainly they shall be questioned on the Day of Resurrection about what that which they forged (29.13).

The first verse stresses that the disbelievers cannot carry the sins of those whom they mislead, whereas the second verse clearly states that the disbelievers carry their own sins as well as "other burdens." These burdens are the sins of the act of misleading others, not the sins of the misled. The following saying of the Prophet states exactly the same thing: "He who introduces a good practice in Islam earns a reward for introducing it and a reward equal to the rewards of those follow it, without their rewards being diminished in any respect. And he who introduces an evil practice in Islam earns a sin for introducing it and a sin equal to the sins of those who follow it, without their sins being diminished in any respect." This is the wording as reported by the scholar Muslim in *The Book of Almsgiving* in his famous collection of Prophetic sayings. This saying has been reported in slightly different wordings by a number of other compilers of Prophetic sayings, including at-Tarmathī in *The Book of the Knowledge from the Messenger of Allah*, an-Nassā'ī in *The Book of Giving to Charity*, Ibn Māja in *The Introduction*, Aḥmad in *The First Authenticated Compilation of the People of Kūfa*, and ad-Daramī in *The Introduction*.

The **third** and last category includes a verse about the substitution of Abraham's son with a sacrifice. Having seen a visionary dream instructing him to slaughter his son, Abraham was about to do so when God ordered him not to kill his son and to have a great animal sacrificed in his stead:

> And We ransomed him with a tremendous slaughtering sacrifice (37.107).

Some have tried to use this verse to suggest that the concept of someone acting as a ransom for someone else exists in the Qur'an. The simple fact is that this verse only states that Abraham's son was ransomed from slaughter with an animal. This event, which is symbolized in the rite of sacrifice in the Muslim annual pilgrimage of Hajj to Mecca, has nothing to do with the Christian concept of a human being sacrificing himself for the whole of mankind.

I should finally talk about the Qur'anic concept of "intercession" which some may mistakenly think have some similarity with the Christian concept of atonement or the bearing of someone's sins by another. Let me first list the statements that the Qur'an makes about intercession and then see what conclusions can be drawn from them. First, like everything else, intercession is completely in the hands of God:

> Say [O Muhammad!]: "To Allah belongs all intercession. His is the kingdom of the heavens and the earth, then to Him you [O people!] shall be brought back" (39.44).

Second, Allah has granted some beings the right of intercession:

> To Him belongs what is in the heaven and the earth. Who is he that can intercede with Him but by His permission? He knows what is before them and what is behind them, and they cannot comprehend anything of His knowledge except what He pleases (2.255).

Third, those intercessors are angels:

> And how many an angel is there in the heavens whose intercession can have no benefit except after Allah gives permission to whom He pleases and chooses (53.26).

Fourth, this verse also shows that God would accept the intercession of angels only for those whom He approves of, i.e. for those whom He considers good enough to receive this help — more or less in the same way that forgiveness is not granted to all but only to those who deserve it.

It is not clear whether this intercession simply means asking God to forgive someone, or having the permission to intervene to help that person in some way. There are verses that talk about the angels asking God to forgive human beings:

> Those who bear the Throne [of God] and those around it celebrate the praise of their Lord, believe in Him, and ask forgiveness for those who believe: "Our Lord! You comprehend all things in mercy and knowledge, therefore grant forgiveness for those who repent and follow Your path, and save them from the punishment of hell" (40.7).

It is clear, however, that this intercession is as far from the Pauline concepts of vicarious atonement and salvation as anything can be. The Qur'an rejects the suggestion that sin can be inherited by, transferred to, or atoned for by someone other than the sinner.

Paul was not a disciple of Jesus nor even met him, yet the influence that he has had in shaping Christianity is more than that of Jesus. This observation is true not only when considering the Jesus of the Qur'an to be the real Jesus, but also if it were the Jesus of the Gospels. As already pointed out by many, "Paulinity" would be a more accurate name for what came to be called Christianity.

Paul openly declared that his knowledge did not come from any scripture or followers of Jesus but rather from God directly: "the gospel I preached is not of human origin. For I did not receive it or learn it from any human source; instead I received it by a revelation of Jesus Christ" (Gal. 1:11-12). His credibility rests wholly on his claim that Jesus appeared to him (Acts 9:3-8, 22:6-10, 26:13-18). Yet even if Paul did indeed experience something strange on his way to Damascus to persecute Christians, that does not justify accepting his teachings as core Christianity. We may not be able to say a lot about Jesus' alleged appearance to Paul, but we know that what Paul ended up teaching has nothing to do with what Jesus preached.

20

A Second Coming?

The Jews do not believe that Jesus is the awaited Messiah, so they are still waiting for the Messiah to come. Christians are also waiting for the Messiah, but for them it is a *return* of Jesus the Messiah who came two thousand years ago. The New Testament claims that Jesus thought that he would return during the lifetime of his audiences, and so the early Christians were expecting him to return shortly after his resurrection.

The Qur'an tells us that Jesus predicted the coming of Prophet Muhammad. This is the truth that was changed to invent the concept of Jesus' second coming. This concept was probably developed by Jesus' early followers in reaction to his very low-key life which was in sharp contrast to their expectations that the Messiah would have enormous influence on the world. They needed an explanation for their master's subdued life, even though they had accepted his corrective message that the Messiah was a spiritual rather than military leader as the Jews thought. Jesus' alleged second coming then marked the time when the Messiah would rule the world. His eschatological return is supposed to coincide with the appearance of powerful but evil figures, such as the antichrist, whom Jesus would destroy.

The Jews believe that the Messiah would come and the Christians believe he would return after the gathering of the historical twelve tribes of Israel in the land that God promised them, Palestine. This belief has given the religious concept of the future coming of the Messiah serious political dimensions.

Muslims also share with the Christians the belief in Jesus' second coming. This belief is not supported by the Qur'an, but it is based on sayings attributed to Prophet Muhammad that talk about Jesus' "descent" from heaven. Jesus' second coming, however, is secondary in importance to the appearance of an apocalyptic, higher status figure known as al-Mahdī. It is clear that the narratives about Jesus' descent and the coming of al-Mahdī are both inspired by the Christian stories.

20.1. The Second Coming in the New Testament

The four Gospels state that Jesus told his followers that he will return in the future, at the end times. This eschatological second coming, which is also known as *parousia* (from the Greek word for "being presence"), would be preceded by changes of cosmic proportion and significance. When asked by some of his disciples on the Mount of Olives about those signs, this is what Jesus had to say:

> Many will come in my name, saying, 'I am he,' and they will mislead many. When you hear of wars and rumors of wars, do not be alarmed. These things must happen, but

the end is still to come. For nation will rise up in arms against nation, and kingdom against kingdom. There will be earthquakes in various places, and there will be famines. These are but the beginning of birth pains. "You must watch out for yourselves. You will be handed over to councils and beaten in the synagogues. You will stand before governors and kings because of me, as a witness to them. First the gospel must be preached to all nations. When they arrest you and hand you over for trial, do not worry about what to speak. But say whatever is given you at that time, for it is not you speaking, but the Holy Spirit. Brother will hand over brother to death, and a father his child. Children will rise against parents and have them put to death. You will be hated by everyone because of my name. But the one who endures to the end will be saved." But when you see the abomination of desolation standing where it should not be (let the reader understand), then those in Judea must flee to the mountains. The one on the roof must not come down or go inside to take anything out of his house. The one in the field must not turn back to get his cloak. Woe to those who are pregnant and to those who are nursing babies in those days! Pray that it may not be in winter. For in those days there will be suffering unlike anything that has happened from the beginning of the creation that God created until now, or ever will happen. And if the Lord had not cut short those days, no one would be saved. But because of the elect, whom he chose, he has cut them short. Then if anyone says to you, 'Look, here is the Christ!' or 'Look, there he is!' do not believe him. For false messiahs and false prophets will appear and perform signs and wonders to deceive, if possible, the elect. Be careful! I have told you everything ahead of time. "But in those days, after the suffering, the sun will be darkened and the moon will not give its light; the stars will be falling from heaven, and the powers in the heavens will be shaken. (Mark 13:6-25)

Then, referring to himself with his favorite periphrastic title of "Son of Man," Jesus went on to talk about his second advent:

Then everyone will see the Son of Man arriving in the clouds with great power and glory. Then he will send angels and they will gather his elect from the four winds, from the ends of the earth to the ends of heaven. "Learn this parable from the fig tree: Whenever its branch becomes tender and puts out its leaves, you know that summer is near. So also you, when you see these things happening, know that he is near, right at the door. I tell you the truth, this generation will not pass away until all these things take place. Heaven and earth will pass away, but my words will never pass away. "But as for that day or hour no one knows it — neither the angels in heaven, nor the Son — except the Father. Watch out! Stay alert! For you do not know when the time will come. It is like a man going on a journey. He left his house and put his slaves in charge, assigning to each his work, and commanded the doorkeeper to stay alert. Stay alert, then, because you do not know when the owner of the house will return — whether during evening, at midnight, when the rooster crows, or at dawn — or else he might find you asleep when he returns suddenly. What I say to you I say to everyone: Stay alert!" (Mark 13:26-37)

His return at the End-time, unlike his departure, would be one of glory and limitless power. He left this world after being judged, but he will come back to judge.

20.1.1. The Unfulfilled Imminence of the Second Coming

Jesus did not tell the disciples exactly when he is coming back, because he did not know it. No one knows it other than God (Mark 13:32; Matt. 24:36). But he made it clear to his disciples that it was "near." In fact, it is so near that he promised his audience that "this generation will not pass away until all these things take place." This imminence is stressed by Jesus' repeated instruction to his disciples to "stay alert."

Each of Matthew (24) and Luke (21) has its version of the speech above, although Luke places it in the temple rather than on the Mount of Olives. Both share the general tone of imminence in Mark's version, and they also confirm that the kingdom of heaven was so near (Matt. 24:33, 24:42; Luke 21:31) that the Son of Man' glorious arrival in a cloud was going to happen in the lifetime of Jesus' generation (Matt. 24:34; Luke 21:32), and that the high priest was going to witness it (Mark 14:62; Matt. 26:64).

Jesus confirmed that his second coming would happen during the lifetime of his audience in an earlier speech to a crowd including his disciples, according to Mark, or to his disciples only, according to Matthew (16:24-28) and Luke (9:23-27). Having explained to them what they need to do to follow him, he went on to say:

> "For if anyone is ashamed of me and my words in this adulterous and sinful generation, the Son of Man will also be ashamed of him when he comes in the glory of his Father with the holy angels." And he said to them, "I tell you the truth, there are some standing here who will not experience death before they see the kingdom of God come with power." (Mark 8:38-9:1)

One passage in Mark's version of the sermon on the Mount of Olives that appears in Matthew also is followed in the latter by a statement in which Jesus confirms his return during the lifetime of his generation:

> Whenever they hand you over for trial, do not worry about how to speak or what to say, for what you should say will be given to you at that time. For it is not you speaking, but the Spirit of your Father speaking through you. "Brother will hand over brother to death, and a father his child. Children will rise against parents and have them put to death. And you will be hated by everyone because of my name. But the one who endures to the end will be saved. Whenever they persecute you in one place, flee to another. I tell you the truth, you will not finish going through all the towns of Israel before the Son of Man comes. (Matt. 10:19-23)

The following passage is not as clear cut about the imminence of the second coming, but it still likely to reflect the author's belief that Jesus meant to say that he was coming very soon:

> Again the high priest questioned him, "Are you the Christ, the Son of the Blessed One?" "I am," said Jesus, "and you will see the Son of Man sitting at the right hand of the Power and coming with the clouds of heaven." (Mark 14:61-62)

A very similar passage from the high priest's interrogation of Jesus is reported by Matthew (26:63-64). In Luke's equivalent passage, Jesus mentions to the Jewish leaders who questioned him his immediate seating at God's right hand but he does not talk about a second coming and that they would witness that glory:

> When day came, the council of the elders of the people gathered together, both the chief priests and the experts in the law. Then they led Jesus away to their council and said, "If you are the Christ, tell us." But he said to them, "If I tell you, you will not believe, and if I ask you, you will not answer. But from now on the Son of Man will be seated at the right hand of the power of God." (Luke 22:66-69)

Apart from this passage, which does not deny or confirm Jesus' second coming, the Jesus sayings above confirm his second advent and stress the imminence of that return during the lifetime of his audience.

There are passages in which Jesus does not mention explicitly his second coming but talks about the nearness of the kingdom of God (Mark 1:15; Matt. 4:17, 10:7). These sayings still imply that his second coming was near because the kingdom of God is supposed to be established when he returns. Interestingly, John the Baptist was also preaching the nearness of the kingdom of heaven just before Jesus' appearance (Matt. 3:2). Luke's (23:51) statement that Joseph of Arimathea "was looking forward to the kingdom of God" also suggests that he was expecting it to be during his lifetime.

The Epistle of James gives clear evidence that the author shared the Evangelists' belief that Jesus would come back during the lifetime of his listeners. This is what he advised his fellow believers:

> So be patient, brothers and sisters, until the Lord's return. Think of how the farmer waits for the precious fruit of the ground and is patient for it until it receives the early and late rains. You also be patient and strengthen your hearts, for the Lord's return is near. Do not grumble against one another, brothers and sisters, so that you may not be judged. See, the judge stands before the gates! (Jam. 5:7-9)

For the author of the Book of Revelation also *the time was near* (Rev. 1:3). He starts his book with a declaration that the events it describes, which include the second coming, "must happen very soon" (Rev. 1:1), and ends with attributing to

Jesus the words that he is "coming soon" (Rev. 22:20). In one particularly interesting vision that is reminiscent of Gospel passages and Daniel 7:13, the author saw Jesus coming in the clouds: "Look! He is returning with the clouds, and every eye will see him, even those who pierced him, and all the tribes on the earth will mourn because of him. This will certainly come to pass!" (Rev. 1:7).

Contrary to the passages that we have seen so far, the Evangelist John records an event that seems to suggest that Jesus' return was not going to happen soon:

> Peter turned around and saw the disciple whom Jesus loved following them. (This was the disciple who had leaned back against Jesus' chest at the meal and asked, "Lord, who is the one who is going to betray you?") So when Peter saw him, he asked Jesus, "Lord, what about him?" Jesus replied, "If I want him to live until I come back, what concern is that of yours? You follow me!" So the saying circulated among the brothers and sisters that this disciple was not going to die. But Jesus did not say to him that he was not going to die, but rather, "If I want him to live until I come back, what concern is that of yours?" This is the disciple who testifies about these things and has written these things, and we know that his testimony is true. (John 21:20-24)

The disciples' conclusion that the special disciple "was not going to die" means that they believed that Jesus' return was a distant future event that would not happen in their lifetime. Even if this particular disciple was very old, the other disciples would have taken Jesus' words to mean that he was coming back soon rather than that the beloved disciple would not die.

This passage, which has been bizarrely misunderstood by some as meaning that Jesus' coming was near, does not mean that John was consistent in his view about the time of Jesus' return. In another passage John makes Jesus tell a Nathanael and others that they "will see heaven opened and the angels of God ascending and descending on the Son of Man" (John 1:51), which suggests that Jesus' return was going to happen during his audience's lifetime.

Paul's letters have many references that Jesus' second coming was near, people were waiting for the return, and they would witness that coming. But these statements cannot be said to *conclusively* mean that Paul believed that Jesus' would return during the lifetime of his own audience. They may be interpreted as meaning that people's experience of Jesus would happen after they are raised from the dead. This is one example from Paul's letter to the Corinthians: "Just as the testimony about Christ has been confirmed among you — so that you do not lack any spiritual gift as you wait for the revelation of our Lord Jesus Christ. He will also strengthen you to the end, so that you will be blameless on the day of our Lord Jesus Christ" (1 Cor. 1:6-8). In the First Epistle to Timothy, whose attribution to Paul is questionable, the writer tells the addressee: "I charge you before God who gives life to all things and Christ Jesus who made his good confession before Pontius Pilate, to obey this command without fault or failure until the appearing of our Lord Jesus Christ" (1 Tim. 6:13-14). This statement also, it may be argued, does not *necessarily* mean that the writer thought that Timothy would be alive when Jesus appears again. Paul's statements about the nearness of Jesus' return may still be seen as implying that Jesus would return during the lifetime of at least some of his audience, but this cannot be concluded with certainty.

However, Paul's passage about the *rapture* does reflect a belief that the second coming was going to be witnessed by at least some of the people who lived in Paul's time. Like the Evangelists, Paul attributes the teaching about the immediacy of Jesus' return to Jesus himself describing it as "the word of the Lord." The term "rapture" denotes the gathering and taking to heaven of the believers by Jesus, hence the derivation of the term from the Latin word *raptura* which means "seizure":

> Now we do not want you to be uninformed, brothers and sisters, about those who are asleep, so that you will not grieve like the rest who have no hope. For if we believe that Jesus died and rose again, so also we believe that God will bring with him those who have fallen asleep as Christians. For we tell you this by the word of the Lord, that we who are alive, who are left until the coming of the Lord, will surely not go ahead of those who have fallen asleep. For the Lord himself will come down from heaven with a shout of command, with the voice of the archangel, and with the trumpet of God, and the dead in Christ will rise first. Then we who are alive, who are left, will be suddenly caught up together with them in the clouds to meet the Lord in the air. And so we will always be with the Lord. Therefore encourage one another with these words. (1 The. 4:13-18)

Clearly Paul taught that the *parousia* or the second coming would take place during his lifetime and the lifetime of his audience. Paul addressed in this letter concerns by the Christians in Thessalonica that fellow Christians, who were expecting to witness Jesus' return, were dying (Fredriksen, 1999: 80; Theissen & Merz, 1999: 94). He dealt with these concerns again in his second letter to the Thessalonians:

> Now regarding the arrival of our Lord Jesus Christ and our being gathered to be with him, we ask you, brothers and sisters, not to be easily shaken from your composure or disturbed by any kind of spirit or message or letter allegedly from us, to the effect that the day of the Lord is already here. (2 The. 2:1-2)

The Gospels also speak about the rapture (also Matt. 24:30-31, 25:1-13):

> Then everyone will see the Son of Man arriving in the clouds with great power and glory. Then he will send angels and they will gather his elect from the four winds, from the ends of the earth to the ends of heaven. (Mark 13:26-27)

> I tell you, in that night there will be two people in one bed; one will be taken and the other left. There will be two women grinding grain together; one will be taken and the other left. (Luke 17:34-35)

> And if I go and make ready a place for you, I will come again and take you to be with me, so that where I am you may be too. (John 14:3)

Except the odd case of John 21:20-24, the Evangelists claimed that Jesus taught that his second coming was going to happen during the lifetime of his audience. Unless one disputes the authenticity of these sayings, it must be concluded that Jesus mistakenly thought that his second coming was to shortly follow his departure. Paul had also said that the rapture was going to be experienced by the first generation of Christians. Assuming that Paul and the Evangelists' belief reflects authentic teachings of Jesus, this is how one scholar reconstructed what happened:

> Jesus originally said that the Son of Man would come in the immediate future, while his hearers were alive. After his death and resurrection, his followers preached that he would return immediately — that is, they simply interpreted "the Son of Man" as referring to Jesus himself. Then, when people started dying, they said that some would still be alive. When almost the entire first generation was dead, they maintained that one disciple would still be alive. Then he died, and it became necessary to claim that Jesus had not actually promised even this one disciple that he would live to see the great day. By the time we reach one of the latest books of the New Testament, 2 Peter, the return of the Lord has been postponed even further: some people scoff and say, "Where is the promise of his coming?" But remember, "with the Lord one day is as a thousand years, and a thousand years as one day" (2 Peter 3:3-8). The Lord is not really slow, but rather keeps time by a different calendar.
> In the decades after Jesus' death, then, the Christians had to revise their first expectation again and again. This makes it very probable that the expectation originated with Jesus. We make sense of these pieces of evidence if we think that Jesus himself told his followers that the Son of Man would come while they still lived. The fact that this expectation was difficult for Christians in the first century helps prove that Jesus held it himself. We also note that Christianity survived this early discovery that Jesus had made a mistake very well. (Sanders, 1995: 180)

One minor point of disagreement that I have with Sander's reading of the text is that he tries to integrate John 21:20-24 about that special disciple with the Synoptists' repeated assertions of the imminence of Jesus' return although the former clearly implies the opposite. My more fundamental disagreement is with Sanders' conclusion that it was Jesus who made the mistaken prediction about his return. The Gospel writers cannot be presumed to have given us accurate accounts of what Jesus said and did. At times they reported authentic sayings and deeds of Jesus, but most of the time their reports were not historical records of his words and actions but reflective of *what they believed he said and did*. The latter is a mix of what they learned from their sources and modifications they introduced based on their different images of Jesus dictated that he would have said or done. Paul does not show any knowledge of the historical Jesus anyway.

As Sanders shows, passages that are embarrassing and awkward to Christians, such as those that attribute failed predictions to Jesus, are considered by New Testaments scholars as more likely to be historical, i.e. reflecting what Jesus truly said or did (Powell, 2000: 53). The reasoning is that Christians would not have made up such uncomfortable passages. This is not a necessary conclusion. The Evangelists did not see in those passages the problems that we clearly see today. They managed to explain them away one way or another. If in this age of critical thinking Christians can accept these and many other awkward and even conflicting passages, then surely the Evangelists who lived in a much less rational time were more than capable of doing the same. If you asked Mark about sayings in which Jesus speaks about his return in the lifetime of his listeners you would find that he has got a ready answer for you. Whether that answer makes sense and is rational or not to you is completely another matter. The answer was reassuring enough to Mark.

Also, the Evangelists, who wrote the Gospels decades after Jesus, were mainly copying from other written and/or oral sources. We already know that Matthew and Luke both probably relied on Mark and Q. Mark himself was not a firsthand witness, so he also must have relied on other sources. The author of John wrote his account even later than Matthew and Luke. The Gospel writers used their sources with liberty, changing, adding, and removing things, but by and large they reported what came to their knowledge and believed to be true. Who the writers of those original sources were and under what circumstances they wrote, we have no way of knowing. But this ignorance does not give us the right to presume that they passed completely accurate and faithful accounts of Jesus' life. If anything, it should make use rather suspicious about the accuracy of the Gospels. Paul spoke about Jesus' imminent return yet he did not see him, and he does not give us any reason to believe that he knew much about or was even interested in the historical Jesus. Paul was interested in talking about the image of the Christ that worked for his salvational theology. The Evangelists' sources were presumably more informed but still not reliable.

The New Testament writers often put the reader in front of a stark choice: either to dispute the authenticity and/or accuracy of some or much of what they say, or accuse Jesus of being contradictory, make terrible mistakes, and/or being naïve.

From the Qur'anic perspective, it is the Evangelists who are wrong, contradictory, and naïve. Jesus could not have made the silly mistake of claiming to be coming back within the lifetime of his audience, which would have meant a few years at most. Prophets talked about the future that God revealed to them, and God could not have misled Jesus. I do not believe that Jesus uttered a single word about a second coming at all.

But if Jesus did not speak about coming back then how did the concept of *parousia* come into being? I think it is unlikely that this was the result of misunderstanding what Jesus said. Had any misunderstanding by his disciples occurred at any point, it would have been cleared up quickly. This would not have been a misunderstanding about a little issue that Jesus' close followers could have entertained while in the company of their master. It must have been made up by people, like many of the things that were attributed to Jesus after he had gone. But why would anyone want to invent such an event?

Jesus was the awaited Messiah. The Jews were thinking of the Messiah as a leader who would liberate them and restore the glory of Israel. In fact, messianic expectations remained widespread among the Jews even long after Jesus had gone. Tacitus (*Histories*, 5.13) and Suetonius (*Lives of the Caesars: Vespasian*, 4.5) both report a Jewish prophecy about Jewish men who would rule the world, although both state that the Jews were misguided as the prophecy pointed to the Roman emperor Vespasian. Josephus (*Jewish War*, 6.5.4) also mentioned the Jewish prophecy that a man from Judea will rule the world, but he also confirmed that the Jews misunderstood the prophecy which he said denoted Vespasian.

Jesus did not rule the world. For most Jews, that proved that Jesus was not the Messiah. A small minority followed him and accepted his corrective teaching that the Messiah was a spiritual not military figure, would liberate people from their sinful lives not Israel from the Romans, and would work to restore the individual's obedience to God not Israel's lost glory. But some of these followers still had a problem. The Messiah, whom people have been waiting for for centuries, had little impact on the world before he left. The Messiah, they reckoned, was surely going to do more than Jesus did, although spiritually rather than militarily. This would have led some to speculate that Jesus must be returning soon to force himself on the world in a spectacular way that reflects his status. Although the Messiah was not going to be involved in military battles, he was going to win the spiritual war.

20.1.2. The Second Coming and Other Apocalyptic Events

New Testament writers have linked Jesus' second coming to other significant figures and events. In his reassuring letter to the Thessalonians, Paul told them that the *parousia* will take place only after "the rebellion comes and the man of lawlessness is revealed, the son of destruction." The "lawless one," as Paul calls this deluding figure, will take his seat in God's temple and display himself as God. When the one who is holding the lawless one back is taken out of the way, this evil character will appear. The lawless one will then work "all kinds of miracles and signs and false wonders," and will lead some people astray. But the Lord will destroy the lawless one by the breath of his mouth and will wipe him out by the manifestation of his arrival (2 The. 2:1-9). In other words, in his second coming, Jesus will destroy the lawless one.

Paul's lawless one is often identified with the "antichrist" of the Johannine Epistles. The term "antichrist" is not found anywhere in the Bible outside the First and Second Epistles of John. These are the five occurrences of the term in John's letters:

> Children, it is the last hour, and just as you heard that the antichrist is coming, so now many antichrists have appeared. We know from this that it is the last hour. They went out from us, but they did not really belong to us, because if they had belonged to us, they would have remained with us. But they went out from us to demonstrate that all of them do not belong to us. Nevertheless you have an anointing from the Holy One, and you all know. I have not written to you that you do not know the truth, but that you do know it, and that no lie is of the truth. Who is the liar but the person who denies that Jesus is the Christ? This one is the antichrist: the person who denies the Father and the Son. (1 John 2:18-22)

> But every spirit that does not confess Jesus is not from God, and this is the spirit of the antichrist, which you have heard is coming, and now is already in the world. (1 John 4:3)

> For many deceivers have gone out into the world, people who do not confess Jesus as Christ coming in the flesh. This person is the deceiver and the antichrist! (2 John 1:7)

John uses the term "antichrist" for more than one person. Many of those antichrists have already appeared, he tells his audience. An antichrist is someone who denies the truth, such as denying Jesus' messiahship. The spirit of antichrist was already in the world. I find it very difficult to identify John's antichrist, which is a term that applies to many people some of whom had already come even by John's time, with Paul's lawless one, who is a single person who is to come before Jesus' second coming. Indeed, down the centuries various individuals were identified as the antichrist, including Popes, religious heretics, and politicians (Nichols, 2001). Even Elvis managed to convince some that he was the antichrist!

Being full of apocalyptic figures and descriptions, the book of Revelation has been a fertile land for those who are eager to learn more about the antichrist. The "dragon" (Rev. 12) and the "beast" (Rev. 13) are among the Revelation figures that have been identified with the antichrist. The beasts mentioned in the Old Testament Book of Daniel (7) are also linked to the antichrist. There are other Old Testament prophecies that are understood by some to be about the antichrist.

Revelation also states that Jesus' return would not be peaceful. It talks about an enormous battle, Armageddon, in which Jesus defeats the antichrist (Rev. 16:16). Some Christians have been seeing in various wars and disasters signs of the nearness of Jesus' second coming and the End-time — a view developed on the basis of Revelation and Gospel passages such as these words that Mark attributes to Jesus:

> When you hear of wars and rumors of wars, do not be alarmed. These things must happen, but the end is still to come. For nation will rise up in arms against nation, and kingdom against kingdom. There will be earthquakes in various places, and there will be famines. These are but the beginning of birth pains. (Mark 13:7-8)

According to the Gospels, Jesus talked about the appearance of many false messiahs and prophets who would perform miracles and mislead people before the coming of the son of man (Mark 13:5-6, 13:21-22; Matt. 24:5, 24:11, 24:24). But he did not speak about an antichrist.

As Jesus knew nothing about the Christ of Paul, he also did not have the slightest idea about Paul's lawless one who is supposed to appear before Jesus returns.

20.1.3. The Dangerous Politics of the Second Coming

The second coming of the Messiah is not only a religious concept, but it has political dimensions which have had an enormous impact on the modern world and is therefore worth talking about briefly.

According to the Old Testament, the kingdom that David established in the holy land, which is dated to 10th century BCE, consisted of the descendants of Jacob, known as the twelve tribes and named after 10 of his sons and 2 of his grandsons. After the death of David's son Solomon, the kingdom split into two separate states. The southern kingdom of Judea, whose capital was Jerusalem, was occupied by the tribes of Judah and Benjamin. The northern kingdom of Israel, which took Samaria as its capital, was occupied by the other ten tribes. When King Hoshea revolted against the new Assyrian king Shalmaneser V, the latter besieged Israel for three years. Shortly after Shalmaneser's death, around 721 BCE, Samaria fell to his successor, Sargon II. The Assyrian king took Israel's inhabitants captives and scattered them. This is what the Bible has to say about this event:

> In the fourth year of King Hezekiah's reign (it was the seventh year of the reign of Israel's King Hoshea, son of Elah), King Shalmaneser of Assyria marched up against Samaria and besieged it. After three years he captured it (in the sixth year of Hezekiah's reign); in the ninth year of King Hoshea's reign over Israel Samaria was captured. The king of Assyria deported the people of Israel to Assyria. He settled them in Halah, along the Habor (the river of Gozan), and in the cities of the Medes. (2 Kings 18:9-11)

More or less the same fate was awaiting Judea and its people. In 597 BCE, the Babylonian king Nebuchadnezzar captured Jerusalem and took its prominent people into captivity in Babylon. In a second campaign in 586 BCE he destroyed Judea. The Old Testament Book of Jeremiah claims that Nebuchadnezzar took Jewish captives to Babylon three times, corresponding to 597, 586, and 582 BCE:

> Here is the official record of the number of people Nebuchadnezzar carried into exile: In the seventh year, 3,023 Jews; in Nebuchadnezzar's eighteenth year, 832 people from Jerusalem; in Nebuchadnezzar's twenty-third year, Nebuzaradan, captain of the royal guard, carried into exile 745 Jews. In all 4,600 people went into exile. (Jer. 52:28-30)

After defeating the Babylonians and reestablishing Judea, the Persian king Cyrus allowed the captive two tribes of Judea to return to Palestine in 539 BCE. The scattered ten tribes of Israel did not have such luck because they had already been assimilated by other peoples and were lost.

The Jews believe that the Messiah *will come* after the twelve tribes have gathered together again in their promised land in Palestine. But Christians believe that the Messiah *has already come*, so they repositioned the gathering of the twelve tribes in Palestine to become a condition for the *second coming* of the Messiah. This is how Jewish Zionism and Christian Zionism have both found in the establishment of the modern state of Israel a sign for the coming of the Messiah, although they believe that each other's Messiah is false! Strengthening the state of Israel, helping and encouraging Jews from all parts of the world to immigrate to Palestine, and usurping more Palestinian lands became noble religious duties for the Zionists.

There are few mentions of the twelve tribes in the New Testament. For instance, James addressed his Epistle to "the twelve tribes dispersed abroad" (Jam. 1:1). In Matthew (19:28) we see Jesus tell his disciples the following: "when the Son of Man sits on his glorious throne, you who have followed me will also sit on twelve thrones, judging the twelve tribes of Israel." Luke (22:30) also has a passage in which Jesus tells his disciples that they would be sitting in his kingdom "on thrones judging the twelve tribes of Israel." These passages imply that the twelve tribes would have been gathered by the time of Jesus' second coming. This is the closest reference that may link the *parousia* to the gathering of the twelve tribes.

20.2. The Second Coming in Sayings Attributed to Prophet Muhammad

An extensive corpus of Islamic literature has developed on the subject of Jesus' second coming, confirming and giving amazingly lengthy details about it. These sources describe Jesus' second coming as a "descent," meaning that he would descend from heaven, where God had taken him to. Keeping in mind our early discussion of the contentious nature and high unreliability of the Prophetic sayings literature (§1.4.1), let's look first at what Prophet Muhammad is supposed to have said about Jesus' second coming.

Al-Bukhārī (810-870 CE) and his student Muslim (c. 817 – 875 CE), whose compilations of Prophetic sayings are highly regarded by Sunni scholars and are referred to as the "correct" compilations, attribute to Prophet Muhammad a number of sayings about Jesus' return. Other compilations that Sunnis consider as highly reliable — such as those of Abū Dāwūd, An-Nassā'ī, and at-Tarmathī — also mention Jesus' second advent. Many of these sayings link the descent of Jesus with the appearance of the antichrist. The latter is called in Islamic literature *al-Masīḥ ad-dajjāl* (the false Messiah) (e.g. al-Bukhārī, 1780; Muslim, 273) or *ad-dajjāl* (the charlatan) (e.g. Al-Bukhārī, 1783; Muslim, 277). The title of "the false Messiah" is reminiscent of the Gospel passages in which Jesus predicts the appearance of false Messiahs and prophets (Mark 13:22; Matt. 24:24). Strangely there are sayings that refer to the antichrist as the *al-Masīḥ* (the Messiah) (Muslim, 1380).

As is the case with Prophetic sayings in general, the sayings about Jesus' second coming are contradictory and inconsistent, with one saying appearing in one form in one book and in another in others. This is reminiscent of the differences between the Gospels. We are not concerned here with detailing the numerous contradictions in the reported Prophetic sayings about Jesus' second coming or the extreme absurdity of many of them, but the references given below should make this task easy for the reader who is interested in this pursuit.

Based on their content, the sayings about Jesus' descent may be grouped into four different categories:

① After descending, Jesus will kill the antichrist (Muslim, 34, 116; Abū Dāwūd, 4324; at-Tarmathī, 2341, 2345). Some sayings have even identified Damascus as the place where Jesus kills the antichrist (Muslim, 110; Abū Dāwūd, 4321). This is similar to Paul's claim that Jesus will destroy the lawless one by the breath of his mouth and wipe him out by the manifestation of his arrival (2 The. 2:1-9).

② Jesus' descent is one of the signs of the Day of Resurrection:

> He (the Prophet) said: "It (the Last Hour) will not come until you see ten signs before." He mentioned "the smoke; the antichrist; the *dābba*; the rising of the sun from the west; the descent of Jesus son of Mary (prayer and peace be upon him); Gog and Magog; and three landslides: one in the east, one in the west, and one in Arabia; and the last sign is a fire that burns forth from Yemen, driving people to the place of their assembly [for the Day of Judgment]." (Muslim, 39)

A very similar saying is reported by Abū Dāwūd (4311). In another two versions of this saying, the descent is described as being the 10th sign of the Last Hour (Muslim, 40, 41). The Prophetic sayings in this group are similar to New Testament statements that link Jesus' second coming to the end times. The *dābba* is usually translated as "the beast" and identified with the similar term that Revelation (13) uses for the antichrist. As the term *dābba* is borrowed from a Qur'anic prediction, I will discuss it in the next section, but I should stress here that this prediction has nothing to do with Jesus' alleged descent. "Gog and Magog" are also mentioned by the author of Revelation who identifies them as "the nations at the four corners of the earth" who will be deceived by Satan to fight against the saints (Rev. 20:8). Gog and Magog appear in the Qur'an as perhaps two old nations (18.94) that would spread again before the Day of Resurrection (21.96).

③ Jesus will "break the cross" and perform other things:

> I swear by He in whose hand is my soul that the son of Mary is about to descend amongst you as a just ruler. He will break the cross, kill the pigs, and abolish the *Jizya* tax. Money will be in abundance so that nobody will accept it [as charitable gifts.] (Al-Bukhārī, 2109; Muslim, 242; at-Tarmathī, 2334)

Again, this saying is also reported in other forms (al-Bukhārī, 3264; Muslim, 242, 243; Abū Dāwūd, 4324), including one that changes Jesus' descent from being *imminent* to happening *before the Last Hour* (al-Bukhārī, 2344).

④ Jesus' descent is linked to leading the prayer of Muslims:

> [The Prophet said:] "A section of my people will not cease fighting for the Truth and prevailing till the Day of Resurrection." He (The Prophet) said: "Jesus son of Mary would then descend and their (the Muslims') commander would invite him to come and lead them in prayer, but he would say: 'No, Allah has honoured this *Ummah* (nation) by making you commanders over each other.'" (Muslim, 247)

In other similar sayings, the second advent is also mentioned in passing as a reminder to people that the son of Mary would come down to them while their leader is *one of them* (al-Bukhārī, 3265; Muslim, 244) or, in other versions, *the son of Mary would become their leader* (Muslim, 245).

Abū Dāwūd (2484) reports a saying that starts like Muslim 247 but it does not mention Jesus, stating that the last of Prophet Muhammad's people, not Jesus, would kill the antichrist. That the last of the Prophet's people kills the antichrist is repeated elsewhere (Abū Dāwūd, 2532).

Some sayings give more details about where Jesus descends (at-Tarmathī, 2341), how long he stays (Abū Dāwūd, 4324), and other details.

Many sayings link Jesus' second coming to the appearance of the antichrist. The latter is dealt with at much more length than Jesus' return. Fanciful details about his coming, wars, and death are given in many sayings, probably influenced by the Gospels (Mark 13; Matt. 24; Luke 21) and Revelation. A large number of sayings report that the Prophet used to pray for refuge in God from the afflictions of the antichrist (e.g. al-Bukhārī, 6710; Muslim, 127; Abū Dāwūd, 984; at-Tarmathī, 3047; an-Nassā'ī). In one saying, the Prophet is reported to have indicated that the antichrist may come during his time or after him (Abū Dāwūd, 4321). Another states that he would appear among the Muslims (Muslim, 117).

The antichrist is said to be one-eyed, with his left eye being blind (e.g. al-Bukhārī, 2892; Muslim, 273; Abū Dāwūd, 4316; at-Tarmathī, 2336). He has the Arabic word *kāfir* (disbeliever) written between his eyes (e.g. al-Bukhārī, 1480; Muslim, 270; Abū Dāwūd, 4316; at-Tarmathī, 2336). The angels would not allow him to enter Mecca or al-Madīnā (e.g. al-Bukhārī, 1782; Muslim, 2927; at-Tarmathī, 2347). He would kill someone and then raise him from the dead (al-Bukhārī, 1783; Muslim, 112). He is barren (Muslim, 38; at-Tarmathī, 2347). He is Jewish (Muslim, 90). He has water that people see as fire and fire that looks to people like water (al-Bukhārī, 3266; Muslim, 105; Abū Dāwūd, 4315). He comes from the east (Muslim, 119, 1380; at-Tarmathī, 2338).

The return of Jesus is also mentioned in some Prophetic sayings in association with the appearance near the end times of someone known as *al-Mahdī* — a title that means "the rightly guided one." While neither al-Bukhārī nor Muslim mention al-Mahdī, Abū Dāwūd has a section dedicated to sayings about al-Mahdī. According to some sayings, al-Mahdī is a descendant of Prophet Muhammad whose name is similar to the name of the Prophet (at-Tarmathī, 2331, 2332) and his father's name is similar to the name of the Prophet's father (e.g. Abū Dāwūd, 4282). He is said to come at a time when the earth had become full of wrongdoing and injustice to replace them with justice (e.g. Abū Dāwūd, 4282). This enforcing of universal justice bears considerable similarity to an Isaiah passage that is linked to the Messiah:

> A shoot will grow out of Jesse's root stock, a bud will sprout from his roots. The Lord's spirit will rest on him — a spirit that gives extraordinary wisdom, a spirit that provides the ability to execute plans, a spirit that produces absolute loyalty to the Lord. He will take delight in obeying the Lord. He will not judge by mere appearances, or make decisions on the basis of hearsay. He will treat the poor fairly, and make right decisions for the downtrodden of the earth. He will strike the earth with the rod of his mouth, and order the wicked to be executed. Justice will be like a belt around his waist, integrity will be like a belt around his hips. A wolf will reside with a lamb, and a leopard will lie down with a young goat; an ox and a young lion will graze together, as a small child leads them along. A cow and a bear will graze together, their young will lie down together. A lion, like an ox, will eat straw. A baby will play over the hole of a snake; over the nest of a serpent an infant will put his hand. They will no longer injure or destroy on my entire royal mountain. For there will be universal submission to the Lord's sovereignty, just as the waters completely cover the sea. At that time a root from

Jesse will stand like a signal flag for the nations. Nations will look to him for guidance, and his residence will be majestic. At that time the sovereign master will again lift his hand to reclaim the remnant of his people from Assyria, Egypt, Pathros, Cush, Elam, Shinar, Hamath, and the seacoasts. He will lift a signal flag for the nations; he will gather Israel's dispersed people and assemble Judah's scattered people from the four corners of the earth. (Isa. 11:1-12)

Some scholars, such as as-Sajustānī and ad-Darquṭnī, have reported sayings to the effect that Jesus would pray behind al-Mahdī. This claim may be linked to sayings in al-Bukhārī (3265) and Muslim (244, 247) that state that at the time of Jesus' return the Muslims will have a leader from among them, although neither al-Bukhārī nor Muslim mentions al-Mahdī. For a detailed study of the Sunni Prophetic sayings about the return of Jesus the reader may consult the Arabic book *The Awaited Messiah and the End of the World* (Ṭawīla, 2004).

Shia scholars add yet more fanciful details to the stories about al-Mahdī by claiming that this mysterious figure is actually their 12th and last Imām (spiritual guide), who was born in 869 CE and disappeared while still a young man. Shias believe that this "absent" Imām will come back and that he is al-Mahdī. Note the striking similarity between the Shia story of al-Mahdī and the Christian story of the Messiah, Jesus. Shias also believe that the triumph of al-Mahdī would return the right to rule the Muslims to a descendant of Imām 'Alī bin Abī Ṭālib whom they think was unlawfully sidelined by the first three caliphs after the death of Prophet Muhammad.

Another saying that talks about Jesus' second coming asks in one of its variations: "How can a nation that I am at its beginning and Jesus is at its end expire?" Prophet Muhammad is supposed to be referring to the nation of believers that he established and which Jesus would come to at the end times. This saying has been reported by the scholar Ibn 'Asākir.

Extra-Qur'anic Islamic literature on Jesus' return is clearly influenced by Christian writings. However, unlike the latter, it does not assign to Jesus a unique and royal role. In fact, Muslim scholars show clear sensitivity about any implication that Jesus might act as the spiritual guide of Muslims — stressing that the Muslims would be praying behind one of their fold, and even having Jesus himself pray behind al-Mahdī.

If the many sayings that detail Jesus' second coming are to be given any credibility and not be seen as complete fabrications, adapted versions of Christian stories, and have nothing to do with Prophet Muhammad, at least the basic event they report has to be confirmed by the Qur'an. However, there is nothing in the Qur'an about Jesus' second coming, an antichrist, or an al-Mahdī.

20.3. The Qur'an's Silence on Jesus' Second Coming

Unlike the sources of Prophetic sayings, the Qur'an does not talk explicitly about Jesus' second advent. There are two verses that exegetes have taken to indirectly talk about Jesus' second coming: 43.61 and 4.159. Let's start with the former, citing it with surrounding verses to clarify its context:

> And when the son of Mary was quoted as an example, your [disbelieving] people [O Muhammad!] turned away from him (43.57). They said: "Are our gods better, or is he?" They raise this only by way of disputation; they are merely a contentious people (43.58). He is only a servant on whom We bestowed favor and whom We made an example for the Children of Israel (43.59). And if We please, We could make among you [O people!] angels to be successors on the earth (43.60). And it is surely a knowledge for the Hour [of Judgment] ; therefore [say, O Muhammad!] "have no doubt about it (the Hour) and follow me: this is the right path (43.61). And let not Satan turn you away; he is a manifest enemy for you" (43.62). When Jesus came with clear proofs, he said: "I have come to you with Wisdom, and to make plain some of what you have disagreed on. So keep your duty to Allah, and obey me (43.63). Allah is my Lord and your Lord. So worship Him. This is a straight way" (43.64). But factions from among them differed. Woe to those who do wrong from the torment of a painful day (43.65). Do they wait for other than the Hour [of Judgment] , which will come upon them suddenly while they are unaware? (43.66). The friends shall on that day be enemies to one another, except those who are dutiful toward God (43.67).

Some scholars have understood the first pronoun "it" in verse 43.61 as "he," and that it denotes Jesus. This is linguistically possible because Arabic does not have neuter pronouns and the Arabic pronoun that I have translated as "it" is masculine. According to this interpretation, verse 43.61 means that Jesus will be a knowledge for the Hour of Judgment because he will return. One problem with this interpretation is that the term "knowledge" is never used in the Qur'an to signify any being. Describing someone as "knowledge" does not make sense. Another problem with this view is that even if the pronoun refers to Jesus, which it does not, there would still be nothing in the verse to support the conclusion that being a knowledge for the Hour means that Jesus will come back.

Recognizing these serious problems is probably what has made some scholars read the Arabic word *'ilmun*, which is translated as "knowledge" above, as *'alamun*," which means "sign." This reading is admitted by a combination of the facts that it only requires changing two diacritical marks, which are used for short vowels, but no change to any letter, and that the script used in writing the early manuscripts of the Qur'an had no *Tashkīl* or use of diacritical marks. The change is equivalent to changing how a word is pronounced but not how it is written, albeit with a change in meaning. However, *'ilmun* remains the common reading of this term and what is used in the printed Qur'an.

This different reading of the word for "knowledge" to mean "sign" may make the meaning more compatible with the concept of Jesus' second coming, but the main problem remains: the change still does not result in the verse stating that Jesus would return. Jesus could be a sign for the Hour, but that would still be too vague and require prior knowledge of and belief in the alleged return to see it in the verse. For instance, Jesus can be considered a sign for the Day of Resurrection because he talked about it and performed miracles that confirmed the verity of his teachings. The concept of Jesus' second coming is being *read into* not *read from* verse 43.61. It is borrowed from outside the Qur'an — from the alleged Prophetic sayings or non-Muslim sources — and forced into the interpretation.

One other obvious problem with the attempts to make verse 43.61, regardless of how it is read, refer to Jesus' second coming is that they make the Qur'an look even more elusive about this rather important event – as if it deliberately avoids stating explicitly that Jesus would return. If we remember that nowhere else in the Qur'an the return is mentioned explicitly, the suggestion that the Qur'an mentions it indirectly and subtly looks even more bizarre and unlikely.

An alternative and more logical interpretation is that verse 43.61 indicates that the *waḥi* (revelation) in the earlier verses, or more generally the "Qur'an," is knowledge that would benefit on the Day of Judgment those who learn from it. Both *waḥi* and "Qur'an" are masculine words so the Arabic pronoun in the verse can refer to any of them. Introducing Prophet Muhammad into the verse might favor interpreting "it" as a referent to the Qur'an. Also, the use of the phrase "and it is" to refer to certain commands or to the Qur'an in general and stress its role is not uncommon in the Qur'an (e.g. 2.149, 26.192). This is one example:

> And if he (Muhammad) had fabricated sayings in our name (69.44). We would have seized him by the right hand (69.45). Then We would have cut off his life-artery (69.46). And not one of you could have held Us off from him (69.47). And it is a reminder for the dutiful [toward God] (69.48). And We know that there are among you those who deny [it] (69.49). And it is a cause of regret for the disbelievers (69.50). And it is the certain truth (69.51). Therefore glorify the name of your Lord, the Great (69.52).

Clearly the pronoun "it" here does not denote Prophet Muhammad but the Qur'an. Similarly, the pronoun "it" in verse 43.61 does not signify Jesus and probably denotes the Qur'an.

Note also that when the Hour is mentioned again in 43.66-67 no mention is made of Jesus' supposed second coming.

Despite the strongly held view of some exegetes, I do not think verse 43.61 has anything to do with the concept of Jesus' second coming.

There is a second verse, 4.159, that exegetes think talk indirectly about Jesus' second advent. Some scholars, such as al-Bukhārī (3264) and Muslim (242), have quoted this verse right after citing Prophetic sayings about Jesus' return, clearly indicating that the verse also refers to the second coming. Similarly, in their commentary on verse 4.159, a number of exegetes, such as Ibn Kathīr, cite Prophetic sayings about Jesus' descent. This verse is cited below, along with verses that surround it to clarify its context:

> The People of the Book ask you [O Muhammad!] to bring down to them a book from heaven. They demanded of Moses a greater thing than that, for they said: "Show us Allah manifestly." Then the lightning overtook them because of their wrongdoing. Then they took the calf [for a god], after clear signs had come to them, but We pardoned that; and We gave to Moses clear authority (4.153). And We caused the Mount to tower above them on account of their covenant, and We said to them: "Enter the door in prostration"; and We said to them: "Do not exceed the limits of the Sabbath"; and We made with them a firm covenant (4.154). Then because of their breach of their covenant, their disbelief in God's revelations, their wrongful killing of the prophets, and their saying "Our hearts are covered [from listening to the call]" — rather Allah set a seal upon them (their hearts) because of their disbelief, so they shall not believe except a minority (4.155). And because of their disbelief and of their speaking against Mary a tremendous calumny (4.156). And because of their saying: "We killed the Messiah, Jesus son of Mary, Allah's messenger." They did not kill or crucify him, but it was made to appear so to them. Those who disagree concerning it are in doubt thereof; they have no knowledge thereof, but a conjecture they follow; they did not kill him for certain (4.157). Allah rather raised him up to Himself. Allah is invincible, wise (4.158). And there is not one of the People of the Book but would believe in him before his death, and on the Day of Resurrection he shall be a witness on them (4.159). Because of wrongdoing of the Jews we made unlawful for them certain good things (food) which had been made lawful for them, and because of their hindering many from Allah's way (4.160). And of their taking usury though they were forbidden it, and of their devouring the property of people falsely, and We have prepared for the disbelievers from among them a painful punishment (4.161).

We should first note that the term "People of the Book" in this passage clearly denotes the Jews, as the cited events are all from their history. The "People of the Book" are also explicitly identified as the Jews in verse 4.160.

Verse 4.159 does not actually talk about Jesus returning to the earth. Those who link it to the concept of Jesus' second coming understand the pronoun in "his death" as a reference to Jesus and *presume* that the term "People of the Book" in the verse denotes those who would witness his return. They take the verse to mean that when Jesus comes back, all the Jews will believe in him before he later dies.

Linking verse 4.159 to the second coming is not the only interpretation of this verse, but it is probably more popular because of the massive corpus of Islamic literature about this event. An alternative interpretation takes "his death" to denote the death of each one of the People of the Book, not Jesus. In this case, the verse would mean that *every* Jew would believe in Jesus as God's prophet and the real Messiah before he or she dies. Advocates of this interpretation say that regardless of how the Jew dies, his/her soul would not depart his/her body before he/she declares faith in Jesus. This fantastic claim is a necessary conclusion of this view

There is a third interpretation that some exegetes cite, but almost unanimously dismiss, which suggests that the pronoun in the phrase "believe in him" in verse 4.159 refers to Prophet Muhammad. In this case, the verse means that *all* Jews and Christians would believe in him before they die, in the same way explained in the previous interpretation. One good reason for rejecting this interpretation is that verse 4.159 and the verses surrounding it do not talk about Prophet Muhammad.

In addition to my rejection of the concept of Jesus' second coming of the first interpretation, I disagree with the identification of the Jews in the phrase "there is not one of the People of the Book" to be *all those who will witness Jesus' second coming*. The second interpretation makes an even much wilder claim suggesting that the verse denotes *every Jew from the time of Jesus to the end of times*! The third interpretation restricts the subject of the verse to all *the Jews from the time of Prophet Muhammad to the Day of Resurrection*. These are more arguments against these interpretations of verse 4.159:

① The Qur'an does not mention any instance of conversion or change of belief that involves every member of a whole people, let alone the kind of conversion just before death that the second and third interpretations talk about! Some may cite two verses that state that Prophet Jonah was sent to about *100,000* people who believed in him (37.147-148), and another stating that the *town of Jonah* believed him (10.98). Clearly those 100,000 are not the population of that town only, and when God says that Jonah's town believed in him, that means the majority did; it does not mean that each and every person in that town believed in Jonah!

② The Qur'an criticizes in many verses the Jews' rejection of Jesus and warns them of punishment on the Day of Resurrection (e.g. 3.55-57). This cannot be reconciled with the suggestion of the second and third interpretations that *every Jew* believes in Jesus before his or her death. This contradiction was noticed by some exegetes, so they suggested that this belief is the kind of useless belief that Pharaoh expressed at the point of drowning and which God rejected (10.90-92). However, Pharaoh's was a very different case. Having been already shown many miracles by Moses, in response to his persistent rejection of Moses' call, Pharaoh was left in no doubt that the last miracle, which at the end killed him, was a divine punishment. So he declared faith in the one God that Moses was preaching that he may be saved. The case of the disbelieving Jews is completely different. Unlike Pharaoh, a dying Jew would have no reason to remember his disbelief in Jesus and change his view at the point of death!

③ It may be argued that, in the case of the first interpretation, Jesus' second coming explains the acceptance of *all* the Jews who will see him that he is the Messiah. Although it is logical to think that the physical presence of a prophet among people would probably increase the number of those who believe him, it is impossible that *all* would accept him. Jesus was rejected by the majority of people of his time anyway. Most Jews thought that he was a charlatan and continued to wait for the Messiah. So why would *all of them* believe in him this time? How would they, and indeed even the Christians and Muslims, know that this new claimant is indeed the Messiah who came over 2000 years ago? Some might believe, but similarly some might never do.

For these reasons, I disagree with how the three interpretations identify the "People of the Book" in verse 4.159.

I also disagree with the suggestion that Jesus is still alive, which is a necessary implication of the concept of his second coming. The Qur'an states that Jesus was born like any child and grew up until he became middle-aged (3.46, 5.110). There is nothing in what the Qur'an, or indeed the Gospels, says about Jesus' life that gives us any reason to suspect that he did not age like other human beings. In other words, there is no reason to think that Jesus would live over 2,000 years, which is what the second coming entails. In fact, stating that Jesus would live until his middle age indicates that this is when he died and that he was mortal. This is the most convincing explanation as to why the Qur'an would mention a particular age range. Like any normal human being, Jesus had to die — the natural kind of death that all people suffer and which they wake up from only on the Day of Resurrection. This is part of what the infant Jesus said to the people of his mother when she took him to them: "Peace is on me the day I was born, the day I shall die, and the day I shall be raised alive" (19.33). Note how this verse uses the Arabic term *amūtu* (die) rather than *tawaffa*, which means that Jesus is talking here about the natural death that all humans experience, not only some temporary loss of consciousness.

Also, while the Old Testament claims that many people in the past lived extraordinarily long, the Qur'an (29.14) confirms only that Noah lived a very long life — 950 years before the deluge. If Jesus was going to live what looks like at least as twice long as Noah, then it is almost certain that the Qur'an would have mentioned this miracle explicitly as it mentioned Noah's miraculous longevity and Jesus' other miracles.

I am inclined to think that verse 4.159 talks about a certain, smaller group of the People of the Book who believed in Jesus before his death. This group must have lived during Jesus' lifetime. I derive this conclusion from Jesus' following words to God after his elevation: "I was a witness over them while I was among them, and when You took me (*tawaffaytani*) You were the watcher over them. You are a witness over all things" (5.117). Jesus clearly says that he can act as witness only over people that he lived with. Since verse 4.159 states that Jesus shall be a witness on that group of the People of the Book on the Day of Resurrection, they must have lived during his lifetime. But I cannot identify this group more specifically. Since I do not have a wholly satisfactory interpretation for the verse I cannot completely rule out the possibility that "his death" may mean *the death of the Jew*, although I find it very unlikely.

The difficulty in interpreting verse 4.159 is no justification for linking it to the concept of Jesus' second coming. As I have already noted, there are serious problems with this connection. This unjustified interpretation is the product of the extensive Islamic literature, including inauthentic sayings attributed to Prophet Muhammad, on Jesus' second coming which itself has been inspired by the Christian concept of Jesus' second advent. The concept of the second coming has no support in the Qur'an.

Having seen that the only two verses that are supposed to refer to Jesus' second coming have nothing to do with this alleged future event, this concept is left with no support in the Qur'an. The Gospels present Jesus as the source of the concept of his second coming, yet Jesus' teachings in the Qur'an make no reference whatsoever to this event. On the other hand, Jesus' Qur'anic prediction of the future coming of Prophet Muhammad (61.6) is not found in the Gospels. We have already seen one corruption of this prediction in the form of the concept of the coming of the mysterious figure of the paraclete. The fictional second coming of Jesus is another form of the corruption of his prediction of the coming of the Prophet whose name is "Aḥmad." The concept of Jesus' return addressed the frustration and disappointment of the early Christians with how little impact the Messiah had even on his small country, let alone the rest of the world. It also dealt with the rather uncomfortable idea that the Messiah was not the climax of God's plan, which is what the Aḥmad prediction meant.

The alleged Prophetic sayings about Jesus' second advent are clearly inauthentic and influenced by the Christian belief. The concept of the coming of al-Mahdī, which is also not found in the Qur'an, seems also to be the product of influence by the Jewish image of the Messiah. The Shias' adaptation of this concept, which identifies al-Mahdī with their 12th Imām, was inspired and driven by a religio-political agenda.

There are other arguments that confirm that the Qur'an does not support the concept of Jesus' second coming or the appearance or return an al-Mahdī:

① If Jesus will come back, it is almost certain that the Qur'an would have mentioned it *explicitly* and presented it as another *miracle*. The two verses that are claimed to mention Jesus' second coming do not do that explicitly or present it as a miracle. Similarly, the appearance of any highly influential figure such as al-Mahdī would have also been mentioned by the Qur'an in an unambiguous way.

Also, the Qur'an would have mentioned these events to make it easier for people to accept the two spiritual figures when they appear. Such a mention would have made their appearances fulfill Qur'anic prophecies.

② According to the New Testament, Jesus said that his second coming and the end times were **linked** and **imminent**. The belief in the imminence of both events and that the second coming would lead to the end times were very important for the early Christian believers. This is where the concept of the second advent drew its religious significance from. A return of Jesus sometime in the distant future would have been completely irrelevant to the early Christians, even if that event was going to be followed by the Day of Resurrection. The Qur'an does not link Jesus to any teachings about imminent eschatology or apocalyptic events. It would be rather strange and difficult to understand that Jesus should tell people about the future coming of Muhammad (61.6) yet remain completely silent on his future return! It may be surmised that the Qur'an's silence is due to the fact that by the time it was revealed over six centuries had already passed on the Christian mistaken prediction. The real reason is that the Day of Judgment in the Qur'an is not imminent. The Qur'an does not link the Day of Judgment to Jesus' alleged second coming or any similar event, which also means no such event has any religious significance. Not even the life or death of Prophet Muhammad is linked to the end times. In fact, when the Qur'an mentioned the then future death of Muhammad, it did not link it to any apocalyptic or eschatological events:

> And Muhammad is no more than a messenger before whom messengers had already passed away. If then he dies or is killed will you [O you who believe!] turn back on your heels? And whoever turns back on his heels will by no means do harm to Allah in the least, and Allah will reward the grateful (3.144).

The Qur'an mentions cosmic signs of the Day of Resurrection — including the destruction of the sun, stars, mountains, and seas (e.g. 81.1-14) — but they do not include or are linked to the birth, appearance, or death of any individual — be it Jesus, al-Mahdī, the antichrist, or anyone else. More broadly, the Qur'an does not present any phase of human history as a sign for the imminence of the Day of Resurrection. The New Testament stresses that increasing wars among nations is one sign on the end times. Muslim scholars have also attributed similar sayings to Prophet Muhammad. These sayings, however, are clearly unauthentic and are influenced like numerous other sayings by Jewish and Christian writings, as the Qur'an does not endorse them. The imminence of Jesus' second coming and its link to the Day of Judgment, which are stressed in the New Testaments, are not supported by the Qur'an.

③ Christians believe that the concept of Jesus' second coming is an essential part of their religion. The same applies to the Shias who consider their very similar concept of the return of al-Mahdī as an intrinsic part of their faith. They usually follow the mention of al-Mahdī with a characteristic venerational expression that means "may Allah speed up his coming." Christians and Shias each think that the belief in the coming of their respective awaited figure is key to salvation. These beliefs are incompatible with the teachings of the Qur'an. The Qur'an states that the Muslim is required to believe in Allah, the Day of Resurrection, the angels, God's Books, and God's messengers. The Muslim is commanded to lead a life that reflects these beliefs. There is nothing in what the Qur'an commands the Muslim to do that reflects any belief in the coming or return of any individual. The concept of someone's return neither constitutes part of the belief system of the Muslims nor is a driver for any actions that the Qur'an commands the Muslims to take.

Although Jesus' second coming and al-Mahdī's reappearance are claimed to start a chain of cosmic and apocalyptic events, these events remain completely irrelevant to the lives of the billions of believers who would die before they happen! Unlike the future event of the Day of Resurrection, which is something that everyone will experience, what Jesus and/or al-Mahdī would supposedly do in the future is no more relevant to the believers who do not witness them than any other future events.

④ The Qur'an describes Muhammad as "the last of the prophets" (33.40). In my view, this rules out not only the appearance of a new prophet but equally the return of any old prophet.

The coming of the antichrist is very much based on the concept of Jesus' second coming, so it is no surprise that there is no antichrist-like figure in the Qur'an and nothing that supports the apocalyptic and eschatological stories found in the Old Testament, the New Testament, and the Prophetic sayings literature.

Also, the suggestion that this future apocalyptic figure is linked to the Christ clearly reflects the Christian belief in Jesus as the last man of God. Muslim exegetes who believe in the concept of the antichrist need to ask why this figure is seen as anti-Christ as opposed by being an anti-Muhammad, given that Muhammad came after Jesus and is the last Prophet? The concept of antichrist makes sense only in the context of Christian theology and is founded on aspects of that theology that the Qur'an rejects.

As mentioned in the previous section, there is one Qur'anic prediction that some exegetes, unjustifiably, consider as one of the signs of Jesus' descent:

> And when the Word [of torment] is fulfilled against them (the disbelievers) we shall bring out from the earth a *dābba* that shall speak to them, because people would not be certain about Our signs (27.82).

The Arabic term *dābba* is used in the Qur'an for living organisms, but more specifically those that can walk, as the verb *dabba* means "walk" or "tread." One verse (6.38) clearly distinguishes between the *dābba* and the bird. It is not clear what kind of *dābba* verse 27.82 talks about, or even whether this *dābba* is necessarily a living being, as opposed to, say, a machine that walks on the earth. This is why I have chosen not to translate the term. The common, inaccurate translation of the term as "beast" is influenced by extra-Qur'anic imageries about the nature of this *dābba*. This translation may have well been facilitated by knowledge of the beast of Revelation. I should also note that the Qur'an uses a different term for "beasts" which is *wuḥūsh* (81.5).

The fact that the appearance of this *dābba* is linked to people's lack of faith in God's signs strongly suggests that this appearance will be miraculous. May be the *dābba*'s ability to speak to people will be a miracle. It is also clear from 27.82 and the verses that follow it that the appearance of the *dābba* will precede the Day of Judgment. Nevertheless, there is nothing in any of the verses to support linking this event to any apocalyptic or eschatological events like those of the coming of the antichrist or the second coming of the Messiah.

21

Christians in the Qur'an

All previous chapters in the book focused on Jesus and his life. It is fitting to conclude this study with a chapter about Jesus' followers, the Christians.

Unlike previous chapters, I will not study what the New Testament says about the Christians. There are countless books on this subject. Similarly, I will not discuss in detail the history of early Christians as reported by Christian and non-Christian writers. I will only look at the two oldest Roman records in which Christians are mentioned. The majority of the chapter will focus on the Qur'an.

The Qur'an talks in 4 verses about a group of Jesus' followers it calls "ḥawāriyyūn." Exegetes usually identify these with his "disciples" in the New Testament, but this cannot be confirmed using the Qur'an.

The Qur'an calls the Christians *Naṣārā*. Although it criticizes those who believe in the divinity of Jesus, it makes it clear that any Christian who has sound faith and does righteous deeds goes to paradise. Like the Jews, the majority of the Christians rejected Muhammad's message, but the Christians were far friendlier to the Muslims.

21.1. The Oldest Roman Mentions of the "Christians"

I will only mention briefly the two oldest references to Christians in Roman writings, both of which record Nero's brutal killing of the Christians.

The first reference comes from the aristocrat Cornelius Tacitus (pp. 420-421). Writing around 117 CE, Tacitus says that in order for Nero to dampen the rumors that it was him who ordered the burning of Rome in 64 CE, he accused the Christians of arson and punished them severely:

> Nero substituted as culprits, and punished with the utmost refinements of cruelty, a class of men, loathed for their vices, whom the crowd styled Christians. Christus, the founder of the name, had undergone the death penalty in the reign of Tiberius, by sentence of the procurator Pontus Pilatus, and the pernicious superstition was checked for a moment, only to break out once more, not merely in Judea, the home of the disease, but in the capital itself, where all things horrible or shameful in the world collect and find a vogue. First, then, the confessed members of the sect were arrested; next, on their disclosures, vast numbers were convicted, not so much on the count of arson as for hatred of the human race. And derision accompanied their end: they were covered with wild beasts' skins and torn to death by dogs; or they were fastened on crosses, and when daylight failed were burned to serve as

lamps by night. Nero had offered his Gardens for the spectacle, and gave an exhibition in his Circus, mixing with the crown in the habit of a charioteer, or mounted on his car. Hence, in spite of a guilt which had earned the most exemplary punishment, there arose a sentiment of pity, due to the impression that they were being sacrificed not for the welfare of the state but to the ferocity of a single man. (Tacitus, *Annals*, 15.44)

A briefer mention of Christians is made by Gaius Suetonius Tranquillus. The work of this prolific biographer and antiquarian that is of interest to us here is the *Lives of the Caesars* which was published in 120 CE. Writing about Nero's abuse of power, Suetonius says:

During his reign many abuses were severely punished and put down, and no fewer new laws were made: a limit was set to expenditures; the public banquets were confined to a distribution of food, the sale of any kind of cooked viands in the taverns was forbidden, with the exception of pulse and vegetables, whereas before every sort of dainty was exposed for sale. Punishment was inflicted on the Christians, a class of men given to a new and mischievous superstition. He put an end to the diversions of the chariot drivers, who from immunity of long standing claimed the right of ranging at large and amusing themselves by cheating and robbing the people. The pantomimic actors and their partisans were banished from the city [Because of their disorderly conduct]. (Suetonius, *Lives of the Caesars: Nero*, 16)

While criticizing Nero and how he used the Christians as scapegoats, both Roman writers are also highly critical of the Christians and their new religion.

In his biography of Emperor Claudius (41–54 CE), Suetonius states that "Since the Jews constantly made disturbances at the instigation of Chrestus, he [the emperor] expelled them from Rome" (*Lives of the Caesars, Claudius*, 25). The spelling of the name or title of this instigator as Chrestus rather than Christus, which is the proper Greek spelling of "Messiah," the suggestion that this troublemaker was still alive at the time Emperor Claudius, and calling his followers Jews not Christians suggest that this passage might have nothing to do with Christ and the Christians, or it is at least very unreliable.

21.2. Christians in the Qur'an

The Qur'an never calls Jesus' followers "Christians." It refers to the Christians with the exclusive title *Naṣārā*. We have already discussed this title in Chapter 12, but that discussion was restricted to mainly showing that, contrary to the New Testament, the Qur'an never uses this title for Jesus himself but applies it exclusively to his followers. We will cover in this chapter all verses in which the term *Naṣārā*. Following the common convention, I will translate the term *Naṣārā* as "Christians."

The Qur'an also refers to the Christians with the non-exclusive term "People of the Book." The latter includes the Jews, who had the Torah of Moses, and the Christians, who had the Injīl of Jesus which complemented the Torah. But as this term is not used exclusively for Christians, is often used for the Jews only, and appears in numerous verses, we will only look at a few of these verses.

We will start first by talking about a particular group of Jesus' followers whom the Qur'an calls *ḥawāriyyūn* — a term that I have translated as "companions."

21.2.1. The Ḥawāriyyūn

The nominative term *ḥawāriyyūn* and its genitive case *ḥawāriyyīn* occur five times in four verses in three chapters (3.52, 5.111-112, 61.14), all in reference to a particular group of Jesus' followers. After citing Jesus' words to people about his miracles, chapter 3 goes on to say:

> "[I have come] to confirm that which was revealed before me of the Torah, and to make lawful some of that which was forbidden to you. I have come to you with a sign from your Lord, so keep your duty to Allah and obey me (3.50). Allah is my Lord and your Lord, so worship Him. That is a straight path" (3.51). But when Jesus perceived disbelief on their part, he said: "Who are my supporters in the cause of Allah?" The *ḥawāriyyūn* (companions) said: "We are Allah's supporters. We believe in Allah, and do you bear witness that we are Muslims (3.52). Our Lord! We believe in that which You have sent down, and we follow the messenger, so write us down among those who bear witness [to the truth]" (3.53). And they (the Children of Israel) schemed, and Allah schemed; and Allah is the best of those who scheme (3.54).

The mention of the *ḥawāriyyūn* in the two verses of chapter 5 also occurs after a reminder of Jesus' miracles:

> Lo! When I inspired the *ḥawāriyyīn* (companions): "Believe in Me and in My messenger." They said: "We believe. Bear witness that we are Muslims" (5.111). Lo! When the *ḥawāriyyūn* (companions) said: "O Jesus son of Mary! Can your Lord send down for us a table of food from heaven?" He said: "Observe your duty to Allah, if you are true believers" (5.112). They said: "We wish to eat of it, have our hearts be at ease, know that you have spoken the truth to us, and be witnesses to it (the table)" (5.113). Jesus son of Mary said: "O Allah our Lord! Send down for us from heaven a table of food, that it may be a feast for the first and the last of us, and a sign from You. Give us sustenance; You are the best of Sustainers" (5.114). Allah said: "I shall send it down for you, so whoever of you disbelieves afterward I will punish him with a torment wherewith I do not inflict on anyone among all the nations" (5.115).

The fourth and fifth mentions of *ḥawāriyyūn* in the Qur'an occur in the last verse of chapter 61. The preceding verses are not related to this verse, so they are not cited:

> O you who believe! Be Allah's supporters, as Jesus son of Mary said to the *ḥawāriyyīn* (companions): "Who are my supporters in the cause of Allah?" The *ḥawāriyyūn* (companions) said: "We are Allah's supporters." Then a party of the Children of Israel believed and a party disbelieved, therefore we aided those who believed against their enemy, so they became the ones that prevailed (61.14).

Verses 3.52-53 and 61.14 recount one event, which I have already discussed in detail (pp. 226-228). Jesus asked for support for him and for his divine cause and the ḥawāriyyūn responded, declaring themselves as supporters of him and God's cause. This probably happened when Jesus felt that the Jews were plotting to kill him as he "perceived disbelief" from them. The ḥawāriyyūn declared their unconditional support and belief in Jesus, and asked him to bear witness to their belief. Their words in verses 3.52-53 depict them as true believers in Jesus who were determined to stand by him and support him. Verse 61.14 even calls on the Muslims to support Prophet Muhammad like the ḥawāriyyūn supported Jesus. Verse 5.111 confirms the faith of the ḥawāriyyūn as it states that it was God who inspired them to believe in Him and in His messenger Jesus.

However, the story of the miracle of table from heaven shows the ḥawāriyyūn behaving rather differently. They asked Jesus whether God can make a table of food descend on them from heaven. Jesus censured them for this request as it suggested that they were testing Jesus' claims, and he reminded them to be dutiful to God. Indeed, the ḥawāriyyūn's reference to God as *Jesus' Lord* confirms that serious doubts were behind their request to see that miracle. They had already seen many miracles performed by him that they should not have any further doubts. The ḥawāriyyūn sought to justify their request citing four things they wanted to achieve: eat from that food, have their hearts full of reassurance and satisfaction, be certain that Jesus has spoken the truth to them, and be witnesses to the miracle. Jesus was right in reprimanding them — as they confessed, probably because he had already exposed them — for wanting to test the verity of his claims. God's answer to Jesus, that He would severely punish any witness of this miracle who would fall in disbelief, confirms that the ḥawāriyyūn's request was not wise to make.

Most Muslim exegetes have tried to deny that the table event portrays a negative image of the ḥawāriyyūn. They have argued that since verse 61.14 calls on Prophet Muhammad's followers to follow the example of the ḥawāriyyūn in supporting him and verse 5.111 states that it was God who inspired the ḥawāriyyūn to believe in Him and in Jesus, they could not have used the table event to test Jesus and his Lord. They have put forward some strange interpretations for the Qur'anic text none of which is even remotely convincing. One attempt to exonerate the ḥawāriyyūn from any wrongdoing was to liken their request to that of Prophet Abraham:

> And when Abraham◎ said: "My Lord! Show me how You raise the dead." He said: "Have you not believed?" He said: "Yes, but I ask so that my heart may be at ease." He said: "Then take four of the birds, then cut them, then place on every mountain a part of them, and then call them, and they will come to you flying; and know that Allah is Mighty, Wise" (2.260).

This very comparison can only confirm that the ḥawāriyyūn's request was sinful. While Abraham confirmed that he had already believed and that he only wanted his heart to feel more comfortable, the ḥawāriyyūn did not say that their request was not triggered by lack of faith, and they even made it clear that they had doubts about Jesus' message which they thought the miracle would address. Note also how Abraham called God "my Lord" whereas the ḥawāriyyūn called Him *Jesus' Lord*. There are clear and explicit references in the Qur'an that the ḥawāriyyūn's request was wrong.

The fact that the ḥawāriyyūn are praised in other verses does not mean that they could not have made the mistake mentioned in the story of the miracle of the table. It is possible, for instance, that something happened that made them develop doubts and ask to see that specific miracle which is similar to the miracle of manna and quails from heaven which happened to the Jews who left Egypt with Moses. It is unlikely that the story of the table took place early in the ḥawāriyyūn's company of Jesus, as Jesus' censure of the ḥawāriyyūn suggests that they had already seen miracles and been in his company for a long time. Also, this miracle is followed immediately by a dialog between God and Jesus that occurred after God elevated Jesus to somewhere in heaven.

But who were the "ḥawāriyyūn" and what is the meaning of this term? Exegetes have suggested four kinds of meanings for "ḥawāriyyūn." The **first** derives the term *ḥawāriyyūn* from the root *ḥawr* which means "intense white." For instance, the man whose eyes have a marked contrast of white and black is called *aḥwar*. Exegetes have therefore suggested the ḥawāriyyūn wore white clothes or that their job was washing and bleaching clothes. The **second** meaning, which is derived from the portrayal of the ḥawāriyyūn in the Qur'an, is "supporters," as the ḥawāriyyūn answered Jesus' call for support. It is claimed that the term also means "the companions that a prophet keeps close to himself and the elite of his followers," or, more generally, "the close companions" of any person, because the ḥawāriyyūn are shown in the Qur'an to be close to Jesus. The term has been claimed to mean "ministers," because the ḥawāriyyūn were to Jesus like the ministers to a king. Some exegetes have taken "ḥawāriyyūn" to mean "those who are suitable for governance," which is concluded from the view that they were Jesus' closest followers. There is a saying attributed to Prophet Muhammad in which he states that "for every prophet there is a ḥawārī (the singular of ḥawāriyyūn), and az-Zubayr is my ḥawārī," which reflects the view that ḥawāriyyūn meant "one's close companions."

The **third** kind of meanings links the first two meanings, so it has been suggested that the ḥawāriyyūn means pure and clean, because they were clean of sins and faults and helped others purify themselves. The **fourth** and last type of meanings seems to be groundless speculation, with "ḥawāriyyūn" is said to mean "kings" or "sons of kings."

It does not look to me that the term "ḥawāriyyūn" is derived from ḥawr, as I do not think that "ḥawāriyyūn" is intended to imply anything about purity or whiteness. If I have to speculate about the linguistic root of the term, I would choose ḥawla, where the "l" has become an "r." This word means "around" and would make "ḥawāriyyūn" mean "companions" or "close companions." Whether or not this is the linguistic meaning of the term, the Qur'anic context fully justifies the view that the ḥawāriyyūn were close and special companions of Jesus, hence my translation of this term as "companions."

Regardless of what meaning an exegete prefers, there is consensus among exegetes that the "ḥawāriyyūn" denotes Jesus' followers that Christian sources, including the New Testament, calls his disciples. Muslim exegetes explicitly equate the ḥawāriyyūn of the Qur'an with the disciples of the New Testament. Clearly the ḥawāriyyūn were disciples of Jesus, but there is nothing in the Qur'an that justifies identifying them with the New Testament disciples. This identification is influenced by the Christian image of Jesus and his disciples. For instance, although the Qur'an does not tell us how many the ḥawāriyyūn were, the number 12 is often cited by exegetes. They also assign the Gospel names of the disciples to the ḥawāriyyūn. One other sign of the influence of Muslim exegetes by Christian sources is the suggestion that the ḥawāriyyūn were fishermen, which is of course inspired by the Gospels' similar claims about some of Jesus' disciples (Matt. 4:18-19; Mark 1:16-17; Luke 5:9-11).

My preference to translate ḥawāriyyūn as "companions" instead of "disciples" does not necessarily mean that the ḥawāriyyūn were not 12 or highlight any specific difference between them and the New Testament image of the disciples. It simply underlines the fact that the Qur'an gives too little information about the ḥawāriyyūn to justify equating them with the disciples of the New Testament. Furthermore, the Qur'an rejects the verity and historicity of some of the behaviors, statements, and beliefs attributed to the disciples in the New Testament, so identifying the ḥawāriyyūn with the disciples, as many exegetes do, would portray the former in a much worse image than that of the table from heaven story, which exegetes have tried hard to explain away anyway.

Additionally, the high historical unreliability of the Gospels and Acts means that the information they give about Jesus' disciples is largely inaccurate or unhistorical. The fact that the earliest Gospel, Mark, was written around 60 CE, with the other Gospels decades afterward, means that these books were written several decades after the events, and by people who did not have firsthand knowledge of Jesus or his companions. These are late, limited, and unreliable accounts, and if we discount them, then we can safely say that we know nothing about Jesus' close companions. Significantly, apart from Peter, who is given some prominence, the Book of Acts, which is supposed to cover what the apostles did after Jesus, almost completely ignores the disciples! This neglect looks even more bizarre when we note that over 60% of the book focuses on Paul — the apostle that persecuted the Christians, never met Jesus but claimed to have seen him in a vision, and ended up preaching a version of Christianity that he created. There is every reason to believe that Jesus' true companions were marginalized, if not persecuted, as Paul took over. This is why it is very difficult to say that we can learn anything about Jesus' disciples from the Christian sources, and, unfortunately, there are no independent sources to supply this information.

From the Qur'anic perspective, all that we know about Jesus' companions is the very limited information given in the verses above.

21.2.2. The *Naṣārā*

As explained in Chapter 12, the Qur'an calls the Christians *Naṣārā* or Nazarenes after the event in which the *ḥawāriyyūn* answered Jesus' call and offered their support to him. Unsurprisingly, most verses about the Christians deal with their response to Muhammad's prophethood and their relationship with the early Muslims. Most of these verses talk about the Jews also.

There are three verses in which the Qur'an makes it clear that the Christians, like any followers of a divine Book, will enter paradise as long as they maintain sound faith and do righteous deeds:

> Those who believe, the Jews, the Christians, and the Sabaeans — whoever believe in Allah and the Last day and does good — they shall have their reward from their Lord, and there is no fear for them, nor shall they grieve (2.62, 5.69).

In the following verse, God states that He will be the judge between and on all those who have received divine Books, those who have not, and the polytheists:

> Those who believe, the Jews, the Sabaeans, the Christians, the Magians, and those who associate others with Allah, Allah will decide between them on the Day of Resurrection. Allah is a witness over all things (22.17).

Most Jews and Christians rejected Prophet Muhammad's message. There was nothing in his message that went against the essence of the teachings of their *authentic* divine books. In fact, his message confirmed the verity of the Torah and

Injīl. They choose not to believe him for reasons that had nothing to do with the truth:

> Say [O Muhammad!]: "O People of the Book! Do you disapprove of us for other than that we believe in Allah and in what has been revealed to us and what was revealed before, and most of you are transgressors?" (5.59).

Muslims shared the Jews and Christians their belief in their books, but the Jews and Christians did not reciprocate — in the same way that the Christians believed in the Torah and the prophets of the Israelites but the Jews did not believe in Jesus and the Injīl:

> And do not [O you who believe!] argue with the People of the Book except in best way, except those of them who act wrongly, and say: "We believe in that which has been revealed to us and revealed to you, and our God and your God is one, and to Him we are Muslims (we submit)" (29.46).

Not all Jews and Christians unjustly rejected Islam and took Muslims for enemies. These are some of the relevant verses, and we will see more later:

> Those to whom We gave the Book before it (the Qur'an) — they believe in it (28.52). And when it is recited to them they say: "We believe in it; it is the truth from our Lord; we were Muslims (have submitted to God) before it" (28.53). These shall be granted their reward twice, because they are steadfast, repel evil with good, and spend [in charity] out of what We have given them (28.54).
>
> They are not all alike; of the People of the Book there is an upright party; they recite Allah's verses in the nighttime, falling prostrate (3.113). They believe in Allah and the Last Day, they enjoin what is right and forbid what is wrong, and they hasten to good works, and those are among the righteous (3.114). And whatever good they do, they shall not be denied it, and Allah knows the dutiful [toward Him] (3.115).

Christians, like Jews, believed that it is only them who will enter paradise. The Qur'an refutes this claim, clarifying the requirements for salvation and stressing that they apply to all people without exception or discrimination:

> And they [the People of the Book] say: "No one shall enter paradise except those who are Jews or Christians." These are [merely] their desires. Say [O Muhammad!]: "Produce your proof if you are truthful" (2.111). Yes, whoever becomes a Muslim (surrenders himself) to Allah and is a doer of good, his reward is with his Lord, and there is no fear for them nor shall they grieve (2.112).

Sound faith and good deeds are what make a person enter paradise.

This belief in getting preferential treatment from God and being His exclusive beloved ones, which is shared by both the Jews and Christians, is rejected in this verse also:

And the Jews and the Christians say: "We are the sons of Allah and His beloved ones." Say [O Muhammad!]: "Why does He then chastise you for your faults? No, you are human beings from among those whom He has created; He forgives whom He pleases and chastises whom He pleases." And Allah's is the kingdom of the heavens and the earth and what is between them, and to Him is the eventual coming (5.18).

Like the Jews who believed that Judaism is the only right way to God, Christians believed the same about their religion. The Qur'an corrects this narrow view by reminding both that it is the monotheistic religion of Abraham — of which Judaism, Christianity, and Islam are different manifestations — that is the true guidance:

And they [the Jews and Christians] say: "Be Jews or Christians and then you will be on the right course." Say [O Muhammad!]: "Rather [follow] the religion of Abraham [which is the real guidance], the upright, and he was not one of the polytheists" (2.135).

Moses, Jesus, and later Muhammad all were prophets who followed the same religion that Abraham had. Singling out Judaism or Christianity as "the" true religion reflects a misunderstanding of the reality of these religions. Only such a misunderstanding could have made Jews and Christians urge people not to follow the last Prophet. "Judaism" is a term that was applied to the religion of Moses and "Christianity" was used to denote Jesus' religion, but these different designations do not make the religions of Moses and Jesus different in essence, nor change the fact that they are different manifestations of one and the same message.

God further exposes the flaw in the claim of the Jews and Christians by reminding them that Abraham, as well as other prophets, lived long before Judaism and Christianity appeared. The one religion of all prophets is Islam, which means "surrender," i.e. surrender to God. Abraham was Muslim, and so were all prophets:

Abraham was not a Jew or a Christian but he was upright, a Muslim, and he was not one of the polytheists (3.67).

Or do you [O People of the Book!] say that Abraham, Ishmael, Isaac, Jacob, and the Asbāṭ (Jacob's sons) were Jewish or Christian? Say [O Muhammad!]: "Do you know best, or Allah does?" And who is more of a wrongdoer than he who conceals a testimony that he has from Allah? And Allah is not unaware of what you do (2.140).

Verse 2.140 also suggests that the Jews and/or the Christian had a testimony in their divine Books to this fact that they chose to conceal.

The Qur'an told the Prophet that the Jews and the Christians would never be pleased with him until and unless he follows their beliefs. This insistence of the Jews and Christians is another aspect of their misunderstanding of the essence of their religions and the message of Prophet Muhammad. However, the Jews and Christians who really understand, honor, and believe in their Books do believe in the Qur'an also:

> And the Jews will not be pleased with you [O Muhammad!], nor will the Christians, until you follow their creed. Say: "The guidance of Allah is the real guidance." And if you follow their desires after the knowledge that has come to you, you shall have no guardian or helper from Allah (2.120). Those to whom We have given the Book read it as it should be read. They believe in it; and whoever disbelieves in it, those are the losers (2.121).

Naturally, the followers of Prophet Muhammad must not seek guidance from the people who rejected his message. Those who did not accept the prophethood of the last prophet were misguided and could only lead others astray:

> O you who believe! Do not take the Jews and the Christians for guardians; they are guardians of each other; and whoever of you takes them for guardians, then surely he is one of them; surely Allah does not guide the wrongdoing people (5.51).

One specific belief held by Jews and Christians that the Qur'an rejects is their claims about certain individuals being sons of God. The Qur'an also criticizes the Jews' blind following of their rabbis and the Christians' of their monks:

> The Jews say: "'Uzayr is the son of Allah," and the Christians say: "The Messiah is the son of Allah." That is a saying from their mouths, imitating the saying of the disbelievers of old. May Allah fight them! How deluded they are! (9.30). They have taken their rabbis and monks as lords besides Allah, and so they treated the Messiah son of Mary, when they were not commanded to worship other than One God; there is no God save Him. Far exalted is He above their attribution of partners to Him! (9.31).

The hostility of the Jews and the Christians was not restricted to the religion of Prophet Muhammad. They vilified and accused each other of heresy and not following the truth:

> And the Jews say: "The Christians follow nothing [true]", and the Christians say: "The Jews follow nothing [true]", while they [both] recite the Book. This is what those who do not know have said. So Allah shall judge between them on the Day of Resurrection concerning what they differed about (2.113).

The Jews and Christians disagreed on whether Jesus was the Messiah and God's messenger. This resulted in them accusing each other of going astray. The reference to the fact that this is what the disbelievers used to say about Judaism and Christianity seems to suggest that the two groups vilified each other's religion completely — something that God disapproves of, as each of the two religions is based on a divine book.

These mutual hostility and accusations between the Jews and Christians are mentioned in verse 5.14 which is cited below with other verses that are of our interest to our current study:

> And Allah made a covenant with the children of Israel, and We raised up among them twelve chieftains; and Allah said: "I am with you; if you keep up prayer, pay the poor-rate, believe in My messengers and assist them, and lend Allah a kindly loan, I will remit your sins, and I will admit you to gardens beneath which rivers flow, but whoever disbelieves from among you after this [covenant], he indeed has lost the right way" (5.12). But because of their breach of their covenant We cursed them and made their hearts hard: they altered words from their contexts, and they forgot a part of what they were reminded of; and you [O Muhammad!] will continue to discover treachery from them, save a minority of them; so pardon them and overlook [their misdeeds]; surely Allah loves those who do righteous deeds [to others] (5.13). And We made a covenant with those who have said "we are Christians," but they forgot a part of what they were reminded of. Therefore We have stirred up enmity and hatred among them (the Jews and the Christians) till the Day of Resurrection; and Allah will inform them of what they did (5.14). O People of the Book! Our Messenger has come to you, expounding to you much of that which you used to hide of the Book, and forgiving much. Here has come to you a light from Allah and manifest Book (5.15).

Verse 5.12 stresses that God made a covenant with the Israelites in which God promised to admit them to paradise if they follow His commands and lead the life He wanted them to have. According to the Qur'an, every man will go either to paradise or hell on the Day of Resurrection. The nature of this covenant is explained in a number of different verses. It involved worshiping none other than God; treating the relatives, the orphans, and the poor kindly; saying good things to people; keeping up prayer; paying the poor-due (2.83); not killing each other and not evicting each other from their houses (2.84); following the revelation (2.93); sharing the Book with people and not concealing it (3.187); not transgressing the Sabbath (4.154); and not telling lies about God (7.169). Verse 5.12 reveals another part of this covenant — that the Children of Israel must believe in God's messenger and assist them. This is clearly something that those who rejected Jesus and his message failed to do. The Jews who did not believe in Jesus broke their covenant with God. These are another two verses that mention the covenant of God with the Israelites and their rejection of His messengers:

> Then because of their breach of their covenant, their disbelief in God's revelations, their wrongful killing of the prophets, and their saying "Our hearts are covered [from

listening to the call]"; rather Allah set a seal upon them (their hearts) because of their disbelief, so they shall not believe except a minority (4.155).

We made a covenant with the Children of Israel and We sent to them messengers; every time a messenger came to them with what their souls did not like, they accused some [of the messengers] of lying and killed others (5.70).

Both Prophets David and Jesus cursed those who would breach God's covenant:

Those who disbelieved from among the Children of Israel were cursed by the tongue of David and of Jesus son of Mary. That was because they disobeyed and used to transgress (5.78).

Verse 5.13 then goes on to explain how God punished those who breached His covenant by cursing them and hardening their hearts, and thus they altered God's words and forgot part of what they had been commanded to observe. Their rejection of Prophet Muhammad is then referred to, as some of the alterations to the divine text aimed at concealing the signs that supported the prophethood of Muhammad, and some of what they forgot was the divine commandment to support and assist him. The Prophet is told that the majority of the Israelites were scheming against him, but he is ordered to pardon and forgive them.

God made a covenant also with the Christians, whom verse 5.14 describes as those who said "we are *Naṣārā*," i.e. who declared their support for Jesus, in reference to the *ḥawāriyyūn's* or companions' declaration of support for Jesus. But the Christians also forgot part of what they were reminded of, which is the commandment to support the last prophet whom Jesus told them about: "And when Jesus son of Mary said: 'O Children of Israel! I am a messenger of Allah to you, confirming that which was revealed before me of the Torah, and bringing good news about a messenger who will come after me, whose name is Aḥmad'" (61.6).

Verse 5.14 then goes on to state that this neglect of the covenant by the Jews and the Christians has created enmity and hatred between them, which is set to continue to the Day of Resurrection. Indeed, in the early days of Christianity, Christians were persecuted by Jews. When they became the powerful party, Christians in turn subjected Jews to persecution, which continued for many centuries until recent times. Much of this Christian hostility toward the Jews was driven by the belief in the Jews' collective responsibility for Jesus' crucifixion which the Gospels advocate (pp. 409-411). Jews often preferred to live under Muslim rather than Christian rule.

Some exegetes have taken the pronoun "them" in verse 5.14 to mean the "Christians," and thus the mentioned enmity and hatred would be between different Christian groups. I find this interpretation rather weak.

Verse 5.15 then addresses the "People of the Book," that is both the Jews and the Christians, reminding them that Muhammad is God's messenger, and that the

Book he has been given reveals some of what they have hidden of God's revelation to them, which includes the references to Muhammad. Muhammad's mission was also an opportunity for the sinners to be forgiven. He was a light that came with a clear Book, the verse concludes.

The majority of the Jews and Christians in Arabia at the time of Prophet Muhammad rejected and did not follow the new message, but there were still significant differences between the attitudes of the two groups to Islam and Muslims. These differences are recorded and explained in the Qur'an:

> You [O Muhammad!] will certainly find the people with most enmity for those who believe to be the Jews and the polytheists. And you will certainly find the nearest in friendship to those who believe to be those who have said "we are Christians," because there are among them priests and monks, and because they are not arrogant (5.82). And when they hear what has been revealed to the Messenger you see their eyes overflow with tears because of the truth that they recognize; they say: "Our Lord! we believe, so write us down with the witnesses [of truth] (5.83). And should not we believe in Allah and in the truth that has come to us and hope that our Lord will admit us to the company of the righteous people?" (5.84). Therefore Allah rewarded them for what they said with gardens in which rivers flow where they will abide; and this is the reward of the good doers (5.85).

The Jews were much more hostile to Muslims, whereas the Christians were their friendliest religious group. The Jews were so hostile to the new revelation that they went as far as forming alliances with various polytheistic Arab tribes to prevent the new message from succeeding and spreading. Their hostility is even mentioned before that of the idolatrous polytheists in verse 5.82. They launched wars against the Muslims and unsuccessfully plotted to kill the Prophet. At one point, an alliance of Jews and Arab polytheists besieged the city of al-Madīnā, where the Prophet and most Muslims lived. The failure of that siege (627 CE), which targeted eliminating Islam, was one of the major turning points in the war against Muslims and led to the ultimate defeat of the Muslims' enemies. The failure of the siege is mentioned in the Qur'an (33.9-20).

The Christians had a much friendlier attitude. In fact, when the Muslims were being persecuted in Mecca, the Prophet ordered some of his followers to immigrate to Abyssinia, where they stayed under the protection of its Christian Negus for a few months. The Negus even rejected the call of a delegate of the Muslims' Arab enemies to have the immigrants sent back to their land. The success of this emigration (614 CE) made the Prophet send his followers again to Abyssinia later. When the Prophet heard of the Negus' death, he offered the funeral prayer for his soul from his residence in al-Madīnā. Some exegetes have suggested that verse 5.82 refers to those Abyssinian Christians who offered shelter and protection to the Muslims who fled Mecca. I do not think this identification is correct. **First**, this verse does not talk about a specific group of Christians, although the following verses about them hearing the Qur'an may suggest that those Christians were living in Arabia. **Second**, this verse was revealed after the Prophet and Muslims emigrated from Mecca to al-Madīnā, i.e. at least 8 years after the immigration to Abyssinia. Ibn Hishām's biography of the Prophet Muhammad also mentions a number of friendly direct contacts that the Prophet had with various Christian individuals and groups some of whom converted to Islam.

The Qur'an gives three reasons for the positive attitude of the Christians toward Islam: their priests, their monks, and the fact that they were not arrogant. The term "priests," which is how the Qur'anic term *Qissīsīn* is usually translated, is taken by some exegetes to denote scholars, meaning that those scholars who had knowledge of their scriptures saw the Qur'an as a book of truth. They were also probably influenced by the Qur'an's recognition of the prophethood of Jesus and the special status it gives to him. This must have made many Christians feel more positively about the new religion and, even if they did not convert, accept that it was a genuine message from the same God that they worshipped.

The mention of the monks probably underlines the fact that these dedicated worshippers promoted peace and sought to look for points of agreement rather than difference with the Muslims. Finally, the Qur'an stresses that the Christians were not arrogant like the Jews. This arrogance might signify the Jews' belief that their ethnicity makes them the chosen people of God and distinguishes them from other people. This would have also influenced the Jews' negative reaction to the new prophet as, contrary to their hopeful expectations, he was not a descendant of Isaac and Israel, but Ishmael.

These verses do not mean that all Christians were good to Muslims or that all monks were righteous people. We have already seen verses that accuse Christians of following the wrong path and of trying to have others, including Muslims, to embrace their beliefs. We have also seen a verse that condemns Christians for following their monks blindly, and in the following verse monks, as well as Jewish rabbis, are condemned for abusing their positions — unfairly and deceptively taking people's money, and piling up wealth instead of spending it on good causes:

> O you who believe! Many of the rabbis and monks eat away the property of people falsely and turn [people] away from Allah's way; and [as for] those who hoard up gold and silver and do not spend it in Allah's way, to them give [O Muhammad!] tidings of a painful chastisement [on the Day of Judgment] (9.34).

Verses 5.83-85 further detail the positive reaction of the Christians to Prophet Muhammad's message. When they hear the new revelation, i.e. the Qur'an, their eyes overflow with tears as they recognize that what they hear is the true word of God, and, unlike those who rejected it, declare themselves as witnesses to the truthfulness of the Qur'an. They state that there is no excuse not to believe in the new revelation which has reached them, and they hope that God would admit them to paradise in the company of the righteous. God then confirms that He will show mercy to these believers and admit them to paradise.

The last verse that we need to study talks about the interesting Christian practice of monasticism:

> Then We made Our messengers to follow in their (Noah and Abraham) footsteps, and followed them up with Jesus son of Mary, and We gave him the Injīl. We placed compassion and mercy in the hearts of those who followed him, and monasticism they invented — We did not ordain for them — only seeking Allah's pleasure, but they did not observe it with right observance. So We gave those of them who believe their reward, but many of them are transgressors (57.27).

Here again God praises Jesus' followers, stressing that He placed compassion and mercy in their hearts. He then moves to name specifically monasticism as a practice that He did not ordain, but one that Jesus' followers introduced as they sought to draw nearer to God. But this practice, the Qur'an points out, was not observed properly. The clause "but they did not observe it with right observance" implies that there is nothing intrinsically wrong with monasticism and that it can be a right practice, so the point that the Qur'an makes is that this practice was misused. It does not explain in what way monasticism was distorted though, so one can only speculate that the reference is to the kind of wrong behavior that this practice has become associated with. For instance, homosexual behavior and sexual abuse spread in some monasteries and in some monk communities, clearly as a result of sexual abstinence going terribly wrong.

This is a concise review of how Christians are portrayed in the Qur'an.

22

The Qur'anic Historical Jesus

This short chapter summarizes what we learned about the historical Jesus as described in the Qur'an and from critically examining Christian and historical sources.

Mary's father, 'Imrān, probably died before the birth of his daughter. When she was still pregnant, Mary's mother vowed to dedicate her newborn to the worship of God. The Lord looked after Mary and made her grow as a righteous person. At some point, probably due to the death of Mary's mother, Prophet Zechariah, who might have been Mary's relative, beat competition from others to win the right to become the guardian of the orphan.

The childless Zechariah, whose wife was both old and barren, had been praying for a righteous child. Living in a hostile environment in which certain unqualified individuals were looking to inherit his high spiritual position, Zechariah asked God for an heir who would protect his prophetic legacy and offer genuine spiritual leadership.

When visiting Mary in the sanctuary Zechariah would notice that she had food that she could have obtained only miraculously. Zechariah was so impressed by the signs of piety he saw on the girl. Seeing Mary made him repeat his prayer for a child, which was finally answered.

Zechariah was one day praying in the sanctuary when the angels called him to give him the good news that he was going to have a child called John, who would have revelation from God and be a righteous prophet. Stunned by the news, Zechariah asked for a miraculous sign that confirms that what he heard was an angelic voice, not a trial by Satan. He was given the sign of losing the ability to speak to people but not to God for three days and nights.

John was given divine wisdom while still a young child. Being pious from his infancy, John is described as having peace on him from birth to death and on the Day of Resurrection. This description is applied in the Qur'an to only one other figure, Jesus, who was miraculously a prophet from birth. No more information is found about John in the Qur'an.

Back to the story of Mary who was living separately to worship God, one day Gabriel appeared to her in the shape of a human being. He delivered to her the good news that she was going to become miraculously pregnant with an illustrious son who is the Messiah. God wanted this child to become a sign for people.

Not surprisingly, the unmarried and chaste Mary was astounded, confused, and disturbed by the news, but Gabriel reminded her that God is capable of everything. Gabriel had a subtle role in Mary's miraculous, non-sexual conception. His visit to Mary was more than an "annunciation." He played a part in inducing the pregnancy. He told her that her son, the Messiah, would also be known as "son of Mary," in reference to the miracle that he would not have a biological father.

In fear of how her people would react to her unexplained pregnancy and their almost certain refusal to believe that her conception was virginal, Mary decided to leave her family. There is no mention in the Qur'an of any man in Mary's life. The clear implication is that she was alone. Similarly, the Qur'an does not deny explicitly that Mary had children other than Jesus but it does imply that.

Away from her family and on her own, Mary found herself in labor under a palm tree. Her extremely difficult circumstances left her distressed to the point of wishing for death. But as soon as she gave birth her newborn started talking to her. Jesus asked his mother not to grieve, and told her that God has miraculously created near to her a stream. He also told his hungry and exhausted mother that God has made dates appear on the palm tree and that she can have them fall to her to eat by shaking the trunk of the tree. She can now eat, drink, and relax, the newborn told his mother. The miraculous infant also told his mother to tell the people she meets that that she has vowed a fast to God not to speak to any human being. Jesus was going to speak on his mother's behalf.

When Mary went back to her people carrying the baby, they reminded her that her family was not known for unchastity, clearly indicating that they thought the child was illicit. As asked by her son, Mary did not say anything but simply signaled to her accusers to speak to the baby in the cradle. People ridiculed her suggestion, but they were stunned when the newborn started speaking. He said that he was God's servant and prophet. He continued to stress his servanthood to God by saying that he was commanded to worship God throughout his life. This miracle may not have convinced everyone that Mary's pregnancy did not involve anything improper, but it managed to spare her the gruesome death by stoning.

The Qur'an does not mention Herod's supposed massacre of young boys that targeted Jesus, which is mentioned in the Gospel of Matthew and other apocryphal sources. It strongly implies that this massacre never took place.

The Jews developed the concept of the Messiah to represent an eschatological figure who would liberate them from heathen occupation and control and reestablish the glory of their lost kingdom. The Messiah in the Qur'an is a completely different figure who has no political agenda. Like other prophets, he is a spiritual teacher whose main message was to call people to repent and worship God. Jesus went out of his way to correct the distorted, political image of the Messiah, but that did not satisfy the majority of the Jews who were waiting for the Messiah to be the savior of Israel. This meant that, during his life, Jesus had only a small number of followers. Even his impressive miracles, which included raising dead people, could not outweigh the Jews' resentment to his correction of their nationalistic concept of the Messiah, and thus did not help him convince many of them of the verity of his message.

While the Jews changed the Messiah into their political and military leader, the Christians turned Jesus, and thus the Messiah, into a divine being. They gave the Jewish concept of "son of God" divine connotations it never had and applied it to Jesus. They made Jesus the special, divine son of God. The Gospel of John was particularly influential in enforcing this distorted image of Jesus. Even Mary was made divine. One consequence of the deification of Jesus is the development of the doctrine of the Trinity.

But Jesus never claimed divinity. He was a Muslim prophet — although a particularly distinguished one — like Adam, Abraham, Moses, and may other messengers of God. He was a faithful servant of God who stressed his servanthood to the Lord. His frequent periphrastic use of the expression "son of man" was intended to head off the future attempts to make him divine. His preemptive action, however, did not stop people from deifying him.

Jesus' appearance was not a unique event in the history of God's messengers to people or some kind of a climax. The appearance of Jesus was a monumental event, but so was the coming of every prophet.

God revealed to Jesus a book called the "Injīl," like He revealed to Moses the Torah. The name of the book, which means "good news," is derived from the fact that it contained the good news about the coming of the last Prophet, Muhammad. The mysterious figure *parakletos* (paraclete) whom Jesus mentions in the Johannine writings denotes Muhammad. This term is a slight corruption of the Greek word *periklytos*. The latter means "highly praised," which is the same meaning of "Muhammad."

The Injīl did not abolish the Mosaic law but modified it. It complemented the Torah. But Paul's high influence on early Christianity resulted in serious demotion of the law in most Christian communities. Paul stressed instead the role of grace in salvation. His approach was objected to by those who knew Jesus, but it was the Pauline version of Christianity that prevailed, simply because he converted a lot more Gentiles to the new religion than the Jews converted by other Christians. Those heathen converts had no attachment to the law and, in fact, abolishing much of its requirements was crucial in attracting them to Christianity. The teachings of those who learned directly from Jesus — that is, his real followers — were overridden by the message of someone who never met Jesus.

Probably at some point in his early teens Jesus started to talk secretly to some chosen individuals about his mission. It might have been some years before he went public with his message. Quickly he found himself very unpopular among the Jews, and particularly the religious authorities. His corrective teachings did not please them. His public mission was probably made very short by the Jews' failed attempt at his life. They misidentified their target but got the wrong man crucified, although they believed that they crucified Jesus. God then lifted Jesus up to a place in heaven, where the then very young man lived until he died as a middle-aged man. Jesus' deification started at some point after he left the earth but before he died.

Paul's dominance over Christian thought meant, among other things, that his doctrine of atonement became one of the main Christian doctrines. Yet Jesus was not killed, so he did not die for the sake of any one. Jesus also had nothing to do with what Paul later taught about him. The theology of the cross not only lacks any historical foundations, but it also contravenes divine justice. In fact, even common sense and natural justice reject this concept.

Jesus was known as "the Messiah" and "son of Mary" but he was not called a "Nazarene." This title was applied only to his followers after a particular historical event that involved Jesus and a group of his followers. This distinct group of the early Christians is given the special name of *ḥawāriyyūn* in the Qur'an.

The inconsistent descriptions of the paraclete are not the only form of corruption of Jesus' prediction of the coming of Prophet Muhammad. This prediction was also changed to the concept of Jesus' second coming. This change addressed the awkward fact that the Messiah was not the climax of God's plan, but it also dealt with a serious concern of the early Christians. Although Jesus' followers, unlike the Jews, accepted that the Messiah was not a political figure, they were still disappointed by the minor impact that he had where he lived, let alone in the world at large. The concept of the second coming addressed the fact that during his life Jesus managed to convert only a small number of people, as his victorious second advent is said would establish the kingdom of God. The fact, however, is that Jesus died, Muhammad came, and there is no return of Jesus. Similarly, the concept of the antichrist, which was adopted by the Muslims also, and the Islamic concept of the coming of al-Mahdī are both unauthentic.

The Christians of the Arabian Peninsula had much friendlier relationships with Prophet Muhammad and his followers than the Jews and the polytheistic Arabs did.

Appendix A

History in the Qur'an

Those who are familiar with the style of the Bible get surprised, and even baffled, when they read a translation of the Qur'an. Unlike the Bible which addresses most issues in the context of relating history, the Qur'an is not a history book. Although it contains historical stories about righteous and sinful individuals and nations, these are very limited. Additionally, the Qur'an has a unique style even in relating history. Understanding this aspect of the Qur'an is vital when studying its historical accounts. This short appendix should be particularly useful to the reader who is not familiar with the Qur'an or expects the Qur'an to have a similar style to other religious or historical texts, such as the Bible.

One attribute that characterizes the Qur'anic text in general and appears in different forms is succinctness. One manifestation of the Qur'an's succinct eloquence is that its text often does not mention explicitly information that can be concluded from or found in another Qur'anic text. This is better explained with examples from the Qur'an, such as the following set of verses which start with God's command to Prophets Moses and Aaron:

> So go you both to him (Pharaoh) and say: "We are two messengers from your Lord; therefore send the Children of Israel with us and do not torment them; we have brought to you a sign from your Lord, and peace be upon him who follows the right guidance (20.47). Verily it has been revealed to us that torture will come upon him who rejects [the message] and turns away" (20.48). He said: "So who is your Lord, O Moses?" (20.49). He said: "Our Lord is He who created everything, then guided it [to its course]" (20.50). He said: "Then what about the former generations?" (20.51). He said: "The knowledge thereof is with my Lord, in a book; my Lord errs not, nor does He forget" (20.52).

The Qur'an reveals in verses 20.47 and 20.48 the essence of the message that God ordered Moses and Aaron to convey to Pharaoh. When it informs us in verse 20.49 of the debate that Moses and Aaron had with Pharaoh, the Qur'an does not mention what the two Prophets said to Pharaoh, because it is the same message mentioned in the previous two verses. The verse starts with Pharaoh's reply to the message. It is as if the Qur'an says implicitly after verses 20.48 "and Moses and Aaron went to Pharaoh and conveyed to him what God had ordered them to tell him."

Note also the Qur'an's use of "He said" without specifying the identity of the speaker in each case. The reason is that the context leaves no ambiguity that the speakers are Moses and Pharaoh, and it makes clear also who said what.

The Qur'an often bypasses details that are given prominence in traditional recounting of history. For instance, it is common for the Qur'an not to mention the names of main characters and places in a story. Examples of prominent characters in Qur'anic stories whose names are not mentioned include Adam's wife and two sons and Joseph's eleven brothers. The latter are referred to throughout chapter 12 of the Qur'an, but never with their names. This is another example of a prophet that the Qur'an refers to but without mentioning his name:

> Have you not considered [O Muhammad!] how the chiefs of the Children of Israel who came after Moses said to a Prophet of theirs: "Set up for us a king and we will fight in the way of Allah." He said: "May it be that you would not fight if fighting was ordained for you?" They said: "Why would we not fight in the way of Allah having been driven out of our homes, and for the sake of our children?" But when fighting was ordained for them, they turned away except a few of them; and Allah knows the wrongdoers (2.246). And their Prophet said to them: "Surely Allah has raised Saul to be a king for you." They said: "How can he hold kingship over us when we have a greater right to kingship than he, and he has not been granted abundant wealth?" He said: "Surely Allah has chosen him in preference to you, and He has increased him abundantly in knowledge and body; Allah grants His kingdom to whom He pleases"; and Allah is Embracing, Knowing (2.247). And their Prophet said to them: "Surely the sign of His kingship is that there shall come to you the Ark, in which there is tranquility from your Lord and a remnant of what the house of Moses and the house of Aaron have left, which will be carried by angels; surely there is a sign in this for you if you are believers" (2.248).

Although God refers to Saul with his name, He refers to the prophet in the three verses with his title only and does not reveal his name.

There are also many instances of places and cities that God refers to in various places in the Qur'an without naming or specifying them explicitly, such as the place to which Adam descended (2.36, 7.24), the village to which Jonah was sent (10.98), and the birthplace of Jesus (19.23).

Let us take another example. The Qur'an mentions in lengthy detail in several places the suffering of a certain prophet at the hand of his disbelieving people, and God's subsequent revenge on those people. Nevertheless, not many details are given about the revenge itself, as often only the type of punishment is mentioned and the perishing of the disbelievers stressed. For instance, God reveals in several chapters various details of the story of Prophet Hūd, but He does not mention many details of the punishment of his disbelieving people:

> So We saved him (Hūd) and those with him by a mercy from Us, and We cut off the last of those who rejected Our signs and did not become believers (7.72).

> And when Our decree came to pass, We saved Hūd and those who believed with him with a mercy from Us, and We saved them from a severe torment (11.58). And that was [the people of] 'Ād; they denied the signs of their Lord, disobeyed His Messengers, and

followed the bidding of every insolent oppressor (11.59). And they were pursued by a curse in this world and on the Day of Resurrection; Lo! Surely 'Ād disbelieved in their Lord; away with 'Ād, the people of Hūd! (11.60).

So they rejected him (Hūd); therefore We destroyed them. Surely there is a sign in this, but most of them (the disbelievers in general) would not believe (26.139).

The punishment represents the end and climax of the struggle of Hūd against his people. Details of this event would have been given particular importance in traditional story telling. The Qur'an, in contrast, mentions only God's aid to His prophet and His destruction of the disbelievers.

Another attribute of the Qur'an's style in recounting historical stories is that the details of any particular story are usually found in more than one place. Building a complete picture of that story in the Qur'an would require compiling all its details from the various chapters. One example is the story of Jesus. The story of Joseph is mentioned in its entirety in the chapter that is named after that prophet; but this is an exception, not the rule.

An event may be described in different, but consistent, ways in different chapters, to reflect what God wants to emphasize and highlight in each chapter. For example, a historical conversation may be cited in different chapters using a number of different wordings to convey the meaning of that dialog. We must not forget that often the original language of a dialog was not the Arabic of the Qur'an, if Arabic at all, such as the dialogs between various prophets and their peoples. The verses below, which come from different chapters, describe the first dialog between God and Moses. They use different wordings to describe the same events. These chapters also differ with respect to the type and amount of information they give about that dialog:

> When Moses said to his family: "Surely I have perceived a fire. I shall either bring you tidings thence, or I shall bring you a burning firebrand so that you may warm yourselves" (27.7). So when he came to the fire he heard a call: "Blessed is Whoever is in the fire and whoever is around it, and glory be to Allah, the Lord of the people (27.8). O Moses! It is Me, Allah, the Invincible, the Wise" (27.9). [And it was said to him]: "Throw down your staff." And when he saw it moving as if it was a snake, he turned away fleeing without retracing his steps; [and it was said to him]: "O Moses! Fear not, for messengers are not to fear in My presence (27.10). Neither he who, after doing wrong, does good instead of evil, for surely I am Forgiving, Merciful" (27.11). [And it was said to him]: "Enter your hand into your bosom, it will come out white, showing no harm; [go with this] as one of nine signs to Pharaoh and his people; surely they are a rebellious people [against Me]" (27.12).

> Then, when Moses had fulfilled the term and left in the night with his family, he perceived [at a distance] a fire at the side of the Mount and said to his family: "Tarry here; I have perceived a fire that I might bring to you tidings thence, or a firebrand that

you may warm yourselves" (28.29). And when he came to the fire, he heard a call from the right coast of the valley in the spot that was blessed because of the tree: "O Moses! It is Me, Allah, the Lord of the peoples" (28.30). [And it was said to him]: "Throw down your staff." And when he saw it move as if it was a snake, he turned away fleeing without retracing his steps. [And it was said to him]: "O Moses! Draw nigh and do not fear for you are one of those who are secure (28.31). Enter your hand into your bosom and it will come out white, showing no harm; and guard your heart against fear, for these shall be two proofs from your Lord to Pharaoh and his chiefs; for they are a rebellious people [against Me]" (28.32). He said: "My Lord! I have killed one of them and I fear that they will kill me (28.33). My brother Aaron speaks better than me, therefore make him a messenger and a helper to confirm me; I fear that they will accuse me of telling lies" (28.34). He said: "We shall strengthen you with your brother, and We shall give to you both authority so they shall not be able to reach you [for harm] on account of our signs; you both and those who follow you will be the victorious" (28.35).

And when your Lord [O Muhammad!] called Moses [saying]: "Go to the wrongdoing people (26.10) — the people of Pharaoh. Will they not act dutifully?" (26.11). He said: "My Lord! I fear that they will accuse me of telling lies (26.12). And my breast will be straitened, and my tongue will not speak fluently, therefore make Aaron a messenger [to help me] (26.13). And they have a charge of crime against me, so I fear that they will kill me" (26.14). He said: "By no means [will they hurt you]. So go you both with Our sings; We shall be with you, hearing (26.15). So, both of you go to Pharaoh and say: 'We are messengers of the Lord of the people (26.16). Let the Children of Israel leave with us'" (26.17).

There is another prominent attribute that characterizes the Qur'an's untraditional style in relating historical stories. Events that are mentioned in successive verses may or may not be related, and if they were related, the fact that they are mentioned immediately after each other does not necessarily mean that the latter event happened immediately before the first. In such cases, starting the narration of the second event with the article *idh* (when), rather than with *thumma* (then) or *fa* ("therefore" or "so"), often indicates the lapse of a period of time since the first event, the unrelatedness of the two events, or both. This is one example of two verses which we studied in detail in the book (§16.4 and §21.2.1). Both events are parts of the Jesus story, but the second event is unrelated to the first and is separate from it temporally, so the second verse is started with *idh* (when):

Lo! When I inspired the companions: "Believe in Me and in My messenger." They said: "We believe. Bear witness that we are Muslims" (5.111). Lo! When the companions said: "O Jesus son of Mary! Can your Lord send down for us a table of food from heaven?" He said: "Observe your duty to Allah, if you are true believers" (5.112).

One last point that should be mentioned is that there are a number of verses that refer to historical details revealed in the Qur'an and stress that this information became known to Prophet Muhammad only through the Qur'an. These verses imply or explicitly state that had Muhammad not been a true Prophet of God, he would not have known these historical accounts. For instance, after relating the story of Prophet Noah, God states:

> Those are some tidings of the unseen which We reveal to you [O Muhammad!]; you did not know them nor did your people before this [the Qur'an]; so be patient; the [prosperous] end is for the dutiful ones (11.49).

The term "tidings" in the following verse denotes the plot of Joseph's brothers to get rid of him — another story that the Prophet learned about through the Qur'an:

> These are some tidings of the unseen which We reveal to you [O Muhammad!], and you were not with them (Joseph's brothers) when they concerted their plans together when they were scheming (12.102).

Another example is God's following words about His revelation to Prophet Moses:

> And We gave Moses the Book, after We destroyed the generations of old, [as] clear testimonies for people, and a guidance and a mercy, that they may remember (28.43). And you [O Muhammad!] were not on the western side [of the Mount] when We handed the matter to Moses, and you were not one of the witnesses (28.44). But We brought forth generations, and their lives dragged on for them; and you were not dwelling with the people of Midian, reciting to them Our verses, but We have sent [you as] a Messenger (28.45). And you were not on the side of the Mount when We called [Moses], but this [knowledge that We have revealed to you] is a mercy from your Lord for you to warn a people to whom no warner before you came, that they may give heed (28.46).

God stresses that the Prophet was not on the western side of the Mount to know about the Tablets of the Torah, which He wrote for Moses there, nor was he living among the people of Midian to know of what happened to Moses there after he left Egypt escaping Pharaoh's wrath. God explains that Muhammad acquired this knowledge because God made him one of His Messengers: "but We have sent [you as] a Messenger." In other words, that knowledge is proof that Muhammad is indeed a Messenger of God. Finally, God reminds His Messenger that he was not on the side of the Mount when God called on Moses, but that He has given him this knowledge as a mercy from Him so that he would warn people who had not had a warner before him "that they may give heed." Confirming the prophethood of Muhammad and the divine source of the Qur'an is one goal that historical accounts in the Qur'an has.

Verse 3.44 makes a similar statement about God's revelation of historical details about Mary's childhood.

Appendix B

Apocryphal Gospels

This book has cited many times, and at times at some length, five apocryphal "infancy gospels." These are briefly introduced below in a possible chronological order.

The Infancy Gospel of James

Also known as the Protevangelion or the "pre gospel," the attribution of this gospel in its more popular name is due its following endnote: "I James wrote this History in Jerusalem: and when the disturbance was I retired into a desert place, until the death of Herod, and the disturbances ceased at Jerusalem." This James is alleged to be Jesus' brother.

The earliest reference to this gospel is found in the writings of the 3rd century Christian theologian Origen. It is generally accepted that this gospel could not have been written by an eye witness and must have been composed around the middle of the 2nd century, whereas that James is thought to have died in 62 CE.

William Wake (1657-1737), Archbishop of Canterbury, whose translation of the *Infancy Gospel of James* is used in this book, has the following to say about the authenticity of this gospel:

> This Gospel is ascribed to James. The allusions to it in the ancient Fathers are frequent, and their expressions indicate that it had obtained a very general credit in the Christian world. The controversies founded upon it chiefly relate to the age of Joseph at the birth of Christ, and to his being a widower with children, before his marriage with the Virgin.
>
> It seems material to remark, that the legends of the latter ages affirm the virginity of Joseph, notwithstanding Epiphanius, Hilary, Chrysostom, Cyril, Euthymius, Thephylaet, Occumenius, and indeed all the Latin Fathers till Ambrose, and the Greek Fathers afterwards, maintain the opinions of Joseph's age and family, founded upon their belief in the authenticity of this book.
>
> It is supposed to have been originally composed in Hebrew. Postellus brought the MS. of this Gospel from the Levant, translated it into Latin, and sent it to Oporimus, a printer at Basil, where Bibliander, a Protestant Divine, and the Professor of Divinity at Zurich, caused it to be printed in 1552. Postellus asserts that it was publicly read as canonical in the eastern churches they making no doubt that James was the author, of it.

It is, nevertheless considered apocryphal by some of the most learned divines in the Protestant and Catholic churches.

Most of the story in this gospel is not covered by any of the canonical Gospels. This gospel starts with the story of the birth of Mary, who is described as being Davidic. It recounts the sense of shame that her parents felt for not having offspring. An angel appeared to Mary's mother to tell her the good news that she was going to conceive and give birth to a child whom the whole world would speak about, so she vowed to devote the child to the Lord. Mary's father was also informed by an angel about the conception of his wife. Mary was born nine months later.

Mary's parents made sure that their little daughter was kept away from any uncleanness. When she became 3 years old, they took her to live in the temple, where she used to be fed by angels.

When Mary became 12 years old and approached the age of puberty, the priests of the temple met to decide what to do about her, as leaving her there would ultimately defile the place. They decided that the high priest should make a special prayer to ask for guidance about this issue. An angel then appeared to him and instructed him to invite all widowers and have each to bring his rod with him, and that God will then reveal who should become Mary's husband. God made a dove come out of a rod and fly upon Joseph's head — a sign that the high priest understood to mean that Joseph is to be the husband.

Joseph argued that, being an old man and with children, he should not get married to the young Mary. But the high priest convinced him that this was God's will. Joseph then took Mary to his house, but he had to go to mind his building business.

One day an angel appeared to Mary to tell her that she was going to conceive, through the descending of the Holy Spirit upon her, and give birth to the Son of God. In a clear convergence with the Gospel of Luke, the angel also told Mary that her barren cousin Elizabeth was already in her 6th month of pregnancy. This is followed by a visit by Mary to Elizabeth that is also very reminiscent of the account in Luke. This is supposed to have happened when Mary was 14 years old — that is, as long as 2 years after Joseph had taken her to his house. The author does not seem to be disturbed by the complete absence of Joseph from the story for all that period.

Having decided to depart with Mary privately, Joseph saw a dream in which the angel reassured him that Mary was pregnant of the Holy Spirit and that she had not committed anything wrong. But a woman who came to visit Joseph and Mary noticed that she was pregnant and told the high priest. Joseph was accused of marrying Mary secretly. It is not clear why much was made of a possible secret marriage when Mary was already betrothed to Joseph (14:4) and supposed to marry him, and living in his house anyway. Joseph and Mary denied the accusation of having a secret relationship, and Joseph passed the test of the water of the Lord by the high priest that confirmed their innocence.

Another convergence point between this gospel and Luke is that here also we meet the story of Augustus' census. While in Luke Joseph and Mary go from Nazareth in Galilee to Bethlehem in Judea, in this gospel they were already in Judea, though in a different city, so they headed to Bethlehem. They were accompanied by a Simon who is mentioned as if the reader already knows him, so the reference might well be to the Simon who is one of Jesus' brothers in Mark (6:3) and Matthew (13:55). If that is the case, then the implication is clearly that Simon was Joseph's son from his dead wife. This Simon is not mentioned again in the story, suggesting that his mention was probably to stress that this brother, and other reported brothers and sisters of Jesus, was Joseph's but not Mary's child.

While on their way to Bethlehem, Mary felt the labor of birth, so Joseph took her to a cave. He went to bring a midwife from Bethlehem, but he saw a vision that is left uninterrupted, but which the author clearly suggests to have been caused by the imminent birth of Jesus.

Having brought a midwife to the cave, it turned out that she was not needed after all, as Jesus appears in a miraculous way from a great light that filled the cave. The midwife, who heard from Joseph the story of Mary's miraculous conception and witnessed the equally impressive miracle of the birth, went and told another woman about this amazing news. Having harbored doubts in her heart about this story, the latter had her hand withered. An angel appeared to the woman and instructed her to carry the child Jesus to be cured. This is the first of Jesus' miracles according to this gospel.

Having recounted events that preceded the birth of Jesus and which are mentioned in Luke, this gospel then relates events that followed the birth and which are found in Matthew. These include the appearance of the star of Bethlehem, the visit of the wise men, Herod's attempt to know the whereabouts of the newborn, and his order for all children who are 2 years old and younger to be killed. One difference with Matthew's account is that Jesus was not smuggled out of Palestine to Egypt, but was rather hidden by his mother who laid him in an ox manger. This is the last time we meet Jesus and his mother in this story, as the last chapter focuses on Zechariah, his wife, and their son.

Unlike Matthew which completely ignores this issue, the Infancy Gospel of James reminds us that not only Jesus was under threat, but also the six month older child John. A miracle in which a mountain was divided allowed John and his mother Elizabeth to hide. Herod refused to accept that John's father, Zechariah, was not aware of his son's whereabouts, so he had him killed.

The Gospel of the Birth of Mary

As suggested by its title, the anonymous author of this gospel focuses on the life of Mary, from the time she was conceived by her mother to her giving birth to Jesus. According to this gospel, the Davidic Mary was born in Nazareth in Galilee, where the family of her father came from. Her mother was from the city of David, Bethlehem.

Introducing his translation to this gospel, Archbishop Wake says the following about this gospel:

> In the primitive ages there was a Gospel extant bearing this name, attributed to St. Matthew, and received as genuine and authentic by several of the ancient Christian sects. It is to be found in the works of Jerome, a Father of the Church, who flourished in the fourth century, from whence the present translation is made. His contemporaries, Epiphanius, Bishop of Salamis, and Austin also mention a gospel under this title.
>
> The ancient copies differed from Jerome's, for from one of them the learned Faustus, a native of Britain, who became Bishop of Riez, in Provence, endeavoured to prove that Christ was not the Son of God till after his baptism; and that he was not of the house of David and tribe of Judah, because, according to the Gospel he cited, the Virgin herself was not of this tribe, but of the tribe of Levi; her father being a priest of the name of Joachim.
>
> It was likewise from this Gospel that the sect of the Collyridians established the worship and offering of manchet bread and cracknels, or fine wafers, as sacrificed to Mary, whom they imagined to have been born of a Virgin, as Christ is related in the Canonical Gospels to have been born of her.
>
> Epiphanius likewise cites a passage concerning the death of Zacharias, which is not in Jerome's copy, viz.: "That it was the occasion of the death of Zacharias in the temple, that when he had seen a vision, he, through surprise, was willing to disclose it, and his mouth was stopped. That which he saw was at the time of his offering incense, and it was a man standing in the form of an ass. When he was gone out, and had a mind to speak thus to the people, 'woe to you, whom do you worship?' He who had appeared to him in the temple took away the use of his speech. Afterwards when he recovered it, and was able to speak, he declared this to the Jews; and they slew him. They add (viz. the Gnostics in this book), that on this very account the high priest was appointed by their lawgiver (by God to Moses) to carry little bells, that whensoever he went into the temple to sacrifice he, whom they worshipped, hearing the noise of the bells, might have time enough to hide himself, and not be caught in that ugly shape and figure."

Despite the considerable similarities that this gospel has with the Infancy Gospel of James and the view of some scholars that both are one and the same book (Ehrman, 2005: 63), it is different enough to be treated as a separate work.

This gospel starts by saying that Mary's pious parents were married for twenty years without having a child, but they had vowed to dedicate their child to the temple should God give them one. An angel then appeared to Mary's father, and later to her mother, to tell him that they will have a girl named Mary, who would be particularly pious and follow the law. He also told him that as she will be born miraculously, she also shall "while yet a virgin, in a way unparalleled, bring forth the Son of the most High God, who shall, be called Jesus, and, according to the signification of his name, be the Saviour of all nations." (BirMary. 2:12). When Mary was 3 years old, her parents dedicated her to the temple.

As she grew up in the temple, Mary was increasing in piety. She started to be visited daily by angels, with whom she used to speak. At the age of 14, Mary's life was destined to change completely. The high priest decided that all virgins who had public abodes in the temple and were approaching this age of maturity must go home and aim to get married. He did not want menstrual girls to defile temple. All virgins obeyed the order except Mary who argued that she and her parents had devoted her to the temple, she had vowed virginity to God, and she was determined not to get married.

In order to solve this problem, the high priest went to consult God, as in the tradition. A divine voice instructed him that he should seek a resolution according to an Isaiah prophecy. He announced that all unmarried but marriageable men of the house of David should bring their rods to the altar, and the spirit of God, appearing in the shape of a dove, would sit on the rod of the person to whom Mary should be betrothed.

Being too old, a Davidic man called Joseph did not volunteer his rod. As the spirit of God did not appear, the high priest went again to consult God, and he was told that the only present person who did not produce his rod is the one who should take Mary. When Joseph produced his rod, a dove descended on it from heaven, and Mary was accordingly betrothed to him. Joseph then went to his hometown of Bethlehem to prepare for the marriage, whereas Mary went back to her parent's home in Galilee.

At her parent's house, Mary was visited by Gabriel. The angel gave her the good news about the birth of Jesus, whom he described as the "son of the Highest," "king of kings," and "lord of lords," among other descriptions. Asking how she could conceive when she had not been touched by a man, Gabriel confirmed that she will conceive, give birth, and give suck while staying a virgin.

Three months after their betrothal, Joseph went from Judea to Galilee to marry Mary, but he was shocked to see signs of pregnancy on her. The pious Joseph did not want to defame Mary, so he decided to end their betrothal privately. God then appeared to him in a dream to confirm Mary's chastity, stress that her pregnancy was not the work of man but the Holy Spirit, and command him to go ahead with the marriage. Joseph obeyed the divine command and married Mary, but he did not have a sexual relationship with her.

When Mary was 9 months pregnant, Joseph took her to Bethlehem, where she gave birth to Jesus. This gospel ends with the interesting remark that Mary "brought forth her firstborn son, as the holy Evangelists have taught." The author seems to suggest that Mary did give birth to other children later on, and his reference to the Evangelists are likely to be Matthew and Luke who described Jesus' birth in Bethlehem, though he may also be referring to other writings.

This gospel stresses Mary's holiness and her unique status among all women.

The Arabic Gospel of the Infancy

This gospel attributes itself to "Joseph the high priest." Its name is derived from the fact that it survives only in Arabic, but it is also known as the *First Gospel of the Infancy of Jesus Christ*.

This is what Archbishop Wake had to say about earlier references to this gospel:

> It was received by the Gnostics, a sect of Christians in the second century; and several of its relations were credited in the following ages by other Christians, viz., Eusebius, Athanasius, Epiphanius; Chrysostom. &c. Sozomen says, he was told by many, and he credits the relations, of the idols in Egypt falling down on Joseph, and Mary's flight thither with Christ; and of Christ making a well to wash his clothes in a sycamore-tree, from whence balsam afterwards proceeded; which stories are from this Gospel.
>
> Chemnitius, out of Stipulensis, who had it from Peter Martyr, Bishop of Alexandria, in the third century, says, that the place in Egypt where Christ was banished is now called Matarea, about ten miles beyond Cairo; that the inhabitants constantly burn a lamp in remembrance of it; and that there is a garden of trees yielding a balsam, which were planted by Christ when a boy.
>
> M. La Crosse cites a synod at Angamala, in the Mountain of Malabar, A. D. 1599, which shows this Gospel was commonly read by the Nestorians in the country. Ahmed Ibu Idris, a Mahometan divine, says, it was used by some Christians in common with the other four Gospels.

This gospel starts with a report of Jesus speaking miraculously while still in the cradle and with a passing reference to Gabriel's earlier good news Mary, before it moves back to recount the birth of Jesus, with considerable similarities with the account in the Infancy Gospel of James. It mentions Augustus' census which had Joseph and the pregnant Mary go to Bethlehem, the city of Joseph's fathers, to be taxed there. When Mary felt that she was about to give birth, Joseph took her to a cave and went looking for a midwife. He met an old woman and brought her to the cave, but they arrived after Jesus was born. To their amazement, the cave was full of light. The newborn was visited then by shepherds who came to praise and adore him.

The author then recounts the visit of wise men from the east of Jerusalem, followed by Herod's attempt to kill Jesus. An angel appears to Joseph in a dream and orders him to take the child and his mother to Egypt. The visit to Egypt triggered a long series of miracles that started with the fall of an idol and continued as the family moved from one city to another. The miracles that this gospel recounts include healing possession, leprosy, impotence, and a man who had been bewitched to a mule. Jesus met two thieves whom he identified as those who will be crucified with him, and he caused a well to spring forth.

This gospel tells us that Jesus met Pharaoh and stayed in Egypt for 3 years. It also states that Jesus performed "very many miracles, in Egypt, which are neither to be found in Gospel of the Infancy nor in the Gospel of Perfection." It is not clear which gospels the author is referring to.

After their sojourn in Egypt and the death of Herod, the family returned to Judea and settled in the Nazareth, where Jesus continued to perform a variety of miracles, including healing various diseases, creating live animals and birds from clay, stretching a wooden throne that Joseph made for the king to the right dimensions, making a viper that bit someone to suck back its venom, raising the dead, causing boys who annoyed him to die, and showing amazing knowledge of the alphabet.

In addition to the two thieves, Judas Iscariot is another character from the story of the future crucifixion of Jesus whom Jesus meets in his childhood. Judas was possessed, and under the influence of the devil he struck Jesus on the right side, the same side which was later pierced by the Jews when he was crucified.

This gospel also contains the story of Jesus in the temple when he was 12 and how he amazed people there by his knowledge of various sciences. It then tells us that from the age of 12 until 30 Jesus hid his miracles. This seems to be an attempt by the author to explain the absence of any account of that part of Jesus' life until he started his ministry. The author implies that it is miracles that publicized Jesus. This gospel then ends with a mention of Jesus' baptism and the descent of the Holy Spirit on him, but there is no mention of John the Baptist.

The Infancy Gospel of Thomas

This gospel attributes itself to an unknown Thomas, hence its name. Bart Ehrman (2005: 58) thinks that this gospel is one of the earliest infancy gospels.

This gospel covers the life of Jesus when he was 5 to 12, focusing mainly on his miracles. It portrays Jesus as a very bad-tempered child, showing little respect even to Joseph, who is described as his father. It claims that Jesus miraculously inflicted violent revenge on those who angered him. He made one child who angered him dry up like a tree, caused another to die, and caused a group of people who complained about his violent behavior to lose their sight. Jesus was so angry and violent that Joseph told his mother at some point not to let the child go outside because he thought anyone who makes him angry would die.

Even when Jesus performs miracles to help rather than hurt people, the miracles described are often to amend his violent mischief. In one miracle Jesus revived a dead child who had fallen down from the house and a man who had died because of the loss of blood as a result an accident by an ax that split his foot. When they came back to life, the child called Jesus "lord" and the man declared that "the spirit of God certainly lives within this child."

Other miracles that the author tells us Jesus performed include fashioning birds out of clay and turning them into real, live birds; carrying water with his cloak; making a one grain of wheat he sowed yield a hundred large bushels which he distributed to the poor; stretching a piece of wood that was too short for what Joseph needed it; curing his brother James who was about to die after a viper's bite, and causing the viper to burst open; and raising a child and a man from the dead.

This gospel relates three encounters that Jesus had with teachers. When the first teacher tried to teach him good manners and the alphabet, Jesus amazed and humiliated him by showing off his knowledge of the alphabet. This gospel says that the teacher declared that the child does not belong to the earth, can tame even fire, and was born before the creation of the whole world. The teacher also praised Mary indirectly, as he was left wondering what sort of womb nourished this prodigious child.

When a second, enraged teacher struck Jesus for his arrogant and humiliating attitude, the child caused the teacher to pass out. But when he felt happy with a third teacher, he caused the second teacher to recover.

The author ends his gospel with his version of the miracle of Jesus amazing the elders and teachers at the temple in Jerusalem, which is also related by Luke (2:42-50).

The Gospel of Pseudo-Matthew

This gospel is said to have been written in Hebrew by Matthew the Evangelist and translated into Latin by Jerome. It is believed that this gospel was probably written around the 8th-9th century. It relates in its first half the story of the birth and childhood of Mary and in the second the story of Jesus. Like the Gospel of Matthew, each now and then it explains some events as fulfilling old prophecies about the Christ.

This book starts with three letters, one addressed from two bishops to Jerome. Expressing their outrage that apocryphal books about the birth of Mary and the infancy and nativity of Jesus contain heretic stories, they urge Jerome to translate into Latin a Hebrew book written by the Evangelist Matthew they heard he had obtained. This letter is followed by Jerome's two-letter reply in which he reveals that Matthew had written this book not for publication like his canonical Gospel, but he concludes that the bishops' request and fighting heretics are good reasons for him to translate it. The inclusion of the three letters is clearly designed to give credibility to this gospel, but they are believed to be forgeries and that Matthew had nothing to do with this book.

There are considerable similarities between this gospel and the Infancy Gospel of James. It starts with Joachim and his wife Anna's lack of offspring and the sense of shame they felt. An angel appeared to Anna and another to Joachim telling them that they will have offspring. When Mary was three years old, her parents devoted her to the temple. She spent her time praying and worshipping God, and she was often seen being visited by angels, who also obeyed her. They also provided her with food.

Mary refused one of the priests' wish to get married to his son, insisting that she would live and die a virgin in devotion to God. The custom was that virgins leave the temple when they become 14 years old and get married, so Mary also had to leave the temple when she reached this age, but she insisted that she would not get married. The high priest, who is called Abiathar in this gospel, called on all unmarried Israelite men from the tribe of Judah to bring their rods to decide by casting lots who would take Mary. Miraculously, a dove came forth from the rod of the old man Joseph — a signal meaning that Mary must be given to him. Joseph was disturbed and argued that Mary was younger than his grandsons, suggesting to the high priest that he would be her guardian until he sees which of his sons would marry her. Clearly, Joseph must have been a widower, as he is described explicitly or implicitly in other gospels. Joseph also asked for other virgins to come with Mary to be her company. The high priest sent with Mary five virgins, but stressed to Joseph that they would stay with her until the day when she gets married to him, as it is he whom she must marry.

While in the house of Joseph, who was away for his building work, Mary was visited by the angel who told her that she would give birth to a unique child. Nine months later Joseph returned to his house to find Mary pregnant. He was extremely upset by the pregnancy, although the other virgins told him that she did nothing wrong that she was made pregnant by the angel. Joseph then saw in a dream an angle who told him that Mary is pregnant of the Holy Spirit and instructed him to take her as his wife.

The news spread that Mary was pregnant, so the high priest brought Joseph and Mary to the temple for a trial. This gospel says that Mary's parents were present at the temple, whereas other gospels do not make any mention of Mary's parents after they devote her to the temple. When Joseph and Mary drunk the water of God and remained unharmed, the crowds knew that they were both innocent and had not committed any sinful act that led to the pregnancy.

Joseph and Mary went to Bethlehem to register there in compliance with a Roman census. During the journey Mary went to give birth in a cavern, which was filled with very bright light because of her presence. When Joseph came back with two midwives, Mary had already given birth. One of the midwives then examined Mary and was stunned to discover her to be still a virgin. The conclusion of the examination was that "a virgin has conceived, a virgin has brought forth, and a virgin she remains." After the second midwife repeated the same examination of Mary, reaching the same conclusion, her hand miraculously started to cause her immense pain. But by touching Jesus' cloth, she was cured immediately. This is Jesus' first miracle in this gospel. After Jesus' birth, shepherds heard praising in heaven, and a star larger than any ever shone over the cave from the morning to the evening.

In another miracle, an ox and an ass worshipped the newborn. After circumcising Jesus on the eighth day, his parents took him to the temple. This is one point of convergence between this gospel and Luke.

The visit of the magi from the east of Jerusalem to Jesus is said to have taken place in the 2nd year, something that explains why Herod wanted to kill all children aged up to 2 years. The story of Herod and the magi here is very similar to Matthew's. After being instructed by an angel, Joseph took Mary and Jesus and headed to Egypt, escaping Herod's wrath and the subsequent massacre of the innocent children. More miracles are then reported in the way to and in Egypt: wild beasts adorned Jesus; Jesus ordered a palm tree to bend and to raise its branches, and made a water spring flow from its root; he shortened a trip from thirty to one day long; and all the idols in an Egyptian temple that Mary and Jesus went to prostrated and were broken. An angel then appeared to Joseph and instructed him to return to Judea, as those who wanted to kill Jesus had died.

More miracles are then reportedly performed by Jesus in Galilee, though these are reflective of the fiery mood of the child and very similar to those found in the Infancy Gospel of Thomas. On three different occasions, Jesus caused the death of a child who annoyed him or spoiled his playing ground, though he later revived two of the dead children. This gospel shows Joseph himself scared of Jesus. Jesus was rude toward Joseph and elderly people. Teachers who tried to teach him did not succeed as he ridiculed them. Both Mary and Joseph call Jesus in this gospel "my Lord."

Other miracles reported in this gospel include Jesus fashioning sparrows of clay and then giving them life. He raised a dead child, carried water with his cloak, sowed little wheat but reaped a lot, had lions adorn him, stretched a piece of wood, and cured the hand of Joseph's son James who was bitten by a viper. This gospel ends with Jesus aged over 8 years old, but probably not older than 12.

Appendix C

Abbreviations

This is a list of the abbreviations used in the book:

1 Chr	1 Chronicles	InThom	Infancy Gospel of Thomas
1 Cor	1 Corinthians	Isa	Isaiah
1 John	1 John	JA	Jewish Antiquities
1 Kings	1 Kings	Jam	James
1 Peter	1 Peter	Jer	Jeremiah
1 Sam	1 Samuel	John	Gospel of John
1 The	1 Thessalonians	Jonah	Jonah
1 Tim	1 Timothy	Josh	Joshua
2 Chr	2 Chronicles	Jub	Jubilees
2 Kings	2 Kings	Judg	Judges
2 Sam	2 Samuel	Lev	Leviticus
2 Tim	2 Timothy	Luke	Gospel of Luke
AraIn	Arabic Infancy Gospel	Mal	Malachi
Bar	Gospel of Barnabas	Mark	Gospel of Mark
BCE	Before Common Era	Matt	Gospel of Matthew
Bera	Berakoth	Mic	Micah
BirMary	Gospel of the Birth of Mary	Nic	Gospel of Nicodemus
CE	Common Era	Num	Numbers
Col	Colossians	Pesa	Pesachim
Dan	Daniel	GoPeter	Gospel of Peter
Deut	Deuteronomy	Phi	Philippians
Ecc	Ecclesiastes	Phm	Philemon
EI	Encyclopedia of Islam	Pro	Proverbs
Enoch	Enoch	Ps	Psalms
Eph	Ephesians	PsMatt	Gospel of Pseudo-Matthew
Exo	Exodus	PsSol	Psalms of Solomon
Ezek	Ezekiel	Rev	Revelation
Ezra	Ezra	Rom	Romans
Gal	Galatians	Sanh	Sanhedrin
Gen	Gensis	Ta'an	Ta'anit
Heb	Hebrews	Yeba	Yebamoth
Hos	Hosea	Zech	Zechariah
InJam	Infancy Gospel of James		

References

These are lists of modern and classical works and religious texts that are cited in the book.

Modern Works

'Ata ur-Rahim, M. (1991). *Jesus, Prophet of Islam*, Omar Brothers Publications PET LTD: Singapore.

Ahmad, M. G. (2004). *Jesus In India: An Account Of Jesus' Escape From Death On The Cross And His Journey To India*, Fredonia Books.

Albright, W. F. (1946). "The Names 'Nazareth' and 'Nazorean,'" *Journal of Biblical Literature*, 65, 397-401.

Al-Kadhi, M. A. (1996). *What did Jesus Really Say*, IANA: Michigan.

Allan, G. (1983). "He shall be called – a Nazirite?" *The Expository Times*, 95, 81-82.

As-Saqqā, A. H. (1972) (In Arabic). *Pereclete: The Name of the Prophet of Islam in the Gospel of Jesus (Peach be upon him) According to the Testimony of John*, Maktabat al-Muti'i: Egypt.

As-Sha'rāwī, M. (1999) (In Arabic). *Mary and the Messiah*, Al-Maktaba al-Tawfiqiyya: Cairo.

Aṭ-Ṭabāṭabā'ī, M. (undated) (In Arabic). *Exegesis of aṭ-Ṭabāṭabā'ī*.

Az-Zarqānī, M. (undated) (In Arabic). *Manāhil al-'Irfān fī 'Ulūm al-Qur'ān (Sources of Knowledge of the Sciences of the Qur'an)*, Dar Ihya' At-Turath Al-'Arabi, Beirut.

Bauer, W. (1996). *Orthodoxy and Heresy in Earliest Christianity*, Sigler Press, Pennsylvania (cited in Theissen & Merz, 1999).

Becker, U. (1976). *New International Dictionary Of New Testament Theology, vol 2*, edited by C. Brown, Paternoster Press: UK.

Behm, J. (1970). *Theological Dictionary of the New Testament, vol 5*, edited by G. Kittel Gerhard, translated by G. W. Bromiley, WM. B. Eerdmans Publishing Company, Michigan, 800-814.

Bock, D. L. (1991), "The Son of Man in Luke 5:24," *Bulletin for Biblical Research*, 1, 109-121.

Brown, R. E. (1970). *The Anchor Bible: The Gospel According to John XIII-XXI*, vol 29, Doubleday: New York.

Brown, R. E. (1993). *The Birth of the Messiah: A Commentary on the Infancy Narratives in the Gospels of Matthew and Luke*, Doubleday: New York.

Bruce, F. F. (2003). *The New Testament Documents: Are They Reliable?*, Wm. B. Eerdmans Publishing Company: Minnesota.

Bruce, F.F. (1982). "The Background to the Son of Man Sayings." In: H. H. Rowdon (ed.), *Christ The Lord: Studies in Christology presented to Donald Guthrie*, Inter-Varsity Press: Leicester, 50-70.

Bucaille, M. (1995). *The Bible, the Quran and Science*, Millat Book Centre: India.

Bullinger, E. W. (1909a). "The Usage of Ruach, Spirit," *The Companion Bible*, Part 1, Oxford University Press: London, 13-14.

Bullinger, E. W. (1909b). "The Usage of Pneuma in The New Testament," *The Companion Bible*, Part 5, Oxford University Press: London, 146-147.

Bullinger, E. W. (1979). *The Giver and His Gifts*, Kregel Publications.

Bultmann, R. (1958). *Jesus and the Word*, Charles Scribner's Sons: New York.

Burkill, T. A. (1972). *New Light on the Earliest Gospel: Seven Markan Studies*, Ithaca: Cornell University Press.

Campbell, J. Y. (1947). "The Origin and Meaning of the Term Son of Man," *Journal of Theological Studies*, 48, 145-155.

Clark, D. H., Parkinson, J. H., & Stephenson, R. F. (1977). "An Astronomical Re-Appraisal of the Star of Bethlehem — A Nova in 5 BC." *Quarterly Journal of the Royal Astronomical Society*, 18, 443-449.

Cragg, K. (1999). *Jesus and the Muslim*, Oneworld Publications: Oxford.

Cullmann, O. (1962). *The Interpreter's Dictionary of the Bible: An Illustrated Encyclopedia*, K-Q, Abingdon Press: New York, 523-524.

Davies, W. D. & Allison, D. C. (1988). *A Critical and Exegetical Commentary on the Gospels According to Saint Matthew, vol. 1: Introduction and Commentary to Matthew*, T. & T. Clark Limited: Edinburgh.

Dawud, A. A. (1994). *Muhammad in the Bible*, The Ministry of Awqaf and Islamic Affairs: Qatar.

Doherty, E. (1999). *The Jesus Puzzle: Did Christianity Begin with a Mythical Christ?*, Canadian Humanist Publications, Canada.

Doherty, E. (undated). "Josephus Unbound: Reopening the Josephus Question". *home.ca.inter.net/~oblio/supp10.htm*.

Durrani, M. H. (1998). *The Forgotten Gospel of St. Barnabas*, Kitab Bhavan: India.

Ehrman, B. (2005). *Lost Scriptures: Books that Did Not Make It into the New Testament*, Oxford University Press: USA.

Ehrman, B. (2007). *Misquoting Jesus: The Story Behind Who Changed the Bible and Why*, HarperSanFrancisco: New York.

Fatoohi, L (1999) (In Arabic). "The concept of 'ladun' in the Qur'an," *Al-Manhal*, 61, no. 560, 26-29. An English translation of the article can be found at *www.quranicstudies.com/article99.html*.

Feldman, L. H. (translator) (1965) *Jewish Antiquities, vol. 9*, Massachusetts: Harvard University Press.

France, R. T. (1978). "The 'Massacre of the Innocents' — Fact or Fiction?" *Studia Biblica 1978*, 2, 83-94.

France, R. T. (1979). "Herod and the Children of Bethlehem," *Novum Testamentum*, 21, 98-120.

France, R. T. (1999). *The Evidence for Jesus*, Hodder & Stoughton Religious, London.

Fredriksen, P. (2001). *Jesus of Nazareth, King of the Jews: A Jewish Life and the Emergence of Christianity*, Macmillan: London.

Friedrich, G. (1971). *Theological Dictionary of the New Testament, vol 2*, edited by G. Kittel Gerhard, translated by G. W. Bromiley, WM. B. Eerdmans Publishing Company, Michigan, 707-737.

Gaster, T. H. (1969). *Myth, Legend and Custom in the Old Testament: A Comparative Study With Chapters from Sir James G.Frazer's Folklore in the Old Testament*, Gerald Duckworth, London.

Guillaume, A. (1955). *The Life of Muhammad: A Translation of Ibn Isḥāq's sirat Rasūl Allāh*, Oxford University Press: London.

Hartman, L. F. (1967). *The New Catholic Encyclopedia, vol. 6*, Catholic University of America: Washington, D. C.

Horbury, W. (1985). "The Messianic Associations of the 'Son of Man'", *Journal of Theological Studies*, 36, 34-55.

Houtman, C. (1996). *Exodus, vol. 1*, translated from the Dutch by S. Woudstra, Kok Publishing House, Kampen.

Irvin, D. (1977). "The Joseph and Moses Stories As Narrative in the Light of Ancient Near Eastern Narrative". In: J. H. Hayes & J. M. Miller (eds.), *Israelite and Judaean History*, SCM Press, London, 180-209.

Kelly, J. N. D. (1999). *Early Christian Creeds (3rd Edition)*, Longman: England.

Kennard, J. S. (1947). "'Nazorean' and 'Nazareth'", *Journal of Biblical Literature*, 66, 79-81.

Kirby, P. (2001). "Testimonium Flavianum." http://earlychristianwritings.com/testimonium.html.

Kitchen, K. A. (1977). *The Bible in its World: The Bible and Archaeology Today*, The Paternoster Press: Exeter.

Lampe, G. W. H. (1962). *The Interpreter's Dictionary of the Bible: An Illustrated Encyclopedia*, K-Q, Abingdon Press: New York, 654-655.

Levenson, J. D. (1997). *Esther: A Commentary*, Westminster John Knox Press: Kentucky.

Lindars, B. (1981). "The Persecution of Christians in John 15:18-16:4a." In: W. Horbury & B. McNeil (eds.), *Suffering and Martyrdom in the New Testament: Studies Presented to G. M. Styler*, Cambridge University Press: Cambridge, 48-69.

Longenecker, R. N. (1969). "'Son of Man' as a Self-Designation of Jesus," *Journal of the Evangelical Theological Society*, 12, 151-158.

Longenecker, R. N. (1975), "'Son of Man' Imagery: Some Implications for Theology and Discipleship," *Journal of the Evangelical Theological Society*, 18, 3-16.

Luard, H. R. (ed.) (1869). *Annales Monastici*, IV, London (cited in Clark, Parkinson, & Stephenson, 1977).

Miller, R. J. (2003). *Born Divine: The Births of Jesus and Other Sons of God*, Polebridge Press, California.

Montefiore, H. W. (1962). *Josephus and the New Testament*, A. R. Mowbray, London.

Moore, G. F. (1920). "Nazarene and Nazareth." In: F. J. Foakes Jackson & K. Lake (eds.), *The Beginnings of Christianity, Part I, vol. 1: Prolegomena I; the Acts of the Apostles*, Macmillan & co: London, 426-432.

Mourad, S. (1999). "On the Qur'anic Stories About Mary and Jesus," *Bulletin of the Royal Institute for Inter-Faith Studies*, 2, 13-24.

Mourad, S. (2002). "From Hellenism to Christianity and Islam: The Origin of the Palm tree Story concerning Mary and Jesus in the Gospel of Pseudo-Matthew and the Qur'an," *Oriens Christianus*, 86, 206-216.

Nichols, S. (2001). "Prophecy Makes Strange Bedfellows: On the History of Identifying the Antichrist," *Journal of the Evangelical Theological Society*, 44, 75-85.

Parrinder, G. (1995). *Jesus in the Qur'an*, Oneworld Publications: Oxford.

Pellett, D. C. (1962). *The Interpreter's Dictionary of the Bible: An Illustrated Encyclopedia*, K-Q, Abingdon Press: New York, 524-526.

Piper, O. A. (1992). *The Interpreter's Dictionary of the Bible, E-J*, edited by K. R. Crim & G. A. Buttrick, Abingdon Press: New York.

Porsch, G. (1993). *Exegetical Dictionary of the New Testament, vol. 3*, edited by H. Balz & G. Schneider, WM. B. Eerdmans Publishing Company, Michigan.

Powell, M. A. (2000). The *Jesus Debate: Modern Historians Investigate the Life of Christ*, Lion Hudson Plc: UK.

Pritchard, J. B. (1950) (ed.). *Ancient Near Eastern Texts Relating to the Old Testament*, Princeton University Press, Princeton.

Redford, D. B. (1992). *Egypt, Canaan, and Israel in Ancient Times*, Princeton University Press: Princeton.

Rhys, J. (2003). *Shaken Creeds: The Virgin Birth Doctrine*, R A Kessinger Publishing: Montana.

Ryan, T. J. (1979). *Encyclopedic Dictionary of Religion*, edited by P. K. Meagher, T. C. O'Brien, M. Aherne, Corpus Publications: Washington, D. C.

Sanders, E. P. (1995). *The Historical Figure of Jesus*, Penguin Books, England.

Smallwood, E. M. (1981). *The Jewish War*. Translated by G.A. Williamson. Revised with introduction by E. M. Smallwood, Penguin Books, England.

Strecker, G. (1991). *Exegetical Dictionary of the New Testament, vol. 2*, edited by H. Balz & G. Schneider, WM. B. Eerdmans Publishing Company, Michigan.

Ṭawīla, A. (2004) (in Arabic). *The Awaited Messiah and the End of the World*, Dar alsalam, Egypt.

Theissen, G. & Merz, A. (1999). *The Historical Jesus: A Comprehensive Guide*. SCM Press: London.

Thompson, T. L. (1977). "The Joseph and Moses Narratives: Historical Reconstructions of the Narratives." In: J. H. Hayes & J. M. Miller (eds.), *Israelite and Judaean History*, SCM Press: London, 149-166.

Tisdall, W. C. (1905). *The Original Sources of the Qur'an*, Society For Promoting Christian Knowledge: London.

Vajda, G. (1971). *The Encyclopedia of Islam, vol. 3*, edited by B. Lewis, Ch. Pellat, & J. Schacht, E. J. Brill: Leiden, 110.

Vermes, G. (2000). *The Changing Faces of Jesus*, Penguin Books, London.

Vermes, G. (2005). *The Passion*, Penguin Books, London.

Von Denffer, A. (2000). *Ulūm al-Qur'an: An Introduction to the Sciences of the Qur'an*, The Islamic Foundation, UK.

Vorster, W S. (1992). *The Anchor Bible Dictionary, vol. 2*, edited by D. N. Freedman et al, Doubleday: New York.

Wells, G. A. (1988). *The Historical Evidence for Jesus*, Prometheus Books, London.

Whiston, W. (1998). *Josephus: The Complete Works*, Thomas Nelson Publishers: Tennesee.

Williamson, G. A. (translator) (1974). *The Jewish War*, translated by G. A. Williamson, Penguin: UK.

Wilson, R. M. (1960). *Studies in the Gospel of Thomas*, A.R. Mowbray & Co.: London.

Witherington III, B. (2003). *The Brothers of Jesus: The Dramatic Story and Meaning of the First Archaeological Link to Jesus and His Family*, Continuum: London.

Classical and Ancient Writings

Africanus (1951). *Chronograph (Chronografiai)*, translated by A. Roberts & J. Donaldson, in: *Ante-Nicene Fathers: Translations of The Writings of the Fathers down to a.d. 325, Volume 5*, WM. B. Eerdmans publishing company: Michigan.

ANET (1950). *Ancient Near Eastern Texts Relating to the Old Testament*, edited by J. B. Pritchard, Princeton University Press, Princeton.

Aṭ-Ṭabarī, M. (undated) (In Arabic). *The Compilation of the Clarification in Interpreting the Qur'an*.

Cicero (1853). *On Divination (de Divinatione)*, translated by C. D. Yonge, Henry G. Bohn: London.

Eusebius (1851). *Ecclesiastical History (Historia Ecclesiastica)*, edited by P. Schaff & H. Wace, in: *Post-Nicene Fathers Of The Christian Church*, WM. B. Eerdmans publishing company: Michigan.

Eusebius (2001). *The Proof of the Gospel (Demonstratio evangelica)*, translated by W.J. Ferrar, Wipf and Stock Publishers: Oregon.

Herodotus (2004). *An Account of Egypt*, translated By G. C. Macaulay, Kessinger Publishing: Montana.

Ibn Hisham, M. (1955). *The Life of Muhammad: A Translation of Ishaq's Sirat Rasul Allah*, translated by A. Guillaume, Oxford University Press: London.

Ignatius (1951). The Epistle of Ignatius to the Smyrnaeans, translated by A. Roberts & J. Donaldson, in: *Ante-Nicene Fathers: Translations of The Writings of the Fathers down to a.d. 325, Volume 1*, WM. B. Eerdmans publishing company: Michigan.

Irenaeus (1951). *Against Heresies (Adversus Haereses)*, translated by A. Roberts & J. Donaldson, in: *Ante-Nicene Fathers: Translations of The Writings of the Fathers down to a.d. 325, Volume 1*, WM. B. Eerdmans publishing company: Michigan.

Jerome (1892). *Lives of Illustrious Men (De viris illustribus)*, translated by E. C. Richardson, edited by P. Schaff & H. Wace, in *A Select Library of Nicene and Post-Nicene Fathers of the Christian Church: Second Series, Volume 3*, The Christian literature company.

Jerome (1893). *Against Helvidius*, edited by P. Schaff & H. Wace, in *A Select Library of the Nicene and Post-Nicene Fathers of the Christian Church: Second Series, Volume 4*, WM.B. Eerdemans Publishing Company: Michigan.

Josephus, F. (1998). *Jewish Antiquities*, translated by W. Whiston, Thomas Nelson Publishers: Tennessee.

Josephus, F. (1998). *Life*, translated by W. Whiston, Thomas Nelson Publishers: Tennessee.

Josephus, F. (1998). *The Jewish War*, translated by W. Whiston, Thomas Nelson Publishers: Tennessee.

Justin (1997). *Epitome of the Philippic History of Pompeius Trogus*, translated by J. C. Yardely, Oxford University Press: Oxford.

Lucian of Samosata (1936). *The Passing Of Peregrinus*, translated by A. M. Harmon: Harvard University Press.

Macrobius, *Saturn (Saturnalia)*. cited in *The New Testament of Our Lord and Saviour Jesus Christ* (1854), Carlton and Phillips: New York, p. 38.

Origen (1994). *Commentary on Matthew*, translated by A. Roberts & J. Donaldson, edited by A. Menzies, in: *Ante-Nicene Fathers: Translations of The Writings of the Fathers down to a.d. 325, Volume 5*, WM. B. Eerdmans publishing company: Michigan.

Origen (2004). *Against Celsus (Contra Celsus)*, translated by A. Roberts & J. Donaldson, Kessinger Publishing: Montana.

Philostratus (1999). *The Life of Apollonius* (*Vita Apollonii*), cited in W. Cotter, *Miracles in Greco-Roman Antiquity: A Sourcebook for the Study of the New Testament Miracle Stories*, Routledge: London, p. 45.

Porphyry (2005). *Against the Christians*, translated by R. Berchman, Brill: the Netherlands.
Suetonius (2004): *Lives of the Caesars (De Vita Caesarum)*, translated by J. C. Rolfe, Kessinger Publishing: Montana.
Tacitus (1962). *Annals (Annales)*, translated by C. H. Moore & J. Jackson, William Heinmann Ltd: London.
Tacitus (1968). *Histories (Historiae)*, Books I-III, Book II, translated by C. H. Moore, William Heinmann Ltd: London.
Tertullian (2004). *Against Marcion (Adversus Marcionem)*, translated by Dr Holmes, Kessinger Publishing: Montana.

Religious Texts

I have made very slight changes to the translations of apocryphal writings — mainly changing archaic pronouns to their modern equivalents.

The Gospel of Barnabas, translated by Lonsdale & Laura Ragg, The Ministry of Awqaf: Duha.
Abū Dāwūd, S. (undated) (In Arabic). *As-Sunan*.
Al-Bukhārī, M. (undated) (In Arabic). *Al-Jāmi' al-Musnad aṣ-Ṣaḥīḥ al-Mukhtasar Min Umūr Rasūli Allah was Sunanih was Ayyamih*.
An-Nassā'ī, A. (undated) (In Arabic). *Al-Mujtaba Min as-Sunan al-Musnada*.
Apocalypse of Peter (VII, 3), translated by J. Brashler & R. A. Bullard. In J. Robinson (ed.), *The Nag Hammadi Library in English*, HarperCollins: San Francisco, 1990, 372-378.
Arabic Gospel of the Infancy, translated by W. Wake, *The Lost Books of the Bible and the Forgotten Books of Eden*, A&B Publishers Group: New York, 1926, 38-59.
At-Tarmathī, (undated) (In Arabic). *Al-Jāmi' al-Mukhtasar Min as-Sunan 'an Rasūli Allah wa Ma'rifat aṣ-Ṣaḥīḥ wa al-Ma'lūl wa ma 'Alayhi al-'Amal*.
Berakoth, *Hebrew-English edition of the Babylonian Talmud*, edited by I. Epstein, Translated by M. Simon, The Soncino Press: London, 1972.
Gospel of Nicodemus, translated by A. Walker, in: *Ante-Nicene Fathers: Translations of The Writings of the Fathers down to a.d. 325, Volume 8*, WM. B. Eerdmans publishing company: Michigan.
Gospel of Pseudo-Matthew, translated by A. Walker, in: *Ante-Nicene Fathers: Translations of The Writings of the Fathers down to a.d. 325, Volume 8*, WM. B. Eerdmans publishing company: Michigan.
Gospel of the Birth of Mary, translated by W. Wake, *The Lost Books of the Bible and the Forgotten Books of Eden*, A&B Publishers Group: New York, 1926, 17-24.

Infancy Gospel of James, translated by W. Wake, *The Lost Books of the Bible and the Forgotten Books of Eden*, A&B Publishers Group: New York, 1926, 24-37.

Infancy Gospel of Thomas, Translated by B. Ehrman, *Lost Scriptures: Books that Did Not Make It into the New Testament*, Oxford University Press: USA, 2005, 58-62.

Muslim, A. (undated) (In Arabic). *Al-Musnad aṣ-Ṣaḥīḥ al-Mukhtasar Min as-Sunan bi Naql al-'Adl 'an al-'Adl 'an Rasūli Allah.*

Pesahim, *Hebrew-English edition of the Babylonian Talmud*, edited by I. Epstein, Translated by H. Freedman, The Soncino Press: London, 1967.

Psalms of Solomon, translated by G. B. Gray, *The Lost Books of the Bible and the Forgotten Books of Eden*, A&B Publishers Group: New York, 1926, 105-120.

Sanhedrin, *Hebrew-English edition of the Babylonian Talmud*, edited by I. Epstein, Translated by J. Shachter & H. Freedman, The Soncino Press: London, 1969.

Second Treatise of the Great Seth, translated by R. A. Bullard & J. A. Gibbons. In J. Robinson (ed.), *The Nag Hammadi Library in English*, HarperCollins: San Francisco, 1990, 362-371.

Ta'anith, *Hebrew-English edition of the Babylonian Talmud*, edited by I. Epstein, Translated by J. Rabbinowitz, The Soncino Press: London, 1984.

Yebamoth, *Hebrew-English edition of the Babylonian Talmud*, edited by I. Epstein, Translated by I. Slotki & M. Litt, The Soncino Press: London, 1984.

Index of Qur'anic Verses

2.3	42	2.216	62	3.53	437, 495
2.4	383	2.234	446	3.53-55	437, 438
2.13	306	2.236-237	92	3.54	437, 495
2.30	129	2.240	446	3.55	437, 446, 447, 448
2.34	130	2.246	514		
2.36	514	2.247	514	3.55-57	486
2.40	251	2.248	514	3.59	96, 97, 105, 127, 131, 294
2.44	36	2.251	80		
2.57	354	2.253	124, 127, 136, 292, 297, 346, 347, 452	3.64	307
2.62	81, 224, 305, 450, 460, 499			3.65	369
				3.67	501
2.65	387	2.255	465	3.71	36
2.67	307	2.260	497	3.78	37
2.75	37, 39	2.285	289	3.79	37
2.78	37	3.3	36, 63, 363	3.80	303
2.79	37, 38	3.4	36, 363	3.83	297
2.80	307	3.28	307	3.84	291
2.83	503	3.33	50, 54, 177	3.112	463
2.84	503	3.34	54, 177	3.113	463, 500
2.87	124, 125, 127, 136, 291, 346, 347, 452, 462	3.35	48, 50, 164, 177	3.114	463, 500
		3.35-37	61	3.115	463, 500
		3.36	50	3.144	367, 489
2.89	383	3.37	52, 55, 56, 61	3.164	80
2.91	462	3.38	53, 61, 62, 63, 66, 67	3.169	445, 448
2.92	308			3.181	438
2.93	503	3.38-41	53	3.187	36, 503
2.97	124, 365	3.39	62, 64, 69, 94, 97	4.1	132
2.98	125, 126			4.14	225
2.101	63	3.40	64, 69, 94, 96	4.15	446
2.102	126	3.41	64, 65	4.33	55
2.107	227	3.42	53, 54, 65	4.43	92
2.111	224, 305, 500	3.42-43	92	4.45	40
2.112	305, 500	3.43	55	4.46	37, 40
2.113	36, 224, 502	3.44	52, 55, 60, 66, 518	4.47	387
2.116	299			4.48	298, 450
2.117	96	3.45	63, 92, 95, 97, 251, 253, 347, 366	4.64	291
2.118	463			4.89	307
2.120	224, 225, 502			4.94	134
2.121	502	3.45-47	105	4.116	298, 450
2.130	288	3.46	96, 178, 308, 347, 366, 448, 487	4.125	308
2.131	288			4.153	308, 485
2.132	288			4.154	387, 485, 503
2.133	288, 383	3.47	95, 96, 117, 143, 347	4.155	438, 485, 504
2.135	224, 225, 501			4.156	119, 485
2.136	291	3.48	80, 347, 364	4.157	251, 253, 435, 436, 438, 439, 440, 445, 446, 447, 485
2.138	83	3.49	131, 253, 291, 349, 351		
2.140	36, 224, 501				
2.146	368	3.49-50	352		
2.149	484	3.49-51	437	4.157-158	447
2.154	445, 448	3.50	295, 351, 383, 385, 386, 495	4.158	435, 447, 485
2.159	36, 346			4.159	451, 483, 484, 485, 486, 487, 488
2.173	383	3.51	351, 352, 495		
2.174	36	3.52	226, 227, 228, 292, 437, 495		
2.183	438			4.160	384, 485
2.185	346	3.52-53	496	4.161	485
2.214	174	3.52-54	437	4.163	289, 291

4.164	289	5.112	352, 353, 495, 516	9.117	227
4.171	97, 105, 124, 125, 127, 251, 253, 310, 311	5.113	352, 495	10.46	446
		5.114	352, 495	10.68	299
		5.115	353, 495	10.72	288
4.172	251, 310, 311	5.116	308, 309, 449	10.90-92	486
5.3	383	5.116-118	450	10.98	486, 514
5.5	383, 384	5.117	308, 447, 448, 449, 451, 452, 487	11.27	293
5.6	92			11.49	517
5.12	503			11.50	176
5.13	37, 503, 504			11.58	514
5.14	224, 227, 228, 503, 504	5.118	308, 449	11.59	515
		5.119	449, 450	11.60	515
5.15	36, 503, 504	6.2	128	11.61	176
5.17	251, 297, 304	6.8	125	11.69-83	54, 290
5.18	224, 304, 305, 501	6.9	126	11.71	366
		6.38	490	11.72	366
5.27	119	6.48	365	11.84	176
5.41	37, 40	6.60	446	12.2	225
5.43	36	6.61	290, 446	12.102	517
5.44	288	6.73	96	12.109	291
5.46	36	6.85	68, 80	13.19	350
5.47	385	6.91	36	13.33	299
5.48	388	6.98	132	13.37	225
5.51	224, 502	6.100	301	13.38	352
5.59	500	6.101	301, 304	13.40	446
5.64	134	6.102	297	14.10	294
5.66	384, 385	6.103	297, 298	14.11	294, 352
5.68	36, 384, 385	6.118-121	383	14.30	299
5.69	81, 224, 305, 460, 499	6.145	383	14.52	383
		6.145-146	384	15.13	40
5.70	504	6.146	383, 384	15.19	134
5.72	119, 251, 310	6.164	461	15.27	300
5.72-75	310	7.12	300	15.28	129
5.73	310, 311	7.24	514	15.29	127, 129, 130, 131, 133
5.74	310	7.26	119		
5.75	251, 291, 310, 311	7.37	290	15.6	41
		7.65	176	15.9	35
5.76	310	7.67	290	15.51-74	54, 290
5.77	310	7.72	514	16.2	134, 135
5.78	310, 504	7.73	176	16.25	463
5.82	224, 225, 227, 228, 505	7.85	176	16.40	96
		7.115	134	16.49	302
5.83	505	7.120	134	16.51	308
5.83-85	506	7.127	200, 211	16.57	299
5.84	505	7.148	308	16.58	299, 366
5.85	505	7.150	134	16.59	299
5.96	383	7.152	308	16.72	132
5.109	450, 451	7.157	296, 368, 387	16.89	365
5.110	124, 125, 127, 131, 136, 199, 200, 308, 346, 351, 352, 436, 437, 441, 449, 450, 452, 487	7.160	353	16.102	40, 124, 127, 365
		7.163	387		
		7.169	503	16.103	40, 225, 226
		7.180	298	16.115	383
		7.189	132	16.124	387
		8.12	134	17.1	452
5.110-115	450	8.17	438	17.15	461
5.110-118	450	9.30	224, 251, 253, 305, 306, 502	17.40	300
5.111	292, 352, 495, 496, 516			17.55	292
		9.31	251, 306, 502	17.70	119
5.111-112	495	9.34	306, 506	17.72	350
5.111-115	450	9.100	227	17.85	136

17.94	293	19.35	96, 180, 303, 307	26.10	516
17.95	293			26.11	516
17.110	298	19.56	445	26.12	516
17.111	302, 307	19.57	445	26.13	516
18.4	302	19.65	69	26.14	516
18.4-5	299	19.81	308	26.15	516
18.15	308	19.88	302	26.17	516
18.9-22	447	19.89	302	26.54	211
19.2	66	19.90	302	26.105	48
19.3	66	19.91	302	26.106	48, 176
19.4	66	19.92	302, 307	26.124	176
19.5	62, 66, 67, 69	19.93	302	26.139	515
19.5-6	66	20.8	298	26.142	176
19.6	67, 68	20.37	200, 210	26.154	293
19.7	68, 80, 82, 94, 366	20.37-39	200	26.161	176
		20.38	200, 210	26.186	293
19.8	69, 70, 94	20.39	134, 200, 210	26.192	484
19.9	70	20.47	513	26.193	124, 127
19.10	71	20.48	513	26.194	124
19.11	71	20.49	513	26.195	225
19.12	80, 81, 82	20.50	513	27.2	365
19.13	81	20.51	513	27.7	515
19.14	81, 144	20.52	513	27.8	515
19.15	69, 81, 180	20.80	119, 353	27.9	515
19.16	52, 56, 91	20.113	225	27.10	515
19.17	56, 61, 91, 95, 124, 125, 127	21.3	293	27.11	515
		21.5	41	27.12	515
19.17-22	105	21.7	311	27.29	134
19.18	92	21.8	311	27.45	176
19.19	92, 93	21.21	308	27.59	81
19.20	92, 96, 117, 143	21.24	308	27.82	490, 491
19.21	93, 117, 143	21.26	302	28.3	209
19.22	94, 143, 173, 177, 184	21.27	302	28.4	209
		21.28	302	28.5	209
19.23	118, 173, 175, 184, 347, 514	21.29	302	28.6	209
		21.30	128	28.7	134, 199, 209, 451
19.23-33	180	21.68	70		
19.24	174, 347	21.69	70	28.8	210
19.25	174, 175, 347	21.83-84	65	28.9	210
19.26	175, 347	21.89	68	28.10	210
19.27	94, 143, 175, 200, 348	21.90	68, 80	28.11	210
		21.91	93, 117, 118, 119, 127, 133	28.12	210
19.27-28	118			28.13	210
19.27-33	105	21.96	480	28.14	210
19.28	48, 143, 176, 200, 348	22.5	294	28.29	516
		22.17	81, 224, 499	28.30	516
19.29	178, 200, 348	22.30	383	28.31	516
19.30	82, 178, 200, 253, 291, 292, 294, 303, 348, 364	22.52	134	28.32	516
		22.71	227	28.33	516
		22.78	288	28.34	516
		23.24	293	28.35	516
19.30-32	118	23.47	293	28.43	517
19.31	179, 200, 252, 294, 303, 348	23.50	118	28.44	517
		23.84-92	299	28.45	517
19.32	144, 179, 201, 303, 348	24.61	350	28.46	517
		25.2	302	28.52	500
19.33	180, 201, 303, 348, 487	25.5	40	28.53	500
		25.7	311	28.54	500
19.34	180, 303	25.20	311	28.86	134
19.34-35	303	25.56	365	29.12	464

29.13	464	40.25	200, 211	53.19	300
29.14	487	40.26	200, 211	53.20	300
29.31-34	290	40.64	39	53.21	300
29.36	176	40.67	446	53.22	300
29.46	500	40.68	96	53.26	465
29.48	41	40.77	446	53.27	300
30.20	294	40.78	352	53.28	300
30.21	132	41.2	363	53.38-39	461
32.7	128, 130	41.3	225, 363	54.23	293
32.8	128, 130	41.41	35	54.24	293
32.9	127, 128, 129, 130, 131	41.42	35	54.25	134, 293
		41.44	225, 226	55.15	300
32.11	126, 446	42.7	225	57.3	297
33.7	291	42.11	39, 132, 297	57.25	346
33.9-20	505	42.13	289	57.27	291, 363, 507
33.40	289, 296, 367, 490	42.49	70	58.3-4	92
		42.50	70	58.22	134, 135, 136
33.49	92	42.51	135	59.22-24	298
34.40	300	42.52	134, 135, 136	59.23	124
34.41	301	43.3	225	59.24	298
35.1	54, 290	43.16	299	61.6	253, 296, 346, 367, 369, 375, 488, 489, 504
35.11	128	43.17	299		
35.18	461	43.19	300		
36.25	445	43.20	300	61.14	227, 228, 437, 495, 496
36.26	445	43.53	134		
36.27	445	43.57	303, 483	66.10	163
36.28	445	43.58	303, 483	66.11	163
36.29	445	43.59	303, 483	66.12	50, 93, 117, 119, 127, 133, 163, 176, 177
36.82	96	43.60	483		
37.11	128	43.61	483, 484		
37.35	35	43.62	483	69.44	484
37.79	81	43.63	294, 304, 346, 483	69.45	484
37.107	464			69.46	484
37.147-148	486	43.64	294, 304, 483	69.47	484
37.149	300	43.65	304, 483	69.48	484
37.150	300	43.66	483	69.49	484
37.151	300	43.66-67	484	69.50	484
37.152	300, 304	43.67	483	69.52	484
37.153	300	43.80	290	70.4	124, 126, 127
37.154	300	43.81	301	72.3	301, 304
37.155	300	43.82	301	72.24	227
37.156	300	46.9	289	73.5	134
37.157	300	46.12	225, 365	75.15	134
38.41-43	65	46.21	176	75.16-19	450
38.71	127	47.2	367	77.5	134
38.72	127, 129, 130, 131, 133	47.13	227	78.38	124, 126, 127
		47.19	35, 297	80.2	350
38.76	300	48.29	35, 367, 368, 369	81.1-14	489
39.2	299			81.5	490
39.3	299	50.24	134	81.8-9	299
39.4	302, 307	50.38	387	93.6	112
39.6	132	51.52	463	97.4	124, 126, 127
39.7	461	51.53	463	110.119	451
39.28	225	52.29	41	112.1	302
39.44	465	52.39	299	112.2	302
40.7	465	53.1-18	452	112.3	302, 304
40.15	134	53.18	300	112.4	302

Index of Biblical Passages

Old Testament

Genesis
1:1-2	129
1:2	122
1:26-27	39
2:2-3	387
2:7	130
2:21-22	133
3:8	122
6:1-4	258
6:3	122
6:17	122
26:35	122
41:46	192
45:27	122

Exodus
1:8-22	208
2:1-10	209
4:19	212
4:22-23	258
12:1-8	390
12:37	211
12:46	404
15:8	122
15:20	176
16:11-15	354
16:11-35	330
40:12-15	231

Leviticus
9:7	454
20:10	105, 178
20:14	412
24:10-16	262

Numbers
9:12	404
24:17	173
26:60	176

Deuteronomy
17:5	412
21:21-23	412
28:30	138

Joshua
2:11	122

Judges
8:3	122
9:23	122
13:7	222
16:17	222

1 Samuel
1:11	49
10:1	232
16:1	239
16:12-13	232
17:56	106
20:22	106

2 Samuel
4:10	358
5:4	192
7:14	258
18:20	359
18:22	359
18:25	359
18:27	359
22:16	122
23:2	121

1 Kings
17:17-24	330
18:12	122

2 Kings
4:42-44	322
5:1-14	330
7:9	359
18:9-11	477

1 Chronicles
1:1-4	141
1:24-17	141
3:19	142
9:24	122
16:15-22	232
23:1-6	68
24:10	68

2 Chronicles
24:20	60
24:20-22	58

Job
1:6	258
2:1	258
4:15	122
19:17	122
38:7	258
41:16	122

Psalms
2:7	258, 270
11:6	122
22:15	403
22:18	403
29:1	258
34:20	404
55:8	122
69:21	403
82:1-7	263
89:6	258
104:4	122
105:15	232

Ecclesiastes
3:19-20	121

Isaiah
1:3	344
4:3	222, 223
7:14	106, 107, 108, 166, 271
7:14-16	107
8:8	107
9:6-7	233
11:1	223
11:1-12	233, 482
26:19	240
29:18-19	241
34:16	122
35:4-6	240
40:3	75
40:9	359
45:1	232
52:7	359
53:4	241
53:12	403
61:1	232, 241

Jeremiah
18:2-3	397, 402
31:15	204
31:15-17	204
32:7-9	402
52:23	122
52:28-30	478

Ezekiel
1:1	192
1:4	122
10:15	122
18:5-20	462
37:9	122
37:14	122

Daniel
7	476

7:13	278, 279, 280, 281, 471	2:7-9	171	9:18-25	323, 327, 336, 339
7:13-14	279	2:11	272	9:18-26	336
8:17	279	2:14	187	9:20-22	323
		2:14-15	203	9:26	338
Hosea		2:15	166, 210	9:27	238, 241
11:1	203, 258	2:16	187	9:27-30	323, 336, 350
11:1-5	203	2:17-18	203	9:30	242, 339
		2:18	166	9:32-33	323
Jonah		2:20	212	9:33	322
1:12	399	2:21	187	9:34	332
1:17	399	2:21-23	221	9:35	323, 338, 358, 359
2:10	399	2:22-23	215		
		2:23	166, 218, 219, 222, 223	10:2	151
Micah		3:1-2	246	10:3	151
5:1	233	3:1-8	74	10:5-6	337, 361
5:1-6	167	3:2	470	10:7	246, 470
5:2	166, 212, 239	3:3	75, 166	10:8	334
		3:11	82, 126	10:19-23	469
Zechariah		3:11-12	74, 76	10:32	283
1:1	59, 60	3:13-17	75, 215	10:32-33	265
6:5	122	3:14	76	10:33	284
9:9	233, 250	3:16	125	10:39	360
11:12-13	397, 402	3:17	264, 272	11:2-3	76, 84
12:1-9	404	4:3	260	11:2-5	240, 331
12:10	404	4:6	260	11:5	358
13:7	403	4:13	219	11:11	74
		4:15-16	166	11:18	284
Malachi		4:17	246, 360, 470	11:20-24	331
2:4-7	456	4:18-19	498	11:21-23	338
		4:23	323, 358, 359	11:27	264, 266
		4:23-24	323	12:1-4	380
		4:24, 325	338	12:10-13	323, 333, 380
New Testament		5:16	263	12:15	338
		5:17-20	378	12:18	294
Matthew		5:17-48	296	12:18-21	166
1:1	139, 140, 238	5:21-44	378	12:22	350
1:16	139, 158	8:1, 338	339	12:23	241
1:17	141	8:2-3	323, 350	12:24	332
1:18	93, 106, 110, 123, 149, 150, 271	8:3	324	12:27	320
		8:4	242, 339	12:38-40	399
1:18-20	100	8:5-13	316, 323, 325, 337, 364	12:38-42	341, 355
1:19	138			12:46-50	142, 147
1:20	87, 93, 106, 110, 271	8:14-15	323	13:14-15	166
		8:16	323, 325	13:41	281
1:21	95, 456	8:16-17	241	13:54-57	332
1:22-23	100	8:17	166	13:55	109, 138, 140, 142, 148, 149, 151, 154, 521
1:23	106, 166, 210, 271	8:20	284		
		8:23-26	326		
1:25	149, 150	8:23-27	336	13:55-56	147, 154
2:1	215	8:27	331	13:57	286, 290
2:1-2	171	8:28-32	325, 329	13:58	337
2:1-6	165	8:28-34	331	14:1	187
2:1-23	196	8:29	260	14:2	77
2:2	212	8:31-32	344	14:3-10	77
2:4-6	210, 239	9:2-8	333, 457	14:14	338
2:5-6	166	9:6	281	14:15-21	317, 326
2:6	166	9:6-7	323	14:21	338
		9:8	330	14:24-31	326, 335
				14:24-33	259

Index of Biblical Passages 545

14:33	260	23:10	238	27:54	261
14:36	325	23:35	58	27:56	148, 398, 401
15:8-9	166	24	469, 481	27:57-60	398
15:10-20	379	24:1-2	393, 414	27:62	390
15:21-28	325, 336	24:4-5	237	28:1	399
15:22	241	24:5	477	28:1-10	401
15:24	337	24:11	477	28:11-15	431
15:24-26	361	24:14	358, 359, 360	28:16-20	401
15:30	324, 350	24:23-24	237		
15:31	331	24:24	333, 477, 479	*Mark*	
15:32-38	317, 326	24:30	280	1:1	260, 358, 362
15:38	338	24:30-31	472	1:2-3	75
16:1-4	355, 400	24:33	469	1:4-5	74
16:4	342, 355	24:34	469	1:6-8	75
16:13	283	24:36	469	1:8	82
16:13-16	285	24:42	469	1:9	215, 219
16:16	259	24:64-65	392	1:9-11	75
16:17	237	25:1-13	472	1:10	125
16:20	237, 245	25:31	280	1:10-11	270
16:21	248, 326, 456	26:2	326	1:11	264
16:22-23	430	26:5	412	1:14	358
16:24-28	469	26:13	358, 359, 360	1:15	246, 358, 359,
16:25	360	26:15	397		360, 470
16:27	280	26:18-30	355	1:16-17	498
16:28	246	26:19-50	390	1:23-26	325
17:1-2	326	26:21	326	1:24	218, 222, 331
17:1-5	272	26:31	326	1:25-26	324
17:5	264	26:31-57	391, 405	1:27	331
17:9	339	26:32	326	1:28	338
17:12	248, 456	26:33-35	326	1:29-31	323
17:14-18	323	26:41	123	1:32-34	323, 325
17:14-20	335	26:47-50	397, 440	1:33	338
17:16	335	26:57-59	392	1:34	339
17:23	430	26:58	398	1:38-39	338
17:24-27	327	26:59-61	406	1:39	325
18:3	244	26:60	392	1:40-42	323, 350
19:28	478	26:61	341, 392, 414	1:44	242, 332, 339
19:29	360	26:63	260, 392	1:45	338
20:17-19	326	26:63-64	470	2:3-12	333, 457
20:25-28	455	26:63-65	261, 407	2:10	284
20:28	284	26:64	237, 280, 469	2:10-12	281, 323, 324
20:29-34	323, 324, 329,	26:65-66	394	2:12	322
	336, 350	26:68	241	2:23-27	380
20:30	241	26:69-74	398	3:1-5	323
21:1-11	250	26:71	218	3:1-6	333
21:5	166	27:3-10	397	3:2-5	380
21:9	413	27:9-10	166, 402	3:10	323, 327
21:11, 219	286, 290	27:11	212, 243, 395	3:11	260
21:12-13	332	27:15	407	3:11-12	339
21:14	324, 350	27:17	237	3:17	151
21:15	241, 332	27:17-26	410	3:18	151
21:18-19	326	27:22	237	3:21	109, 147, 150
21:18-22	334, 336	27:29	243	3:22	332
21:19	344	27:37	243, 396	3:23-26	332
21:21	335	27:40	261	3:31	109, 147
21:46	286, 290	27:42	247	3:31-35	146
22:16-21	245	27:44	397	4:26-29	368
22:21	285	27:45	423	4:35-39	326
22:41	140	27:45-50	396, 399	4:35-41	336
22:41-46	141, 239, 245	27:46	364	4:41	331

5:1-13	325, 329	9:10	430	14:57-58	341
5:1-17	331	9:12	248, 456	14:58	414
5:7	260	9:17-26	323	14:61	284, 392
5:9-13	344	9:18	335	14:61-62	470
5:18-20	338	9:29	335	14:61-64	261, 407
5:20	331	9:31	429	14:62	237, 280, 469
5:22-42	323, 327	9:31-32	336	14:63-64	406
5:25-29	323	9:32	430	14:64	394
5:25-34	336	9:38-40	334	14:66-71	398
5:35	336	10:15	244	14:67	218
5:41	364	10:29	358, 359	15:1	392
5:42	331	10:29-30	360	15:2	212, 243, 395
5:43	242, 339	10:32-35	326	15:6	407
6:1	169	10:33-34	429	15:7	408
6:1-3	332	10:41-45	455	15:10	409
6:3	109, 142, 147, 148, 151, 154, 309, 521	10:45	284	15:12	244
		10:46-52	323, 324, 329, 336, 350	15:14-15	409
				15:18	243
6:4	286, 290	10:47	218, 241	15:25	396
6:4-6	337	10:48	238	15:26	243, 396, 412
6:5	323, 324	11:1-11	250	15:31-32	247
6:7-13	334, 337	11:9	413	15:32	241, 243, 397, 412
6:14	77, 338	11:12-21	326		
6:15	286, 290	11:13-20	344	15:33	396, 423
6:17-27	77	11:20-25	334	15:33-37	399
6:35-44	317, 322, 326	11:23	335	15:34	364
6:44	338	11:25	263	15:34-37	396
6:47-51	259, 326, 335, 336	11:28	332	15:39	261
		12:14-17	245	15:40	148, 151, 398, 400
6:56	323, 324, 338	12:17	285		
7:3	378	12:35	140	15:42	390
7:15-19	379	12:35-37	141, 239, 245	15:42-46	398
7:24-30	325	13	481	16:1	399, 400
7:25	123	13:1-2	393, 414	16:6	218
7:26-27	361	13:5-6	237, 477	16:7	401
7:27	337	13:6-25	468	16:9	400
7:32-35	323	13:7-8	477	16:15	358, 359, 361
7:34	364	13:10	358, 359, 360	16:19	401
7:36	242, 338, 339	13:21-22	237, 477		
7:37	331	13:22	333, 479	**Luke**	
8:1-9	317, 322, 326	13:26	280	1:1	362
8:9	338	13:26-27	472	1:1-4	31, 202
8:11-12	342, 354	13:26-37	468	1:5	67, 68, 140, 201
8:22-25	323, 350	13:32	264, 469	1:5-25	58
8:27	283	14:2	391	1:13	63
8:27-29	285	14:6-8	326	1:22	71
8:28	77, 331	14:9	358, 359, 360	1:26	215, 219
8:29	259, 284	14:12-46	390	1:26-27	59
8:29-30	236, 245	14:16-26	355	1:26-38	87
8:31	248, 326, 429, 456	14:18	326	1:27	100
		14:27	326, 398, 403	1:28	55
8:32-33	430	14:28	326, 429	1:31	95, 100
8:35	358, 359, 360	14:29-31	326	1:32	140, 244, 271
8:38	280, 283, 284	14:30-53	391, 405	1:34	138
8:38-9:1	469	14:36	364	1:35	100, 126, 271
9:2	339	14:43-46	397, 440	1:36	84, 140
9:2-3	326	14:53-55	392	1:42	55
9:2-8	271	14:53-65	392	1:47	123
9:7	264	14:54	398	1:57-64	73
9:9	339, 429	14:56-58	406	1:59	386

1:59-61	69	5:24-25	323	12:32	263
1:61	69	5:26	333	13:10-14	380
1:80	74	6:1:4	380	13:10-16	333
2:1-2	201	6:1-11	333	13:11-13	324
2:1-7	188, 216	6:35	263	13:31-32	338
2:1-20	168	6:35-36	264	14:2-4	324
2:4	219, 239	6:6-10	323	14:3-4	380
2:5	138	6:7-10	380	17:11-19	337
2:7	150	7:2-10	316, 323, 337	17:12-14	324, 350
2:11	236, 239, 247	7:12-15	325, 351	17:14	332
2:21	386	7:16	286, 290, 331	17:25	248, 456
2:23	216	7:18-22	240, 331	17:34-35	473
2:25	198	7:19	84	18:17	244
2:25-26	242	8:2	324, 325	18:29-30	360
2:29-32	242	8:19-21	142, 147	18:31-33	326
2:33	109	8:22-24	326	18:34	336, 430
2:39	216, 219	8:22-25	331, 336	18:35-42	323, 324, 329, 350
2:40-41	216	8:27-33	325, 329	18:35-43	336
2:41	138	8:28	260	18:36	338
2:42-50	526	8:30-33	344	18:37	218
2:48	109, 140	8:39	338	18:38	238, 241
2:51	219	8:41-55	323, 327	19:29-41	250
3:1	187, 191	8:43-44	323	19:38	242, 413
3:1-2	74	8:43-48	336	20:22-25	245
3:2	406	8:50	336	20:25	285
3:3-7	74	8:56	242, 339	20:41	140
3:4-6	75	9:1-2	334	20:41-44	141, 239, 245
3:15	74, 249	9:1-5	337	21	469, 481
3:16	82	9:7	77	21:5-6	393, 414
3:16-17	74, 76	9:7-8	331	21:27	280
3:18-22	76	9:9	77	21:31	469
3:19-20	77	9:12-17	317, 326	21:32	469
3:21-22	271	9:14	338	22:7-54	390
3:22	125, 264, 271	9:18	283	22:10-38	355
3:23	74, 191, 432	9:20	240	22:15	248, 456
3:23-38	139	9:20-21	236, 245	22:19	455
3:38	142, 263	9:20-22	326	22:21	326
4:3	260	9:22	248, 456	22:24-27	455
4:9	260	9:23-27	469	22:27	284
4:16	169, 219	9:24	360	22:30	478
4:22	138, 140, 142, 147, 154	9:26	280, 284	22:31-34	326
		9:28	339	22:37	403
4:24	169, 286, 290	9:28-29	326	22:47-48	440
4:25-27	330	9:35	264	22:47-54	397
4:33-35	325	9:36	339	22:50	406
4:34	218, 331	9:38-42	323	22:50-51	324
4:36	331	9:40	335	22:54	398, 406
4:37	338	9:49-50	334	22:54-60	398
4:38-39	323	10:1-17	334	22:66	391, 392
4:40	323	10:13	330	22:66-69	470
4:40-41	240	10:22	264, 265	22:66-71	393
4:41	237, 245, 260, 325	11:14	324	22:67	237
		11:14-20	355	22:70-71	261, 407
5:2-7	326	11:15	332	22:71	394
5:9-11	498	11:16-20	342	23:2	237, 243, 395
5:12-13	323, 350	11:19	320	23:3	212, 243
5:14	242, 339	11:29-30	400	23:4	410
5:15	338	11:30	342, 355	23:5	395
5:17-26	333, 457	11:51	58	23:8	338
5:24	281	12:8	280, 284		

23:13-24	410	2:18-22	341, 355, 393	9:1-7	324, 350
23:14	395	2:23	391	9:1-34	333
23:18	407	3:3-7	123	9:6-7	324
23:25	408	3:13	281	9:16	333, 380
23:35	247	3:14-16	281	9:17	286, 290, 331
23:37	243, 247	3:16	264, 455, 462	9:31-33	333
23:38	243, 396	3:18	264	10:6	336
23:39	247	4:7-29	327	10:17-18	266
23:39-43	398	4:16-19	327	10:24-25	237
23:44	423	4:19	286, 290, 331	10:30	267
23:44-46	396, 399	4:24	123	10:32-36	261, 262
23:49	398	4:25	158, 236	10:33	406
23:50-53	398	4:25-29	240	10:36	286
23:51	399, 470	4:25-30	237	10:38	267
23:54	390	4:42	247	10:41	77
24:1	399, 402	4:44	286, 290	11:4	260
24:1-12	401	4:46-53	324, 325	11:9	396
24:7-8	429	4:48	330	11:17-27	240
24:10	148	4:54	328	11:27	260
24:13	402	5:5-9	324	11:38-44	325, 351
24:13-16	401	5:5-10	380	11:45-48	330
24:13-27	248, 419	5:16-17	333	11:47-53	392, 394
24:19	218, 286, 290	5:16-18	261, 265	11:49	407
24:20	394, 395, 410	5:21-30	266	11:49-53	395
24:21	248	5:26-27	281	11:51	407
24:21-22	402	6:2	324	12:9-11	330
24:26	248, 456	6:3	391	12:10-11	333
24:36-42	336	6:5-13	317, 326	12:12-15	250
24:46	248	6:10	338	12:13	242
24:46-47	248, 457	6:14	286, 290, 331	12:16	336
24:50-51	402	6:14-15	244	12:17	338
		6:18-21	326, 336	12:34	249, 282
John		6:27	281	12:49	269
1:1-2	268	6:28-33	342, 354, 355	13:1-3	269
1:9-11	268	6:31	330	13:1-17:26	355
1:14	268	6:40	266, 456	14:3	473
1:15	74, 268	6:41-42	102	14:6	265
1:19-25	74	6:42	137, 140	14:7-11	267
1:23	75	6:62	281	14:14	371
1:26-27	76	7:1	340	14:15-16	372
1:29	391, 397, 456	7:3-4	339	14:16	370, 371, 373, 376
1:29-34	76	7:5	109, 147, 150	14:26	370, 371, 372
1:30	74, 76	7:6-8	339	14:28	269
1:30-33	84	7:10	340	14:31	269
1:31	74	7:11-12	339	15:23-27	374
1:32	125	7:14	340	15:24	322, 334
1:33	82	7:22-23	386	15:26	370, 371, 373, 377
1:36	391, 397, 456	7:27	239		
1:41	236	7:31	239	15:26-27	372
1:44-46	224	7:38	23	16:5-11	370
1:45	137, 140	7:40	286, 290	16:7	370, 371
1:45-46	219, 220	7:41-42	169, 216, 224	16:7-11	371, 372
1:46	169, 216	7:41-43	239, 246	16:8-11	371
1:49	242, 260	7:42	140, 238	16:12-14	372
1:51	281, 471	7:52	169, 216, 224	16:13	371
2:1-10	326	8:31	263	16:13-15	371
2:11	328, 336	8:37-41	105, 114	16:15	266
2:12	146	8:41	263	16:27-28	269
2:13	391	8:42-44	263	17:4-5	268
2:18-20	192	8:57	432		

17:11	267
18:2-12	397
18:3-9	441
18:5	218
18:7	218
18:12-13	392
18:13	407
18:15	398
18:15-16	407
18:15-22	392
18:16-17	398
18:19	394, 398, 407
18:24	392, 406
18:24-28	395
18:25-27	398
18:26	406
18:28	391, 405
18:30	395
18:31	395, 406
18:33-38	243
18:36	396
18:38	410
18:39	407
18:40	408
19:3	243
19:4-16	411
19:7	394, 396, 407
19:11	411
19:12-15	243
19:14-16	396
19:18	398
19:19	218, 243, 396
19:23-24	403
19:25	148, 398
19:26	398
19:26-27	147
19:28-29	403
19:31	390
19:31-37	404
19:36	391
19:38-42	399
20:1	399
20:14	401
20:17	263
20:21	269
20:27-28	267
20:30	328
20:30-31	240, 261
20:31	260
21:1-25	401
21:3-7	326
21:20-24	471, 473
21:25	328

Acts

1:1-3	402
1:13	154
1:14	148, 154
1:18-20	397
1:22	105

2:4	126
2:22	218, 321
2:43	322, 334
3:1-9	322, 334
3:6	218
3:13	294
4:6	407
4:10	218
4:27	294
4:30	294
5:12	322, 334
5:16	322, 334
5:36	321
5:36-37	190
5:37	190
6:8	322, 334
6:11-14	393
6:14	218
8:6	322, 334
8:29	123
9:3-8	104, 321, 466
9:20	261
9:32-34	322, 334
9:36-40	322, 334
10:11-16	379
10:37-38	271
10:38	219
11:26	252
12:17	154
13:11	322, 334
13:24-25	77
13:27	395
13:27-28	394
13:29	399
13:33	270
14:8-10	322, 334
15:2	151
15:13	154
15:29	151, 380
16:16-18	322, 334
19:6	322, 334
19:11-12	322, 335
20:9-12	322, 335
21:8	362
21:18	154
22:6-10	104, 466
22:8	218
24:5	218, 219, 221
26:9	218
26:13-18	104, 321, 466
26:28	252

Romans

1:3	104, 140, 267, 270, 295, 322
1:3-4	270
2:16	458
2:25-29	380
3:21-26	295, 453
3:29-30	380

5:6-21	295, 454
8:6	123
8:15	123
8:29	146
8:32	454
9:4	263
9:5	104, 267, 270, 322
14:3	381
16:25	458

1 Corinthians

1:6-8	471
1:10	146
5:7	454
6:17	123
7:18-19	380
9:5	145, 156
11:23-25	355
11:23-27	152
12:4-11	123
12:9-10	322, 335
12:28-29	322, 335
15:4-8	401
15:5-8	151
15:6	146, 340
15:17	453
15:22	453
15:45	123
15:45-50	295
15:47	267, 270

2 Corinthians

11:2-6	458
11:12-14	459
11:21-23	459
12:7-9	104, 322
12:12	322, 335

Galatians

1:11	458
1:11-12	153, 466
1:13-24	153
1:19	145, 151
2:9-10	380
2:9-12	151
2:11-15	381
2:21	381, 386
3:5	322, 335
4:4	103, 322
4:10	381
5:4	386

Ephesians

2:5-15	386
2:15	386, 454
4:11	362

Philippians
1:14   146
2:5-11 270
4:15   458

Colossians
1:2   146

1 Thessalonians
4:13-17 246
4:13-18 472

2 Thessalonians
2:1-2   472
2:1-9   476, 479

1 Timothy
6:13-14 471

2 Timothy
2:8   104, 322, 458
4:5   362

Philemon
1:16   146

Hebrews
7:14   140

James
1:1   154, 478
4:5   23
5:7-9   470

1 Peter
4:16   253

2 Peter
3:3-8   473
3:16   458

1 John
2:1   370, 371
2:18-22 476
2:29   264
3:8   261
3:9   264
4:3   476
4:9   264
5:1   264
5:11-13 265

5:12-13 456
5:18   264

2 John
1:7   476

Jude
1:1   154

Revelation
1:1   470
1:3   470
1:7   471
12   476
13   476, 480
14:14   280
16:16   477
18.94   480
20:8   480
22:16   140
22:20   471

Index of Other Religious Texts

Ḥadīth (Prophetic Sayings)

Abū Dāwūd
984	481
2484	480
2532	480
4282	481
4311	479
4315	481
4316	481
4321	479, 481
4324	479, 480

Al-Bukhārī
1480	481
1780	479
1782	481
1783	479, 481
2109	480
2344	480
2892	481
3264	480, 484
3265	480, 482
3266	481
6710	481

At-Tarmathī
2331	481
2332	481
2334	480
2336	481
2338	481
2341	479, 480
2345	479
2347	481
3047	481

Muslim
34	479
38	481
39	479
40	479
41	479
90	481
105	481
110	479
112	481
116	479
117	481
119	481
127	481
242	480, 484
243	480
244	480, 482
245	480
247	480, 482
270	481
273	479, 481
277	479
1380	479, 481
2927	481

Christian Writings

Apocalypse of Peter
N/A	442

Arabic Gospel of the Infancy
1:2	214
1:2-3	179, 345, 348
1:4	191
1:4-11	216
1:4-5	188
1:5-11	171
3:1	198
4:1-3	198
4:11	179, 259, 349
4:15-16	343
4:21	179, 261, 349
5:1	198
6:5-7	343
6:11-14	343
6:16-17	343
6:25-34	343
7:2-3	343
7:13-26	343
8:6-7	344
8:8-11	181
8:10	344
8:13	342, 363
8:14-16	198
8:16	216
9:1	216
9:2-5	343
9:8-10	343
10:3	343
10:6-7	343, 344
10:9-10	343
11:5-6	343
11:8	343, 363
12:5-6	343
12:9-20	343
12:14	216
13:10	216
13:17-19	343
15:1-6	345
15:2-4	349
15:6	349
15:13-14	344
16:2	318, 344
16:16-14	318, 344
17:10	345
18:14-17	343, 344
18:19	363
19:1	149
19:2-3	343
19:6-11	343
19:16-19	345, 349
19:20-21	343
19:22-24	343
20:11	344
20:15-16	344
21:5-21	344
21:27	216

Gospel of Barnabas
37	444
216-217	444
217	444, 445

Gospel of the Birth of Mary
1:1	217
1:6	49
2:5	48
2:9	48, 49
2:12	523
3:2	48, 49
3:3	49
3:11	49
6:1	149
6:6	217
7:1-10	88
7:3	100
7:9-10	100
7:15-21	88
7:16	139
7:17-19	100
7:19	93
8:13	138
8:15	217

Gospel of Nicodemus
2	115

Gospel of Peter
11:4	411

Gospel of Pseudo-Matthew

1	48
2	49
4	49
6	53, 54
7	47
8	91, 149
9	90, 91
10	53, 90, 93
11	90, 101
12	47
13	113, 188, 191, 217
14	344
15	95
16	166
16-17	197
17	205
19	344
20	181, 344
22	345
26	217, 343
27	345, 349
28	343
29	343
31	345
32	343
33	344
34	344
35	217
36	344
37	318, 344
40	343
41	217, 343
42	149

Infancy Gospel of James

2:1	48
3:1	48
4:2	48, 49, 50
5:9	49
8:2	53
8:3-5	59
8:6	61
8:6-8	149
9:1-4	91
9:3	61
9:7	89
9:9-15	89
9:11-13	139
9:13	93, 100
9:14	95
9:15-16	59
9:23	89, 94
10:9	53
10:11-12	89
10:19	89
11	105
11:9	53
11:11-20	90
12	217
12:1	191
12:1-5	188
12:3	138
14:18-19	113
15:1	171
15:1-16:2	197
15:7	172
16:2	183
16: 3-16	73
16:16-20	60
16:27-28	198

Infancy Gospel of Thomas

2	345, 349
3	343
4	343
5	343
8	344
9	343
10	343
11	344
12	344
13	318, 344
14	344
15	343
16	343
17	343
18	343

Jewish Writings

1 Enoch
37-71	278, 279, 282

4 Ezra
13	278, 279

Berakoth (Mishnah)
17b	259
33a	316
34b	316

Jubilees
1:21-24	258

Pesachim (Mishnah)
112b	318

Psalms of Solomon
17	235, 259

Sanhedrin (Mishnah)
32a	405
43a	425
49b	412
55b	262
56a	262
60a	262

Second Treatise of the Great Seth
N/A	443

Ta'anit (Mishnah)
23a	315
24b	259, 317
25a	317, 318
23a	259

Yebamoth (Mishnah)
121b	317

Index of Ancient Texts

Christian Writings

Africanus, *Chronograph*
18   423

Eusebius, *Ecclesiastical History*
2.23   150
2.23.19-20   161

Eusebius, *The Proof of the Gospel*
3.5.124   416
9.1   172

Ignatius, *Epistle to the Smyrnaeans*
2.1   441

Jerome, *Against Helvidius*
9-17   149

Jerome, *Lives of Illustrious Men*
13   161, 417

Origen, *Against Celsus*
1.28   116
1.32   116
1.47   160, 417
2.13   160

Irenaeus, *Against Heresies*
1.24.3   442
1.26.1-2   106
2.22.5   433

Origen, *Commentary on Matthew*
10.17   161, 417
15.14   25

Tertullian, *Against Marcion*
4.19   150, 190

Roman Writings

Cicero, *On Divination*
1.47   172

Josephus, *Jewish Antiquities*
2.9.2   210
8.2.5   320
13.14.2   412
14.2.1   315
15.11.1   192
17.6.5   205
18.1.1   188
18.3.3   78, 158, 313, 417, 416
18.4.1   321
18.5.2   78
20.5.1   321
20.8.6   321
20.9.1   157, 417, 419
20.9.3   408

Josephus, *Jewish War*
1.21.1   192
3.5.8   162
6.5.4   475

Josephus, *Life*
65   162
75   431

Lucian, *The Passing of Peregrinus*
N/A   421

Macrobius, *Saturn*
2.4.11   207

Philostratus, *The Life of Apollonius*
4.45   320

Porphyry, *Against the Christians*
2.12   389

Suetonius, *Lives of the Caesars, Nero*
16   494

Suetonius, *Lives of the Caesars: Augustus*
94   172

Suetonius, *Lives of the Caesars: Vespasian*
4.5   475

Tacitus, *Annals*
15.44   420, 494

Tacitus, *Histories*
5.13   475

Index of Names and Subjects

'Alī bin Abī Ṭālib, 34, 482
'Imrān (Mary's father), 48, 50, 54, 55, 117, 119, 127, 133, 163, 164, 176, 177, 509
'Uthmān bin 'Affān (caliph), 34
Aaron (Prophet), 48, 57, 118, 176, 177, 231, 235, 288, 289, 293, 296, 454, 513, 514, 516
Abraham (Prophet), 12, 50, 54-56, 70, 114, 139, 140, 141, 177, 232, 238, 273, 287-291, 307, 308, 363, 366, 369, 382, 458, 459, 464, 497, 501, 507, 511
Abraham (Prophet), 497
Abū Bakr aṣ-Ṣiddīq (caliph), 34
Abū Dāwūd, 479, 481
Abyssinia, 505
Adam (Prophet), 50, 54, 55, 97, 99, 127-134, 141, 142, 177, 263, 267, 278, 288, 290, 294, 295, 444, 453, 454, 460, 461, 511, 514
ad-dajjāl, 479
ad-Daramī, 464
ad-Darquṭnī, 482
Adoptionism, 270, 275, 307
Africanus, 193, 219, 423, 423, 424
Agrippa II (king), 252
aḥādīth qudsiyyah, 32, 33, 35
Ahaz (king), 107
Bin Ḥanbal, Aḥmad, 464
aj-Jalālayn, 447
Akkadian, 364
Al-Bukhārī, 32, 479, 482
Janneus (king), Alexander, 412
Alexander the Great, 172, 273
Alexander (bishop), 276
Alexandria (Egypt), 157
al-Madīnā (city), 227, 481, 505, 506
al-Mahdī, 467, 481, 482, 488-490
al-Masīḥ ad-dajjāl, 479
al-Qummī, 69
al-Qurṭubī, 83, 251, 252
Amenhotep III (Pharaoh), 111
American Standard Version Bible, 123, 369
Annas, 74, 115, 392, 394, 395, 398, 405-407, 432
An-Nassā'ī, 464, 479, 481
antichrist, 467, 476, 477, 479-482, 489-491
Antioch, 252, 253, 380, 381
Apocryphon of James, 24
Apollo (god), 21, 182, 183, 185, 273
Apollonius of Tyana, 273, 320
Aramaic, 361, 364, 365
Aretas (king), 78, 79
Arianism, 276
Arius, 276
Armageddon, 477
Asbāṭ, 501
as-Sajustānī, 482
Assyria, 107, 167, 203, 233, 477, 482

Athanasius (bishop), 24, 524
atonement, 435, 453-457, 459, 460, 465
aṭ-Ṭabarī, 69, 83, 301, 350, 440, 447, 450
aṭ-Ṭabāṭabā'ī, 51, 53, 65, 67, 69, 82, 95, 125, 175, 179, 252, 385, 440, 447, 448
at-Tarmathī, 464, 479
Attis (god), 111
aṭ-Ṭūsī, 83
Augustus (emperor), 74, 170, 172, 187-192, 207, 273, 358, 524
Authorized Version Bible, 121
Babylon, 204, 478
Babylonians, 364
Barabbas, 408, 409, 410
Barnabas (apostle), 151, 252, 380, 381
Baruch (book), 23
Basilides, 441, 442, 443
Benjamin, 477
Bethlehem, 46, 115, 165, 166, 168-171, 173, 182, 186, 187-189, 191, 193, 195-198, 202, 204, 206, 207, 213, 215-218, 224, 238, 239, 246, 521-524, 528
Buddha, 21, 111, 181, 185
Bultmann, Rudolf, 30, 31, 373
Caiaphas (high priest), 74, 115, 392, 394, 395, 405, 406, 407, 432
Canaan, 232
Capernaum, 217, 330
Celsus, 116
Cephas (Peter), 145, 151, 153, 380, 381, 401
Chalcedon Council, 277
circumcision, 151, 380, 381, 382, 386
Claudius (emperor), 494
Clement of Alexandria, 192
Cleopatra, 192
Constantine (emperor), 25, 276, 412
Constantinople Council, 277
Constantinople, 277
contextual displacement, 39, 40, 50, 53, 55, 60, 61, 179, 186, 349, 355, 369
Council of Trent, 23
Cyrus (king), 232, 478
Damascus, 153, 232, 321, 466, 479
Daniel, 23
Day of Judgment, 484, 489, 491
Day of Resurrection, 35, 42, 81, 82, 254, 290, 300, 365, 387, 437, 446-450, 463, 464, 479, 480, 484-487, 489, 490, 499, 502-504, 509, 515
Dead Sea Scrolls, 235, 240, 364, 405
Decius, 413
Dionysos (god), 111, 112
Docetism, 275
Easter, 272, 284
Ebionites, 105, 106
Ecclesiasticus, 23

Egypt, 110, 111, 115, 116, 168, 170, 180, 185, 187, 189, 192, 195-198, 203, 208, 210-217, 233, 497, 521, 524, 525, 528
Elijah, 271, 285, 330, 331
Elisha, 330
Emmanuel, 100, 106, 271
Emmaus, 248, 401, 419
English Standard Version Bible, 369
Epiphanius of Salamis, 149, 519, 522, 524
Epiphany, 193
Epitome of the Philippic History of Pompeius Trogus, 173
Esther, 18, 19, 23, 39
Eucharist, 1, 373
Eusebius, 25, 149, 150, 157, 158, 160, 161, 172, 192, 219, 416, 419, 424, 441, 524
Eve, 99, 132, 133, 458
Ezekiel, 461
Faustus Socinus, 224
First Maccabees, 23
Gabriel, 54, 55, 65, 87, 88, 91-95, 97, 110, 117, 118, 244, 252, 271, 292, 347, 348, 352, 452
Galilee, 46, 60, 74, 75, 77, 89, 110, 138, 168, 169, 170, 187-191, 196, 215-217, 221, 223, 224, 229, 239, 246, 250, 319, 326, 328, 330, 336, 338, 364, 382, 396, 398, 401, 521-523, 528
Gentiles, 115, 151, 153, 242, 337, 361, 380-382, 386, 416, 455, 511
Gilgamesh, 17
Gog and Magog, 479, 480
Gospel of Thomas, 24
ḥadīth, 31, 32, 33
Hāmān, 18, 19, 39, 40, 209
Hanina ben Dosa, 259, 316-319, 320
Helvidius, 149
Heracles (god), 273
Heraclitus, 269
Reimarus, Hermann Samuel, 430, 431
Herod Agrippa, 421
Herod Antipas, 74, 76-79, 187, 189, 396, 410
Herod Archelaus, 187, 190, 196, 221, 421
Herod Philip, 74, 77, 187
Herod the Great, 57, 77, 83, 110, 138, 165, 166, 168, 170-172, 180, 183, 187-190, 192, 193, 195, 196, 221, 521, 525, 528
Herodias, 76, 77, 78, 79
Honi, 259, 314, 315, 316, 318, 319, 320
Hosea, 203
Hoshea (king), 477
Hour of Judgment, 479, 480, 483, 484
Hūd, 290, 514, 515
Ibn ʿAsākir, 482
Ibn Hishām, 374, 375, 506
Ibn Isḥāq, 374, 375, 376
Ibn Kathīr, 485
Ibn Māja, 464
Idrīs, 445
Ignatius, 441
Ilyās, Prophet, 68, 80

Immaculate Conception, 99, 278
Incarnation, 270, 307, 359
Injīl, 35-40, 51, 65, 81, 110, 178, 186, 199, 288, 296, 297, 346, 347, 349, 351, 352, 355, 436, 448, 495, 500, 507, 511
intercession, 465
International Standard Version Bible, 369
Irenaeus, 105, 432, 433, 441-443
Isaac, 55, 232, 274, 288, 289, 291, 366, 501
Isaiah, 222
Ishmael, 55, 288, 289, 291, 501
Isrāʾ (night journey), 452
Israel, 165, 166, 172, 173, 191, 195-199, 203, 210, 212, 231-235, 239, 241-244, 247-250, 253, 254, 258, 260, 296, 303, 310, 315, 321, 337, 338, 344, 346, 349, 351, 353, 361, 367, 375, 384, 436, 437, 438, 444, 461, 462, 467, 469, 475, 477, 478, 482, 483, 495, 496, 503, 504, 506, 510
Jacob, 139, 232, 288, 291, 366, 459, 501
Jeremiah, 222, 285
Jericho, 323, 324, 329
Jerome, 149, 157, 158, 160, 161, 522, 526
Jerusalem, 45, 107, 138, 151-153, 155, 160-162, 165, 168, 171, 195, 196, 198, 216, 217, 222, 232, 242, 248-250, 254, 314, 319, 321, 333, 336, 340, 341, 380, 394, 397, 399, 401, 404, 407, 408, 411, 413, 422, 440, 457, 477, 478, 519, 525, 526, 528
Jesse, 232, 481
Joash (king), 58
Job, 65, 289
Mill, John, 25
John the Baptist, 57-60, 62-65, 67-69, 71, 102, 168
Jonah, 289, 341, 342, 355, 399, 400, 486, 514
Jordan River, 74, 75, 79, 215, 216, 217, 321, 344
Joseph of Arimathea, 398, 431, 470
Josephus, 73, 78, 79, 82-84, 205-207, 210, 219, 235, 316, 319, 321, 358, 407, 408, 412, 416-420, 425, 431
Judaism, 50, 231, 234, 249, 252, 254, 257, 259, 261, 262, 267, 273, 280, 287, 306, 389, 411, 412, 429, 457, 501, 503
Judas Iscariot, 269, 389, 397, 402, 440, 441, 444, 445, 525
Judea, 60, 87, 89, 110, 138, 165, 166, 171, 187-191, 195-198, 204, 215, 216, 221, 234, 238, 271, 407, 408, 414, 416, 420, 421, 423, 432, 433, 468, 475, 477, 478, 493, 521, 523, 525, 528
Judith, 23
Verne, Jules, 14
Justin Martyr, 28, 115
King James Version Bible, 26, 123, 369
Last Supper, 355, 370, 455
lawless one, 475-477, 479
Lazarus, 240, 260, 325, 329, 332, 351
Lot (Prophet), 54, 163, 290

Lucian, 421, 422, 426
Macedonia, 246
Macrobius, 207
Malachi, 456
Mandaeans, 80, 81
Mani, 373
Marcion, 24
Mariolatry, 278, 309, 311
Mary Magdalene, 148, 398, 400, 401
Mecca (city), 227, 452, 465, 481
Mi'rāj (ascension), 452
Midian (city), 517
Midrash, 219
Mirza Ghulam Ahmad, 431
Mishnah, 138, 405, 406, 412, 424
Montanus, 373
Robertson, Morgan, 15, 16
Mosaic law, 152, 378, 380, 511
Moses, 11, 12, 18, 21, 35, 36, 40, 48, 71, 80, 151, 176, 177, 195, 199, 200, 208-214, 220, 224, 228, 258, 262, 271, 274, 281, 287-291, 293, 296, 308, 330, 344, 346, 353, 354, 363-365, 368, 380, 382, 386, 393, 435, 451, 454, 459, 460, 462, 485, 486, 495, 497, 501, 511, 513-517
Mother Shipton, 14
Mount of Olives, 237, 249, 467, 469
Muslim, 32, 464, 479
Nag Hammadi, 24, 442, 443
Nazareth, 59, 75, 168, 169, 170, 188, 189, 196, 198
Nebuchadnezzar, 232, 234, 478
Negus, 505
Nero, 413, 420, 493, 494
New American Standard Bible, 369
New English Translation Bible, 106, 123, 133, 232, 362, 369
New International Version Bible, 123, 369, 370
New King James Version Bible, 369
Nicea Council, 276
Nineveh, 399, 400
Noah, 17, 50, 54, 55, 163, 177, 288, 289, 363, 487
Origen, 25, 157, 158, 160, 161, 417, 519
original sin, 99, 254, 278, 373, 460, 462, 463
Palestine, 150, 162, 203, 204, 205, 280, 282, 364, 389, 421, 452, 467, 478, 521
Pantera, 116
paraclete, 127, 488, 511, 512
Parthenogenesis, 113, 114
Passover, 138, 192, 243, 268, 389-391, 397, 404, 405, 407, 408, 411, 423, 424, 425, 432, 454, 456
patripassionism, 275
Pekah (king of Israel), 107
Peter, 236, 240, 271, 284, 321, 323, 326, 327, 334-336, 339, 358, 379-381, 398, 401, 407, 411, 430, 442, 458, 471
Pharaoh, 18, 19, 39, 163, 195, 199, 200, 208-213, 258, 486, 513, 515-517, 525

Pharisees, 58, 196, 216, 330-333, 338, 341, 342, 354, 355, 378, 379, 394, 399, 400, 412, 440, 444
Philo, 269, 358, 405, 407
Pilate, 115
Pius IX (Pope), 99, 278
Pius XII (Pope), 278
Plato, 273
Pompey, 280
Pontius Pilate, 74, 115, 158, 191, 237, 243, 244, 321, 389, 390, 394, 395, 396, 403, 406, 408-414, 416, 418-421, 425, 432, 433, 436, 493
Porphyry, 389
Prophetic sayings, 32, 33
Protevangelion, 519
Pythagoras, 273, 422
Quirinius, 187-191, 193, 407
Rachel (Jacob's wife), 196, 203, 204
Rama (god), 111
redemption, 439, 453, 457, 459
Revised Version Bible, 121
Rezin (king of Syria), 107
Rome, 190, 280, 282, 493, 494
Sabaeans, 80, 81, 305, 460, 499
Sabbath, 265, 317, 318, 332, 333, 378, 380-382, 387, 394, 403, 405, 485, 503
Sabellianism, 275
Sabellius, 275
Sadducees, 331, 342, 355, 400
Ṣāliḥ (Prophet), 293
Samaria, 477
Sanhedrin, 157, 159, 241, 284, 391, 392, 394, 395, 405, 406, 407, 411, 419
Sargon II, 477
Sargon of Akkad (king), 21
Satan, 51, 65, 70, 71, 322, 325, 332, 355, 480, 483, 509
Saul, 232, 252, 358, 514
Second Maccabees, 23
Secret Book of John, 24
Sepphoris (city), 364
Septuagint, 106, 250, 359, 369, 376
Serapion, 422, 423, 426
Shalmaneser V, 477
Shias, 33, 34, 482, 488, 489
Shu'aib (Prophet), 293
Solomon (Prophet), 288-290, 319, 341, 477
son of Pantera, 424
son of Stada, 424
Stada, 116
Stephen, 392, 393
Suetonius, 494
Sunni, 479
Sunnis, 33, 34
Syria, 153, 187-189, 207, 407
Syriac, 372, 374, 375
Tacitus, 493
Talmud, 116, 219, 316, 319
Tatian, 28

Ten Commandments, 380
Tertullian, 150, 190, 192, 275, 276, 373
Thallus, 423, 424, 426
The Companion Bible, 121
Thessalonica, 246, 472
Thomas (disciple), 267
Tiberius (emperor), 74, 191, 192, 420, 493
Titanic, 15, 17
Titus (emperor), 162
Tobias (book), 23
Torah, 35-37, 39, 40, 80, 110, 199, 253, 288, 316, 346, 347, 351, 352, 436, 448, 495, 499, 500, 504, 517
Trinity, 122, 127, 287, 309, 310, 311
two-source hypothesis, 22
Uzayr, 502
virgin birth, 99, 111, 113
Wisdom (book), 23
Zechariah, 509
Zeus (god), 111, 112, 273
Zionism, 478

www.ingramcontent.com/pod-product-compliance
Lightning Source LLC
Chambersburg PA
CBHW060327240426
43665CB00047B/2567